ECDL®/ICDL® 4.0
Study Guide

D1216495

John Lancaster

Bill McTaggart

David Penfold

David Stott

San Francisco • London

SYBEX

Associate Publisher: Neil Edde
Acquisitions Editor: Elizabeth H. Peterson
Developmental Editor: Colleen Wheeler Strand
Production Editor: Mae Lum
Technical Editor: James Kelly
Copyeditor: Sarah Lemaire
Compositor: Scott Benoit
Graphic Illustrator: Scott Benoit
Proofreaders: Emily Hsuan, Laurie O'Connell, Nancy Riddiough. Monique van den Berg
Indexer: Ted Laux
Book Designers: Bill Gibson, Judy Fung
Cover Design and Illustration: Richard Miller, Calyx Design

Manufactured in the United States of America

10 9 8 7 6 5 4 3 2 1

SYBEX

To Our Valued Readers:

Thank you for looking to Sybex for your ECDL®/ICDL® exam prep needs. We at Sybex are proud of the reputation we've established over the past ten years for providing IT certification candidates with the practical computer knowledge and skills in demand by companies around the world. It has always been Sybex's mission to teach individuals how to utilize technologies in the real world, not to simply feed them answers to test questions. Just as the ECDL Foundation is committed to establishing measurable standards for validating computer skills, Sybex is committed to providing individuals with the means of acquiring the skills and knowledge needed to meet those standards.

Sybex is proud to have partnered with the British Computer Society, the leading professional and learned society in the field of computers and information systems, to produce this Study Guide for the Syllabus Version 4.0. The authors, editors, and technical reviewer have worked hard to ensure that this Study Guide is comprehensive, in-depth, and pedagogically sound. We're confident that this book will meet and exceed the demanding standards of the certification marketplace and help you, the ECDL/ICDL certification exam candidate, succeed in your endeavors.

Good luck in pursuit of your ECDL/ICDL certification!

Neil Edde
Associate Publisher—Certification
Sybex, Inc.

Contents

Introduction

Welcome to this study guide, which is intended to help you successfully complete the individual tests for all seven modules of the European/International Computer Driving Licence (ECDL/ICDL).

However, before you go any further, let's quickly look at exactly what the ECDL/ICDL is, why so many people believe that it is such an important qualification, and how this book is structured to give you the best possible chance of achieving this qualification.

What Is the ECDL/ICDL?

The European Computer Driving Licence (ECDL) is an internationally recognised qualification that enables people to demonstrate their competence in computer skills. Also known as the International Computer Driving Licence (ICDL) for countries outside of Europe, this certification programme has seen tremendous growth on a global basis and now spans some 60 countries.

The ECDL/ICDL qualification certifies the candidate's knowledge and competence in personal computer usage at a basic level. It is based upon a range of specific knowledge areas and skill sets that are broken down into seven modules. Each of the modules must be passed before the ECDL certificate can be awarded; although they may be taken in any order, all modules must be completed within a three-year period.

Testing of candidates takes place at audited test centres, and successful completion of the test demonstrates the holder's basic knowledge and competence in using a personal computer and common computer applications.

In order to ensure that the ECDL certification programme reflects current trends and practices, the Syllabus is updated on a regular basis. This study guide covers Syllabus Version 4.0.

The ECDL Modules

The seven modules that make up the ECDL certificate are as follows:

Module 1: Concepts of Information Technology   Module 1 covers the physical makeup of a personal computer and some of the basic concepts of information technology (IT) such as data storage and memory and the uses of information networks within computing. This module also looks at the application of computer-based software in everyday life, together with the health and safety issues and environmental factors involved in using computers. Some of the more important security and legal issues associated with using computers are also addressed.

Module 2: Using the Computer and Managing Files   Module 2 covers the basic functions of a personal computer and its operating system. In particular, this module looks at adjusting the main settings, operating effectively within the Desktop environment, managing and organising files and directories, and working with Desktop icons. An understanding of computer viruses and the use of anti-virus software is also included.

Module 3: Word Processing   Module 3 covers the use of a word processing application on a personal computer. This module looks at the basic operations associated with creating, formatting, and finishing a word processing document ready for distribution. It also addresses some of the more advanced word processing features such as creating standard tables, using pictures and images within a document, importing objects, and using mail merge tools.

Module 4: Spreadsheets   Module 4 covers the basic concepts of spreadsheets and the ability to use a spreadsheet application on a personal computer. Topics included in this module are the basic operations for developing, formatting, and using a spreadsheet, together with the use of simple formulas and functions to carry out standard mathematical and logical operations. Instructions on how to create and format graphs and charts are also included.

Module 5: Databases   Module 5 covers the basic features of databases and the ability to use a database on a personal computer. This module addresses the creation and modification of tables, queries, forms, and reports, and the preparation of output for distribution. The retrieval and manipulation of information from a database through the use of query, select, and sort tools is also covered.

Module 6: Presentation   Module 6 covers the use of presentation tools on a personal computer, in particular, creating, formatting, and preparing slide show presentations. The tools used to duplicate and move text, pictures, images, and charts within and between presentations, and the features that for implementing various slide show effects are also addressed.

Module 7: Information and Communication   Module 7 is divided into two main sections. The first section covers basic web search tasks using a web browser and search engine tools, together with an appreciation of some of the security considerations of using the Internet. The second section addresses the use of electronic mail software to send and receive messages, to attach documents, and to organise and manage message folders and directories.

Why Become ECDL Certified?

There is obviously a lot of time and effort required to complete the ECDL certification process. So why would you want to put yourself through this—what can you expect to actually gain from it?

Well, there are a number of very good reasons for becoming ECDL certified, including the following:

- Many governments, learning institutions, and large corporations around the world are now endorsing it.

- Employers are increasingly viewing it as the leading formal computer skills qualification, so it really can improve your employment prospects.

- Employers are also using it to benchmark the IT skills of their current staff, so it can help with your internal promotion prospects.

- It has been evaluated and approved by many governments as a framework for the development of IT in schools and can, therefore, provide a passport to higher-level IT education.

- From an organisation's point of view, it can help to ensure a consistent level of IT ability throughout its staff.

How to Obtain the ECDL

Each country has a licensee that administers the ECDL (or ICDL) programme locally; these can be found on the ECDL website (www.ecdl.com). The licensees, in turn, appoint a network of independent test centres to conduct the actual testing of candidates.

Your first step, therefore, is to register with any of these accredited test centres near you, at which point, you will obtain a skills card (sometimes referred to as a logbook) on which your progress through the seven tests is recorded. As each module is passed, the accredited test centre will endorse the skills card, indicating the passing of that module. When all modules have been successfully completed, the skills card is forwarded to the licensee, and an ECDL or ICDL licence/certificate is issued to you.

How to Use This Study Guide

The purpose of this guide is to take you through all of the knowledge areas and skill sets specified in the ECDL Version 4.0 Syllabus. The use of clear, non-technical explanations and self-paced exercises will provide you with an understanding of the key elements of the Syllabus and give you a solid foundation for moving on to take the ECDL test relating to each of the individual modules.

 All exercises contained within this study guide are based upon the Windows XP operating system and Office XP Professional software.

Each chapter has a well-defined set of objectives that relate directly to the ECDL Syllabus. Because the study guide is structured in a logical sequence, you are advised to work through the chapters of each part one at a time, from the beginning.

At the end of each part, there are various review questions, so that you can determine whether you have understood the principles involved correctly prior to moving on to the next step. These questions are a great way to review your understanding of the topics covered in each module.

This ECDL approved courseware product incorporates learning reinforcement exercises. These exercises are included to assist the candidate in their training for the ECDL. The exercises included in this courseware product are not ECDL certification tests and should not be construed in any way as ECDL certification tests. For information about Authorised ECDL Test Centres in different national territories, please refer to the ECDL Foundation website at http://www.ecdl.com.

In addition, there is a bonus glossary of key terms posted on the Sybex website (http://www.sybex.com). Type this book's ISBN (4308-3) in the Search box at the top of the web page and press Go. On the right side of the web page for this book, click Downloads to obtain the glossary in Adobe Acrobat PDF format.

Conventions Used In This Study Guide

Throughout this guide, you will come across notes alongside a number of icons. They are all designed to provide you with specific information related to the section of the guide you are currently working through. The icons and the particular types of information they relate to are as follows:

These notes represent information supplemental to the text, of which you should, well, take note.

These tips include some additional bit of information that may make your computing experience easier, faster, or more efficient.

These warnings inform you about the risks associated with a particular action, together with guidance—where necessary—on how to avoid any pitfalls.

Should a given example require you to type in information, that text will appear in **bold**. New terms are italicised and their definitions can be found in the Glossary.

Where to Go for More Information

You can find out more about the ECDL/ICDL certification from the ECDL foundation website at http://www.ecdl.com/. Good luck on your exams!

ECDL Module 1: Concepts of Information Technology

PART

I

Chapter

1

General IT Concepts

IN THIS CHAPTER YOU WILL LEARN HOW TO

✓ Understand the general concepts of hardware and software and how these are related to the field of information technology.

✓ Understand and be able to distinguish between the different types of computer systems.

✓ Know the main parts of a personal computer system.

✓ Know the factors that impact a computer's performance.

There is a great deal of jargon used within the field of computing and information technology. It is not necessary to know all of this jargon to be able to adequately function within these fields. However, knowing some jargon can help you to communicate with others concerning your use of computers. The first two terms to consider are hardware and software.

Hardware/Software and Information Technology

Hardware is commonly thought of as all the computer items you can touch. This is an over-simplified definition, as well as a little worrying. I prefer to think of hardware as all the physical items of a computer system. Some of these physical items you definitely should not touch! Hardware is discussed at length in Chapter 2.

Software refers to the programs you run on a computer to perform certain tasks. Computer programs are as wide and varied as your imagination, performing all types of different tasks. Software also enables the various computer hardware devices to function together. Software is discussed at length in Chapter 3.

Information technology (IT) refers to the use of this hardware and software to store and process raw facts and figures into an organised form that we call information. With the right human knowledge, IT can be a powerful tool. Information technology can be regarded as the use of technologies to collect, process, store, and communicate information. Within the education sector, the term "information technology" has been widened to *information and communication technology (ICT)*. This has been done to recognise the growing importance of computers and similar technology in world communication.

Before going on, there is one distinction you should understand. The term *data* refers to the raw facts and figures. *Information* is data that is processed within context. A number is seen as *raw data*; once the number has been processed, it may have much more meaning as perhaps a date, a part number, or an order number.

Types of Computer

Computers can be grouped together broadly according to their use and complexity. Starting with the most complex, there are

Supercomputers   Supercomputers are very powerful, very expensive computers that are capable of processing billions of instructions in an instant. They usually have specialised scientific or engineering functions. Examples of the uses of supercomputers are for weather forecasting or monitoring the wind flow and airframe stress of full-size experimental designs in huge wind tunnels. Such computer systems are designed specifically for this use, and consequently their cost is considerable.

Mainframe computers   Mainframe computers usually occupy the whole of a specially air-conditioned room. They would be used by large multinational organisations with great data-processing needs such as banks and large insurance companies. Today they have found a relatively new role as Internet servers. Mainframe computers can vary in size, but each is quite costly.

Personal computers (PCs)   In the late 1970s, Intel Corporation managed to put the main functioning parts of a computer onto a single integrated circuit. IBM thought that there might be a need for a computer that would be small enough to fit onto a desktop. In 1981, they incorporated Intel's microprocessor into the first personal computer. Many other manufacturers made clones of this computer, but the name *personal computer* stuck. Today they are simply referred to as *PCs*. Today's PCs have significant processing power and an immense range of uses in the workplace, at home, and within schools. PCs cost from around £500 to £2,000, depending on their quality and capability.

Portable computers   Portable computers may not be any less powerful than personal computers, but they have many different characteristics. Within this category, we can place *laptops, notebooks,* and *personal digital assistants (PDAs)*. The common characteristic is that they are all battery powered. The rechargeable battery packs can be quite heavy; early designs certainly were. Today they are considerably lighter, and once charged, they can function for a few hours.

Laptops tend to be about the size of an A4 pad, whilst notebooks are smaller and are sometimes referred to as *palmtops*, as they are small enough to sit in the palm of your hand. This is really the smallest type of design because they are restricted by the requirement to provide a useable keyboard. PDAs get around this problem by providing a pen or a stylus in order to select characters. PDAs are designed to be truly hand-held whilst in use. There is a conflict of interest with PDAs, having something that is small enough to perhaps fit in your pocket whilst at the same time having something that has a big enough screen and keyboard to work with. Some PDAs have add-on keyboards. Whilst it is quite possible to upgrade PCs, it is not usually possible to upgrade a PDA.

Portable computers are useful to provide computing power whilst on the move or at a business meeting. They provide a solution for any situation where *mains power* is not always available or convenient. Such computers usually provide some method of transferring files between themselves and a larger PC. The cost of portable computers tends to be more than that of a PC. For example, you can expect to pay nearly twice as much for a laptop with the same capabilities of a PC.

Network computers   A *network* is a set of computers connected together so that they can communicate with and transmit data between each other. Today the use of computer networks is commonplace within many organisations. Controlling such a network would be a central computer, known as a *file server* or simply *server*, with many other computer terminals connected to it in a certain configuration. These other computers are normally PCs, although a modern network can allow for the connection of portable computers. The server could possibly be a mainframe computer. On commercial networks, people are usually given a username and password, which they must enter before they can use the system.

Main Parts of a Personal Computer

All computers, of whatever size, have the same basic components: input devices, the processor, output devices, and auxiliary storage. Each device that makes up a computer system can be put into one of these categories. When trying to understand a system, it helps to be able to break it down in this fashion. Figure 1.1 shows how these four components work together.

FIGURE 1.1   Components of a computer

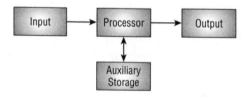

This model is sometimes referred to as the *four-stage model. Auxiliary storage* is sometimes called *secondary storage* and covers all the components used to store your data whilst you are processing it and used to store this data for possible retrieval at a later time.

Figure 1.2 shows the most common setup of a personal computer system. Inside the base unit are all of the electronics and circuits for the functioning of the computer. The main component that many of you have probably heard of is the processor, often referred to as the *CPU (central processing unit)*. This is one of the components that dictates the capability of the computer system. The base unit also contains the computer's memory.

FIGURE 1.2 A common computer system

Memory is basically divided into two different types: *RAM (random access memory)* that can be both read from and written to, and *ROM (read-only memory)* that can only be read from. Devices such as the CPU and memory are plugged into a main board called a *motherboard*. It is this motherboard that contains the electronics that enable all the devices to work together.

The disk drives that store the information either cannot be seen as they are inside the base unit or they are accessible from the front of the base unit. Some drives are completely external devices connected to the computer with a trailing lead. The disk drives that are accessible from the front are floppy drives, CD-ROM drives, and DVD drives. The drive unseen inside the computer is the hard disk drive. An *LED (light-emitting diode)* on the front of the base unit usually indicates when this is being accessed. *Hard drives* are where the programs that run on the computer are stored. Hard drives can also be used to store personal computer data such as work files and documents. The capacity of a hard drive is far greater than that of a CD-ROM or a floppy disk.

There are more input and output devices used than the ones shown in Figure 1.2. You can use a microphone for direct voice input, a bar code reader, a scanner, or even a digital camera. Output can take the form of sound and video. You can use a plotter that draws with pens rather than prints. There are other specialist forms of input such as for bank cheques that have magnetic ink on them and are read by a dedicated reader.

All the devices that attach to the base unit are termed *peripherals*. They are provided to perform a specific function. Some peripherals, such as speakers, may be provided as part of a computer package when it is purchased. Others, such as a microphone, may not.

Computer Performance

There are many factors that influence a computer's performance. The performance of a computer is judged on such factors as how quickly and efficiently an application runs and how long it takes to save a file to memory and to hard disk. If the computer is to be used for graphic-intensive work, the quality of the display and how quickly it is refreshed are considered. These types of criteria are often termed *benchmarks* and are used to compare one system with another. Such comparisons can be found in many popular computer magazines.

The type of microprocessor has an obvious effect on the overall performance. The faster a processor "runs," then potentially, the better the performance of the PC. The faster processors have larger numbers indicated in their name or in their specification. This number is usually followed by the symbol *Hz (hertz)*. A 600MHz *(megahertz)* processor is going to outperform a 166MHz processor. Other considerations are as follows:

More memory generally improves the performance of a PC so it can pre-load more program code into memory where it can be accessed quicker.   This is usually indicated as RAM size. Having constantly to go back to the hard disk drive for more program code slows down a system.

The type of hard drive fitted can affect the system performance.   Hard drives have a stated access time. This is the time taken from when a signal is issued to read data from the drive to when data has been reliably read. Access times are stated in milliseconds (msec), with typical values of current drives being between 7 and 11 msec. This may not sound like much, but compared to the speed that a microprocessor runs at, a few milliseconds can seem like a lifetime.

Using a hard drive that is nearly full to its capacity can affect performance.   Popular operating systems such as Windows create a temporary file on the hard drive to help it whilst it is running. This file is deleted when Windows is shut down. If there is not enough free hard drive space, a file of less-than-optimum size is created, meaning more time-consuming passing of data.

When running more than one program at once, the performance of a PC can visibly suffer. Running multiple programs at once is called *multitasking*. The more programs that are run at the same time, the greater the decrease in performance. The computer needs to remember where it was up to in the program that it was running so that it can pick it back up cleanly as well as restore the data it was using. All of this requires intensive memory usage.

A powerful graphics card can improve computer performance by displaying the screen contents more quickly and clearly.   These are specialised cards that today have their own type of processor and memory on board. This relieves some of the burden off the main processor and memory. Some programs involve complex graphics that can change quite rapidly whilst being shown on the computer screen. With such graphic-intensive programs, a powerful graphics card can provide a distinct improvement.

It is not just any one of these components that makes a computer seem to speed along but a balance between all of them. It's no use having a very fast processor struggling with very little memory. It will simply spend most of its potential transferring data from disk to memory. Likewise, a particularly slow hard drive can cause a bottleneck in an otherwise well-specified system.

Summary

In this chapter, you had a general overview of IT concepts. Hardware is any physical part of a computer system. Software refers to the programs that run on a computer system and allow you to do work. IT refers to the broader category of information technology.

You learned about the different types of computer systems: supercomputers, mainframe computers, personal computers, and portable computers. Each type is basically classed according to its capability and use.

A network is a set of computers connected together and able to communicate with each other. These are usually under the control of a central server.

Computer systems consist of input devices, processors, output devices, and auxiliary storage. Peripheral devices are devices that can be attached to the processing unit to carry out a specialised job. Not all peripherals are necessarily provided as a standard part of a computer system.

Computer performance depends upon the type of microprocessor, the amount of memory installed, the type of hard drive, and the type of graphics card fitted. Optimum performance can be gained by achieving the correct balance of these components.

Chapter

2

Hardware

IN THIS CHAPTER YOU WILL LEARN HOW TO

- ✓ Recognise the functions of the CPU and how its speed is measured.
- ✓ Understand the different types of computer memory and how memory is measured.
- ✓ Identify some of the main devices for inputting data.
- ✓ Identify some of the common output devices for displaying the results of processing.
- ✓ Understand that some devices are both input and output devices.
- ✓ Compare the different storage devices in terms of speed, capacity, and cost.
- ✓ Understand the purpose of formatting a disk.

As noted in the previous chapter, the term *hardware* refers to the physical parts of the computer. This chapter takes a closer look at some of the hardware components in a computer system.

Central Processing Unit

The central processing unit (CPU) lies at the heart of any computer system. It is the main component that is responsible for executing, or running, the software. The software programs are translated into a series of codes made up from 1s and 0s that the CPU can understand. A certain code means a certain operation needs to be carried out. A CPU has various discrete units to help it in these tasks. For example, there is an *arithmetic and logic unit (ALU)* that takes care of the mathematics and logical data comparisons that need to be performed. A *control register* makes sure everything happens in the right sequence. An important task of the CPU is to access memory for the purpose of placing data there—writing data, and looking at what data is stored—reading data.

In the early days of computing, all of these separate functions performed by the CPU were on separate circuit boards. It was in the late 1970s that the Intel Corporation managed to put all of these functioning parts onto a single integrated circuit that became known as a *microprocessor*. These much smaller devices led to the development of the personal computer. The microprocessor resides within a specially designed slot on the motherboard. The *motherboard* is the main circuit board inside a PC. All the other components are either slotted into or soldered to this board.

The microprocessor communicates with the rest of the system by means of three types of buses. These *buses* are really no more than sets of parallel electronic conductors, sets of wires, or tracks on the circuit board. The actual data travels along a *data bus*. The information concerning the exact location of where data is stored travels along an *address bus*. Signals to synchronise access to the various devices, such as whether to read or write data, travel along the *control bus*.

Microprocessor Performance

The type of microprocessor installed within a system can greatly affect its performance. It is rare that a system would have more than one processor installed; a file server is perhaps a good example of a system that may have two processors. In the past, microprocessors were given numbers rather than names. Each development was a significant improvement on its predecessor.

Originally, the first IBM personal computers had an 8080 microprocessor that was quickly superseded by the 8086. Subsequently, the 80286, 80386, and 80486 have followed these. (It is common to drop the 80 and just call them 486s, for example.) Today, as you can see in Figure 2.1, we've moved away from numbers, and we have the Pentium, Pentium II, Pentium III, and Pentium 4 (P4) processors. (Intel produces Pentiums, whilst AMD produces 586s and Athlon processors, which are essentially variations on the same theme.)

FIGURE 2.1   The continuous improvement of microprocessors

8080 ➤ 8086 ➤ 80286 ➤ 80386 ➤ 80486 ➤ Pentium ➤ Pentium II ➤ Pentium III ➤ Pentium 4

All microprocessors are not created equal. The later versions were all improvements upon earlier designs. These improvements invariably involved an increase in the amount of data handled at any one instance and an increase in clock speed.

The speed at which a microprocessor executes its instructions is governed by the speed of an internal clock. The number of clock pulses per second is measured in hertz (Hz), with one pulse per second referred to as 1Hz. Early microprocessors ran at around 8MHz (8,000,000 pulses per second). Pentium III processors run at speeds of up to 1GHz (1,000,000,000Hz), and Pentium 4 processors run at speeds of up to 3.06GHz (3,066,666,666Hz). In theory, a 1GHz Pentium processor executes instructions twice as fast as a 500MHz Pentium processor.

There are a variety of factors that influence a computer's performance other than just pure clock speed. Don't forget to consider all the factors.

With the modern processor running at these speeds, it is quite easy to appreciate that hard disk access times of milliseconds (msec = 0.001 of a second) can seem like an age. Also, processors that run at these top speeds generate considerable heat, so such computers therefore require elaborate cooling systems. Some of these cooling systems can seem quite noisy.

The unit hertz (Hz) was adopted in the 1930s in honour of German physicist Heinrich Hertz. Hertz completed work in the late 1880s on electromagnetic waves. He was the first person to send and receive radio waves. It is used to indicate a measurement of the number of cycles per second.

Memory

The next major element of a computer system is *memory*. Whilst the concept of memory in the everyday world is an abstract one, in the computer realm the term refers to specific bits of hardware.

Types of Memory

Memory is divided into two main types: ROM and RAM. Both are electronic components contained within the computer's base unit. ROM contains programs and data that are written into it at the time of manufacture. The data and programs can be read and used by the computer, but not altered in any way. They are *read only*. There is ROM inside the computer that "wakes up" the system when the computer is first switched on. It checks the computer's own components to make sure they are working properly. It is responsible for loading other aspects of the system that then largely take over. This process is referred to as *booting up*, the action of the computer "pulling itself up by its bootstraps." ROM contains important data that ensures the system runs smoothly. When power is removed, the data in a ROM is not lost.

RAM is the main memory. The microprocessor uses RAM to both read data from and write data to. Data may be taken from RAM, altered by the processing that takes place and then stored back into memory. Parts of the operating system are copied into RAM when the computer is switched on. Application programs are initially loaded into RAM when they are selected for use. Whilst the program is being executed, the work you produce is also stored in RAM. RAM is said to be *volatile*. When the power is removed from a computer, all the work that you've done since you last saved your work will be lost! Remember to save your work at regular intervals. Data loss in the event of a power cut can be minimised with the use of an *uninterruptible power supply (UPS)*. This is basically a device containing a battery. If a power failure occurs, the battery supplies enough power to enable any open files to be saved and the computer to be closed down properly without the loss of any data.

When investigating the specification of a computer system and the type of microprocessor, you may come across the term *cache memory* (pronounced *cash*). Cache memory is a form of RAM that is very fast but expensive in comparison to ordinary RAM. Cache memory is situated between the processor and main memory and is used to store frequently used or recently used program instructions. As access to this cache is much faster than access to main memory, computer performance is enhanced.

Memory Size

The stated size of computer memory can be confusing at first glance. Why is a kilo 1024 and not 1000? A little time spent studying the origins and design development of computer systems can help to unravel this mystery.

Computers are essentially digital devices. They work with data that is physically at one of two different voltage levels. In practice, these two levels are referred to as 0 and 1. For our purposes, it doesn't really matter if the levels are 0V and +5V, which are typical values, merely that there are two different entities. The computer just needs to detect a certain level that is some distance from the other. This is sometimes likened to the brain receiving pulses of energy via our nervous system.

As we use just these two levels, binary arithmetic has been adopted to help when working at this machine level: 0 to represent one level, or perhaps false, and 1 to represent the opposite level, or perhaps true. A single binary digit, a 1 or a 0, is called a *bit* (for example, 1). Eight bits are called a *byte* (for example, 10011101). Four bits, half a byte, are called a *nibble* (for example, 1001).

Eight bits (a byte) are important because some of the first basic microprocessors could only work with data eight bits long. They were said to have a word length of eight bits. It is from this premise that further design work was based and has since developed.

Each memory location is capable of holding a byte of data (eight bits) and must be given a discrete address. This is just the same as the way in which each phone number needs to be unique. As with phone numbers, we need to add more digits if we want to have more capacity for unique numbers.

In computing a kilobyte, KB is actually 1024 bytes. It doesn't really matter if you cannot remember the exact values. If it is easier, think of them with their correct values of kilo = 1000; mega = 1,000,000; giga = 1,000,000,000; and tera = 1,000,000,000,000. It may be simpler to remember that a kilo is a thousand, a mega is a million, a giga is a billion (a thousand million), and a tera is a trillion (a million million).

To get an idea of how all of this relates to your work, you need to understand that it takes one byte to hold the binary code for each letter on the keyboard; for example, 01100101 is "A" and 10010111 is "a". Each *character* is represented by a byte of data. A word contains lots of bytes, one for each character. A sentence further increases the bytes used—don't forget about the spaces and punctuation marks. Information containing the layout and fonts used also needs to be stored. A whole document saved as a file on a floppy disk can take up kilobytes of space.

A *field* of information may be of a certain format, consisting of a number of characters. A whole number may actually take two bytes of storage. A complete set of fields related to a single entity, for example, a person, form a complete *record*. This record can be many bytes. If you have a lot of these records stored within a *file*, 1KB of data is starting to seem quite small. It is for these reasons that today we have storage devices that are measured in gigabytes. In order to help organise such storage devices, related files are kept in *folders* or *directories*. If the files can grow quite large, then these folders can be even larger.

 A record may be quite empty, with many of the fields left blank or not totally filled, yet the storage space for this record can still be as great as a record that's totally filled. This is because the computer's filing system may reserve the same space for each record whether all the fields are full or not. This can seem like wasted space, but that's the way it is. If a field is declared as being 50 characters long, then space for 50 characters is reserved even if they are not all used. Good initial design can overcome some of this waste.

RAM is measured in MB. PCs today have a minimum of 128MB of RAM, a more common value being 256MB. PCs can have much more RAM installed. It is the need for the software to function adequately that can influence the amount of RAM that's necessary. Windows 98 functions with 32MB of RAM. But if a memory-intensive program is run from within Windows 98, the system may slow down appreciably, so a user may wish to install more RAM.

Cache memory is measured in kilobytes (KB) rather than in megabytes (MB). 128KB and 256KB are typical cache sizes.

Input Devices

The need to capture data quickly and accurately has led to the development of many different input devices, each designed with a specific purpose in mind. These peripheral devices need to be able to capture the data and present it in a form that is readable by the computer system.

Some of the common input devices are described in this section.

Keyboard

Keyboards are perhaps the most common input devices used with personal computers and therefore the most easily recognised. Keyboards are set out in a QWERTY layout, just as a typewriter, for efficient use. Although there are no standard keyboards, a common layout used to have 102 keys. Today this has slightly increased, with the inclusion of specialist keys such as those to access the Windows Start menu.

Mouse

The mouse is used to control the position of the cursor on the screen and to make selections. It is possible to control the position of the cursor by using the keyboard, but many users prefer to use a mouse. New users can find a mouse a little difficult to use initially, but many soon become proficient. The cursor can change shape depending on the task being performed.

TABLE 2.1 Cursor Shapes

Cursor	Name	Occurs
↖	Pointer	To select menu items, file icons, or graphics
I	I-beam	To place the cursor into text in order to add or delete
┼	Crosshairs	To draw lines, boxes, circles, and so on

A single click on the left-hand mouse button inserts the I-beam cursor into text or selects an icon or graphic. A double-click on the left-hand button opens a file or selects a word for editing. Clicking and holding down the left-hand mouse button whilst the mouse is moved is called *dragging*. This enables items to be moved around the desktop. Clicking the right mouse button often makes visible a context-sensitive shortcut menu.

Keyboards and mice do not necessarily have to be attached to the computer's base unit. Some now use infrared, or radio, waves to connect to the computer. These are generally termed *cordless* or *wireless*.

Other Input Devices

Beyond the standard mouse and keyboard, there are a variety of other tools that can be used to input data into a computer.

Trackballs

These are used just like a traditional mouse, but unlike a mouse, the ball is on top (see Figure 2.2). The user rolls the ball to move the cursor on the screen. These input devices are commonly used on computers where there is not enough space to use a traditional mouse.

FIGURE 2.2   A trackball input device

Scanners

A scanner enables you to input graphics, photographs, and text into the computer. If text is scanned, it is merely a picture of the text that is captured; the text cannot be edited. OCR (optical character recognition) software can be used to make the text capable of being edited as if it had been keyed in via the keyboard. Scanners are widely used by graphic-intensive businesses.

Optical Mark Readers

Optical mark readers (OMRs) scan a pre-printed form using infrared light for simple marks made in specific places on the form. They are used for things such as marking test answers and for some lottery entries. They provide a very quick method of ascertaining choices made from quite an extensive list of options.

Bar Code Readers

Striped bar codes are now found on most products in our shops. The different thicknesses of the lines of the bars correspond with different numbers. These carry information on the country of origin, the manufacturer, and the article itself. The reader gathers this information by measuring the bars and spaces and converting them to a machine-readable form.

Magnetic Strips

Strips of thin magnetic tape are attached to plastic cards. They are used in conjunction with a specialist reader through which the card is swiped. Playback heads—similar to those in a tape recorder—read the information encoded onto the strip. These are used extensively on cash and debit cards. They are thought to have added security as they can only be read with specialist readers and dedicated software.

Touchpads

Touchpads are essentially pressure-sensitive switches that are placed under a protective plastic film. They can often be seen in two forms: as a keyboard and as a replacement for a mouse. On portable computers, an area can be provided for the user to run one's finger over to imitate the movement of a mouse. Tapping the pad can perform the equivalent of a mouse click.

Touchpads can be used instead of conventional keyboards where there is a risk of dirt or liquids causing problems. They are particularly useful in hostile environments such as at sea where sea-salt spray may damage an ordinary keyboard. They are also used to aid people with physical disabilities to select items. Such keyboards are sometimes termed a *concept* keyboard. They were originally designed for use by young children, enabling them, for example, to press on a symbol rather than have to try spelling a certain item. Today, touchpads are used widely in restaurants to speed up data entry and improve accuracy.

Light Pens and Graphics Tablets

Drawing with a pen on a tablet is more natural for artists or designers who may be used to using more traditional types of tools, such as pencils and brushes, than drawing by moving a mouse around. The graphics tablet can have certain libraries attached, enabling an architect, for example, to select a pre-drawn graphic such as a door or light fitting. A light pen looks like a pen with a wire connecting it to the computer. These devices are mainly found in graphics studios and architects' offices.

Joysticks

Joysticks, illustrated in Figure 2.3, consist of a lever that can be moved in any direction to control a pointer, or more likely, the direction of movement within a computer game. They function in a similar fashion to a mouse; however, with a mouse, the pointer stops when the movement of the mouse stops. With a joystick, the movement continues in the same direction the pointer is moving until the lever is returned to a central position. Speed of movement increases the further away from the central position the lever is moved. Joysticks have at least two buttons used in games for such things as to fire, change views, or increase acceleration. Joysticks are said to give a more realistic feel to games and simulations.

FIGURE 2.3   A joystick input device

Digital Cameras

Digital cameras are used just like traditional cameras. However, instead of using film, the images are stored in the camera's memory or directly to a floppy disk. Many digital cameras have a small screen on which the photographs can be displayed. Unwanted pictures can be deleted directly from the camera.

Microphones

Sound can be input into a computer system via a microphone. The sound is stored as digital data within a file that can be played back through certain applications. It is possible to edit the sound in a variety of ways once it is stored. Voice recognition systems exist where a spoken word is analysed and compared with those voices that the computer knows. If a match is found, the word is recognised. Speech recognition software enables the spoken word to be directly input into an application such as a word-processing package. This has obvious advantages for the speed of data input and for those with physical difficulties.

There is, at present, a great deal of difference in speech recognition software packages between the less-expensive end of the market and the high-priced top end of the market. The less-expensive packages have a limited vocabulary and are not very good at distinguishing between words that sound similar. These packages also require the user to speak more slowly, with a pause between each word. The user needs to train the software to the sound of their voice by reading set passages and phrases, thus enabling the software to work with different users. Specialist vocabularies are available for such users as pathologists and accountants.

Output Devices

Output devices are peripherals that enable you to interpret the results of the computer's processing or present those results in a form that is suitable for reprocessing by a computer at a later date. Without any output devices, the computer becomes no more than an electronic pinboard. Like input devices, there are many output devices, each designed for a particular purpose. The more popular output devices are described in this section, starting with the most common: the visual display unit.

Visual Display Units (VDUs)

The term *visual display unit (VDU)* is used to describe any output unit that displays the result of processing in a visual form on an electronic output unit.

Cathode Ray Tube (CRT) Monitors

Computer screens that use a cathode ray tube are referred to as *monitors*. A *cathode ray tube (CRT)*, contains an electron gun at the rear of the tube that fires electrons at phosphor dots on the back of the screen. These dots glow when the electrons hit them. The dots are very small; they cannot be seen by the naked eye. There needs to be a certain distance between the gun and the screen that increases as the size of the screen increases. This is why large screen monitors are also quite deep. This is a hindrance to the development of large screen monitors using this technology.

CRT monitors can be colour or monochrome. Monochrome monitors can be white, orange, or green on a dark background. Orange and green are supposed to be easier on the user's eyes than black and white. There are very few monochrome monitors used today.

Most computer systems are set up to display a certain number of colours on a monitor. The more colours displayed, the closer to real life the images seem. The more colours displayed, of course, the greater the need for a high-specification system. Not all systems can display all depths of colour.

Like conventional TV screens, monitors are measured diagonally from corner to corner. The standard screen has a size ratio of 4:3, width to height. Common sizes are between 14" and 19".

Resolution is a measure of the clarity of the computer display. It involves a unit known as a *pixel*. A pixel or *picture element* is the smallest unit that can be displayed on a screen. A pixel on a colour monitor consists of three phosphor dots: one to display the colour red, one for the colour green, and a third for the colour blue. Using a mixture of these three, all other colours can be constructed. For a monitor to be able to create millions of colours, it must be capable of displaying 256 different shades of each of these three colours. A typical distance between pixels is 0.28 mm.

The resolution is usually expressed in terms of the number of scanned lines high by the number of pixels wide. Three standards have emerged: VGA (Video Graphics Array), SVGA (Super Video Graphics Array), and XGA (Extended Video Graphics Array). The respective resolutions are

VGA	640×480 pixels
SVGA	800×600 pixels
XGA	1024×768 pixels

Low resolution can give a jagged look to text and graphics as a result of the small number of large pixels used to form the picture. High resolution gives greater clarity and sharpness by displaying text and graphics with many smaller pixels. The difference can usually be seen on curved edges. A high resolution is therefore particularly important for design and graphic work.

The quality of a monitor also depends on its *scan rate*, also referred to as the *refresh rate*. The scan rate is a measure of the number of times the screen is refreshed, or redrawn, per second. This is necessary because the phosphor dots that are illuminated to give the display fade rapidly. Most modern monitors can operate at different scan rates and are known as *multiscan* or *multisync* monitors. A low scan rate causes flickering and can cause eyestrain. A minimum refresh rate is said to be 75Hz.

Liquid Crystal Display (LCD) Panels

LCD stands for liquid crystal display. These displays rely on the fact that certain liquids alter their ability to reflect light when a voltage is applied to them. This type of display is found in digital watches and in some domestic appliances. They were once only commonly used for laptop computers, but today they are becoming popular for conventional PCs. LCD screens are much slimmer than a cathode ray tube (CRT) type monitor and therefore take up much less space on a desk top. Technology has advanced so that screens of 15", 17", 18", and 19" are available, but presently the cost of these is higher that the CRT equivalent.

Printers

Printed computer output is referred to a *hard copy*. Printers can be categorised under two main types: impact printers and non-impact printers. Paper can be fed into either type of printer in a number of ways. The three main categories of printers are as follows:

Friction feed   As in a typewriter, friction feed is where a single sheet of paper is gripped between two rollers. Standard printing paper can be used with these printers.

Traction feed   In a traction-feed printer, specially designed paper with holes along the edges fits over wheels with corresponding spokes for the holes. As the wheels revolve, the paper is pulled through the printer. Continuous stationery needs to be used with these printers.

Cut sheet feed or tray feed   The type of paper is automatically drawn one sheet at a time through the printer. Standard printing paper can be used with these printers.

Impact Printers

Impact printers have a carbon ribbon, and characters are "hammered" onto the paper through that carbon ribbon, just as with a typewriter. There can be problems with noise when impact printers are used.

A dot matrix printer is an inexpensive impact printer that has lines of pins programmed to hammer a carbon ribbon onto paper to make a dot. The characters are formed from either 9 or 24 pins. 24-pin versions produce a higher quality of print. They are quite noisy and slow and produce medium-quality text and graphics. Dot matrix printers are very economical to use.

Non-Impact Printers

Non-impact printers use electrostatically charged paper to create a printed character, as in the case of laser printers, or a spray of ink, as in the case of ink-jet or bubble printers.

Ink-jet or bubble printers are non-impact printers. A jet of quick-drying ink is forced from a nozzle and acquires an electrical charge. The jet then passes between charged plates that deflect it to the right spot on the paper. These printers can produce cheap colour output. They are quiet but not very fast. They are best used when a relatively low, good-quality output is required. These are a popular choice for home use.

A laser printer is a fast and quiet non-impact printer. They are quite expensive but produce high-quality text and graphics. Colour laser printers are particularly expensive. A toner cartridge inside the printer releases fine powder that sticks to the paper wherever it is electrically charged during the printing process. They function in a similar fashion to a photocopier.

Plotters

A plotter is used to produce large drawings created on the computer using one of the many computer-aided design (CAD) programs. Plotters have groups of pens of different thickness, with barrels containing ink in different colours that are each selected in turn. On smaller plotters, up to A2 in size, the paper remains stationary and the pens move over its surface. On larger plotters, the pens move simply up and down whilst the paper is rolled underneath it (see Figure 2.4). These output devices are mainly found in the offices of architects or engineers.

FIGURE 2.4   A plotter output device

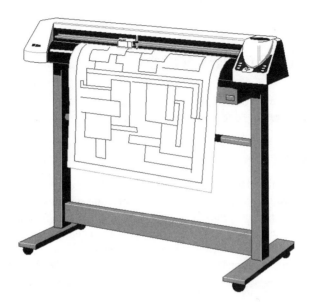

Audio Output

Aside from visual data, a computer can also house and organise audio data such as music, speech, and various other audio signals.

Speakers

Speakers can be attached to a computer system in a similar way to a stereo system. They are usually small in physical size and may be built into the monitor case. Some have their own power source and amplifier. They vary in output capability but can be of a very high quality. Computers fitted with DVD drives can have high-quality surround-sound speaker systems attached. Speakers usually require that the computer be fitted with a sound card.

A *sound card* is a hardware device in the form of a circuit board that fits into a slot on the motherboard. The purpose of the card is to take care of all the sound processing for both input and output.

Speech Synthesisers

This is the production of speech by electronic methods. This is achieved by a combination of software and hardware. Synthesised speech can often be heard when making telephone directory enquires. When the operator has located the desired number, it is often delivered to the caller by a computer-generated voice.

Input/Output Devices

Some devices can perform as both input and output devices. They can both obtain input from the user for further processing and subsequently provide a means of output.

Touch Screens

Touch screens are specially adapted screens that let you select from the available options by the press of your finger (see Figure 2.5). It's a little like selecting with a mouse. The disadvantage with such screens is that the information and options available are often limited. These are not the sort of interfaces to use if large amounts of information need to be portrayed or if multiple selections need to be made. The screen is able to show further output depending upon the input made by the user.

FIGURE 2.5   A touch screen device

Such screens are criss-crossed by horizontal and vertical beams of infrared light. When a finger is placed on the glass screen, two of these intersecting beams are broken and the position of the finger can be detected.

These screens are very user friendly and can be seen in such places as shopping precincts and tourist centres. They are often used in cinemas for the sale of tickets by credit card. In a shopping precinct or tourist centre, they are used as a POI (point of information).

Storage Devices

When working with applications, the work completed is stored temporarily in RAM. As this work would be lost when the computer is switched off, there needs to be some way of saving it. The work is saved in what is known as *secondary storage*. Computer memory is referred to as *primary* or *main storage*. Secondary storage covers all other forms of storage such as disks and tapes:

Hard disks   The main type of storage medium used at the present time is the disk. The terms *hard disk* and *hard drive* are often used interchangeably when referring to the same type of medium. Hard disks with a capacity on the order of gigabytes are usually located within the computer's base unit and are used to store the operating system and the application programs. Hard drives are in-built into a computer system when new. Additional hard drives can be added to give greater storage area, supplementing the original drive. Hard drives are not portable devices, although there are some available that are external devices that plug into the computer in the same way a printer does. Programs, or at least parts of them, are loaded into RAM from the hard drive for use by the microprocessor. Some programs set up temporary files on the hard drive whilst the program is running and erase them when the program is shut down. Hard disks are slower to access by the computer than RAM.

Floppy disks   Floppy disks, 3.5", are used to store work and data files on. They have a capacity of 1.44 megabytes. Floppy disks are much slower to access than hard disks. The greatest advantage of these disks is their portability. The ability to take a 3.5" floppy disk between different personal computers and be able to use it holds great appeal and is perhaps the main reason they are still in widespread use today.

Compact discs (CDs)   As 1.44MB is actually quite a small storage capacity, CDs have become more popular, especially for distributing software. At present, many CDs are ROMs—they can only be read from, and you cannot store any additional data on them. They are said to be WORM devices—written once and read many times. However, we ought to simply refer to them as CDs now that recordable and rewriteable CDs are becoming more popular.

Recordable CDs can be written to once and then read many times. A rewriteable CD can be written and overwritten many times. The capacity of most CDs is around 650 megabytes or 74 minutes. There are larger capacity CDs available that are 700MB or 80 minutes. CDs can be accessed more quickly than floppy disks, but they are slower than hard disks. CDs are of course very portable devices. CD drives are rated in different speeds: ×4, ×8, ×24, or ×40, for example. These speeds relate to audio speed. In computing, data needs to be read much faster than when reproducing audio. ×4 means 4 times faster than audio speed.

Digital versatile disks (DVDs)   A more recent innovation has been the digital versatile disk (DVD) drive. These are high-capacity CD-ROM disks that can store up to 17GB of data. The latest disks have two layers, and the drives use two different lasers—each with a different focal length to read each of the layers. Each layer holds 4.7GB of data. It's therefore said that a dual-sided, dual-density disk holds approximately 17GB of data. Such disks are used to store entire feature-length films. Some drives are able to write to such disks. Some DVD drives that can write to such disks can only be read back on similar drives. Computers today are being sold with dual CD-ROM and DVD drives. DVD technology seems destined to be popular and to a great extent has already replaced videotape.

Tape or data cartridges   Tape or data cartridges have large storage capacities, but they can be slow to access the data. They cannot go directly to data as on a disk. The tape is very similar to audiotape but of a much higher quality, as they need to be accelerated and decelerated at much higher speeds in order to try and improve access time. To access just two or three records on a tape can mean a great deal of winding and rewinding. Tape drives are used to back up or to archive large amounts of data where access might only be necessary in an emergency or on a rare planned interval.

Zip drives   Zip drives are another example of a high-capacity yet portable storage medium. Zip disks are a little larger and heavier than 3.5" floppies but have a capacity of between 100MB and 750MB. They can be included within a personal computer system as an internal device, or as something that can be plugged in when needed. They are not as portable as CDs or floppy disks because there are just not that many of these drives around. The advent of the rewritable CD-ROM and DVD drive may have sealed their fate. They are mainly used for backup and archive functions, not something one would constantly run programs from.

The relative cost of each of these storage options varies considerably, and that cost is further influenced by the hardware investment required to use a particular media. Installing a drive to write and rewrite to a CD may be only slightly cheaper than a recordable DVD drive, but the actual recordable media for a DVD is much more expensive. In terms of the cost of portable media, generally a floppy disk is the cheapest, then a recordable CD, and finally DVD and Zip disks. Hard drives can be the most expensive, especially for the larger capacity drives, but it is probably unfair to directly compare the cost of these with more portable devices.

We've chosen not to list actual cost values, as it is impractical given the rate at which costs differ with geography and inevitably change over time.

The following table is provided for comparison of the various storage media.

Media	Capacity	Cost	Speed
Hard disk	20GB–250GB	Most expensive	Fastest
Tape cartridge	2GB–100GB		
Zip disk	100MB–750MB		
DVD	17GB		
CD	650–700MB (74–80 minutes)		
Floppy disk	1.44MB	Least expensive	Slowest

It should be noted that the relative speed of access is provided only as a guide, as this is dependent upon external factors such the number of software applications running at the time of access and the hardware the media is used with. The difference in speed between DVDs and CDs is relatively small. For instance, DVDs tend to be accessed for large volumes of data (DVDs are often used for storing such data as video in digital form). Therefore the relative access time to read a whole data item can be seen as slower in comparison to CDs. Today computers tend not to be fitted with hard drives of less than 20GB. Older machines may have smaller capacity hard drives. Speed of access for media such as Zip disks and tape cartridge is dependent upon the actual physical location of the data. If a lot of winding of the tape is necessary to reach this location, this will cut down access time.

Applications that run on the computer are commonly distributed on portable storage media, but they often need to be copied, or installed, on a computer's hard drive.

Formatting Disks for Use

Before floppy disks and hard disks can be used, they need to be formatted. This is done by the operating system that they are to be used with. The disks are magnetic devices in that the data is written to them and read from them using tiny heads that detect changes in magnetic fields. These changes correspond to the 1s and 0s of the raw data. However, the disk needs to be marked out so that the computer knows where it has stored the files. Formatting a disk does just this; it marks out the disk magnetically so that the data can be written and read from a known place on the disk. 3.5" disks are often purchased pre-formatted.

The formatting procedure sets the disk out in a series of circular tracks broken up by radial sectors. Each intersection gives a block into which data can be written. The first track on a disk is special and holds what is called the *file allocation table (FAT)*. This holds an index of which blocks contain which particular items of data and which blocks are free for use. If the FAT becomes corrupted, the whole disk cannot be used until it has been reformatted. Formatting results in the loss of any previously stored data.

Summary

In this chapter, you learned about the major hardware features of computer systems. The central processing unit (CPU) is the main component of any computer system. It is responsible for executing the software. An important task of the CPU is to access memory for the purpose of placing data there—writing data, and looking at what data is stored—reading data.

All the main components of a CPU are found on one integrated circuit known as a microprocessor. The clock speed of a microprocessor is measured in hertz. One hertz is one cycle per second.

There are two main types of memory: ROM and RAM. ROM is read only and contains programs and data that are written into them at the time of manufacture. RAM forms the computer's main memory and can be both read from and written to. Copies of programs are written into RAM from where they can be accessed by the microprocessor. RAM is volatile, and any data that is not saved will be lost when power is removed.

Cache memory is fast RAM that is situated between the processor and main memory with the main purpose of improving computer performance.

Input devices are peripherals that are able to capture data and present it in a form that is readable by the computer system. Examples of input devices are keyboards, mice, trackballs, scanners, optical mark readers, bar code readers, magnetic strips, light pens, joysticks, digital cameras, and microphones.

Output devices are peripherals that enable you to interpret the results of the computer's processing or present these results in a form that is suitable for reprocessing by computer at a later date. Examples of output devices are monitors, liquid crystal displays, printers, speakers, plotters, and speech synthesisers.

Some devices such as a touch screen can operate both as an input device and as an output device.

Primary or main storage is the computer memory. Secondary storage covers all other forms of storage such as disks and tapes. In this chapter, you learned about various types of storage media: hard disks, floppy disks, CDs, DVD, tapes, data cartridges, and zip drives.

Chapter

3

Software

IN THIS CHAPTER YOU WILL LEARN HOW TO

- ✓ Distinguish between application and system software.
- ✓ Understand the reasons for software versions.
- ✓ Understand the functions of an operating system.
- ✓ Be aware of the different operating systems.
- ✓ Be aware of the common software applications together with their uses.
- ✓ Understand the term graphical user interface (GUI).
- ✓ Understand how computer systems are developed.

Software is the name given to a set of instructions, or programs, that can be run on a computer. There are two types of software: *system* software and *application* software. System software is concerned with controlling the operation of the computer's hardware. Application software is any program that has been written to do a particular job—in other words, calculate a company payroll, manipulate text, and so on. Both types of software interact with each other in order to complete useful work.

There can frequently be different versions of the same software. An original version is usually version 1 or V1.0. If there are small changes made to the software, maybe to get rid of minor bugs or to add support for new hardware, then an upgraded version is released and the number after the decimal point is increased, in other words, version 1.1 or V1.1. These upgrades are sometimes released as *patches* that can be obtained free of charge. It's often possible to download these patches from the Internet. A user with a licence for version 1 can usually upgrade for free as long as it is only a version change after the decimal point, for example, from V1.0 to V1.2.

When major changes are made to software, a whole new version is released and the version number before the decimal point increases, in other words, version 2.0 or V2.0. These versions may look and feel similar to earlier versions, but they perhaps have greater functionality in certain areas. For example, Excel V4.0 added a spell-check capability that was not in Excel V3.0. Such version upgrades need to be purchased, even if a user has an earlier version. It is expected that these later releases are *backward compatible* with earlier versions. This means that data and documents constructed under earlier versions can still be used with the new versions.

Operating System Software

The most important type of system software is the operating system itself. This software loads automatically when the computer is switched on. It controls all of the hardware and ensures that the different components work with each other. For example, the operating system checks for the presence of a keyboard when the computer is first switched on. The *operating system* provides an interface between the user, the applications, and the computer's hardware. Examples of operating systems are

- MS-DOS
- Windows 3.1
- Windows 95
- Windows 98

- Windows 2000
- Windows XP
- Windows NT
- Linux
- Unix
- IBM OS/2
- MacOS

Most of the tasks an operating system performs are invisible to the user; for example, when a key is pressed on the keyboard, it displays the correct character on the monitor. If the operating system fails to load, the computer cannot be used. The number of tasks that the operating system performs varies depending on the size and power of the computer. The operating system of a large mainframe computer that looks after hundreds of users as well as the communication links between them is different from the operating system of a typical personal computer that only deals with one user and a single communication link. Having said this, the tasks that they perform are quite similar in many ways. Some tasks carried out by an operating system are

- Allocating internal memory (RAM)
- Transferring programs and data between disk and RAM
- Controlling input and output devices
- Booting up (starting) the computer
- Checking and controlling user access to prevent unauthorised access
- Logging errors

 There are different types of operating systems, and software bought for one operating system may not run on another. For example, MacOS is designed particularly for Apple Macintosh computers and will not run on a conventional PC.

Graphical User Interfaces

Different operating systems offer different user interfaces. The *user interface* is the way in which the user communicates with the computer. This includes both the hardware and software. A certain type of operating software provides a certain user interface.

The first IBM personal computers came with MS-DOS (Microsoft Disk Operating System). MS-DOS is typified by a black screen, a C prompt, and a flashing cursor awaiting a command to be typed by the user:

```
C:\> _
```

This is not very user friendly because the user has to remember a whole range of commands in order to achieve anything, that is, to achieve anything other than the message, "Bad command or filename." In order to run a program, the user needs to know the name of the application's file and then type this in correctly. There are other commands that need to be learnt, for example, to view the contents of a directory, stopping each time the screen is full, one would type **dir /p**. For some users, remembering all of these commands and their actual syntax is not easy. This type of operating system is often referred to as a *command-line interface*.

Today it is more common for personal computers to use a version of the Microsoft Windows operating system. These utilise *graphical user interfaces (GUIs)*, pronounced "gooeys." Such systems use a combination of pictures (icons) and menus in order to run programs and achieve certain tasks. A mouse is useful to navigate through such systems, although not essential. They are sometimes referred to as a *WIMP environment* as they utilise windows, icons, menus, and pointers.

FIGURE 3.1 The Microsoft Windows XP operating system

The advantage of such operating systems is that all programs are run in exactly the same way, and once users have learned to perform a task within one application, they can usually perform it within another. All Windows-type applications have the same look and feel about them. All of the menus are arranged in the same order and often contain the same commands. By becoming proficient with one application, a user can be partly proficient in another. The user develops what is known as *transferable skills*.

GUIs were the first environment that allowed users of personal computers to multitask—run different applications in separate windows at the same time. This enables users to more easily copy data between applications. GUIs need a more capable machine to be able to run. People who are competent with a command-line interface sometimes criticise GUIs for being slow and cumbersome.

The system software also includes what are known as *drivers*. These are programs that are related to a certain piece of hardware, such as a certain brand of CD drive or a certain printer. Drivers ensure that the hardware runs with a particular operating system. There can be many different drivers for a single hardware device—one driver for each of three versions of an operating system, for example. If you wish to use a certain device, you must ensure that the driver that you are supplied with is for the operating system you intend to use it under.

Application Software

Application software is the term applied to any program that has been written to do a particular job, for example, calculate a company payroll, manipulate text, or produce a drawing. Application software is usually broken down into two sections: general-purpose or generic application software, and specialised application software. These applications can only be run once the operating system has successfully loaded.

Generic or general-purpose application software not only includes word processing, databases, and spreadsheets, but packages such as web browsing, desktop publishing, accounting, graphic packages, and presentation packages.

Word Processing Packages

Word processing applications are used to produce documents such as letters, reports, books, and articles. Today's more powerful computers with increased memory have allowed modern word processing packages to include many extra features that may not have been present in earlier packages. Perhaps the greatest advantage of such a package is that the document can also be saved on disk for future amendment or use.

A modern word processing package allows a user to

- Type, correct, delete, and move text
- Change font size; align text left, right, or centre; set tabs; and set italics and bold
- Find and replace text
- Insert graphics and wrap text around them
- Check spelling and grammar
- Set up templates with type styles for different types of documents
- Work in tables or columns
- Add headers and footers to each page
- Create indexes and tables of contents
- Type equations with mathematical symbols
- Mail merge to send personalised letters to people selected from a list

For more information about word processing applications, please see Part 3 of this book.

Spreadsheet Packages

Spreadsheets are used to store and manipulate tables of numerical data. Text, data, and formulae can be entered so that the data is automatically calculated and can be recalculated if it is altered. They are ideal for storing, calculating, and displaying numerical information. One of the most useful features of a spreadsheet is its ability to perform "What If" calculations. These calculations allow the user to enter or change one or more values and to see how this affects the outcome. Spreadsheets are often used in financial modelling. They are used extensively by such people as engineers, bank personnel, and financial planners.

A modern spreadsheet package allows a user to

- Contain many related sheets within a workbook
- Enter and copy complex formulae
- Set up several different types of graphs
- Use predefined mathematical functions
- Record and create macros
- Allow extensive formatting
- Allow data to be filtered according to multiple criteria
- Trace sources of error

For more information about spreadsheet applications, please see Part 4 of this book.

Database Packages

Databases are used for the storage and retrieval of information. Database programs, or *database management systems (DBMSs)* as they are called, are extremely powerful. These packages allow users to set up tables of data and link them together. These sets of linked data can then be searched according to certain criteria stipulated by the user. More sophisticated database packages include wizards to help the user set up the database, import data from other packages, and customise the database to hide the workings of the package from an inexperienced user. Databases can hold many thousands of records.

A few examples of database application use are

- Details of the books in a library giving the author, title, and subject of each book and allowing books of a particular interest to be found.

- Names and addresses of possible customers sorted by location and interest.

- Details of the items stored in a warehouse, giving location, cost, number currently in stock, and supplier. Items below a stock reorder level can be highlighted.

- Details of students enrolled at a college. Class lists and tutor groups are generated from this information.

For more information about database applications, please see Part 4 of this book.

Web-Browsing Packages

Web-browsing packages are the software that allows users to view pages constructed for use on the World Wide Web. An *Internet service provider (ISP)* often provides a browser as part of the software they supply to the end user, or it may come as part of an operating system. The term *browser* is related to a person "browsing through a magazine." Rather than browsing the Web, many people use the term *surfing*. Surfing the Web is achieved through web-browsing software. The two main packages used are Microsoft Internet Explorer and Netscape Navigator.

These browser packages are distinct from features that allow a user to search the Internet; these are often referred to as *search engines*. A search engine is a piece of software that allows the user to enter search criteria, upon which it then carries out a search of the World Wide Web and returns the results for the user to continue to browse the Internet.

Desktop Publishing (DTP)

Desktop publishing (DTP) packages allow the user to lay out a page exactly as he or she wants it. They allow the entry of text, diagrams, and photographs in a variety of formats. It is easy to change fonts and write in columns. Often a document is prepared using a word processor and then imported into a DTP package, where it can be put into columns, and different typefaces can be used or diagrams added. Text is placed in boxes that can be positioned virtually anywhere on the page. Text from one box can be made to flow into another. Complex pictures and graphics can be prepared in other specialised drawing packages and then imported onto the page before printing.

The edges are now becoming a little blurred between powerful word processing packages and some of the less-expensive DTP packages.

Accounting Packages

These are specialist software packages aimed at small- and medium-sized companies, enabling them to more easily manage their accounts. A larger company may actually have accounting software written especially for them, commonly referred to as *bespoke software*. Knowledge of accounting procedures is required to use these packages effectively to their full capability.

Accounting software produces a balance sheet and a profit/loss statement. The package helps to maintain a General Ledger and Chart of Accounts. The General Ledger allows for a number of accounts and sub-accounts within a company. It assists in the production of a transaction journal and allows this to be broken down in different ways; for example, it may allow VAT to be recorded separately. Transactions are usually automatically reflected in the General Ledger.

It is important that balance sheets and profit/loss statements are produced annually. Account packages allow trial balance sheets to be produced as a check before the end-of-year report is due. Some accounting packages allow a complete audit trail to be completed so that a transaction can be tracked.

It's possible to purchase integrated accounting packages. These packages also take care of purchase and sales order processing, integrating these functions into the whole accounting procedure. Some of these integrated packages also incorporate online banking, employee payroll, inventory management, and time and billing capabilities.

Presentation Packages

These packages are used for presenting information to an audience. They allow for the inputting of text, numerical data, graphs, and images, along with the use of basic animation effects and sound. They allow for quite extensive formatting, usually coming with some standard templates for the user to customise if they wish. The presentation is constructed on a number of slides. The resulting presentation can be shown in a variety of formats. The presentation can be run full screen on a computer system with automated or remote progression through the slides. Alternatively, the slides can be printed onto OHP transparencies, with a set of speaker's notes produced separately. Microsoft PowerPoint is an example of a presentation package.

Integrated Packages

In the past few years, many integrated packages have been produced. These are often called *suites* or *works*. An integrated package contains several generic programs, probably a word processor a graphics package, database, communications (e-mail) software, and spreadsheet. Examples include Microsoft Office, Lotus Smart Suite, Microsoft Works, and ClarisWorks. All the component parts have the same look and feel, and it's very easy to transfer data from one component to another. These integrated packages can prove to be more economical than purchasing each package separately if one intends to use each of the individual packages.

Specialised Application Software

Application software that is not bought "off the shelf" but written especially for a user is called *bespoke software* or *tailor-made software*. Bespoke software can either be developed in house by programmers employed by the user's company or by using an outside agency. Software to produce a particular company's accounts would be of no use for other companies who are likely to run their business in a different manner.

Specialised applications software is designed to carry out a specific task, usually for a particular industry. It is of little use in other situations. Examples include payroll processing, timetabling, and attendance monitoring. With the rise in computers within the home, there's been an increase in specialist software to support a wide variety of interests. These include family tree programs, menu planners, flight simulators, route planners, maps, and city guides.

Systems Development

A computer system may be changed for a number of reasons. It may be that the current system is no longer suitable for its intended purpose. Originally, it may have been fine, but changes in working practices or the expansion of a business can render a system less than ideal. The technology used may have become out of date. A company may wish to take advantage of new services offered by new technology such as online ordering and payment.

There are recognised stages in the development of a computer-based system: analysis, design, programming, testing, and evaluation. This development cycle is known as the *systems life cycle*. A systems analyst would be heavily involved in the initial stages. It is good practice, especially for bespoke software, to involve the intended end user in the various stages of the software development. Feedback from the end user during the specification, design, and testing stages of the system is crucial.

First, an analysis of the problem or situation is carried out for which the software is required. The type, amount, and frequency of the data to be processed are considered at this stage. A feasibility study is carried out to see if it is technically and economically possible to complete the work within the required timescale.

If it is decided to continue with the project, the systems analyst produces a specification for the project to be constructed against. Designs for the software can now be produced. This design covers proposals about designs for the user interface and how any data will be processed. The user interface covers how the software will look and feel. The software is then written.

Once the program has been written, it is tested to ensure that it meets the prescribed specification. Software producers need to demand very high standards for the testing of software. No one would want to purchase a less-than-perfect product. The people testing the system should try to deliberately make it fail in some way. It is vitally important to discover any serious shortcomings in the new system before it is released. Colleagues who have not been involved with the actual production themselves should test a program in house. This is often termed *alpha testing*.

The next stage is to release the software to selected users to test and report bugs before the final release date. This is termed *beta testing*. This stage gives the developers the opportunity to test the software on different hardware. Differences in microprocessors, memory size, and sound and video cards, for example, can all affect software performance. The developers receive feedback on this performance during the beta testing stage.

An evaluation report is produced on the performance and limitations of the new system or software.

Summary

There are two types of software: system software and application software. System software is concerned with controlling the operation of the computer hardware. Application software is any program that has been written to do a particular job. Examples of system software are the various versions of Windows, MS-DOS, Linux, and Unix. Hardware drivers are examples of system software that relate to the particular functioning of a hardware device. Today, most operating systems provide a graphical user interface (GUI).

Application software packages include word processing, spreadsheet, database, desktop publishing, web-browsing, accounting, and presentation packages.

An integrated package contains several generic programs. These can prove to be more economical than purchasing each package separately if you intend to use each of the individual packages. Data should be more easily transferred between the different elements of an integrated package.

The processes of analysis, design, programming, testing, and evaluation are all involved in the development of computer-based systems.

Software needs to be extensively tested. This may involve both in-house testing, termed alpha testing, and testing outside of the company on a wide variety of systems by selected people, termed beta testing.

Chapter

4

Information Networks

IN THIS CHAPTER YOU WILL LEARN HOW TO

- ✓ Understand the terms local area network and wide area network.
- ✓ Understand the term client-server.
- ✓ Know the reasons for using a network.
- ✓ Understand the term intranet.
- ✓ Understand the term extranet.
- ✓ Understand the concept of the Internet and its uses.
- ✓ Understand the use of the telephone network in computing.
- ✓ Understand the terms analogue, digital, modem, and transfer rate.

Many computers do not stand alone but are connected to other computers for the purpose of communication in what is termed a *network*. It is impossible to ignore computer networks in your daily life. They are in the smallest of offices to the largest of banks, and with the advent of the Internet, they are truly worldwide. With such wide usage, there are significant benefits to be had:

- Networks can provide a hierarchically organised storage area where people can store files they need to share with others. Rather than passing around files on a floppy disk, for instance, co-workers can be given access to a common place on the network (known as a drive) where they can swap files with one another. These drives can be organised by department or subject matter so that people can efficiently locate the files they need.

- There can often be bottlenecks when more than one person needs access to information. Letting more than one person have access to a database at one time can improve productivity. If there is a lot of data to be manually entered into a database, shared access has an obvious advantage. As long as controls are put into place, this type of sharing can be achieved efficiently whilst at the same time maintaining the integrity of the data.

- Printers and other expensive peripheral devices that are not always in constant use can be shared. Each computer does not need to have an individual printer attached. Access to expensive peripherals such as a colour laser printer can be granted to many users.

- Telecommunication services can be accessed and shared. Sharing a modem between many users avoids the need to purchase multiple units.

- The security of access and of data files can be improved with the implementation of different levels of passwords with different access rights. Dividing the network into drives based on department or subject matter allows network administrators to restrict access to only the specific files required by a group or individual.

LANs and WANs

Networks are classified according to the number of users that they support and the size of the area that they cover. There is, however, a lot of confusion in categorising some networks, as there are no hard and fast rules that make the categories distinct. The two broad categories are

LAN and WAN. A *local area network (LAN)* is often defined as one where the users are relatively close together, within a single room, floor, or building. A *wide area network (WAN)* is one that covers a wide geographical area, connecting computers that are quite remote.

Sometimes it's hard to distinguish between the two: some LANs span more than one building, and some networks that span only one building are termed a WAN! The key to being able to distinguish between the two is to consider the medium by which they communicate. A LAN communicates by "normal" network cable, because the distances can be physically small, thus enabling a direct connection to be made. WANs involve the use of a range of connection methods, including the telephone system and communication satellites. Satellite communications are now fairly common and provide a better alternative medium for transmission across oceans than undersea cable.

It can be easier to think of networks in terms of the number of users. A small LAN with between 5 and 50 users that does not employ any dedicated IT staff is termed a *workgroup*. The next level is an *intermediate* or *departmental LAN*, serving up to around 200 users. These are corporate networks installed within a large-sized company. Joining workgroups together can create a departmental LAN. An enterprise network serves around 500 users spread across multiple offices, floors, or buildings. There are other names that crop up when talking about computer networks such as *campus networks* installed within academic institutions.

Data travels around a network split up into small parcels called *data packets*. Each packet is divided into discrete sections known as *fields*. Each network packet can be different, but there are some common fields. Most have start and end fields, containing information relating to the source and destination for the data, the length of the data being sent, and a field to enable error checking.

The Internet

The Internet was started in the late 1960s as an experiment in the United States by the Advanced Research Projects Agency that later became the Defense Advanced Research Projects Agency (DARPA). They developed the ARPAnet, which was a network consisting of a small number of computers situated geographically remote from one another. The aim was to establish the feasibility of building a network that could survive in the event of a nuclear strike. Such a network must still be able to function if a number of the hosts are not working.

This successful experiment was then used by scientists to store and communicate scientific documents amongst each other. This became a popular means of sharing information and keeping abreast of new developments. Later, universities, academic institutions, and commercial organisations gained use of the technology. The Internet is actually the physical resource used to form this worldwide network. Today the Internet is a truly global network of computer networks, linking together millions of computer systems. The Internet is not run or owned by any one organisation. The Internet allows access to basically three types of service: electronic mail (e-mail), file transfer, and the World Wide Web.

During this development, it became quickly apparent that there needed to be some method of linking the vast array of scientific text documents that were floated on the Internet. A system of linking and finding a particular document was developed in the early 1990s called *hypertext*. Hypertext is simply text that, when selected by a mouse click, transports the user to the destination pointed to by the hypertext link. This interface was later developed into the *World Wide Web (WWW)*, a system that provides for easy movement from one Internet resource to another as well as a method of searching for a particular topic. The WWW is the actual software interface that allows you to search and view information held at specific *websites* on the Internet.

> The Internet is the physical worldwide network links allowing for communication between computers. The World Wide Web is the collection of information stored as web pages on websites. Web pages are available to users of the Internet.

Today these websites do not just hold pages of simple text, but they also have the capability to display pages with images, sound, and video. There are many, many sites available today covering an array of subjects beyond most people's imagination. With so much information on the many sites available, finding the right information can be very difficult.

Search engines such as Google, Yahoo!, Excite, and Lycos enable users to search the Internet for selected keywords. These search engines search the websites available according to the keywords stipulated by the user. A search on one keyword may provide thousands of links. The search engine lists the first set of most likely hits, possibly the top 10. Hyperlinks are provided directly to the site(s) selected.

> A more complete discussion of the Internet and the Web can be found in Part 7, "Information and Communication."

Although the user may be involved in global communication when using the Internet, the cost is reduced to that of a local telephone call. The user is actually only connected to their Internet service provider (ISP), who is usually just a local phone call away. The costs of the telephone calls are now usually integrated into a monthly cost that the user pays to the ISP for Internet access. This fee paid allows the user access at any time of the day or night, or at off-peak times only. The length of time that a user is online during these periods does not affect the monthly charges that they pay. Some people still prefer to simply pay for their Internet telephone calls by the minute.

ISPs often allocate to a subscriber a certain amount of web space so that they can set up their own web page for others to view.

Intranet and Extranet

Intranets and extranets are both private networks for use by businesses, organisations, or enterprises. Both use Internet technology to display the information, and therefore they look and feel just like the Internet. There can be various levels of accessibility to users who can only gain access if they have a valid username and password. A person's identity determines which parts of the system they can access.

A *firewall* is used to fend off unwanted intruders from outside a network. A firewall is a set of related programs that protect the resources of a private network from outside users. On an intranet that allows its users access to the Internet, a firewall is used to prevent outsiders from accessing its own private data and also for controlling what outside resources its own users have access to.

An *intranet* is an internal network, for example, within a company or organisation, whose main purpose is to share company information and resources between employees. Often an internal e-mail system is part of the intranet. An intranet is only accessible to people who are members of the same company or organisation.

An *extranet* is similar to an intranet, but it allows part of a company's or organisation's information to be shared with outside agencies such as suppliers, partners, customers, or other businesses. It can be seen as extending part of a company's intranet to outside users. There can be various levels of accessibility to outsiders.

Extranets are becoming a very popular means for business partners to exchange information. They allow companies to share product catalogues with others that work in the same area, collaborate with other companies on joint development and training programs, and access services offered by one company to a group of others.

The Telephone Network in Computing

Without the use of the public telephone system, WANs would be very limited. In order to communicate across any appreciable distance, it is not practical to install network cables, especially when an adequate alternative already exists.

The telephone network has, over the years, undergone a series of metamorphoses, much of which has been invisible to the user. The *public switched telephone network (PSTN)* was originally designed for voice transmission, using analogue electrical signals.

 NOTE A telephone mouthpiece functions like a speaker in reverse. It contains a diaphragm that vibrates when struck by sound waves. These vibrations are converted into electrical signals that are sent over the network.

Many people are surprised to learn that the telephone system actually handles more computer data traffic than voice traffic. Much of the main network is now geared up to work with digital traffic. The analogue connections are mainly confined to local links to homes and businesses. Here are some of the technologies used to transmit computer data over the telephone system:

Leased lines In the UK, a dedicated line can be leased from British Telecom and provide a permanent connection for devices in a network. Users are charged a flat rate for the lease of the line no matter how much or how little it is used. They are cost-effective if there is a need for a permanent connection or for high-volume data transmission.

Integrated Services Digital Network (ISDN) A key element in the development of this network is the Integrated Services Digital Network (ISDN). Such lines are designed to carry a variety of digitised data, all integrated into a single connection. They are designed specifically for the integrated transmission of text, sound, graphics, and video. Such connections are completely digital and provide for fast and reliable transmission.

ADSL (asymmetric digital subscriber line) ADSL technology has been developed to revolutionise Internet access for the home and business user. It utilises existing copper phone lines to transmit digital data faster than modems and ISDN lines. It is termed *asymmetric* because the transmission rate between the telephone exchange and the user is faster than the other way around. Speeds of between 512 kilobits per second and 6 megabits per second between the exchange and the user are quoted. In the opposite direction the speed is 256 kilobits per second. Because most people use the Internet for downloading data, it is seen as a great advantage to have the faster speed in this direction. This type of connection allows the home user to have simultaneous use of the Internet and the telephone down the same line. The user is often required to fit micro filters to the phone sockets in the home that split the voice data from the computer data. Internet access need no longer tie up the phone for normal voice use.

Analogue vs. Digital Signals

In electronics, there are actually two quite distinct fields: one dealing with digital signals and one dealing with analogue signals. A digital signal is one that is seen to be physically in one state or its opposite, at one of two opposite extremes. These states are represented by the binary digits 1 and 0. They are usually represented by a square wave (see Figure 4.1). A switch or LED indicator can be seen as digital devices.

FIGURE 4.1   Example of a digital signal

Digital

Analogue signals can be at either extreme or at any value in between. Such signals are usually represented with a sine wave (see Figure 4.2). Our senses for heat, light, and sound function in an analogue fashion.

FIGURE 4.2   Example of an analogue signal

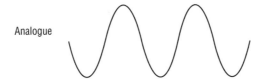

Analogue

Connecting to a Communications Network

To transmit computer data over analogue sections of the PSTN requires the use of a *modem*. Modems are used to connect a computer to a dial-up line. The term modem comes from the fact that it is used to modulate and demodulate the signals that are transmitted over the PSTN. This functions in much the same way as normal radio signals. To listen to a radio station, you tune in to the carrier frequency that has been modulated with the signal of the music or voice transmitted. The carrier frequency gives the signals the power to be transmitted—it carries them. A radio demodulates this signal, removing the carrier frequency so that the music and voice can be heard.

In terms of computer data, two different frequencies are used to represent the digital 1s and 0s. These frequencies, in the audible range, can be transmitted in the usual fashion over the PSTN. When receiving data, the modem demodulates the two frequencies into the 1s and 0s that the computer understands.

The power of your personal computer does not affect too much the speed at which you can access the Internet. It is the modem speed that has the most effect. The speed of a modem is specified by its baud rate. The *baud rate* is simply the number of bits per second that can be transmitted or received. Currently, 56 kilobits per second is the fastest baud rate for a standard dial-up modem. This rate is significantly increased with the use of ADSL. A faster baud rate can save on telephone call charges, as the time spent waiting to receive data is reduced. Less time waiting to view a web page can also make using the Internet far easier.

WAP (Wireless Application Protocol) is designed by the mobile telecommunications industry to allow mobile phone users access to basic Internet functions. It is a global standard that is a combination of a communication protocol and an application. As it is difficult to view a standard Internet page on a mobile phone, WAP pages are pared-down equivalents. Not all Internet pages are yet WAP compatible.

Summary

People use networks of computers to share files and devices and to communicate with each other.

Networks can be broadly classified as local area networks (LANs), where a number of computers that are physically close to each other are connected together, and wide area networks (WANs), which cover a wide geographical area.

The topology of a network describes how the cabling is laid out and the manner in which the terminals are connected to this cabling. Common topologies are bus, ring, and star networks.

Client-server networks utilise a central dedicated computer that serves files and resources to other computers on the network that are termed clients. Peer-to-peer networks utilise computers that act both as clients and servers, with no one computer in overall control.

Intranets and extranets are private networks used by businesses, organisations, and enterprises. Intranets are for internal use only. Extranets can allow access to outside related agencies.

The Internet is a global network of computers. The World Wide Web provides an interface for easy location and movement between resources that are stored on the Internet. Search engines are software tools that locate resources on the Internet according to keywords specified by the user.

WANs often use the public switched telephone network (PSTN) in order to communicate across appreciable distances. This extensive use has led to the development of Integrated Services Digital Network (ISDN) lines in order to speed up transmission rates.

Asymmetric digital subscriber lines (ADSL) enable users to access the Internet at much faster speeds than before. The download speed is much greater than the upload speed.

Digital signals are in one of two physical states, at one of two opposite extremes. These states are represented by the binary digits 1 and 0. Analogue signals can be at one of these extreme states or at any value in between.

A modem is needed to connect the digital computer to the analogue telephone lines. The speed of data transmission is measured in bits per second (bps).

Chapter 5

Use of IT in Everyday Life

IN THIS CHAPTER YOU WILL LEARN HOW TO

- ✓ Identify situations where a computer system may be appropriately used.
- ✓ Recognise some of the uses of computer applications in business, government, hospitals and healthcare, and education.
- ✓ Understand the term teleworking.
- ✓ Understand the term electronic mail.
- ✓ Understand the term e-commerce.
- ✓ Be aware of the advantages of purchasing goods and services online.

When you consider the vast array of activities that computers are involved in, you might ask, "Is there nothing a computer cannot do?"

Computers undoubtedly have many advantages. They never get tired, frustrated, hungry, or angry; they can produce an extensive range of documents that can be easily recalled and edited; and they can cross-reference facts derived from many different sources.

Computers also have many disadvantages. They break down (usually at the most inopportune moment); training and recruiting people to use computers can be difficult and expensive; some information systems need to be set up and maintained by highly trained staff; and some people are fearful of computers, which can cause undue stress in the workplace.

Computers at Work

So what makes computers good for some tasks? To answer this question, you need to consider the desirable attributes of a computer system. The first attribute that usually comes to mind is speed. Computers can carry out tasks at lightning speed that would take an age to do manually. Consider sorting a list of thousands of names alphabetically. A computer can merge the names and addresses of hundreds of people into a standard letter in an instant. To do this manually would possibly negate the job being performed at all. A calculation can be performed on many, many sets of data over and over again in an instant.

Computers are very consistent in their actions. Once information is entered correctly, a computer processes it consistently. If you consider the merged letter example in the previous paragraph, a different letter could be merged with the same names and addresses and then sent to exactly the same list of names and addresses.

Computers are also very accurate. Calculations are performed with great precision in a consistent manner. A computer would never tire of completing calculations, being able to perform them over and over again as many times as necessary.

The computer can only produce correct output if it receives correct input. The frequently used saying is "garbage in, garbage out."

A computer and its associated peripherals can hold vast amounts of information in a very small space. Thousands of personal records would perhaps take up a great deal of space in filing cabinets, yet they could be stored on a single hard disk. The ability to quickly search and sort records stored on a computer has helped to make records stored in filing cabinets obsolete in many instances.

Computer-controlled devices can carry out dangerous tasks or enter dangerous environments where humans cannot or would prefer not to enter. They can also help provide round-the-clock service, with minimal human resources performing boring and arduous tasks.

However, computers are not always the answer. It can be a surprise to some people that humans are considered superior in many situations. A human is better when the situation calls for a particularly "human touch." Humans are better where creativity is required, where judgement and experience are needed, and where human feelings need to be taken into account. Humans are also adaptable and better in situations where the tasks to be performed are different each time. Knowledge that comes with experience is something that is not easily programmed into a computer system. Could a robot cuddle a baby when it cries?

Computers—fast, accurate, and stupid.

Man—slow, slovenly, and smart.

As you have seen, computers are not always the perfect answer to every problem. You need to consider carefully the nature of the problem and how the application of a computer system might benefit the solution. There are a great many real-world situations where computers are used. In many instances, without the use of a computer, a job could not be competed.

Computer Applications in Business

There are many applications of large-scale computer systems that are used in business today. They include systems to help with the administration within businesses, more specialist systems for activities such as the booking of theatre and airline tickets or processing insurance claims, and systems for the provision of online banking.

On a smaller scale, some businesses in fact use quite a limited range of general application software packages to help in their administration. The most commonly used of these are word processing, spreadsheets, and e-mail packages. Database use can be on a small, local scale, or on a large, shared scale. There are other applications that are specially designed to help with the administration of business:

Management information systems (MIS) *Management information systems* are designed to provide the right information to the right manager at the right time. Different levels of management require different information, perhaps in a different format, in order to be effective at their job. This information is then used to support a structured decision-making process influencing, for example, budgets or sales targets.

Decision support systems (DSS) *Decision support systems* are integrated systems that use data from a variety of different sources. They are primarily aimed at senior managers who make strategic decisions. They utilise sophisticated data analysis techniques on an interactive basis to aid the decision-making process. The information they provide may not routinely be provided by an MIS. For example, a company director may wish to know the effect on profits if the sales increase by 10% and the costs increase by 6%.

Many large-scale computer systems are likely to have a database at their heart. Systems that support the booking of airline and theatre tickets can be large and complex. In order that several "agents" can make such bookings, the system needs to be shared. This requires that only certified agents have access to the system and that the double booking of seats cannot be made. Such large systems are supported by a WAN that uses telecommunications media to provide the links to the agents. In order to ensure that a double booking cannot be made, *record locking* needs to be implemented. This means that when an agent has access to say, a certain flight, a second agent cannot access these flight details until the first one has closed the record. This preserves the integrity of the data. If record locking were not instigated on a large system with many users, two people could conceivably open a record at the same time. The last one to close the record would have their changes saved, over-writing the changes made by the first person.

Insurance companies rely heavily on the use of computer systems. When one considers the requirement for the storing of policies for car, house, and contents insurance, you can get an idea of the scale of the systems necessary. This information is often shared between the company and insurance brokers. The company grants partial access to customer and contract data. It is now possible, for example, to pay for car insurance, and instead of waiting for the certificate to be mailed through the post, the brokers can print a certificate instantly. When a claim is made, this claim is tracked through its many different stages to settlement. The transfer of damage information, reports, cost calculation, digital photos, invoices, and settlements can all be made electronically. Information and communication technologies can play an important part in decentralising the processing of an organisation. At any time, an individual claim can be retrieved and its progress reviewed and updated.

For years now, financial institutions have used large computer systems to manage millions of daily transactions. For many people, the only paper-based record has been a receipt at the point of sale. Banks have adapted some of their internal processes and made some of them partially available for home use. With the advent of the Internet and the popularity of PCs in the home, banks are now offering their customers the opportunity to bank online. They view online banking as a way of attracting new customers and retaining existing ones, whilst at the same time cutting down on costly teller interaction and paper handling.

Online banking is seen to hold many advantages for the customer. The possibility to transfer money, pay bills, and apply for an overdraft are all available, as well as merely viewing personal account details. It can save the customer time, as there is no more waiting in a queue after having travelled to a branch. It is convenient, with access available 24 hours a day, seven days a week, all year around. Often there is help online, with the additional support of a help desk that you can call in order to obtain further guidance.

Many people worry about the security aspects of banking using the Internet. Banks have employed elaborate security to support this facility. Many are so confident that they offer 100 percent protection in the unlikely event of fraud.

Computer Applications in Government

The government of a country can be enhanced through the use of computer systems that necessarily need to be of a large scale. As already stated, computers are very useful for storing large amounts of data and for searching and sorting this data. This makes the tasks of public record keeping ideally suited to computerisation. The actual details stored vary depending upon which country a person is living in. The minimum information a person might reasonably expect a government agency to hold on them would be their name and address together with their Social Security number or a national identification number. Each time someone is involved in an activity such as paying tax or voting, details are added to many different registers.

Computers can also be used to store other types of government records. For example, in the United Kingdom there have been many national censuses, each of which has resulted in a great deal of information that needs to be stored. Not all records are stored in digital format. Some of the older types of records that may be damaged by constant handling are stored on microfiche. There are efforts being made to store these in a digital format. Recently the whole of the 1901 census data has been made available online. This site can be accessed from local libraries as well as from the home. A basic search for people within a certain area can be undertaken free of charge. More detailed information on people is available, and this can be downloaded for a small charge. The charge can be paid for by obtaining vouchers from local libraries.

Records need to be kept for every person who holds a driving licence and for each vehicle used on public roads. A driver and vehicle licensing agency needs to store, process, and update thousands of records. The registered owner of a vehicle is particularly difficult to track. A vehicle may pass through several owners throughout its life before it is scrapped. These large computerised systems can assist in the fight against vehicle crime.

A particular car crime problem is the re-registering of stolen vehicles with the identity of vehicles "written off" for scrap, thus disguising the true identity of the vehicle. In England, systems are being developed that will enable salvage dealers and the motor trade to notify the authorities of those cars that have been scrapped and those cars that are stored within the motor trade, without a registered keeper. This, it is hoped, will help to maintain the accuracy of the records kept. Number plate suppliers need to be electronically registered. They are required to carry out simple checks before supplying number plates. Auditable records of number plate transactions need to be kept in order for a supplier to keep their registered status.

Many records need to be kept for revenue purposes. The storage, calculation, and processing of the many facets of tax payments paid and due is a huge undertaking, requiring the use of very large computer systems. Online revenue sites can make available free advice to people who may feel intimidated obtaining it by other means. There are different types of taxation and rules that need to be adhered to. Many of these rules and parameters are difficult to understand and consequently make the calculation of tax payable difficult. In many countries, it is not only possible to get advice online directly from the government agency, but also to submit tax returns and make payments online. Many of the calculations are automatically performed when online submission is made.

Governments make concessions to certain sections of society with regards to taxation. Online services provide information on such concessions and offer the ability to claim for them. For instance, in the United Kingdom, such concessions include the Child Tax Credit for families and the Working Tax Credit for working families on low incomes.

One particular area of government has not kept pace with the IT environment in which we live: voting in public elections. Many people who live in a democratic society have seen little change in way they vote over the past 100 years. A vision of being able to vote online has been prompted by the expansion of information and communication technology into everyone's lives. In the United Kingdom, it is hoped to offer this as an alternative method of voting. In the year 2002, some local elections in the United Kingdom successfully piloted a method of e-voting. E-voting covers voting by fixed and mobile phones, digital television, and the Internet. It is hoped that by the year 2008, and certainly by the year 2011, general elections in the United Kingdom will utilise e-voting. Large-scale e-voting has already taken place in the Netherlands, Belgium, and Brazil, based in supervised locations. In Arizona, USA, the primary elections of 2000 allowed voting by the Internet.

It is envisaged that such voting will be based around a secure electronic electoral register that will verify voter details and record who has voted in real time. There are still some concerns over security that need to be addressed, but once implemented, it would make the voting system more robust and electoral fraud less likely. The benefits of such a system include increasing voter turnout, particularly amongst younger voters. For elections where there are a large number of voters, vote counting could be automated, reducing time and costs.

Computer Applications in Hospitals and Healthcare

There are many, many patient records that need to be stored, retrieved, updated, and searched. Systems in hospitals and medical centres can be linked so that these records can be shared. The enhanced accessibility of these records can assist in the care of a patient. For example, they can help with speedy receipt of laboratory data. Many medical records updated in this fashion do not allow for the deletion of details, thereby removing any suspicion of malpractice. Within hospitals, computer systems are used widely to run appointment systems and other areas of patient administration. There are specialist uses such as those involving patient body scans and monitoring.

Computers can prove an invaluable source of information for the doctors themselves. Details on complex procedures can be posted by more expert practitioners, and these can then be made available to others. Access to drug databases, reference materials, and current medical advances can all help in keeping a doctor informed of global developments. There are many online medical databases, journals, and library sites that can be accessed.

This sharing of expert knowledge can also aid in the diagnosis of problems. These do not have to be complex problems. An initial enquiry by telephone can be dealt with, and a preliminary diagnosis can be made with the help of a computerised system. The symptoms of a problem can be entered and certain paths followed depending upon the answers gained to prompted questions. This preliminary diagnosis can perhaps put at rest the mind of a person who made the enquiry, or filter enquiries so that those who are in need of more urgent treatment can be seen sooner by a possibly overstretched health service.

When an ambulance is called, the speed of reaction can have a direct effect on the well-being of the patient. Real-time ambulance control systems have been developed that help to dispatch the nearest and most appropriate vehicle, with the correct equipment on board, to a situation. Often, locating addresses and physical access to these addresses can be difficult. Details on exact locations can be linked into such a system so that guidance can be given to the ambulance crew. The more routine booking of ambulances for hospital visits also benefits from computerisation.

With the advancement of virtual reality techniques, new or complex procedures can first be tried and tested without risk to anyone. This may encompass the use of new instruments or the training of new personnel. Computer systems can also be used to analyse vast amounts of biological data that can help in research. The modelling of DNA strands is accomplished via computers. A whole new field of bio-informatics is emerging.

Computer Applications in Education

Computers are widely used in many schools, colleges, and training institutions. They are used not only for common administrative, recording, and production purposes, but they also play a role in the process of education itself.

There is a need for today's educational institutions to carefully track student attendance and achievement with reports on an individual or a group of students to be accessed instantly. The use of computers can easily carry out these tasks, as long as the information is correctly entered in the first place. In order to track and total attendances, there are electronic registration systems that can be linked up to a main central system.

As educational institutions grow larger and offer many different courses, on perhaps more than one site, the timetabling of these courses becomes complex. There are several specialist timetabling software packages on the market today. These allow a user to enter staff details, including the subjects that they teach, as well as the times and locations of teaching slots. The software allows the manual placing of taught sessions and staff, or it can be set to automatically timetable both staff and students in the most efficient manner possible. Any session that cannot be placed is reported to the user. The better systems offer the flexibility for the user to set key sessions and let the systems place the rest. Timetables can be printed for an individual student or staff member, or for whole groups. Such systems have proven their worth in maximising the utilisation of staff and facilities.

A computer can be the primary means of delivering a course or section of learning. The computer can be a single stand-alone machine or part of a network. This delivery method is referred to as *computer-based learning* or *computer-based training (CBT)*. CBT is popular for delivering training on a wide variety of subjects. Many larger companies employ CBT for educating their workforce. It is possible to study a wide variety of subjects this way. For example, there are training packages that cover such things as forklift truck driving. (This type of instruction would of course be accompanied by some practical learning as well.) CBT is extremely popular for learning computer software-related subjects. Often the software used to deliver the training is integrated with the package they are trying to learn so that the student can practice using the application as they learn.

CBT is sometimes referred to as *computer-aided learning (CAL)*.

Many CBT packages enable the student to obtain information, ask questions, and even obtain a marked score on a test. Some find the instant feedback gained from computer-marked tests encouraging. The learning material can be enriched with sound, images, and video to provide a more stimulating environment. A student can work at their own pace, perhaps taking a different route through the material, according to their ability. If difficulties are encountered, an exercise can be repeated as many times as the user wishes without the computer getting tired or irritable.

There are disadvantages of CBT, and overuse can serve to highlight some of these. It can be laborious reading large amounts of information from a screen. The valuable interaction between teacher and student is missing. A student cannot ask for something to be explained from a different viewpoint. A lesson cannot therefore be easily changed to suit a certain group of individuals. Some students need the discipline and motivational skills of a human teacher as well as the constraints of a set timetable.

However, it is not always possible for a student to attend classes at the time they are scheduled. This may be because the student is in full-time employment, or that the physical distance from the place of study is prohibitive. Online learning, often referred to as *distance learning*, can overcome these problems. There are many types of distance learning courses, from modular degree courses to short courses of only a few hours. Students are able to study when they want, 24 hours per day, 7 days a week, fitting it in around their schedule. Students can be allocated a tutor online with whom they can freely contact and gain feedback from. Often students can contact other students on the course, thus removing the feeling of isolation.

For the younger family member possibly studying a much wider curriculum than their parents, a computer becomes a valuable homework tool. With a computer's production capabilities and the use of multimedia CD-ROMs, the research and presentation of projects can become a fascinating endeavour rather than a laborious task. Access to the Internet is an invaluable asset for gathering information on any topic covered within a school's curriculum. There are even specialist websites for that vital examination revision.

Teleworking

The division between work and home is becoming increasingly fine. For some, the development in computer technology can make this division indistinguishable. *Teleworking*, or *telecommuting* as it is sometimes called, has given people the opportunity to work at home via a computer linked to their office. The home computer becomes just an extended terminal on the company's network.

This can be ideal for some employees. The obvious advantage is the reduction of commuting time or not having to commute at all. This can be a great benefit for some people who have to suffer a daily slog through busy traffic to get to work. Many cities are now introducing congestion charges to try and cut down traffic in city centres. There is flexibility of working time, and there's no need for employers to provide office space, lighting, and heating. There is no need, for example, for a salesperson to travel into a busy city centre office to pick up documentation and then travel back the way he or she came to carry out their business. The documents can be downloaded at home and the day's work begun immediately. At the end of the day, the documentation can be uploaded to the office without physically having to visit it. Contact with colleagues can be made by telephone, fax, or e-mail. Many people who work from home in this way are able to be more focused on the task in hand without any of the many distractions of a busy office environment. In addition, an employer can recruit employees from a much wider geographical area.

For others, teleworking can prove to be an unpleasant experience. The distractions of the home can prove too much. A meter reader, a salesperson, lost courier, and hungry pet can all seem like larger-than-life distractions, not to mention the young child home from school! There is the feeling of always being at work, and not just because you work at home. An organised person, who may be able to cope with the home environment, can come up against other difficulties. Colleagues do not know your working hours and might think nothing of phoning, faxing, or expecting e-mails to be read at all times of the day and night. "Sorry, didn't know you were on holiday," is no comfort when a week's work has just downloaded. Teleworkers can feel pressured into over-performing in an effort to keep up with office-based colleagues.

Teleworkers can feel isolated from colleagues. In fact, some companies will insist that workers gather in the office at a specified time of the week just to get over this feeling of isolation. This can also help to foster a sense of corporate identity and instill a sense of loyalty as well as providing important human contact. Teleworkers can become isolated within the home, especially for those without an active social life. For some projects that rely on teamwork, teleworking may not be the best way of working. There are means of communicating with the rest of the team, but these are not spontaneous, and aspects of some team qualities are lost. There is less emphasis on teamwork with teleworking.

The Electronic World

For many people, we seem to be living in an electronic age. Activities such as letter writing, banking, and shopping are being carried out in a different manner. Some people argue that the art of letter writing is dead as more and more people use e-mail. Many people shop via the Internet. Even collecting the weekly groceries may not involve a trip to the actual supermarket anymore. Most people today survive with only the use of a minimal amount of hard cash.

Electronic Mail

E-mail stands for electronic mail. E-mail provides the facility for both one-to-one and one-to-many communication. It is used in much the same way as conventional postal mail, but the information being sent is electronic and therefore much quicker. In some respects, it is similar to a fax, but there is actually no need for a hard copy (printed output) of material to be sent.

E-mail users refer to conventional postal mail systems as *snail mail*.

In order to send e-mail and access the Internet, the user needs to have a computer system connected to a phone line, usually via a modem. In addition, an account with an Internet service provider (ISP) is needed. The ISP provides the user with mail software such as Microsoft Outlook, Internet software, and mail facilities. At the time of sign up, the user is given an e-mail address. This e-mail address is usually in the form of your_name@ISPname, all in lowercase letters. Each e-mail address needs to be unique. This often necessitates some alterations being made to your name to avoid duplication of common names; for example, one might end up as john.lancaster8@myisp.com.

To send e-mail, the sender logs on to their ISP and sends their message to the ISP's mail server. The message can be text or a simple message with a computer file or files attached. Once sent to the ISP, the sender can forget the message; the ISP's mail facilities take over, automatically sending the mail to the receiver's e-mail server. When the receiver next logs on to their server, they can download the message, read it, and open any files attached.

E-mail removes the need for both the sender and receiver to actually be in direct contact with each other; only the mail servers come into contact. Mail servers are always available to send and receive mail, so mail can be sent when ready and downloaded to be read when convenient. The relatively low cost, speed, and relative confidentiality of e-mail compares favourably with the use of everyday postal mail systems.

An additional advantage of e-mail is that one message can be sent to many receiving computers simultaneously. There can be perhaps just a few people receiving the message, within perhaps a single organisation, or many people on an extensive mailing list, without the sender having to make more than one copy. Abuse of this facility to send multiple e-mails at once by sending unwanted material to others can cause annoyance and is termed *spamming*.

E-Commerce

The term e-commerce applies to the buying and selling of goods and services on the Internet. It is sometimes referred to as *e-business*. There has been an increase in the number of people shopping this way. The most commonly bought items are computer-related products, books, and travel tickets.

Online shopping has some similarities to mail-order purchasing in that customers are required to supply personal details and pay for the goods before they receive the products. Normally, products are delivered within the next few days. Larger supermarket chains now offer the service of being able to do the weekly shop online. The selection is made by browsing through the goods on offer via the company's website. The goods, after being collated by an in-store shopper at a local store, are conveniently delivered to your door. There is of course an additional charge on the bill for shopping this way.

A relatively new concept is the online auction. This resembles a traditional auction, but without the pressure of a man with a mallet rushing people into a bid. Goods for sale are often posted in the auction room to be sold by a certain time and date. The goods go to the person with the highest bid submitted at this time. To submit a bid, people have to leave personal and payment details. If they submit the highest bid, they are committed to the sale.

The usual way to pay for products purchased in this way is by credit card. Many people are a little worried about sending out their credit card details over the Internet. In fact, as long as you use a little caution and submit details only on secure sites, this method of payment is much more secure than giving out details over the telephone or letting a waiter disappear into the back of a restaurant with your card.

 Users can usually tell if a site is secure by the appearance of the picture of a closed padlock in the bottom right-hand corner of the browser software. On an unsecured site, this is replaced with a picture of an open padlock.

When purchasing online, it is important to be aware of your statutory rights. Consumers have the basic right to return unsatisfactory products. Consumers in the United Kingdom, for example, have the same statutory rights whether they purchase from a shop, online, or by mail order.

Advantages and Disadvantages of E-Commerce

The most obvious advantage of e-commerce is that the services are available 24 hours a day, 7 days a week. For many users with a busy lifestyle, this is enough, but there are other advantages. When purchasing goods online, some companies give customers a username, password, and order ID. This allows the customer to track the progress of their order online. For the purchase of computer software, there may be no actual waiting for delivery. Some software products can be paid for online and then downloaded directly. The Internet can be seen as a vast marketplace that is easy to travel through. This enables the potential customer to compare prices and buy from the most competitive, no matter where the store is situated.

The disadvantages of online shopping include having to purchase from a virtual store, without actually seeing or feeling the goods. Sometimes it is only a description and a photograph that can be viewed. To overcome this, some users view goods in a high-street shop and then look for a better price online. Of course, this cannot be done for many products. Some people prefer the human contact when buying goods. People like to listen to a salesperson and ask questions about the goods. As stated, many people are still not confident paying for goods and services over the faceless Internet.

Summary

This chapter discussed some of the uses of computers in the real world and some of the appropriate applications for using and not using computers.

On one hand, computers never get tired, frustrated, hungry, or angry; they can produce an extensive range of documents; and they can cross-reference facts derived from many different sources. Computers can consistently carry out tasks at high speed with accuracy. A computer system can hold vast amounts of information in a very small space. Computers can carry out dangerous tasks or enter dangerous situations. They can provide round-the-clock service.

However, computers have many disadvantages. They break down; training and recruiting people can be difficult and expensive; information systems need to be set up and maintained by highly trained staff; and some people are fearful of computers, which causes undue stress. A human is better than a computer when the tasks to be performed are different each time. Humans are better when creativity is required, where judgement and experience are needed, and where human feelings need to be taken into account.

This chapter also discussed how computers have been put to use by businesses, governments, hospitals, and educational institutions. In the home, computers are now also being put to work by teleworkers, who no longer need to visit the office to perform their jobs.

You also learned some of the ways that people are using computers in their lives. E-mail stands for electronic mail. It is used in much the same way as conventional postal mail, but the information being sent is electronic and therefore much quicker. E-mail removes the need for the sender and receiver to actually be in direct contact with each other; only the mail servers come into contact. One message can be sent to many receiving computers.

The term e-commerce simply applies to the buying and selling of goods and services on the Internet. Online shopping has some similarities to mail-order purchasing in that customers are required to supply personal details and pay for the goods before they receive the products. The usual way to pay for products purchased this way is by credit card. Consumers have the basic right to return unsatisfactory products. Consumers in the United Kingdom have the same statutory rights if they purchase from a shop, online, or by mail order.

Chapter 6

Safety and Security: Protecting Your Health, Data, and Rights

---

IN THIS CHAPTER YOU WILL LEARN HOW TO

✓ Understand what can help create a good working environment.

✓ Know the common health problems associated with using a computer.

✓ Understand some safety precautions when using a computer.

✓ Be aware of practices associated with computers that can help the environment.

✓ Understand the term information security.

✓ Know the benefits to an organisation of being proactive in dealing with security risks.

✓ Know about privacy issues associated with the use of computers.

✓ Know about the purpose and value of backing up data and software.

✓ Be aware of the possible implications of theft of portable devices.

✓ Understand the term virus as used in computing.

✓ Know about anti-virus measures and what to do in the event of infection.

✓ Understand good practice associated with avoiding virus infection.

✓ Understand the concept of copyright when applied to software.

✓ Understand copyright issues with using and distributing materials.

✓ Check the product ID number for a software product.

✓ Understand the terms shareware, freeware, and end-user licence agreement.

✓ Know about data protection legislation or conventions in your country.

With the introduction of a new tool or media, you must always consider the health and safety of the user. You also have a responsibility to consider its impact on the environment. When the use of such a tool concerns the public, there are other issues you need to consider. With a widely used and powerful tool such as a computer system, these items need particularly careful consideration.

Health and Safety Issues

Whilst your computer might not seem as inherently dangerous as, say, a chain saw or jack-hammer, you must still consider some safety precautions when working with computers.

Ergonomics

Ergonomics refers to the design of the environment in which you live and work so that it is safe and comfortable to use. If you spend a long time at a computer, either by choice or as a necessary part of your work, a good workspace is essential to your well-being. In the United Kingdom, the Health and Safety Executive have published guidelines for the use of display screen equipment. These regulations can help a computer user create a good workspace and adopt good working practices. Such guidelines exist in many other countries as well.

The computer screen is an important aspect of a computer system. Care should be taken concerning its comfortable use. It is the item that people spend most time looking at. It should be of adequate size, displaying a stable image in a suitable resolution. In order to make viewing easy on the eyes, a screen needs to be adjustable for brightness and contrast. When a screen has been switched on for a period of time, it warms up a little and the screen increases in brightness. Users should remember to make appropriate adjustments after a period of use. The ability of the screen to swivel and tilt not only makes it easier to view but can help to eliminate glare. It may be necessary to install a window covering or reposition a computer in order to avoid screen glare. A monitor filter can help to cut out screen glare.

Try to sit with the top of the screen at eye level, approximately 60 cm from your eyes. People who wear bifocal spectacles may find that they are less than ideal for use with a computer system, having to constantly raise and lower their heads to see the screen easily.

A *monitor filter* is a device that is attached to a monitor, covering the screen. It covers the viewable area of the monitor with a high-quality glass filter. They are said to absorb a high percentage of reflected glare in addition to the small amount of electromagnetic radiation that emanates from a monitor.

Because the keyboard is the most common method of inputting data into a computer system, data input is much easier and more pleasant if a keyboard is able to tilt and there is space in front of the keyboard for the user's hands and arms. This can be more of a problem with notebook and laptop computers. It is recommended that these types of computers not be used for inputting large amounts of data. A matt keyboard with clearly-defined letters is a must. The keyboard should sit comfortably at your fingertips with your arms and hands sloping down slightly. Holding your wrists at a sharp angle can cause discomfort with prolonged use. Money spent on a good-quality keyboard is a sound investment.

Having spent a good deal of money on a computer system, many people give little thought to where they are going to use it and onto what they are going to place it. The work surface itself should be stable and have a matt finish. There needs to be adequate room for movement of the mouse on a mouse mat. The use of a good-quality mouse and mat can make this important input device a joy to use, making the movements smooth as well as cutting down the amount of movement necessary. There ought to be adequate space for all other equipment and any documents that one might work from.

Being able to adopt a comfortable position at the workspace on an appropriate chair is important. The chair should have a five-point base to protect from overbalancing and be adjustable in height and able to tilt. A conscious effort should be made to sit so that your back is adequately supported. Your feet should be firmly on the ground or on a suitable footrest.

Adequate room lighting should be provided both to view the screen and other documents. This should be moderate and indirect, providing low contrast between the screen and other lighting. Some users like to work in a dim light to achieve better screen contrast. It is not good to have too much of a contrast as this can contribute to eyestrain and make it difficult to see documents you may be working from. Any lighting should take into account the possibility of glare on the screen.

Computer systems, like most large electrical devices, emit a degree of heat. This heat can make the air seem drier, and some contact lens wearers can find this uncomfortable. Where there are perhaps several computers within one room, adequate ventilation and control of humidity levels may be necessary. Many large companies and institutions provide air-conditioned rooms in situations where many computer systems are used in close proximity to each other.

Users can help themselves in planning their work schedules. If possible, take frequent breaks from the screen, about every $1\frac{1}{2}$ hours. An employee could perhaps punctuate computer work with filing or telephone work. If such breaks are not possible, move your eyes frequently away from the screen, focusing them at a different distance.

Health Issues

It is difficult for many to appreciate how a poorly designed workspace and bad working practice can cause serious health and safety problems. Computers are directly blamed, often wrongly, for a wide range of health problems. Opinions do differ on the extent of the problems that can occur from long-term use of computers. For instance, there is no real consensus of opinion between professional bodies on such problems as repetitive strain injury (RSI) (see the next paragraph for more on RSI). However, computers do not affect eyesight, they do not have detrimental effects on pregnant women, and they do not give out harmful radiation. Only a small amount of electromagnetic radiation is emitted from the screen, well below safe levels set out in international recommendations.

As in other occupations, computer work can be monotonous. A data entry clerk performs many repeated movements throughout a typical working day. *Repetitive strain injury (RSI)* is a term applied to problems that arise from such work. It usually manifests itself as numbness, stiffness, or tingling in the neck, shoulders, arms, hands, and fingers. A user suffering from RSI finds it difficult to pick up or lift items. Intensive use of the mouse can cause such problems. (Mouse work concentrates the activity on one arm, one hand, and just one or two fingers.) Taking frequent breaks can help to avoid these risks.

Aching shoulders and arms, as well as an aching back, may not be caused by RSI but by bad posture. It is essential that a person who is going to sit for long periods of time at a computer system adopt a correct posture. Avoid slouching or bending and have your back supported to help avoid problems.

Eyestrain is a common complaint that is levelled against the use of computers. Again, there is no evidence to suggest this is true. Long spells of work at a computer can lead to tired eyes. Subjecting your eyes to such demanding tasks can highlight eyesight problems a person may not have otherwise have noticed. A properly adjusted monitor in adequate lighting with a screen that is free from glare should not affect a person's eyesight. A flickering screen, as with a flickering television, can cause nausea and affect people with photosensitive epilepsy.

As well as physical difficulties, it is worth considering the stress that the use of computers can cause. Change of any kind causes stress in people. Changing to a computer-based environment can cause great stress in some workers who do not feel competent or comfortable using computer systems. Senior colleagues can feel threatened by a more computer-literate, possibly younger, person. In a less direct way, computers are often used to monitor the productivity of workers. The ability of computers to process data at high speed and present vast quantities of information can lead to a feeling of information overload. People can experience stress in the workplace if they perceive that they have more work than they can finish in the time allocated, and equally, if they are bored with nothing to do. Working with computers in this respect is no different from many other working practices where a correct balance needs to be struck. There are numerous working days lost each year through stress.

Safety Precautions

In addition to the health and safety aspects already covered, there are some common potential dangers that apply to the use of any electrical device. Computer equipment ought to be connected to the power supply with suitable cables that are in good condition, not frayed or worn. A full computer system generates the need for many electrical outlets. The computer base unit, monitor, printer, scanner, and modem all need access to an electrical socket. There is an obvious temptation to overload a socket using multiple adapters. Overloading instead of supplying suitable outlets leaves users liable to electrical shock and generates a real risk of fire within the property.

Computer cables connecting different hardware devices ought to follow a proper course. Leaving trailing cables near to where people work and across walkways is dangerous practice. There is an obvious risk of injury through tripping. A cable trailing off the end of a desk can catch a passing person, potentially causing injury, but it can also cause damage to the equipment. This trailing of leads across pathways is particularly evident in the use of portable computers. Users often place the computer on their desk and trail the lead across a pathway to the nearest socket in order to charge the battery. Other office users may not be aware of this temporary obstruction.

The Environment

In order to protect the environment, many companies and their employees need to be aware of how they can make a difference. The smallest consideration can have a huge overall effect. The concept of recycling is not new, but it can be applied to the use of computers in different ways. Computer systems can produce a large amount of paper output. Unfortunately, sometimes some of this output is produced in error; perhaps an image is in the wrong place or spelling and grammatical errors have been overlooked. If you make an effort to recycle this paper, you can help the environment. In a large company, this wasted paper can be considerable.

One item that is constantly replaced in a computer system is a printer cartridge. A laser printer toner cartridge can be refilled rather than simply throwing it away and replacing it with a new one.

The most power-hungry device of any computer system is the monitor. The monitor can be configured to shut itself down after a certain period of inactivity. After a further period of inactivity, the whole system can be configured to essentially put itself to sleep. The press of a key can restore system activity. Shutting the monitor down when not in use can save money for a homeowner, and this is considerably multiplied when you consider a large company with many computers.

Energy Star is a US programme requiring all computer equipment to conserve electrical power. A device complying with these requirements is deemed "Energy Star Compliant." As well as requiring that the hardware put itself into suspended animation after a specific period of disuse, this programme also limits the amount of power computers and printers can draw.

Large companies can further reduce printed materials by communicating in an electronic format. Within a typical company, many internal memos, for example, are circulated. If this is achieved via internal e-mail, then as well as being more efficient, a great deal of paper can be saved. The workforce needs to be educated in the use of such a system with regard to being environmentally friendly; many workers simply print out the e-mail in order to read it. The use of e-mail can be extended to external agencies, further reducing the need for printed output.

There are some concerns about the disposal of computer equipment, especially items such as CRT monitors. People wishing to dispose of these should check local regulations or with waste recycling centers as to the correct method of disposal.

Information Security

In addition to protecting users and the environment, it is also important to protect the information created and stored on computers. *Information security* is a general term used to cover the protection of data from accidental or malicious loss. It also includes ensuring the integrity and privacy of the data. Data integrity is concerned with ensuring the correctness of data during and after processing. Data may not be physically lost, but it can be altered so that it is no longer of use. It is necessary in many cases to keep a degree of privacy regarding information stored in computer files, preventing them from being disclosed to unauthorised individuals or organisations.

For many businesses, the real value of their computer files is not in the applications they run but in the information stored. If a system fails, the applications can quite easily be reinstalled from the original media supplied by the software producers. However, unless measures have been taken, it is much more difficult, if not impossible, to retrieve the personal information generated by the business. It is therefore of great benefit to a business if they can be proactive in the security of their data. Businesses need to ensure that the data remains safe, cut down possible risks, and be able to restore personal data in the event of loss. Simply losing electronic address books and records of e-mails can ruin a business.

Security Policies

Valuable data can be lost if a computer system is subjected to intrusion from unauthorised personnel. Measures to stop unauthorised access should be taken to protect sensitive or confidential information. In fact, in some instances people have a legal obligation to take measures to protect data.

There are several measures that can be taken. These may include physically locking the computer within a cabinet or room and allowing only certain people to have keys. Entry to a room can again be restricted by the use of swipe cards. For many organisations, a more practical solution is the use of passwords to access individual computers.

Many businesses adopt an information security policy that employees agree to abide by on acceptance of a position within a business. Such policies usually outline employees' responsibilities with respect to information security. Common aspects include: ensuring that they are authorised to use a computer; familiarising themselves with the system and its security; and being familiar with the backup procedures, in other words, a description of procedures to follow in the case of a real or suspected security breach.

As e-mail and Internet access is available within many businesses and institutions today, it is usual for such policies to cover the correct use of these facilities. A company needs to adopt a policy that encourages good business use and discourages improper personal use. It is common practice to prevent staff from using these facilities for any personal use. Use of the Internet is often further restricted, covering time wasted and the downloading of dangerous or unwanted files onto a company's system. Companies can often employ systems to monitor e-mail and Internet traffic. The posting of salacious material is a problem for many businesses.

Employees who breach such company policies are usually asked to leave the business at once without being required to work any period of notice of dismissal. A disgruntled employee with access rights to vital business information is a grave security risk.

Privacy and Access Issues

The use of networks is extremely widespread, especially within businesses, no matter if they are small or large. The first function that a potential user needs to perform is to log on in order to gain access. This usually involves having to enter both a user ID and a password. These are entered in two separate boxes.

The user ID is visible as it is typed in. It identifies a particular user on the network, and as such, user IDs are unique. A network administrator can track the activities of a user via this user ID. The network administrator allocates the user ID to the user. A password, when entered, usually appears as a series of stars, *****. Initially, a network administrator allocates a temporary password, requiring the user to change it when first logging on. The users themselves choose, and change, their own passwords. These passwords are private to the individual and cannot be seen by the network administrator.

The user IDs and passwords can allow access at various levels. Access to a certain drive, a folder, or a single file can be restricted. An administrator may have full access to all drives and applications along with the ability to set, edit, and remove other people's level of access. At the other end of the spectrum, a guest password may only allow access to one application and the use of a removable drive. These access rights are an important method of retaining security over some areas of a system, allowing only designated individuals right of access. In order to maintain data integrity, only certain users are given the right to read and write data, whilst most others may only read the information without being able to make any changes. More than one level of access can be set on a single computer. Different people logging on to a system with the same level of password may see a different, personalised desktop, but the same restrictions on drives and folders still apply.

In order for a password system to be effective, the users need to adopt an effective policy. Users should remember that the purpose is security and that passwords should never be revealed. Passwords of at least five characters need to be remembered and not written down. They ought to be changed on a regular basis. This change can be enforced by the computer system itself, with passwords that have been used previously not allowed. When changing a password, the user usually has to enter it twice in order to verify its correct entry.

Common bad practice is simply adding a number to the end of a password and incrementing this number when requested to change it. This is ineffective if the original password has been compromised. Choosing the name of a child, a favourite team, a favourite player, or even a location whose name appears below a photograph on the person's desk, is again not a good idea. The often-used mother's maiden name can be compromised if people know a little of your history.

Backing Up Data and Software

As computer files can hold important data for an individual, perhaps an essential project, vital account information, or examination coursework, it makes sense to make copies of these files in case the original files become corrupt. Files can become corrupt for many reasons such as operating system failure, power being removed from the computer before it has been closed properly, network problems, virus infection, and perhaps malicious damage.

Routine backups of an entire computer system, individual folders, or files can be made so that they can be re-created to the last backup taken if the working files fail. Files of a small size can be backed up to 3.5" floppy disk that holds 1.44MB of data. Larger files can also be stored to 3.5" floppy disk, but they first need to be compressed using special software so that they take up less space than the originals. Larger files or a large number of files need special consideration. It is difficult and not very practical to back up a hard disk drive onto many floppy disks. A more practical solution is to use another hard disk or a tape backup system. Restoring files for a whole hard drive from tape can take quite a while.

The location of the backup copies is important. There is little use in keeping backups in close proximity to the originals, as whatever catastrophe befalls the originals may also damage the backups. Copies of important files should be saved regularly onto portable storage media and clearly labelled. If the originals are then lost or damaged, they can be recovered from the backup storage. It is a wise policy to keep backup copies of files in a different physical location than the originals. Really valuable data should preferably be stored in a safe fireproof location to guard against the premises containing the files being destroyed by a fire or other natural disaster.

Implications of Theft

Today there is a widespread use of portable devices, including laptop computers, PDAs, and mobile phones. These devices are used to hold personal and confidential information in varying degrees. It is not only devastating that the device is actually lost, but there is also the issue of losing the data stored on it. Mobile phones and PDAs can contain electronic phone books and contact details within them. It is not always possible to back up data from these devices. When such a device is stolen, you might worry that the unscrupulous person who stole the device will misuse the data stored on it. Misuse of telephone numbers can at best be an annoyance, at worst a serious invasion of a person's privacy.

Many people take extravagant measures to protect data on a desktop computer, but take few, if any, measures to protect data on a portable computer. Sometimes a thief's initial intention may be to steal a portable computer itself, but they subsequently find that the data stored on the computer is actually of more value. This can lead to misuse of these files, or extortion for their return.

There are measures that can be taken to limit the vulnerability of portable devices. Travelling with such devices clearly on show is not a good idea. Laptop computers should be locked away out of sight. Implementing password systems to access a laptop computer can offer some protection. If the data is of a particularly sensitive nature, it can be encrypted. Encryption makes the data appear meaningless and unintelligible, both on screen and in the way it is stored. Access to the correct decryption device is needed to access the data.

Computer Viruses

A computer *virus* is a piece of computer code that has been written to cause damage, recover data illegally, or simply cause annoyance. Virus is an apt term, as the main goal of such code is to survive, reproduce, and damage a computer system, just like a biological virus in a living body. Computer viruses can travel at lightning speed. In the year 2000, the "I Love You" virus utilised the Internet to travel; originating in the Philippines, it had spread globally within hours. It also highlighted the vulnerability of computer systems despite sophisticated protection measures. A virus originating from a small personal computer had within hours closed down networks within government agencies and multinational companies.

There are many different forms of computer viruses, and new ones are being produced all the time. Boot viruses infect the boot sector of a disk. The *boot sector* is where files are located for loading the operating system when the computer is switched on. Such viruses load themselves into memory when the disk is accessed and can prevent the computer from starting at all. Program viruses usually attach themselves to executable files, enabling them to spread each time the file is opened. There are multi-particle viruses that are a hybrid of boot and program viruses. They infect program files, and when these are executed, they also infect the boot sector. When the computer is next booted, the virus becomes effective.

Viruses can entwine themselves within certain popular software packages. These are mainly macro viruses that affect documents or templates containing macros. When the document is opened, the virus is activated, affecting the application by making changes to all other documents created within this application. Some mail viruses travel via the Internet using a person's personal e-mail address book to reproduce and spread. These are often referred to as a *mail virus*. A common ploy of a mail virus is to send itself to everyone in a person's address book. This rapidly spreads the virus, whilst at the same time increasing traffic to such an extent that the system slows down. A WORM-type virus (write once read many) may not actually physically damage any particular type of file, but simply grind a system to a halt by repeatedly reproducing itself. There are other viruses that attach to a certain type of file, corrupting the data within the file but not actually reproducing.

A *macro* is an automated routine that carries out a set of commands within an application. This prevents the user from having to repeatedly carry out difficult or onerous tasks. A macro virus is one that carries out a series of destructive or disruptive commands automatically when a file is accessed within an application package.

Viruses spread either via contaminated removable disks being passed between computers, or they are innocently downloaded via a network or Internet connection. Simply copying text or images from a computer cannot transmit viruses. The virus program itself needs to be run. This can often be done unintentionally.

Sometimes users are unaware that their system has been infected. Symptoms that may indicate infection are: the computer may run very slowly, files may disappear, files are reported as being corrupt, areas of memory become inaccessible, or applications simply won't run because they no longer fit into RAM. Some types of virus are not so subtle and inform the user by displaying some kind of message on the screen.

A good virus software package is an excellent guard against infection. It is important to use the latest version and make sure that it is kept up to date. Anti-virus software is effective only against strains of virus that it is aware of; it cannot detect and clean viruses that it is not told about. A good package from a reputable source rapidly offers free updates for registered users in order to deal with new viruses. These can often be downloaded from the Internet. Virus protection software can be set to constantly scan your system for any changes. It can then warn the user if a virus is present before it has any chance to do any damage. The anti-virus software itself should be able to clean disks and rid a system of infection; this cleaning is termed *disinfecting*. The software allows the user to scan a certain drive on demand and then allows the user to disinfect files that have been infected.

If a system is clean from the start, the only way that infection can occur is from the outside. Accepting this fact, users can take some simple precautions to help protect themselves. A user ought to virus-check any unfamiliar disks before using them, in addition to checking one's own disks that have been used outside their own system. Because viruses spread by attaching themselves onto existing files, simply write-protecting a disk can stop infection. If a disk is write-protected, it can only be read from and not written to. Commercially produced software is unlikely to be infected, and even less likely if it is distributed on CD-ROM. Some people still scan such software in an effort to be safe rather than sorry.

There are certain precautions that apply particularly to e-mail viruses. Users should be wary of opening any e-mails that have come from an unknown source, especially if they have file attachments. A good anti-virus software package scans e-mails before they are opened. Never open e-mails that contain executable files. In fact, many mail servers do not handle mail that has executable files attached due to the high risk of infection.

Protecting Copyright

The authors of computer software have the same copyright protection as music, literary, and dramatic authors. In the United Kingdom, this extends for the life of the author, and for 50 years after death. Copyright is the legal right to be the only one to reproduce, publish, and sell the content and form of a work.

When buying commercial software, what you are actually purchasing is a copy of the software and the right to use it. You are not buying ownership of the software; you're simply purchasing a licence that gives you the right to use it. All commercial software contains an *end-user license agreement*. This is an agreement that is included as part of the electronic software installation process, in which the user of the software agrees to adhere to particular terms for its use. Read all licence agreements carefully and make sure that your use of the software is in compliance with the licence issued with it. Otherwise, you could be breaking the law. Often, software is supplied in a sealed wrapper on which the terms and conditions of the licence are stated. By opening the package, you are agreeing to abide by the stated terms and conditions.

The most common licence is a single-user licence for use by one person at a time on one machine. Some single-user licence agreements allow the purchaser to install the software onto a portable computer as well as on a desktop computer, as long as both are not used at the same time. This allows for the fact that a user may be out and about during the day working with an application on a laptop, but may wish to download data to a desktop once back at the office.

When there are many users within a company who wish to use the software at the same time, then either multiple copies of the software can be purchased, or a site licence or multi-user licence agreement can be bought if one is available. Multi-user and site licences are usually offered at a much-reduced cost from that of purchasing numerous single licences. However, they may come with limited sets of documentation and user manuals. Additional manuals are usually available to be purchased separately. Sharing files across a network is deemed to be multiple use. A licence must be purchased to cover the maximum possible numbers of users of the software at any one time.

Copyright protection not only applies to whole software applications, it can also apply to individual files, or certain parts of these files. It is quite possible that text, a graphic, or an audio or video clip contained within a document is copyright protected. Copyright protected images and video usually contain a copyright symbol, ©. Care must be taken when downloading and using information from the Internet. It is very easy to download and save images and audio and video clips; perhaps there are more of these downloaded than anything else. All of these can be copyright protected and therefore cannot be freely used and distributed. The copyright belongs to the artist or photographer. There is great concern from the music industry about copyrighted music that is downloaded from the Internet without payment.

Using and Distributing Materials

It is quite common for commercial software to be distributed on CD, less so on floppy disk. It is common to have to install the software to a hard drive in order for it to run. By installing the program, you are agreeing to the licence terms. Some applications, mainly games software, require that the original CD be in the CD drive when the software is run. The purchaser may be allowed to make one copy of legally purchased software as a personal backup, but this must be checked against the end-user licence agreement. Copying for any other purpose is software piracy, which is illegal. It is illegal to knowingly use pirated software, even though you may not have copied it yourself.

CDs, floppy disks, and Zip disks may contain personal backups of software. To further copy these is illegal. It is also illegal to copy installed software from a hard disk onto these portable devices for use on any other computer. Using these portable devices as a means of distributing illegally downloaded or copied music has become a major problem for the music industry. Copyright issues relate to the actual software itself; they do not apply to documents or data created by a software application.

Product ID Numbers

Each piece of software sold has a unique product ID number. Most commercial software applications require the user to input this number during the installation of the software. If the number input does not match the one supplied with the software, the installation does not continue. You can usually find the product ID number of an installed package from the Help menu. From this menu, click About. This brings up a dialog box similar to the one in Figure 6.1. It contains basic copyright information, the name of the person to whom the product is licensed, and the product ID number.

FIGURE   6.1   The product ID number

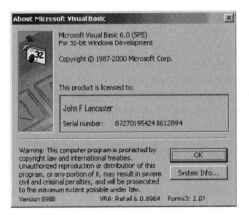

There is usually a registration card included with a software package. Fill in this card and send it back to the address in the documentation. Alternatively, you can usually register online via the Internet. When you register your software, the distributor has a record that you have purchased their product and, via the product ID number, exactly what product has been purchased.

Being a registered user has its advantages. You could be eligible for upgrades to later versions of the product for free or at considerably less cost than purchasing the new version. Many software producers also send relevant information to their registered users with details of the software purchased or other information that may be of interest. Even though you may have taken great care of the original program disks, accidents do happen. If at a later date these originals are damaged, the distributor may be prepared to help registered users.

In addition to this strictly commercial software, public domain software is available. This is usually distributed on disk or can be downloaded from the Internet. Public domain software is often referred to as either shareware or freeware. The authors of *shareware* allow you to try their program for free. If you like it and want to continue to use it, they ask you to pay a fee. Some shareware programs are time limited and cease to function a short period of time after installation, perhaps one or two months.

Freeware can be freely copied and used. It is quite rare and always contains a notice within the program stating that use of the software is free of charge. Large commercial companies sometimes distribute cut-down freeware versions of applications that they wish to sell. These cut-down versions do not have full functionality available; often the ability to save files has been disabled.

Data Protection Act

Computers are very efficient tools at gathering and sorting data. For this reason, it was felt that there needed to be some legislation to protect the rights of the individual whenever personal data is stored or processed automatically. Many countries now have in statute a Data Protection Act—a misleading title because it is really about protecting the individual—the data subject—not the actual data. Employers and employees are legally obliged to protect other people's privacy. For example, compliance with the Council of European Convention on Data Protection enables data to flow between European countries.

Interpretation of the Data Protection Act can be a little confusing. At present, it applies only to data that is processed automatically, although in the future, full compliance will extend to paper-based documents that are processed manually. Information relating to living identifiable individuals is covered, not information relating to a company or organisation. Personal data covers statements of fact and expressions of opinion about an individual. Confusion arises when exemptions are considered.

There are some quite straightforward reasonable exemptions. Exemption is made over

- Data that is needed to safeguard national security or enforcement of the law
- Data held for the payment of wages and pensions
- Data held for the recording of purchases and sales
- Personal data held by an individual for personal, family, and household affairs and for recreational purposes

Care must be taken over exemptions such as

- Personal data held for distributing articles or information to people. This exemption is small and really relates to only names and addresses.
- Personal data held by members of a club. Each person must be a member of the club and asked if they mind the data being held for this purpose.
- Word-processed data. The act does not cover information entered onto a computer for the sole purpose of editing text and printing out the document.

The Data Protection Act stipulates that users of personal data, the data holders, must register certain facts with a data registrar. Personal data must be

- Obtained and processed lawfully and fairly
- Only used for the purpose stated when registering the intentions with the data registrar
- Only disclosed to those people described in the register entry
- Adequate, relevant, and not excessive
- Accurate and kept up-to-date
- Held no longer than is necessary
- Accessible to the individual concerned who has the right to have the information corrected or erased
- Held securely

Personal data is put to a wide spectrum of uses. Some examples of situations where privacy should be respected concern medical reports, accounts recording credit ratings, and employee assessments. In each of these instances an individual would, in addition to privacy, expect that the information is accurate, relevant, and kept up-to-date.

If the Data Protection Act is breached by accident or by deliberate misuse, the person in control of the data could be required to pay considerable financial penalties. For some companies, this may pale in comparison to a loss of public confidence.

Summary

This long chapter discussed a variety of safety and security issues surrounding the use of computers.

It began with user safety. For people who spend a long time at a computer, a good workspace is essential to one's well being. A computer user can create a good workspace and adopt good working practices by considering the computer screen viewed, the keyboard used, the work surface the system is placed on, adopting a comfortable seating position, and working in suitable lighting. This chapter also discussed health issues that arise from computer use, such as repetitive stress injury, and the safety issues with respect to electrical power and cabling.

You also learned about safety issues regarding computers and the environment. Recycling printed output and printer toner cartridges, along with the use of a monitor that consumes less power, can help the environment. Using electronic documents can help to reduce the need for printed materials.

There are a variety of issues with regard to protecting information stored on and created by computers. Information security is a general term used to cover the protection of data from accidental or malicious loss. It also includes ensuring the integrity and privacy of the data.

For many businesses, the real value of their computer files is not in the applications they run, but in the information stored. Many businesses adopt an information security policy that employees agree to abide by on acceptance of a position within the business. It is usual for such policies to also cover the correct use of e-mail and the Internet.

User IDs and passwords can allow access at various levels. Access to a certain drive, a folder, or a single file can be restricted. These access rights are an important method of retaining security over some areas of a system, only allowing designated individuals right of access.

As computer files can hold important data for an individual, for example, an essential project, vital account information, or perhaps examination coursework, it makes sense to make copies of these files in case the original files become corrupt. Routine backups of an entire computer system, individual folders, or files, can be made so that they can be re-created to the last backup taken if the working files fail.

With the widespread use of portable devices, care must be taken to protect the data therein. It is not only devastating when such a device is actually lost, but also that the data stored within it is lost. It is not always possible to back up data from these devices. Sometimes a thief's initial intention may be to steal a portable computer itself, but they may subsequently find that the data stored on the computer is of more value. This can lead to misuse of these files or extortion in exchange for their return.

This chapter also discussed protection against viruses and the measures that can be taken to avoid viruses.

Finally, you learned about copyright protection. All commercial software contains a software end-user licence agreement that sets out the terms and conditions under which you are entitled to use it. By installing the program, you are agreeing to the licence terms. The purchaser is usually allowed to make one copy of legally purchased software as a personal backup.

Copyright protection not only applies to whole software applications, but it also applies to individual files, or certain parts of these files. It is quite possible that text, a graphic, or an audio or video clip contained within a document is copyright protected. Care must be taken when downloading and using information from the Internet.

Module Review Questions

1. Which of the following devices does not constitute computer hardware?

    A. CD-ROM drive

    B. Printed document

    C. Monitor

    D. Mouse

2. Which of the following is not a type of computer?

    A. Laptop

    B. PDA

    C. Mainframe

    D. Minorframe

3. A computer network is:

    A. A group of computer specialists sharing a common interest

    B. A set of computers connected together and able to communicate with each other

    C. A set of computers that all share the same printer

    D. A set of computers you have to log on to

4. Which of the following is not a basic function that a microprocessor performs?

    A. Running applications

    B. Accessing memory

    C. Defining the number of colours displayed on a monitor

    D. Performing arithmetic and logical comparisons necessary for running programs

5. Which of the following is not a form of computer memory?

    A. Random access memory (RAM)

    B. Write-only memory (WOM)

    C. Cache memory

    D. Read-only memory (ROM)

6. Which of the following terms is commonly used to measure computer RAM?

   A. Bit

   B. Kilobyte

   C. Byte

   D. Gigabyte

   E. Bitbyte

   F. Megabyte

7. Which of the following devices can be used for both input and output?

   A. Scanner

   B. Touch screen

   C. Mouse

   D. Speaker

8. Which of the following application packages would you use to carry out financial modelling?

   A. Database

   B. Spreadsheet

   C. DTP

   D. Word processing package

9. What is the purpose of an extranet?

   A. Keep out all external users

   B. Keep all company data secure from outside users

   C. Allow part of a company's information to be shared with outside agencies

   D. Only allow access to external users

10. Which of the following are not applications of large-scale computer systems within business?

   A. Word processing employee references

   B. Online banking

   C. Processing insurance claims

   D. Booking of airline tickets

11. Which of the following do governments widely use large-scale computer applications for? (Choose all that apply.)

A. Revenue collection

B. Electronic voting

C. Storing census data

D. Vehicle registration

12. Which one of the following statements is false concerning product ID numbers?

A. Product ID numbers are often entered during installation.

B. Product ID numbers often appear on software packaging.

C. Product ID numbers are never needed when registering software.

D. Product ID numbers can often be seen by using the Help, About menu item.

Answers to Module Review Questions

1. B.
2. D.
3. B.
4. C.
5. B.
6. F.
7. B.
8. B.
9. C.
10. A.
11. A, C, D.
12. C.

ECDL Module 2: Using the Computer and Managing Files

PART

II

Chapter

7

First Steps with the Computer

IN THIS CHAPTER YOU WILL LEARN HOW TO

✓ Start the computer.

✓ Shut down the computer.

✓ Restart the computer.

✓ Utilise the Windows XP user options.

✓ Adjust the Desktop.

✓ Find system information.

✓ Find basic Desktop information.

✓ Find information about your disks.

✓ Format a floppy disk or a Zip disk.

✓ Understand why backing up files is important.

✓ Use the Help facility.

As you have already learned in the first part of this book, the first module of the ECDL is all about information technology in general. This module looks at how to use your computer, in this case what is referred to as the *PC*, and how to manage your files.

PC stands for personal computer. What we generally call PCs today are based on the PC first developed by IBM in about 1980. Before long, other companies began to manufacture and sell similar machines, generally built around an Intel processor and initially called *clones*, but more recently referred to as IBM-compatible computers. These are the computers that the majority of people and businesses use on their desktops. There are other types of computers, most notably the Apple Macintosh, which is also a personal computer, although it is not usually referred to as a PC. The Mac, as it is generally known, has a very loyal following and is still widely used in the graphic arts industries.

First Steps with the Computer

Obviously, the first thing you need to be able to do is start your computer and understand what is happening when you do so. This section assumes that you have connected everything up correctly or that someone else has done this for you. If in doubt, consult the manual or someone with experience. Today, when most PCs are sold as boxes, consulting your supplier may not be a very helpful approach.

Starting the Computer

In most, but not all, cases, the various components of your computer have separate switches, so you need to power on the monitor (screen), the speakers, and any other peripherals—for example, an external Zip drive—before you switch on the computer itself. Incidentally, while it is probably a good idea to switch on a scanner or a printer at the same time, it's not usually essential, because they will work satisfactorily if you switch them on later.

Windows XP includes what is called "Plug and Play," which means that when you plug in a new hardware device, the operating system usually recognises it immediately.

The monitor and speakers can usually be switched on once the computer is running, but as far as the monitor goes, there is little point in switching on the computer if you cannot see what's happening on the screen! When you switch the PC on, you initially see a screen of (usually) white characters on a black background. What this tells you is that the system is running a series of checks on your hardware and the system software, some of which is stored on read-only memory (ROM) chips and the rest of which is stored on your computer's hard disk. You can intervene at this point to make changes, but this is outside the ECDL syllabus; don't make any changes without expert advice or until you have learnt more about the system.

If all is well, eventually you see a Windows XP introductory screen, followed in due course by the Windows XP Desktop. How long this takes—perhaps as long as a few minutes, but probably less for a new system—depends on factors such as the speed of your processor and how many programs have been set up to start automatically when you switch on your PC.

The images that you see while your computer is starting up probably depend on either the manufacturer of the computer or how your company has set up its PCs and its network.

If there is more than one user set up to use your computer or you are on a network, you do not go directly to the Desktop; you need to log on first with a username and password. If you have any problems, ask whoever set up your system. You will also be advised to log off, when you have finished using the system.

Which programs start when the computer starts up can also be changed by you, but this is outside the ECDL syllabus. Figure 7.1 shows a typical Windows XP Desktop.

FIGURE 7.1   A typical Windows XP Desktop

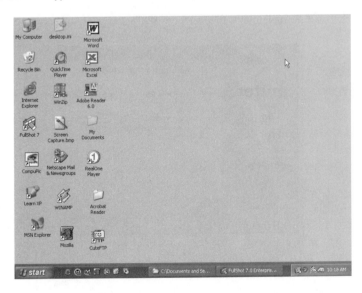

The next two chapters look at the Windows Desktop in more detail, but note that when you first use your computer, you may see a window that offers you the opportunity to follow a tour of Windows XP. If it does not appear as shown in Figure 7.1, open it from the Start button at the bottom left of the screen. Click Start with your left mouse button and the window shown in Figure 7.2 opens.

FIGURE 7.2 The Start menu. Note that the programs on the left-hand side, apart from the first two, are the programs that you have used most recently.

Select All Programs (at the bottom of the pop-up menu) ➢ Accessories ➢ Tour Windows XP. Once you start, notice that there are various options (see Figure 7.3), but these do not need additional explanation. More guidance on specific topics can be obtained by using *walkthroughs*, which are accessed from the Help screen.

FIGURE 7.3 The options in the Windows XP tour

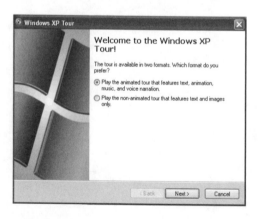

It's a good idea to take the XP tour before you start to use your computer. There will, of course, be some overlap with what we talk about here, but the tour (and Help) should make matters easier to understand.

Note that you can use the version of the tour with sound and animations (which makes life easier for you). If it's not practical for you to have sound on, try the text and images version instead, which you view in Internet Explorer, the Windows web browser. Internet Explorer opens automatically when you choose this option. If you have not previously used a web browser, you may find it useful to look at the sections on navigation in Part 7 to help you understand how to use this.

Shutting Down Your Computer

Before you turn off or shut down your computer, it's a good idea to close down all the applications you're running. If you do not, then there may be various effects:

- You will probably see a series of prompts asking you if you want to save files you have been working on if they are still open.

- You may see a message saying that an application is still running, giving you the option of waiting or cutting short its operation and possibly losing changes you have made.

- Finally, when you choose to start the computer again (either by using the Restart option or when you next turn it on), you may find that some of the windows you had open when you shut down your computer have reopened automatically, which you may not want.

So make sure to close all the programs you can see on your Desktop before you shut down your PC.

Once you have closed applications in the usual way, click the Start button (in the bottom-left corner of the screen). Then click Turn Off Computer, and a window opens in the centre of the screen asking what you want to do (see Figure 7.4). If you want to shut down the computer, click the appropriate button and watch the screen until the system switches your computer off automatically. You may also have to turn off the monitor and any peripherals, depending on whether they operate from separate power supplies.

FIGURE 7.4   This dialog box appears when you request to turn off your computer.

Restarting the Computer

If, instead of shutting down, you want to restart your computer, click the Restart button. The system goes through the same shutdown procedure, but this time your PC then goes through the startup procedure, just as if you had switched off and switched on again.

Why should you want to restart? There are two main reasons:

- You have installed new or updated software, and it's necessary for the computer to be restarted for the software to be usable or the updates to be effective. In fact, this restart may be part of the installation procedure, although you are always asked to confirm whether you want to restart.

- An application is not working as it should; this unfortunately still happens. In such a situation, restarting your PC can often solve the problem, because essentially you are exiting from the problem situation. (Chapter 9, "Working with Windows," explains what to do if an application "freezes," in other words, does not respond to the mouse or the keyboard.)

Another option in the Turn Off Computer dialog box is Stand By. This turns off the monitor and the hard disk, but pressing the Start button (or some other action) brings the system alive again.

Exactly what action you need to take to "wake up" your system depends on the system hardware.

You may also see a Hibernate option, which is most useful on laptop computers, although this may be activated by using the Start button or by just closing the lid of the laptop. This closes down the system completely, but keeps a record of all the current settings, so that when you come out of hibernation (usually by using the Start button), your position before hibernation is restored.

Just as for Turn Off and Restart, make sure to save all your work before activating the Stand By and Hibernate options, because if the power fails, any changes you made since you last saved will be lost. Note that if you are on a network, you may not be able to use these options.

The Basics of the Windows Operating System Interface

If you successfully followed the directions for starting your computer in the previous section, your computer should now be displaying the Windows Desktop. Windows is what is known as your computer's operating system. The *operating system (OS)*, put simply, is the software that allows the user to interact with the processor using a series of commands in something like natural language. This section discusses the components of the operating system that allow the user to interface with the system, and how to adjust that interface to what suits you best.

The operating system upon which this book (and the ECDL syllabus) focuses is Microsoft Windows XP. Windows XP comes in two versions: Home and Professional. This section discusses the Professional version, but most of the features that come within the scope of ECDL also apply to the Home version.

Each of these components is discussed at length in their respective chapters, but for now you need a basic working knowledge of them in order to accustom yourself to working in the Windows environment.

A Brief History of Operating Systems

When IBM started to develop the PC, they selected a small software company called Microsoft to design the operating system. They called this operating system PC-DOS (DOS = Disk Operating System). Subsequently, IBM and Microsoft parted ways and the operating system was then called MS-DOS (and often just DOS).

DOS went through a number of versions, but it remains what is called a *command-line interface*, so that to carry out any operation, you have to type a command followed by the Enter key. An example of a DOS screen is shown here:

Then in the mid-1980s, Apple developed the Macintosh, which had what is called a *graphical user interface (GUI)*, using windows, icons, and a mouse. How much this influenced Microsoft was the subject of several court cases, but at about the same time, Microsoft developed the first version of Windows, which has itself gone through a number of versions, the latest of which is Windows XP. This has many differences from earlier operating systems—Windows 2000, Windows 98, and Windows 95—which are still widely used. Although specialists still write programs that require you to use DOS, all the major commercial PC software is now written for Windows (or for Linux or Unix; see below). Consequently, for all the software discussed in this and subsequent modules, you only need to know about Windows.

Windows 95 and later versions are operating systems in their own right, whereas earlier versions, of which Windows 3.1 was the last, were effectively programs run from DOS, so it is important to understand the relationship between the two. Here we mention DOS for completeness. Although you can open a DOS window in Windows XP, you can access all the information you need to know from within Windows.

You may also hear of operating systems called Unix and Linux. These can be run on PCs, but they are not discussed in this book.

The Desktop

You saw the Windows Desktop earlier in Figure 7.1; it was the screen that was visible on the computer after you successfully started it up. Note that it takes up the whole screen, and, unlike any other window, you cannot make it smaller than the visible screen.

You can technically make your Desktop smaller than the screen, but that is fairly pointless. You may also be able to make the Desktop bigger than the screen, which can sometimes be useful. Indeed, you can also spread your Desktop over more than one screen, but we shall not consider either of these options here.

You can change the background of the Desktop, as you'll see later in this chapter. When you first use your computer, it's probably a single colour or *default* background. On this background, you see a number of *icons*. They may not appear exactly the same as shown in Figure 7.1, because what appears depends on your system setup. But there are two icons that nearly always appear: Internet Explorer and the Recycle Bin (see Figure 7.5). In addition, you may also see My Computer and My Documents. Whether you see these depends how your system has been set up; you can also access them from the Start menu (explained in the next section).

FIGURE 7.5   Icons that nearly always appear on the Windows Desktop

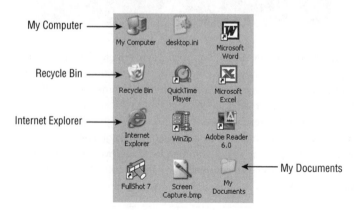

Here's what these icons do:

Internet Explorer   The Microsoft Internet Explorer (IE) web browser comes with Windows XP. While there are advantages in using IE in the context of Windows XP because they are closely integrated, some people prefer to use other browsers such as Netscape Communicator or Opera.

 See Part 7, "Information and Communication," for more information on the Microsoft IE browser and other browsers.

Recycle Bin   The Recycle Bin is important, because by default any file you delete from your hard disk is not actually deleted, but is sent to the Recycle Bin, from where you can retrieve it if you find that deletion was not what you wanted to do. However, the Recycle Bin has a fixed size (although you can change it) and once it is full, the oldest files are automatically deleted to make room for the new files. So if you want to retrieve a file from the Recycle Bin, don't wait too long after you've deleted it! Note that when you delete a file from a removable disk, you really delete it and you're not able to retrieve it.

My Computer   `My Computer` is physically the "root" folder of the disks on the computer, as you will see in the next section. Note that the logical "root" folder of the system is the Windows Desktop.

My Documents   `My Documents` is exactly what it says it is, a place (a virtual folder) where you can store your documents. While you can put them anywhere you like on the system, putting them here—usually in subfolders with names that make sense to you—is a good idea. Apart from anything else, it makes backing them up much easier. Note that Windows XP allows several users to use the same computer, although you can set up options to share files.

Click each of the icons on your Desktop to see what you find. (Close the items that open by clicking the X button at the top-right corner.)

Taskbar

Along the bottom of the screen is the Taskbar (see Figure 7.6).

FIGURE 7.6   The Taskbar is located at the bottom of the screen.

The Taskbar is made up of the following items (from left to right):

The Start button   Clicking this button opens the Start menu, which is discussed in detail in the next section.

The Quick Launch bar   The Quick Launch bar contains icons for specific programs, which can be launched from here with a single click. You can add programs to or remove them from the Quick Launch bar. Note that if the Quick Launch bar is not displayed, you can display it by right-clicking a blank part of the Taskbar and selecting Toolbars and then Quick Launch. Note also that this Quick Launch bar is of a fixed length, and items that do not appear on the bar itself can be accessed by clicking the double arrow on the right-hand side. Mousing over the icons that do appear opens a box telling you what each one is.

Mousing over an icon or a filename simply means moving your mouse over it. You can choose an option so that doing this selects the file. Without setting this option, mousing over an icon or tool often opens a box giving you information about that tool. See, for example, Figure 7.11 (shown later in this chapter), where the icon has been moused over. In addition, mousing over a filename or icon opens a pop-up box giving information about the file or folder.

Running tasks   These are the programs that are currently running, or to be strictly correct, the windows that are currently open, even if they are minimised. This means that the entry on the Taskbar is the only visible evidence that they are running. The active window—in other words, the one you can see (or the one on top if you can see several)—is highlighted. Clicking any other activity makes that the active window. If the window is maximised—in other words, it fills the full screen—then the new window overlays the previously active window. If the window is not maximised, clicking it simply brings it to the front. Note that changing the active window does not affect anything that is happening in any of the other windows. Activities in different windows are effectively independent. Note that you can also switch between active windows by holding down the Alt key and pressing the Tab key, as you'll see shortly.

Notification area   The Notification area (previously called the System Tray) contains screen information, the volume control and time, and icons representing various background tasks. These appear on the right-hand side, but usually only the time appears (mousing over it shows the date). You may need to click the arrow to the left of the time to reveal the rest of the Notification area.

The Start Menu

The Start menu is opened by clicking the Start button on the Taskbar. At the top, it says who the user is, in this case, David. On the left-hand side, in the top in what is described as the *pin area*, above the separator rule are the labels Internet and E-mail. Note that you do not have to use these programs; you can remove them from the pin area and add other programs if you wish. It probably makes sense to add programs that you use frequently. Of course, programs that you do use frequently are displayed in the area below the separator rule.

At the bottom of the left-hand side of the Start menu is All Programs. If you click this, a list of all the programs on your computer is displayed (see Figure 7.7).

Classic Start Menu

The "classic" Windows Start menu (from Windows 95) is still around. You can switch to the "classic" Start menu by right-clicking Start and selecting Properties.

FIGURE 7.7   The result of clicking All Programs in the Start menu, with subfolders shown

Strictly speaking, what you see is a list of all the programs that are stored in the Program Files folder, which you can access from the Hard Disk Drives section of the My Computer folder (described shortly). If programs are stored elsewhere (and sometimes programs install themselves in their own folders), they do not appear here. You can start a program from here (and some programs you can start only from here) by moving your cursor onto the program and clicking. Those entries that have a right-pointing arrow alongside them are folders; if you move your cursor onto them, you open the folder. There may be several levels of subfolders, as shown in Figure 7.7.

On the top right-hand side of the Start menu, the following are listed:

My Documents   Clicking this opens the folder called My Documents, which is set up automatically for each user (see Figure 7.8). It is difficult to specify what is stored here, except to say that the files are those that you create. The nature of these, of course, depends on what you do. They could be letters, accounts spreadsheets, databases, or documents of different kinds. And, although there are other special folders for them, there is no reason why you shouldn't store pictures, music files, or even programs here.

FIGURE 7.8   The My Documents folder

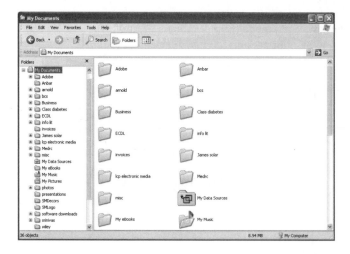

My Pictures   Similarly, clicking this opens the folder called My Pictures (see Figure 7.9). Note that subfolders here appear in a different style. If you open such a subfolder, you can choose the Filmstrip view in which you see thumbnails of the pictures (see Figure 7.10), together with a larger version of the selected picture, the ability to step through the pictures, and the facility to rotate them.

FIGURE 7.9   The My Pictures folder

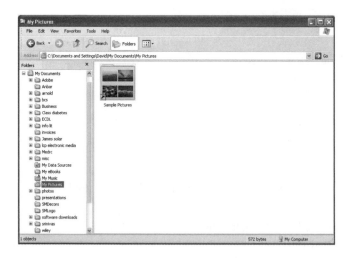

FIGURE 7.10   A folder containing pictures, with the Filmstrip view enabled

My Music   Clicking this opens a folder called My Music (see Figure 7.11). Incidentally, this is a good example of the information displayed when you mouse over the icon for a piece of music.

FIGURE 7.11   Two icons in the My Music folder showing the information displayed if an icon is moused over

My Computer   Clicking this opens what is effectively the top-level folder of your computer (see Figure 7.12). This is divided into three sections. The first is Files Stored On This Computer, which shows Shared Documents (documents available to all users) and, in this case, David's Documents. If any other users were created, there would also be folders for their documents. The title is slightly misleading, because this section does not include all files stored on the computer, only those in the two folders shown. To access all files, you need to go to the second section, Hard Disk Drives, which does indeed give access to all the folders on the computer, including those containing system files and programs. The final section, Devices With Removable Storage, shows devices such as floppy disks, Zip disks, CDs, tape drives, or even memory cards that can be used with digital cameras.

FIGURE 7.12   The My Computer folder

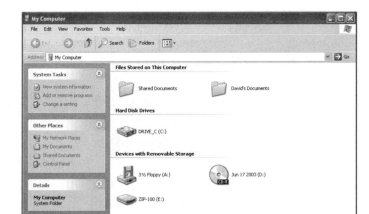

The next section on the right-hand side of the Start menu has two entries:

Control Panel   Control Panel allows you to change the settings for almost every aspect of the way your computer runs. However, many of these settings are outside the scope of this book.

Printers And Faxes   This entry allows you to add printers and fax machines to your system and to control how they operate. We shall return to this feature in Chapter 13, "Printing."

The bottom section of the right-hand panel of the Start menu includes three items:

Help And Support   We will come back to this entry later in this chapter. It is important to know about the Help and Support options so that you can find out about Windows features and get help when you have a problem.

Search   This entry provides you with ways of locating files and information within files on your system. We shall consider searching in detail in Chapter 10, "Working with Files and Folders."

Run   If you select this entry, a dialog box opens that allows you to start applications. This is effectively an alternative to using the All Programs option at the bottom of the Start menu.

At the bottom of the Start menu are the entries Log Off and Turn Off Computer. Logging off is the reverse of logging on. If you are working on a network or there are others who use the same computer, you log off when you have finished using the system. This means that your files are no longer accessible unless you log on again or you have allowed any of your files to be shared with others.

See what happens when you select different options, particularly the options on the right-hand side. You're very unlikely to change your system unless you click OK after making any changes. To avoid making any unintentional changes, do not click OK; always click Cancel.

Basic Information and Operations

Now that you know your way around the Windows Desktop, you can start to find out more about your computer and learn how to perform basic operations such as disk formatting and backing up.

Classic View

Windows 95 offered only one interface option or view; in Windows 98, this was referred to as the *Classic* view. It shows how fast things change in this area that a style can become a classic in only a few years. The first version of Windows appeared only about 10 years ago, but the interface changed quite significantly with Windows 95, so it became "classic" in only three years! Windows XP provides you with many options. The two different views are shown in Chapter 9, "Working with Windows." You can switch between the views by using Folder Options in Control Panel (described in the following section).

How to Look At Basic System Information

You may want to know about the operating system, the processor type, or the amount of memory (random access memory—RAM) installed. Most of this information you access via Control Panel, which you open from the Start menu. A window appears that may look confusing, but most of the icons are either self-explanatory or have complex names that probably mean that you'll never have to be concerned with them.

Click the one that (by default) looks like a computer and is labelled System. A System Properties window opens that looks like Figure 7.13. The first view (called a tab) is called General and tells you about your operating system, your processor type, and who supplied it. This information may be useful when talking to dealers or support people.

FIGURE 7.13   The General tab under System Properties

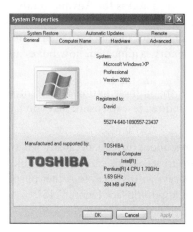

There are six other tabs in this window:

Computer Name   This tab allows your computer to be identified if it is attached to a network.

Hardware   This tab allow you to set up and manage hardware, but you are unlikely to need to access this yourself. As noted earlier, adding hardware to a system running under Windows XP is easy because of the Plug and Play facility.

System Restore   This tab controls how you store system information and track harmful changes to your computer to help the system recover from a problem. You should only access this under expert guidance or with careful attention to the Help files.

Automatic Updates   You may wish to access this tab, because here you can determine whether automatic updates to your operating system are downloaded if you are connected to the Internet (see Figure 7.14).

FIGURE 7.14   The Automatic Updates tab under System Properties

Advanced   You should not need to access the Advanced tab, although you can look at it. It concerns user profiles (so that you can be recognised when you log on to different systems), system performance (how the processor in your system operates—giving priority to programs or background tasks), how memory is allocated, how boxes and menus appear, and changes to startup and recovery.

Incidentally, if you do access any of these settings out of interest, always click Cancel rather than OK when you leave the window, just to ensure that you have not inadvertently made any changes.

Remote   You may need to know about this tab, because it lets you allow access to someone else to look at your system, perhaps to see if they can solve a problem for you. The bottom part of the window allows others to access your system for other purposes. You should only use this if you are sure about what you are doing (see Figure 7.15).

FIGURE 7.15   Remote tab under System Properties

How to Look At and Set Basic Windows Information

You may also want to look at information about the Desktop, including screen settings, the time and date, and other options, such as the (sound) volume settings. Again, you access Control Panel. There are two views of Control Panel, called by Microsoft the Classic view and the Category view. You can switch between them by clicking the first entry in the left-hand window of Control Panel. For simplicity, let's use Classic view. The following list covers some of the things that you can view and change:

Folder options   You can use one of two views of folders and files. To set Classic view globally, choose Folder Options, and the Folder Options window opens. You can also open this window from any folder; to do this, go to Tools in the top line of the window, click it, and select Folder Options from the menu. Check that the General tab is showing. The information on this tab is divided into three sections. In the top section, you can choose to view your folders either with the common tasks listed on the left-hand side or in the Classic view. In the bottom section, you can choose whether to use a single click or a double-click to open a file. In the former case, the file is selected simply by mousing over it; in the second case you have to (single) click the icon or filename to select it. Once you have selected a file (but not opened it), you can carry out various operations on the file or find out information about it.

Date and time settings   Click Date And Time, which, not surprisingly, opens the Date and Time Properties window (see Figure 7.16) where you can set the date and time. A second tab, Time Zone, allows you to change the time zone in which you live. You can also set the system to automatically correct the time for daylight savings. Incidentally, when the clocks change, the computer informs you about it and asks you to check that everything is correct. If you just want to see the time, it is usually displayed in the bottom-right corner of the screen. In addition, mousing over the time displays the date. The third tab, Internet Time, allows you to synchronise your computer's time with a clock on the Internet, but we shall not discuss this further here. To change the display format of the date and time, go to Regional and Language Options (described shortly).

FIGURE 7.16   The Date And Time Properties dialog box enables the user to set the date and time.

    It is not a good idea to change the date and time to settings that do not correspond to the actual date and time, particularly if you are on a network. This is partly because of the way that network settings are synchronised, and partly because many of the settings on your computer pick up the date; setting the wrong date may cause you problems.

Screen settings   Click Display and then the Settings tab (see Figure 7.17). Here you can see how the screen area (or resolution) and the colour scheme have been set. The screen area shows the number of *pixels* displayed, for example, 800 × 600, and the colour scheme specifies how many colours are used on your Desktop; the more colours used, the more natural any photograph appears. Note that the options you are given, and indeed how the screen will appear, depends on your system (desktop or laptop, for example), your physical screen size, and on the software used to control the screen. There is a button for Advanced settings, of which there are many. You may wish to have a look at these, in particular, General, if you find the screen typeface too small, and Displays, if you are connecting a second monitor, for example, a data projector.

FIGURE 7.17   The Settings tab under Display Properties

Desktop colours and fonts   Click Display and select the Appearance tab in the Display Properties window (see Figure 7.18). Here you can choose the styles, fonts, and colours used on the Desktop. Clicking Advanced allows you to change the colour and font for different parts of the Desktop. Clicking Effects allows you to change a number of other effects, which are self-explanatory and you can investigate for yourself. Fonts for use within applications are handled using the Fonts option in Control Panel, but this is outside the scope of this book.

FIGURE 7.18   Choosing fonts and colours using the Appearance tab

Desktop wallpaper   Wallpaper is the background to the icons on the Desktop. Click Display and then the Desktop tab in the Display Properties window (see Figure 7.19); you can also open this window by right-clicking the Desktop background and selecting Properties. Changing the settings will illustrate the effects. Note that you have three options: You can centre a pattern or picture, which is probably preferable if you have a picture, you can stretch it to fill the screen (which may or may not be appropriate), or you can tile it so that it repeats across the screen in both directions.

FIGURE 7.19   Selecting the Desktop wallpaper using the Desktop tab

If you don't like what you see, just change the settings again; you can do no harm. If you don't like anything that Microsoft or your computer manufacturer provides, you can use any graphics file or even a web page. To do this, click the Browse button and find the file you want to use. Click Open and the file appears in preview. If you want to use it, click OK. Windows XP also allows you to choose Desktop themes, but this is outside the ECDL syllabus.

Screensavers   Screensavers have two main purposes. The original purpose was to avoid *burn-in*, an effect in which a picture displayed for too long became permanently etched on the screen. However, this is not really a problem with modern screens. The second reason is that screensavers act as a security device, hiding what you are doing from prying eyes if you leave your desk. And, of course, they can be fun to look at. You choose them in a similar way to choosing wallpaper. Click Display and choose the Screen Saver tab in the Display Properties window (see Figure 7.20). You can scroll through the available options, adjusting settings if there are any available and previewing them if you wish. Note that you can also set a password and determine how long before the screensaver comes into effect. There is a reference to power saving; this is when the screen goes completely blank in order to save power. Exactly how this is set up varies from system to system.

FIGURE 7.20   The screensaver options

Regional and language options   Clicking this icon in Control Panel displays the Regional Options tab in the Regional and Language Options window shown in Figure 7.21. In this window you can view (and change) the currency symbol in use, the character used for the decimal point, and the time and date formats. Click Customize to see the options.

FIGURE 7.21   The Regional And Language Options window

The Languages tab in the Regional And Language Options window allows you to set up your system to use different languages. If you go to this tab and click Details, the Text Services and Input Languages window opens. Before you can change the language, it is necessary to add the languages that you wish to use (in addition to the default). In Figure 7.22, French (as used in France; for many languages, there are several different options) and German (as used in Germany) are added.

FIGURE 7.22   The Text Services and Input Languages window with French and German added

There are two other settings that you can change to make it easy to switch between languages. If you click Language Bar, you have the option to display the language options in different ways.

However, you may find it easier to switch between keyboard language settings by using the keyboard shortcut. This is achieved, by default, by holding down the Shift key and then striking the left-hand Alt key. You can cycle through the languages you have available. If you have many, you can set up direct keyboard shortcuts by clicking the Key Settings box shown in Figure 7.22, which opens a window where you can also change the default shortcut. (Be careful, however, when you set up keyboard shortcuts, that you are not overwriting other shortcuts that are already set up.) Note that there is also an option here to change how you exit from Caps Lock. The Advanced tab in the main Regional and Language Options window is concerned with setting up your computer when using languages that either do not use what is referred to as the Western alphabet or use extensions to this alphabet, such as diacritical marks. These are generally outside the scope of this book.

Sound volume   The simplest way to control the sound volume is to use the volume control on the Taskbar. (If necessary, click the left arrow first to reveal the Taskbar.) Just select the volume control, and a slide bar is displayed like those on a hi-fi system. Move the slider to a comfortable volume and then click elsewhere to close the window. Note that there is also a Mute option, which can be useful in certain circumstances.

If you do not see the symbol on the Taskbar, then click Sounds And Audio Devices in Control Panel. The Volume tab in the Sounds and Audio Devices Properties window is active by default (see Figure 7.23), and among other controls, a slide bar appears, on which you can adjust the volume. Below this is a box that allows you to display the volume control on the Taskbar. If you also want to change the balance, click Advanced. You only need to change the Master settings (the other settings are outside the scope of this book). When the volume and balance are as you want them, close this box by clicking the X in the top-right corner. To close the Sounds And Audio Devices Properties window, click OK.

FIGURE 7.23   Adjusting the sound volume

Note that these are just some of the settings you can view and change via Control Panel. You will learn about others if and when you need them.

Finding Information about Your Disks

To find information about your disks, the simplest way is to open My Computer and select the disk that you are interested in. You can then see the size of the disk and how much free space there is on it. Exactly how this is displayed depends on which Desktop view you are using; the default view is shown in Figure 7.24.

FIGURE 7.24   Checking information about your disks using the default view in My Computer

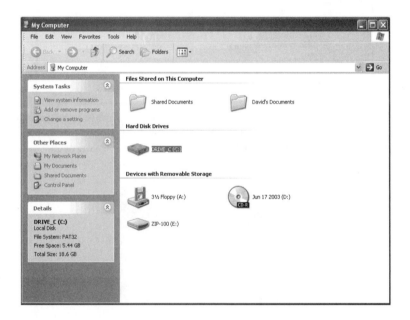

Look at any other disks on your system, for example, floppy disks, Zip drives, or even network disks. Try changing to the Classic view as well.

An alternative way to look at disk information is via Windows Explorer, which you can open by right-clicking Start and selecting Explore. When the window has opened, slide the scroll bar in the left-hand window to the top and select Drive C:. Your window should look like the one in Figure 7.25.

FIGURE 7.25 Looking at system details via Windows Explorer

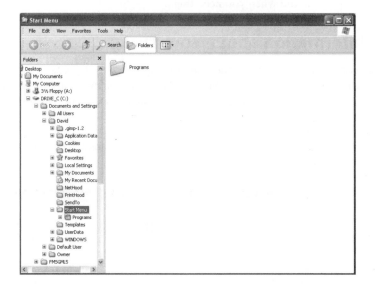

Select the disk that you're interested in and choose File ≻ Properties. A Properties window like the one in Figure 7.26 opens, which gives you the information you need.

FIGURE 7.26 Obtaining disk information

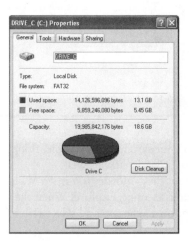

Formatting Removable Disks

While you may never have to format a hard disk (and this is not covered within ECDL), you may frequently have to format a removable disk, either a floppy disk or a Zip disk. (What *format* means technically is to organise the magnetic sectors on the disk surface so that they store data in the format recognised by the Windows operating system, which organises the data differently from a Macintosh system, for example.) What this means from a practical perspective is that the disk is ready to store files.

Formatting a Disk

To format a disk, use the following steps:

1. Open My Computer and select, but not open, the disk drive—usually labelled 3.5-Inch Floppy (A:).

2. Choose File ➢ Format. A Format window opens (see Figure 7.27) with various options. (Alternatively, you can right-click the disk icon and select Format.)

FIGURE 7.27   The floppy disk formatting dialog box

3. Choose the type of disk and its capacity. Today, most 3.5-inch disks have a capacity of 1.44 megabytes (MB), but you may have a disk that has only 720 kilobytes (kb) or even an old-style 5.25-inch disk (these really are floppy!).

4. Choose the type of format:

  ▪ Quick can only be used if the disk has been previously formatted; this option just erases any existing data. So for a new disk or one about which you have little information, do not select Quick.

  ▪ The Create An MS Startup Disk option is only used if you want to create a disk from which you can boot (start) your system. You may find that you need this if you have problems with your hard disk. Windows XP usually prompts you to create such a boot disk when you install the operating system. Alternatively, you may have been supplied with a recovery disk with your system.

     Leave the other options (FAT and Allocation Unit Size) at their defaults.

5. If you want to, give the disk a label. You do not have to do this, but it can be useful.

6. Click Start, and you see a record of the progress being made and a summary when the formatting is complete.

Formatting a Zip Disk

To format a Zip disk, use the following steps:

1. Open My Computer and select, but not open, the Zip drive—labelled something like ZIP-100 (E:). The letter in parentheses may vary.

2. Choose File ➤ Format. This opens the Format Disk window (see Figure 7.28) with two options. (You can also right-click the disk icon and select Format.)

FIGURE 7.28   The Zip disk formatting dialog box

3. Choose the type of format:

- Short Format can be used only if the disk has been previously formatted and just erases any existing data.

- For a disk on which there may be errors or for which you have forgotten the password, select Long Format.

   All new Zip disks come formatted.

4. If you want to, give the disk a name. You do not have to do this, but it can be useful. The default name is ZIP-100 (or ZIP-250 or ZIP-750 if you are using higher-capacity disks).

5. Click Format, and you see a record of the progress being made and a summary when the formatting is complete.

Backing Up Your Files

You have seen how to format removable disks, floppy and Zip disks. You can also write to recordable CDs and to the memory cards that are used in digital cameras. There are now even storage devices that you can put on your keyring.

There are two main reasons why you need removable storage devices. The first is to be able to transfer files between computers. Even when computers are connected via the Internet, it is often much easier to send a CD through the mail than to e-mail large files over the network.

The second reason is security. However well you protect your system, there is always a chance that something will go wrong with the software. And certainly things can go wrong with the hardware as well.

So, it's important to back up your files. If you are on a company network, you may find that the systems people back up your work files; they almost certainly back up program and system files. If you either use a stand-alone computer or run your own system, you need to devise a backup strategy.

It is likely that your system came with a recovery disk or you were prompted to create one when you installed your operating system. However, it is still a good idea to make a backup of your complete system onto a CD if you can. This can be done either manually—in other words, you copy the files—or with special software. Windows XP includes a backup program, but it can only be run under DOS and is not for novice users. It's possible to buy software packages that handle backups, but manual backup can be quite reliable.

If your system does fail, then, once you have repaired it or have a new system, you have to reinstall the operating system and any software supplied to you on disk. Make sure that you have held a record off the system of the serial numbers and other important information. However, you will need to restore any software that you have downloaded from the Internet and any data or text files, so you should copy these files to a removable storage device at regular intervals. Depending on what you are doing, this can be as often as once a day.

How To Use Help Functions

Your system has extensive help built into it, and you should get used to using this. These days, you do not get the large printed manuals that used to be provided; being able to use Windows Help properly will make your life much easier.

There are two ways to access Windows Help:

Choose Start ➤ Help And Support.   This takes you in at the top level of Help (see Figure 7.29). Note that while the main screen remains the same, the label at the top right may vary, depending on the make of your computer and possibly your company, as may the details of your hardware at the top left of the main window.

FIGURE 7.29   The Help window

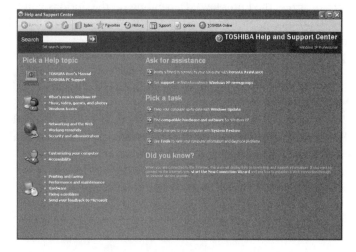

Press the function key F1. This provides you with context-sensitive help, in other words, help about the part of Windows XP that you are currently using. This is often the better solution. Figure 7.30 shows the window that opens when F1 is pressed in Control Panel. Note that if you press F1 within an application, you open the help for that application.

FIGURE 7.30 Context-sensitive help

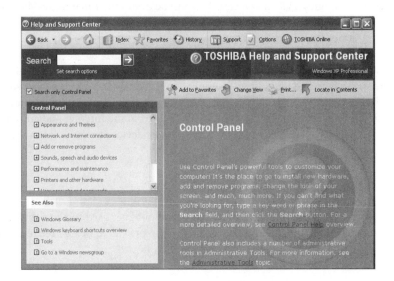

As you can see from Figure 7.30, Help is self-explanatory, as indeed it should be if it is going to be much use. Some additional explanation may be helpful, however. You can access topics from the table of contents that you see in the figure. However, there are two other ways that you can find information on your computer: Search and Index.

To use Search, you enter a term in the box at the top left of the Help screen and click the arrow on the right (or press the Enter key). Depending on the options you have set (see the line below the Search box), a list of relevant items is returned under four headings (see Figure 7.31):

- Suggested Topics

- Overviews, Articles, And Tutorials

- Full-Text Search Matches, which are articles in which the term or terms you have entered appear in the text. These are quite often the same as under Suggested Topics.

- Microsoft Knowledge Base, which contains articles that you can access on the World Wide Web. Note that you have to be connected to the Internet to access these.

FIGURE 7.31   The result of a search in the Help window

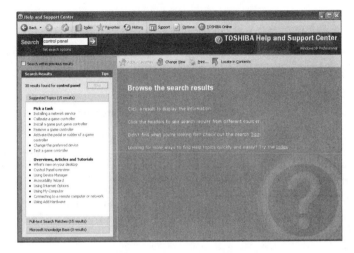

The Index is simply that, an index to the Help files (see Figure 7.32). As you can see, you simply type in the term that you are looking for or scroll down the list provided. Note, however, that the term that you think is correct may not always be the one that Microsoft uses, so Search may be a better option.

FIGURE 7.32   The Help index window

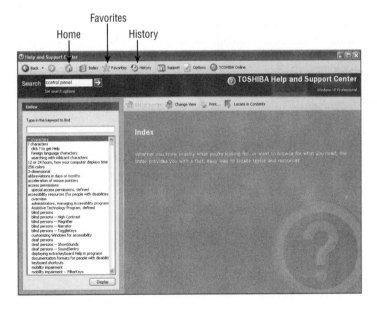

Along the top of the Help screen is a toolbar, including Back and Forward arrows, plus the following icons:

Home   The Home option takes you back to the Help opening screen.

Favorites   The Favorites option allows you to easily access pages that you reference often.

History   The History option allows you to review the pages you have looked at and access them again.

(There may also be other icons, put there by your computer manufacturer.)
There are two other ways in which you can get help:

- Right-click what you don't understand. While you may get a series of options, you may also get a box saying What's This? Click this box to get an explanation, although it may not always be the explanation that you want or tell you as much as you hoped for!

- In some windows (and most applications), there's a question mark on one of the toolbars at the top of the window. Click this and then click in the area where you are confused; an explanatory window opens.

Summary

This chapter covered the basics of working on a computer in the Windows environment. First, you learnt the first steps of starting, shutting down, and restarting a PC. Next, you explored the Windows Desktop and learnt how to make adjustments using Control Panel. You also went over how to obtain and modify information about your system.

Whilst formatting a hard disk is outside the scope of this book, you've seen how to format a floppy disk and a Zip disk. You also learnt how important it is to create backup files, for security and preservation reasons.

Finally, you looked at the Help system and learnt different methods of locating information about unfamiliar functions.

Chapter

8

Working with Icons

IN THIS CHAPTER YOU WILL LEARN HOW TO

✓ Open a file, folder, or application from the Desktop.

✓ Select and move icons.

✓ Recognise basic types of icons such as folders and applications.

✓ Create a shortcut icon or desktop alias.

If you've worked through this book so far, you already have a good idea what icons are. Originally, icons were religious images, usually stylised, and most commonly used in the Orthodox churches. However, in recent years, an *icon* has come to mean any image that represents an idea or an organisation. In computing terms, they are little pictures that represent programs, files, folders, commands, and so on.

Within the Windows environment, clicking or double-clicking an icon triggers an operation of some kind. In order to help you, icons are generally designed to illustrate the operation they represent. After all, if they were all the same, they would not be much help. Indeed, in early versions of Windows, files, for example, were all represented by the same icon, and you had to rely on the filename (usually shown below the icon) to identify the type of file.

When you open a window representing a folder, you see icons within that window that represent either other folders or individual files (see Figure 8.1). By clicking (or in some cases double-clicking) these icons, you open the file or application they represent.

FIGURE 8.1 Icons representing files appear within an open window.

If you try to open an individual file, one of two things can happen. If the file is a program (an application such as Word 2002, for example), the application opens in its own window. If, however, you try to open a file that is not a program, then once again one of two things can happen. If the file is associated with an application (for example, it is a word processing document in Word format), the file opens in the window of that application. If there is no such association, you are asked what application you want to use. This is really outside the scope of this book but useful to know.

Selecting, Moving, and Arranging Icons

You may like to move icons around on your Desktop according to how you use the programs they represent. To select an icon without opening the file it represents, either click the picture once with your mouse or simply mouse over it (depending on which option you are using). You can then use the drag-and-drop method to move it. *Drag and drop* means that, instead of clicking an icon, you place the cursor on the icon and depress the left mouse button. Keeping the button depressed, move the cursor, dragging the icon with it, to its new position. Then let go of the mouse button and the icon stays in the new position as long as this is allowed. (You may, however, get a warning message.)

You can also use drag and drop to move files between folders and move text in a word processing program.

To arrange all the icons on your Desktop at once, right-click the Desktop or within any folder and select Arrange Icons By (see Figure 8.2). By default, icons are arranged in rows and columns. If you select Auto Arrange, you remove the tick by it and turn off this automatic ordering. Then you can move the icons around using drag and drop or using the other options on the menu to arrange icons by type, size, or date. To tidy up the arrangement, just select Auto Arrange again. There are also other options that you can try, for example, Align To Grid, although you cannot change the grid except by changing the size of the icons.

FIGURE 8.2   Selecting how to arrange icons

Changing the Size of Icons

Align To Grid gets the spacing between icons about right, but if you feel the icons are too small, then carry out the following procedure:

1. Right-click the Desktop and select Properties (or choose Start ➤ Control Panel ➤ Display). The Display Properties dialog box opens.

2. In the Display Properties dialog box, select the Appearance tab. Click Effects and the Effects window shown in Figure 8.3 opens.

FIGURE 8.3   The Effects window

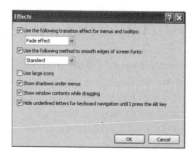

3. Check the box for Use Large Icons.

4. Click OK.

   The sizes of the icons change. Note that you're changing the size of all icons in all windows. You can also change the size of the icons in your Start menu or on your Taskbar:

1. Right-click the Start button and select Properties.

2. Make sure that you are viewing the Start Menu tab and click Customize.

3. The Customize Start Menu window shown in Figure 8.4 opens, where you can change the icon size and other settings.

FIGURE 8.4   Changing the icon size via the Start menu

Basic Types of Icons

You've already met a few icons, but there are quite a number of standard ones shown in here.

Icon	Label	Description
	My Computer	Clicking this icon opens an overview of your system.
	Any hard disk	Clicking this icon opens a hard disk so that you can see what is stored on it.
	Floppy disk	Clicking this item opens the floppy disk that is in the drive that the icon applies to.
	A CD (CD-R means recordable)	Clicking this icon allows you to see the contents of a CD in the CD drive.
	Any folder or directory	Clicking this icon opens up the folder in question so that you can see the files within it.
	My Documents	This is the folder in which it is suggested that you store your work, whatever that may be.
	A printer	Clicking this icon allows you to see the status of the jobs sent to the printer it refers to.
	The Recycle Bin	Clicking this icon allows you to see the contents of the Recycle Bin.
	Microsoft Word	Clicking this icon launches Microsoft's word processing application.
	Microsoft Excel	Clicking this icon launches Microsoft's spreadsheet application.
	Internet Explorer	Clicking this icon launches Microsoft's web browser.
	Adobe Acrobat	Clicking this icon launches the application for reading PDF files.

Whether you click or double-click the icon depends on which option you have chosen (see "How to Look At and Set Basic Windows Information" in Chapter 7).

When files are created by a particular application program, they have a file-name extension (the part of the filename after the full stop). These extensions are automatically associated with a program (not necessarily the one used to create them, so be careful), and the icon representing a file carries a modified version of the program icon.

Shortcut Icons

Shortcuts are icons that you put, for example, on the Desktop to give you easier access to a particular program, folder, or file. In other words, they are pointers, also referred to as *desktop aliases*, to the real icon that starts an application, which usually sits in a folder inside another folder called `Program Files`. You can recognise a shortcut icon by the small arrow in the bottom-left corner. If you delete a shortcut, it is not important, because you can always re-create it. However, if you delete the real icon, you delete the application, which is not usually what you want.

If you delete the file or folder to which the shortcut points, any shortcuts to it are not deleted automatically. If you click what might be called "orphan" shortcuts, you see a message saying that Windows is searching for the file to which the shortcut points, but if you want to, use Browse to locate it yourself. This is because, rather than deleting the file, you may just have moved it, while the shortcut still points to the original location. If you know you have removed the application, you can simply delete the shortcut.

Creating Shortcut Icons

Shortcuts can be created to any file, although usually they are to a program or a folder. The Create Shortcut option appears in many places, including the following:

- On the Desktop pop-up menu (accessed with the right mouse button) as New ➢ Shortcut
- On various drop-down menus
- On the pop-up menu you see if you right-click an icon

 Originally, the term *shortcut* meant a keyboard shortcut. But when Windows 95 was released, pointers—in other words, icon shortcuts—were introduced. So, when we say shortcut, we mean an icon. Keyboard shortcuts will always be referred to by the full term.

There are various ways to create a shortcut. (You must be realising by now that in Windows, there is nearly always more than one way to perform any task.) If you can see an icon on the

Desktop, in a folder, or in Windows Explorer, or even the filename in Windows Explorer, then do the following:

1. Point to the object and right-click, keeping the button held down.

2. Drag the object to the Desktop; you will probably see an outline or ghost version of the object move, while the original stays where it was.

3. Release the mouse button, and a menu appears like that shown in Figure 8.5, although sometimes it looks like Figure 8.6. This is because you are not allowed to move some icons, such as disk drives, because they form the structure of the filing system, as you shall see in more detail in Chapter 10, "Working with Files and Folders."

FIGURE 8.5   Right-clicking and dragging an icon to the Desktop produces this menu.

FIGURE 8.6   Releasing the right mouse button produces this menu if you are not allowed to move the icon.

4. Select Create Shortcuts Here, and a shortcut icon is displayed. If you right-click the icon and do not hold the button down, a menu like the one shown in Figure 8.7 opens. (It may not be exactly the same, because in this case installing the antivirus software, PC-cillin, has added an entry to the menu.)

FIGURE 8.7   Right-clicking (and not dragging) an icon produces this menu.

5. If you then select Create Shortcut, you create a shortcut in the same folder as the real icon, if you are allowed to. Sometimes you get a message that you cannot do this and are asked

if you want to create a shortcut on the Desktop. Of course, a shortcut in the same folder as the real icon is not very useful, but once you have created it, you can always drag it to the Desktop or to a toolbar. Alternatively, you can cut and paste the icon.

If you cannot currently see the icon you want, rather than using My Computer or Windows Explorer to locate it, you can do the following:

1. To create a new shortcut on the Desktop, right-click in a blank area and select New. To create a shortcut in any other folder, either right-click or go to the menu bar at the top and select New. In either case, the window shown in Figure 8.8 opens.

FIGURE 8.8   The shortcut menu with the New window selected

2. Click Shortcut and the Create Shortcut window opens (see Figure 8.9).

FIGURE 8.9   The Create Shortcut window

3. Now you need to indicate what application the shortcut is pointing to. If you know the folder containing the application, type it in the box. In most cases, however, you won't know it. Anyway, you have to be sure to type the full path without making any mistakes, so it's easier (even if it takes longer) to use Browse. This opens the Browse For Folder window (see Figure 8.10).

FIGURE 8.10   Browsing for a folder when adding a shortcut

4. You then need to move down the hierarchy, first opening `My Computer`. It is most likely that your application file will be on Drive `C:`, which is the label always given to the main hard disk of your computer.

5. Again, most application files are stored in the `Program Files` folder, although not always. There is no easy way of finding the folder you want, except that the folders usually have names that give some guidance. When you open a folder containing files, they are displayed as shown in Figure 8.10. Simply select one and click Open (or simply click or double-click it, depending on how your system is set up). Note that you usually want a file with a file-name extension (the letters after the stop or period) of **exe**, which denotes an executable file, in other words, a program. However, you can create shortcuts to particular files, so, for example, if there is a Word file that you access frequently, you can create a shortcut to that file.

6. The path is then displayed in the box in the Create Shortcut window. Click Next and enter a name for the shortcut. For a program, this is usually the name of the program, but you can call it what you like (see Figure 8.11), so a Word file might be called `Monthly Agenda` or `Sales Report`. Click Finish and your shortcut is created.

FIGURE 8.11   Naming a shortcut

Note that when you install new software (as you will in Chapter 9, "Working with Windows"), you are usually offered the option of having a shortcut placed on the Desktop as part of the installation, so you do not have to go through this procedure.

Try creating shortcuts to applications and/or files that you access frequently using the different approaches outlined. If you don't like what you create, delete the icon (select the icon and press Delete; as noted earlier, you delete only the shortcut, not the application) or change the icon, as described in the next section.

There are various shortcuts—that is, icons—that are useful to create. For example, creating a shortcut on the Desktop to a disk drive provides you with a quicker way of seeing the contents than using Windows Explorer or My Computer. Similarly, if you are on a network, you can add other computers to the Desktop. If you access the Internet frequently, a shortcut to the Dial-Up Launcher is useful, although putting it on the Quick Launch bar would be even better (just drag and drop it onto the bar).

Altering Shortcut Icons

You may find that shortcuts are allocated names automatically. However, if you want to rename a shortcut (or, indeed, any icon), just right-click it and select Rename. Type in the new name and, to finish, click somewhere else or press the Enter key. Since Windows 95, there have been no practical limits on the length of filenames or icons, so it makes sense to use a description that you will understand. However, remember that the following characters are not allowed in icon names or filenames: " * : | \ < > / ?.

You can change the *properties* of a shortcut by right-clicking the icon, selecting Properties, and then choosing the Shortcut tab. Most of these options are outside the ECDL syllabus, but a useful one may be the Shortcut key, which allows you to create a *keyboard shortcut* to, say, a program file. If you type in a letter, the system adds Ctrl+Alt. Thus, if you enter F for a program, then the keyboard combination to start that program becomes Ctrl+Alt+F. As usual, click OK to finish.

 WARNING   Be careful: If you define a keyboard shortcut that has been used in a program previously, you will no longer be able to use that in-program shortcut.

You can also change the image of an icon. While it is not a good idea to change the "real" icons for applications and system functions (and you may not be allowed to), you can change the icons for shortcuts, selecting others from amongst those stored on your system. The procedure is as follows:

1.   Right-click a particular shortcut and select Properties.

2.   Because the shortcut selected in this example is to Microsoft Word and is called "Shortcut to WINWORD", the Shortcut to WINWORD Properties dialog box opens (see Figure 8.12).

Note that the Properties dialog box takes on the name of the shortcut. Click the Change Icon button. The Change Icon dialog box opens (see Figure 8.13).

FIGURE 8.12   The shortcut Properties window

FIGURE 8.13   The Change Icon window

3.   In the Change Icon dialog box, you can choose another icon. If you are not happy with any of the choices provided, click Browse to see what is provided on the system. First, a window opens. (Exactly which folder opens depends on previous operations on your system.) Try and open any of the files shown. If there are icons stored in the file you select, they are displayed. However, you may see a message that tells you that there are no icons in the file you selected. If you then click OK, the file `Windows\system32\SHELL32.dll` opens, as shown in Figure 8.14.

FIGURE 8.14 Selecting new icons from the system options

4. Select the icon that you want and click OK.

You can, of course, try opening any file on your system, browsing through the file hierarchy. However, icons are generally only in executable (or program) files, with a file extension of .exe, or in what are called dynamic link library files (with a file extension of .dll). In general, it's probably not a good idea to change the shortcut icons for programs (or applications), but you may wish to do so for specific files.

Try changing some icons. When you browse in the Windows\system32 folder, try opening any file that has an extension .dll (dynamic link library) or .exe (an executable file or program). Either of these file types may incorporate icons, although not all such files do.

Summary

In this chapter, you learned about icons that are used to activate files and programs in Windows. You also learnt about the more prevalent types of icons. You now understand how shortcut icons are used, and you know how to create and modify those shortcuts.

Chapter

9

Working with Windows

IN THIS CHAPTER YOU WILL LEARN HOW TO

- ✓ Recognise the different parts of a desktop window.
- ✓ Reduce, enlarge, minimise, and close a window.
- ✓ Recognise the characteristics that all application windows generally have in common.
- ✓ Move between windows and between applications.
- ✓ Install and uninstall a software application.
- ✓ Capture the screen and paste it into a document.
- ✓ Shut down a non-responsive application.

What is a *window*? This may sound like an unnecessary question to ask, but it's important to be clear. Windows are essentially of several kinds:

- Windows that represent a folder or directory, in which you can see the subfolders and files that are contained within that folder (the ECDL calls these *desktop windows*). (Chapter 10, "Working with Files and Folders," looks at folders in more detail.)

- Windows that are menus or dialog boxes. You have already seen some of these in previous chapters.

- Application, or program windows, that open when a program is started and represent the program environment. There are almost certainly further windows that open within that window; these will be dealt with in other parts of this book, although in Chapter 12, "Editing Text Files," you will briefly look at a simple text editor and a word processor. In the previous chapter, you spent some time looking at the main desktop window, and much of what was said there applies to all windows.

You have already seen what windows look like; for example, clicking My Computer opens a window that shows the disk drive icons and various other folders and files.

Notice that we refer to windows with a small *w*, although of course these windows are an integral component of Windows XP.

When you open a window (and you will soon see how to do this), note that it represents either a folder or an application such as Microsoft Word. When you open a window representing a folder, you see icons (or possibly the names of files; you will see later how to switch between the two) within that window that represent either other folders or individual files.

The Parts of a Desktop Window

Figures 9.1 and 9.2 show a desktop window for the C: drive. This window has been chosen because there is more information than can easily fit in the window as shown. Figure 9.1 shows the default view and Figure 9.2 shows the Classic view. The main difference is that in the default view, the main area of the window is split, providing you with information in the left-hand pane. Sometimes this is useful, but using the Classic view fits more files or information about them into the window. As explained previously, you can choose which view you prefer and switch between them at will. You shall also see shortly that there are various different ways of displaying the information within the window. The options are the same for both views.

FIGURE 9.1   Desktop window for the C: drive using the default view

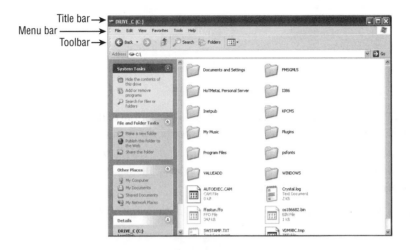

FIGURE 9.2   Desktop window for the C: drive using the Classic view

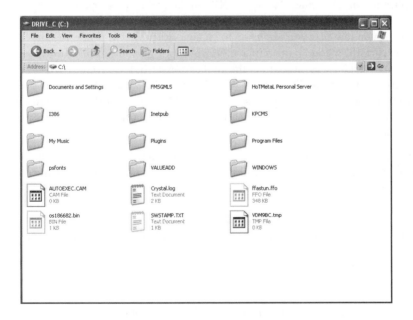

At the top right of almost every desktop window are three buttons, identified in Figure 9.3.

FIGURE 9.3   The top right corner of most desktop windows

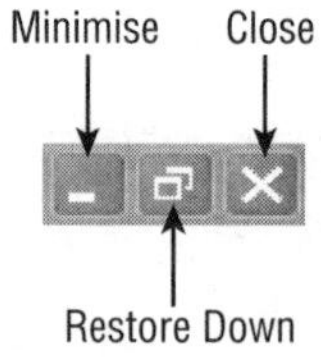

Minimise   Close

Restore Down

These icons perform the following tasks:

Minimise   The Minimise button looks like a flat line at the bottom of the box. If you click this icon, the title of the window appears in the Taskbar at the bottom of the screen, but no window is visible.

Restore Down   If the window occupies the full screen, you see the Restore Down button, which looks like two boxes overlapping. If you click this button, the window size is decreased and the button changes to the Maximise button.

Clicking this Maximise button makes the window fill the whole screen again.

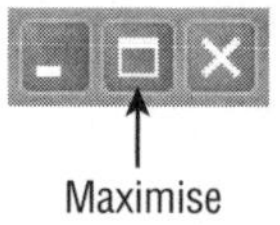

Maximise

Close application or Close file   Windows XP, unlike earlier versions of Windows, has two Close buttons. In general, if you click the first of these (white on red), you close (exit from) the application or window that you are using to change either system properties or, for example, icons. If you click the second button (black on white) within some applications, you close only the file you are working on, rather than the application itself. However, in Word 2002 (the version of Microsoft Word usually supplied with Windows XP), each file opens as a separate window, so clicking the first Close button closes only the file you are working on, and not the Word application, unless it is the only file open. This may sound confusing, but it does not cause any real confusion in practice.

Note also that if you click either button within an application, depending on what you are doing, you may see a message on the screen, asking, for example, if you want to save the file or files on which you have been working.

If a window does not fill the screen, it is a good idea to click the Maximise icon so that the window fills the screen. Even then, the Taskbar is still at the bottom of the screen.

At the top of each window is the title bar, which usually contains the name of the document, file, or program that you have open, or some combination of the three. The title bar tells you which window you have open. On the left, there is an appropriate icon. If you click that, the tasks you can perform are self-explanatory. If you click Move or Size (available only if the window is not maximised), then the cursor changes shape and allows you to move either the window as a whole or one of its edges. Maximise, Minimise, and Close have the same effect as the symbols at the top right of the window.

On the second line of the screen within an application or folder, there is also a menu bar, a (usually grey) bar which contains various menus of frequently used commands arranged by command type: File, Edit, and so on. When you select a particular menu from the menu bar, the appropriate list of commands drops down. (In this case, whichever view you're using—Classic or default—mousing over them selects the menu and clicking opens the menu.) Moving the arrow away deselects the menu if the menu is not open; clicking the menu title again or elsewhere in the window closes the menu. Anything you can do with the window or the files within that folder can be accessed from these menus. You'll be looking at many characteristics of menus as you go through this chapter.

Below the menus are one or more toolbars. Note that the toolbars contain icons that are graphical equivalents of the commands on the menus. Clicking an icon is often quicker than accessing the menu. What the icon does is often printed alongside it in Desktop menus, while in application menus you often have to mouse over the icon to reveal its name. Some of these operations will be discussed later, but those that appear at the top of folders (see Figure 9.4) are worth looking at now.

The icons that are displayed can be changed by selecting View ➤ Toolbars ➤ Customize.

FIGURE 9.4   Some Desktop toolbar icons

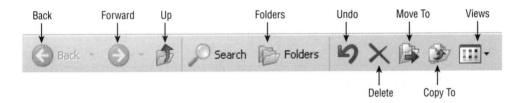

These icons perform the following functions:

Back   The Back icon takes you to the last window you looked at. If the one on the screen is the first or only window that you have looked at, this icon is *greyed out*, which means that it is not operational.

Forward   The Forward icon is greyed out when you open the window initially. However, if you move to another window and then back to the first window, clicking this icon takes you to the second window. If you have moved forward several windows and then back several windows, you can use the Forward icon to move forward to one of those previously viewed windows.

Up   The Up window moves you up the directory structure, which you'll learn more about in Chapter 10. So if you're looking at the window for drive C:, clicking Up moves you to My Computer.

Folders   If you click the Folders icon, a list of folders is displayed in the left-hand pane of a folder window. This allows you to move to any other folder on the system. Effectively, you are opening Windows Explorer. Note that the effect is the same whether you are using the default view or the Classic view. In the former, the pane on the left replaces the usual pane, while in the latter, it simply reduces the width of the main pane. In either case, clicking the Close icon at the top right of the left-hand pane restores the window to its previous state.

Undo   The Undo icon is a very important operation and applies everywhere in Windows. You can also access the Undo option from the Edit menu. It cancels the last operation you carried out (the keyboard shortcut is Ctrl+Z). If you repeat Undo several times, you can work backwards through the operations you have carried out within a folder. There is also a Redo operation, which is accessed either by typing Ctrl+Y or by pressing the function key F4 on your keyboard. Note, however, that these operations apply to editing operations, such as Delete, and not to display options, in which you just choose another option. The difference is that display options, like changing a window size, affect only what you see. Editing operations actually change the files on your system!

Delete   If you select a file or folder within the window and then press the Delete icon, press the Delete key on your keyboard, or go to the File menu and select Delete, you see a message asking you if you want to delete the file or if you want to transfer it to the Recycle Bin (with Yes and No options in each case). Which message you see depends upon which folder you are looking at. If it is a folder on your hard disk, as discussed in Chapter 7, "First Steps with the Computer," deletion just means copying to the Recycle Bin. However, if you're looking at a removable disk, then deletion means exactly that and the file is not recoverable—so be careful!

Move To   The Move To icon is active only when you select a file or folder. If you click this icon, you see a window asking where you want to move the selected file to. Once you have moved a file, it is deleted from its original location.

Copy To   This option is similar to Move To and is active only when a file is selected. Again, a window opens, asking for a destination when you click the Copy To icon. A copy of the file is created in the designated destination, but the original file remains unchanged. Note that Move To is really Copy To and then delete.

Views   Clicking the down arrow to the right of the Views icon not only allows you to choose how to view files and folders, but also what information you view (see Figure 9.5).

Let's look at the options under Views in detail:

Thumbnails   In the Thumbnails view (see Figure 9.6), a folder icon shows images from the folder, so that you can more easily identify the contents of that folder. These may be pictures or they may be slides from a presentation, for example. By default, Windows displays up to four images, but you can choose a picture to identify a folder in Thumbnails view. (Right-click the thumbnail, select Properties, select the Customize tab (see Figure 9.7), and select the picture that you want by browsing in the usual way). The complete folder name is displayed under the thumbnail.

FIGURE 9.5   Options available under Views

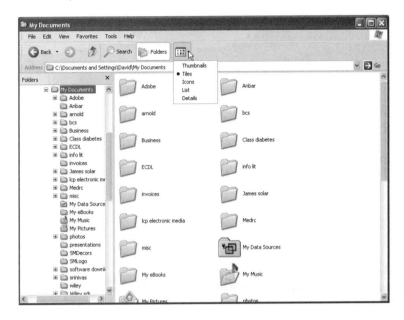

FIGURE 9.6   Selecting the Thumbnails option

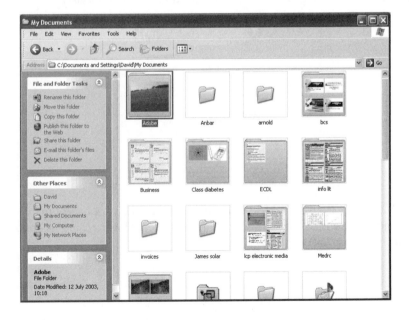

FIGURE 9.7 Choosing a picture to show on a thumbnail

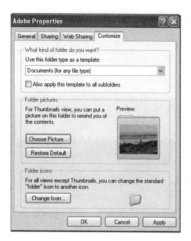

Tiles The Tiles view is similar to the Icons view described next, except that the icons are larger than those in the Icons view, and the information for sorting the order in which files and folders are displayed is shown under the file or folder name. To choose what order to use, go to the View menu and select Arrange Icons By (see Figure 9.8).

FIGURE 9.8 Choosing which information to sort by in the Tiles view

Icons The Icons view (see Figure 9.9) is similar to the Tiles view except that the icons are smaller and only the filename is displayed under the icon. However, in this option, you can also display items in groups.

FIGURE 9.9   The Icons view

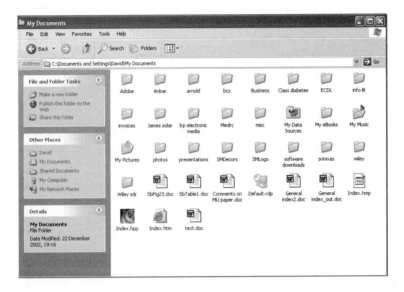

List   In the List view (see Figure 9.10), a list of file or folder names is shown, each preceded
by a small icon. This view can help if you know the name of the file you want to select or open.
While you can sort your files and folders in this view, you cannot display your files in groups.

FIGURE 9.10   The List view

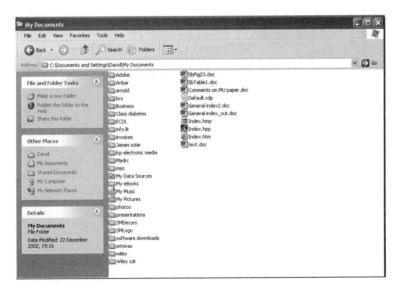

Details   In the Details view (see Figure 9.11), the list of files and folders is shown, including name, type, size, and date last modified. You can add other information by going to the View menu and selecting Choose Details to open the Choose Details window (see Figure 9.12). Within this view, you can sort by the different types of information and show your files in groups. Note that a quick way of sorting by a particular type of information is to click the column heading.

FIGURE 9.11   The Details view

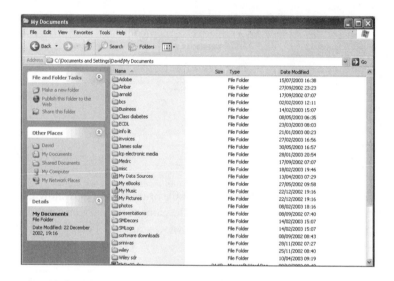

FIGURE 9.12   Choosing the details to display under the Details view

There is also a Filmstrip view for picture folders. Pictures appear as a row of thumbnails. You can move from one picture to another using the left and right arrow buttons. The picture selected is displayed at a larger size above the thumbnail.

> Remember that in the Classic view, you see one pane, and in the default view, two panes. Choose Tools ➢ Folder Options to switch.

Compare the different views of information in windows. Remember that you can switch at any time, so you do not need to keep to one view. Each view is useful in different contexts.

Below the toolbars in a folder window is the Address toolbar, which gives you the full address of what you're looking at. To move to another window, you can either type the new address in this window or, what is probably easier, browse by clicking the down arrow at its right-hand side to display the structure of your system in a similar way to Windows Explorer.

> If the Address toolbar is not showing, choose View ➢ Toolbars and click Address toolbar. It is probably a good idea to confirm that Lock Toolbars is not checked. If it is, then the Address toolbar may not appear where you want it, and you won't be able to move it.

If a window contains more information than can actually be seen in the window, then on the right-hand side of each pane in the window is a vertical *scroll bar* that can be used to display the rest of the files. You can use the scroll bar in several ways:

- Put the cursor on the sliding box and hold down the left mouse button. Then drag the mouse, and thus the box, up or down until you reach the line that you want in the window.

- Move the sliding box by pointing either at the single arrow at the top to move up, or at the single arrow at the bottom to move down the document, and hold the left mouse button down until you reach the line that you want.

- Click in the space above or below the sliding box, and the document moves up or down one screen at a time; repeat until you reach the line that you want.

There may also be a horizontal scroll bar at the bottom of the window. You can use this in the same way; just substitute left and right for up and down in the preceding description.

There may be a third button or a scroll wheel on your mouse. Both are intended to make scrolling easier.

At the bottom of a folder window there are three boxes, which may contain various pieces of information:

Left-hand box   This box contains the number of objects in the window, information about the file selected, or the number of objects selected (if a folder or folders or more than one file is selected). More information is given in the Details section of the left-hand pane in the default view.

Centre box   This box contains the size of the file(s) selected. If a disk is selected, it contains the size of the disk and how much free space there is on the disk. If nothing is selected, it shows the total size of all the files in the folder. If a folder is selected, the box is blank, as it will be if the folder contains only other subfolders.

Right-hand box   This box says where in the system you are, for example, My Computer.

Note that application windows have many different kinds of information, which depend on their function.

Even when a window is set for full screen, you can still see the Windows Taskbar at the bottom of the screen. Depending on how your system is set up, there may also be an Office toolbar (or maybe a Desktop or Accessories toolbar) down the right-hand side of the screen (although these can be moved to anywhere on the screen that you wish). For example, you can keep the Office toolbar floating and minimised for most of the time, opening it only when required (see Figure 9.13). You can add other shortcuts to the bar and thus use it as an alternative to the Start menu. Note that the shortcuts on this bar do not include the arrow in the bottom left-hand corner.

FIGURE 9.13   A floating Microsoft Office toolbar

Moving and Resizing Windows

You have already looked at how you can resize a window using the icons in the top right-hand corner of every window. You can also resize a window by placing the cursor on the edge of the window (if it does not occupy the full screen); the cursor turns into a double-headed arrow (see Figure 9.14). You can then move in either of the directions indicated by the arrow to move that boundary of the window. If you place the cursor at a corner of the window, you can move both of the boundaries that meet at that corner. Selecting the icon in the top left-hand corner and then choosing Size allows you to do the same thing, but it is an unnecessary step.

FIGURE 9.14   The cursor turns into a double-headed arrow when resizing the window.

To move a window (providing it does not occupy the full screen), simply place the cursor on the title bar at the top of the window and drag and drop. Again, using the icon at the top left and the menu produced by selecting it allows you to do the same thing, but this is unnecessary.

As you've seen, this menu also allows you to maximise, minimise, and close the window (repeating the icons at the top right). Occasionally using this menu may be useful because another window is obscuring your access to the top-right corner of the window. (Some windows can be set so that they are always on top.)

Open some windows on the Desktop and change their sizes by the various methods described in this section.

Applications Windows

Applications windows are similar to desktop windows, except that they usually contain more toolbars, menus, and so on, that are specific to their application. They are usually customisable and so may look different on different computers.

For standard applications such as Word, Excel, Access, and Internet Explorer, the windows are explained in the appropriate module.

This section looks briefly at the Microsoft Word window (see Figure 9.15) to obtain a generic idea of the typical characteristics of an applications window. Most other applications have a similar window layout, but vary in the details.

FIGURE 9.15   The Microsoft Word window

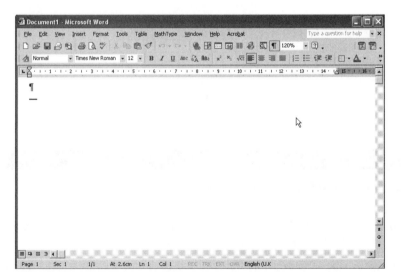

Parts of a Word Application Window

Before we go on to describe the different areas of the screen, notice that, when Word starts up, it opens a new document called Document1 for you. The name is given at the top of the window after the Word file icon (a page with the Word icon superimposed) and, just to remind you, the words "Microsoft Word." In most cases, you won't use the name Document1, but you can do so, typing in the text area and saving the document, giving it whatever name you wish.

At the top right of the screen are the three icons—Minimise, Maximise (or Restore Down), and Close—common to all Windows applications and described previously.

On the second line of the screen are the menus, which are similar to those for the desktop windows. Anything you can do with Word can be accessed from these menus. See Part 3 for further details about using Microsoft Word.

Below the menus are one or more toolbars. Note that the toolbars on your system may not be exactly the same as shown earlier in Figure 9.15. As you now know, the toolbars contain icons (tools) that are graphical equivalents of the commands on the menus; there are also a few icons at the bottom left of the screen. Clicking the icon is often quicker than accessing the menu; if you mouse over an icon, the meaning of the icon is displayed in a small box, as you saw in Chapter 8, "Working with Icons."

Toolbars within applications do not have to be at the top of the screen; they can also be moved around the screen so that they float. If you want to use them in that way, you can, although most people leave them fixed at the top of the screen; the benefit in doing this is that a tool is always in the same place. To move a toolbar that has been "docked" at the top of the screen, put your cursor in the vertical broken line at the left of the toolbar and drag and drop (see Figure 9.16). To move a floating toolbar, put your cursor in the title area at the top and drag and drop. If you move the toolbar back to the top of the screen, it will "dock" again.

FIGURE 9.16 Moving a toolbar

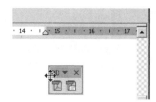

EXERCISE 9.1

Practising with Application Windows

You may not have Microsoft Word, but every Windows system has the more basic word processor, WordPad. Open WordPad and try mousing over the icons and opening the menus so that you start to understand the window and its contents.

To open WordPad, choose Start ➢ All Programs ➢ Accessories; WordPad is the bottom entry in the drop-down menu that opens. Move your cursor to it and click. To close WordPad, click the Close button at the top-right corner. If you are asked whether you wish to save any files, answer No. Open another applications (perhaps Word, Excel, or Microsoft Works) and see the differences from, and similarities with, the WordPad window.

Below the toolbars is the ruler, immediately above the text window, which shows the margins you are using and any tabs you have set for the line you are on in the text. At the left, there is a box showing the type of tab you can currently set. If you are in Page view, there is also a ruler down the left-hand side of the page.

There are probably scroll bars on the right-hand side and at the bottom of the window; this depends on whether the whole document or page can be seen within one window.

Within the Word window, you have a line—the status bar—that gives you more information such as the page and section showing on the screen, the total number of pages, and whether, for example, you are in Insert or Overtype mode.

Applications obviously differ, because they are designed to fulfill different functions. However, virtually all applications have windows with a similar appearance to the Word layout, with menus and toolbars. What the menus and toolbars do varies widely between applications, but generically they are the same. Similarly, scroll bars always work the same way.

Moving Between Windows and Between Applications

Windows is what is called a *multi-tasking system*, in that various different operations can be carried on at the same time. As you work, you may wish to switch between these various tasks.

In fact, systems programs and the applications you have open all take turns using the central processor, but this happens so fast that the user is not usually aware of it, at least in principle. Sometimes, however, depending on what you are doing, how much random access memory (RAM) you have, and how powerful or fast your processor is, the sharing is obvious, and you have to wait for a response from the computer. However, in this section, we are concerned only with how to move between applications that are running and between windows.

If you have a number of windows visible on the screen, in other words, none of them occupy the full screen, the active window's title bar is highlighted. *Active* means that any commands you type on the keyboard will apply to that particular window. *Highlighted* refers to the title bar, which is a dark blue in Windows XP as it is supplied (but this can be changed, so your system may be different).

The title bars of all non-active windows are greyed out. If one window occupies the full screen (and you can see no other smaller windows), then this is the active window.

To make a different window active, you simply click in it if you can see it. While clicking anywhere in the window makes the window active, it is safer to click in the title bar if you can. You then know that you cannot select a file or instigate a process inadvertently by holding down the mouse button for too long.

If you cannot see the title bar or if your active window occupies the full screen, there are two ways to move to another window. The first involves using the Taskbar along the bottom of the screen, where all open windows are represented. To make another window active, just click the box on the Taskbar that represents it, and the new window opens. This also applies if you have windows minimised, that is, they appear only on the Taskbar. If you're not sure which window is which, just select until you have the one you want. Note that a full-screen (maximised) window immediately occupies the full screen if selected, while any window that is not full screen opens on top of whatever was displayed before you made the selection (see Figure 9.17), unless you have a window set to be always on top.

FIGURE 9.17   An example of windows opening on top of each other

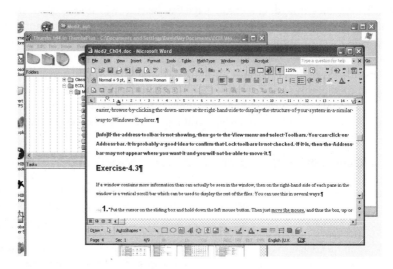

 If you click the box on the Taskbar that represents the window that is currently open, you minimise that window. This can be useful, but, if your system slows up, for whatever reason—for example, you are waiting for a web page to load in Internet Explorer—you may find that, until the system sorts itself out, it is not very clear which page is selected. All you can do here is wait or, if any delay is excessive, take one of the actions described in the next section.

In previous versions of Windows, the boxes on the Taskbar became narrower and narrower as more windows were opened. In Windows XP, windows for applications are combined. This is also necessary because in Word, for example, each file now opens in its own window, rather than there being one window for Word. Thus, if you have a number of files open within one application, the box on the Taskbar tells you how many, and if you click the down arrow on the right-hand side of the box, you can choose which window you want (see Figure 9.18).

FIGURE 9.18   Choosing windows within an application

The second way of changing the active window is to use the key combination Alt+Tab. This opens a small window in the centre of your screen (see Figure 9.19) showing the open windows, with the active window surrounded by a square and its title displayed below. If you hold down Alt and press Tab again, the square moves to the next application, and the title changes appropriately. You can cycle through all the open windows; if you also hold down the Shift key, the square moves backwards. To make a window active, simply release the keys when it is surrounded by the square. It is useful to note that although you cycle through the operations, if you press Alt+Tab a second time, the previously active window becomes active again. This can be useful if you are switching backwards and forwards between two applications or windows.

FIGURE 9.19   The active window surrounded by a square

You can, of course, also minimise the currently active window, but you can't usually predict which window then becomes active.

You may wish to look at the Desktop and minimise all windows. To do this, click the arrow at the right-hand side of the Quick Launch bar on the Taskbar and click Show Desktop. Alternatively, you can right-click a blank part of the Taskbar and click Show The Desktop on the pop-up menu. If you're viewing the Desktop and you right-click in a blank part of the Taskbar, Show The Desktop has changed to Show Open Windows. Clicking this restores the position that you were in before showing the Desktop, which can be useful and is not an option accessible from the Quick Launch bar. Whenever you change the active window, it's a good idea to save the file you're working on in the active window. While in principle you should be able to go back and save it, things sometimes go wrong; even though Windows has ways of restoring files that have been lost or corrupted, they are not foolproof and anyway, it's better not to need them!

Shutting Down a Non-Responsive Application

Occasionally, for one of a number of reasons, an application stops responding. This usually means that when you use the keyboard or click the mouse, nothing happens or perhaps whatever operation the system was carrying out just stops. You can usually tell because you can no longer hear the disk drive operating, or the light that indicates that the disk drive is operating stops flashing. If this happens, try the following, in the order shown:

- Press the Esc (Escape) key on your keyboard. This may stop the operation in progress and let you enter another command.

- If pressing the Esc key has no effect, then hold down the Ctrl and Alt keys together and press the Delete key. This brings up the Applications tab of the Windows Task Manager window as shown in Figure 9.20 (don't worry about the other tabs). Often the program you're using is at the top of the list, followed in brackets by "Not responding." In this case, click End Task. This closes the program you are running. You will lose any changes you made since you last saved the file(s) you were working on. You may then just be able to start the application again. If another program shows "Not responding," scroll down to that program and close it as well. In such a case, because the result is unpredictable, it's a good idea to save your work and close any application you are running and restart the computer as described in Chapter 7. Indeed, you may find that even if it is the program you are running that has hit problems, they may recur, so restarting the computer is a good idea.

FIGURE 9.20 The Applications tab of the Windows Task Manager window

- If you cannot close the program, either because the Windows Task Manager has no effect or because the cursor does not respond to the keyboard or the mouse, try Ctrl+Alt+Del again. This restarts your computer immediately without going through the shutdown procedure. If Ctrl+Alt+Del has no effect, you can achieve the same result by pressing the Reset button on your computer, if it has one. As a last resort, switch the computer off and on again.

- Finally, there may be a serious problem with your system or your disk. While these are much rarer than they used to be, they do happen, particularly as systems get older. It is best to consult someone who knows about hardware. To maximise the benefits from their advice (for which you may have to pay), make sure you have a recovery disk to hand.

Capturing the Screen Image and Pasting It into a Document

Sometimes you want to capture what is on the screen and include it within a document. While there are various programs that allow you to do this in more complex ways, Windows XP provides a simple way of doing so: Hold down the Windows key and press PrtSc (Print Screen). To include the image in a document, you simply execute the Paste command in an application.

 You may want to save the image you have captured. While this can be done in, for example, a Word file, the image is then not accessible to other programs. However, if you paste the image into a picture-editing program, you can save it under whatever name you wish and in an appropriate format. While outside the scope of this book, it's useful to know that there are various image formats that are used in different contexts.

Installing and Uninstalling Software Applications

Although your computer comes with some software applications installed, you may wish to install other applications and, of course, you may decide that you wish to uninstall some applications that are installed.

Installing Applications

To install a new application (or program), you can get the required software in one of three ways:

- It may come supplied on a removable disk of some kind (usually a CD, but it could be on a floppy disk or a Zip disk).
- It may be downloadable from the Internet.
- It may be elsewhere on a network to which your system is connected.

As with other Windows operations, there are various ways in which you can initiate the installation of a new application:

- A CD may incorporate a program that runs automatically when you insert the CD.
- You can use the Run command from the Start menu.
- You can use Add Or Remove Programs in the Control Panel.

All of these are ways to start a special installation program that copies the files that an application needs from the source, whether they are on a removable disk or in some compressed format in a file that you have downloaded.

If the program is supplied on CD, it's possible that the CD will *autorun*, that is, execute automatically when the CD is put in the drive. If this does not happen, or if your software is supplied on a floppy or indeed downloaded as an executable file from the Internet (a file with a filename extension .exe), then choose Start ➢ Run, which opens the Run window shown in Figure 9.21.

FIGURE 9.21   The Run window

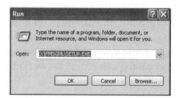

The Open box usually contains the name of the last file that was run in this way, so browse to find the file that you want on a CD, on a floppy, or even on your hard disk, where it may have been saved as a download from the Internet. What happens when you run the program varies from program to program. Usually special installation software opens, and you follow the instructions on the screen, which almost always includes agreeing to abide by the software licence.

While you can use the Run command on the Start Menu, you do not need to do so. You can simply browse, either using Windows Explorer or starting from My Computer (or any other folder), find the folder and program you want, select the icon, and choose Open. Alternatively, once you have found the program you want, you can open it by clicking or double-clicking.

To use the standard Windows XP route for installing software, click Start and open the Control Panel. Choose Add Or Remove Programs so that you see the Add or Remove Programs window shown in Figure 9.22.

FIGURE 9.22   The Add Or Remove Programs dialog box

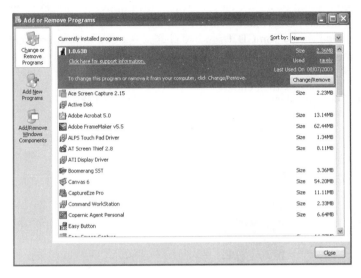

Click Add New Programs on the left-hand side to display the window in Figure 9.23.

FIGURE 9.23   Adding new programs

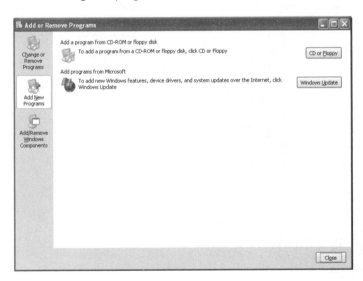

Click the first option to open the Install Program From Floppy Disk Or CD-ROM window shown in Figure 9.24 and then click Next to search the floppy and/or CD in their respective drives. The Run Installation Program window shown in Figure 9.25 opens. Clicking Finish in this window is then just the same as if you had clicked Run from the Start menu. The other option shown earlier in Figure 9.23 connects you to the Internet to download software, but this is outside the scope of this book.

FIGURE 9.24   Installing a program from a CD or floppy disk

FIGURE 9.25   The Run Installation Program window

Uninstalling Applications

Uninstalling software is in some ways more complicated than installing. Some applications come with Uninstall routines, which you can access from the Start menu, using All Programs (see Figure 9.26, for example).

FIGURE 9.26   Opening an uninstall program from All Programs on the start menu

Click Uninstall and follow the instructions. There are two caveats, however. First, the Uninstall program may ask for the installation disk, so have this to hand. Second, you may see a warning like that shown in Figure 9.27 about shared components; if you are in any doubt about what to do, click No To All, as the window suggests.

FIGURE 9.27   A warning about removing shared files during the uninstall process

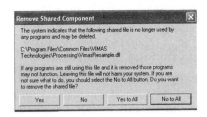

As you did for installing software, use the standard route shown earlier in Figure 9.21. Clicking a specific program changes the window to that shown in Figure 9.28 and clicking Change Or Remove Programs opens an uninstall routine. You're asked (probably more than once) if this is what you want to do. If so, then simply follow the instructions.

FIGURE 9.28   Add or Remove Programs: Removing a program

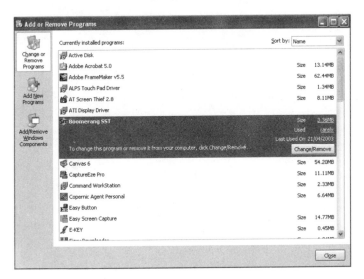

WARNING   If you are connected to a network, check with the network administrator before you add or remove programs. It's likely that you will not be allowed to do so for several reasons. Uninstalling software obviously may affect not just yourself, but also others using the network. The prohibition on adding software is perhaps not quite so obvious, but network administrators and companies in general need to ensure that software that is added to the network is virus-free. While good-quality anti-virus software should detect any viruses, restricting software to that which is approved is quite common. In addition, companies need to be sure that the software is properly licenced, so that no illegal software is installed on their systems.

Summary

This chapter explained the parts of a desktop window—icons, buttons, views, menus, and toolbars. You also learnt how to move and resize desktop windows.

You also learnt a few things about application windows, including how to move between them. You now understand the various ways to shut down non-responsive applications and how to capture screen images and paste them into a document.

The final topic of this chapter described how to install and uninstall applications using the tools available in the Windows operating system.

Chapter

10

Working with Files and Folders

IN THIS CHAPTER YOU WILL LEARN HOW TO

- ✓ Utilise file and folder structures.
- ✓ Create folders and subfolders.
- ✓ View the properties of a folder, including the number of files of each type.
- ✓ Change the read-only status of a file.
- ✓ Recognise the different types of icons that represent files and folders.
- ✓ View the properties of files.
- ✓ Rename files and folders using the appropriate filename extensions where applicable.
- ✓ Create, access, and extract compressed files.
- ✓ Select files.
- ✓ Copy and move files and folders.
- ✓ Delete files and folders, using the Recycle Bin properly.
- ✓ Copy files to a disk as backup.
- ✓ Use the Search tool to locate a file or folder.
- ✓ Use different properties of a file to locate it.
- ✓ View recently used files.

All computer systems use the concepts of files and folders to operate and organise the information stored on the system. As you've seen, there are various kinds of files, with different file-name extensions. Some of these are programs, others are data files, and still others are files used by the operating system as part of the way it runs. All files are held in *folders* (also known as *directories*), which are generally organised in a logical fashion, either by the installation program if they are program files or (hopefully) by you if they are the files that you create as part of your work. The latter may be word processing documents, spreadsheets, digital photographs, music files, or whatever else you decide to create.

The files and folders are physically stored on storage devices, known as drives. The main storage device is the hard (internal) drive on your system (and you may have more than one of these). In addition, you can store data on floppy disks, Zip disks, CD-ROMs and DVDs, although in each case you must have the appropriate disk drive and software to read and write to the removable medium. You can even store data on other devices, which the system sees as disks, but are physically different. An example is the data cards used in digital cameras.

Logically, these drives form part of My Computer and when you click that icon (either on the Desktop or on the Start menu), you will see the icons representing the disks displayed. Clicking a disk icon will show the folders stored on that device or, in the case of a removable device, the medium in the device.

If your computer is part of a network, you can also store data on (and read files from) the drives on other computers on the network, as long as you have permission to access them. To see these drives, you click My Network Places (again either on the Desktop or on the Start menu).

File and Folder Structures

To look at folder structures, you really need to understand the overall structure of the file system. The concept is very simple: Think of files as folders within other folders within filing cabinet drawers within the cabinet, within the filing room, and so on. Alternatively, think of files as leaves growing on twigs, growing on branches, growing on bigger branches, growing from the root. (For some reason, the trunk never features.) Remember that, from a practical viewpoint, there is no limit to the number of levels of subfolders you can create, although you will find that unless you are systematic and use a structured approach, creating too many levels makes it difficult to remember where specific files are.

When you look at your system, you see an organised structure. In fact, the files are not stored like that at all. They are scattered in small sections all over your hard disk, and the operating system handles the task of linking all those pieces together and relating them to the filenames that you (and Microsoft and other vendors) have given them. After some time, the pieces can become so scattered (the files are described as *fragmented*) that access to them slows down. Windows provides what is called a *defragmentation tool* to sort out this situation. If you think this may be a problem, talk to someone with experience about it.

You have already seen how opening a window that represents a folder shows you the files and other folders within that folder. You shall look again at this in the next section.

Examining a File or a Folder

Open a window representing a folder by going to My Computer or My Documents. Open folders and subfolders until you find the folder or file in which you are interested. Select this item; a *selected* item appears with a different-coloured background. In the default view, to get information about the selected folder, look at the Details section in the left pane (see Figure 10.1). If the information is not shown, click the arrows at the top left of the Details section, which point down when no details are shown and up when they are shown. In the Classic view, you need to select a folder to obtain information. Remember that you can switch between views by choosing Tools ➤ Folder Options.

FIGURE 10.1   Accessing folder information in the default view

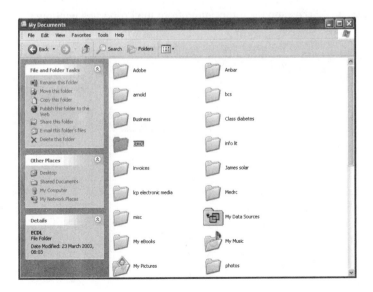

Similarly, if you select a file, information about the file is shown under Details (see Figure 10.2). To get more information (and in the Classic view to get any information), right-click the selected file or folder or go to the File menu. In either case, select Properties to open the Properties window (see Figure 10.3).

FIGURE 10.2 Accessing file information in the default view

FIGURE 10.3 Accessing file information from the Properties window

Note that to get properties information about a folder, you need to move up into the parent folder and then select the folder of interest, as shown in Figure 10.4.

FIGURE 10.4   Accessing folder information from the Properties window

    Notice that the information displayed for a folder is slightly different from that displayed for a file. The reasons for this should be obvious; essentially, you can modify and update files, whereas once folders are created, they do not change (except in their content).

The Properties window for a folder tells you how many files and subfolders there are within that folder. If you want to know how many files of each type there are, open the folder and either sort by file type or perhaps display them in groups (View ➢ Arrange Items By), as discussed in Chapter 9, "Working with Windows." If you then select all the files of one type or in one group, the number of selected files is shown in the Details panel of the left-hand pane.

The other information that you can view and change in the Properties window (look back at Figure 10.3) is the file attributes—whether a file is read-only, hidden, or (the default) archive. *Archive* means that anyone can access the file, and *hidden* means that it cannot be seen in folder windows unless the option to do so is chosen in the Folder Options section of Control Panel. *Read-only* means that you may view a file, but you cannot save any changes. (Note that, although it is outside the scope of this book, you can also share files—in other words, decide which other users should have access to them.)

If a file has read-only status, you can usually change this to read-write status, by selecting (but not opening) the file and then either right-clicking it and selecting Properties or selecting Properties from the File menu. At the bottom of the Properties window, you will see check boxes for Attributes. The first of these will be checked if the file is read-only. Simply click it to remove the check mark and make the file read-write. Note that for some files you may not be able to do this, because you are not the owner and the owner wishes the file to remain read-only.

As you've seen, the name of a folder or file is displayed below its icon in the parent folder window and, of course, it is displayed in the title bar of its own window.

> If you use the Details view, you can see much of the same information about the files and folders as you do in the Properties window, but in a more compact form. The previous chapter explained that you can choose which information to display. You can always obtain the same information in the same format via Windows Explorer, so the option you take depends on what you find simplest.

Select a file and then a folder and see what you can find out about them using the approaches described in this section. The basic properties are as follows:

Filename   The filename is not as absolute as you might think, because you can change the name of a file, as you shall see shortly, without changing the contents and nature of the file. However, if you try to change the filename extension (and by implication, the file type), Windows asks you if you mean to do this. As you know, the filename is preceded by an icon.

File size   The file size is given in bytes, where effectively a byte represents a character or a code. Thus, although a text file may contain 400 words with perhaps 2,500 characters (including spaces and carriage returns), a formatted Word file of the same text may have a size that is ten times as great because of the inclusion of the formatting information.

Keep an eye on file sizes, because eventually you may run out of disk space, although disks are now so large that this becomes increasingly unlikely. Size can also be important, however, if you are transferring a file, either on disk or over the Internet.

Type   The file type is almost redundant, but it confirms what the icon shows you about the file.

Modified   This shows the date and time that the file was either created or last modified. If this is a file that you have created, then it is straightforward. However, sometimes files that have come from elsewhere may show the date and time when they were transferred onto your system or even some other date. So do not put too much trust in this information, except for your own files, which are likely to be the ones where this information is most significant for you because you may need to be able to identify when you saved a file. If the date and time are shown in a format that you do not like, you can change it using International Settings—not Date/Time—in Control Panel.

However, you can also display other file properties. As well as choosing View ➢ Choose Details, you can right-click the headings in the Details window, as shown in Figure 10.5. Click to select and deselect different properties. Some of these properties are obvious, but most are outside the scope of this book.

Now that you have a basic understanding of file types, open a folder on your own computer and examine the properties of different kinds of files. Are some types of files smaller than others? Are the system files older? Find some files that have never been modified. In all, try to understand what the file properties tell you.

FIGURE 10.5   Selecting which file properties to display in the Details view

Common Types of Files

You've noticed that files have different icons associated with them. While these can be chosen at random, in fact they represent the application that is associated with that type of file. The file icon may be related to the program used to create the file, but not necessarily. There is occasionally confusion, because the association is based on the filename extension, the letters—usually three—after the dot in the filename. These were originally specified under the old DOS (pre-Windows) system to specify what sort of file the file was. Sometimes you find that two applications use the same extension. On the whole, though, this is not common and certainly not so for the most frequently used files.

Common file extensions and icons include the following:

.exe   This is an executable file, in other words, a program. Many programs tend to have a particular icon associated with them, as we have seen for Microsoft Word.

.doc   This is usually a Microsoft Word file. However, the icon can also represent an RTF file, which is also usually a word processing file in Rich Text Format. (This is considered in more detail in Part 3.) RTF files are in a form such that the formatting commands can be read as text. This format is often used as an exchange format between word processing programs and as a safe way of sending a word processing file via e-mail, especially if viruses are likely to be a problem.

.txt (or sometimes .asc)   This is usually a plain text file. The .asc is short for ASCII, which is the name of the coding system used for the alphabet, numerals, and a few other symbols.

.xls   This is almost always a Microsoft Excel spreadsheet file.

.mdb   This will usually be the file extension for a Microsft Access database file. Note that there are other database programs and these will have different file extensions.

.ppt   This is usually a presentation file produced using Microsoft PowerPoint.

.pdf   This is almost always a file in Portable Document Format that is produced and read with Adobe Acrobat software.

Files in the PDF format are effectively screen images of printed documents. They are generated by printing from an application as though to a printer, but actually to a file. The full version of Adobe Acrobat or a similar program is required to create such files, but Adobe Acrobat Reader can be used to view them. The latter can be downloaded free from the World Wide Web. In addition, Acrobat Reader is often already loaded on new computers or given away free on cover disks provided with computer magazines.

.zip   This is a compressed file format, which is frequently used to transfer large files either on disk or across the Internet. Note that the icon shows that Windows XP treats zip files as folders, which of course they are (see the folders with zippers in Figure 10.6). You will learn about zip files in more detail later in this chapter.

FIGURE 10.6   A folder containing zip files, which Windows XP treats as folders

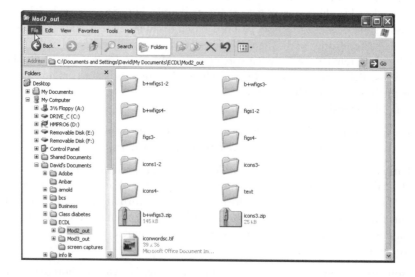

.htm   This file type is an HTML (HyperText Markup Language) file that represents a World Wide Web document. Note that the icon given here is that of Microsoft's web browser, called Internet Explorer. There are other browsers, the most common of which is Netscape Navigator. If your system is set up to use Navigator as the default web browser, rather than Internet Explorer, then you will see the Navigator icon.

.jpg   This is an image file in JPEG format. This format, named after the Joint Photographic Experts Group, is widely used for photographs on the World Wide Web. In some views of folders, you see the icon, while in others, as discussed in the previous section, you see a thumbnail of the image. Because there are many different picture editors available, the icon that you see associated with this type of file will depend on how your system is set up.

.gif   This is another kind of graphics format, used for graphics such as logos on the World Wide Web. Again, you see an icon or a thumbnail of the picture, depending on which view of a folder you are using.

.tmp   This is the file extension given to temporary files, which are files created by Windows or by an application as a way to store data or other information as part of their operation. Usually temporary files are deleted when the operation or Windows itself is closed. However, this is not always the case and special programs can be obtained to clean up your system from lingering temporary files.

Video and audio files   These file types are usually associated with one of the three main playing programs: Windows Media Player, RealPlayer, and QuickTime. The filename extensions include, for audio, **.wav**, **.aif**, **.mp3**, **.ra**, **.ram**, and **.wma**. The filenames for video include **.mpg**, **.avi**, **.mov**, **.cpt**, **.wm**, and **.wmf**. Which files are associated with which player depends very much on how your system has been set up, because, in many cases, all players can play most types of file.

This is just a sample list of common file types. If you go to either My Computer or Windows Explorer and choose Tools ➢ Folder Options, you open first the window in which you can choose the view that you want to use. However, if you click the File Types tab, a Folder Options window opens (see Figure 10.7), which indicates what each of the icons represents.

FIGURE 10.7   The File Types tab in the Folder Options window

If you select one, as has been done in Figure 10.7, in the bottom half of the window you see the icon, the filename extension, and the program that opens this file by default, in other words, if you open it in a window or in Windows Explorer. You can change these, remove them, and add new ones, but that is outside the ECDL syllabus. Another way of seeing a (shorter) list is to right-click an icon, select Properties from the pop-up menu that opens, and click Change (alongside Opens With). You will then see a Open With window (see Figure 10.8).

FIGURE 10.8   An alternative list of application icons

 In some of the windows that you have seen in the figures in this section there is a tab concerned with viruses. This has been added by the anti-virus software used and so may not appear on your system or, if it does, it may be different because you are using different anti-virus software. For more on viruses, see the next chapter.

If a file has the generic Windows icon associated with it, this can mean one of two things: No icon has been allocated or Windows does not recognise the file type and therefore when you open the file by clicking it, a window opens (rather like Figure 10.9) in which you are asked to select the application that you wish to use to open the file. Note, however, that Windows XP is able to detect internal information within files and may well open in the correct application a file that simply has an incorrect extension.

FIGURE 10.9   Windows cannot find an appropriate application to open a file.

Creating Folders and Subfolders

Now that you have a basic understanding of files, you'll use what you know to create your own folder. There are two ways to create folders and subfolders: using desktop windows and using Windows Explorer.

From the Windows Desktop, do the following:

1. Open My Computer and select and open folders until you reach the folder where you want to create a new subfolder. Of course, if you already have a shortcut on your Desktop to this folder, you can open it directly. Alternatively, you can type the full path name in the Address toolbar.

2. Choose File ➢ New. Another menu appears to the right, with Folder and Shortcut at the top (see Figure 10.10).

FIGURE 10.10   The menu for creating new folders

3. Select Folder, and a new folder appears in the window labelled, not surprisingly, "New Folder" (see Figure 10.11). Generally, unless you have chosen to view by groups, the new folder appears at the end of the list of files, irrespective of the view that you have chosen. However, the words "New Folder" are highlighted, so you should have no problem locating it.

FIGURE 10.11   Creating a new folder

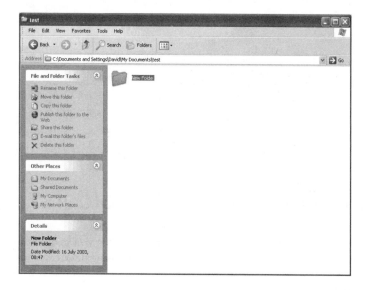

4. Type the name you want to give the folder and then press the Enter key or click somewhere else. The new folder has the name you have given it.

If you do not give it a new name, perhaps clicking somewhere else inadvertently, you can still rename it (as described in more detail shortly). The next time you open this folder window, the file will be in the correct place, depending on how you have decided to view the files (by date, name, and so on).

To create a new folder from Windows Explorer, the steps are very similar:

1. Open Windows Explorer (right-click the Start button and click Explore).

2. Select the folder within which you wish to create a new folder.

3. Open the File menu and select New.

After this, the steps are the same again. The new folder appears in the pane of the Explorer that shows the folder content. Again, how the new folder appears depends how you are displaying the filenames. Figure 10.12 shows the folder window with the Tiles view selected. Figure 10.13 shows Windows Explorer with the Details view selected.

As noted previously, there is no practical limit on the number of levels you can nest folders, so to create a folder within your new folder, you simply open the new folder and repeat the process.

Try creating a file system for ECDL. My Documents is a good place to put it, so start by creating a folder called ECDL (or something similar) in My Documents. Inside the ECDL folder, you can add subfolders for each of the modules: Word Processing, Databases, and so on.

FIGURE 10.12   A folder window using the Tiles view

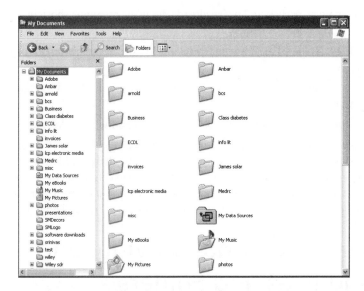

FIGURE 10.13   Windows Explorer with the Details view

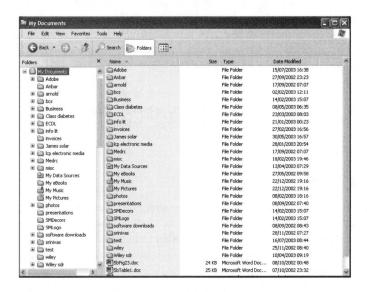

Renaming Files and Folders

We mentioned renaming earlier, and we've already discussed renaming shortcuts. The procedure for renaming files and folders is very similar:

1. Select the file or folder that you want to rename, either in My Computer or in Windows Explorer.

2. Choose File ➢ Rename or choose Rename from the menu produced by right-clicking. The existing name is highlighted.

3. Type the new name, and either click elsewhere or press the Enter key.

The next time you open the window or change the order to alphabetical, the new file appears correctly under its new name. As noted earlier, if you try to change a filename extension, Windows asks you if you really want to do this, because the file may not function correctly if you do.

Experiment with renaming files. See what happens when you try to rename a program file. (It is probably better to follow the advice given and cancel the name change.)

Selecting, Copying, Moving, and Deleting Files and Folders

This section is mainly about doing what one might call secretarial or administrative tasks with files and folders. In other words, think of a file in conventional terms—as a bundle of papers that you can choose from the filing cabinet, move around, throw away, and even copy without actually referring to the contents of that file. Just as you can do these things with a real file of papers, so you can do them—more easily and certainly with less effort—with files and folders on your computer.

 To save repeating the phrase "file or folder," throughout this section, when we say "file," this means either a file or a folder.

Selecting Files

If you want to carry out an action on a file, the first thing you need to do is to *select* it. You have already seen some examples of how this is done, by clicking once or mousing over. It is obviously easier just to move the cursor to the file, rather than to have to click it. However, if you then move the cursor onto another icon, that icon is selected instead. In contrast, if you click to select, the file that you have selected remains selected until you make a decision to select another file or you decide to deselect the first one by clicking it again or clicking in a blank area of the window. If you simply mouse over to select, just moving the cursor to a blank area deselects the file.

Before you consider what you can do once you have selected a file, let's look at ways in which you can select more than one file.

Selecting Multiple Files at Once

You'll find that there are times where you need to select more than one file at a time. There are several techniques to use, depending on what you want to achieve.

To select all the files in the active window, choose Edit ➢ Select All. Even easier is to use the keyboard shortcut and press Ctrl+A.

To select adjacent files, you can select one and then hold down the Shift key as you select others. All those you either moused over or clicked are then included in the selection.

If you are looking at icons, you can also use the marquee select. This means that you draw a box in the window by clicking an appropriate blank spot in the window and holding down the left mouse button until the box includes all the files you want to select. Release the mouse button and those files are selected (see Figure 10.14).

To select non-adjacent files, select the first one you want and then hold down the Ctrl key while you either click the others you want in turn or pass the cursor over them. The latter is more difficult because you have to take what may be a rather complex path with the cursor in order to avoid all the files that you do not want to select. Clicking to select certainly seems simpler.

To deselect a particular file, you effectively repeat the process on the files that have been selected. Thus, to deselect a series of adjacent files (and they have to be at the beginning or the end of the selection), deselect the first or last file and, keeping the Shift key depressed, click or mouse over the file for each of the other files you want to deselect.

In fact, it is generally easier to hold down the Ctrl key and deselect files one by one, and they do not have to be at the beginning or end of the selected list.

Experiment with different methods of selecting and deselecting files to see which you prefer.

FIGURE 10.14 Using the marquee select feature

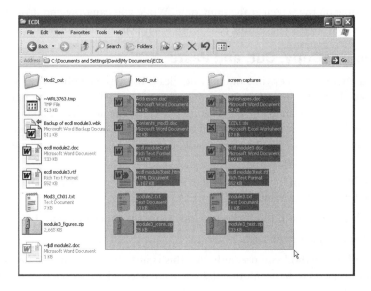

Copying and Moving Files

Copying the complete contents of a folder can be achieved with a few clicks of the mouse button. There are two ways to move and copy files: drag and drop and using the Clipboard.

Drag-and-Drop Methods

You've already seen that you can move icons by using drag and drop. (Drag and drop is when you select a file and then, holding down the mouse button, drag the icon or filename until it is where you want it and release the mouse button.)

In fact, you can carry out drag and drop in more than one way. If you use the left mouse button, then if the target window is on the same disk drive (in other words, it has the same letter such as C:), the file is moved. However, if the disk drive has a different letter (for example, a diskette A:), then a copy takes place. While you have the button held down, if a copy is due to take place, a small plus (+) sign appears next to the icon. Also note the ghost effect as the icon is moved; try this for yourself. If the file is a program file, instead of the plus sign, the shortcut arrow appears, because instead of either a copy or move, a shortcut is created. This is because moving program files can mean that they will not operate properly. In fact, if you open the Program Files window, a warning to this effect appears in the Web view.

An alternative approach is to use the right mouse button when you drag and drop. This time (whatever the target window), when you release the mouse button, you have four options: Copy Here, Move Here, Create Shortcut(s) Here, and Cancel. This is probably the easiest and least risky approach, other than using the Clipboard (described in the next section).

Selecting and moving or copying groups of files is not always as simple as it sounds. Unless you're careful, you can find that you have changed your selection without intending to do so, just because your timing was not quite right. So if you plan to use this approach, it is a good idea to practise.

In addition, drag and drop really requires you to have both the source window and your target window visible on the screen at the same time. While you can drag and drop off the screen by moving the cursor to the edge of the screen, what happens then is not always easy to control.

The Clipboard: Copy, Cut, and Paste

Another useful method for copying and moving files is using the Clipboard. Think of the Clipboard as a special area in the computer memory that temporarily stores files until you decide where to put them. The term "Clipboard" is used because the actions are analogous to taking a piece of paper and adding it to a clipboard until you decide where it should be refiled.

To copy a file or group of files from one folder to another, first select what you want to copy and then use one of three methods:

- Choose Edit ➢ Copy in the window where you are viewing the file(s). (This can be done in either My Computer or Windows Explorer.)
- Right-click the selected file and choose Copy from the shortcut menu that appears.
- Press Ctrl+C on your keyboard.

Regardless of the method you use, although this is not obvious from what you see on the screen (nothing appears to happen), the files you have selected are stored (usually described as *placed*) on the Clipboard.

If you decide that instead of copying a file, you want to move it, then instead of choosing Copy from the Edit menu or the pop-up menu, choose Cut (or press Ctrl+X on your keyboard). This time something does happen; the selected file changes in appearance, becoming faded with the outlines dotted (see Figure 10.15). Again the file has been copied to the Clipboard.

FIGURE 10.15   The result of selecting Cut from the Edit menu

In either case, you then open your target window (using My Computer or in Windows Explorer) and go again to the Edit menu or the pop-up menu produced by right-clicking and select Paste (or press Ctrl+V on your keyboard). The file (or its icon) then appears in the new window. You'll also notice that, if you cut the original file, it now disappears from the original window.

When you use the Clipboard, it does not matter whether the target window is on the same disk or not; the operation is the same. Also note that the Clipboard retains a filename (and in fact, other types of data, for example, text from a word processing program) until you either turn your computer off or carry out another Cut or Copy operation. Thus, you can paste the contents of the Clipboard in more than one place (this is more useful with text than with files). But remember that if you do cut or copy something else, then what was previously on the Clipboard is lost (although you can use Undo—Ctrl+Z). Of course, if you copied, then this is not a problem. However, if you are cutting, then you need to be careful; that is why the faded image is shown until you have pasted the file. It is possible to obtain programs that allow more than one item to be retained on the Clipboard, and within Microsoft Office XP, a number of items can be stored on the Clipboard at a time.

Because the keyboard shortcuts for Copy, Cut, and Paste are probably some of the most widely used, we repeat them here:

Copy	Ctrl+C
Cut	Ctrl+X
Paste	Ctrl+V

Note that, along with Ctrl+Z (Undo), they are at the bottom left of the keyboard, making them easy to access, even for one-finger typists.

The other point worth noting is that Undo (Ctrl+Z) can reverse all move-and-copy operations.

Copying Files to a Removable Disk as Backup

Chapter 7, "First Steps with the Computer," stressed how important backing up your files is, just in case something goes wrong with your computer system or you perhaps delete a file inadvertently.

Although special software is obtainable for handling backups, you can simply copy the files from your working window (probably within the My Documents folder) to the window that represents the removable medium that you wish to use for backup. Indeed, all you need to do is select the files or folders that you want to back up and drag and drop them to the new window. Remember that because this is a different disk, the result will automatically be a copy rather than a move.

If you are moving files to a disk that already contains files or folders with the same names, you will receive a message asking if you want to replace the files or folders with the new ones. This message even gives you the dates on which the two files of the same name were last updated (see Figure 10.16); all you have to do is click Yes or No. There is also sometimes a button that allows you to indicate Yes To All, which saves you having to look at every file individually. However, to use this, make sure that you do want to replace the old files with the new ones. For backup purposes, this usually is the case.

FIGURE 10.16   A dialog box requesting confirmation of file replacement

Deleting Files and Folders

Deleting files is similar to copying and moving, except that once you have selected the file(s) you want to remove, you either click the right mouse button and select Delete or choose File ➤ Delete in the window containing the file(s) you want to delete. Even simpler is to select the file and depress the Delete key on your keyboard. Whichever of these three options you take, you see a message asking you to confirm the deletion (see Figure 10.17). This message varies depending on where the file is situated. As noted earlier, files deleted from the hard disk are actually moved to the Recycle Bin, so that you can get them back again, if necessary. Files deleted from a Zip disk or a floppy disk (see Figure 10.18) are actually deleted—even Undo does not work here—so make sure that you do indeed want to delete these files.

FIGURE 10.17 Files deleted from the hard disk are sent to the Recycle Bin.

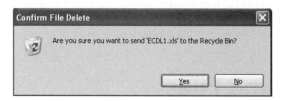

FIGURE 10.18 Files deleted from Zip disks (and floppy disks) are erased immediately.

If you indicate that you want to delete a folder, a message appears asking if you want to delete/move to the Recycle Bin the folder and all its contents, just to remind you that this is not just a single file that you want to remove. You can also drag and drop a file to the Recycle Bin window (or onto its icon), but, if you do that, you don't see the message asking you confirm the operation.

To empty the Recycle Bin, right-click the Recycle Bin icon on the Desktop and choose Empty Recycle Bin. You see a message asking if you do indeed want to do this. Click OK.

To restore a file from the Recycle Bin, open the Bin from the Desktop. Select the file you want to recover (in other words, restore to the folder from which you deleted it) and right-click it. The pop-up menu in Figure 10.19 opens. Choose Restore, and the file disappears from the Recycle Bin window and goes back to where it came from; Windows remembers this.

FIGURE 10.19 Restoring files from the Recycle Bin

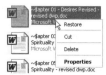

If, when you use a menu to delete, you hold down the Shift key when you select Delete, then irrespective of which disk the file is situated on, you delete rather than copy the file to the Recycle Bin. This may be useful if you have a confidential file that you want to remove, but again be very sure that you do want to remove that file completely.

Compressing Files

Every file has a size, in other words, it occupies a certain amount of space on the medium on which it is stored. The size of a simple text file is almost the same as the number of characters and spaces, while the size of a word-processed file is much larger because it includes formatting information. Similarly, a graphics file with high resolution contains more pixels than the same picture at low resolution and therefore has a larger file size. However, there is a considerable amount of redundancy in the way the information is stored. For example, a large stretch of the same colour in an image or perhaps the instances of the word "the" can be coded in a more efficient way so that the file size is reduced. This technique is called *file compression*.

There are many techniques for compressing files, but for the purposes of ECDL, you do not need to understand how they work, only how to use them. Here we shall be concerned with what are called zip files.

Note that zip files and Zip disks are not the same thing. Zip files are compressed files, while Zip disks are a proprietary form of removable storage medium. You can, of course, store zip files on Zip disks, but you can also store them on any other kind of storage medium as well.

To create and access zip files in previous versions of Windows, it was necessary to have special software. Windows XP, however, incorporates the zip format and treats zip files as a special kind of folder. To create a zip file (or a zip archive), go to the File menu in the folder in which you want to create the zip archive, just as you would to create an ordinary new folder. This time, however, go to the bottom of the list and click Compressed (Zipped) Folder (as you saw back in Figure 10.10). This creates a new (zipped) folder, labelled New Compressed (zipped) Folder.zip. Type the filename you want to use (remembering that you have to keep the extension .zip).

To add files to your new zipped folder, copy and paste them or drag and drop them, either onto the file icon or after opening it into the folder window; zip archives open exactly like ordinary folders.

To access a file in a compressed archive, simply open the archive and select and open the file in the usual way. You can also drag and drop a file from a compressed folder to a non-compressed folder.

Searching for Files and Folders

Although it is important to organise your directory structure so that you know where different files are, even in the best regulated systems there comes a time when you want a file and you cannot be sure where on the system it is. And the larger hard disks become and the more space software takes up, the more likely this is to happen.

Fortunately, Windows provides you with an important tool called Search to look for files and folders. While you can use this to search the World Wide Web as well, there are other tools for doing this, which are discussed in Part 7.

Performing a Standard Search

To open Search, choose Start ➢ Search. (You can also click the Search icon—the magnifying glass—at the top of each folder.) The window shown in Figure 10.20 opens. The left-hand pane lists your options. You have two ways to search: standard and advanced. If you use standard, which is what is shown in Figure 10.20, you are prompted through the options.

FIGURE 10.20   The standard Search window

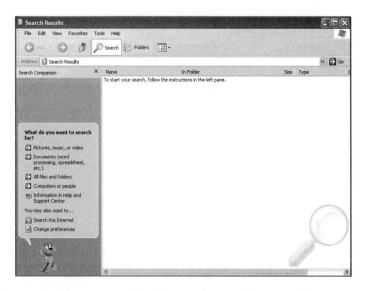

If you click Pictures, Music, Or Video, the Search pane changes to the view in Figure 10.21. Similarly, clicking Documents (Word Processing, Spreadsheets, Etc.) changes the Search pane to that shown in Figure 10.22, which allows you to specify when you last modified the document. In both these cases, notice that you are given the opportunity to use advanced search options, which are described shortly. You'll see what happens when you enter filenames or parts of filenames in the box provided.

FIGURE 10.21 Searching for pictures, music, or video

FIGURE 10.22 Searching for documents

If you click All Files And Folders, the Search pane shown in Figure 10.23 opens. As you can see, there are two main ways in which you can search: by the name of the file you are looking for or by a string of text that occurs within the file you are looking for. You can also combine the two.

Let's look at a simple search first. Enter **keyboard.sys**—the name of a file that is an important part of Windows—in the top box and press Search. As the search continues, the current status is displayed (see Figure 10.24).

FIGURE 10.23   Searching in all files and folders: Setting up

FIGURE 10.24   Searching in all files and folders: Ongoing status

When the search is complete (or you stop it), the Search pane changes to a final report, as shown in Figure 10.25, which contains the results of the search. Note then that you are given various options as to what to do next. We will discuss this search in more detail later.

If you click Computers Or People, you can either access an Internet search, or in the latter case, a search in your address book (see Part 7).

Finally, if you click Information In Help And Support Center, you open the Help screens that you saw in Chapter 7.

FIGURE 10.25 Searching in all files and folders: The final report at the end of the search

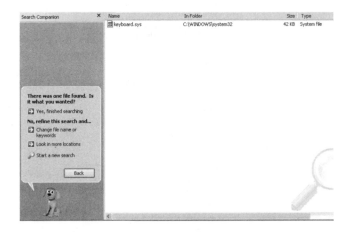

Using the Advanced Option in Search

This section uses the advanced option for searching because this gives you much more control over what you are searching for. To move to the advanced search, choose Change Preferences and select Change Files And Folder Search Behavior. The Search pane changes to the one shown in Figure 10.26. (The other preferences will be discussed shortly.)

FIGURE 10.26 The advanced search window

First, just look for a file by name. Type **keyboard.sys** in the box that asks for All Or Part Of The File Name. You also need to tell the system where to look by making a selection in the Look In box. By default, you are usually given the name for your hard disk (C:), but you can browse your system in the usual way to make the search more specific and, incidentally reduce the search time. On the other hand, you increase the scope of your search if you include removable disks such as CDs, and other computers on the network.

The result (see Figure 10.27) is very similar to that shown in Figure 10.25. However, this time, as the search goes on, you do not see a status report or a final report; there is simply a scroll bar at the bottom of the Search pane (and the animated screen character, if you have one displayed, keeps on moving). Incidentally, this also means that you do not get the option of a new search; to start a new search, simply enter what you want to search for and search again.

Incidentally, if you click More Advanced Options, you see that, by default, the box Search Subfolders is ticked (see Figure 10.28). If it isn't, then the search only looks for files within the top-level folder. So, if you have specified that the system should look in disk C: and the box had not been ticked, then the system would only have looked for files within C: and would not have found the file.

FIGURE 10.27 Results of the search for keyboard.sys using the advanced search option

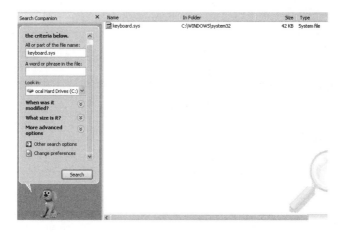

FIGURE 10.28 Search Subfolders is ticked when you choose More Advanced Options.

If you do not know the full filename, you can enter any part of it, and the system finds all those files with names that contain this string. Figure 10.29 shows that just searching for "keyboard" brings up many more results, while searching for ".sys" (see Figure 10.30) gives even more.

FIGURE 10.29 Results of search for "keyboard"

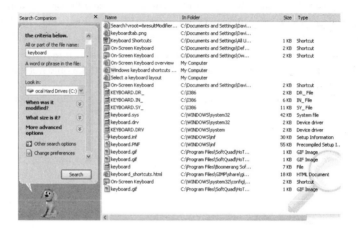

FIGURE 10.30 Results of search for ".sys"

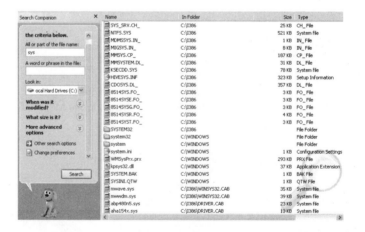

To locate a folder, you proceed in exactly the same way. Indeed, the search results include both files and folders. Note that the file type is listed, so you can tell which are folders. Note also that if you select any file or folder and go to the File menu, clicking Open Containing Folder does just that—opens the folder containing the file or folder you have found. Try putting in partial filenames of some of the common filename extensions described earlier in this chapter. See what anomalies this may produce.

Text Strings

The second box in the Search pane allows you to specify a text string that occurs within a file. Just type the string into the box. If you go to More Advanced Options, you can narrow down the range of folders and files where you want the system to search if you wish (see Figure 10.31).

FIGURE 10.31   Choosing the file type in the Search pane

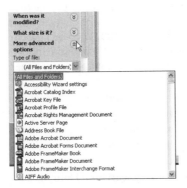

Say you write letters to someone called Jones, and you store these in a folder called `letters`. You want to find all the references to Brown in letters to Jones (which you called `jones01.doc`, `jones02.doc`, and so on). The Search pane would look like Figure 10.32, where you have also narrowed the search to the `My Documents` folder (and all subfolders).

FIGURE 10.32   A search box with the options specified as in the text

However, this search also results in all files that include any occurrence of "brown," including, for example, the phrase "brown shoes." So, under More Advanced Options, you can choose Case Sensitive, which means that if you enter **Brown** (rather than **brown**) in the A Word Or Phrase In The File box, you will be given only files in which "Brown" (with a capital *B*) appears. Of course, if "Brown shoes" happens to appear at the beginning of a sentence, then the file containing that will appear as well, but case sensitivity helps in most cases.

The case-sensitivity option does not apply to filenames, because although Windows appears to allow case-sensitivity in filenames, this is not really so. Therefore Keyboard.sys, KEYBOARD.SYS, and keyboard.sys all describe the same file. This is not really a problem, because Windows always warns you if you are in danger of overwriting a file with the same name.

You can also use what are known as *wildcard characters* in search boxes, either for the filename or for the word or phrase. If you use the asterisk (*), this substitutes for zero or any number of characters, so **can*** will find can, cane, canal, cannot, candle, and so on. If you use the question mark (?), this substitutes for a single character, so **can?** will find cane, cant, and cans, but not can or candle.

Add some text to the text box and try searching Help files. Note that if you put nothing in the File Name box, then you will find every file containing the word or phrase that you have specified.

Date Options (When Was It Modified?)

If you click the double arrows next to When Was It Modified? in the Search pane, the Search pane changes to the view shown in Figure 10.33. If you click the white circle beside Specify Dates, then you can do just that. Note that if you do specify dates, then you can change Modified to Created or Last Accessed by clicking the down arrow at the right-hand side of the box and selecting the appropriate option.

FIGURE 10.33   Specifying the When Was It Modified? criteria when searching for files

You can then put in specific dates (check which date convention your system is using—see Chapter 7—or else you may confuse 5 March and 3 May, for example) or specify the period in months or days. This information works together with the information in the first tab. If you close Search and reopen it, it reverts to the default settings. However, if you leave Search open on your Desktop and come back to it later to carry out another search, then if you do not have the When Was It Modified? section open, there is nothing in the pane to tell you that you narrowed the date range. It is worth checking this, or you may find that the search does not give you the result you want. For practise, try searching for all the files you have modified in the last week and in the last month.

Size Options

You can also search for files of a certain size. Click the double arrows next to What Size Is It?, and the pane changes to what you see in Figure 10.34. As for the date, if you click the circle next to Specify Size (In KB), you can specify At Least or At Most.

FIGURE 10.34   Searching for a file by size

These options can be used separately or together and are used in conjunction with the settings discussed previously. Just as for the date, the settings are cancelled when you close the Search pane, but while the window is open, they remain in force, so you need to check them if you are coming back to reuse an open Search window.

Other Search Options and Preferences

There are one or two other options under More Advanced Options concerned with hidden and system files, but these are not covered by ECDL.

You can change your preferences by clicking Change Preferences in many of the screens you've seen in this chapter. This produces the pane shown in Figure 10.35. Most of these options are self-explanatory. You have seen that Change Files And Folders Search Behavior allows you to switch between standard and advanced behaviour. With AutoComplete on, as soon as you enter the beginnings of a search term, you see previous entries that began with the same letter(s) (see Figure 10.36). You have the option to switch this on or off. The option Change Internet Search Behavior is outside the scope of this section.

Experiment with the different search options and preferences so that you get used to what is possible and can decide which search options you find easiest to use.

FIGURE 10.35   Search preferences

FIGURE 10.36   The effect of having AutoComplete on

Saving Searches

You may well want to carry out the same search on a regular basis. To save you having to enter the options each time, you can save the search. This is particularly useful if the search is fairly generic, such as find all files modified in the last seven days. Choose File ➢ Save Search, and you're given the usual options for where you want to save the file. An entry is then created in the folder you choose (with the search icon). If you subsequently click this, the search (with all its settings) is updated.

Recently Used Files

You may wish to view a list of files that you have recently used. You can, of course, do this by using Search as described in the previous section, and most applications give you the option of viewing the most recent files that you have opened within that application.

However, if you wish to look at a list of all the files that you have opened recently, add this option to the Start menu (if it is not there by default). If it is already there, choose Start ➤ My Recent Documents (see Figure 10.37).

FIGURE 10.37   Recently used files

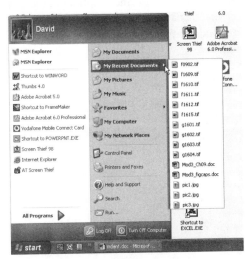

If the option My Recent Documents is not on the Start menu, right-click Start and click Properties. On the Start Menu tab, click Customize and Advanced and check the box List My Most Recently Opened Documents (see Figure 10.38). Note that you can also clear the list from here. Finally, click OK in this window and in the Properties window.

FIGURE 10.38   Setting the recently used files option

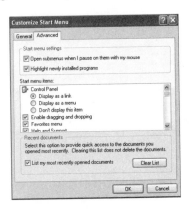

Summary

This chapter looked at directory structures containing files and folders. You've learnt how to create folders and subfolders. You have also seen how you can obtain information about folders and files. You have considered common types of files, how to rename files and folders, and how to compress them to save storage space.

You also learnt a bit about how to work with files and folders, including how to select files and groups of adjacent and nonadjacent files, and a variety of methods for copying, moving, and deleting files.

This chapter explained the standard and advanced options of the Search facility. You examined the various options for specifying filenames and text that is included in the file. Additionally, you looked at the date conditions and file-type conditions that can be applied to your searches, and you saw how to save a search.

Chapter

11

Viruses

IN THIS CHAPTER YOU WILL LEARN HOW TO

- ✓ Understand what viruses are and the effects they can have.
- ✓ Recognise how viruses can be transmitted onto a computer.
- ✓ Use anti-virus software for checking and disinfecting your system.
- ✓ Understand why anti-virus software needs to be updated regularly.
- ✓ Understand virus hoaxes.

Just as there are biological viruses that can be transmitted from person to person, so there are, by analogy, computer viruses that can be transmitted from computer to computer. Unlike biological viruses, computer viruses do not occur naturally, but are the work of programmers (often called *crackers*). Perhaps originally, programmers developed these viruses as a way of showing how clever they were, but viruses are now developed in order to disrupt systems for political or other reasons.

A virus is a program or piece of code that is attached to or embedded in another program. Note that viruses can only be associated with program files (not simple text files), but a macro in a word processing files is a kind of program, so viruses can be found in word processing files.

What Effect Can Viruses Have?

It is impossible to provide a complete list of what viruses can do, because virus writers invent new effects on a regular basis. Viruses do many different things. Some are instantaneous, that is, they happen as soon as the program with which the virus is associated is run. Other viruses are *moles* and wait until an event triggers them; for example, one early virus went into action on a Friday the 13th.

Some effects of viruses are as follows:

- They copy themselves to other files.

- They make your screen image degrade or disappear.

- They erase files from your hard disk.

- They send files from your computer at random to people in your e-mail address book and, at the same time, transfer the virus to them.

- They overwrite parts of files.

The list goes on. In fact, almost anything bad that you can think of that can happen to your computer (apart from hardware failure) can be triggered by a virus. More subtle effects, which you may not be aware of, are caused by what are called *Trojan horses*. These are programs that sit within your system and carry out operations that you would not wish to happen. For example, they can make your system accessible to specific computers elsewhere on the Internet, so that they can see what you are doing or even send files routinely to another computer, perhaps simply for purposes related to advertising, but possibly for more damaging reasons. An effective way to control this is to add a firewall to your system.

All this should illustrate that viruses are bad news and that you do not want them on your system. However, if you do find a virus on your system, you need a way to get rid of it; this is often called *disinfecting* files. This chapter looks at anti-virus software, but first you need to understand where viruses come from.

How Do Viruses Arrive on Your System?

If you never connect to the Internet and never accept removable disks from anyone else, you should remain virus-free, particularly as it is reasonable to expect that commercial software does not contain viruses. However, you should not be complacent, and anyway, if your system remains sterile, then you are missing a lot of the advantages of having a computer, whether for business or leisure.

Viruses are transmitted to your system by transferring files onto it. This may be by transferring them from external media (floppy disks, Zip disks, CDs, or even data cards), but most commonly today, viruses are transferred within e-mail messages. These may be part of a quite genuine message, but one that comes from someone who has a virus on their system and has not taken adequate precautions to detect and destroy the virus. However, many viruses come as part of what is called *spam*, which is another term for junk or unwanted e-mails. Spam is becoming very common. Indeed, it is estimated that before long, half the messages on the Internet will be spam. Sometimes this may be intentional (because this is a good way to get a virus to a large number of systems) or it may just be that the spammers have a virus on their system. In fact, it doesn't really matter whether it is intentional or not. What it means is that, although outside the scope of this book, it is a good idea to look at ways of handling spam so that the messages are never opened, and, ideally, never reach users at all, as well as installing anti-virus software.

A third way that viruses can be transmitted is via the World Wide Web. Many web pages are now much more than simple files containing text and figures; they may well include programs or scripts that can contain viruses. Admittedly, this is not that common, but it is a potential threat. If you use the Web, you need anti-virus software that detects any viruses arriving by this method.

It is sometimes said that you only need anti-virus software if you regularly accept files from other people, on disk or via e-mail. However, as communications become universal, that is a situation that will apply to almost everyone, so everyone needs to have anti-virus software on their system.

Anti-Virus Software

The principal way to combat these insidious programs is to use anti-virus software. Windows XP does not come with anti-virus software, but there are a number of reputable suites of such software. Within company networks, anti-virus software may execute on a special computer, so that all e-mails, for example, have been scanned for viruses before they reach you. (However, this may not stop you using infected files from an external storage medium; companies should have security policies that cover this situation as well.) If you need to select some anti-virus software, it is a good idea to talk to an expert or read reviews in computer magazines or on the World Wide Web (ideally using a system that already has anti-virus software installed).

The system on which this chapter was written uses anti-virus software called PC-cillin. One of the things that PC-cillin does on installation is add options to some of the menus that are used to access and change file information. However, its main functions are as follows (and most other anti-virus programs provide the same functionality):

- You can scan your whole system for viruses (and set up a schedule so that this happens automatically at regular intervals).

- Rather than scan the whole system, you can select a specific drive (or drives) to scan. Before you try to access any of the files on a removable disk that has been supplied to you by someone else, it is a good idea to scan that disk or drive. When checking your system, you need to scan only the hard drives. Note that while you can scan read-only disks, such as CD-ROMs, you cannot clean or quarantine files on that disk. It is, however, very rare for commercially supplied CD-ROMs to include files carrying viruses.

- You can scan individual files and folders; in fact, every time you open a file, it is automatically scanned. If the software finds a virus, it disinfects the file, in other words, removes the virus. If it is unable to do this, the software "quarantines" the file to a special area, where you can decide what to do with it. The safest thing is to delete the file, and, if appropriate, notify the person who provided it.

- E-mails downloaded using the POP3 protocol, which is probably the most widely used protocol today, are scanned as they arrive, and are either disinfected or quarantined if a virus is found.

- Web files are scanned as they are downloaded to check that they do not contain viruses. They are either disinfected or quarantined if a virus is found.

- There are a large number of options that you can set, for example, making sure that files with zip archives are cleaned. In addition, PC-cillin has some firewall functionality and can block specific websites, but these capabilities are outside the scope of this chapter.

While PC-cillin can handle Trojan horses, not all anti-virus software do, so you may need to obtain special software to handle this problem.

How you scan individual files and folders varies from program to program, so we shall not give details here. If how you do this is not obvious from the main window for your software (often accessible from the System Tray on the Taskbar), you need to look at the Help files, or discuss this with an expert or someone with experience with the program you are using.

Other anti-virus software suites for PCs include McAfee, Norton, AVG, and Kaspersky. In addition, there are products that are designed to protect whole networks and products that are specifically used for checking that both incoming and outgoing e-mail is virus-free. The latter are more often used by companies than by individuals.

Keeping Anti-Virus Software Up to Date

It is all very well to install your anti-virus software, but if you don't keep it up to date, then whilst being partially effective, it may certainly miss a significant number of viruses. Why is this? Because virus writers are active all the time, and new viruses are propagated almost every day. Some even make the main television news programs.

However, if you keep your virus software up to date, you don't need to worry too much about new viruses. Of course, it's always possible for viruses to slip through (reading reviews of anti-virus software will give you a good idea of how reliable programs are), but if you update regularly (at least once a week and maybe even daily), your potential problems will be minimised.

The only practical way to update regularly is via the Internet. Indeed, some programs, such as PC-cillin, are updated automatically. When you are connected to the Internet, the program goes to the manufacturer's server (the computer that sends out the files) and checks that your anti-virus files are up to date. If they are not, you're asked if you wish to download the latest file(s). When you accept, the files are downloaded and updated automatically. If you carry out a manual download from a website, the operation is similar.

Virus Hoaxes

Although not within the ECDL syllabus, we should not end this chapter without referring to *virus hoaxes*. These are e-mails that are sent round, usually telling you to delete a specific file from your system or else it will wipe clean all your disks (or something of this nature). The specific file is usually a Windows system file, which may or may not have an important role in running your system, so that, if you do delete it, your system may not start or may run incorrectly. While this is not strictly a virus, the effect can be almost as irritating. So beware of such hoaxes. They usually start by saying that they have been told about the file that needs to be deleted. A list of virus hoaxes can be found at Symantec's website: www.symantec.com/avcenter/hoax.html. If you receive a message that looks like a hoax, then it is a good idea to check this site.

Summary

This chapter explained what viruses are and how they are transmitted. It discussed steps that can be taken to protect your computer against viruses, such as using anti-virus software and updating that software regularly. It also described virus hoaxes, which can be damaging in their own way.

Chapter 12

Editing Text Files

IN THIS CHAPTER YOU WILL LEARN HOW TO

✓ Launch a text-editing program or word processor.

✓ Open a file or create one and save it.

✓ Enter text into a text file.

✓ Close the file and the application.

This chapter explains the creation of a simple text file. Windows provides you with a text editor called Notepad and a very basic word processor called WordPad. However, for any serious word processing, you need to look at Microsoft Word (see Part 3 of this book), a similar program such as WordPerfect or WordPro, or, for less demanding applications, Microsoft Works. This chapter simply looks at Notepad and WordPad.

Opening a File in Notepad and WordPad

The first thing you need to do is open a Notepad file or create a new one. An existing text file usually has the filename extension .txt or .asc. When you click to open a text file in My Computer or My Documents, or by using Windows Explorer, it will most likely open in Notepad (see Figure 12.1). Notepad is very basic in its operation. Because Notepad has a limit on the length of the file that it can open, you sometimes see a message that tells you that the file you want to open is too large for Notepad and asks you if you would like to use WordPad instead.

FIGURE 12.1 The Notepad text editor

Alternatively, if you want to open Notepad directly, choose Start ➤ All Programs ➤ Accessories ➤ Notepad. Incidentally, WordPad is opened in the same way; WordPad is

lower down the Accessories list. Once you have opened Notepad, try entering a few paragraphs of text. Alternatively, try opening an existing file with the filename extension `.txt`.

Using Notepad to Edit and Create Files

The Notepad program includes some simple text-formatting tools. If you open the File menu,
you can choose Page Setup, which allows you to specify the size and orientation of paper and
the margins; note that the formatting is not stored with the file.

Notepad includes a few page-formatting features in case you want to print
a file.

The Edit menu has the usual Cut, Copy, Paste, and Select All options that you have seen in
previous sections. Here, however, if you select, then you select strings or blocks of text, and, if
you cut or copy, then you cut or copy the text you have selected; the same applies if you paste.
Try this with a file that you already have on your system.

One other entry in the Edit menu that is of interest is Time/Date, which inserts the system
time and date into the file. In the Format menu, you find Word Wrap, which, if switched
on, wraps the lines (in other words, inserts temporary carriage returns) so that the text all
fits within the editing window. If Word Wrap is switched off and there are only carriage
returns at the end of each paragraph, you see only the first few words of each paragraph in
your editing window. You can, of course, use the horizontal scroll bar, just like the ones you
saw in Chapter 9, "Working with Windows," but if the text wraps, it makes reading much
simpler. In the Format menu, you also find the Font option, which determines which font
Notepad uses. Remember, however, that this is simply for display and is not stored with the
file when you save it. What it does is determine the format that every file opened in Notepad
is displayed in. Search allows you to look for sequences of letters and is self-explanatory.

If you already have a file open in Notepad, you can make any changes by adding or deleting
characters using the keyboard. In fact, in many ways you can think of Notepad as an electronic
typewriter. Once you have finished your editing, you can save the file, using either one of two
methods:

- By choosing File ➤ Save, your new version will overwrite the old version.
- By selecting File ➤ Save As, you can give the file a new name or you can save it under the
  same name (or a new name) in a new folder (see Figure 12.2).

The Encoding box at the bottom of the window determines how characters that do not fall
within the standard ASCII character set (essentially the Western alphabet, numbers, and punctuation) are to be encoded. This is outside the scope of this book.

FIGURE 12.2   Saving a Notepad file

In this way, your original file is preserved. Saving to a removable medium simply involves browsing through the system until you find the disk drive that you want. Then you just save your file in the usual way, ensuring of course that you have the right disk in the drive.

Note that you can have only one file open at a time in Notepad, so if you choose File ≻ Open or File ≻ New, you will be asked if you want to save any changes to the file that is currently open. (If you have not made any changes, you won't see this message.) To open a file, choose File ≻ Open, and the Open window is displayed (see Figure 12.3). This window is rather like the My Computer window and not unlike the Save As menu. Browse until you find the file you want, which you open by selecting it and then clicking Open or by double-clicking.

FIGURE 12.3   Opening a file in Notepad

If you want to create a new file, choose File ➢ New. The Notepad window goes blank and the filename Untitled appears in the window title bar. Just type your text in the window and, when you are ready to save, choose File ➢ Save. A window appears much like the Save As window. Browse to where you want to save the file and type in the filename you want to use. Note that if you leave the Save As Type box showing Text Documents, the system automatically adds the .txt filename extension for you.

Using WordPad to Edit and Create Files

The WordPad window is shown in Figure 12.4. Although WordPad allows you to format files—setting the typeface (font), type size, and various aspects of layout such as bullets—if you are editing a text file, these features are irrelevant, because when you save the file, they are lost. However, what WordPad does allow you to do (as indeed does Microsoft Word) is open a file formatted in Word or one that is in Rich Text Format (RTF) and save it as a text file. To balance this, you can save a text file as a Word document (where the formatting is preserved). You also have the page setup controls that you find in Notepad, but unlike a full-featured word processor, the page setup is not retained as part of the file when you save it.

FIGURE 12.4   The WordPad window

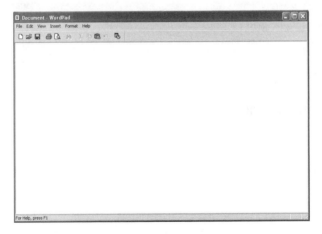

To open a file, select File ➢ Open. The Open window is displayed (see Figure 12.5). In the Files Of Type drop-down list, select the type of file that you want to open, and these filenames are displayed. You also need to browse until you find the appropriate folder. If you open a Word file, it appears formatted (see Figure 12.6), while a text file will be unformatted and the formatting bar disappears (see Figure 12.7). However, you can add formatting using the Format menu and then save the file as a Word file (with a filename extension of .doc), and the formatting bar reappears.

FIGURE 12.5 The Open Window.

FIGURE 12.6 WordPad opens Word files with formatting.

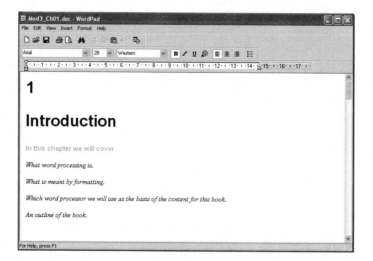

FIGURE 12.7   WordPad opens plain text files without formatting.

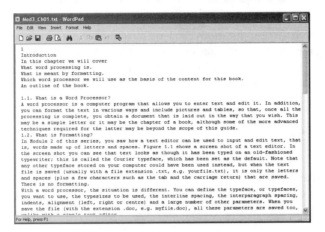

Similarly, if you open a Word file and save it as a text file, the formatting bar disappears, although the formatting remains on the screen. If you close WordPad (and WordPad is like Notepad in that you can only close the file by closing the application, opening another file, or creating a new file) and then reopen the text file in WordPad, the formatting disappears. You use Save and Save As in exactly the same way as you would with Notepad.

You may find that using WordPad gives you a simple introduction to word processors, because it is much simpler than Word. In practice, it is generally used only to edit text files that are too large for Notepad.

Using Notepad and WordPad

To practise using Notepad and WordPad, try these steps:

1. Find a text file on your system (use Search, as described in Chapter 10, "Working with Files and Folders"). Open it in Notepad.

2. Switch on word wrap if you can only see the beginnings of lines. Do not make any changes.

3. Click Save As in the File menu and save the file under a name of your choosing in your ECDL folder.

4. Select File ➢ New and open a new file. Type something into it, but do not save the file.

5. Select New again and see what message you get. It's up to you whether you save what you have done.

6. Repeat this exercise, but open the file in WordPad. Try adding some formatting to your new file and saving it as a Word file.

Closing Notepad or WordPad

As already noted, both these applications can have only one file open at a time. Thus closing the file means closing the application, while opening another file means closing the current file.

To close either application, choose File ➤ Exit. If you have unsaved changes in the current file, you are asked if you want to save the file. Otherwise, the application simply exits.

Summary

This chapter described how to open, edit, and save text files in Notepad and open, edit, and save text and Word files in WordPad. (Both Notepad and WordPad, simple word processing applications, come standard with Windows XP.) Note that only in WordPad can any formatting be saved.

Chapter

13

Printing

IN THIS CHAPTER YOU WILL LEARN HOW TO

- ✓ Carry out printing.
- ✓ Print a document from a text-editing application.
- ✓ Change the default printer.
- ✓ Install a new printer on your computer.
- ✓ View the progress of a print job.
- ✓ Use the Desktop Print Manager to pause, restart, or delete a print job.

Even in this age of electronic communication, it is more than likely that you will need a printed version of a file you have been working on. Windows can store the details of many printers, and you can switch between them if they are attached to your system. However, there is always a default printer, which is the one to which documents are automatically sent unless you indicate otherwise.

Basic Printing

It is possible to print from a desktop window or from within an application.

Printing from a Desktop Window

You can print directly from a desktop window if a file has an application associated with it. Strictly speaking, however, the associated application opens and moves straight to printing. If you select a file using My Computer and then choose File ➤ Print, the application associated with that file opens and the file is printed immediately by the default printer. If there is no associated application, Print does not appear on the File menu.

Printing from within an Application

In practice, most printing is done from within applications. As you saw in the last chapter, you can use the Print command from the File menu of Notepad or WordPad. Virtually every application, including web browsers, has a Print command on its File menu.

Exactly how printing works within an application, in other words, exactly what options you see to print all the pages, some of the pages, left-hand pages, right-hand pages, and so on, varies from application to application.

Notepad, for example, gives you no options and prints directly, while WordPad is more complex and typical of many applications. When you select Print, you see the menu shown in Figure 13.1. This allows you to choose which printer to use, how many copies to print, and how to collate them. (The default printer is highlighted and has a tick by it, but you can select any other printer that is installed or even install a new one, as described later in this chapter.)

FIGURE 13.1   The Print dialog box for selecting the desired printer

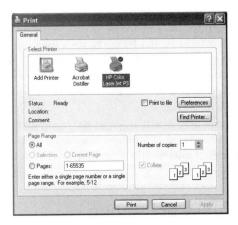

If you click Preferences, the Printing Preferences window opens (see Figure 13.2); this window varies depending on the printer. Each printer has its own driver software, which determines what you see here. What always appears, however, is the option to change the paper size (many applications use the US letter size by default, so you may need to change to A4) and the orientation of the page on the printer, that is, portrait (long side vertical) or landscape (long side horizontal). Once you have made your selection, click OK and then click OK in the main printer window.

FIGURE 13.2   The Printing Preferences dialog box

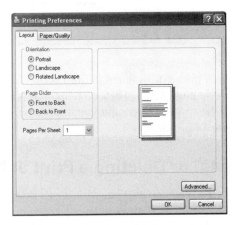

Using the Desktop Print Manager

When you send a file to be printed, it does not go directly to the printer, but to a print queue. The main reason for this is as follows: If a file, perhaps a long one, is being printed and you or someone else on your network sends another file to be printed, the queue manages this. The second file is printed when the first one is complete. If there were no queue, the second print operation would not be allowed and the person sending the second file would have to wait until the first file had finished printing, which is not a very practical way to work.

The Desktop Print Manager allows you to monitor and manipulate the queue of print jobs that you have sent to the printer. In addition, the queue allows more control over printing, so that you can pause, restart, or even delete a job from the Print Manager. You can also move urgent jobs up the queue to be printed earlier.

Viewing the Progress of Printing

If you have sent a number of documents to be printed, you may wish to review their progress. You can do this from the Desktop Print Manager. There are two ways to do this:

- Open the Printers window (Start ➤ Printers And Faxes) and select the printer that you are currently using and open it. A window appears like that shown in Figure 13.3, which shows you the progress of the various print jobs you have sent to this printer.

FIGURE 13.3   Monitoring the progress of print jobs

- When you start to print, a printer icon opens in the Taskbar at the bottom right of your screen (next to the clock, in most cases). The icon remains on the Taskbar as long as there are files being printed. When printing is complete, it disappears. Clicking the icon opens the window shown in Figure 13.3.

Pausing, Restarting, or Deleting a Print Job

From the Print Manager screen, you can also pause or purge printing. This can be useful if, for example, you have a long print queue and suddenly have something urgent to print, or if the printer jams and you need to stop printing. To do this, either click the Printer menu or right-click a specific file. In either case, select what you want to do.

Printer Setup

For a printer to operate on your system, it must have the matching printer driver program installed. With Windows XP, adding a new printer can be very easy or it can be quite complicated.

Installing a Printer

If your new printer is Plug and Play, then if you plug it into the correct port (the connector at the back of the computer) and turn it on, Windows automatically detects it and installs it. The different types of printer port are outside the scope of this book, but the documentation with your printer should make clear which port to use—the plugs and sockets are different for each kind of port.

If you do not have a Plug and Play printer, you can use the Add Printer Wizard. Choose Start ➢ Printers And Faxes. If you are using the default view, the pane at the left side of the Printers and Faxes window (see Figure 13.4) has the option Add A Printer at the top. If you are using the Classic view, you see an Add New Printer icon.

FIGURE 13.4   The Printers and Faxes window

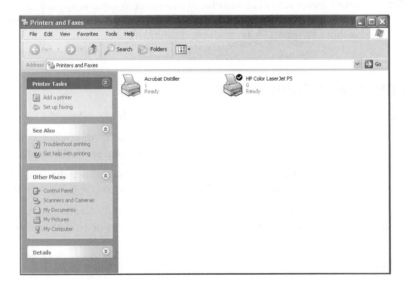

In either case, click this option to open the Add Printer Wizard and follow the instructions. You will be asked (see Figure 13.5) for the manufacturer and model of printer. You may also be asked to insert the installation disk that came with your printer. You may also be asked if you want to share the printer with other network users, and you will be given the option to print a test page.

FIGURE 13.5   Selecting the printer manufacturer and model

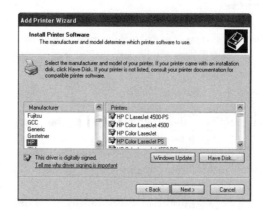

When you have completed the installation, a new icon appears in the Printers and Faxes window shown earlier in Figure 13.4. You may need to check whether it has become the default printer.

 Although adding new hardware such as a printer to a system has been made much easier with Plug and Play, if you are at all unsure, speak to someone who is experienced with printers. If you are on a network, don't install a new printer without speaking to the system administrator.

Changing the Default Printer

Your system always has a default printer, but you can change this by taking the following steps:

1. Choose Start ➢ Printers And Faxes. The Printers and Faxes window shown earlier in Figure 13.4 opens. Which printers are listed depends on how your system and network has been set up.

2. Select the printer that you want to make the default. (Perhaps you have changed your printer, installed another, or want to run a series of jobs on a printer that is currently not the default.)

3. Choose File ➢ Set As Default Printer or right-click the printer icon and select Set As Default Printer from the menu that displays. If there is a tick alongside this, then this printer is already the default printer.

4. Close the Printers window. The next time you print from an application, your new default printer will be highlighted.

Summary

This chapter explained how to print from a desktop window and from within an application. Then it described how print queues work and how to review and modify the progress of printing. You also learnt how to add a new printer and how to change the default printer.

Module Review Questions

1. How do you turn off your computer?

2. If you go to the Start menu and click My Computer, what do you see?

3. What are the two views of folders and files that you can choose, and what is the difference between them?

4. What should you do if a program appears to freeze?

5. When you delete a file from a fixed disk, are you able to retrieve it? If so, how?

6. What usually happens when you right-click your mouse?

7. When does a vertical scroll bar appear?

8. If you see a file called, for example, letter.doc, what are the three letters after the stop (in this case, doc) called and what is their purpose?

9. What kind of file is one that has htm after the stop, for example, myfile.htm, and what kind of application is it most likely to open in?

10. If you have a file called myfile.doc in a folder, can you create another one called MYFILE.doc? If not, why not?

11. Why should you be careful about files that you add to your computer, either from disk or by e-mail?

12. What normally happens to a file when you send it for printing?

Answers to Module Review Questions

1. Go to the Start menu, select Turn Off Computer, and then click Turn Off.

2. My Computer is a folder that contains all the disks and other storage devices on or attached to your computer.

3. The default view is when additional information about the open window is displayed in a pane on the left. The Classic view is where you have to select an icon before you can obtain information about the file or folder it represents.

4. First, press the Esc key on your keyboard. If this has no effect, press Ctrl+Alt+Del and see if the application is labelled as "Not responding." You can then shut down that application.

5. Yes. If you open the Recycle Bin, you can restore a recently deleted file.

6. A context-sensitive drop-down menu opens when you click the right button on your mouse.

7. A vertical scroll bar appears when the window you are viewing contains more icons or other information than can be displayed within the window.

8. The three letters after the stop in a filename are called the filename extension, which tells you (and the system) what kind of file it is, and therefore what program to use to open it.

9. This is an HTML (HyperText Markup Language) file, and it will open in a web browser such as Internet Explorer.

10. No, you cannot create MYFILE.doc in the same folder as myfile.doc, because file-names in Windows are not case-sensitive; it doesn't matter whether letters are upper-case or lowercase.

11. Any files you add to your computer may contain viruses.

12. The print file is added to a print queue.

ECDL Module 3: Word Processing

PART

III

Chapter

14

First Steps With Word Processing

IN THIS CHAPTER YOU WILL LEARN HOW TO

- ✓ Open and close Word.
- ✓ Open an existing document.
- ✓ Open more than one document at the same time.
- ✓ Create a new document.
- ✓ Save a document onto different media.
- ✓ Save a document as a simple text file.
- ✓ Save a document for use in other versions of Word and other word processing applications.
- ✓ Save a document in Rich Text Format (RTF).
- ✓ Save document as a template.
- ✓ Save different versions of a document.
- ✓ Save a document in a form that can be put up on the World Wide Web.
- ✓ Close a document.
- ✓ Use Word Help functions.
- ✓ Change the basic settings in Word.
- ✓ Change the page magnification.
- ✓ Modify the toolbar display.
- ✓ Modify basic options and preferences.

A *word processor* is a computer program that allows you to enter text and edit it. In addition, you can format the text in various ways and include pictures and tables. Once all the processing is complete, you have created a document that is laid out in the way that you wish. This may be a simple letter, or it may be the chapter of a book, although some of the more advanced techniques required for the latter may be beyond the scope of this book.

One of the key features of a word processor is the ability to *format* the text in various ways. In Part 2 of this book, you saw how a text editor can be used to input and edit text words made up of letters and spaces. You'll recall that in a text editor, the text looks as though it has been typed on an old-fashioned typewriter; this is the Courier font, which has been set as the default. When the text file is saved (usually with the filename extension `.txt`, for example, `yourfile.txt`), it is only the letters and spaces (plus a few characters such as the tab and the carriage return) that are saved. There is no formatting.

With a word processor, the situation is different. You can define the fonts you want to use, the type sizes to be used, the inter-line spacing, the inter-paragraph spacing, indents, alignment (left, right, centre, or justified) and a large number of other parameters. When you save the file (with the extension `.doc`, for example, `myfile.doc`), all these parameters are saved too, unlike with a simple text editor.

You can even group all these changes together to form a *style*, to which you can give a name. You can then group these styles, together with other details such as the page layout into a template, which you save as a special kind of file (with the extension `.dot`, for example, `mystyle.dot`) and use again to provide a structure for other documents. You'll learn more about styles and templates in Chapter 16, "Formatting."

This module is based on Word 2002, the version of Microsoft Word that forms part of Office XP, which runs on a PC under the Windows XP operating system. But there are other word processors as well. There are earlier versions of Word, many of which are still used, including Word 97, Word 2000, Word 2002, and versions of Word that run on an Apple Macintosh. There are also word processors provided by other software suppliers. Aside from Microsoft Word, probably the most widely used on the PC platform are Corel WordPerfect and WordPro (previously called AmiPro), which forms part of the Lotus SmartSuite. Although some of the commands are different in these programs, in general they can be used to achieve the same effects as Word. If you follow and understand the chapters in this guide, you should be able to use any other word processor without too much difficulty, particularly if you use the Help files intelligently.

From here on in this book, we shall generally just refer to Word, rather than Word 2002, although you know that this is what is meant.

 These guides are based on Windows XP Professional. If your system uses Windows XP Home, there may be some differences. As far as word processing is concerned, Windows XP Home is often supplied with Microsoft Works rather than Microsoft Office. Works now includes Word 2002, but some of the options that you will see in menus, particularly concerning templates, may be slightly different. However, the functionality is usually similar.

This chapter is rather long, so you may find it easier to consider it in three sessions:

- The first session covers starting Word, opening or creating a file, and finding out about the Word window.
- In the second session, you can look at saving and closing files.
- In the third session, you will experiment with Help and learn how to adjust some basic settings in Word.

Getting Started in Word

The first thing you need to do is start the application. There is no one way to open Word. Indeed, there are almost too many ways, but the three simplest are as follows:

- Click or double-click (depending on which view you are using; see Part 2 of this book) the Word shortcut icon on your Desktop.
- Click the shortcut icon in the Microsoft Office Shortcut Bar that is created if you installed Word as part of the Windows XP Office suite.
- Click Start (at the bottom left of your Desktop). If you have used Word recently, the program is listed (as WinWord, plus its icon) on the left-hand side of your Desktop. All you need to do is click this.

There are many other ways to start Word. You will certainly develop your own preferred method, if you have not already done so, possibly from the following options:

- If you find the Word file that you want to edit (by using any of the methods described in Part 2), opening the file (by clicking or double-clicking) opens Word itself so that you have access to the file.
- You can choose Start ➤ Run. You can then browse through the directories until you find the application file (`Winword.exe`). It's probably in `C:\Program Files\Microsoft Office \Office10`, but not necessarily.

- Open up the directories on your system by double-clicking My Computer on the Desktop (or on the Start menu, produced by clicking Start). Then successively open directories until you find the Word icon or the application filename (`winword` or `winword.exe`), depending on how your windows display the files.

- You can use Windows Explorer (right-click Start and choose Explore) and then select Explore, either by clicking with the left mouse button or by just moving your cursor to Explore; this depends again whether you are using the Classic view or the Web view of your system, as discussed in Part 2. Go down through the directory structure in the same way as for the two preceding approaches.

For obvious reasons, while opening a pre-existing document is a common way of opening an application, none of the last three approaches is a good way to start an application that you use frequently. However, there may be times when any one is appropriate.

If, for any reason, you do not have an obvious icon available on your Desktop, on the Office toolbar, or amongst recently used files, then try the following approach:

1. Click Start and move your cursor up to All Programs, when the programs stored on your system are shown on the right.

2. Move your cursor to Microsoft Word and open it (by clicking or double-clicking, depending on the view you are using).

However, if you are working on a networked system, check with your system administrator if you have not already been told the recommended way to start Word.

Caution: Opening Word by Launching an E-mail Attachment

If you have a Word file as an attachment to an e-mail (see Part 7 of this book), opening the file opens Word. Note, however, the warnings in both Part 2 and Part 7 about security and viruses and check any attachments for viruses before you open them. Remember that Word files can contain viruses.

Word macros are combinations of editing commands, and because they are effectively computer programs that run within Word, they can carry viruses. Although macros are beyond the scope of this book, it is a good idea to check the macro security level by taking these steps:

1. Go to the Tools menu and select Options.

2. Click the tab labelled Security and then the button labelled Macro Security.

3. Set your level to Medium or High to minimize the risk of any macro-based viruses affecting your system (see the following graphic). Of course, if your virus checker is checking incoming e-mails (and it is up-to-date), it should have already detected a virus if one is present. Nevertheless, setting the Word macros security level provides a second level of defence. Again, if you are working on a networked system, talk to your system administrator before making any changes.

Incidentally, Word is not entirely reliable in reporting whether a virus scanner has been installed; this depends on which anti-virus software you are using.

When you start Word, certainly for the first time and maybe every time, the Office Assistant appears. We will not look at this yet, so for now, hide it. Right-click the Office Assistant and select Hide or click Options and uncheck the line stating Use the Office Assistant. We will come back to it later in this chapter.

Understanding the Word Window

Now Word is open, and the screen looks like Figure 14.1. You can see that the screen is divided into various areas. You generally only use one command at a time, so there's no need to feel intimidated (each icon or button represents a command); some of them you will use a lot, while others you may hardly ever use.

Because different people use Word in different ways, Microsoft has made it so that you can customise your Word window, as you'll see in various chapters in this module. Additionally, when you install other programs that integrate with Word, you find that they add toolbars or icons to Word. This means that no two users have Word looking exactly the same.

FIGURE 14.1   The opening screen in Word

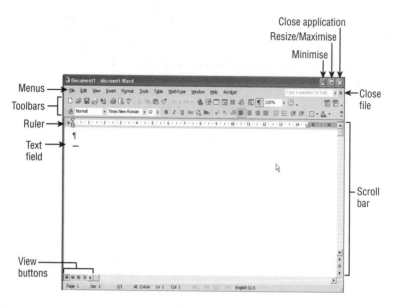

Before the different areas of the screen are described, notice that when Word starts up, it opens a new document, called Document1 (which disappears if you open an existing file). The document name is at the top of the window after the Word icon and just to remind you, the words *Microsoft Word*. At the top right of the screen are the three buttons common to all Windows applications: Minimise, Maximise or Resize, and Close.

If your Word window does not fill the screen, click the Maximise icon to maximise the window so that it fills the screen. The Taskbar at the bottom of the screen is still visible, showing the Start button, any open applications (Word is highlighted), and at the bottom right, various icons representing background tasks in what is called the *System Tray*. To switch between windows and applications, click the appropriate place on this bar.

If you are not familiar with the Minimise, Maximise, and Close buttons, review their functions in Part 2 of this book.

In Word 2002, each document that you open appears as a separate application, so you can switch between documents using the technique for switching between applications described in Part 2 (using the Alt key and the Tab key). This was not true for all earlier versions of Word (and is not true of many other applications), in which you have to go to the Window entry in the main menu bar (described shortly) and choose the document you want. You can, of course, still do this in the current version.

As noted earlier, you can switch between documents by clicking the appropriate tab on the Taskbar at the bottom of the screen. However, if you have several applications open and several documents in each, Windows combines them onto a single tab for each application and when you click it, you can choose the document you want.

The Close control button at the right-hand side of the second line of the screen applies to the open file. Because each document opens in its own window, you can change the size of the window by using the icons on the top line. Clicking the Close button on the second line closes only the document that you are working on.

 You can close any application by holding down the Alt key and pressing function key F4 (Alt+F4).

To get started, open Word (choose your method) and examine the Word window. Mouse over icons. Open menus. Try typing some text into Document1 if you have not done so already, but do not save. If ever in doubt, when you see a screen that requires an answer, click Cancel. (You can do no harm, as long as you do not open an existing document and save it after making any changes.) Once you have finished, close Word by clicking the Close control button in the top-right corner. (Click No when asked if you want to save changes to Document1.)

Adjusting the Window Size

Try the following tasks to familiarise yourself with resizing the Word window:

- Click the Word file icon (in the top left-hand corner of the screen) to see various commands that allow you to change the document window. Depending on the actual size and status of the window, some of these may be greyed out, which means you cannot use them.

- Click Restore and the document window probably becomes smaller. Even if it does not, the centre icon at the top right of your screen changes from the Resize icon to the Maximise icon. You can use drag and drop to move the window so that you can change its size.

- Click Move or Size, and the cursor changes shape and allows you to move either the window as a whole, by clicking in the title bar and moving the cursor and the window (using drag and drop) or one of its edges.

- Click Maximise or Minimise. These have the same effect as the symbols at the top right of the window.

Working with the Menus

On the second line of the screen is a list of words: File, Edit, and so on. These are *menus*. If you click them, the menu drops down. Click again (or elsewhere in the window) and the menu closes.

In Word 2002, this can be a two-stage process. The most common (and recently used) commands appear on the first click, but at the bottom of the drop-down menu is a double arrow. If you click this arrow (or even just move the cursor over the arrow), the rest of the menu is displayed, as you can see in Figure 14.2. Anything you can do with Word can be accessed from these menus. This book looks at many functions of these menus.

FIGURE 14.2   The full version of the File drop-down menu

In each of the menu names, there is nearly always a letter underlined. What this denotes is a *keyboard shortcut*, so that entering this letter while holding down the Alt key has the same effect as selecting the menu. Within the menus, each command also has an underlined letter within it. To select that command, you can just enter that letter (do not use the Alt key) as long as the menu is showing. Finally, some menu items have an arrow pointing to the right; if you move your cursor over that arrow, a fly-out menu appears showing various options (see Figure 14.3).

FIGURE 14.3   The fly-out menu for Send To

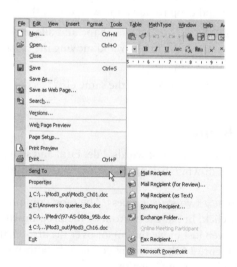

Word is similar to Windows XP in that it allows you to select an icon or tool when you mouse over it. If, in Word, you put your cursor on a menu name (or any icon), it is surrounded by a box. To open it, you click once. Similarly, once you have a menu open, as you move the cursor down it, the entries are surrounded by a blue box, although your system may have been set up to show a different colour. To select that option, you only need to click, rather than double-click. Other approaches are described in this and subsequent chapters.

Using the Toolbars, Ruler, and Scroll Bars

Below the menu names are one or more toolbars. As you saw earlier, the toolbars on your system may not be exactly the same as shown in this figure. The Standard and Formatting toolbars are shown by default (see Figures 14.4 and 14.5).

FIGURE 14.4 The Standard toolbar in its default state

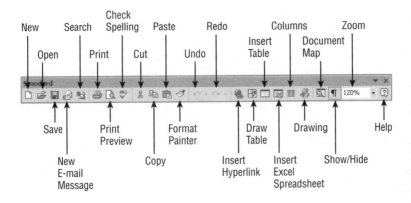

FIGURE 14.5 The Formatting toolbar in its default state

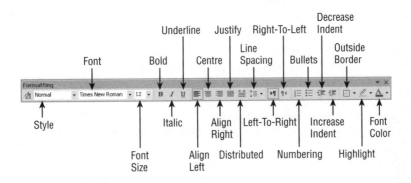

Chapter 16 looks at toolbars in more detail, but it's worth repeating here that the toolbars contain buttons that are graphical equivalents of the commands on the menus.

There are also a few buttons at the bottom left of the screen, as you saw in Figure 14.1. Clicking the button is often quicker than accessing the menu, and if you mouse over a button, the meaning of the button is displayed in a small box. As well as the buttons, most commands also have a keyboard equivalent, which is even quicker than clicking a button. However, you have to remember what the keyboard command is, so you'll probably use keyboard commands for operations that you carry out frequently, toolbar icons for common operations that you do not need all the time, and menus for less common operations. You will see examples as you go along, and you will develop your own preferred way of accessing different commands.

Toolbars do not have to be at the top of the screen; they can be moved around the screen so that they float. If you want to use them in that way, you can, although most people leave them fixed at the top of the screen; that way, an icon is always in the same place. However, sometimes it's useful to display a specific toolbar for a particular task, for example, editing pictures, and sometimes toolbars open automatically. In such cases, a floating toolbar can be helpful, because it isolates the operations of current interest. You can also have, say, the Drawing toolbar along the bottom of the document window.

Below the toolbars, immediately above the text window (as shown earlier in Figure 14.1), is the *ruler*, which shows the margins you are using and any tabs you have set for the line in the text on which the cursor is currently placed. At the left, there is a box showing the type of tab or the indent you can currently set. (You'll learn more about this in Chapter 16.) If you are in Page Layout view (discussed later in this chapter), there's also a ruler down the left-hand side of the page.

On the right-hand side of the text window is the vertical scroll bar, which you use to move through the document. You can use this in several ways:

- In Document1, press the Enter key (add some text if you wish) until you see the sliding box in the scroll bar start to move down.

- Put the cursor on the sliding box and hold down the left mouse button. Just move the mouse, and thus the box, up or down until you reach the line that you want in the text.

- Move the sliding box by pointing at either the single arrow at the top, to move up the document, or the single arrow at the bottom, to move down the document, and hold the left mouse button down until you reach the line you want.

- Click in the space above or below the sliding box, and you move up or down the document by one screen-full. Repeat until you see the line you want.

If you have a third button or a wheel on your mouse, you can also use one of these to control scrolling, but this is outside the ECDL syllabus.

Above the top vertical scrolling arrow is a small horizontal bar, which can be used to split the screen, but this is outside the scope of the ECDL syllabus. We mention it for completeness.

Below the bottom vertical scrolling single arrow are two double arrows with a circle between them. If you mouse over (that is, move your mouse over) either of the arrows, a box opens telling you what will happen if you click the double arrow. By default, you go to the next page.

You can change the action of this double arrow. Mouse over the circle, and it says Select Browse Object. Clicking the circle opens a menu containing 12 icons (see Figure 14.6), from which you can select what you want to happen when you click the double arrow. (If you mouse over an icon, it is highlighted and in a box below the icons, you can see what the option means.) For instance, you can set the double arrows to find the next table or graphic.

FIGURE 14.6   Selecting the action for the double arrows

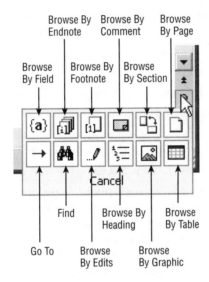

You may not understand some of these options at this stage, but we will come back to many of them as we go through the book. Note that if you are using Find, the browse object is automatically set to what you are looking for. (This can be disconcerting if you are expecting to go to the next page.)

There is a small toolbar at the bottom left of the screen containing the view options. Alongside this is the horizontal scroll bar, which you can use if your text is wider than the screen. You can use this to move horizontally in exactly the same ways as described for the vertical scroll bar.

Open Word again (try a different method this time). Type a few sentences. Zoom in to make the text larger (click the down arrow by the percentage—probably 100 percent—on the Standard toolbar. Now type some more and see what happens to the text in the window. Try to read the text you have typed using the horizontal scroll bar to take you back and forth across the page width.

Unless your document is very wide, we suggest that you change the magnification (described in the last section of this chapter), so that your text fits in the screen window. Although the horizontal cursor moves automatically if you are inputting, this can be very irritating. This is even more the case if you are editing or reading the text, because you have to scroll left and right on every line. It is also worth considering choosing Tools ➤ Options. Click the View tab and remove the tick from Horizontal Scroll Bar; this saves you inadvertently moving the text off to the left of screen. However, Word allows you to customise so much that you will have to develop what is most convenient for you.

Reading the Status Bar

Finally, within the Word window, you have a line that gives you information known as the *status bar*. From left to right, you see

- The current page number (for example, Page 4).

- The current section number (for example, Sec 1). (Sections are outside the ECDL syllabus.)

- The page number and the total number of pages (for example, 4/16).

- The cursor position on the page (for example, At 17cm). The unit depends on what units you have chosen in the menu Tools ➤ Options ➤ General.

- The line number where your cursor is placed on the current page (for example, Ln 25).

- The column number where your cursor is placed on the current line (for example, Col 79). In fact, this is not really the column number, but the number of characters to the left of the cursor minus one. However, if you have some sort of numbering or bullet style applied, the column number does not have an obvious meaning. When you go to a new line, the column number generally goes to 1 (before you type anything new). The terminology is really a hangover from the days when all characters were the same width. (See Chapter 16 for a discussion of fonts.)

- Four labels—REC, TRK, EXT, and OVR—describe the current operating mode(s). As you mouse over them, you'll see that these stand for Record Macro, Track Changes, Extend Selection, and Overstrike. When any of these modes is engaged, the letters are dark; otherwise, the letters are greyed out.

  In Overstrike mode, when you type, you overwrite the characters that are already there. When Overstrike mode is off, if you type something anywhere except at the end of a paragraph, the text moves to the right to make room for the new material. You can turn Overstrike mode on and off by hitting the Insert key on your keyboard or double-clicking the OVR letters on the status bar. Decide for yourself which mode you wish to work in. However, the danger with Overstrike mode is that you may overwrite text that you wish to keep, so consider working in Insert mode for most of the time.

There are three final items on the Word status bar:

- The first item shows the language that you have set for the spelling dictionary.
- The second item has an open book in it, which shows the Grammar and Spelling status. (See Chapter 15, "Basic Text Operation," for more explanation of this feature.)
- The last item is an icon of a disk, which displays only when Word is saving your file, either because you decided to save or because Word is saving in the background. Background saving is a security measure; if your system crashes, you can get back your work up to the last background save, even if you haven't saved what you have done. To set how often background saves take place, choose Tools ➤ Options ➤ Save. You can also turn off background saves, but this is not a good idea. It's also a good idea to leave Always Create Backup Copy ticked, so that you have the previous version of a file to go back to.

WARNING   Word saves a security copy that can be used for recovery after a crash only if you have saved the file at least once. If you do not give the file a name, you will lose your work!

Even when the Word window is set for full screen, you can still see the Windows Taskbar at the bottom of the screen. Depending on how your system is set up, there may also be an Office toolbar (or maybe a Windows toolbar) down the right-hand side of the screen, although you can move this to the top or bottom of the screen or even allow it to float (when it takes on a more compact shape).

Opening and Creating Word Documents

As you have seen, when you launch the Word application, you are given a temporary file called Document1. Now that you are familiar with the basic Word interface, you can move on to opening an existing document and creating a new one.

Opening an Existing Document

In this section, you'll learn how to open an existing file from within the Word application. If you do not appear to have an existing Word document, reopen WordPad, as described in Part 2, and type some text. You can then save it as a Word file (with a .doc filename extension) and close WordPad. Alternatively, you can ask someone who is experienced with Word to create a file for you. In either case, save the file in a subfolder within the My Documents folder.

To open an existing document, choose File ➤ Open. The Open window is displayed (see Figure 14.7) that looks similar to the ones you saw when opening files in Part 2.

FIGURE 14.7   Opening an existing document

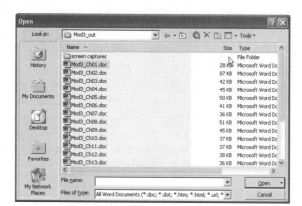

Next, you need to see if you are in the folder where the file you want is stored. The first time you open a file in a Word session, by default, you'll probably be in the My Documents folder. If you need to browse to other folders, use the same technique as for looking for the Word application file. This assumes that you know where the file is that you want to open. More often than not, this will be the case, particularly if you have organised your directory structure in a logical way, as described in Part 2.

However, if like all of us, you sometimes cannot remember exactly what the filename was that you gave to a file or where you saved it, the Open dialog box provides various ways that you can find the file.

Once you have found the folder you want, you may wish to find out more about the files therein. The Views icon on the right-hand side above the file window allows you to view different aspects of the file. The views are similar to those used in Desktop windows. Two new views are Properties and Preview. The Properties view lists information the file, for example, when it was created and when it was last modified. While this information is useful, it is outside the scope of this book. The Preview view shows you the top of the file so that you can check that you have the right file.

The other icons or menus here either are described later in this book or are outside the ECDL syllabus.

The Open dialog box contains a large number of ways to specify a file, but we will look at only some of the options. First, because you are going to open a Word document, go to the box at the bottom of the window—Files Of Type. If it already shows Word Documents, you do not need to change anything. If it says anything else, click the down arrow on the right of the box and a list of options is displayed, which you can scroll down. Choose Word Documents by clicking it, and only Word files are displayed in the main filename window. You can achieve the same thing by typing ***.doc** in the box labelled File Name and pressing Enter.

In older versions of Word, the filename extension was almost always displayed. Word XP uses a more graphical approach; the extensions are still there, however, even if you do not see them.

In the drop-down box showing the file types, there is an All Word Documents option. While the Word Documents option shows only the files saved in Word format, the All Word Documents option displays all the files that Word can open without translation, for example, Rich Text Format (RTF) and HTML files. You can find more out about a file by mousing over it.

Once you have decided which file you want to open, you can double-click it or select it with a single click and then click Open. If you know the full name of the file you wish to open, enter it in the File Name box and press Enter. One file is listed in the filename window, so all you need to do is click Open.

> Instead of clicking the Open button in the Open window, you can just press Enter. This is always the case when you have a sub-window open, when pressing Enter is the same as clicking the button that is highlighted. Be careful, however, if you use this approach, which is undoubtedly faster, to ensure that the option you want is indeed highlighted!

To open a file that you have worked on recently, click File on the menu bar and almost at the bottom (immediately above Exit and even in the shorter display), you'll see a list of recently accessed filenames. (How many filenames appear depends on how your system has been set up. The number can be changed by choosing Tools ➤ Options ➤ General; the maximum number is nine.) These are the last files that you saved; the most recent file is listed first. To open one of these files, just click the filename. If a file is not in the directory in which the file you are currently working on is stored, then the path (disk drive name plus directory tree) is given, although if this is long, parts of it may be replaced by dots, for example, C:\...\ECDL\module3. Again, unlike earlier versions of Word, the filename extension is not shown, which can sometimes be a disadvantage.

> Instead of choosing File ➤ Open, you can type Ctrl+O or click the Open File icon on the toolbar. All of these actions display the Open dialog box.

Opening Several Documents

You can open almost as many documents in Word as you like at the same time. The size of the memory on your computer is the main factor limiting the number; along with the number of other applications you have open.

You open each file in one of the ways described in the preceding section. Alternatively, to open several documents in the same directory, you can select more than one by depressing either the Shift or the Ctrl key when you select files after selecting the first file. Pressing the Shift key selects contiguous files, in other words, the file you first clicked and all files down to and including the file you clicked with the Shift key held down. Clicking another file (with the Shift key still held down) either extends or shortens the selection, making the latest file clicked the final file selected, whether it is before or after the initial file selected. If you hold down the Ctrl key as you click subsequent files, you select files one by one. Clicking a file for a second time (with the Ctrl key held down) deselects that file. Then click the Open button. You can also, of course, open individual files in turn.

You've already learnt how to move between files. The way that Windows XP operates means that moving between Word documents is very similar to moving between applications. In earlier versions of Word, you had the option only of going to the Window menu and then selecting the file that you wanted to view (effectively bringing a file to the top). Now, because each Word document is in a separate system window (rather than just in a window within Word), you can use the tabs at the bottom of the screen or the combination of the Alt and Tab keys to move between windows. By using the split screen and changing the sizes of the document windows, you can view more than one file at the same time (but this is outside the ECDL syllabus).

Creating a New Document

There are three ways to create a new document:

- Click the New icon on the toolbar. This immediately opens a new document in whatever view you are currently using.

- Type Ctrl+N. This is the keyboard shortcut for the New command, and the effect is the same.

- Go to the File menu and select New. This opens a window on the right-hand side of the screen that looks like Figure 14.8. (If Word has been supplied as part of Microsoft Works, probably under Windows XP Home, you will see a different window, but one that has similar functionality.) This gives you various options that determine the way your document will appear. (Templates will be discussed in Chapter 16.) For now, choose Blank Document in the New section.

FIGURE 14.8   Creating a new document via the File menu

Open Word and type a letter, putting your address (or whatever address you want to use at the top) and using the usual forms of address. Perhaps you could tell a friend about doing the ECDL course. Do not be concerned with formatting or fonts yet. Just use the font that appears when you type and allow everything to align left. Now that you've created a file, in the next section you'll learn how to preserve it.

Saving and Closing Documents

When you perform a Save command in Word, you are telling Word to preserve the document as it currently exists. Before you close a document, you often want to save the work you've done. There are a variety of file types you can choose for your document's saved format.

Saving a New Document

Take the following steps to save your document:

1. Use any of the following methods for saving the file that you created in the previous section:

    -   Click the Save icon on the toolbar.

    -   Go to the File menu and select Save. This has the same effect as clicking the Save icon.

    -   Type Ctrl+S. This is the keyboard shortcut, and again the effect is the same.

2. Regardless of how you issue the Save command, because the document is new, the Save As dialog box opens (see Figure 14.9). To save your document as a Word file, all you need to do is make sure that the name suggested is acceptable, change it if it is not, and ensure that the file is saved in the desired folder. This window is similar to the Open window, and the icons mean the same.

FIGURE 14.9   Saving a Word document

3. If you have not already carried out the exercise in Part 2 in which you created a subfolder in your My Documents folder called ECDL, with subfolders for each module, we suggest that you do so now:

    -   Make sure that you are in the My Documents folder and click the Create A New Folder icon, which allows you to create a new subfolder within the current folder.

    -   Type in the name **ECDL**, press Enter, and then open that directory by double-clicking or single-clicking and then clicking Open. (If you wish, you can then create a subdirectory called Module 3.)

4. Once you're in the desired directory, decide what you want to call your file, perhaps **letter01.doc** or **test01.doc**, and click Save. (When you have a directory selected, this button changes to Open.).

You will come back to this file as you go though this book and we shall refer to this file as test01 (and others as test02, and so on). Please also save this file as test02.doc, perhaps after making a few changes.

Once you have determined the name and place for the file you want to save and you have clicked OK, an expanding bar appears at the bottom left of the Word window, tracking the progress of the save. If you were saving a file that had previously been saved, then you would only see the progress bar and not the Save window.

Saving a File Under a New Name, in a Different Directory, or on a Different Medium

If you are working on a file that has been saved before, instead of selecting Save, you can select Save As in the File menu to change the name of the file and/or the directory in which you saved it. The procedure is the same as if you were saving a new file.

You can also save onto a different medium from the Save As window. You can keep pressing the Up One Level icon to eventually reach My Computer, and you see the drives on your system listed. Select the drive that you want (making sure, if appropriate, that there is a formatted disk in the drive) and move down the directory structure, creating directories if you wish. When you reach the level where you want to save the file, click the Save button. Alternatively, if you click the down arrow at the right-hand side of the box showing the current directory, you will see a Windows Explorer–type layout, from which you can select the top-level directory you want.

If you want to use a file as a kind of unofficial template, for example, you are using one letter as the basis for another, it is a good idea to save it under a new filename before you make any changes. If you do not do this and go ahead and make the changes, there is always the chance that you will click Save and over-write your original file. While your system may have been set up to keep a backup of the original file, it is much easier if you do not have to use it.

Saving Documents in Other File Types

You may not always want to save your document as a Word document. For instance, you may want a web version, or you may want to send it to someone who has an earlier version of Word, or someone who is using, for example, WordPerfect or Word on a Macintosh. Word provides ways of saving documents in other formats.

Saving a Document as a Simple Text File

Word documents include formatting information when they are saved, so that the next time you open the file, it has the same appearance as before. However, there are times when you want to save only the text, in other words, the letters and spaces, plus punctuation, carriage returns, and tab characters. These are known as *simple text files* (usually with the filename extension .txt, although other extensions are used as well).

To save a file in text format, choose File ➢ Save As. This time, however, as well as selecting the filename and the directory where you want to save it, go to the drop-down menu Save As Type (see Figure 14.10) to see a list of various file type options. If you scroll down, you will see various options, including

- Text Only

- MS-DOS Text With Layout

- Text With Layout

FIGURE 14.10   The Save As Type drop-down list

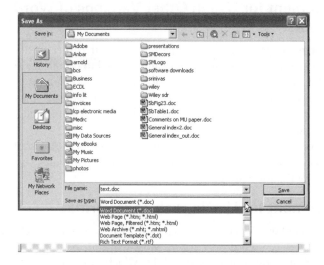

The second and third of these options are effectively shortcuts, because when you select Text Only and then click Save, you bring up a window that includes a whole range options, almost all of which are outside the scope of this book. Text With Layout includes a carriage return at the end of each line, as it appears in the Word document. MS-DOS Text With Layout is much the same, except that the coding for accented and some other characters is different.

These formats may be useful if you are going to use the text file in some application where the text is not automatically wrapped (although such applications are less common today than they used to be). Choosing one of these file types adds the filename extension .txt, although in this version of Word, you do not see the extension unless you wish to. What you see when you open the file is the program associated with the file type. This is outside the scope of this book, but Word 2002 and Windows XP use it much more than earlier versions.

If you are using Word 2002 as part of Microsoft Works, the Save As Type options are slightly different.

When you save a file as text, the existing formatting remains on the screen. However, if you close the file and reopen it in Word, all the formatting you added has disappeared.

The other thing to note (and this applies to all saves in different formats) is that the filename and the file extension in the title bar have changed. You are now looking at the new file, not the Word file. If you want to go back to working on the Word file, you need to reopen it. If you want subsequent changes saved in the new format, you need to choose File ➢ Save As again. When you do so, a message appears asking you if you wish to overwrite the previous file or not. Click OK to accept.

Open `test01.doc`. Although it has very little formatting, it will almost certainly be in a font such as Times. Save it as `test01.txt` and (with line breaks) as `test03.txt`. Close the file(s) and then reopen them and notice the differences.

Saving a Document for Use in Other Versions of Word and Other Word Processors

Word makes it extremely easy to save a document for use with earlier versions of Word or with certain other word processors. You may, for example, need to do this if you are sending your file to someone else who has an earlier version of Word, or who perhaps uses WordPerfect.

Choose File ➢ Save As and look through the Save As Type list until you see what you want. This list contains various versions of WordPerfect and Word 6.0/95 (as well as RTF and HTML, which we shall consider in the following sections).

Choose the option that you want, as for text files, and click Save. Again, the correct filename extension is added if you do not include it. If you save in certain formats, you see a warning that you may lose some of the formatting.

Saving a Document for Use in Rich Text Format

Rich Text Format (RTF) was invented by Microsoft as a document interchange language for moving documents between word processors. Most word processing programs—and some other programs—can now open files saved as RTF, which can be useful. As noted earlier, an RTF file is actually a text file with all the formatting instructions spelt out as codes. Part of the file of this section as originally entered looks as follows in RTF:

```
\par }\pard \ltrpar\ql \li0\ri0\sb144\sl360\slmult1\nowidctlpar\faauto
\outlinelevel0\rin0\lin0\itap0\lisb60\pararsid13398795 {\rtlch\fcs1 \ab\af36
\afs56 \ltrch\fcs0 \b\f36\fs56\cf1\insrsid6968703 Saving}{\rtlch\fcs1 \ab\af36
\afs56 \ltrch\fcs0
\b\f36\fs56\cf1\insrsid13398795   }{\rtlch\fcs1 \ab\af36\afs56 \ltrch\fcs0
\b\f36\fs56\cf1\insrsid6968703 Documents in}{\rtlch\fcs1 \ab\af36\afs56 \ltrch
\fcs0 \b\f36\fs56\cf1\insrsid13398795   }{\rtlch\fcs1 \ab\af36\afs56 \ltrch\fcs0
\b\f36\fs56\cf1\insrsid6968703 Other Formats
```

Before this passage, which is near the start of the text, there is a very long section—often called the *preamble*—that specifies almost all aspects of the layout. This is often longer than the file itself! As you can see, RTF is not a reader-friendly language, but it doesn't need to be because it needs to be understood only by other word processing programs (and occasionally by programmers!). If you open an RTF file in Word, you may be asked to confirm that it is RTF, or it may just open like a Word file; this depends on how your system is set up, but normally you will never see coding like this, unless you want to.

To save a file in this format, use File ➢ Save As and this time select Rich Text Format from the Save As Type list. Word automatically changes the filename extension to `.rtf`.

Word can be set up to ask for confirmation when a file is opened in a format that is not Word. Choose Tools ➢ Options and click the General tab. One of the entries is Confirm Conversion At Open. If this is ticked, then you are asked to confirm that a file is indeed RTF, for example. You can simply click Open or you can select Text Only instead and then click Open. You then see the RTF as text. The same can be done for HTML files. If you do this with other file types, you simply see a screen of characters that makes no sense to you. If you try to open a file in an incorrect format, other than as a text file, then Word tells you that this is not possible.

Open your file `text01.doc` and save it as RTF. Close it and then reopen it. Did it open immediately or ask you to confirm? If the latter, click Open. In either case, you should find that the file appears identical to the original Word file. If you want to see the RTF file, ensure that Confirm On Open is selected and then select text in this box, as discussed. As your file is quite short, go to the end of the file and work up until you find the start of your file. Looking at the position of the box on the vertical scroll bar gives you an idea of what proportion of the file the preamble takes up.

Saving a Document as a Template

Chapter 16 discusses document templates in more detail; all you need to know now is that a template stores all the formatting information that you have created. It can contain text, but it doesn't have to. When you create a new document by choosing File ➢ New, you have a choice of templates.

If you want to save a file as a template, you can delete all the text that is specific to the document, but leave, for example, your address in a letter template and then go to Save As and choose Document Template in the Save As Type box. Two things occur, as you can see in Figure 14.11:

- The filename extension changes from `.doc` to `.dot`. You may also want to change the filename to something that is more generic and describes the template type rather than this particular file.

- The folder changes to one called `Templates`. Until you have more experience, it is wise to accept this and store the new template in this directory. In this way, when you open a new document by choosing File ➢ New, your new template is one of the choices offered to you.

FIGURE 14.11 · Saving a file as a template

While you can open `text01.doc` and look at saving it as a template, we recommend that you only look and do not save it. The file as yet contains too little formatting information to make saving it as a template worthwhile.

Saving Versions of a Document

There may be situations where you want to save different versions of a document without changing the filename.

If you go to the File menu and select Versions, you can save different versions of a document all in the same file, which saves space. A Versions window like Figure 14.12 appears (but with a blank window). You can open earlier versions of a file by selecting them and clicking Open. You can also delete previous versions.

FIGURE 14.12 · The opportunity to review earlier versions of a Word document

When you click Save, you have the opportunity to add comments to each version, as shown in Figure 14.13. When you reopen the file, you see the latest version. Note that you can also have Word save new versions automatically, rather than continuing to overwrite the original file.

FIGURE 14.13   The option to add comments to file versions

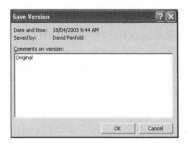

Open `text01.doc`. Make a few changes and then save the new version. Make a few more changes and save another version. Review your versions. When you have finished, delete all versions except the original and the most recent version.

Saving a Document for Use on the World Wide Web

The World Wide Web (WWW) uses a coding system called *Hypertext Markup Language (HTML)* with which to describe formatting. A web browser such as Internet Explorer or Netscape Navigator interprets this language in just the same way as Word interprets RTF, so that you do not see the coding on the screen. HTML carries out a similar task to RTF and is also a text file, but it is much simpler. The same text you saw earlier looks like the following in HTML:

```
<p class=MsoNormal style='margin-top:7.2pt;mso-para-margin-top:.6gd;line-height:
150%;mso-pagination:none;mso-outline-level:1;mso-layout-grid-align:none;
text-autospace:none'><b><span style='font-size:28.0pt;line-height:150%;
font-family:Helvetica-Black;mso-bidi-font-family:Helvetica-
Black;color:black'>Saving
Documents in Other Formats<o:p></o:p></span></b></p>
```

This extract is taken from near the beginning of the file. As in RTF, there is a preamble, although it is not usually described in this way. The preamble includes information about how the document should be formatted. However, you do not ever need to see this coding.

In earlier versions of Word (and earlier versions of HTML), most of the formatting information was stored in the web browser, so the HTML file was much simpler than in the preceding example. However, recent versions of browsers use style sheets in a similar way to Word (described in Chapter 16). While this makes the HTML file more complex, it allows you as the author of a document to specify how your web pages will appear. How this is done is outside the scope of the ECDL syllabus.

You can also open HTML documents in Word and save them as Word files.

To save a document in HTML format, choose File ➤ Save As and in the Save As Type drop-down list, choose Web Page. When you save a Word document as a web page, the screen layout changes to look more like a web browser. This is the web layout and the style is built into the template, which changes when you open an HTML file. You can switch to other layouts in just the same way as for an ordinary Word file.

There are also two other options that are relevant here. The first is Web Page, Filtered. If you use this option, a warning appears that certain (Microsoft) Office-specific tags will be removed, so that if the file is reopened in Word, some information may be lost.

The final option is Web Archive, which includes features that are not supported by earlier web browsers.

Open `text01.doc` and save it as Web Page. See what happens to the screen. If you have a web browser available, you can try opening the HTML file—which now has the filename extension `.htm`—to see what it looks like. Because it has very little formatting, it will probably look very uninteresting.

Closing a Document and Closing Word

To close a document, you can do one of the following:

- Go to the File menu and select Close (File ≻ Close).

- Click the Word document icon on the left of the filename in the title bar and then click Close.

- Click the Close control button at the top right-hand corner of the document window (not the one at the top of the screen, which exits from the Word application).

- Type Ctrl+**W**.

If the document you are closing has not been saved, you will be prompted to save it.

Adjusting Basic Settings

One of the great advantages of Word (and many other modern programs) is that, in many ways, you can choose to use them as you want to, rather than as the software designer felt was the right way. This section describes some of the settings you can adjust to your liking.

Changing Display Modes

Word allows you to view a document in different ways, called *display modes*, each of which serves a specific purpose. If you look at the View menu, four display modes are listed:

Normal This is probably the easiest to view work with, at least for basic text entry, in that the text fills the Word window (see Figure 14.14), and page breaks are just indicated by a broken line across the screen. However, neither drawings and artwork in boxes nor page headers and footers appear in this view, so you need to be careful if you have these elements in your document.

FIGURE 14.14   Normal view

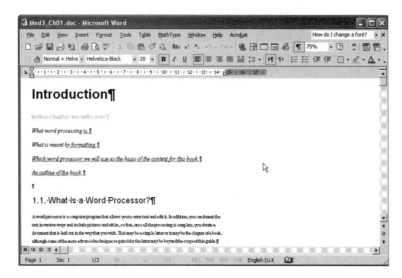

Web Layout   Use this view if you are creating a web page or, more probably, if you are converting an existing Word document for use on the Web. Backgrounds are displayed, text is wrapped to fit the window, and graphics are placed as if they were in a web browser (see Figure 14.15).

FIGURE 14.15   Web Layout view

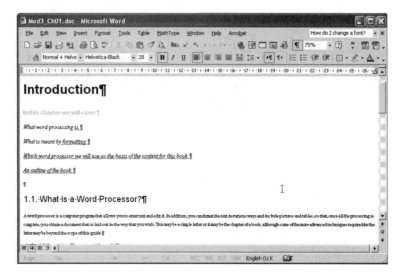

Print Layout   This view shows you how your document will appear when printed, with all the graphics, page breaks, and so on (see Figure 14.16).

FIGURE 14.16 Print Layout view

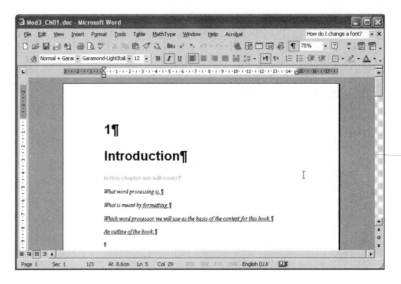

Outline The different levels of heading in a document are usually distinguished by different typographic styles and, as you will see in Chapter 16, these can be given names and stored. In the Outline view (see Figure 14.17), you can view only the hierarchy of the headings, so that you have an overview of the structure of the document without seeing the pargaraphs of text.

FIGURE 14.17 Outline view

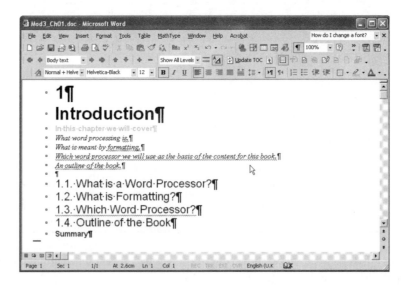

These views can also be accessed from the toolbar at the bottom left of the window.

On the View menu, you also see the Document Map option. If you click this, a window opens on the left of your screen showing what is effectively a table of contents of your document (see Figure 14.18). It is important that you use styles to take advantage of this. (Styles are described in detail in Chapter 16.) If you click one of the headings in this window, you jump to the appropriate place in the document. To close this window, click Document Map again.

FIGURE 14.18   Using the Document Map feature

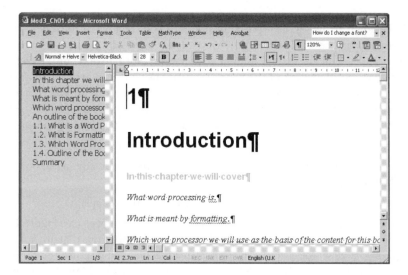

To become familiar with the different view modes, open `test01.doc` or `test02.doc`. Experiment with the Normal and Print Layout views. The latter will give you a good idea, for example, if your letter will fit on a single page.

If you have access to a longer Word file that includes headings and other advanced elements, open it and experiment with the Online Layout and Outline views, as well as Document Map.

Changing Page Magnification

You can change the page size of a document, as well as the font sizes within it, as you'll see in Chapter 16. However, it is convenient to be able to see the text at a larger size, perhaps to make editing easier. You may also wish to see a number of pages at a smaller size to obtain an overall impression of the layout. Remember that in either case, you are changing how you look at the document and not the document itself.

The first way to set the page magnification is as follows:

1.   In the toolbar, you can see the box illustrated in Figure 14.19, which allows you to specify the view size as a percentage; the current percentage is already shown.

FIGURE 14.19   Zoom options on the toolbar

2.   Click the down arrow on the right-hand side, and you see a list of fixed percentages, plus for Normal, Print Layout, and Outline views, Page Width. If you choose Page Width, the system calculates the percentage so that your text (in Normal view) or the page (in Print Layout view) fills the width of the page. If you are using Print Layout, you also see Text Width, Whole Page, and Two Pages, which are self-explanatory. In Web Layout, you see only the percentages; this is because the text wraps to fit the screen—that is, the line length adjusts to fill the width of the window, so Page Width has no absolute meaning.

3.   Click one of these percentages, and the magnification changes.

4.   Alternatively, you can type the percentage you want to use directly in the box and then press the Enter key.

The second way to set the page magnification is to take these steps:

1.   Go to the View menu and select Zoom. The Zoom window opens (see Figure 14.20) with a selection of percentages. Again, the options available (the options that are not greyed out) depend on the view you are in. They are the same as when you use the toolbar Zoom option. In addition, if you're using Print Layout, there is also a Many Pages option.

FIGURE 14.20   The Zoom options

2.   Your present percentage is shown halfway down on the left, and you can type directly into this box or pick from the list. The option Whole Page, of course, shows the whole page on the screen. If you choose the option Many Pages, click the computer icon to choose from a series of preset layouts, as illustrated in Figure 14.21. You can also see a preview of your choice.

Although you are specifying percentages, it is not clear exactly what they are percentages of. If you choose 100 percent, the font size on screen is not the same as it would be on paper. It partly depends on the size and resolution of your screen. Thus, it is unwise to use what you see on the screen as a final guide to font sizes in the final printed document. Although zooming is referred to, this is not a graphical zoom like those in many graphics programs, where the area of interest is selected and zooming changes the view so that the area of interest fills the screen window.

FIGURE 14.21   Preset multi-page Zoom options

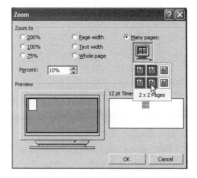

3. Click OK when you are happy with what you have.

Each layout view retains its own magnification, so that if you change the magnification in Normal view, you do not alter it in, for example, the Print Layout view.

Continue with the files you created earlier in this chapter and change the magnification in the different views to see what the effects are and whether larger sizes are helpful or present a problem.

Changing the Toolbar Display

Toolbars are sets of icons that represent tools (or operations that you can carry out). Word comes with a number of toolbars already prepared. To see a list of what is available on your system, go to the View menu and select Toolbars (see Figure 14.22). To see what is on each toolbar, select one and it is displayed at the top of the screen. (Those toolbars that are ticked are already showing.) To remove a toolbar, open the Toolbars window again and deselect it. It is obviously impractical to have all the toolbars on the screen, so you need to choose which ones are most useful to you. Indeed, depending on what you are doing, you may change your selection from task to task.

FIGURE 14.22 List of available toolbars in Word

In Figure 14.22, the three bottom toolbars are not part of Word. However, if you install other applications, they add toolbars to Word so that you can access them directly. For instance, Copernic Agent allows you to access a web search tool, MathType is for producing mathematical equations, and PDFMaker is added by Adobe Acrobat for creating files in the Portable Document Format (PDF), which is a format that allows you to transfer to others a printable version of a document.

With a few exceptions, such as the Layout toolbar in the bottom left of the Word window, most toolbars can be moved around the screen. If a toolbar is *docked* at the top of the window, then place the cursor on the broken line at the left and just drag and drop. If the toolbar is floating, place the cursor in the title bar at the top of the toolbar window (see Figure 14.23). When the toolbar is floating, you see what it is called, which is not the case when it is locked at the top of the window (see Figure 14.24). You may find it helpful to use floating toolbars when you are carrying out a specific task.

FIGURE 14.23 A fixed toolbar

Formatting toolbar is docked

FIGURE 14.24   Moving a floating toolbar by dragging its title bar

Formatting toolbar is floating in window

You may have noticed that it says Customize at the bottom of the Toolbars window. This is outside the ECDL syllabus, but it is worth experimenting with once you are more confident. You may want to add to the toolbars icons that are appropriate to the work you do. You can even create your own toolbar if you wish! Customize also appears on the Tools menu. (If you find that the Customize is greyed out, this is probably because you have another window open, such as Find.)

The icons on the toolbars are not really self-explanatory, except perhaps in a few cases. However, to find out what they mean, just move your arrow over (mouse over) the icon, and a small box appears telling you what it means. There is a certain knack in doing this, so move the cursor around over the icon if the box does not appear immediately. You will get to know the icons you use regularly.

Look at the list of toolbars in the View menu. Select as many as you can and mouse over the icons, so as to familiarise yourself with what they mean. Try moving the toolbars so that they are fixed and floating.

Modifying Basic Options and Preferences

There are various basic options that you can set in Microsoft Word:

User name   Although doing so is outside the scope of the ECDL syllabus, you may wish to change this name, because it is linked to files and appears in a variety of ways. For example, Word uses this information to list the author in the Properties screen and to identify the writer of a given comment. To change this, go to Tools ➢ Options and select the User Information tab in the Options window. Figure 14.25 shows the information that can be changed.

FIGURE 14.25 The User Information options

Default directory The *default directory* is the one that appears in the boxes, such as those shown earlier in this chapter, when you click Open or Save. Choose Tools ➤ Options and select the File Locations tab in the Options window (see Figure 14.26). You may want to change this to a directory that you use frequently. To change this, select Documents in the window and click the Modify button (or double-click Documents). The Modify Location window opens, as shown in Figure 14.27. It looks like the Save window. You can either select an existing folder and click OK or click the Create New Folder icon and enter a new name. The next time you open or save a file in Word, this is the directory that is shown. As you can see in Figure 14.26, there are various other defaults that you can change, but we will not discuss these here.

FIGURE 14.26 The File Locations tab in the Options window

FIGURE 14.27   Changing the default directory

Using Help

If you find that you need assistance, there are various ways you can obtain help using Word. With earlier versions, you would have received a large printed manual, but today almost all help is provided electronically, which means that it's easier to locate what you want to know. Even now, however, there are different approaches you can take.

The first of these is called the Office Assistant, which usually appears the very first time you use Word. The rather sly-looking character, based on a paper clip, is called Clippit.

To open Office Assistant, if it is not already open, click the Question Mark icon on the Help menu, press the function key F1, or choose Help ➢ Show The Office Assistant. Clippit opens, asking you what you would like to do. If you type in a question and click Search, Clippit does its best to answer it.

> If you click the Question Mark icon on the toolbar, the Office Assistant opens only if you have elected to use Office Assistant. If you have not, then the conventional Help window appears, as discussed shortly.

Some Help options are now displayed. If you select one of these, a relevant Help screen is displayed, as shown in Figure 14.28.

Once you have read that screen and any others that may be linked to it, you can close it by clicking the Close control button at the top-right corner. To reactivate the Office Assistant, just click it (or press function key F1) and you see the same display. You can then click a different option.

FIGURE 14.28 A Word Help screen

If you do not like Clippit, the paperclip character, there are a number of other characters that you can use. To access these, and to customise the Office Assistant in other ways, click Options in the Office Assistant window. The Gallery tab allows you to move through the various alternative characters.

But more important are the options themselves. Most of these are fairly self-explanatory, but let's talk about the tips.

Depending on which options you have selected, when Office Assistant thinks that you could do what you are doing more efficiently, a lightbulb appears in the top-right corner of the Office Assistant window. If you click that lightbulb, you see the tip (see Figure 14.29).

FIGURE 14.29 A tip from the Office Assistant

If you no longer find Office Assistant helpful or you prefer a more formal approach, you can close it. Right-click the Office Assistant, choose Options, and uncheck Use Office Assistant. This window also allows you to change other options if you continue to use the Office Assistant. When you are using the Office Assistant, all messages appear in the Office Assistant message box, so it's possible that you may miss them because the Office Assistant has become a feature that you tend to ignore. On the other hand, there is usually a sound cue to draw your attention to any message. You have to choose which option you prefer.

You can also obtain information by clicking the question mark at the top right of the windows shown in most figures. Clicking the question mark changes the cursor to the Question Mark icon (a question mark is added to the cursor), but this applies only within the window in question. Click the area of interest to open an information box, although you may see a message telling you that no Help topic is associated with the item you have clicked; clicking elsewhere returns the cursor to normal.

You may have a What's This? option, with the Question Mark icon, on the Help menu; this can also be added to the toolbar. It provides you with context-sensitive help, in other words, help about the part of Word that you are currently using. If you choose What's This?, your cursor changes to the Question Mark icon. Then when you click any part of the Word window, a window opens to give you information. For example, the window in Figure 14.30 was produced by selecting What's This? when the cursor was over the word *text*, which had previously been selected.

FIGURE 14.30   A window produced by selecting What's This?

If the Office Assistant is in use, when you go to the Help menu and select Use Microsoft Help (or press F1 or click the Question Mark icon on the toolbar), the Office Assistant opens. However, if the Office Assistant is not being used, then selecting Use Microsoft Help opens a Help window, as shown in Figure 14.31.

FIGURE 14.31   The Help screen showing Contents

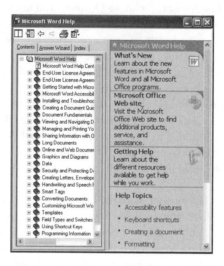

Help is self-explanatory, as indeed it should be if it is going to be of much use. A little explanation may be helpful, however, specifically for the Contents, Answer Wizard, and Index elements:

- Contents gives you the view shown in Figure 14.31. If you are learning about the system or are not really sure, this is probably the easiest approach. Clicking the plus sign at the side of an item opens up the contents of that item; if a minus sign is shown, then clicking it closes that section of the Contents.

- The Answer Wizard provides the same functionality as the Office Assistant, but without the graphics. Just type in your question, click Search, and you get a list of places where you can look for more information (see Figure 14.32).

FIGURE 14.32   Using the Answer Wizard

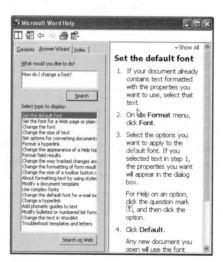

- Index gives you a back-of-the-book type index. This is good to use if you know what you are looking for and if you know the term Microsoft uses, which may not always be obvious! The Search facility helps here, however. Again, click the item in the box below that you hope will provide the information you want and a new screen opens on the right (see Figure 14.33).

FIGURE 14.33   The Help screen showing Index

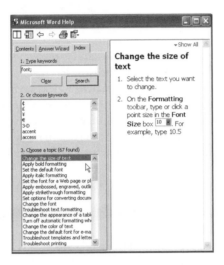

The Index facility in Word 2002 is rather limited compared to that in earlier versions of Word (for example, Word 97), in which an index of all the significant words in the Help files was created. Here you are limited to the keywords defined by Microsoft.

Whether you are using the Office Assistant or not, you can type in a query at the top right of your Word window.

Other options in the Help menu are:

- Office On The Web, which links you to Microsoft pages on the World Wide Web, which compensates somewhat for the limitations on Index. However, it does require a connection to the Web at the time when you need the information, which is not always possible.

- Activate Product, which you need only when you first install Word, so you can probably ignore this.

- Detect And Repair, which is self-explanatory, but arguably outside the ECDL syllabus.

- WordPerfect Help, which may or may not be installed on your system.

- About Microsoft Word, which gives you information on various aspects of the program, and indeed your system, if you click System Info. Note that there is also a Technical Support button that opens special Help screens that tell you about Microsoft Technical Support.

Experiment with the different ways that you can find help. Don't worry about finding information about a specific topic (although you may want to do that). Just make sure that you are happy about the ways in which help can be obtained, so you can decide which approach you prefer.

Summary

In this chapter, you saw how to open Word and examine the window that appears. You learnt how to open one or more existing documents and how to create a new document. Once a document contains text, you can save it in Word format, as well as saving existing documents under a new name, in a new directory, or on a different storage medium. It's also possible to save a document as a text file, for use in other versions of Word and other word processors, in RTF format, or for use on the Web. You saw that a document can be saved as a template, so that certain aspects of a document can be easily repeated for future documents. You saw how to close a document and how to close Word.

You can make several changes to the way in which documents are viewed within Word to meet your personal preferences. This includes changing the display mode (or view), changing the page magnification, and changing the toolbar display. You can also modify some basic preferences by choosing Tools ➤ Options.

There are several different ways of using Help if you need help using Word. The Office Assistant is one way, while if you do not use the Office Assistant, there are three tabs—Contents, Answer Wizard, and Index—in the Help window that provide ways of accessing help.

Chapter

15

Basic Text Operations

IN THIS CHAPTER YOU WILL LEARN HOW TO

- ✓ Insert and delete characters, words, sentences, paragraphs, and special characters such as fixed spaces or mathematical symbols.
- ✓ Display and hide non-printing characters.
- ✓ Use the Undo and Redo commands.
- ✓ Select text.
- ✓ Copy and move text within and between documents.
- ✓ Delete text.
- ✓ Search for characters or text strings.
- ✓ Replace characters or text strings with other characters.
- ✓ Use a spell-check program and make any necessary changes.
- ✓ Use a grammar-checking program and make any necessary changes.

Most of this chapter is about the basics of word processing, getting text (characters and spaces) onto the page in the order you wish them to be. Of course, if you open a new document, all you need to do initially is type, just as you would on a typewriter. You have already seen that when you reach the right-hand margin that has been set up for you, the next word automatically appears on the next line. When you press the Enter key, you generate a carriage return (paragraph marker) that starts a new line. Similarly, you can enter tab characters, and the cursor moves to a fixed pre-set position in the line, just as it does with a typewriter.

This is fine as long as you want to type only the characters you can see on the keyboard and you do not need to change anything. But this chapter considers how to change the text you have already entered and how to enter characters that are not on the keyboard. You will also learn how to undo an edit.

Inserting, Editing, and Deleting Text

The first thing you need to know when editing text in Word is where you are. When you are working on a document, there are effectively two cursors on the screen. There is the *mouse cursor*, which looks like a capital I (with bars at the top and bottom); this moves around the screen as you move your mouse. There is also the *text cursor*, which is a flashing vertical line that shows you where in the text you are; in other words, where the next thing you enter at the keyboard will take effect. You need to be clear about the difference between these two cursors.

If you click the left mouse button (left-click, or just click) with the mouse at any position in the text, you move the text cursor to that position. As you'll see shortly, there are other ways that you can move the text cursor, but the big advantage of the mouse is that you can move anywhere in the text, particularly if you also use the scroll bars. Once you have clicked, the text cursor stays where you put it, irrespective of where you now move the mouse cursor to.

Incidentally, if you click the right mouse button (right-click), a pop-up menu appears that duplicates parts of the menus at the top of the Word window. This is context-sensitive—what appears depends on where you right-click.

There are various other ways in which you can move the text cursor:

- You can use the arrows that are usually included on the numeric keypad, although exactly where they are depends on the design of your keyboard. There are always four arrows (up, down, left and right) and sometimes eight of these; the additional four are diagonal (up left, up right, down left and down right). Depressing one of the first four arrow keys moves your text cursor one line up or down or one character to the left or right. Depressing one of the other keys combines two movements. If you also hold down the Ctrl key, then instead of moving by a line or a character, you move by a word or a paragraph.

- You can use the Home and End keys. Home takes you to the beginning of your current line, and End takes you to the end of it. If you hold down the Ctrl key at the same time, Home and End take you to the beginning or end of your document.

- You can use the Page Up and Page Down keys. These usually take you up or down a screenful rather than a text page, although this depends on which view you are using.

Adding and Deleting Characters

To insert characters in the text, for example, if you've missed a character out of a word, just place the text cursor at the position where you want to add the character(s) and type. Usually when you open Word, you're in Insert mode, which means that typing inserts the new characters into the text. However, you may have switched to Overstrike mode, intentionally or even inadvertently, by depressing the Insert (Ins) key. If you are in Overstrike mode, instead of inserting the new characters, each character replaces that to the right of the cursor as you enter it. Sometimes, of course, this may be what you want. If you are in Overstrike mode, then OVR at the bottom of the window is dark, as shown in Figure 15.1. In Word, the text cursor does not change; in some other, particularly older, word processors, in Overstrike mode the cursor changes to a block covering the current letter; the letter is then white on black—or its colour equivalent.

FIGURE 15.1   The Overstrike mode status

REC   TRK   EXT   OVR   English (U.K

To insert more than one character (in Insert mode), just keep on typing. If you want to add a new paragraph, just type at the beginning or end of an existing paragraph, adding carriage returns appropriately.

If you want to delete characters one by one, simply place your text cursor before the first character you want to delete or after the last one. To delete the character after the cursor, press the Delete key (Del). To delete the character before the cursor, press the Backspace key. You do this as many times as there are characters you want to delete. You can also hold down the Del or Backspace key, but, if you do this, be careful that you do not delete more characters than you intend to.

You can, of course, insert and delete hard and soft carriage returns. We shall see below how to show and hide the characters representing these and it is easier to see what is happening if you have the characters showing. However, you simply insert a hard paragraph mark by striking the Enter key and a soft paragraph mark by holding down the Shift key when you strike the Enter key. Entering a new soft paragraph mark just creates a new line, while the style produced by creating a hard paragraph mark will be the same as the style of the current line unless you add it at the end of the line, when the style of the new paragraph created will depend on what has been defined in the style for the paragraph you had originally. Styles are discussed in more detail in Chapter 16.

Deleting a soft paragraph mark simply removes the new line, while if you delete a hard paragraph mark, the following paragraph will now run on and take on the style of the paragraph at the end of which you deleted the paragraph mark.

Open the latest version of your test file. Edit it by adding additional paragraphs and words and sentences within paragraphs. Delete some text. Press the Insert key and then overtype some text. Remember to press the Insert key again to come out of Overstrike mode. Save the file as a new version (or even save it as a new file, say, `test03.doc`), so that you have a series of versions or files that represent the stages that you have gone through.

Inserting Symbols and Special Characters

One of the big advantage of a word processor over an old-fashioned typewriter (and there are many) is that you can include in your document many more characters than you can type directly on the keyboard. Keyboards generally used in the U.K. and U.S. are not, for example, designed so that you can enter accented characters directly (unlike those used, say, in France). However, you can still enter such characters, as well as all kinds of symbols. There is also a special way to enter characters that have traditionally been used in printed books but not in typed documents. These include curly quote marks (" and "), en and em rules (– and —), and many more.

There are various ways of inserting symbols and special characters. The simplest way is to choose Insert ≻ Symbol. The Symbol window opens (see Figure 15.2). You can then do two things to find the symbol you want:

- Scroll through the fonts. (You may also find that you can scroll through subsets; exactly what appears depends on the font of the characters on which your text cursor is placed.) The top font is always called normal text.

- Look at the characters; it may unfortunately take you some time to find the character you want if this is the first time you have used it.

FIGURE 15.2   The Symbol window

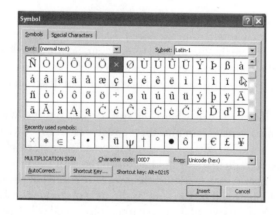

At the bottom of this window are various other features. First, Microsoft helps you by listing recently used symbols; this is a very useful feature. On the next line, you see what the character is called, its character code in three different formats; the only one that you need to be concerned with here is the ANSI coding. There are also two buttons: AutoCorrect and Shortcut Key. AutoCorrect is outside the ECDL syllabus, but it allows you to automatically correct common mistakes; you'll see references to it in later chapters. If you click AutoCorrect, the corrections are listed. A Shortcut Key allows you to set up a keyboard shortcut, which you can use instead of the menu. This is quicker once you know the shortcuts, but it means you have to remember them. If, in the Symbols box, you select a character and a shortcut key has already been set up, it is shown next to the Shortcut Key button, as you can see in Figure 15.2. As discussed in Part 2, be careful about setting up new shortcuts because you may overwrite existing standard shortcut keys.

To make life easier for you, in the Symbol window there is a second tab, labelled Special Characters (see Figure 15.3). Here are listed a number of characters that occur quite frequently in well-formatted material.

FIGURE 15.3   The Special Characters tab in the Symbol window

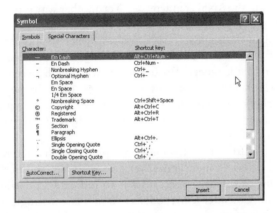

Most of these are characters that used to be the province of the typesetter in the days when secretarial work was done on typewriters, but now they are available to everyone. Because the symbols are listed on the left, they should be self-explanatory. However, a few need some explanation:

- The em space and en space are fixed spaces that are the same width as the em and en dashes above them. They are called em and en because they are, respectively, the width of a capital M and a capital N in the font you are using.

- The optional hyphen is a hyphen that appears at the end of lines only if you allow the text to be automatically hyphenated (to keep the inter-word spaces within a fixed range); see Chapter 16 for more details on hyphenation.

- The non-breaking space allows you to keep two words with a space between them on the same line. The non-breaking hyphen is similar.

- Your program can be set up to produce opening and closing quotes that look like ' and ' at the appropriate positions, even though you type the straight quote ' (Format ➢ AutoFormat As You Type ➢ Options ➢ Autoformat As You Type ➢ "Straight Quotes" with "Smart Quotes"). Sometimes, however, the autoformatting gives you the wrong characters, for example, when you want a single closing quote mark by itself (with a space on either side), so you can use this menu to allow you to put in the character you actually want.

You again see the Autocorrect and Shortcut Key buttons, and the shortcuts are listed in the main menu. The coding is not shown, but all the characters in the Special Characters window also occur in the Symbol window.

Another way of inserting non-keyboard characters is to use the character number, entered on the numeric keypad while holding down the Alt key (you must have the Num Lock on). This is quite efficient, but requires you to know these numbers and effectively applies only to characters that are in the basic Windows character set (often known, although incorrectly, as the *ANSI character set* after the American National Standards Institute). For example, entering Alt+0233 gives the character é. (Note that you have to put a 0 before the number given in the Symbol window.) For other characters, such as those in the Symbol font, you still need to know which is the equivalent character in the ANSI character set. Yet another way is to use the Alt Gr key and a keyboard character, so that, for example, Alt Gr+a gives à. Again, you have to know which character to enter. And, of course, if you wish, you can switch to another language, so that the keyboard allows you to enter accented characters directly. Then, of course, you need to know the keyboard layout for that language. For details of switching between languages, see Part 2.

Finally, for Greek characters and symbols, enter the character in the normal font and then change the font. Entering **m** and changing the font to Symbol gives a μ. This also applies to Cyrillic (Russian) characters, but once you get away from alphabetical characters, remembering the equivalents becomes difficult.

Open one of your test files. Insert some non-alphabetic characters using the methods described previously. Add a French quotation, for example, and perhaps an en rule to replace a hyphen. (One of the uses of en rules is to indicate a relationship; for example, the parent–child bond.) Consider a Greek letter to indicate an angle, say θ (letter *q* in the Symbol font). See which method you find easiest to use. Save your file as `test04.doc`.

Displaying and Hiding Non-Printing Characters

The most common non-printing characters are spaces, carriage returns (paragraph marks), line breaks (soft carriage returns), and tab characters. (For more on carriage returns and soft carriage returns, see Chapter 16.) You have a choice of whether you wish to show these on the screen or not. Go to the Tools menu, select Options, and click the View tab in the Options window, as illustrated in Figure 15.4.

In the Formatting Marks section are boxes for three types of non-printing characters, plus Hidden Text (outside the scope of this book, although easy to implement by choosing Format ➢ Font), Optional Hyphens, and All, which is self-explanatory. All non-printing characters can be displayed or hidden by using the toolbar Show/Hide icon. As you'll see in Chapter 16, there is also an option to do this when selecting styles. Figure 15.5 shows a Word document with all the formatting characters showing.

FIGURE 15.4   The View tab in the Options window

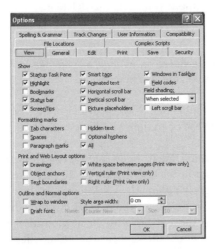

FIGURE 15.5   A Word document with formatting marks shown

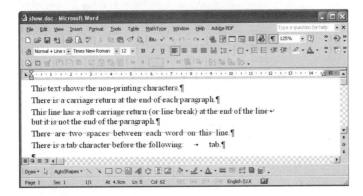

Whether or not you display formatting characters is entirely your own preference. However, if you do not show the marks, you have less control over your documents, because, for example, double spaces are not always obvious, and why the formatting appears as it does may not always be apparent.

Open your test file and change the options between showing the formatting marks and not showing them. Then do some editing and see which option you find easier to use.

Using Undo (and Redo)

One of the most useful Word commands is Undo. This is accessed from the Edit menu (or you can enter Ctrl+Z or click the Undo icon on the toolbar). What this does is reverse the last editing operation you carried out. Thus, if you have inserted some text and then decide that you did not want this, Undo removes it without you having to delete it.

While the Undo command reverses editing changes, it does not reverse changes of view, scale, and so on. It works on changes you have made to the file and not on changes you make to how you are viewing it.

What is even more important is that Word provides multiple Undos. If you keep selecting Undo, you successively undo the operations you have carried out, in reverse order. This can sometimes be very helpful.

A command closely linked to Undo is Redo (press Ctrl+Y, the toolbar icon, or the function key F4) This allows you to repeat the last operation you carried out. The toolbar icon and the keyboard shortcuts work slightly differently. Clicking the toolbar icon simply reverses the last Undo, while the keyboard shortcut allows you to carry out the same operation at several places in a document. You just move the text cursor to the new position and type Ctrl+Y or press F4.

If you choose Edit ➢ Redo or use the keyboard shortcut (click the down arrow to the right of the symbol), you are given a clue as to what you will be undoing or redoing. Using the icon is actually more explicit (look at Figure 15.6) and allows you to carry out several actions at one go. It is also worth noting that if you are undoing or redoing typing, you need to check carefully exactly how much text has been affected.

FIGURE 15.6   Using the Undo command from the toolbar

Open your latest test file. Try carrying some edits and undoing and redoing them. Look at what the toolbar icon tells you rather than always using Ctrl+Z or Ctrl+Y (F4).

Selecting, Copying, Moving, and Deleting Data

One real advantage of a word processor over a typewriter is that you can use text over and over again by copying it, and you can move it around very easily. This section explains how to do that and how to delete larger sections of text instead of just the one-character-at-a-time method that you learned in the last section.

Selecting Text

If you want to carry out an action on a piece of text, which can be anything from a single character to the whole text of your document, the first thing you need to do is to *select* it. As with many tasks in Word, there is more than one way to do this.

Open your latest test file and try the following methods of selecting text:

- To select the complete text, choose Edit ➤ Select All. Even easier, use the keyboard shortcut and type Ctrl+A. The text changes to reverse (also called *inverse*) video; in other words, negative white on black if you are using black type on a white background, as shown in Figure 15.7; otherwise, the colours change.

FIGURE 15.7   Selected text in reverse video

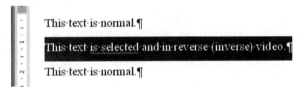

- Place the cursor (the mouse cursor) at the beginning of the text you want to select and, holding down the left button, move the cursor to the end of the text you want and release.

- Place the cursor (the mouse cursor) at the beginning of the text you want to select, click and hold down the Shift key. Move to the end of the text you want to select and click again; you can go up or down the document. In fact, you don't have to keep the Shift key held down; just hold it down when you click for the second time. If you have to scroll, in other words, the beginning and end of the text you want do not appear on the screen at the same time; this is much easier than holding down the mouse button (or even the Shift key) while you scroll. You can also use this approach to extend a selection, but only in the direction in which the selection was originally made.

- To select a single word, double-click that word. If you click three times, you select the whole paragraph. If you click once while holding down the Ctrl key, you select the sentence.

- Use the arrow keys and the Home and End keys. These keys move you around the document. If you hold down the Shift key at the same time as you press one of these keys, you select from the position of the text cursor. Thus, pressing Shift plus a single arrow selects a single character (left and right arrows) or the line from the cursor position to the same position in the line below (up and down arrows). Holding down Ctrl as well selects words or paragraphs.

- Shift+Home selects from the text cursor position to the beginning of the line and Shift+End selects from the text cursor position to the end of the line (including the carriage return if there is one). Holding down Ctrl as well selects to the beginning or end of the document (and takes you to the beginning or end of the document). Similarly, if you hold down Shift and press either Page Up or Page Down, you select the page above or below the current cursor position (although, as noted previously, a page is really a screenful, even in the Print Layout).

- Use the function key F8. Press the F8 key once and the (mouse) cursor selects the text between the position when you struck F8 and wherever you click next. Click again, and you extend the selection. Click within the selection, and you shorten the selection. Pressing F8 a second time selects the paragraph, and a third press of F8 selects the whole document (or section, but these are outside the scope of this book). Pressing F8 together with Shift reduces the selection in a similar way. To "switch off" F8, press the Esc key or double-click the EXT on the status bar.

To deselect text selected by clicking or double-clicking, just click it again. If you have selected text by using a combination of keys (Home, End, or arrow keys), you can deselect part of the text; hold down the Shift key and click at the point where you want the deselection to start/end. This works from the end of the selection if you selected the earlier point in the document first, and from the beginning if you selected the later point in the document first. You'll find that you develop your own preferred way of selecting text. Once you start using Word in earnest, selecting text is something you'll do all the time.

Although at the moment you will be doing nothing with what you select, try to familiarise yourself with the various approaches and see which you find easiest. For example, some people think that using F8 is a great approach, while others find it confusing or inconvenient. See what you think.

Copying and Moving Text

One of the main advantages of using a word processor over a typewriter is the ability to copy and move text around. As you've discovered with other tasks, there are many ways to go about this task.

Drag and Drop

In principle, the easiest way to move text is to use drag and drop. You select some text and then, holding down the mouse button, you drag the cursor until it is where you want to put the text, when you release the mouse button (see Figure 15.8).

FIGURE 15.8   Drag-and-drop editing

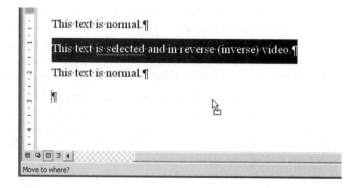

However, this is easy only if the amount of text is not too large or you are dragging within what you can see on the screen. While you can drag and drop off the screen by moving the cursor to the edge of the screen, what happens then is not always easy to control.

When you drag and drop, you can decide on the formatting of the repositioned text. An icon (the paste icon in a square) appears below and to the right of the position where you dropped the text. When you mouse over the icon, a downward-pointing arrow appears that allows you to open a drop-down menu (see Figure 15.9), the options in which are self-explanatory. If you click the bottom option, Apply Style Or Formatting, you open a window that allows you to add formatting.

FIGURE 15.9   Formatting text following drag and drop

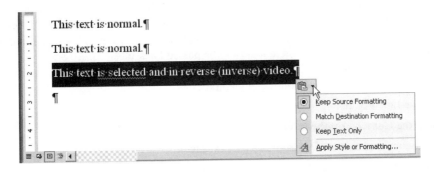

 If you have a window open on the screen such as Find or Replace, you cannot drag and drop text.

Drag and drop also allows you to copy text rather than move it. If you hold down the Ctrl key when you drag and drop, then you copy the selected text. You can also drag and drop with the right mouse button and, as you saw in Part 2, you then have the option of moving or copying (as well as creating a hyperlink, but this is outside the scope of this book). Again, these methods are useful when the place you are copying from and the place you are copying to are on the visible screen.

However, an alternative method is necessary for copying and moving large amounts of text (a method that can, of course, be used for short selections as well). This uses what is called the Clipboard and techniques called Copy, Cut, and Paste.

The Clipboard, Copy, Cut, and Paste

To copy text from one place in a document to another or between documents, you first select what you want to copy and then choose Copy. There are four major ways to perform a copy operation:

- Choose Edit ➢ Copy.
- Click the Copy icon on the toolbar.
- Right-click and choose Copy from the context menu.
- Type Ctrl+**C** on your keyboard.

What happens then, although this is not obvious from what you see on the screen within your document, is that the text you have selected is stored (usually described as *placed*) on the Clipboard, which you can think of as a special area in the computer memory. The term "Clipboard" is used because, if you think of the physical analogy, you can take a piece of paper and add it to a clipboard until you decide where it should be pasted back in.

If you decide that, instead of copying some text, you want to move it, then instead of choosing Copy, choose Cut via one of the following methods:

- Choose Edit ➢ Cut.
- Click the Cut icon on the toolbar.
- Right-click and choose Cut from the context menu.
- Type Ctrl+**X** on your keyboard.

This time, the text vanishes from the screen. Again, it has been copied to the Clipboard. You can see that Copy and Cut work in just the same way within Word as they do for files (see Part 2).

In the latest version of Word, you can view the Clipboard and the last 24 items that you cut or copied. Go to Edit and click Office Clipboard. The Clipboard window opens (see Figure 15.10), showing the contents of the Clipboard.

FIGURE 15.10   The Office Clipboard

In either case, you then move to where you want to place the text you have copied or cut. This can either be within the same document or within a different document. To move between open documents, go to the Window menu and select the document you want. You can even open a completely new document to paste your text into.

To paste the selection in its new location, you perform the Paste command by using one of these techniques:

- Choose Edit ➢ Paste.

- Click the Paste icon on the toolbar.

- Right-click and choose Paste from the context menu.

- Type Ctrl+V on your keyboard.

The last item you cut or copied is then displayed. Alternatively, if you have the Clipboard window open, you can select the item you wish to paste. As with drag and drop, the Paste icon appears below the place where you pasted, allowing you to choose the options shown in Figure 15.9. You may still have to adjust the font or type size to match the new position. You should also check the inter-word spacing (and possibly the number of carriage returns) before and after the passage you pasted in to make sure that you have neither left no space nor left a double space (or carriage return).

Note that it is not just text you can copy, cut, and paste. Part 2 discusses moving and copying files, but you can also copy and move illustrations. And you are not limited to copying within an application. You can copy and move text and illustrations from or to, for example, an Excel file in an Excel application window. Within Office applications, you have access to the last 24 clips, but when pasting into other applications, the Clipboard may only retain an object (filename, text, picture, and so on) until you either turn your computer off or carry out another Cut or Copy operation. And, even with Office applications, when you copy or cut more than 24 items, the first item is lost.

You can paste the contents of the Clipboard in more than one place (this can be very useful with text). But if you do cut or copy something else, then what was previously on the Clipboard may not be accessible. Of course, if you copied, then this is not a problem. However, if you are cutting, then you need to be careful, although you can use Undo to reverse a Cut, which is sometimes useful if you used Cut when you meant to use Copy! It is possible to obtain programs that allow more than one item to be retained on the Clipboard.

Open your latest test file. Select passages by whatever method you found easiest in the previous exercise and then see what happens when you cut them or copy them and then paste them elsewhere in your document, both directly and using the Clipboard. You can also drag and drop (with and without holding down the Ctrl key) and compare the ease with which this can be done for a word, a sentence, and a paragraph.

Deleting Text

Deleting text is similar to copying and moving, except that once you have selected the text you want to remove, you either click the right mouse button or go to the Edit menu of the window containing the text you want to delete and select Clear. Even simpler is just to depress the Del (Delete) key on your keyboard. You can, of course, also delete by using the Delete and Backspace keys without previously selecting any text, as discussed earlier, or by choosing Cut and never pasting.

Open your test file again, and this time delete some of the text you select. You can always use Undo to restore it.

This is probably a good point at which to review your test document and check that the text makes some sense. All the changes you have made may have moved it away from what you originally intended. You can, of course, simply revert to an earlier version. Did you save versions of the test document?

Searching and Replacing

Another convenient text operation is being able to search for and replace a particular word or phrase. You will often want to find a word or phrase in a document, either when you are writing and want to see what you have already put or when you are reading or editing a document. Word provides you with extensive facilities for doing this. This section describes only the simpler aspects.

Remember that you can also use the more general Search facilities of Windows, as discussed in Part 2.

Finding Characters

There is a special Find menu (see Figure 15.11) that you can open from the Edit menu or by pressing Ctrl+F. To find a string of characters, you simply type them into the box and click Find Next (or press Alt+F).

If the string exists in the document, the next occurrence is highlighted. (If you click the Highlight All Items Found In box, all occurrences are highlighted.) If the string does not exist in the document or you have found all the occurrences, you see a message telling you so.

In Figure 15.11 is a button labelled More. If you click this button, the window expands so that it looks like Figure 15.12.

FIGURE 15.11   The Find tab: Basic

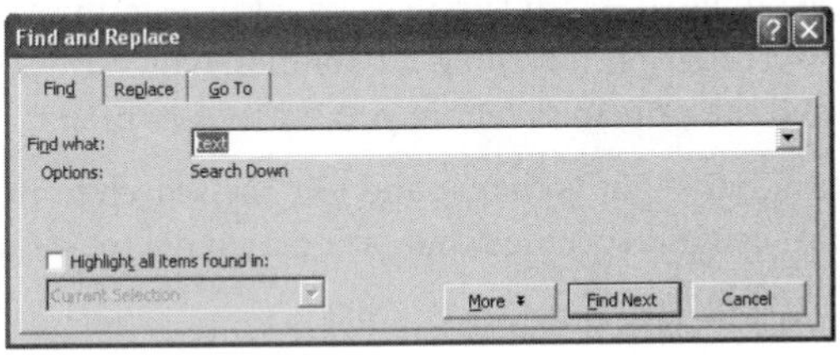

FIGURE 15.12   The Find tab: Expanded

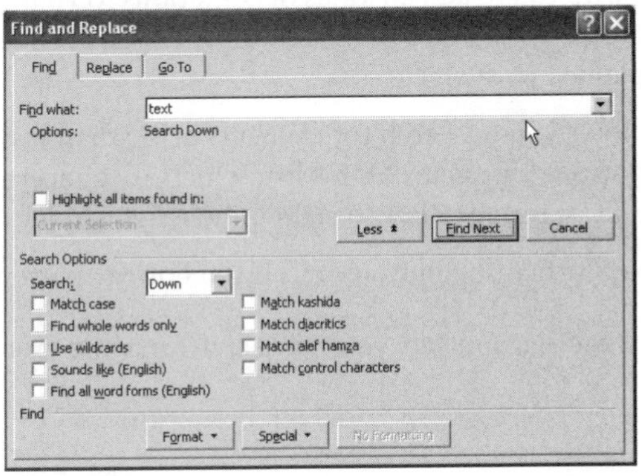

There are various boxes in the expanded Find and Replace window, representing options. The right-hand column you can ignore for the purposes of the ECDL, but those in the left-hand column are as follows:

Search drop-down list   This can say All, Down, or Up. If you select Down, you search from the present position of your text cursor to the end of the document. Correspondingly, with Up selected, you search back to the beginning. With All, as you would expect, the search goes through the whole document, going to the end and then starting again at the beginning until it gets back to the original position of the text cursor. If you select Up or Down, Word, unlike some other programs, tells you that it has reached the beginning or end of the document and gives you the option to search the rest of the document.

Match Case   Unless this box is selected, a search finds all occurrences of a string, irrespective of whether it contains capital or small letters. If you select this box, you find only occurrences corresponding to the case you enter. For example, if this box is selected and you search for "brown", you won't find occurrences of "Brown". Similarly, if you search for "Brown", you won't find "brown".

Find Whole Words Only   If this option is selected, searching for "can", for example, will not find "scan" or "candidate"; it finds only the word "can".

Use Wildcards   This allows you to search for more complex strings, for example, all strings beginning with "iz" and continuing with "a", "e", or "i", so that one can change them to "-isa", "ise", or "-isi", depending on the style that you're using. However, this is outside the scope of this book. Word has some powerful string-searching capabilities, which are described in the Help files, but you need to understand the principles before you try to use these.

Sounds Like   This option finds words that sound like the search term that you have entered. Here the language you are using is specified, but you may have to allow for American pronunciation when you use this option.

Find All Word Forms   If this is selected, when you search, for example, for "stay", you also find "stays", "staying", "stayed", and so on. Again, the language you are using is specified.

At the bottom of the Find and Replace window are three buttons:

Format   This button allows you to add all kinds of conditions to your search, for example, the characters have to be italic or bold or in a particular font. This is outside the scope of the ECDL syllabus, but is well explained in the Help files.

Special   This button allows you to search for elements other than just letters, as listed in Figure 15.13. (Ignore the bottom four items of this list, which are concerned with non-European languages—LTR and RTL stand for "left to right" and "right to left," respectively.)

No Formatting   The No Formatting button cancels the Format button.

FIGURE 15.13   Special characters you can search for in the drop-down list opened with the Special button

Open your latest test file (or perhaps an earlier version that you want to clean up). Search for words or strings that you know are there, and just to see what happens, words or strings that you know are not there. Try out the different search options to see their effect.

Replacing Characters

Earlier, in Figure 15.11, you saw two other tabs in the Find and Replace window: Replace and Go To. You can access these by clicking them once you are in Find, or you can get to them directly from the Edit menu. Replace (strictly speaking, Find and Replace) can also be accessed using the keyboard shortcut Ctrl+H.

The Replace menu is shown in Figure 15.14, and like Find, it can be expanded by using the More button.

FIGURE 15.14   The Replace tab: Basic

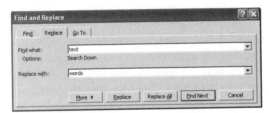

The Replace tab is similar to the Find tab, except that it has a Replace With box and additional buttons, Replace and Replace All. The option to highlight all instances of the search string is no longer available. The selectable options all work in the same way as for Find, although, if you use Special Characters when the text cursor is in the Replace With box, the list is different and shorter. Comparing Figures 15.13 and 15.15 shows you why. It does not make sense, for example, to replace with any number, although you may well wish to search for any number.

FIGURE 15.15   Special characters that you can use in Replace

If you enter text in the Find What and Replace With boxes, say, "cats" in Find What and "dogs" in Replace With, then if you click the Replace button, you replace the first instance of "cats" with "dogs" and highlight the next instance (or Word tells you that the whole document has been searched). Clicking the Replace button again repeats the process. If you click Replace All, every instance of "cats" in a document is replaced by "dogs".

You need to be careful when using Replace, because searching for "can", for example, and replacing it with "could" will not only change "can" to "could", but also changes "scan" to "scould", which you don't want. In that case, you can either select the Find Whole Words Only option or enter the string with spaces, for example, " can", but the latter would also change " canvas ", while putting a space at the end would mean that you would not find examples of "can" followed by punctuation. It is therefore important to think about what you are doing!

Now replace words, characters, and strings with other words, characters, and strings in your test document. One very useful replacement is to replace all double spaces with single spaces. (Although traditionally, secretarial usage is to put a double space after a full stop, this does not normally happen in typeset material.) Repeat this until you get a zero result, when you no longer have any double spaces in your document. Try using the Special Characters in the Find What and Replace With boxes. You can always use Undo if you wish (but be sure that your cursor is in the document text, rather than in the Find or Replace window). Alternatively, when you close the file, you can decide not to save the changes.

Remember that when you use Find or Replace, the browse object changes to what you last looked for, so you can find the next instance by clicking one of the double arrows below the vertical scroll bar.

Go To

The third tab that can be seen with Find and Replace is Go To. This is outside the scope of this book, but allows you to go to a page or some other named location in a document.

Checking Spelling and Grammar

Another basic task in word processing is using the tool that Word provides to check your spelling and your grammar. The first thing to be sure of is whether Word is talking the same language as you are. To do this, choose Tools ➢ Language ➢ Set Language. The language that is already set for your document is highlighted. You can change this if you wish.

Note that there are various versions of English; U.K. English assumes that you want to spell words with *-ise, -ising, ised*, and *-isation* at the end, rather than using *-ize, -izing, ized*, and *-ization*. This means that you have to be careful if you want to use British spelling for words such as *colour*, but the *-ize* option as well (which some publishers such as Oxford University Press recommend). While you can set up customised dictionaries, this is outside the scope of the ECDL.

Checking and Correcting Spelling

In early versions of Word, you had to run the spelling checker to see if Word thought you had made any errors. While Word now underlines apparent spelling errors with a wavy red line (see Figure 15.16), you can still run the spelling checker by pressing function key F7, by clicking the Spelling And Grammar icon, or by choosing Tools ➢ Spelling & Grammar. You can also specify whether to check the grammar at the same time using one of two methods:

- By choosing Tools ➢ Options ➢ Spelling & Grammar ➢ Check Grammar With Spelling
- By clicking the Check Grammar box in the window that is displayed when a potential error is found, as shown in Figure 15.16. If you have some text selected, the check takes place only on the selected text.

FIGURE 15.16   A possible spelling error is found.

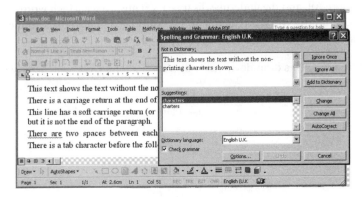

If the spelling checker hits a word that it thinks is wrongly spelled, a window like that shown in Figure 15.16 opens. You can choose from the following options:

Ignore Once   Go on to the next possible spelling error; make no change. If you do not click this but click back in your document, this button changes to Resume.

Ignore All   Go on to the next word; do not make any change and do not query this word again if it occurs in the document.

Add To Dictionary   Add to your custom dictionary. You can also edit this dictionary by choosing Tools ➢ Options ➢ Spelling & Grammar and clicking the Dictionaries button.

Change   Change to the suggestion highlighted in the Suggestions box. You can select the right word if it is there. If it is not and you still need to make a change, you can overtype in the box at the top. If your new word is also not in the dictionary, then another message is displayed, and you have to decide whether to ignore the word or add it to your custom dictionary. You can also choose Ignore All, which allows you to use the highlighted word in the present document, but not add it to the dictionary.

Delete   Delete the highlighted word; this option occurs when Word finds a repeated word. Of course, the repeated word may be not be incorrect, but this is a useful check.

AutoCorrect   This makes the correction and adds it to the list of words that are automatically corrected as you type. Be careful about using this option in the spelling checker, because you may find that you add changes that are wrong! Fortunately, you can access and edit the Auto-Correct list by choosing Tools ➢ AutoCorrect.

Dictionary Language   This drop-down box allows you to choose the language for the word, which is useful if you are working with multi-language documents. Any change here applies only to the word selected.

Note that the Options button takes you directly to Tools ➢ Options ➢ Spelling & Grammar. There is also a tick box that allows you to decide whether to check grammar or not.

More recent versions of Word make life easier for you in that, if you have indicated so in the Options menu, all words that Word thinks are wrongly spelled have a wavy red underline. To view alternative spellings, right-click the word (see Figure 15.17). To leave the word unchanged, just click away from the pop-up menu (although it retains the wavy underline). Alternatively, you can click Ignore All, and the underline disappears. Thus, to see which words may be spelled "incorrectly" according to the Word dictionary, you just need to scan the document by eye. The other options are similar to those discussed earlier and elsewhere.

FIGURE 15.17   This drop-down list is displayed after a word with a wavy red underline is right-clicked.

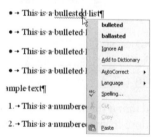

It is worth remembering that all a spelling checker is doing is comparing the words you use with a dictionary. The spelling checker may be incorrect from your point of view and it makes some odd, and sometimes amusing, suggestions for proper names. Furthermore, it does not find misused words (for example, *principle* instead of *principal*, *effect* instead of *affect*), so spell-checking needs to be used intelligently and with caution. Nevertheless, spelling checkers are extremely useful utilities if used properly.

To try this out, open your text file. If you have made any potential spelling errors, they will, by default, already be underlined with a wavy red line. Right-click these and decide what to do. You can also choose Tools ➢ Spelling & Grammar (or just press F7). At present, uncheck the Check Grammar box and work through the document. If you wish, you can introduce deliberate spelling errors or proper names to see what happens. Save your corrected document.

Checking and Correcting Grammar

The grammar checker works in exactly the same way as the spelling checker as far as the interface is concerned. Indeed, you cannot run the grammar checker independently of the spelling checker. Grammatical errors are underlined with a wavy green line, rather than a red one, so right-clicking an example brings up the possible grammar error, as illustrated in Figure 15.18.

FIGURE 15.18   This drop-down list is displayed after a phrase or sentence with a wavy green underline is right-clicked.

If you choose Tools ➢ Spelling & Grammar, the options that you have are similar to those with the spelling checker, but fewer (see Figure 15.19).

FIGURE 15.19   A possible grammar error is found.

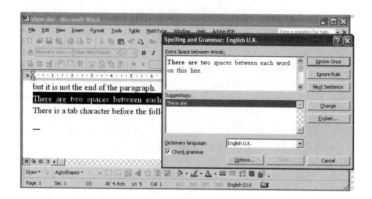

The grammar checker gives you the following options:

Ignore Once   Go on to the next possible grammar (or spelling) error; make no change. If you do not click this but click back in your document, this button changes to Resume.

Ignore Rule   Ignore the rule throughout the document.

Next Sentence   Move on to the next grammar error.

Change   Change as suggested or as you re-enter. Note that if the main window makes a suggestion such as "Consider revising" rather than suggesting a specific corrected text, this button is greyed out.

Explain   Clicking this opens the Office Assistant with an explanation. Note that you see the Office Assistant here whether or not you are using it for Help.

In the Tools ➢ Options ➢ Spelling & Grammar window (see Figure 15.20), Word allows you to select various writing styles and even to generate your own style, but only by selecting from the list of settings provided.

FIGURE 15.20   The option to choose writing styles

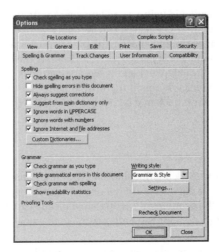

If you click the Settings button and select the Grammar & Style option, the Grammar Settings window opens (see Figure 15.21), and shows you some of the grammar options.

FIGURE 15.21   Some of the grammar-checking options

If care is needed in using a spelling checker, then even more care is needed in using a grammar checker. It can certainly be useful in throwing up obvious errors such as double spaces, misplaced punctuation, and so on, but it often suggests unnecessary changes (for example, the Word grammar checker does not like passive clauses) and is even sometimes wrong. For example, it can sometimes wrongly recommend singular or plural verbs because it does not look far enough back in a sentence. So use the grammar checker, but use it intelligently!

If you double-click the Spelling And Grammar Status icon on the status bar (and your cursor is not on a grammar or spelling error), you move to the next instance and open the drop-down menu that you can also open by right-clicking on the "error." If you cursor is on an "error," you simply open the drop-down menu.

To experiment with the grammar checker, open your text file. If you have made any potential grammar errors, they are already underlined with a wavy green line. Right-click these and decide what to do; you may well disagree with the advice given! You can also choose Tools ➤ Spelling And Grammar (or press F7). This time, check the Check Grammar box and work through the document. You will almost certainly find something that the grammar checker does not like. You'll also see any spellings that you left uncorrected in the last exercise. Save your corrected document.

Summary

This chapter explained how to create basic text, how to carry out simple editing operations, and how to use some of the tools provided by Word.

The discussion of formatting included inserting, overwriting, and deleting characters, and inserting symbols and special characters. The coverage of basic editing operations included displaying and hiding non-printing characters, using Undo and Redo, and selecting text. Once you have selected some text, you learnt how it can be moved, copied, and deleted within a document, using drag and drop or Cut, Copy, and Paste, together with the Clipboard.

Editing tools discussed in this chapter were Find, Replace. and Go To. You also learnt how to use the spelling and grammar checkers.

Chapter

16

Formatting

IN THIS CHAPTER YOU WILL LEARN HOW TO

- ✓ Change the appearance of text, including changing the font, font size, style (italic, bold, and underlining), and the colour.
- ✓ Change the alignment of text.
- ✓ Apply subscript and superscript formatting to text.
- ✓ Change the case of text.
- ✓ Apply styles.
- ✓ Use automatic hyphenation.
- ✓ Insert and remove paragraph marks and soft carriage returns.
- ✓ Change the alignment (left, right, centre, and justified) of paragraphs.
- ✓ Adjust the indentation of paragraphs.
- ✓ Change the line spacing and add space above and below lines.
- ✓ Apply and remove bullets and numbered lists.
- ✓ Add borders to paragraphs.
- ✓ Change the document's orientation and paper size.
- ✓ Insert or delete a page break.
- ✓ Modify headers and footers.
- ✓ Apply automatic page numbering.
- ✓ Copy the formatting from a selected piece of text to another.
- ✓ Use and set tabs.
- ✓ Use lists.
- ✓ Add borders to your document.
- ✓ Use styles.
- ✓ Use templates.
- ✓ Add page numbers.
- ✓ Set up and use page headers and footers.
- ✓ Use Word's Page Setup facility.
- ✓ Change page size, page orientation, and margins.

In many ways, what you shall look at in this chapter is at the heart of word processing—how you actually make your document look the way you want it to.

The Importance of Content and Design

While this book is essentially about how to produce documents using a word processor, there are two other essential issues to producing documents. The first is obviously the content, and while no two readers are likely to use their word processor to handle identical content, every user needs to ensure that the content is what they intend and that it is produced in the clearest and most accurate way possible. In order to achieve this, you need to use a good design for your document, but you also to check it carefully, *proofreading* in publishing parlance.

The second issue is document design. There are many different aspects of document design, and it is unreasonable to expect those who use word processors to become design experts overnight. However, it is important to ensure that your layout looks good, with the right margins, readable (and not too many) fonts, not too much use of boxes and shading, and so on. Microsoft provides a considerable amount of assistance to you in this respect, with predefined templates and style galleries, but it is your document that you are producing, and you have to make the final decision. If in doubt, try and discuss the design with someone who is experienced in this area.

There is considerable confusion in many people's minds between editing (or copyediting) and proofreading. Copyediting should be done first and may include deciding what design to use. However, it is mainly concerned with checking the grammar and spelling (although you can use Word to help you here), as well as deciding which headings should go into which style, how tables should be laid out, and so on. In other words, copyediting is about preparing the document for formatting.

Proofreading, in contrast, is about checking that the document is how you intended it to be. It can include checking spelling (or typing errors) as well as ensuring that the headings are correct (have you kept to your rules on capitalisation in headings, for example) and do not, say, come at the bottom of a page. In fact, when you proofread a document, you should be checking that all the formatting that is discussed in the later chapters of this book has been carried out in the way you want. Only when you are happy that this is the case, should you make your document public.

Formatting Fonts

What is a *font*? The term derives from the days when metal type was used and had to be cast, the French word being *fonde*. In fact, British usage was generally *fount*, rather than font, but US usage has taken over with the spread of computers. There has also been some disagreement over exactly what a font is. Does it include the size or just the typeface? Are italic and bold of the same typeface the same font or not? However, these arguments are all rather sterile, so here we shall refer to font and font size, with italic, bold, and so on, referred to as *font style* where we need a generic term.

Although the title of this section refers to formatting fonts, the formatting that we'll discuss is actually applied to single letters, individual words, lines of text, or even whole documents. You can select any amount of text using your favorite method (double-clicking a word, dragging the mouse across the desired selection, or even typing Ctrl+A to select your entire document), and then apply the styles discussed here to that whole selection.

Choosing the Font and the Font Size

The basic choice of font and font size is usually controlled from the toolbar. Figure 16.1 shows the drop-down menu for fonts. Those at the top, above the double line, are the fonts you are currently using in your present editing session. The remainder of the available fonts are listed in alphabetical order. If the font appears in this list, you can use it in your document. To use a font for a particular piece of text, select that text, go to the list of fonts, and click the one you want to use.

FIGURE 16.1   The Font drop-down list

In the drop-down list, the icon on the left of the font name describes how the font is encoded. For the purposes of the ECDL, you do not need to know about that, except that fonts with the TrueType (two Ts overlapped) icon always appear on your printer exactly as shown on the screen.

Similarly, there is a font size drop-down list. Select the text you want to change and click the size you want. If the size you want is not shown, simply type it in the box at the top and press Enter. Font sizes are given in *points*, which is a longstanding typographic unit. Word allows you to specify font size to a precision of half a point, but not more precisely (unlike page makeup programs). If you really want to, you can go up to a size of 999 points, and, in practice, 6- or 7-point type is the smallest size that is comfortable to read when printed; on screen you can always use a larger magnification.

Setting a Font Style

You can also set the *font style* from the toolbar—italic, bold, or underline as you can see in Figure 16.2; the corresponding keyboard shortcuts are Ctrl+I, Ctrl+B, and Ctrl+U.

FIGURE 16.2   Font style icons on the toolbar

$$\textbf{B} \quad \textit{I} \quad \underline{\text{U}}$$

These are what is described as *toggle commands*, so that if your original selection is not italic, then pressing Ctrl+I or selecting the appropriate icon makes it italic. Similarly, if your selected text is already italic, pressing Ctrl+I or selecting the appropriate icon removes the italic style. If you select a sentence that begins in italic, but is not fully italic throughout, then clicking the italic icon or pressing Ctrl+I removes all the italics. In contrast, if the sentence does not begin in italic, but includes some italics, then clicking the italic icon or pressing Ctrl+I makes the whole sentence italic. The bold and underline commands work in the same way, although all three are independent and can be combined.

Using the Format Menu

More detailed font formatting is controlled by the Font dialog box (see Figure 16.3), which is displayed when you choose Format ➤ Font. First, you can set the font, the font size, and the font style. (You can ignore the boxes dealing with Complex Scripts; they apply only to languages set right to left.)

FIGURE 16.3   The Font tab of the Font dialog box

You can set the colour from the Color drop-down menu. You can also do this by using the toolbar icon shown in Figure 16.4. You can set a variety of what Word calls *effects*, which are fairly self-explanatory and include subscript and superscript. You can also add subscript and superscript buttons to your toolbar if you wish. The Preview window shows a sample of the font you've chosen, and underneath is a brief explanation of the font type (which corresponds to the icon in the font listing). Once you have made your choice, click OK.

FIGURE 16.4   Changing the colour of the text

Setting the Character Spacing

The Font dialog box has two other tabs: Text Effects, which you can ignore for the purposes of the ECDL, and Character Spacing (see Figure 16.5), which is more important for your purposes.

FIGURE 16.5   The Character Spacing tab in the Font dialog box

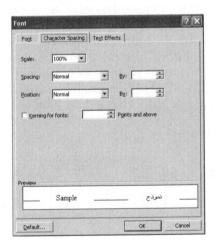

The Character Spacing tab contains these options:

Scale   The Scale option allows you to change the type size within a line without changing the inter-line spacing (which is related to the main font size, but can be changed in the Paragraph dialog box, as described in the next section).

Spacing   The Spacing option allows you to contract or expand the spacing between characters. This can be useful for fitting text into a limited space.

Position   The Position option allows you to move characters up and down relative to the base line (the line that is formed by the bases of the letters without descenders, in other words, not letters such as p, q, y, and g). For subscripts and superscripts, it often looks better if you use the subscript and superscript options (effects) in the Font dialog box, because these also reduce the character size, rather than just moving the characters relative to the base line.

Kerning   Kerning is the inter-character spacing between certain characters for aesthetic reasons. A good example is the space between A and W (AW), which if not kerned, looks disproportionately large. You do not usually need to make any adjustments here as it happens automatically.

Open the latest version of your test file. You can start to make it look better. Try changing the font and the font size until you find a combination that you like. Notice that some fonts look larger, even though they are nominally the same size as others, and there are two main types of font: serif and sans-serif (or sanserif). *Serifs* are the small hooks at the ends of the strokes that make up letters and "sans" is the French word for "without," so serif fonts have serifs and sans-serif fonts do not. Times is a serif font and Helvetica is a sans-serif font.

You may also want to add bold or italics (adding underlines is not generally regarded as good style, but add them if you wish). Save the file when you like what you have.

Changing Case

You can also change the case from the Format menu. *Case* refers to whether letters are uppercase or lowercase. The term comes from the days when compositors took lead type from type cases. The upper case held the capitals, and the lower case held the small letters, and the terms have been carried over to our days of electronic formatting.

To change case, choose Format ➤ Change Case, and the Change Case dialog box (see Figure 16.6) opens; select the option you need. Sentence case means only an initial capital for the first word of a sentence, whilst title case means an initial capital for every word. The other options are obvious. You can also add a Change Case button to the toolbar.

FIGURE 16.6   Changing case

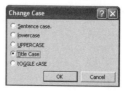

Formatting Paragraphs

Sometimes, you want to apply specific formatting that applies to an entire paragraph, rather than just to individual characters or words that you formatted at the font level. As with font formatting, you can set some paragraph formatting from the toolbar.

Before formatting a paragraph, it's important to define precisely what Word means by a paragraph. A paragraph starts with a new line and ends with a paragraph mark. All paragraph formatting applies throughout the paragraph, whereas font formatting can be changed for shorter selections within a paragraph. It is possible to have new lines within a paragraph by using the line break or soft carriage return. This, as you saw in Figure 15.5 in Chapter 15, shows on the screen as a backward-turned arrow and is entered by holding down the Shift key when you press the Enter key. This soft carriage return simply adds a new line in the text, without ending the paragraph or affecting the formatting.

As described in Chapter 15, "Basic Text Operations," you can hide these (and other) non-printing characters by choosing Tools ➢ Options ➢ View and changing the selection or by using the Show/Hide Paragraph button on the toolbar. (Non-printing characters are also called *formatting marks*, although strictly a soft carriage return is not a formatting mark.) Remember, as also described in Chapter 15, you can delete these marks the same way you would delete any character, thus changing the overall formatting and delineation of any paragraph.

Setting the Alignment of a Paragraph

One type of formatting that applies to an entire paragraph is how the text is aligned horizontally relative to the page. Figure 16.7 shows the icons you can use to adjust the text alignment:

FIGURE 16.7   Paragraph alignment icons on the toolbar

The following text is left aligned:

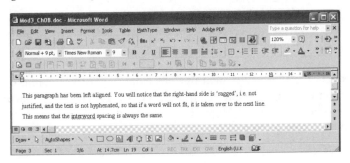

The following text is right aligned:

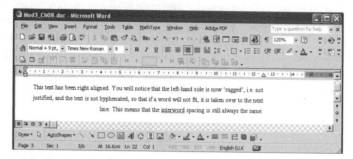

The following text is centred:

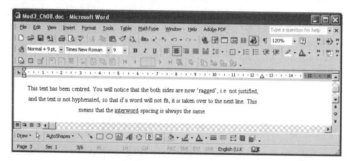

The following text is justified and indented on both sides:

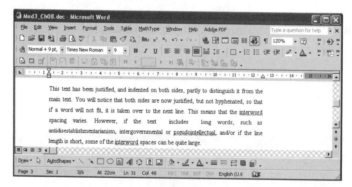

You can also choose these alignment options from the Format menu. Choose Format ➢ Paragraph, and the Paragraph dialog box opens to the Indents And Spacing tab (see Figure 16.8). Next to the box labeled Alignment is a drop-down menu that lists the alignment options described in this section.

The Outline level relates to what you see in the Outline view of the document, but is not covered in the ECDL syllabus.

FIGURE 16.8   The Indents And Spacing tab in the Paragraph dialog box

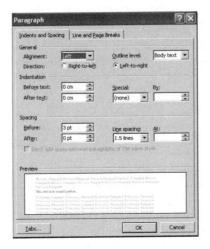

FIGURE 16.8   The Indents And Spacing tab in the Paragraph dialog box

Setting the Indentation

The other formatting feature that you can adjust in the Indents And Spacing tab of the Paragraph dialog box shown earlier in Figure 16.8 is the paragraph indentation. By default, any paragraph has its sides aligned with the sides of the text area specified for the page size you are using. (You'll see how to set margins later in this chapter). However, sometimes you want text indented from one or both margins, or you want to indent just the first line (for a new paragraph, perhaps), or you want to use what is called a *hanging indent*, which is when lines after the first line are indented, perhaps for a list or a set of definitions. The simple versions of these indentations can be set from the indentation icons on the toolbar, which are shown in Figure 16.9. The Decrease Indent icon moves the indentation of the current paragraph to the left side of the document, stopping at the pre-set left-hand margin. The Increase Indent icon moves the indentation of the current paragraph toward the right side of the document.

FIGURE 16.9   The Decrease Indent (left) and Increase Indent (right) icons on the toolbar

The following indentation is available in the Indents And Spacing tab of the Paragraph dialog box:

Left Indent   The most common indent is the left indent, which means indenting every line of a paragraph by the same amount from the left-hand margin, as shown in the following graphic. You can adjust the left indent in three ways:

- By using the icons on the toolbar (see Figure 16.9).
- By entering a value in the Indentation Before text box in the Paragraph window (see Figure 16.8)

- You can move indent marker on the ruler at the top of the text window, as shown in the following graphic.

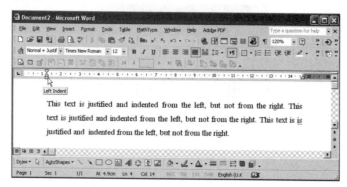

Right Indent   Right indents, that is, indenting every line from the right-hand margin, as shown in the following graphic, are less common. You can use the Paragraph window or the indent marker on the ruler (as shown in the following graphic) in the same way as for the left indent.

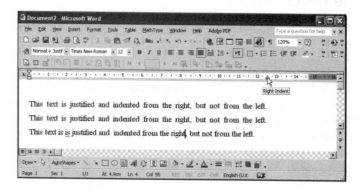

First Line   First line indent means having the first line of a paragraph indented and the remaining lines aligned with the left margin. This is set in the Special box in the Indents And Spacing tab of the Paragraph window. Select First Line in the Special box, and in the By box, enter the amount by which you want to indent the first line. You can also do this by adjusting the top marker on the ruler (see the following graphic).

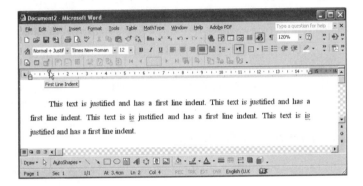

Hanging   A hanging indent is really the reverse of the first line indent, in that the first line aligns with the left-hand margin of the page while the remaining lines are indented. This is also set by using the Special and By boxes in the Indents And Spacing tab of the Paragraph window, or by using the marker on the ruler (see the following graphic).

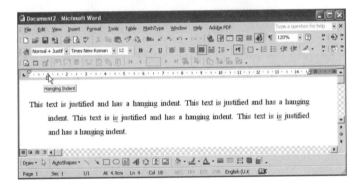

Setting the Paragraph Spacing

Another aspect of paragraph formatting is the amount of space within and around the paragraph. Open the Paragraph window by choosing Format ➢ Paragraph. On the Indents And Spacing tab, in the Spacing section, you have the following options:

Before   The Before option lets you specify the amount of space before the paragraph.

After   The After option lets you specify the amount of space after the paragraph.

Line Spacing   The Line Spacing option lets you specify the amount of space between each line within the paragraph. If you choose single spacing, the line spacing will be determined by the font size of the paragraph. Choosing 1.5 lines or double increases the spacing by half or doubles it, while choosing multiple allows you to specify the factor by which the spacing is increased in the At box. If you choose Exactly, or At Least, or Multiple from the drop-down menu, you can specify the exact amount of space in the At box. Note that, unless you choose Exactly, the spacing of any line will be determined by the size of the largest font size used in the line.

You can see a preview and can click OK if you are happy with your choices. Making these changes affects only the current paragraph. Place the text cursor somewhere within the paragraph for the changes to apply; you do not have to select the whole paragraph. Alternatively, you can select a number of paragraphs to which the changes are to apply.

Setting Line and Page Breaks

The other tab in the Paragraph window is Line And Page Breaks (see Figure 16.10).

FIGURE 16.10   The Line And Page Breaks tab

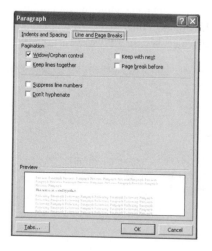

The page break options are as follows:

Widow/Orphan Control   This option stops odd lines being left at the top and bottom of pages. In Word, you cannot control the minimum number of lines, as you can in some programs.

Keep With Next   This option always keeps a paragraph on the same page as the one following. Note that it makes sense to use this only occasionally, for example, with headings, because otherwise you can have some very short pages or may not be able to even paginate at all.

Keep Lines Together   This option ensures that all the lines in a paragraph are included on one page.

Page Break Before   This option causes a paragraph to start on a new page.

The other two options in the Line And Page Breaks window are

Suppress Line Numbers   For this option to have any effect, you have to indicate that you want line numbering as the default. You do this by choosing File ➤ Page Setup and then the Layout tab (described later in this chapter).

Don't Hyphenate   Again, for this option to have any effect, you have to have hyphenation set for the whole document. You do this by selecting Tools ➤ Language ➤ Hyphenation, where you can also set the parameters that control when hyphenation takes place. If you have hyphenation set, the paragraph shown earlier (with the text changed appropriately) now looks like the one in Figure 16.11.

If you do not like the hyphenation breaks, you can add optional hyphens, as you saw in Chapter 15.

FIGURE 16.11   The justified paragraph after changing the hyphenation setting

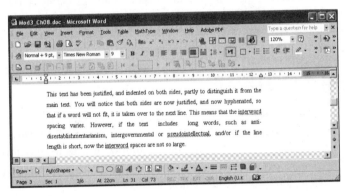

Inserting and Deleting a Page Break

As well as formatting paragraphs, you can always add a manual page break to your document. Sometimes you want your text to continue at the top of a new page, so Word allows you to insert a page break.

Choose Insert ➤ Break to display the Break window (see Figure 16.12). Page Break is selected by default, so all you need to do is click OK. Exactly what you then see on the screen depends on which layout you are using, but when you choose View ➤ Print Layout, you'll see that the text cursor has moved to the top of the next page. If you choose View ➤ Normal, you see a dotted line across the page with Page Break typed in the middle. Once the page break is in place, you can remove it using the same techniques you learned for deleting other characters and paragraph marks. The simplest way is to place the cursor on the page break and then hit the Delete key.

You can also add section breaks from the Break window. While this is outside the scope of the ECDL, it is useful to know about. Section breaks allow you more flexibility in handling your documents, because sections can be formatted independently. For example, you can have one section with a portrait orientation (long side vertical) and the next section with a landscape orientation (long side horizontal). You can also change the page headers and footers from section to section, as you will see shortly.

FIGURE 16.12   Adding a page break

Open your most recent test file and insert a page break at a point where it makes sense. Save the file again.

Now continue the operation with your test file and add some formatting to your paragraphs. Because your test file is a letter, the address and the date should probably be right aligned. You may also want to change the inter-line spacing in the paragraphs and perhaps the spacing before and after the paragraphs. Do you need spacing both before and after? You may also want to add some indents.

Copying Formats

There may be times when you want to copy the character or paragraph format of one piece of text to another piece. To do this, you use the Format Painter icon on the toolbar. This is one of the few commands that does not exist in the menus. Take the following steps to copy formatting:

1. Place your cursor within the text from which you want to copy the format. You do not need to select a whole paragraph or even a whole word.

2. Click the Format Painter icon. Double-click it if you want to copy the formatting to more than one location. The cursor changes to look like a paint brush.

3. Select the (first) text to which you want to copy the format. If you only clicked once (rather than double-clicked) the Format Painter icon, the reformatting takes place and the cursor changes back to normal.

4. If you double-clicked the Format Painter icon, select the next section that you want reformatted. Do this as many times as is necessary.

5. Click the Format Painter icon to cancel when you have finished.

6. Continue this operation with your test file and copy the style from one paragraph to another. Save your file when you are happy with the results.

In Word 2002, you can also remove formatting. Choose Edit ➢ Clear. Click the arrow at the side; one option you'll see is Formats. If you click this, the formatting is removed from any selected paragraphs.

Tabs, Lists, and Borders

Now that you understand the basics of simple formatting, let's move on to more complex tasks. Some information is much more understandable if it is laid out as a table or list. This section looks at using tab markers and list commands to align text and describes how to add a border or box to some text in order to make it clearer.

Using and Setting Tab Markers

There are four different tab markers you can set so that the text aligns to the left, to the centre, to the right, or to a decimal point. You can use these markers to set simple tables. (More complex tables are better handled with table formatting, as discussed in the next chapter) Aligning to a tab marker is similar to aligning the paragraph text, except that you can define alignment points (tab markers) at any point in a paragraph. Figure 16.13 illustrates the four different tab settings.

FIGURE 16.13   Tab settings

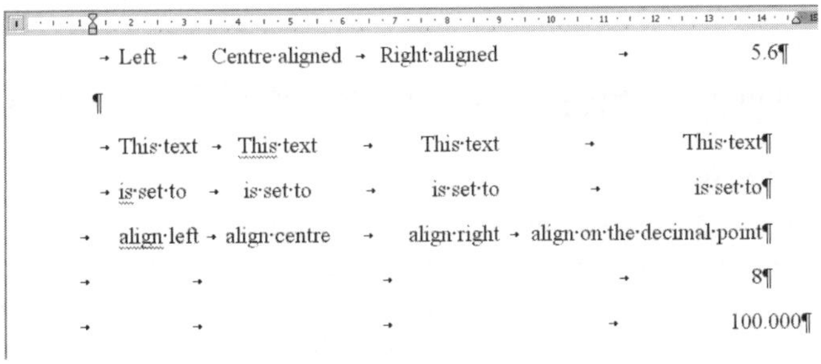

If you look at Figure 16.13, on the ruler above each alignment point you can see where the tab stop (or tab marker) has been set; the shape tells you what kind of tab stop it is. (It is known as a *tab stop* because in the days of the typewriter, this was physically a stop that prevented the carriage from moving further, though there were only left tab stops in those days.) The L shape is a left stop, the inverted T is a centre stop, the reversed L is a right stop and the inverted T followed by a decimal point is a decimal tab. With a decimal tab, any line that does not include a decimal point or full stop aligns as though the decimal point is at the end (just as though it were a number). You also see a vertical line, which is discussed shortly. You have already seen how the indent markers on the ruler operate.

It is important to understand that tabs apply line by line; if the text goes past the next tab stop, that tab stop is ignored. Thus it is important to understand that, while tab characters are ideal for aligning short pieces of text or numbers, they are not a good way to align paragraphs that spread over more than one line. This is because you have to enter the text line by line. If, for example, you decide to change the type size of your document (or even the font), you may find that your text no longer fits and has to be re-entered, which is something best avoided.

Although we are referring here to the decimal point as a *full stop*, the character to be used as a decimal point (along with various related settings) can be set differently by choosing Control Panel ➢ Regional Settings (see Part 2). The French, for example, generally use the comma as a decimal point.

Setting Tabs Via the Ruler

Setting tabs involves two types of operation: setting the position and inserting the tab character in the text. Take the following steps:

1. Type a line (or lines) of text and insert tabs before the text you want to align. At this stage, the text probably aligns to a series of default positions (which do not appear as tabs on the ruler).

2. Click the box to the left of the ruler until it shows the type of tab stop you want to set. The settings indicator rotates as you click (Left, Centre, Right, and Decimal). Note there are three other symbols, one of which (a vertical bar) sets a bar tab, while the other two provide an easy way of setting the indents for a paragraph.

3. Make sure that the text cursor is in the paragraph in which you want to set a tab. This may sound obvious, but it is very easy to overlook. You can, of course, select a number of paragraphs, and the settings apply to all of them.

4. Click the menu bar at the positions where you want the tab stops. If you need more than one type of tab stop, return to step 2 between each click. However, you can set all the left tabs first and then all the decimal tabs, for example. You do not have to work from right to left. The tab stop may not go exactly to the position you want, locking onto an invisible grid. To place the stop exactly, you can hold down the Alt key as you adjust the position. As you set each tab stop, the text aligns. If you're unhappy with any of the tab stops, either drag and drop them along the bar (holding down the Alt key if necessary) or drag and drop them off the bar altogether to remove them. Remember that if the text goes past a tab stop, that tab stop is ignored.

If you are typing in a paragraph with the tab stops set, and you enter a carriage return, the settings also apply to the new paragraph you create. As you saw in step 1, if you have no tab stops set, entering tabs aligns the text to a series of default positions. The spacing of these can be set, as discussed in the next section.

You can change the units of measurement you are using by choosing Tools ➢ Options and then the General tab. At the bottom is a window where you change between inches, centimetres, picas, and points.

Formatting Tabs via the Format Menu

Instead of using your mouse and setting tabs by eye, choose Format ➢ Tabs. A Tabs window opens (see Figure 16.14).

FIGURE 16.14   The Tabs window

The first box to note is at the top right, Default Tab Stops. Here you adjust spacing of the default tab stop positions, repeated across the page at the interval shown in the box. These can be useful if you want the same alignment throughout your document. You adjust the spacing value by entering a new figure or by clicking the up or down arrow at the side of the box. However, as soon as you set just one tab stop in a paragraph, the default positions no longer apply.

Near the bottom of the window are three buttons: Set, Clear, and Clear All. If there are no tab stops shown in the box on the left, type the position where you want to set the tab into the box at the top left. You can overwrite what is already there, because it's just a copy of what is in the larger box below. Select the type of tab stop you want and click Set. You can do this as many times as you want. When you have finished, click OK. If you just set one stop, you can skip clicking Set and just click OK. However, if you set more than one stop, you must click Set after entering each position except the last. You can also select the alignment of each stop. Just as with setting stops on the ruler, the new tab positions apply to the current paragraph or to all the paragraphs selected.

There is an additional type of alignment called Bar. If you set this, you get a vertical bar the height of the paragraph at the tab stop position. However, this is not a real tab stop, because the tab key does not recognise the position, even though a vertical bar also appears on the ruler that makes the bar easy to move or remove. So if you want text aligning to the left of a bar, you need to set the bar and a right tab stop just before it.

Before you click Set, you can also set a leader character. This means that, instead of space between the text aligned at the different tab stops, you get whatever leader character you specify. Figure 16.15 shows the text shown earlier in Figure 16.13, with periods as leader characters and bar stops included.

To remove stops, open the Tabs window and select the tab you want to remove by clicking the setting in the large box. The setting is then copied to the smaller box above. Click Clear, and that tab stop no longer applies to the current paragraph (or any paragraphs selected). If you want to get rid of all the stops in the selected paragraphs, just click Clear All.

FIGURE 16.15   Tab settings with leaders and bars

→ Left →	Centre·aligned	→ Right·aligned	→	5.6¶
¶				
→ This·text	→ This·text	→ This·text	→	This·text¶
→ is·set·to	→ is·set·to	→ is·set·to	→	is·set·to¶
→ align·left	→ align·centre	→ align·right →	align·on·the·decimal·point¶
→	→	→	→	8¶
→	→	→	→	100.000¶

WARNING   Although you can move tab stops on the ruler, you cannot edit tab stop positions in the Tabs window. You have to clear a stop and enter a new stop in a new position.

In the following exercise, you will repeat what you did via the ruler, but this time use the Tabs dialog box:

1. Type a line (or lines) of text (or take some text you have already entered) and insert tabs before the text you want to align. At this stage, as before, the text probably aligns to a series of default positions or to any tab positions you have previously set.

2. Make sure that the text cursor is in the paragraph in which you want to set a tab. You can again, of course, select a number of paragraphs, and the settings will apply to all of them.

3. Choose Format ➤ Tabs. If any tab positions are showing, click Clear All to get rid of them.

4. By reference to the ruler at the top of the text area, decide the positions of the tab stops you want to add.

5. Add tab stops (and their alignments) as described earlier, clicking Set between each one and then OK when you have finished. The tab stops appear on the ruler at the top of the type area.

Open the latest version of your test document and add some information with tab stops included. Perhaps you can add information about when you started each ECDL module or how long each chapter took you (include a decimal tab). Try adding leaders and bar stops. Once you have set up the tabs, try adjusting them (with and without the Alt key held down). Save the version that you are happy with.

Formatting Lists

A different way of aligning text is to use a list. Figure 16.16 shows a bulleted list and a numbered list.

The simplest way to create these is to ensure that the text cursor is in the correct paragraph (or a selected number of paragraphs) and then clicking the appropriate toolbar icon (Figure 16.17).

FIGURE 16.16   A bulleted list and a numbered list

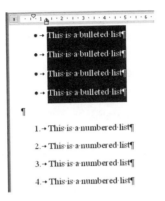

FIGURE 16.17   The toolbar icons for numbered (left) and bulleted lists (right)

These are toggles, so if you have selected a bulleted list and you click the Bullets icon again, you remove the formatting. However, if you have a bulleted list and you click the Numbering icon, you convert the list to a numbered list (and vice versa). If you click the Numbering icon again, you remove the list formatting all together. You do not have to increment the numbers in a numbered list (or, indeed, even type them); this is done for you.

You can change the style of bullets or numbers in your list by choosing Format ➤ Bullets and Numbering. This brings up a screen (with separate tabs for bullets and numbers) where you can choose from some built-in options, including choosing alpha or numeric characters for a numbered list. You can customise list formats from this screen as well, but this is outside the scope of the ECDL syllabus.

Open the latest version of your test document and add a numbered and a bulleted list. It is a good idea to only use numbers when they actually mean something, for example, a series of sequential steps. Otherwise, it is simpler to use bullets. However, add an extra paragraph in the middle of your numbered list and see what happens to the numbers of the following paragraphs. Save the version that you are happy with.

Adding Borders

You can apply borders to almost anything within your document. The simplest is to apply a border (or box) to a paragraph. Select the paragraph (or paragraphs) you want included and click the Outside Border icon on the toolbar. You can change the border you select (and what is shown initially on the icon) by clicking the arrow to its right to open the box, as shown in Figure 16.18. If you click a particular style, you not only apply that style to the current paragraph or to a group of paragraphs selected, but you also change the rule on the main icon. If you select a bottom rule, for example, and you have a number of paragraphs selected, the rule appears only below the last paragraph. If you want a rule after each paragraph, you have to treat each one separately.

FIGURE 16.18   Adding a border or box around some text

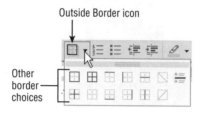

If you click a rule style a second time, you reverse the style change, but if you click another rule style, that rule style is added or removed, depending on what is currently shown. Thus, if you click a box rule and then click the left-hand side rule, you end up with a box rule without its left-hand side. You can remove all the rules by clicking the last style shown (all broken lines), which does not toggle. You can vary the style of border and add borders more selectively by choosing Format ➢ Borders And Shading to open the Borders And Shading window (see Figure 16.19). On the left, you can change the style of the border, its width, and its colour. The Horizontal Line button at the bottom gives you even more choices. You can also use the Tables And Borders toolbar to add a border around text (see Figure 16.20). (Chapter 17, "Tables, Graphics, and Other Objects," discusses tables in detail.)

FIGURE 16.19   The Borders and Shading window

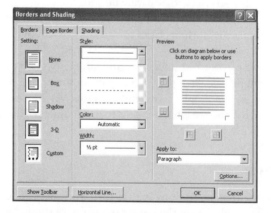

If you select some text before you open the Borders and Shading window, the Apply To drop-down menu allows you to apply the border to either the whole paragraph or to the selected text. In this way, you can apply underlines, overlines, and boxes to individual words or phrases.

FIGURE 16.20   The Tables and Borders toolbar

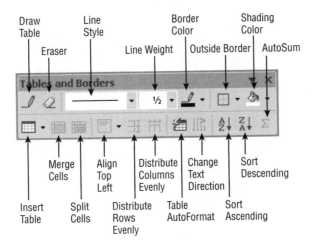

Selecting the Page Border tab in the Borders and Shading window (see Figure 16.21) allows you to opt for a page border similar to those described earlier and specify its position.

FIGURE 16.21   The Page Border tab in the Borders And Shading window

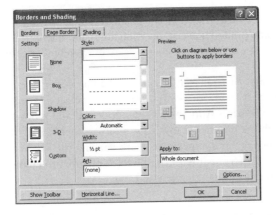

 WARNING   Most desktop laser printers do not print to the edge of the paper. There is a narrow strip around the edge of the print area on which it is impossible to print anything. Thus, if you want to include page borders in your documents, experiment with your printer to see what it will print and what it will not.

The final tab in the Borders And Shading window is Shading (see Figure 16.22), which allows you to change the shading within a border. Although you cannot see them because this book is in black and white, the Fill section allows you to choose a colour (or a level of grey). The Patterns section makes it possible to vary the level of tint (how much colour) in your shading. The Horizontal Line button lets you choose the colour (or pattern) of a line, which can of course be thick enough to reveal a pattern.

FIGURE 16.22 The Shading tab in the Borders And Shading window

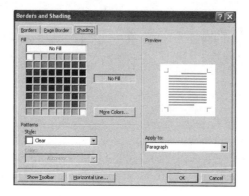

 Facilities such as borders and shading should be used with restraint. Have a look at some printed books to give you ideas about when such features enhance the text and when they are unnecessary or even hinder comprehension.

Open the latest version of your test document. Add a border to a paragraph by using the toolbar. Remove part of it (you can always use Undo). Select a word or a few words in the text and then go to the Borders And Shading window and add a border to the selection. For example, enter a telephone number below your address; then select this and add a border to it. Add a border to the page and experiment with varying the thickness and type of the rule being used as a border. Experiment with shading. (Remember to change the formatting back, however, unless you want to keep the new settings.)

Using Styles

The last few chapters have talked about applying formats to paragraphs and explained that styles, alignment, and tab settings apply only to the current paragraph or to any selected paragraphs. It is probably obvious that applying these formats over and over again to different paragraphs would not only take a great deal of time and possibly lead to errors, but it would also not take advantage of the storage and processing capabilities of the computer. Just as you can store documents, you can also store and use combinations of formatting, which are called *paragraph styles*, or usually just *styles*.

It should by now be clear that styles are combinations of formatting instructions (you will see exactly what shortly) that can be applied to a paragraph. So how can you see and apply these styles? Choose Format ➢ Styles And Formatting, and the Styles and Formatting window (or what Microsoft calls a *task pane*) opens (see Figure 16.23).

FIGURE 16.23   The Styles And Formatting window

The top of the window shows the style that you are currently using. The Select All button allows you to select and highlight all the styles in the document that have this style. In the main panel, a list of styles is shown, each displayed in the style it specifies. Using the Show drop-down menu at the bottom (see Figure 16.24), you can choose which formats to display. As with the font formatting discussed earlier, these existing styles can be applied to any letter, word, line, or paragraph that you have selected. Selecting a style from the list displayed applies the style to any selected text or to the whole paragraph if no text is selected.

FIGURE 16.24   Choosing which styles to list

Some of these style options have already been discussed; you'll learn about others in future chapters or else they are outside the scope of the ECDL. If you select Reveal Formatting (which you can also select from Formatting on the main menu bar), a Reveal Formatting window opens (see Figure 16.25). The Reveal Formatting window describes all the font, paragraph, and section formatting for the text you have selected (the first few characters are displayed in the box at the top) or the word in which your cursor is placed (when that word is displayed in the box).

FIGURE 16.25 The Reveal Formatting window

You need to scroll the main window to see all the detail. Note that the plus sign or minus sign alongside the headings allows you to display or hide the details. Figure 16.26 shows the top of the box with all the details hidden. You also have the option to compare the style of one selection with that of a second selection by clicking Compare To Another Selection below the sample box.

FIGURE 16.26 Part of the Reveal Formatting window with all the details hidden

There are two boxes at the bottom of the Reveal Formatting task pane. By clicking Distinguish Style Source, you can distinguish the style source; that is, does the style come from the paragraph style or have you applied it directly? The second option, Show All Formatting Marks, allows you to display (or not) the formatting marks (non-printing characters), as discussed in Chapter 15.

While defining styles is outside the scope of the ECDL, Word provides a set of predefined styles within each of the templates it provides. These include various levels of headings and bullet points.

Applying a Style to a Selection

You've already looked at the boxes on the toolbar where you can set the font and type size. To the left of these is another box, in which the style name of the current paragraph is shown. It may, for example, say Normal or Heading 1. If you click the down arrow to the right of the box, you can see (or scroll down to) the available styles, as shown in Figure 16.27. Alongside the box is a button that opens the Styles And Formatting window.

FIGURE 16.27   The Style drop-down box

To apply a style to a paragraph, click the drop-down list and your current paragraph, or any selected paragraph, changes to the new style. If you select only part of a paragraph (for example, a word or a line), then the style change that takes place will depend on exactly what the new style is. The type size and alignment will certainly change to the new style and, if the style is a list style, the whole paragraph will adopt the list format. You may need to experiment to see exactly what happens. Remember that you can always use the Undo key. In general, however, it is probably better to apply formatting, in other words, type size and font changes, directly within paragraphs rather than using styles.

You can, of course, make direct changes to the formatting of individual paragraphs (and this shows in the Reveal Formatting window if you clicked the Distinguish Style Source check box), but applying the style elsewhere does not take those changes into account. If you want to make overall changes to a style, you need to either learn how to edit a style or get someone who understands styles to provide you with a new template. These are outside the ECDL syllabus.

Using Style Themes

There is yet another way that you can choose styles. Choose Format ➢ Theme, and the Theme window opens (see Figure 16.28).

FIGURE 16.28   The Theme window

You can choose any theme to preview and then click OK to apply the style to your document. You can also click the Style Gallery button to review the styles in different themes (see Figure 16.29). You can choose to look at sample text or note that you need to use the predefined styles (Normal, Heading 1, and so on) in your document if you want to see how changing themes affects the document.

FIGURE 16.29   The Style Gallery window

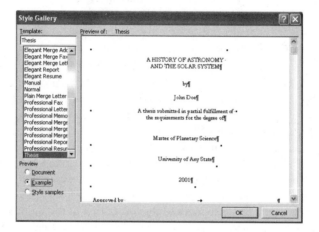

There is an option on the Format menu, AutoFormat, which effectively analyses your document and applies styles appropriately. Again, this is really beyond the scope of the ECDL syllabus and needs to be used with great care, or you may find that changes that you did not intend have been made to your document.

Open the Styles And Formatting window for your new document and click various styles in the list in turn. You should see the details for each style as it is selected. Click Cancel when you have finished looking at the window. Try applying themes and use the Format Gallery and AutoFormat. Unless you want to keep one of the styles you create, close your document without saving, or save a new document or version.

Look again at your new document. If you have moved or copied paragraphs to where you want them, you can now apply the appropriate styles by using the drop-down box from the toolbar. Save your new file as, say, letter01.doc.

Using Templates

Combinations of these styles and other aspects of document formatting such as the page size, layout, margins, and so on (covered in the next section) can be housed in *document templates* (or just *templates*).

The ECDL syllabus does not cover the questions of setting up and changing styles and templates, simply choosing and using them. Chapter 14, "First Steps with Word Processing," already mentioned saving documents as templates.

There are two ways you can use a particular template for a document. One is when you create a new document; in the other case, you may not realise that this is actually what you are doing. This happens when you save a document under a new name and delete or change parts of it so as to use the styles and formats in that document. The document you have used as a pattern may well have a specific template associated with it. This template includes a list of styles and also determines the page size, layout, margins, and so on.

In fact, every document has a template associated with it. In Chapter 14, when you created a new document, we said that you should select a template, which in that case was the Blank Page. This associates the default template, called normal.dot, with the document.

All templates have the filename extension .dot, as you saw in Chapter 14. That chapter also explained that when you saved a file for use on the Web, the page layout changed. This was because a new template, more appropriate for the Web, was then associated with the document.

Selecting a Template

Let's go back to creating a new document. Choose File ➢ New or click the New icon on the toolbar. The New Document window opens on the right-hand side of the screen to provide you with various options (see Figure 16.30).

FIGURE 16.30 The New Document window

Clicking General Templates in the New From Template section opens the Templates window (see Figure 16.31). Select the Memos tab.

FIGURE 16.31   Selecting a template for a new document

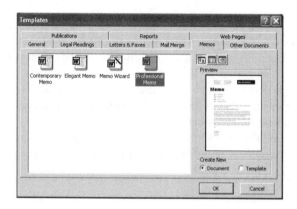

Choose Professional Memo and a new document is displayed (see Figure 16.32). This template is relatively simple, and it's important to be professional! Note that the window in Figure 16.31 allows you to preview the template before you select it.

FIGURE 16.32   The blank document produced when the Professional Memo template is selected

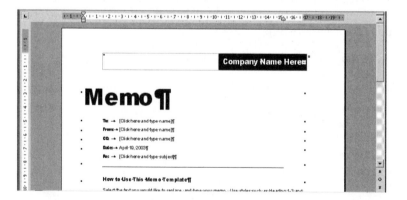

Notice that Microsoft has included some text for you to overwrite. This not only tells you what goes where and what to do, but it also gives you an idea what the final document will look like. It is not necessary for a template to include text (and, of course, the blank page by definition does not), but it can be helpful. If you had chosen a different template, the page would, of course, have looked quite different. But if the sample text had not been there, you might not have found that out until you started applying the styles. Indeed, even here, although the text refers to the heading styles, you cannot immediately see from the document what those styles will look like. You'll carry on with this in the next section.

We already mentioned (in Chapter 14) saving documents as templates. Any document can be saved as a template (with or without text), but it is a good idea only to save as templates those files that are indeed different from existing templates or those that have a specific purpose.

So let's create a new document and choose a template. Because your previous test document was a letter, we suggest that you choose a letter template. You can either follow the instructions in the template, or you can try opening the latest version of your test document and cutting and pasting paragraphs from that letter into your new letter. Select the whole of your test document (choose Edit ➢ Select All, or press Ctrl+**A**) and then copy and paste it at the end of the new document. You then need to move parts of the pasted text to the right place (using Cut and Paste or drag and drop).

Whichever approach you use, you may find that the style does not change to the new style. Indeed, as shown in Chapter 15, when you drag and drop, you see the paste options. If you decide not to keep the formatting, you can apply the skills you learned about using styles to achieve the appropriate style.

Document Formatting

You've looked at formatting paragraphs and imposing styles. This section discusses formatting options that pertain to an entire page or document. You can use formatting to add page numbers and headers and footers (which are discussed shortly) to your pages. You can also set the overall layout of the document, page size, paper size, and so on.

Adding Page Numbers

It is almost certainly unnecessary to explain why page numbering is useful. Of course, you could enter page numbers as part of the text on each page. However, that would not be a good idea, because if you change the formatting or add or delete text, your page breaks may no longer be in the required place. In addition, if you add your own headers and footers, they form part of the text and upset the text flow, stopping paragraphs running on from one page to the next.

Fortunately, Word provides special routines to handle the inclusion of this aspect of a book or report (as indeed do all top-level word-processing and page makeup programs). You can add page numbers (or *folios*, as they are known in publishing) to pages without setting up headers and footers as such.

In the Print Layout view (View ➢ Print Layout), choose Insert ➢ Page Numbers, which opens the Page Numbers window shown in Figure 16.33. You can choose where on the page the number is to go and how it should be aligned. The Position box allows you to select the top or bottom of the page, while the Alignment box includes the options Left, Center, and

Right, as well as Inside and Outside to cater to left-hand and right-hand pages. You can also choose whether or not to include the page number on the first page by using the Show Number On First Page check box.

FIGURE 16.33   The Page Numbers window

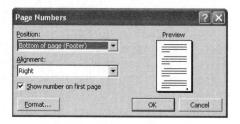

If you click the Format button, the Page Number Format window opens (see Figure 16.34). Most of these options are self-explanatory, except perhaps the reference to section numbers. Although outside the ECDL syllabus, as noted earlier, you need to know that a document can be divided into sections (and indeed it has to be if you mix, for example, portrait and landscape pages). Here you have the option to restart the numbering of each section (which is another reason for dividing the document into sections) or running it on.

FIGURE 16.34   Page Number Format window

Page numbers are displayed only in Page Layout view (you can switch to any other view once you have added the page numbers); notice that the page number is greyed out. If you want to edit it (and there is no real reason why you should, unless you are perhaps unhappy with the type size), you have to treat it as a footer. Double-click it, which brings up a window/toolbar that we will discuss shortly. The page number may appear as {PAGE}, because it is what Word calls a *field*; it depends on how your system is set up whether field codes are shown or not. You can change this by choosing Tools ➢ Options ➢ View. Incidentally, to be sure that you see the actual page number, choose Print Preview.

Notice that various new styles have been added to your drop-down list, including Page Number, and several referring to headers and footers, described in the next section. These are applied automatically, and you would not normally use them in any other context. However, if you know how to do so, they can be changed just like any other style. This is outside the scope of the ECDL.

Open your letter file. Add text to ensure that it at least runs on to two pages. Then insert page numbers. Try the different options. (You can insert page numbers in only one place, so changing the options moves them, rather than adding yet another folio.) Again, it may be worth looking at letters from large organisations to see which styles are clear and which are not. Save your file again as a new file or a new version.

Using Headers and Footers

You are probably familiar with page headers and footers, which may contain the page number, but also include information about a book title and chapter or section title. In reports, the headers and footers might include the name of the organisation, a reference code, and the date of the revision.

Strictly speaking, in Word documents, headers and footers (otherwise referred to as *headlines* and *footlines* or *running heads* and *running feet*) are present all the time, although you are not aware of them because they are empty. This is why, if you want to add them, you have to go to the View menu, rather than to the Insert or Format menu.

When you select Header And Footer in the View menu, three (or perhaps four) things happen:

- If you were not using the Page Layout view, Word automatically switches to this view. In fact, headers and footers are visible only in this view.

- The main page text is greyed out.

- The header area is displayed.

- A Header and Footer window, effectively a toolbar, opens.

All these effects are shown in Figure 16.35. If you mouse over each of the icons on the toolbar, you see an explanation of what each means. On the left is Insert AutoText, which is shown with its drop-down menu displayed. The entries are self-explanatory; AutoText entries can be edited and added by choosing Tools ➤ AutoCorrect and then the AutoText tab. The use of AutoText is outside the scope of the ECDL syllabus, but some aspects are useful in the context we are discussing here. The insertion takes place at the position of the text cursor.

FIGURE 16.35 Viewing headers and footers with the AutoText options displayed

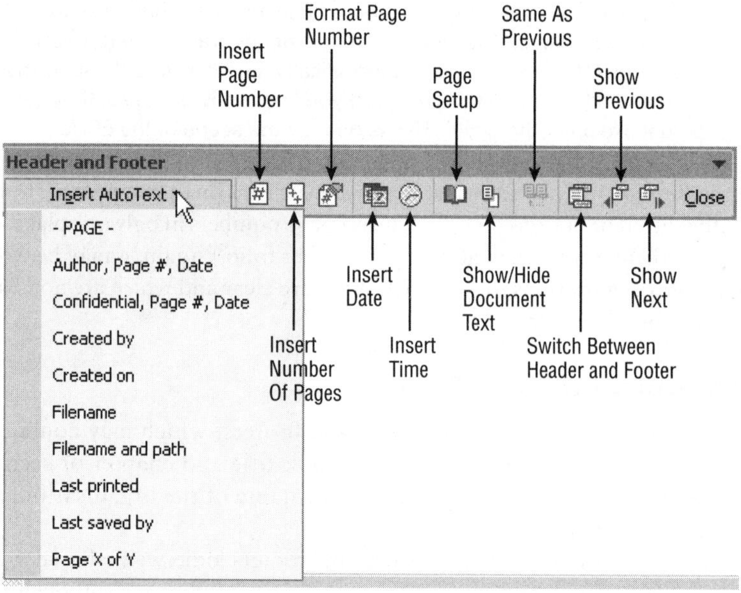

The icons fall into the following groups:

- The first and third icons (Insert Page Number and Insert Number Of Pages) effectively duplicate the page number commands discussed earlier. The middle icon allows you to insert the total number of pages in your document.

- The next two icons (Insert Date and Time) allow you to insert the current date and time. These options can also be used by choosing Insert ➤ Field, where you see many other fields. All of these can, of course, be inserted anywhere in a document.

- The next icon (Page Setup) allows you to access Page Setup (discussed later in this chapter). The other icon in this group (Show/Hide Document Text) allows you to hide or show the main text while you are editing the header and footer. This has no effect on the file itself.

- The next icon (Same As Previous), in a group of its own, allows you to make the header the same as the previous one, that is, the same as the header in the previous section. If there is no previous section, the Same As Previous icon is greyed out.

- The first icon of the last group before Close (Switch Between Header and Footer) allows you to move between the header and footer, while the other two icons (Show Previous and Show Next) allow you to move between sections.

The implication of some of these icons is that different sections can have different headers and footers, although they do not have to be different. Having different headers and footers is often a good reason for splitting a document into a number of sections. For example, the "prelims" of a book (title page, table of contents, preface, and so on) are often numbered with Roman numerals, and the main book pagination is in Arabic numerals.

You can also have different headers for odd and even pages and also for the opening page. These are changed in the Layout tab of the Page Setup dialog box (File ➤ Page Setup). If you choose Different Odd And Even, the word *Header* at the top of the header box in Figure 16.35 changes to *Odd Header* on odd pages and *Even Header* on even pages; if you choose Different First Page, the word *Header* changes to *First Page Header*.

When you click Close after entering the header and footer information, you return to the view you were in before you opened the headers and footers.

Other than these options, you handle text in headers and footers just as you would other text. You can apply any style to text in a header or footer and can also use all the usual formatting options.

Headers and footers expand if the contents becomes greater than the original size (and headers and footers can contain pictures as well as text), so you need to handle them with care. The position of the header and footer is set in the Page Setup dialog box (described shortly).

We said that if you add a page number, it can appear only in one place. This is true if you use the Insert Page Number facility. If you include a page number in a header or footer as well, then you get duplicate page numbers. If that's what you want, this is fine, but be careful. It's a good idea to insert a page number or, if you want a more complex layout, to use headers and footers; using both in the same document can lead to confusion. In general, use simple page numbering when that's all you need. Use headers and footers when the situation is more complex. Remember that you cannot see either in the Normal view!

Open the version of your letter file in which you included page numbers. Add headers and footers to see what happens. If you include a page number field in the header or footer as well as inserting a page number, you end up with two folios, which is generally not a good idea. Do not save this file.

Open the version of your letter file without page numbers. Add an appropriate header and/or footer. Save this as a different version or file from the version in which you simply added page numbers.

Page Setup

You've looked at formatting paragraphs and imposing styles, but so far you haven't learned how to define the overall layout of the document, page size, paper size, and so on. These are all defined and modified by using the Page Setup window (File ➤ Page Setup).

Setting Paper Size and Paper Source

When you open the Page Setup window, the first tab is usually Margins. However, we will look first at the Paper tab (see Figure 16.36), because logically it makes sense to define your paper size and orientation before you choose your margins.

FIGURE 16.36   The Paper tab of the Page Setup window

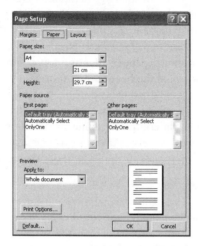

The Paper tab is divided into three sections. The top one, Paper Size, lets you set the size of the paper that you (or more correctly your printer) is using. The paper size you see is based on the Normal (standard) template set up for Word. You can change this by clicking the Default button at the bottom of the window, but this changes the setting for all documents. You are, therefore, asked to confirm whether you want to do this. If you go ahead, for example, to change your default paper size to A4, then it is a good idea only to make this change of paper size at this time, so that all other settings are retained.

What appears in the Paper Source section depends on the printer that you have set up on your system. You have the option of taking paper for the first page from one tray and the paper for the remaining pages from another tray. This is to cater for letters where the first page and the continuation pages use different notepaper. It depends on what you are doing (and whether your printer allows this) as to whether this facility is useful to you. In general, however, you don't need to make any changes to this section.

The third section, Preview, allows you to choose which parts of the document you apply the changes to. Exactly what you see in the drop-down box depends on whether or not you have sections in your document. If you do, you can choose to apply the changes only to a single section. This means that you can print different sections on, for example, different-sized paper if your printer supports this.

At the bottom of the Preview section is a Print Options button. Clicking this opens a window in which most of the options are either obvious or outside the scope of the ECDL. One option that it is useful to have checked is Allow A4/Letter Resizing. If you have this checked, you don't see an error message if you try to print a document with a US Letter page size on A4 paper.

Open your letter file, choose File ➢ Page Setup, and click the Paper tab if it is not already showing. If the paper size is not already set to A4, change it so that it is; this is almost certainly the size of paper you'll be using if you are in the U.K. or any other part of Europe. It's probably a good idea to change the default as well. Save the document if you have changed the page size. You can also experiment with the Allow A4/Letter Resizing in the Print Options window, but here it is not a good idea to change the default or save your document. Look at the Paper Source section, but you're unlikely to want to change anything here unless you are on a network, in which case you should talk to your network manager.

Margins

The Margins tab of the Page Setup window is divided into four sections (see Figure 16.37). The first four entries in the Margins section are self-explanatory and indicate the distance from the edge of the paper to the edge of the text area. The margins are shown in the Preview section at the bottom of the window.

FIGURE 16.37   The Margins tab of the Page Setup window

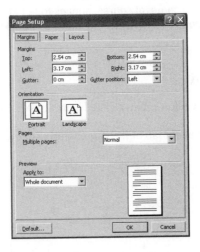

The Gutter box needs some explanation. It refers to what is also called a *binding margin*, which is the extra margin allowed to take account of the part of the page that is effectively lost when a book is bound. It is added to whichever margin you have selected in the Gutter Position box.

In the Orientation section, you can set whether your document is to be portrait (long side vertical) or landscape (long side horizontal). Incidentally, when you change between portrait and landscape, the dimensions in the Paper Size section of the Paper tab are interchanged. As for the paper, you can apply these settings to the whole document or just from this point on. If you have sections in the document, you can apply the change just to one section (useful if you want one section to be landscape and the rest to be portrait). Again, a preview is available in the Preview section.

The next section of the Margins tab is called Pages. It allows you to decide how to handle documents with more than one page. The book options are outside the scope of the ECDL, so the only one we will discuss is Mirror Margins. If you have the Mirror Margins option selected, the gutter is added to the right-hand side of left-hand (verso) pages and to the left-hand side of right-hand (recto) pages, as the preview shows. The visual effect when a reader opens a bound document is that the text is centered on the page. You can also see the effect in Page Preview. Note that the Top, Left, and Right options have changed to Inside and Outside.

You can also change the left and right margins of a page by dragging the page markers on the ruler. You usually need to select the whole document (choose Edit ➢ Select All, or press Ctrl+A), or you will change the margins only for the paragraphs selected. If you do the same thing in Print Preview, you can move all the margins, both horizontal and vertical. This is equivalent to changing them in the Page Setup window.

The Preview section of the Margins tab is the same as that in the Paper window, except that it does not have the Print Options button.

Remember that most printers do not print right up to the edge of the paper, so make sure that you do not site your header and footer too near to the edge of the page. The same, of course, applies to left and right margins, but aesthetic and filing considerations usually make this unlikely anyway.

Setting Up Layout

The last tab in the Page Setup window is Layout (see Figure 16.38). This is divided into four sections.

FIGURE 16.38   The Layout tab of the Page Setup window

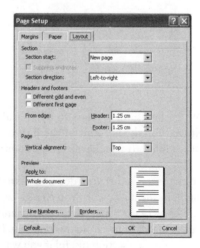

The Section area of the Layout tab applies only if you have sections in your document; it allows you to specify how to break between them. It also lets you have some sections in languages that read from left to right and other sections that read from right to left. However, this is outside the scope of the ECDL.

The Headers and Footers section of the Layout tab has to do with and headers and footers and duplicates some of the settings we discussed earlier.

The Page section allows you to vertically justify a page, in other words, position text at the top, middle, or bottom of a page. The justified option affects only full pages and varies the spacing between paragraphs so that the bottoms of pages align.

The Preview section of the Layout tab is similar to those in the Page and Margin tabs. It also allows you to add a border to your pages and to specify line numbering if you wish.

Open the latest version of your letter. Try changing the margins and, if you included a header and footer, the distance from the edge of the page. Set what you think may be reasonable. Add a binding margin if you wish. Are you planning to print the second page on the back of the first? If so, then set Mirror Margins. You can also experiment with different headers for odd and even pages using the Layout tab. Again, once you are happy, save the latest version.

Ideally, the format that you now have is one you want to use for a real letter. If you wish, save this as a template, calling it `Myletter.dot`. It's probably a good idea to delete all the text except your address (and telephone number), unless of course you want to modify it so that it tells you what to type in the template. You can always edit this template later if you wish.

Summary

The first section in this chapter went over basic formatting techniques, including how to format characters, change the case of text, format paragraphs, copy paragraph formatting using the Format Painter, and clear formatting.

The next section covered tabs, lists, and borders. You examined the use of tabs and tab stops and numbered and bulleted lists. This section also explained how to add borders and shading to paragraphs, selected text, and pages.

The third section covered styles and templates. Styles are combinations of formats, and you saw how to apply them to paragraphs and to the whole document. You also learnt how templates are used, particularly when setting up a new document.

Finally, you saw how to make formatting changes to pages and entire documents. This included inserting page numbers (folios), adding headers and footers to a document, and using Page Setup. In Page Setup, you saw how to change the page size and orientation, how to set the default page size, and how to change the paper source if necessary. Page Setup also allows you to modify and mirror the page margins and the positions of the header and footer, add a gutter or binding margin, and add line numbers and a page border.

Chapter 17

Tables, Graphics, and Other Objects

IN THIS CHAPTER YOU WILL LEARN HOW TO

- ✓ Set up a table in various ways.
- ✓ Edit and format a table.
- ✓ Add an image or graphics file to a document.
- ✓ Format, move, and copy a picture.
- ✓ Delete a picture.
- ✓ Resize and crop a picture.
- ✓ Import spreadsheet files.
- ✓ Import image files, charts, and graphs.

So far we have only discussed formatting and editing text made up of pargaraphs. However, word processors belie their name to some extent in that they are also able to handle complex tables, graphics of various kinds, and other objects such as data imported from a spreadsheet program. This chapter explains how to handle these.

Using Tables in Word

The last chapter explained the use of tab stops and noted that their use was good for short items, but not for blocks of text, because tabs only handle text on a line-by-line basis. Tables in Word, however, are based on a cellular approach; a table is essentially a block of cells, to each of which separate formatting can be applied. You can also apply formatting to the whole table, or to either a given column or row.

Creating a Table

As with most things in Word, there is more than one way to create a table.

Using the Create Table Toolbar Button

You'll start by creating a table from the toolbar button. Click the Create Table icon, which opens a grid (see Figure 17.1) on which you can by default choose up to five columns by four rows.

FIGURE 17.1 Table options shown when using the Create Table toolbar option

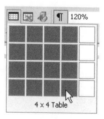

However, if you drag and drop with the right mouse button, starting in the top left cell, you make the table any size you like. Figure 17.2 shows a table of four columns and four rows produced in this way.

If you select text before you click the icon, you convert that text into a table with the number of columns corresponding to the number of tabs you have set in the paragraph, although the result is not always easy to predict.

FIGURE 17.2   An example of a table created with the Create Table toolbar option

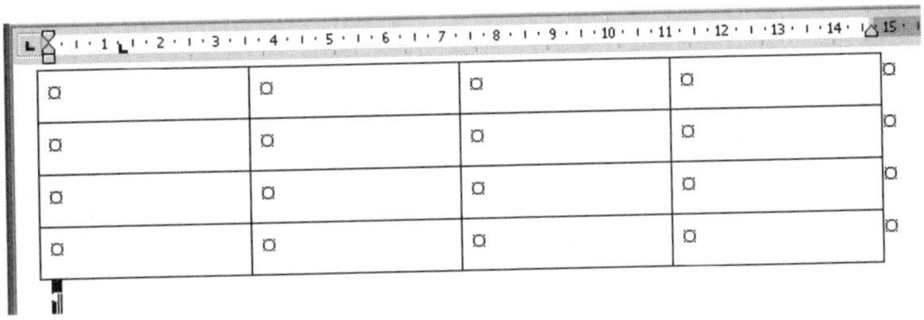

Using the Insert Table Command

Another way to create a table is to choose Insert Table from the Table menu (tables have their own menu). The Insert Table window opens (see Figure 17.3). In the Table Size section, choose the number of columns and rows. Below that is the AutoFit Behavior section. This allows you to choose the column widths if you wish, although Auto is a good first choice (and is what the icon approach generates automatically), providing equal widths with the total table width equal to the page width. If you make your columns wider, some of the table may be off the edge of the page! The other options are to fit the table to the window or to the contents.

FIGURE 17.3   The Insert Table window

You can also select the AutoFormat button in the Insert Table window. Unless you use Auto-Format (also available by choosing Table ➤ Table AutoFormat), each cell of the table initially takes on the format of the paragraph in which you create the table. Thus, if you choose another table of four columns and four rows, it appears below the first table, as shown in Figure 17.4. Note that the two tables are identical.

FIGURE 17.4 Tables created via the menu and toolbar options

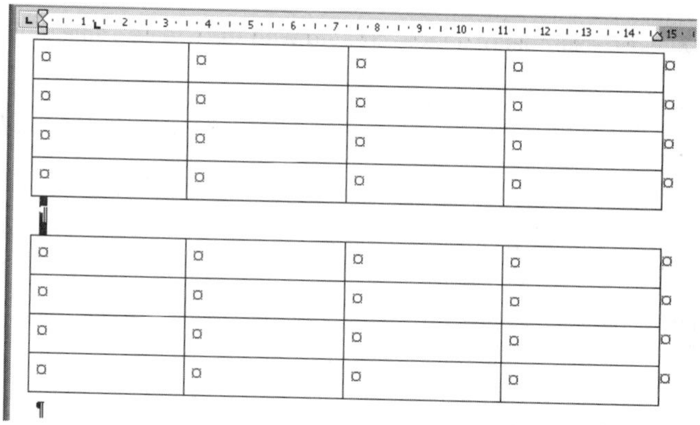

Now create a new file (with a blank page template). Try creating a table using either of the two approaches. See which one you find easier. For use later in this chapter, create seven columns and head the columns as follows: **Title, Firstname, Surname, Address 1, Town, County,** and **Postcode**. Enter some text in those columns corresponding to the column headings. Create at least five rows in addition to the heading row. It does not matter whether you use real names and addresses or not. Save the file as `table_test01.doc`.

Drawing a Table

Word also allows you to draw a table. To create a table using this method, take the following steps:

1. Either click the pencil button at the left of the Tables And Borders toolbar or choose Draw Table from the Table menu. Your (mouse) cursor turns into a pencil and the Tables And Borders toolbar opens, if it is not already showing (see Figure 17.5). The view changes to Page Layout.

FIGURE 17.5 The Tables And Borders toolbar

2. Click where the top-left corner of the table is to go.

3. Drag and drop until the overall size of the table is about right, as shown in Figure 17.6.

FIGURE 17.6   Drawing the outside of a table

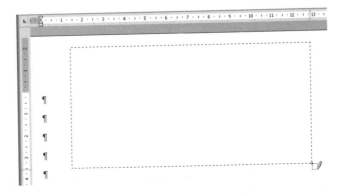

4. Click at the top of the box you have created, roughly where you think the boundary between the first two columns should be, and draw a line to the bottom of the box, as shown in Figure 17.7.

FIGURE 17.7   Indicating the first column boundary of the table

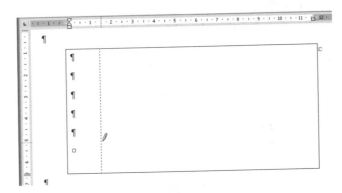

5. Repeat this for as many columns as you want.

6. Click the side of the box or a column boundary for the position of the first row and draw a line across the box, straddling as many columns as necessary.

7. Repeat for as many rows as you want, as shown in Figure 17.8.

FIGURE 17.8   Indicating the last row boundary when drawing a table

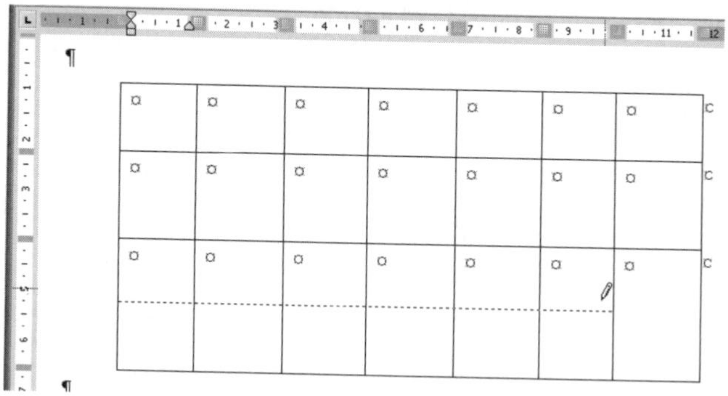

8. Click the Pencil icon again and click anywhere in the main text or press the Esc key on the keyboard to exit from drawing mode.

You can then tidy up your table and add formatting in the ways discussed in this module. Now open a new file. Create the same table as you did in the first exercise, but this time by drawing. See which approach you prefer. You can save this file if you wish, but do not overwrite your last table file (`table_test01.doc`).

Modifying a Table

Once you have created your table, the first thing to note is that there are various selections you can make in a table. You can choose Insert, Delete, or Select from the Table menu and then make a further selection from the fly-out menu that opens.

You use Insert to insert rows or columns above or below (or to the left or right) of the cell in which your cursor is placed. If you choose Insert ➢ Table, you can insert a nested table within an existing table cell. If you choose to insert cells, you get various options in the Insert Cells window (see Figure 17.9). However, the result is not always predictable.

FIGURE 17.9   Inserting cells into a table

Use Delete to delete the row or column in which the cursor is situated (or the whole table). If you choose to delete cells, you get similar options to those for Insert, and again the results are not always easy to predict.

WARNING Unless you are very experienced, it makes sense always to insert or delete only rows and columns and then use the Merge Cells option to insert and delete cells. This is because if you insert or delete cells, the columns—and perhaps also the rows—cease to align. Making changes in terms of the rows and columns, which is a great advantage of handling information as tables, is much more predictable.

Choosing Table ➤ Select or using the mouse in the usual way, you can perform the following tasks:

- You can select the whole table from the fly-out menu that opens when you choose Table ➤ Select, or you can use the mouse. If you use the mouse, make sure to include the column marker for the end of the row(s), which looks as though it is outside the table (see Figure 17.10). If you do not do this (see Figure 17.11), you've selected the cells making up the row, not the whole row or table.

FIGURE 17.10   A row selected

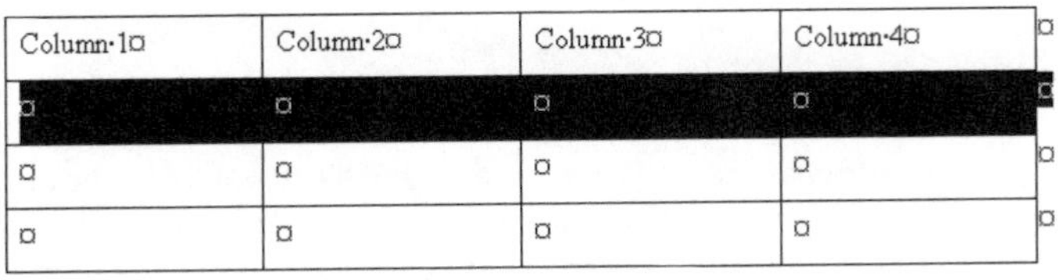

Column·1□	Column·2□	Column·3□	Column·4□	□
□	□	□	□	□
□	□	□	□	□
□	□	□	□	□

FIGURE 17.11   Cells in a row selected

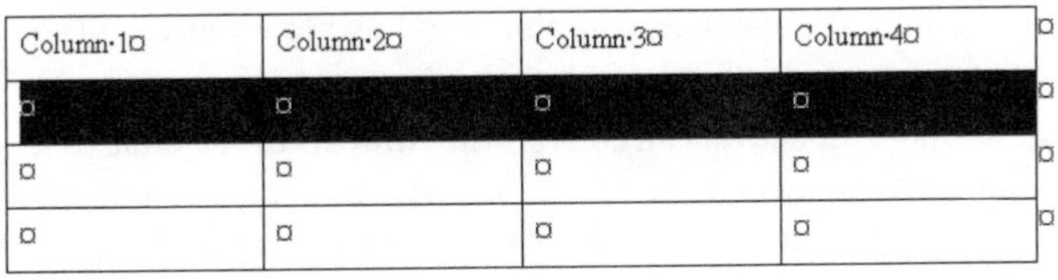

Column·1□	Column·2□	Column·3□	Column·4□	□
□	□	□	□	□
□	□	□	□	□
□	□	□	□	□

- You can select a row. Again, it is important to make sure that you include the last column marker.
- You can select a column. You can also do this by moving your mouse cursor over the top of the column. The cursor changes to a broad arrow, and the column is selected when you click (see Figure 17.12).

FIGURE 17.12   Selecting a column

Column·1□	Column·2□	Column·3□	Column·4□	□
□	□		□	□
□	□		□	□
□	□		□	□

- You can select a cell or cells. You can use the mouse, and the cursor changes to a broad arrow. This time, point up and right, and the cell is selected if you then click. You can also double-click in a cell to select it.

Once you have made this selection, you can edit that selection in the same way as any other selection in a document. However, there also some other things that you can do:

- If you select a row or column, you can move the boundaries with the mouse. While this is a convenient way of adjusting column widths, adjusting row heights in this way can lead to a rather untidy appearance. Using paragraph formatting and/or the AutoFit options discussed shortly is a better approach.

NOTE   To add a row at the end of a table, the easiest way is to click in the last cell of the table (placing the text cursor in that cell). Then press the Tab key, and the text cursor moves to the next cell, creating a new row in the process. This illustrates the role that the Tab key plays in tables. It does not insert a Tab character as such. It moves the cursor from cell to cell, starting at the top left and going along the rows until it reaches the bottom right. Holding down the Shift key while pressing the Tab key moves the cursor in the opposite direction. To enter a Tab character within a table cell, for example, to align a column on the decimal point, you have to enter Ctrl+Tab.

- If you select the whole table, you can convert the contents of the table to text (with or without tab stops) or sort entries in it. These two options are outside the scope of the ECDL syllabus, but are useful techniques. By selecting text and going to the Table menu, you can also convert the text to a table, which can be very convenient. This is a more controllable approach than selecting the text and using the Insert Table icon.

- If you select a cell, you can of course format this cell, delete it, and insert additional cells (although note the caution earlier in this section). You can also move the cell boundaries, but it is better to do this for whole columns and perhaps rows to avoid any problems with appearance. You can also merge cells, so that you are able to produce cells that straddle either vertically or horizontally or alternatively split a cell into a number of other cells, as illustrated in Figure 17.13. This approach is easier to handle than deleting and adding individual cells.

FIGURE 17.13   Splitting a cell

In Word 6, an earlier version of Word, when you selected two columns in a table and then chose Merge Cells, the two columns were merged cell by cell, so that two columns became one. Unfortunately, in more recent versions of Word, merging two columns gives one enormous cell, which is not very helpful. There are ways around this, but they involve various tricks. If you have a specific requirement to merge columns, for example, to make three columns containing honorific (Mr., Mrs., Ms., and so on), first name, and surname into a single column containing the full name with honorific, then, although this may be increasingly difficult, see if you can obtain a copy of Word 6 to run on your system alongside the latest version of Word!

You can change column widths with the mouse even if a column is not selected. If you move the cursor to one of the grid lines indicating a column boundary, it changes into a double vertical line with an arrow on each side (see Figure 17.14). If you now drag and drop the cursor, the column boundary moves to a new position.

FIGURE 17.14   Moving a column boundary

Column·1□	Column·2□	Column·3□	Column·4□	□
□	□	□	▣‖◆	□
□	□	□	□	□
□	□	□	□	□

If no cells are selected, the whole column boundary moves; if one (or both) of the cells adjacent to the boundary is selected, only the boundary of that cell or those cells moves. In either case, it is simply the boundary that moves, so if one column becomes wider, the adjacent column becomes narrower. Getting column widths correct can therefore be an iterative operation.

You can also change the column width, as well as the row height, by choosing Table Properties from the Table menu. This is the only way to adjust cell height (although AutoFit allows you to distribute rows evenly). If you know the width of the information that you want to put into the cells, this is a better way of adjusting the width. AutoFit (see Figure 17.15) repeats some of the options available when you create a table. Note that if you use the commands Distribute Rows Evenly and Distribute Columns Evenly, the actual row spacing is not completely under your control. The rows are averaged over the table depth or width.

FIGURE 17.15 The AutoFit options

The Table Properties window has four tabs—Table, Row, Column, and Cell—that allow you to modify appropriate properties. Try them out with these steps:

1. Place your cursor somewhere in the table you want to modify. To change the properties of the whole table, it doesn't matter where in the table you click. However, to modify the properties of a row, column, or cell, click in the appropriate cell. If you select a number of rows or columns, the changes you make apply to all those rows or columns.

2. Choose Table ➤ Table Properties. The first tab you see is probably Table (see Figure 17.16). If it is not the one on top, select it.

FIGURE 17.16 The Table tab of the Table Properties window

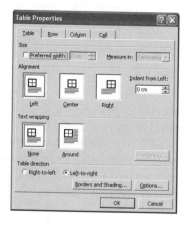

3. The Table Tab has these options:

   - The Preferred Width option sets the overall width of the table
   - The Alignment and Text Wrapping options are the same as for normal paragraphs.
   - The Indent From Left box applies to the whole table.
   - Clicking the Borders And Shading button opens the Borders And Shading window (to be discussed shortly).
   - The Options button opens the Table Options window shown in Figure 17.17, in which cell dimensions can be set.

FIGURE 17.17   The Table Options window

4. Choose the Row tab of the Table Properties window (see Figure 17.18). This also has various boxes you can complete:

   - Specify Height—While you can set this exactly, if you do so, you may find entries disappearing, because either the type size is too large for the height or the text goes onto two rows, for example. Leave it unchecked, so that Word calculates the height automatically, or specify At Least, so that the row expands to take whatever is entered into it.
   - Allow Row To Break Across Pages—This is a question of style and personal preference.

FIGURE 17.18   The Row tab of the Table Properties window

5. Go on to sort out the next row or group of rows.

6. Choose the Column tab of the Table Properties window (see Figure 17.19). This is even simpler than the Row tab, with just the column width to complete. Again, if you leave the box unchecked, Word calculates the column width automatically.

FIGURE 17.19   The Column tab of the Table Properties window

7. Choose the Cell tab in the Table Properties window (see Figure 17.20). This is also self-explanatory.

FIGURE 17.20   The Cell tab of the Table Properties window

8. Clicking the Options button in the Cell tab opens the Cell Options window (see Figure 17.21), where you can format the text in a given cell or in a group of cells.

FIGURE 17.21   The Cell Options window

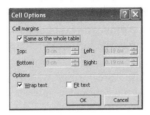

Open your table file. Try inserting columns, rows, and even cells to see what the effect is. Delete some columns, rows, and cells. Once you are happy with carrying out the operations, close the document and do not save it.

Open your table file again. Change column widths and row heights and even the font size in columns and rows until you feel that the table is as readable as you can get it. Then save it as a new file or a new version.

Formatting and AutoFormat

As noted earlier, you can format table cells as you wish, using all the formatting facilities used in normal text. It is also possible to save special table cell styles in a template. However, to make life easier for you, Microsoft has developed a series of standard formats.

These are accessed by selecting AutoFormat, either when creating the table or from the Table menu. The Table AutoFormat window opens (see Figure 17.22).

FIGURE 17.22   The Table AutoFormat window

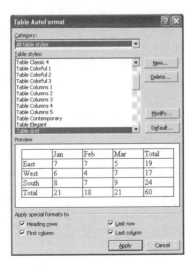

The Table Styles box at the top left lists the formats; if you select them in turn, you can see what each one looks like in the Preview box. At the bottom of the Table AutoFormat window, you can decide what to do about the first and last row and/or column, which may be a heading or a total, for example. If you click Apply, your table takes on the formatting that you have selected. If you are creating a new table, the format you have chosen now shows in the original Insert Table window.

Open your first table file again. Use AutoFormat to see if you can achieve a better effect than you did in the last exercise. Save the file again as a new file or a new version.

Splitting a Table

If you click in any row of a table and then select Table ➤ Split Table, the table splits above the row in which you clicked, creating a blank line, in other words, a carriage return, between what are now two tables.

Open your first table file again. See what happens when you split the table. Do not save it.

Adding Borders and Shading

Word offers a number of ways to achieve borders and shading for your table. To add borders, you can use the Tables And Borders toolbar, or click the normal boxing button that you've used previously, which is the same as the one on the Tables And Borders toolbar. Select the appropriate cells, rows, or columns—or even the whole table—and then choose the rules you want to add. It is a good idea to use Print Preview to check that the rules are where you want them. The grid lines in a table are very useful, but they can be confusing. You can hide them if you wish (see the Table menu), but that can also cause confusion if you're not careful.

To change the weight and type of rule you are using for the border, you can use the icons on the Tables And Borders toolbar or you can choose Format ➤ Borders And Shading, as described in Chapter 16, "Formatting." Similarly, you can change the colours of the rules and the fill (or shading) of a table cell. If you use the toolbar, click the pencil icon for the rules or the paint can icon for the fill and choose what you want from the selection now displayed (see Figure 17.23). Remember, however, that you may also need to change the colour of your font if your text is to be visible.

FIGURE 17.23   The fill selection on the Tables And Borders toolbar

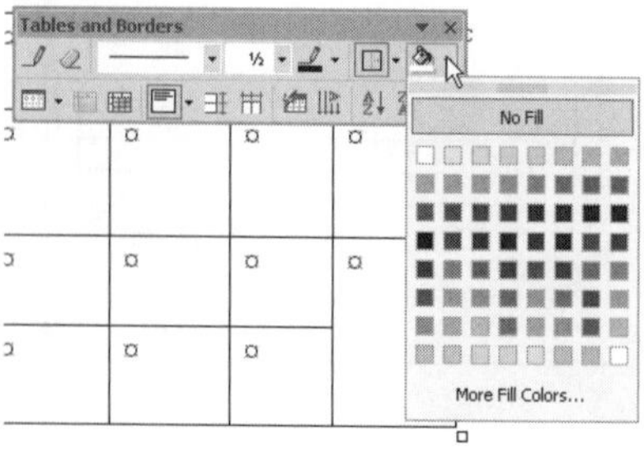

Open your latest formatted table file again (not the one where you used AutoFormat). Add some rules and perhaps some shading. How does it look in comparison with the table formatted using AutoFormat? Save this file if you wish.

Adding Pictures in Word

Many documents contain illustrations. From a technical point of view, there are two kinds of illustrations: bitmaps and vector graphics. *Bitmaps* are images, often digital photographs, made up of many small dots, known as *pixels*, either black and white or coloured, as shown in Figure 17.24.

FIGURE 17.24   A bitmap image

Vector graphics (see Figure 17.25), in contrast, are based on a combination of lines and shapes that can be described mathematically and redrawn each time they are shown on screen or sent for printing.

FIGURE 17.25   A drawing or vector graphic

In some ways, the two types of artwork are handled similarly, while in other ways, they are treated quite differently, so it helps if you understand the difference. One important factor, for example, is that the file size of a piece of vector artwork is almost independent of the size at which it is output. In fact, the same illustration can be reproduced at any size because it is *scalable*.

In contrast, a bitmap is created at a *fixed resolution*, in other words, with a fixed number of dots (pixels) per unit length in each direction. Put simply, each dot contains the information about the colour at that point and over its own small area. If you enlarge a bitmap, you may be able to create more dots, but you cannot increase the information content; the quality of the picture gradually gets worse and the impression of continuous tone cannot be sustained. To obtain a larger bitmap at the same resolution, you need more dots, with each dot containing its own information. Another effect of this is that the larger a bitmap is, the larger its file size is.

Strictly speaking, these differences are not part of the ECDL syllabus, but they will help you understand why the two types of artwork are handled differently. Indeed, you will find that there are different types of program for handling the two types, although there is some overlap.

More important, understanding the difference will help you to use artwork more sensibly. For example, a letter containing a photograph has a large file size, so it takes a long time to print and takes longer and therefore also costs more to transmit electronically, quite apart from taking up more space on your system.

There are ways to compress files so that their file size is smaller, but these methods do not affect the time taken to print. These compression techniques are also not as appropriate for files used for printing as they are for files viewed on screen. You will see more about images for viewing on screen in Part 7, but this chapter looks only at how to add illustrations to documents, format them, and move and resize them.

Adding an Illustration

There are essentially two ways in which you can include a picture in your document: You can draw it yourself or you can bring it in (import it) from somewhere else, in just the same way as you would if you were generating a paper document in the old-fashioned way. Just as with a paper document, even if you draw the picture, you may choose not do it directly within the document, but complete the drawing somewhere else and insert the finished drawing into your document.

 Word includes a facility called AutoShapes, which helps you create frequently used shapes, but this is no longer in the ECDL syllabus.

If you add either a bitmap image or a drawing to a Word document, the techniques you use are the same, because you are simply including another file within your document file. While it is useful to understand the differences between the two types for practical reasons, importing a file is importing a file. In fact, we shall see more about importing other types of file in the next section.

You can either add an illustration directly in the text of your document, or together with some additional text, you can put it in a text box, which is a box that is separate from the main flow of the document text and can be moved independently. The use of text boxes is outside the ECDL syllabus, but it is a good idea to understand the principle.

To include an illustration, you need to decide where it should go, placing your text cursor at that position. Then choose Insert ➤ Picture. This section covers three of the entries in the Picture menu that opens (see Figure 17.26): Clip Art, From File, and From Scanner Or Camera. In fact, the first two options only distinguish the source of the image and the method of inclusion, while the third option is outside the scope of the ECDL.

FIGURE 17.26   The Insert Picture menu

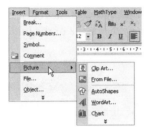

If you select Clip Art, the Insert Clip Art window opens (see Figure 17.27). From here, you can search for all kinds of media, including movies and sound (although these are not within the ECDL syllabus). These can come from the Office Collection, which is installed from a separate CD, or from a collection that you have set up using Clip Organizer (which, as its name implies, is a facility that allows you to store images in a logical way).

FIGURE 17.27   The Insert Clip Art window

One of the problems with Word is that the exact position of the picture is not always predictable, although as you will see shortly, you can specify the rules for placing a picture. Do not be surprised initially if the picture does not appear where you expect it to. The position depends partly on the size of the picture and partly on your page size and where the callout was on the page. However, once it is part of your document, you can move it around.

Rather than using Insert Clip Art, you can choose Insert ➤ Picture ➤ From File. Alternatively, you can click the Insert Picture icon in the Picture toolbar and move to a directory that you know contains pictures. The Insert Picture window opens (see Figure 17.28). In fact, you can access the Clip Art library this way as well if you know the folder it is in. This is rather like many of the other Open windows, except that instead of filenames, you see the directories that contain pictures (of whatever types you specify at the bottom of the window) or the pictures themselves. Note that, when you see directories, it can sometimes be determined what pictures they contain by viewing the smaller thumbnails on the image of the folder.

FIGURE 17.28   The Insert Picture window

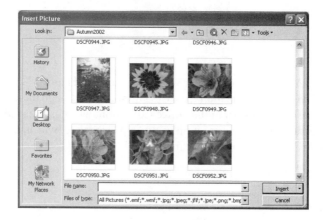

 If you see only a file list rather than thumbnails, click the View icon and select Thumbnails.

You can search (either by filename or by text or property) by choosing Tools ➤ Search. This is outside the ECDL syllabus, however.

Once you have the picture you want, select Insert in the Insert Picture window. Note that the drop-down box has two other options as well as the simple Insert:

Link To file   If this box is ticked, then a link to the picture is added instead of the picture being inserted in the file. This has advantages and disadvantages. Of course, it keeps the file size down, but if the document is passed to someone else, you have to remember to include a copy of the artwork file and update the link. In addition, when you look at the file on the screen, the picture has to be called in each time you scroll, which can slow down the scrolling. What may or may not be an advantage is that if the picture is changed, you see the latest version in your document.

Insert And Link   This option includes the picture in the document, but also means that any updates to the picture appear in your document.

You can of course always copy an illustration from another document and paste it into your document. While this is not the place to discuss it at length, remember that the copyright of almost all illustrations belongs to someone, and so their use in any commercial or widely distributed document without permission or payment is infringing the copyright owner's rights.

Try placing an image in a new file; you'll need some text, although it does not matter what it is about. Copy the text from anywhere—a Help file perhaps. If you prefer, you can open your letter file. Choose Insert ➤ Picture ➤ Clip Art. If you've opened the letter, see if you can find an appropriate picture to include; otherwise, just select any picture you fancy. You can use either Search or the Clip Organizer. Once you have found a picture, see what happens when you add it.

Choose Insert ➤ Picture ➤ From File. Do you have any photographs on your system? If so, try inserting one. If not, browse through directories, download a photograph off the Web, or find a CD that has photographs or clip art on it. Use Browse (or Search) to locate files with an extension such as .jpg, .bmp, .gif, .tif, .png, or .pcx and try the different options available.

Moving and Placing Images within and between Documents

As noted earlier, the placement of images in Word is not exact, but there are some tools you can use to adjust the placement of your image. Images can be sited in three ways. They can float between paragraphs, they can be fixed, or they can overlap the text. In addition, you can always move (or copy) an image by using Cut (or Copy) and Paste or drag and drop. Some of the adjustments can be made from buttons in the Picture toolbar shown in Figure 17.29.

Images can be moved not only within documents, but also between them. Using Cut (or Copy) and Paste is the best option because dragging and dropping between documents requires both documents to be visible on the screen at the same time, which means that they cannot be maximised and this may be a problem, particularly if the images are large.

FIGURE 17.29 The Picture toolbar

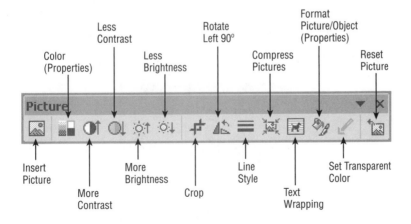

Many of the adjustments that the Picture toolbar allows you to make are not covered in the ECDL syllabus. Furthermore, whilst the toolbar provides some basic functionality, there are much better tools than Word for handling pictures.

If you want to reformat a picture, either right-click the picture and choose Format Picture from the pop-up menu that opens or click the Format Picture icon on the Picture toolbar. The Format Picture window opens (see Figure 17.30).

FIGURE 17.30   The Picture tab of the Format Picture window

We shall not describe most of the options here, but we will look at the Layout tab (see Figure 17.31), which allows you to position the picture relative to the text. The illustrations in the window show you what happens. You can have the text wrap in line with the text; you can have the text form a square around the picture, either at the boundaries of the whole image (including the white space surrounding the subject) or tight up to the subject itself; and you can place the picture behind or in front of the text. For all except the first option, you can choose the horizontal alignment (Left, Center, or Right). There is also an alignment option called Other, which really means leave the picture where you inserted it.

FIGURE 17.31   The Layout tab of the Format Picture window

You can also access these options (although not the alignment options) by clicking the Text Wrapping icon on the Picture toolbar.

Open your file with the pictures. Experiment with the options in the Format Picture window or in the Picture toolbar to see the ways in which you can place your pictures relative to the text. You can also try moving and copying pictures. Save the file if you wish.

To select an image, picture, or chart, you simply click on it and a frame and four handles will appear (as shown in Figure 17.32).

FIGURE 17.32   Resizing a picture

Sizing and Cropping Images

To size an image, select the object (picture or AutoShape) and then drag one of the *handles* (the small boxes on the sides and corners) to the size you want, as shown in Figure 17.32. Using one of the handles on the sides distorts the aspect ratio (height to width). If you use a corner handle, you retain the aspect ratio as long as you hold down the Shift key at the same time.

Cropping a picture means removing part of the picture (as if you were cutting it off). To do this, you either specify the crop in the Picture tab of the Format Picture window or select the Crop icon from the Picture toolbar. The cursor shape changes to the shape of the Crop icon. In the same way as sizing, drag one of the handles. This time, the size of the picture does not change. If you use a corner handle and hold down the Shift key, you retain the aspect ratio. When you finish cropping, just click in a blank part of the screen to cancel the cropping task. The end result is shown in Figure 17.33.

FIGURE 17.33   Cropping a picture

Try resizing one or more of your pictures and try cropping one or more of your pictures. (You can always use Undo or close the file without saving.)

Deleting Images

To delete an image, simply select it and press the Delete key. However, if you click the picture rather than the frame, you delete the picture and leave the frame, which you can again select and delete.

Adding Other Elements in Word

You have seen earlier in this chapter how tables and images can be inserted into a document. However, these are not the only objects that can be inserted, and the approach used in the previous sections is not the only approach possible. One of the advantages of Windows is that you can insert an object such as a spreadsheet into a Word file in such a way that when you want to edit it, selecting it also opens the application that is associated with it (often the application that it was created with).

> **NOTE**   How applications are associated with file types is discussed in Part 2. For example, files that have the filename extension .doc are almost always associated with Word and files with the extension .xls are almost always associated with Excel.

There are a number of ways in which you can transfer text and pictures from another application into Word. The simplest way is by copying and pasting—this works from many applications. The second approach is to choose Insert ➤ File. This only works for file types for which Word has an input filter, including Excel. The third approach is to use what is called OLE (Object Linking and Embedding) by choosing Insert ➤ Object.

Word 2002 provides ways of generating charts, organisation charts, and what it calls WordArt without going to other programs. While these are outside the scope of the ECDL syllabus, you may find it interesting to look at them. They are all accessed by choosing Insert ➢ Picture.

Let's deal with the three approaches in turn.

Copying and Pasting from Other Applications

You looked at copying and pasting in detail in Chapter 15, "Basic Text Operations." The approach is just the same here, except that you have to open the other application first. Figure 17.34 shows a small spreadsheet in Excel (see Part 4 for more information on spreadsheets). If you select the cells containing the data and then use the Copy option (enter Ctrl+C), the material is added to the Clipboard.

FIGURE 17.34 A small spreadsheet in Excel

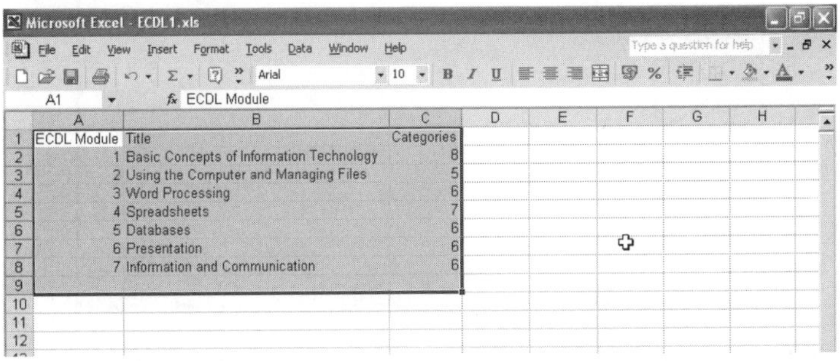

Next you have to transfer the table to Word. Open Word if it is not already open and ensure that you have the right target document open. (Moving/switching between applications is described in Part 2.) Once you are in the Word document at the position where you want the table to be inserted, you simply paste (enter Ctrl+V or click the Paste icon). The Excel data appears as a table (see Figure 17.35) that can be edited in the ways discussed earlier in this chapter. Copying in this way breaks the link with the original application.

FIGURE 17.35 The Excel spreadsheet pasted as a table into Word

However, there is a way of copying that does not break the link, which is described shortly in the section "Inserting Objects."

Once you know how to use Excel, create a small file, then create a Word file, and try copying the Excel file yourself. You could also try with other applications such as graphics and drawing programs.

Inserting a File

The second way to include a file from another application (usually just the Microsoft applications and one or two others such as WordPerfect and Lotus 1-2-3) is to choose Insert ➤ File. The Insert File window opens (see Figure 17.36), and is almost the same as the Open window.

FIGURE 17.36   Inserting a file

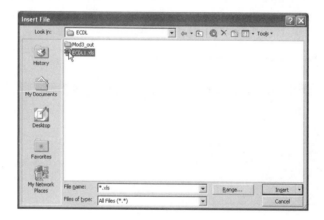

Assuming that you saved your spreadsheet as ECDL1.xls, if you find this spreadsheet to insert, the Open Worksheet window opens and asks you for information on how much of the spreadsheet you want to import (see Figure 17.37).

FIGURE 17.37   The Open Worksheet window for selecting which part of a spreadsheet to insert

The imported file (below the one you copied and pasted) can be seen in Figure 17.38. It may need some formatting, but you can see that the information is identical.

FIGURE 17.38   The Excel spreadsheet imported into Word

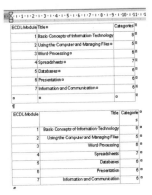

 Only certain file types can be inserted into a Word document (and that make sense to do so). If you try to insert a type that Word does not recognize (or one that may need conversion), a conversion window opens. This is outside the scope of the ECDL.

This approach also breaks the link with the original application. There are advantages in using the Insert method and in using Copy and Paste. For the whole file, particularly if it is large, the Insert approach is probably better. If you want only part of a file, then using Copy and Paste is probably the better approach.

 If you use Insert, you can include only the part of the file that you want to insert by using the Range button in the Insert File window. For Excel files, this is straightforward because you simply insert the range of cells that you need (this is in addition to the option shown in Figure 17.37). For other documents such as Word documents, you need bookmarks in the file to be inserted to identify the range. This is not only outside the scope of the ECDL, but it involves you changing the file to be imported, which you may not wish to do.

Inserting Objects

The third approach to adding other elements in Word allows the link to the original application to be retained. Choose Insert ≻ Object. The Object window opens (see Figure 17.39) with the Create New tab active. The Object Type list includes essentially the software that you have available; if you select, for example, Microsoft Excel Worksheet, you open an Excel spreadsheet within your Word document.

FIGURE 17.39   The Create New tab in the Object window

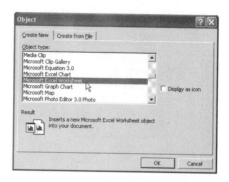

Although it forms part of the Word document, this object is edited with Excel, which provides you with increased functionality. And of course you can choose any of the programs that are compatible.

Here, however, you are concerned with importing an existing application file, which will at least in principle continue to be updated in Excel. So choose the second tab, Create From File, as illustrated in Figure 17.40. This assumes that you know what you want to insert and where it is, so browse until you find your Excel file. The Result section tells you what is going to happen.

FIGURE 17.40   The Create From File tab in the Object window

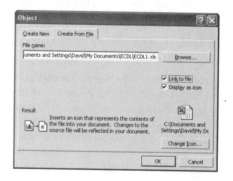

Note that there are two check boxes in the Create From File tab:

Link To File   If this option is not ticked, the effect is the same as it was with the first two methods.

Display As Icon   In this option, only an icon is shown in the document. This is mainly of use if the document is not to be printed. Clicking the icon opens the linked document.

You can achieve the same result with the link by using Copy in Excel, but then in Word, instead of simply using Paste, you choose Edit ➢ Paste Special. (There is no keyboard shortcut for Paste Special.) There are various options that you can choose in the Paste Special window (see Figure 17.41), but these are all explained. While the principle is within the ECDL syllabus, the detail is not.

FIGURE 17.41   The Paste Special window

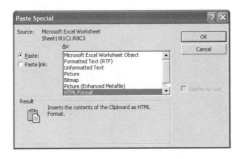

Now repeat the exercise where you used Insert menu earlier in this chapter, but this time choose Object from the list of items to be inserted. Once you have inserted the object, click it to edit it and see what happens.

Repeat this exercise once again, but this time use Paste Special instead of Paste. Once you have done this, click the object to edit it and see what happens. It should be the same as when choosing Insert ➢ Object.

Pasting Charts

Within Excel, it's possible to generate charts based on the data (see Part 4 for further details). For these purposes, a chart has been generated from the ECDL spreadsheet data, as you can see in Figure 17.42. You can copy this chart and then use either Paste or Paste Special in the same way you did for the spreadsheet data itself. If you use Paste Special, the data in the chart (see Figure 17.43) is linked back to the original spreadsheet and is updated as and when the spreadsheet is updated.

FIGURE 17.42   An Excel chart

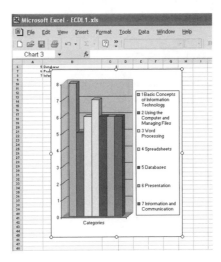

FIGURE 17.43   An Excel chart pasted into a Word document

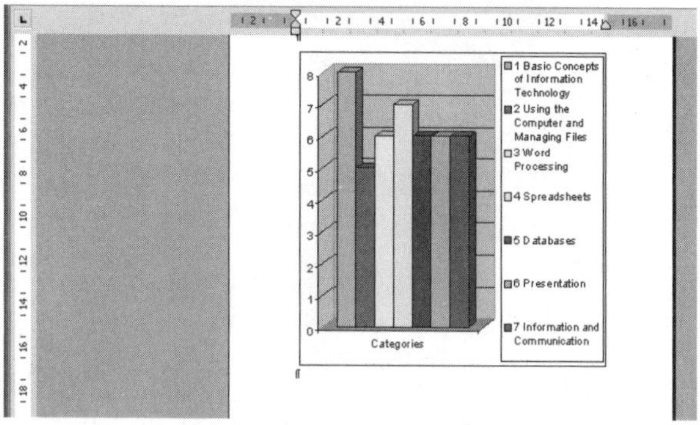

As noted earlier, Word now provides the facility to generate charts, but using existing data does not seem all that straightforward.

Repeat the previous exercise in this chapter, but this time, before you do that, create a chart in Excel, using the instructions in Part 4. Then copy the chart into a Word document. Once you have inserted the chart in Word, click it to edit it and see what happens.

Charts are selected in the same way as images, by clicking them. To delete a chart, simply select it and then hit the Delete key.

Placing Charts and Moving Charts within and between Documents

All the options available for placing pictures are available for charts. The only difference is that, when you select a chart, you will find that on the Format drop-down list, Picture has changed to Object. Similarly, you can use Cut (or Copy) and Paste or drag and drop to move or duplicate charts.

Sizing and Cropping Charts

Charts are resized and cropped in the same way as images. To resize, select the chart and drag one of the handles to the size you want, as shown in Figure 17.44.

FIGURE 17.44   Resizing a chart

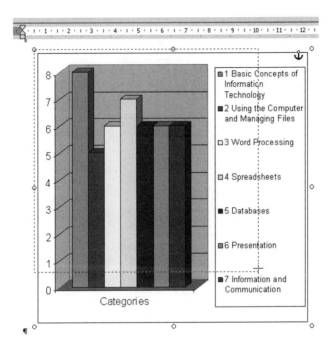

Again, if you use the corner handle and hold down the Shift key, you will retain the aspect ratio. It is also worth noting that, even if you do not maintain the aspect ratio for the chart as a whole, any text on the chart remains undistorted, although if you make the chart too small, the text becomes unreadable. You may also find that some of the text no longer fits within the frame of the chart.

To crop a chart, you can either specify the crop in the Picture tab of the Format Object window or select the Crop icon from the Picture toolbar in the same way as for an image. The final result is shown in Figure 17.45.

FIGURE 17.45 Cropping a chart

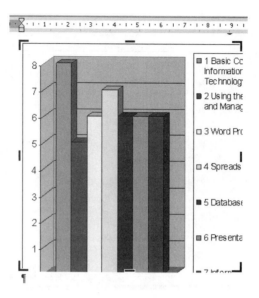

Summary

This chapter explained that there are three different ways of adding tables to a document. Once you have a table, it's possible to select cells, columns, rows, and complete tables. These elements can then be modified, reformatted, or deleted. You can merge and split cells and tables and add borders and shading to table cells.

The next section described the differences between vector graphics and bitmaps. It also explained the different ways to add a picture, move and place images relative to text, delete images, change their size, and crop them. Note that the copyright of almost every illustration is owned by someone.

The final section of this chapter described how to import a spreadsheet and a chart from Excel into Word in various different ways, including retaining the link with the original application by using Paste Special.

Chapter

18

Word Processing Output

IN THIS CHAPTER YOU WILL LEARN HOW TO

- ✓ Preview a document.
- ✓ Use the basic print options.
- ✓ Print a document from an installed printer.
- ✓ Create a data file such as a mailing list for use in a mail merge.
- ✓ Create a letter for mail merging.
- ✓ Create a label document for mail merging.
- ✓ Carry out the mail merge.

Managing your text, images, charts, and tables on your computer is efficient and easy in Word. But often you may need to produce output from your Word files, so that your work can leave the confines of your computer and function in the world at large. This chapter goes over how to print Word files and how to use a special tool called Mail Merge.

Printing Documents

Even in this age of electronic communication, it is more than likely that you will need a printed version of a file you have been working on. Windows is able to store the details of many printers, and you can switch between them if they are attached to your system. However, there is always a default printer, which is the one to which documents are sent unless you indicate otherwise.

Although the printers are installed from Windows itself, all control of the printing of documents is done from within Word. And not only can you print from within the program, but you can also preview what you are going to print. As we saw in Chapter 14, "First Steps with Word Processing," the Page Layout view may not give you a true WYSIWYG (What You See Is What You Get) view, whereas the Print Preview does. Indeed, Print Preview is a very useful tool, because it allows you to check your document before it's printed out, potentially saving both paper and time.

Print Preview

To see a print preview of your document, click the Print Preview button on the toolbar or choose File ➤ Print Preview. Your view switches to Print Preview (see Figure 18.1). There are various tools shown on the special toolbar:

- You can print directly from this preview.

- You can select the magnifying glass and zoom in and out by simply clicking the page.

- You can show a single page or up to six pages at the same time.

- You can choose the exact magnification that you want to use. Type below a certain size may appear as a pattern block if the magnification is too small. However, this may be all you need to gain an overall idea of what the page looks like.

- You can display both horizontal and vertical rulers if you wish. These allow you to modify the margins, as discussed in Chapter 16, "Formatting."

- You can shrink the view to fit.

- You can use a full-screen view, so that the menu bar disappears.

FIGURE 18.1   The Print Preview window

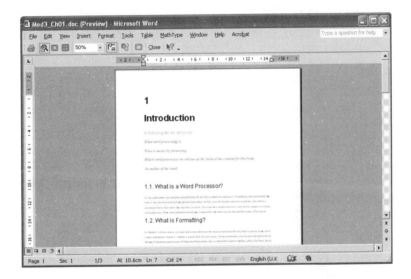

When you exit from Print Preview, you return to the document view you had previously. You do not close the file. If you print directly from Print Preview, you open the Print dialog box, described shortly.

Open the latest version of your letter file and then choose File ➢ Print Preview. Zoom in and out and vary the magnification. Change the number of pages you can view. Show the rulers and experiment with the margins. (If you do this, either use Undo or better yet, make sure that you do not save the new version of your file.) Try some of the other options. Do not print your document at this stage. You can close the Print Preview and even the file, if you wish, when you have finished.

As discussed in the box at the beginning of Chapter 16, it is important to check or proof your document before you make it public. This includes not only checking the content of the document (that is, what you have said, the grammar, and the spelling), but also the layout. For example, have you used the correct heading and text styles and are the margins correct? Indeed, you need to check all the formatting discussed in this module. While you can do this on-screen, perhaps using Print Preview, it is much safer to print out the document and check the printed version, because documents do not always look the same when printed as they do on the screen.

Using Basic Printing Options

There are four ways to print a file:

- Choose Print from the Print Preview window.
- Select the Print icon on the toolbar.
- Choose File ➢ Print.
- Use the keyboard shortcut (Ctrl+P).

Whichever option you choose, when you decide to print, the Print window opens (see Figure 18.2).

FIGURE 18.2   The Print window

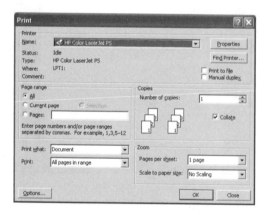

In this window, you choose which printer to use (the default printer and other installed printers are listed), which pages to print, how many copies to print, and how to collate them. You can also determine whether you print the document itself or certain related information, but this is not within the ECDL syllabus. Other options that you can change here are:

- Print just odd or just even pages
- Zoom so that you print more than one page per sheet of paper
- Scale to fit the paper
- Duplexing (printing on both sides of the paper)
- Collating

Collating is an option that is useful only for very simple printers. If you have the Collate box ticked, multiple copies are sent to the printer one by one, which takes a long time. As long as your printer can handle multiple copies, it is better not to tick Collate.

If you want to use a printer that is not the default, click the down arrow at the side of the default printer and choose your alternative. Only those that are installed are shown.

If you click the Properties button, the printer Properties window opens. We have not included a figure, because this window is different for different printers. Each printer has its own driver software (see Part 2), which determines what you see in the printer Properties window. What always appears, however, is the option to change the paper size, because as already mentioned, you may find that many applications use the US letter size as default. You probably need to change this to A4; this is a separate setting from that in Page Setup, which sets the page size for the document rather than for the printer. You will also be able to change the orientation of the page on the printer—portrait or landscape. Once you have made your selection, click OK in the printer Properties window and then click OK again in the Print window.

The Options button displays the same window accessed from Page Setup (see Figure 18.3), which was discussed in Chapter 16.

FIGURE 18.3   Print options

You will also see a Print To File check box in the Print window. This allows you to create a print file, but not send it to a printer. You may need to use this facility if you don't have a printer accessible from your computer. You do need to know which printer the file will be printed on, which means having the correct printer driver installed. There are two ways around this. The first is to produce what is called a PostScript file, which should print on any PostScript printer. The second (and much easier option, although you do need special software installed) is to create a PDF (Portable Document Format) file by using Adobe Acrobat or similar software. This can then be read and printed by using the (free) Adobe Acrobat Reader. These topics are, of course, not within the ECDL syllabus, but are useful to know about.

Open your final letter document and, by whatever method you prefer, print it on your default printer (or another one). Are you happy with what you get? If not, you may need to go back and change some of the things you set in previous exercises.

 NOTE   To review the progress of your printing, refer back to Part 2.

Try printing several documents and then opening the Print Manager window. Relate what is happening there to what is coming out of the printer. Note that sometimes, because a printer may take some time to process the page internally, it may be even a few minutes after a print job has disappeared from the Print Manager window before it is actually printed.

Mail Merge

One great advantage (or disadvantage, depending on your viewpoint) of computers is that they can do things over and over again, very fast. Thus, if you have a list of names and addresses, creating an individualised letter to each person on the list or a set of labels is very straightforward. This is known as *mail merging*, because the production of such letters and labels was its prime purpose.

Creating the List

The first thing to note is that you do not necessarily have to create the list. You can do this, of course, and you will see how, but in most cases the list comes from a spreadsheet, a database, or a Word file in which the fields (that is, the different parts of the name and address) are separated in a standard way. The list may be in a table (like the one you created in Chapter 15), but it can even be what is called a *delimited text file* that looks something like this:

Title|Firstname|Surname|Address 1|Town|County|Postcode

Mr|John|Smith|1 Church Street|Bradford|West Yorks|BD22 3XL

Ms|Gloria|Brown|22 High Street|Bath|Wilts|BA34 9ZZ

Notice that there are the same number of fields in each entry, and the top line describes the fields. This can probably be seen more clearly if it is converted to a table, which is an equally usable format for mail merging:

Title	Firstname	Surname	Address 1	Town	County	Postcode
Mr	John	Smith	1 Church Street	Bradford	West Yorks	BD22 3XL
Ms	Gloria	Brown	22 High Street	Bath	Wilts	BA34 9ZZ

With many addresses that match this format (and of course, many addresses do not, so in reality the format has to be more complex, in other words, more fields), you can carry out a mail merge. You can create the list using whatever approach you prefer.

Setting Up Mail Merge

You can carry out mail merging either directly by using the Mail Merge toolbar (see Figure 18.4) or by using the Mail Merge Wizard. We will look at the two approaches in parallel.

 Mouse over the icons on the Mail Merge toolbar to see what they do.

FIGURE 18.4   The Mail Merge toolbar

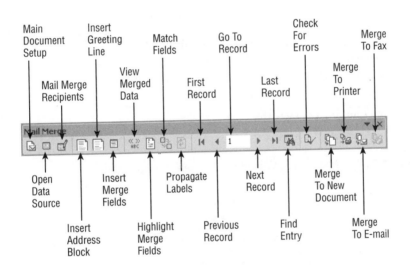

To use the Mail Merge Wizard, choose Tools ➤ Letters And Mailings ➤ Mail Merge Wizard. The Mail Merge Wizard opens (see Figure 18.5). (Only the top half of the window is shown; at the bottom are navigation links to take you backward and forward through the steps.) The first thing you have to do is decide what kind of document you are working on. For the purposes of this example, choose Letters.

FIGURE 18.5   Mail Merge Wizard, step 1: Select document type

At the bottom of the window, you can move to the next stage, Select Starting Document. In Step 2 (not shown here) you can use your current document, start from a template (in other words, create a new document), or use an existing mail merge document and modify it. If you use the Main Document Setup icon on the Mail Merge toolbar to do this step, you'll see a slightly different window for this step.

Create a new letter, which at the moment you should leave blank. (Note that, if you decide to do this and you have another document open, the contents of the open document are deleted, so it probably makes sense to open a new document first.)

The next step—shown in Figure 18.6—allows you to specify the *data source*, in other words, where the list of recipients is to be taken from. There are three options:

- Use an existing list.

- Select from Outlook contacts (see Part 7).

- Type a new list.

FIGURE 18.6   Mail Merge Wizard, step 3: Select recipients

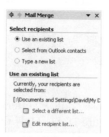

If you choose to use an existing list, browse through the system in the usual way until you find the file you want and open it, producing the Mail Merge Recipients window (see Figure 18.7). (For briefness, there are only two records in this file.) This window can also be opened from the Open Data Source icon on the Mail Merge toolbar.

FIGURE 18.7   The Mail Merge Recipients window

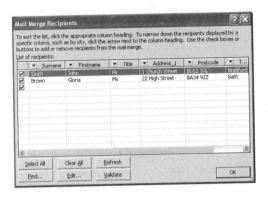

If you decide to create a data source (that is, type a new list), the New Address List window opens (see Figure 18.8), in which you can enter data. Microsoft has provided a standard set of fields, but they are based on U.S. addresses. You can, however, customise this by selecting the Customize button, which opens the Customize Address List window shown in Figure 18.9. This means that you can use some of the Microsoft fields, rename them, or even start from scratch by deleting them all and adding new ones. Once you are happy with the fields, click OK, which returns you to the previous window (which has, in fact stayed open). Now you can go ahead and enter data. When you click Close, a Save window is displayed like those you've seen previously.

FIGURE 18.8   The data entry screen open in Mail Merge

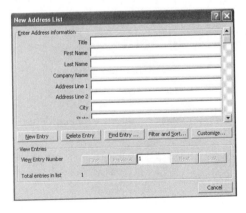

FIGURE 18.9 Choosing fields for the data source

You can also edit existing data, whether you create a new file or use an existing one. Click Edit Recipient List in the Mail Merge Wizard or click the Mail Merge Recipients icon on the Mail Merge toolbar. In either case, you see the Mail Merge Recipients window (see Figure 18.7). If you then select a record and click the Edit button, the Data Form window shown in Figure 18.10 opens.

FIGURE 18.10 Editing data

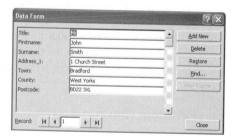

Creating the Main Document

Add the fields that you've created into the main document using the following steps.

1. Move to Step 4 of the Mail Merge Wizard, titled Write Your Letter (see Figure 18.11).

FIGURE 18.11 Mail Merge Wizard, step 4: Write your letter

2. Write your letter, which is the open document, in the usual way, but when you want to insert information from the list (in other words, information that is different for each recipient), you have two options: use an address block and/or greeting line, or use the More Items option.

3. Clicking Address Block (or the Insert Address Block icon on the Mail Merge toolbar) opens the Insert Address Block window shown in Figure 18.12. This allows you to define what is included in the address block. The preview at the bottom shows what it will look like. Microsoft has defined a series of fields.

FIGURE 18.12 Formatting the address block

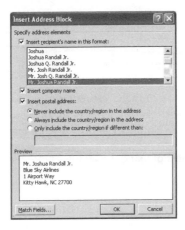

4. However, in case your fields are not the same, there is a facility by which you can match your fields to the Microsoft fields. Click the Match Fields button (or the Match Fields icon on the Mail Merge toolbar) to open the Match Fields window (see Figure 18.13). If you click the down arrow alongside one of the boxes on the right-hand side, you can decide which of your fields should match the Microsoft field in question. When you click OK in the Match Fields window and then OK in the Insert Address Block window, you insert the address block in the form that you have chosen.

FIGURE 18.13 Matching fields

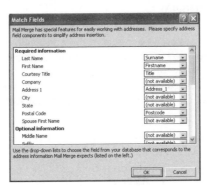

5.   Click Greeting Line in the Mail Merge Wizard to open the Greeting Line dialog box shown in Figure 18.14. (The dialog box can also be opened by clicking the Insert Greeting Line icon on the Mail Merge toolbar.)You can choose the greeting line format you want and preview it at the bottom of the dialog box.

FIGURE 18.14   Formatting the greeting line

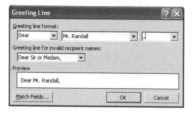

6.   Click the Match Fields button in the Greeting Line dialog box to open the Match Fields window. When you're finished, a form letter is produced that looks like Figure 18.15. You can of course add other text. You'll see shortly what a merged letter looks like.

FIGURE 18.15   The effect of using the address block and greeting line options

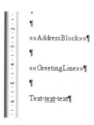

7.   You do not, however, have to use these facilities. Click More Items in the Mail Merge Wizard to see a list of all your fields. You can insert them directly, as well as using the Microsoft address fields; you can again access Match Fields. (This window can also be opened by clicking the Insert Merge Fields icon on the Mail Merge toolbar.)

WARNING   While there are some aspects of the address block that you can customise, others appear to be fixed. For example, the postcode follows the city on the same line, but without a comma (in spite of what the preview shows). Thus, inserting fields individually is probably worth the very small extra time required, because you can design the document to look exactly as you want it.

Using the Insert Fields window, you can insert only one field at a time, so this can be rather tedious. A better way is to customise the Mail Merge toolbar and add the Insert Merge Fields icon (or get someone to do it for you). This provides a much easier way of inserting fields directly. When you click the icon, you get a drop-down list from which you can select fields.

The form letter then looks like Figure 18.16. There are also Word fields, which are outside the scope of the ECDL, but which allow you to make Mail Merge much more powerful, for example, by adding conditions.

FIGURE 18.16   The form letter after customising the fields

Note that you enter the fields in the same way whether you use an existing list or create a new one.

Once your letter is complete, you can save it. You may also see messages asking if you want to save the associated mailing list. If it is a new mailing list, you probably want to do this. If you have made changes to an existing list, you need to review your options.

Now move to step 5 of the Mail Merge Wizard (see Figure 18.17) to preview your letters.

FIGURE 18.17   Mail Merge Wizard, step 5: Preview your letters

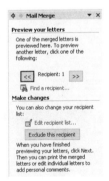

If you don't like what you see, go back to the previous steps. Two options in the Mail Merge toolbar are useful here, both of which toggle. The first is View Merged Data, which allows you to switch back and forth between seeing the fields and the actual merged data. The second is Highlight Merge Fields, which does what it says—highlights the merge fields, whether or not you are viewing the fields or the merged data. It is obviously more useful if you are looking at the data.

Note in step 5 that you can move through the recipients and, if you wish, exclude particular ones, although of course this is probably practical only for a relatively short list of recipients.

Let's review the steps of mail merging:

1. Open your letter file. Select Tool ➤ Letters And Mailings ➤ Mail Merge and select Letters in step 1 of the wizard.

2. Move to step 2 and choose what to use as the text of your letter. We suggest that you choose Use The Current Document so as to use your letter.

3. In step 3, choose a source for the recipients. Again, you can choose Type A New List, but we suggest that you use the table file that you created earlier. Select Use An Existing List and then browse to find it.

4. In step 4, insert the fields that you want to use, either using address blocks and greeting lines or inserting the fields individually using the More Items option.

5. In step 5, you can preview your merged document and go back to previous steps if you are unhappy.

6. Finally, in step 6, you carry out the merge. Try merging to a file (Edit Individual Letters), so that you can see what has happened. You can then print the document if you wish.

Producing Address Labels in Mail Merge

If, instead of producing a letter, you want to produce a set of address labels, choose Labels in step 1 of the Mail Merge Wizard (shown earlier in Figure 18.5) and select (or create) a file, just as for a mailing letter. For now, use the same file you used for the letter. Going to step 2 of the wizard now produces some different options.

The Label Options window opens (see Figure 18.18) where you can choose the type of label you want to use. Unfortunately, there is no preview, and the file does not tell you how many labels per sheet. However, the dimensions are given, and from these, you can work out which label you need.

FIGURE 18.18   Choosing the label type

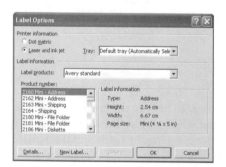

Once you have selected an appropriate label size—and remember to select the A4 and A5 size, rather than the (US) standard—a window opens (see Figure 18.19, where the merge fields are also shown) that does show you the size, so you can go back and change it if you wish. Note that, if you change the label size, you have to re-enter your merge fields.

FIGURE 18.19   The chosen label type

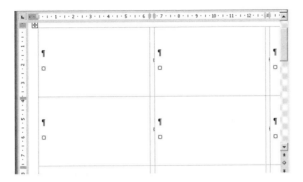

In step 3, choose the recipient list in the same way as for a letter. In step 4, enter the merge fields, in a similar way to that which you used for the letter (see Figure 18.19). A useful option is to be able to replicate the fields on every label (Update All Labels).

When you first see your main document, it looks like Figure 18.19. However, if you switch back to it after merging, the second and subsequent records have acquired an extra field <<Next Record>> (see Figure 18.20). The reason for this should be obvious.

The Populate Labels icon on the Mail Merge toolbar does the same as Update All Labels and adds the text <<Next Record>> at the same time.

Do not use the Envelopes And Labels option on the Tools ➤ Letters And Mailings menu. This has a somewhat different use, which is outside the scope of the ECDL.

FIGURE 18.20   The chosen label with fields replicated

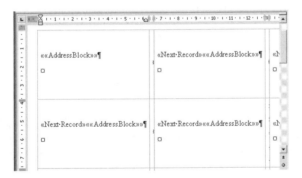

Options for Mail Merge Output

The final part of mail merging is the actual merge, which is carried out in the same way for both letters and labels.

Move to step 6 of the Mail Merge Wizard, shown in Figure 18.21. You can either merge straight to the printer or to a file, which you can edit. These options, as well as merging to an e-mail or to a fax (if you have a fax connection set up) are also available from the Mail Merge toolbar.

FIGURE 18.21 Mail Merge Wizard, step 6: Complete the merge

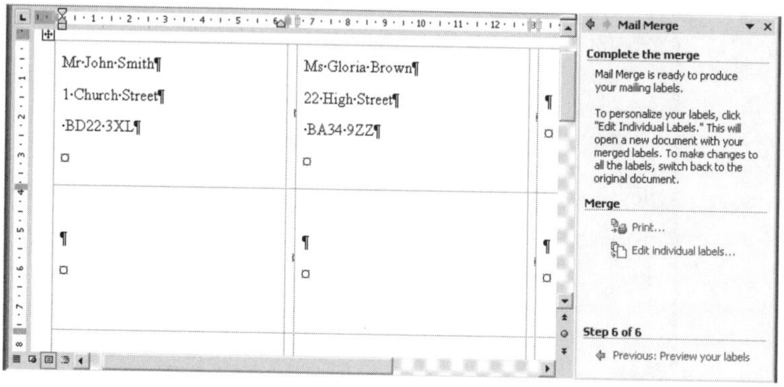

When you click Merge, another dialog box opens, allowing you to choose which records to merge.

In previous versions of Word, you could, at this stage, choose whether to leave blanks if a field is empty. Now, by default, Word does not leave blank lines, probably because in most situations where you are producing letters or labels, this is what you would choose anyway. It is possible to use Word fields to handle this, but this is outside the scope of the ECDL.

There are also options on the Mail Merge toolbar for launching the merge directly and checking that the merge is doing what you want. Once you are happy, launch the merge and get ready to put everything into (window) envelopes and stick on the stamps! Of course, if you have also created labels, you can use these instead of window envelopes!

You can always go back and try other options to see how these change what happens. Experiment with using the toolbar buttons instead of the Mail Merge Wizard.

Before you go on to the next exercise, save your document, calling it, for example, `letter_merge1.doc`.

Summary

The first part of this chapter looked at outputting the documents you have produced. The Print Preview option allows you to check your document before you print it. You can set the print parameters and the printer properties so that the document is printed as you wish.

The second part of this chapter described Word's Mail Merge facility. You saw how to set up a mail merge for a letter and for labels.

Module Review Questions

1. When do you use a scroll bar?
2. What is the difference between changing font size and zooming in or out?
3. What happens if you type in (a) Overstrike and (b) Insert modes?
4. How does a text file differ from a Word file?
5. What does the Print Layout view show that the Normal view does not?
6. What is meant by non-printing characters?
7. What are the keyboard shortcuts for Cut, Copy, Paste, Undo, and Redo?
8. Why should you be careful if you want to use Replace to change "cat" to "dog" in the following text: "The cat jumped at the birds and scattered them"?
9. Why should you only use tabs (rather than tables) for short items?
10. If you plan to put a border around the pages in your document, what should you take into account and why?
11. If you are resizing a figure with the mouse, what should you do to ensure that the aspect ratio (the ratio of width to height) is unaltered?
12. What is meant by *special characters*?

Answers to Module Review Questions

1. Use a scroll bar when the document you are viewing is larger than the screen on which you are viewing it.

2. Changing font size changes the size of the text in the document, while zooming in or out changes the magnification at which you are viewing the document (which is itself unchanged).

3. In Overstrike mode, you write over (replace) the characters that already exist at the cursor position. In Insert mode, you add characters at the cursor position, displacing but not replacing the characters that are already present.

4. A text file contains only the words and spaces (and a limited amount of formatting information, such as carriage returns and tabs). A Word file contains detailed formatting information in addition to the words and spaces.

5. The Print Layout view shows formatted pages, including graphics.

6. Non-printing characters control the way text appears but do not appear in the printed document. Examples of non-printing characters are the carriage return, the tab marker, the soft carriage return, and the space.

7. The keyboard shortcuts are Ctrl+**X** (Cut), Ctrl+**C** (Copy), Ctrl+**V** (Paste), Ctrl+**Z** (Undo), and Ctrl+**Y** (Redo).

8. If you simply replace "cat" with "dog", you will get "The dog jumped at the birds and sdogtered them".

9. Only use tabs for short items, because tabs work on a line-by-line basis, and if the text overlaps the next tab position, that position is ignored and the alignment is no longer correct.

10. Make sure to take into account the page size relative to the paper size, because most laser printers do not print to the edge of the paper, and a border too near the edge of the paper will not be printed.

11. Hold down the Shift key to retain the aspect ratio of a figure.

12. Special characters are characters such as curly quotes ("") and en and em rules (– and —, respectively) that do not appear on the keyboard.

ECDL Module 4: Spreadsheets

Chapter

19

Using the Spreadsheet Application

IN THIS CHAPTER YOU WILL LEARN HOW TO

✓ Open and close a spreadsheet application.

✓ Make modifications to an existing spreadsheet.

✓ Save a new or existing spreadsheet.

✓ Use the application Help functions.

✓ Switch between worksheets and open a workbook.

✓ Change the spreadsheet view mode.

✓ Use the page view magnification tool/zoom tool.

✓ Modify the toolbar display.

✓ Save an existing spreadsheet under another file format.

This module is concerned with the subject of spreadsheet applications and is based on Microsoft's Excel XP software. Before embarking on the task of learning how to use Excel, it is important to understand what spreadsheet packages are and what role they play in modern PC-based computing.

The modern *spreadsheet* package is a tool that can be used to create, edit, modify, process, and display information in tabular form. Essentially this means data that is normally arranged in rows and columns, as, for example, in an accounting ledger. However, spreadsheet software is not only suitable for dealing with accounting data; it can be used for practically any task that involves the need to process numbers or perform calculations.

Like most other spreadsheet packages, Excel is based on the principle of providing the user with a very large virtual sheet of paper on which to record and manipulate information on screen. This concept of using a large sheet of paper is a fundamental characteristic of the typical spreadsheet package. If you were to compare Excel's virtual spreadsheet to a physical piece of paper, the paper would be approximately 5 metres wide and 325 metres long! Computer spreadsheets are generally divided up into rows and columns in the form of a grid of small rectangles called *cells*, where data is recorded.

However, the primary feature of the spreadsheet is its ability to perform calculations on the data stored in cells, and the fact that once "programmed," a spreadsheet can update itself automatically.

Most modern Windows-based spreadsheet packages such as Excel provide extensive formatting capabilities so that data doesn't have to appear in rather plain-looking tables. Using these capabilities, it is possible to produce spreadsheets with an attractive and professional-looking appearance. In addition, Excel can also be used to process raw data and present it in a pictorial form such as charts and graphs.

This part of the study guide is structured in chapters that are designed to be followed in a logical sequence. Therefore you are advised to work through this part one chapter at a time from the beginning.

First Steps with Spreadsheets

Before you begin, you need to check whether Microsoft Excel is already installed on your PC. Click the Start button and select the All Programs option. You should see a list of installed programs. Excel may be listed here, or it may be under the Microsoft Office option; this depends on how your system has been set up, as in the example in Figure 19.1.

FIGURE 19.1   Opening Excel using the Start button

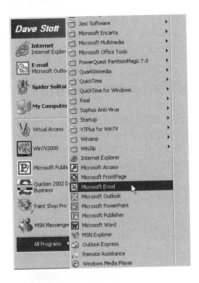

Note that there may be other Microsoft Office programs also installed on your PC such as Word, Access, or PowerPoint. However, it should be fairly obvious whether Excel is installed or not.

 If Microsoft Excel is not already installed on your PC, follow the instructions for setting up the software as detailed in the Office XP "Getting Started" guide. These instructions are quite straightforward, but if you have any difficulty installing the software, seek advice from your computer supplier or system administrator.

Assuming that Excel is installed on your PC, you're now ready to start learning how to use it to create and edit spreadsheets. Excel is an extremely flexible package and can be used to create a wide variety of spreadsheets that can be used for many different purposes. Your Excel spreadsheets can be as simple or as complicated as you like; you'll soon learn how to create basic spreadsheets that can be enhanced to produce professional-looking reports.

In this initial chapter, you'll learn some basic procedures that allow you to open and save spreadsheet files, create new worksheets, use the online Help facilities, and perform basic adjustments.

Getting Started with Excel

In this exercise, you'll look at what happens when you start Excel, and you'll learn how to open, close, and save spreadsheets (also referred to as *workbooks*). You'll also learn how to save a spreadsheet in another file format and how you can access the online Help facilities within Excel when you need them.

Whilst Excel is recognised as a *spreadsheet* application, Microsoft has adopted the terms *workbook* and *worksheet* to describe two different aspects of the package. The term *workbook* refers to the actual spreadsheet file; a workbook can consist of a number of separate *worksheets*. In other words, a workbook is a collection of spreadsheets. Things will become clearer when you look at each of these elements in turn.

Understanding Excel's Hieroglyphics

When you initially open and as you eventually use Excel, you'll see a myriad of different buttons and images that you'll need to interpret. Microsoft has attempted to make these images as intuitive as possible, but sometimes they can seem like obscure hieroglyphics. Before you get started, Table 19.1 lists some of the buttons and icons that you might see in Excel and what they mean.

TABLE 19.1 Descriptions of Excel's Graphical Images

Excel Image	Description
	New document (workbook) icon tool
	Open document (workbook) icon tool
	Save icon tool
	Spelling icon tool
	Border (cell-formatting) icon tool
	Paste icon tool
	Copy icon tool
	Cut icon tool
	AutoSum icon tool
	Undo icon tool
	Clock icon tool. Used when formatting headers and footers.
	Tick icon. Used to accept changes when entering or editing in the Formula Bar.

TABLE 19.1   Descriptions of Excel's Graphical Images *(continued)*

Excel Image	Description
	Sort Ascending icon tool
	Sort Descending icon tool
	Paste Function icon tool
	Center (data within cell) icon tool
	Print icon tool
	Print Preview icon tool
	Chart Wizard icon tool
	Redo icon tool
	Format Painter icon tool
	Merge and Center icon tool
	Format Chart Area icon tool
	Window close control button
	Up/Down scroll buttons
	Smart Tag alert button
	Drop-down list control button
	Taskbar Start button
	Cursor pointer displayed when expanding column widths or row heights
	Crosshair plus cursor

TABLE 19.1 Descriptions of Excel's Graphical Images *(continued)*

Excel Image	Description
⊕	Cross pointer
+	Cursor (crosshairs)

Creating a New Workbook

To create a new workbook in Excel, take the following steps:

1. Open Excel by selecting it from the Start ➤ Programs option on the Taskbar, as shown earlier in Figure 19.1.

   Each time you start Excel, a new blank workbook is automatically created at the same time. By default, this workbook contains three separate worksheets, shown as tabbed sections at the bottom of the screen and labelled Sheet1, Sheet2, and Sheet3, as in Figure 19.2.

FIGURE 19.2 Excel opens a new blank spreadsheet when it is started.

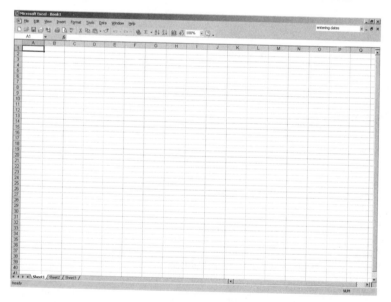

You can use the blank workbook to create your own spreadsheets from scratch, or you can open an existing workbook.

2. For the moment, let's ignore the creation of new spreadsheets and concentrate on opening an existing workbook instead. To open an existing workbook, choose File ➤ Open on the menu bar at the top of the screen. The Open File dialog box opens, and by default, the folder My Documents is displayed, as in Figure 19.3.

FIGURE 19.3   The Open File dialog box showing the My Documents folder

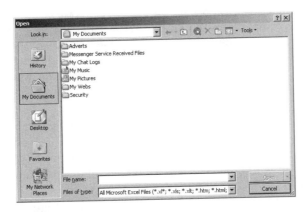

Don't be alarmed if there are no workbooks displayed for you to open. The chances are that if this is the first time you have run Excel, there are no workbooks in the My Documents folder, so you need to look somewhere else to find an existing workbook to open.

Using the Look In drop-down list, select the `C:\Windows\Program Files\Office\Office10\` folder. Once selected, you should see an entry called `SAMPLES.XLS`. Select this and click the Open button. The SAMPLES workbook is loaded into Excel, and your screen should look like Figure 19.4.

FIGURE 19.4   The Excel main screen after opening the SAMPLES workbook file

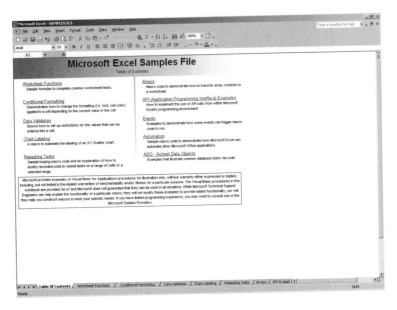

The preceding instructions assume that when Microsoft Office was installed on your computer, the standard default locations were used. If this is not the case, then the file SAMPLES.XLS may be located somewhere else, and you'll have to use the Find options in the Open dialog box to locate it. If the file does not exist on your hard disk, you can open it from the OFFICE1.CAB folder on the Microsoft Office XP CD-ROM.

Once SAMPLES.XLS has been opened in Excel, you may think that it doesn't look much like a spreadsheet. You're right because this particular workbook consists solely of examples of various Excel functions and operating techniques. For the moment, however, you'll use this workbook to demonstrate some of the file-management procedures available in Excel.

3. Before proceeding any further, make a copy of the workbook SAMPLES.XLS by saving a new version of it in the My Documents folder via the next steps.

4. On the menu bar, choose File ≻ Save As. The Save As dialog box opens, as in Figure 19.5.

FIGURE 19.5   The Save As dialog box with the filename highlighted

5. Select the My Documents folder using the Save In drop-down list and type the filename **Excel1** in the File Name box. Check that the Save As Type box says Microsoft Excel Workbook (*.xls) and click the Save button.

You can open several different Excel workbooks at the same time by following steps 1 and 2 and selecting the appropriate folders from which to load files. Similarly, you can save any Excel workbooks by following steps 4 and 5, changing both the folder and filenames as appropriate.

6. To close a workbook, choose File ➢ Close. If you've made any changes to an open work-book, when you try to close it you'll be asked whether you wish to save the changes you have made to the file, as shown in Figure 19.6.

FIGURE 19.6   The warning displayed if you attempt to close an unsaved workbook

If you click Yes, the file is saved with the existing filename, overwriting the original version. Choosing No will close the file without saving any of your changes. If you wish to keep the original version of the file as well as save your changes, click Cancel and use the File ➢ Save As option from the menu bar to save the current open workbook with a different filename from the original.

Getting Help from the Office Assistant

Let's look at the Help facilities available in Excel, which can provide you with online assistance when you need it. There are several different ways to trigger the Help functions within Excel; we'll deal with each method in turn.

When you started Excel, you may have noticed a small window, as shown in Figure 19.7. (If this window doesn't appear, simply press the F1 key on your keyboard.)

FIGURE 19.7   The Office Assistant

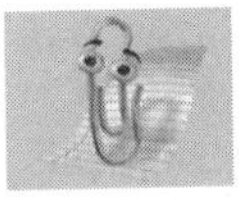

This is the Office Assistant, and it is designed to provide you with help if you encounter problems when using Excel. The Office Assistant, like the normal Microsoft Help facilities, is context-sensitive, which means that it tries to provide you with help based on what you are actually doing at the time.

There are several different "characters" available to act as Office Assistants. Depending on how your version of Microsoft Office has been configured, you may see any of the characters shown in Figure 19.8.

FIGURE 19.8 The various Office Assistant characters

If you click the Office Assistant, the pop-up dialog box in Figure 19.9 appears.

FIGURE 19.9 The Office Assistant asks you what you would like to do.

As you can see from the example in Figure 19.9, one of the best features of the Office Assistant is that you can simply type in a question and it tries to find the most appropriate help for you.

For example, type the words **Saving my work** and click the Search button. The Office Assistant displays a list of topics similar to those shown in Figure 19.10 for you to choose from.

FIGURE 19.10 Performing a query using the Office Assistant

Clicking an item in the list displays the text of that Help topic.

As well as the Office Assistant, you can access Help by choosing the Help ➤ Microsoft Excel Help option on the menu bar. As you can see in Figure 19.11, a window appears with three tabbed sections: Contents, Answer Wizard, and Index.

FIGURE 19.11   The Microsoft Excel Help window with the Contents tab showing sub-sections

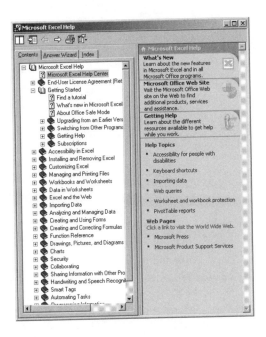

The Contents tab presents a list of Help contents for you to select from. Note that the main sections may have sub-sections. Clicking any of the topics displays the results on the right-hand side of the Microsoft Excel Help window.

The Index tab displays a list of indexed keywords that are available in the Help system. Simply click the index word you want and then click the Search button, as in Figure 19.12.

The Answer Wizard tab in the Microsoft Excel Help window allows you to search for a word or phrase; the Help system then shows you any matches that it finds. Once again, simply click a found topic and click Search to see it, as in Figure 19.13. Note that if your computer is connected to the Internet, you can also search for help using the Search On Web button in the Answer Wizard tab.

FIGURE 19.12 You can search for keywords in the Index section.

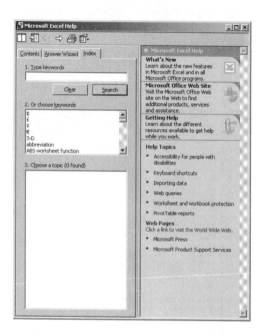

FIGURE 19.13 The Answer Wizard section allows you look for words or phrases.

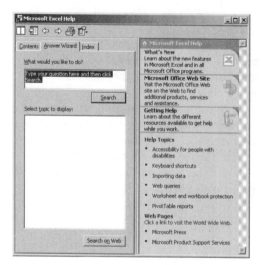

Help is always available in Excel no matter what task you are performing. The quickest way to get help is to press the F1 key on your keyboard.

Whichever method you use to access the Help system in Excel, you can see step-by-step help on most topics, as in Figure 19.14.

FIGURE 19.14 A specific Help topic on how to open a workbook.

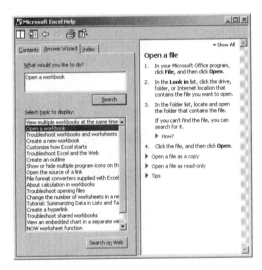

Switching between Open Worksheets

As mentioned previously, a single Excel workbook can consist of several separate worksheets that are shown as tabbed sections at the bottom of the screen. Try out these steps:

1. If the sample workbook (which you saved earlier with the name Excel1.xls) is not still open on your PC, open it by choosing File ➢ Open from the menu bar. Notice that there are a series of tabbed sections, as shown in Figure 19.15.

FIGURE 19.15 Tabbed sections in the Excel1 workbook

2. Now if you click the tab labelled Conditional Formatting, the contents of that worksheet are displayed, as in Figure 19.16.

FIGURE 19.16 The Conditional Formatting worksheet displayed in the Excel1 workbook

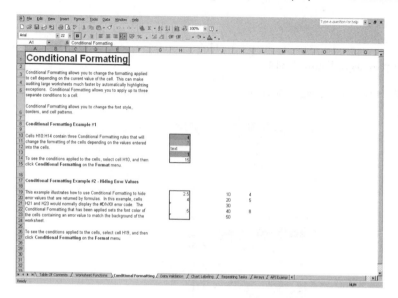

 Simply clicking a tab allows you to access different worksheets within a workbook.

Microsoft Excel also allows you to open several different workbooks at the same time:

1. With the Excel1 workbook still open, choose File ➢ Open. A new window called the Task Pane appears on the right-hand side of your screen, as shown in Figure 19.17.

FIGURE 19.17 The Task Pane window

2. The Task Pane shows a list of tasks that you can perform, in this case either opening an existing workbook or creating a new workbook. Click the Blank Workbook task, and a new empty workbook appears, as shown previously in Figure 19.2.

3. Notice that the original Excel1 workbook seems to have disappeared. In fact, it is still there, but it is no longer the active application. If you look at your Windows Taskbar (normally at the very bottom of your screen) there are now two versions of Microsoft Excel running with a workbook open in each one, as shown in Figure 19.18.

FIGURE 19.18   The Taskbar shows two Excel sessions running.

 You can have many copies of Excel running at the same time and switch between them simply by clicking the appropriate item on the Windows Taskbar.

Adjusting Basic Settings

Now that you've learnt how to start Excel and open, close, and save workbooks, let's investigate the main Excel screen in more detail.

In this section, you'll learn how to use the magnification/zoom tools, modify the toolbar display, freeze row and/or column titles, and modify your basic Excel preferences. You'll also look at how you can alter the way that Excel displays information and how you can alter the appearance and behaviour of Excel itself.

If it is not already open, start Excel, and, if for some reason a blank workbook isn't displayed, simply choose File ➢ New from the menu bar; the Task Pane shown earlier in Figure 19.17 appears.

Click the Blank Workbook option to create a new blank workbook; your display should now look like the example in Figure 19.19. If the Office Assistant window is displayed, close it by clicking the Close button in the top right-hand corner.

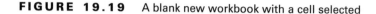

FIGURE 19.19   A blank new workbook with a cell selected

Using the Zoom and Magnification Tools

The example in Figure 19.19 shows the Normal view of an open workbook, but there are some options available for changing the display. First, you should know how to adjust the magnification level. Excel offers a Zoom feature that allows you to magnify the current worksheet being displayed. To use the Zoom feature, take the following steps:

1.   First, click cell reference E9 with the mouse, type the word **Test**, and press the Return or Enter key on your keyboard.

2.   Controlling the magnification or zoom level can be achieved in two ways:

   ▪   By using the Zoom icon drop-down list on the Standard toolbar, as in Figure 19.20.

FIGURE 19.20   Using the Zoom icon to change magnification

- By choosing View ➤ Zoom from the menu bar, which opens the Zoom window, as shown in Figure 19.21. Here you can select one of several pre-set levels of magnification or type your own preference in the Custom box.

FIGURE 19.21   The Zoom control window

Whichever method you use to adjust the zoom level, the area of the screen displaying the worksheet magnifies or shrinks the image relative to the main Excel window, as in Figures 19.22 and 19.23.

FIGURE 19.22   Zoom at 200%

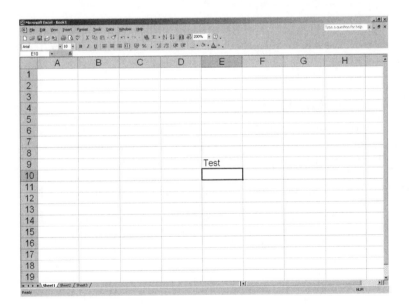

FIGURE 19.23   Zoom at 50%

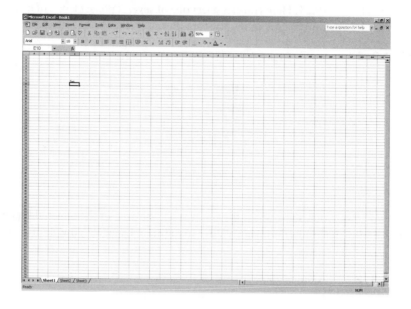

Notice that the menu bar and the toolbars are the same size, but the spreadsheet area being displayed is a different size.

Modifying the Toolbar

Excel has a total of 19 separate toolbars available. However, by default, only two of these are displayed at the top of the screen. The topmost toolbar is normally the Standard toolbar (Figure 19.24) and just below it is the Formatting toolbar (Figure 19.25).

FIGURE 19.24   The Standard toolbar (at the top of the screen by default)

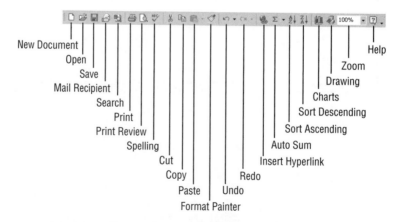

FIGURE 19.25   The Formatting toolbar (just below the Standard toolbar by default)

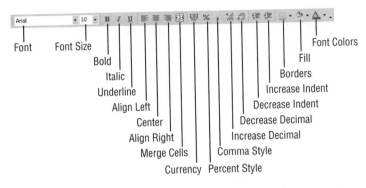

You can control which of the 19 toolbars are visible by using the View ➢ Toolbars option on the menu bar. Toolbars currently displayed are shown with a tick next to them, as in Figure 19.26. To add a toolbar to your display, simply select it from this menu. To hide any of these toolbars, simply click them again to remove the check mark; this will remove the toolbars from your display.

FIGURE 19.26   Selecting toolbars to be displayed

Freezing Panes

Excel has a way of locking selected columns or rows so that they are always visible, regardless of where you scroll in the worksheet. Take the following steps to freeze panes:

1. On the currently open worksheet, select cell A1 by clicking it with the left mouse button. Type the word **Date**. Select cell B1 and type the word **Time**. Select cell C1 and type the word **Task**. Your worksheet should now look similar to Figure 19.27, with the word **Test** still showing in cell E9.

FIGURE 19.27   Text entered in cells A1, B1, and C1

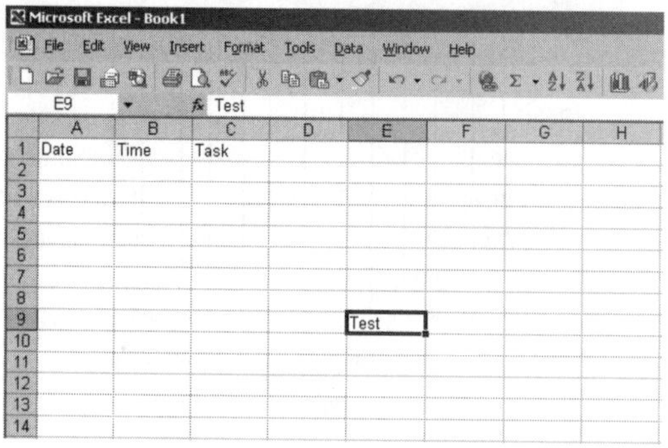

	A	B	C	D	E	F	G	H
1	Date	Time	Task					
2								
3								
4								
5								
6								
7								
8								
9					Test			
10								
11								
12								
13								
14								

2. Use the scroll bar on the right-hand side of the worksheet to move downward. Notice that the text entered on the top row disappears off the top of the screen, and you can no longer see the column headings. Fortunately Excel has a way of "locking" or "freezing" rows or columns so that they that are always displayed.

As well as using the scroll bar, you can move up and down within a worksheet by pressing the Page Up and Page Down keys on your keyboard or by using the up arrow or down arrow cursor control keys.

3. To freeze the top horizontal pane, you need to select the row underneath the row you want to freeze. Use the scroll bar to move back to the top of the worksheet and then click on the number 2 to select the entire second row, as shown in Figure 19.28.

FIGURE 19.28   Selecting the entire second row in the worksheet

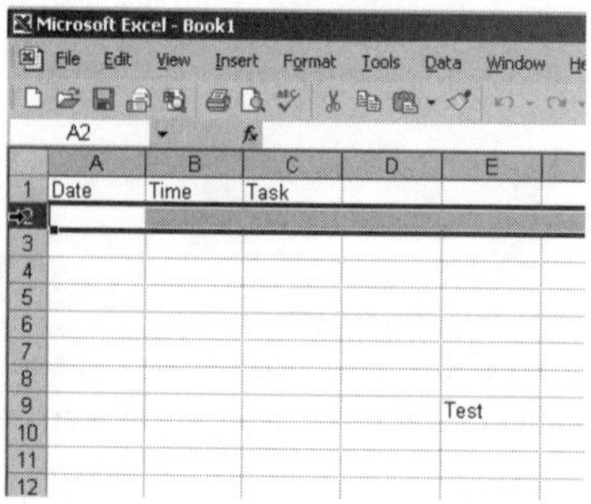

	A	B	C	D	E
1	Date	Time	Task		
2					
3					
4					
5					
6					
7					
8					
9					Test
10					
11					
12					

4. Choose Window ➤ Freeze Panes. Now when you use the scroll bar to move downward, the top row (row 1) of the worksheet remains visible, as shown in Figure 19.29. When you're finished scrolling up and down the worksheet, select Window ➤ Unfreeze Panes to unlock the top row of the worksheet.

FIGURE 19.29   Worksheet with row 1 frozen

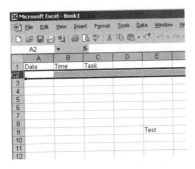

To freeze a column, select the column to the *right* of the column you want to freeze and select Window ➤ Freeze Panes.

Setting User Preferences

Excel has a series of options that are used to specify preferences for things such as the name of the user, where to look for worksheets to open, and which folder to save files in. To set these preferences, take the following steps:

1. Select Tools ➤ Options. The Options dialog box opens, as shown in Figure 19.30.

FIGURE 19.30   The Options dialog box

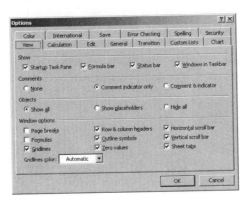

2. By default, the View tab is shown. Click the tab labelled General, as shown in Figure 19.31. Notice the User Name, which identifies the author of any workbooks created, and the Default File Location, which specifies where workbooks will be opened from and saved in. Normally the default file location is C:\My Documents, but it could be set to any folder. Change your settings as you require and click the Cancel button to close the Options window.

FIGURE 19.31   The General tab in the Options dialog box

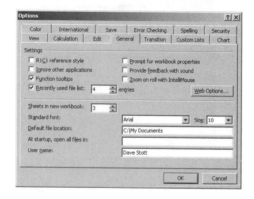

3. Finally, close the workbook by choosing File ➢ Close.

4. Despite the fact that this spreadsheet has only a few entries in a couple of cells, you'll use it in the next section. So when you're asked whether you want to save the changes you made to Book1.xls, click Yes and save the workbook in the My Documents folder with the name Test.xls.

Saving Documents in Different Formats

Excel uses its own file format with the file extension .xls for storing workbooks. However, there may be occasions when you need to save a spreadsheet in a different format, for example, to transfer text into a word-processing package or to use spreadsheet data in a database.

In this section, you'll learn how to save an existing spreadsheet under another file format: a text file, a document template, a software type, or a version number. You'll also learn how to save a document in a format appropriate for posting to a website.

Options for Saving in Excel

Take the following steps to save Excel spreadsheets, or parts thereof, in different formats:

1. If it is not already open, start Excel and open the Test.xls workbook that you saved in the My Documents folder in the previous section.

2. When you choose File ➤ Save As, the Save As dialog box opens, as in Figure 19.32.

FIGURE 19.32 The Save As dialog box, where you can decide on the target folder and filename

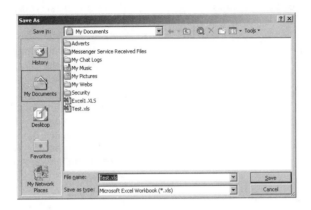

3. As well as being able to specify a filename and a location (folder) for saving the workbook, you can also specify the file type by clicking the drop-down list on the Save As Type box, as in Figure 19.33.

FIGURE 19.33 Using the Save As Type option to save a worksheet in a different file format

Excel allows you to save a spreadsheet in a variety of file formats that are listed in Table 19.2.

TABLE 19.2 File Format Options in Excel

Save as type	Extension	Used to save
Microsoft Excel workbook (Microsoft Excel 2002)	.xls	A normal Excel workbook.
Template (Microsoft Excel 2002)	.xlt	A workbook as a template for creating similar spreadsheets.
Workspace (Microsoft Excel 2002)	.xlw	A file format that saves display information about open workbooks so you can later resume work with the same window sizes, print areas, screen magnification, and display settings. A workspace file doesn't contain the workbooks themselves.
Microsoft Excel 97–2002 & 5.0/95 workbook	.xls	This format saves two versions of a workbook—one with the Microsoft Excel 97–2002 file format and one with the Microsoft Excel 5.0/95 file format—in the same .xls file.
Microsoft Excel 5.0/95 workbook	.xls	Saves the workbook in Microsoft Excel 5.0/95 format only.
Microsoft Excel version 4.0 workbook	.xlw	Saves the workbook in Microsoft Excel 4.0 format only; saves only worksheets, chart sheets, and macro sheets.
HTML	.htm	Saves the workbook using the standard markup language used for documents on the World Wide Web. HTML uses tags to indicate how web browsers should display page elements such as text and graphics and how to respond to user actions.
Web archive	.mht	Used to save multiple web pages as a single archive file.
XML spreadsheet	.xml	Saves a workbook using the Extensible Markup Language (XML) as a method for putting structured data (such as that in a worksheet) in a text file that follows standard guidelines and can be read by a variety of applications.

TABLE 19.2   File Format Options in Excel *(continued)*

Save as type	Extension	Used to save
Microsoft Excel version 4.0 sheet formats (including Microsoft Excel macro or international macro sheets)	`.xls, .xlc, .xlm`	Formats that save only the active worksheet rather than the entire workbook.
Microsoft Excel version 3.0 formats	`.xls, .xlc, .xlm`	Formats that save only the active worksheet rather than the entire workbook.
Microsoft Excel version 2.x formats	`.xls, .xlc, .xlm`	Formats that save only the active worksheet rather than the entire workbook.
Lotus 1-2-3 file format 4.0	`WK4 (*.wk4)`	Saves the entire workbook.
Lotus 1-2-3 file format 3.x and Lotus 1-2-3/W	`WK3 (*.wk3), WK3 FM3 (*.wk3)`	Saves only worksheets and chart sheets.
Lotus 1-2-3 file format 2.x	`WK1 (*.wk1), WK1 (FMT) (*.wk1), WK1 (ALL) (*.wk1)`	Saves only the active worksheet.
Lotus 1-2-3 file format 1.0 and 1.0A	`1.0 and 1.0A`	Saves only the active worksheet.
Formatted text (space-delimited)	`*.prn`	Lotus space-delimited format. Saves only the active worksheet.
Text (tab-delimited) (Windows), Text (Macintosh), Text (OS/2 or MS-DOS)	`*.txt`	Used to save spreadsheet data in a format for use with other applications. Saves only the active worksheet.
CSV (comma-separated values) (Windows), CSV (Macintosh), CSV (OS/2 or MS-DOS)	`*.csv`	Used to save spreadsheet data in a format for use with other applications. Saves only the active worksheet.
DIF (Data Interchange Format)	`*.dif`	Used to save spreadsheet data in a format for use with other applications. Saves only the active worksheet.

TABLE 19.2   File Format Options in Excel *(continued)*

Save as type	Extension	Used to save
DBASE II, III, and IV	*.dbf	Opens and saves only the active worksheet.
Quattro Pro for MS-DOS	*.wq1	Opens and saves only the active worksheet.
Microsoft Works version 2.0 for Windows and Microsoft Works for MS-DOS	*.wks	Opens only Microsoft Works version 2.0 for Windows or Microsoft Works for MS-DOS spreadsheets.

In addition, you can save the data in an Excel workbook in a format that is suitable for publishing web pages on the Internet.

Closing Down Excel

Closing down the Excel application is very similar to closing any other Windows-based application. You can click the right uppermost Close Window control button or choose File ➢ Exit from the menu bar to close your spreadsheet application. If any document you are working on at the time has not been saved in its current form, Excel will ask you if you want to save the changes before closing the application.

Summary

In the initial section on Excel in this chapter, you learnt the procedures necessary to start the application and to open any existing workbook files. You also learnt how to save workbooks and how to use both the Office Assistant and the Help facility to obtain help relevant to the procedures being carried out. Finally, you learnt how to switch between worksheets and any open workbooks.

The second section of this chapter explained how to use the Zoom controls to increase or decrease the size of the worksheet image being viewed. In addition, you looked at how to control the displaying of toolbars in Excel. You also saw how it is possible to freeze an area of a worksheet (for example, the top row) so that its contents always remain visible when scrolling through the worksheet. Finally, you explored how to modify the your basic preferences within Excel.

In the final section of this chapter, you learnt about the ways that you can save Excel spreadsheets in various formats so that the information they contain can be used in other applications such as Microsoft Word or other spreadsheet packages such as Lotus 1-2-3. You also saw how to generate web pages so that Excel spreadsheet data can be used on the Internet.

You should now have a better understanding of the main elements of the Excel screen—how to control the display of information and how to manage where Excel stores and loads worksheets from. You should also be able to save your Excel documents in a variety of formats.

Chapter

20

Cells

IN THIS CHAPTER YOU WILL LEARN HOW TO

✓ Enter numbers, dates, text, and simple formulas into a cell.

✓ Select cells, rows, and columns.

✓ Insert and delete rows and columns.

✓ Modify column widths and row heights.

✓ Edit data in cells.

✓ Use the Undo command.

✓ Use the Copy and Paste tools to duplicate and move cell contents.

✓ Use the AutoFill tool to copy and increment data entries.

✓ Move or copy cell contents between active worksheets and workbooks.

✓ Delete cell contents in a selected cell range.

✓ Search and replace specified cell content.

✓ Use the Replace command to change content in a worksheet.

✓ Sort selected data in alphabetic or numerical order.

Now that you've become familiar with the basic concepts of spreadsheets, it's time to look in more detail at how the cells in Excel are used to store data.

However, before delving into the package too deeply, you need to understand a few preliminary concepts regarding navigating around spreadsheets.

Spreadsheet Navigation

As described in the introduction, spreadsheets consist of a vast number of cells arranged in the form of a grid. In Excel, each cell is referenced by a set of coordinates based on its column and row position, for example A1, D12, AD1020, and so on. Each worksheet has a total of 256 columns referenced as A through IV and 65536 rows numbered consecutively 1 through 65536. This means that a single Excel worksheet has a total of 16,777,216 individual cells for you to use.

By default, in Excel, gridlines are used to display the individual cells on a worksheet; the currently active cell is evident by means of a border and shading of the associated column and row headings, as shown in Figure 20.1.

FIGURE 20.1   The current active cell marker, which in this case is cell B2

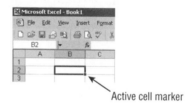

Active cell marker

There are several different ways to refer to cells and areas of the worksheet in Excel:

To Refer To:	Use:
The cell in column A and row 10	A10

To Refer To:	Use:
The range of cells in column A and rows 10 through 20	A10:A20
The range of cells in row 15 and columns B through E	B15:E15
All cells in row 5	5:5
All cells in rows 5 through 10	5:10
All cells in column H	H:H
All cells in columns H through J	H:J
The range of cells in columns A through E and rows 10 through 20	A10:E20

You can move the active cell marker in two ways:

- Use the four arrow cursor control keys on the keyboard to move to a cell that's above, below, to the left, or to the right.
- Click any inactive cell with the mouse.

Note that the mouse pointer is displayed as a thick outlined plus (+) sign when moved across the grid of cells. As you change from one active cell to another, the cell reference is automatically updated, as shown in the white box just above the column heading in Figure 20.1. Try out these two different methods so that you become familiar with both. Understanding how to navigate around a spreadsheet is a basic skill that's essential for the next step of this guide.

Inserting Data

You've now reached the point where you can start to insert data into a worksheet and see how Excel can be used for a variety of different tasks. In this section, you'll learn how to enter numbers, dates, and text into a cell.

Entering Data in a Cell

To create a new workbook and look at the options available for entering various types of data, take the following steps:

1. If it is not already running, start Excel and create a new workbook by selecting File ➢ New from the menu bar. Your screen should now look like the example in Figure 20.2.

FIGURE 20.2   Excel with a new workbook opened

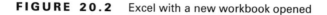

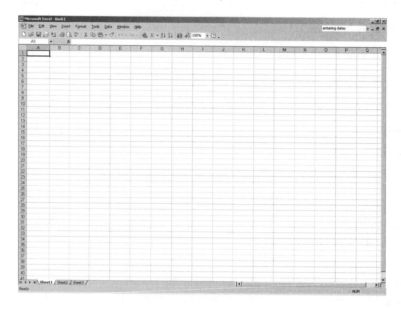

2. With the active cell marker at position A1, type the digits **34** and press the Return or Enter key on your keyboard. The active cell marker should automatically move down to cell A2. (If A2 is not the active cell, use the cursor keys or the mouse to make it active.)

3. Following the same procedure, enter the following numbers into these specific cells:

Cell Reference	Value
A2	11
A3	25
A4	9

Your worksheet should now look like the example in Figure 20.3. Notice how the numbers that you've entered have been aligned on the right-hand side of the cells; this is the default action in Excel when you enter numeric values.

FIGURE 20.3   Entering numeric data into a worksheet

4. Move the active cell marker to position B1 either by using the cursor keys on the keyboard or by clicking cell B1 with the mouse. Once cell B1 is active, type the word **Apples** and press the Return or Enter key on your keyboard. Again, the active cell marker should automatically move down so that cell B2 becomes active.

5. Following the same procedure, enter the following text in these specific cells:

Cell Reference	Value
B2	Oranges
B3	Bananas
B4	Melons

Your worksheet should now look like the example in Figure 20.4. Notice how the text has been aligned towards the left-hand side of the cells; this is the default action in Excel when you enter text.

FIGURE 20.4   Entering text into a worksheet

 When you enter digits into a cell, Excel recognises them as numbers. Conversely, when you enter letters, Excel interprets them as text. Mixing digits with letters always results in Excel interpreting the entry as text. However, on occasions you may need to enter digits so that they are treated solely as text. To do this simply place a single quote character (') at the beginning of the numbers you wish to enter, like this: '1999 or '2000; they appear as text in the cell.

6. As well as entering numbers and text in cells, you can also enter dates, which are treated differently by Excel. Select cell C1 and enter **21/05/03** and then press the Return or Enter key. Notice how Excel automatically formats the data you entered as "21/05/2003," as shown in Figure 20.5.

If you do not have your computer set up to recognise the international date format, you need to use the correct date format for your region; otherwise Excel will not interpret the data entered as a valid date. This also applies anywhere else in this module where dates are used.

FIGURE 20.5   Entering dates into a worksheet

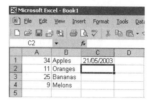

7. Next enter **5/2003** into cell C2. Once again, Excel recognises that you have entered a date and formats it automatically, as shown in Figure 20.6. Also notice how Excel assumes that the date should be the first of the month.

FIGURE 20.6   The first day of the month is assumed.

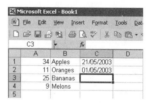

8. Now enter **22-5** into cell C3. This time Excel formats the data entered as 22-May, as shown in Figure 20.7.

FIGURE 20.7   Day and month format

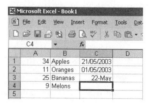

9. If you now enter **5/2003** into cell C4, notice that Excel formats the date as May-03, as shown in Figure 20.8.

FIGURE 20.8   Month and year format

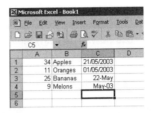

 If you wish to enter today's date into a cell, all you need to do is hold down the Ctrl key and press the semicolon (;) key on your keyboard.

10. Save the current workbook in the My Documents folder using the filename Fruit.xls.

Selecting Data

Now that you have a simple spreadsheet of your own to work with, you can start looking at the various ways to select areas of a worksheet in order to perform actions on complete ranges of cells. In this section, you'll learn how to select a cell or a range of adjacent or non-adjacent cells, select a row or column, select a range of rows or columns, and select the entire worksheet.

Selecting Data in Excel

To select data in Excel, take the following steps:

1. If it is not already running, start Excel and open the workbook from the last section called Fruit.xls, which you saved in the My Documents folder. Your screen should look like the example shown earlier in Figure 20.8.

2. You can select any single cell in an Excel spreadsheet by simply clicking on it. To select multiple cells, simply click any cell and whilst holding down the left mouse button, drag the cross pointer across the grid of cells and they turn blue-grey as they are selected. Release the mouse button when your selection is complete. On the Fruit worksheet, use this method to select all the cells in the range D6 to G14; your display should look like Figure 20.9.

 When selecting cells with the mouse, if you drag the pointer to any of the window boundaries, Excel simply scrolls the worksheet automatically to allow you to extend the selection beyond the area that's normally visible.

To deselect a selected range of cells, simply click once with the left mouse button on any non-selected cell, and the selection disappears.

An alternative method of selecting a range of cells is by using the keyboard. If you hold down the Shift key and use the cursor control keys, you can extend the range of selected cells outwards from the current active cell.

FIGURE 20.9   Cells D6 to G14 selected

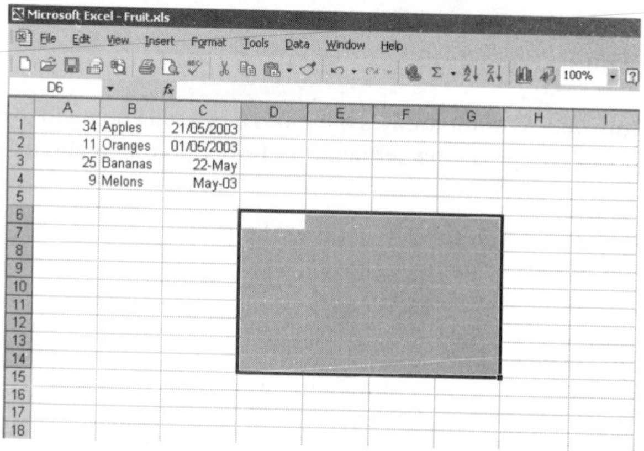

3. Normally, cell range selection is done on adjacent cells, but if you need to select non-adjacent cells, simply hold down the Ctrl key on the keyboard and then click the desired cells with the cross pointer, as shown in Figure 20.10.

FIGURE 20.10   Selecting non-adjacent cells of a worksheet

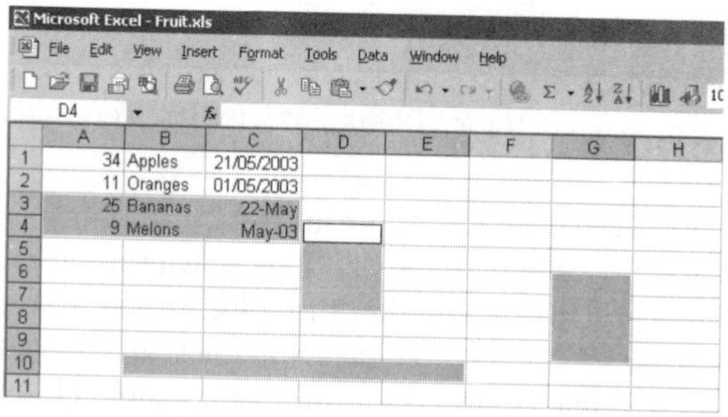

Once again, clicking any non-selected cell after releasing the Ctrl key deselects everything.

4. To select an entire row of cells, simply click any row number with the pointer. Similarly, to select several adjacent rows, drag the left or right arrow pointer across the row numbers

in the vertical row headings on the left-hand side of the screen. Try selecting rows 6 through 8, as shown in the example in Figure 20.11.

FIGURE 20.11   Selecting several entire rows of a worksheet

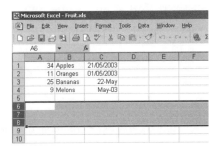

5. Likewise, if you need to select a complete column of cells, just move the cursor onto a column letter header at the top of the worksheet and click with the down arrow pointer; an entire column is selected. Similarly, to select several adjacent columns, drag the up or down arrow pointer across the column letters in the column headings. Try selecting columns B through E8, as shown in the example in Figure 20.12.

FIGURE 20.12   Selecting several entire columns of cells

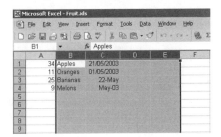

You can always tell when entire rows or columns have been selected because their respective heading labels are shown as white text on a black background, as opposed to the black text on a grey background when just a range of cells is selected.

6. Now suppose you need to select multiple non-adjacent rows or columns. You can do this by holding down the Ctrl key whilst clicking with the cross pointer on the rows or columns that you want to select, as shown in Figure 20.13. You can even select non-adjacent rows and columns at the same time, as in the example in Figure 20.14.

FIGURE 20.13 Selecting non-adjacent rows

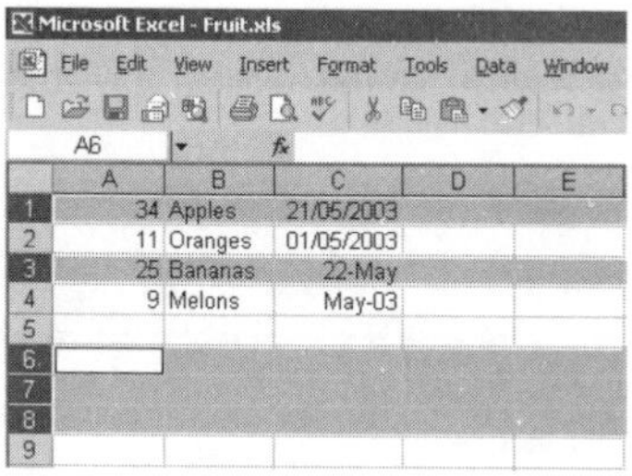

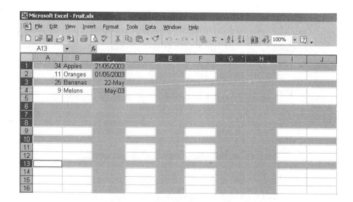

FIGURE 20.14 Selecting multiple rows and columns, both adjacent and non-adjacent

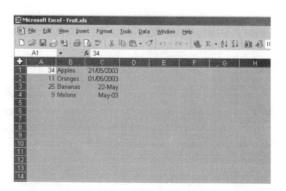

7. Finally, on the subject of selecting cells, there is a quick and easy way to select the entire worksheet. Simply click once with the cross pointer on the small grey box called the Select All button at the junction of the row numbers and column letters, as shown in Figure 20.15, and all the cells will be selected.

FIGURE 20.15 Selecting the entire worksheet

8. Save the current workbook, along with all the changes you've made so far by either clicking the Save icon on the Standard toolbar or by selecting File ➤ Save on the menu bar.

Editing Data

Previously, you've seen how to enter data into the cells of a worksheet. But it is just as important to know how to edit or change any existing data. Similarly, mistakes can be made when entering or editing data, and it's a good idea to learn how to correct any mistakes you make as quickly and easily as possible. In this section. you'll see how to insert additional data in a cell.

Inserting Additional Data in a Cell

Excel provides two methods for editing the contents of cells: using the Formula Bar and direct cell editing. The following steps teach you how to use both methods:

1. If it is not already running, start Excel and open the workbook called Fruit.xls that you saved in the My Documents folder. Your screen should now look like the example in Figure 20.16.

FIGURE 20.16   The Fruit workbook

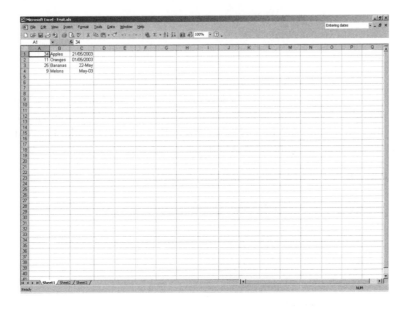

2. First, let's use the *Formula Bar*. Start by selecting cell B1. When you select a cell that has existing data stored in it, the contents are displayed in the Formula Bar next to the Paste Function icon, as shown in Figure 20.17.

FIGURE 20.17   The Formula Bar showing the contents of the selected cell B1

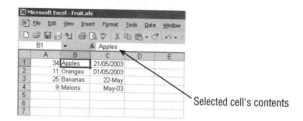

Selected cell's contents

3. If you now click in the Formula Bar to the right of the word Apples, notice that a small vertical flashing cursor appears immediately after the letter *s*. Using the left arrow cursor control key on your keyboard, move the vertical flashing cursor so that it appears exactly between the two letter *p*'s in the word *Apples*. Now type **ricots**. Your Formula Bar entry should now look like Figure 20.18. Notice how the contents of cell B1 change when you type the letters.

FIGURE 20.18   The Formula Bar showing the editing of the contents of B1

4. Now move the cursor to the end of the text in the Formula Bar, press the Backspace key on your keyboard four times, and remove the spurious letters left over from the word *Apples*. Press the Return or Enter key to apply the changes that you have made. The contents of cell B1 should now read *Apricots*, as shown in Figure 20.19.

FIGURE 20.19   The new edited contents of cell B1

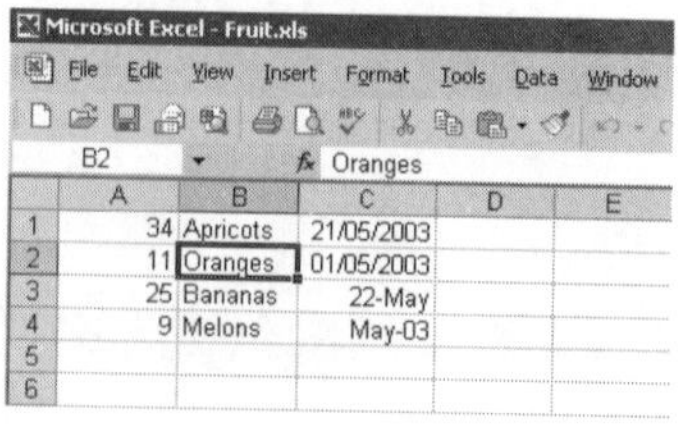

5. The second method of changing or modifying the contents of a cell involves the use of direct cell editing. Double-click with the left mouse button on cell A4. Notice that a vertical flashing

cursor appears just to the left of the number 9, as shown in Figure 20.20. As with the previous method, you can use the cursor control keys to move the flashing cursor to the left and right within the cell's text.

FIGURE 20.20   Using direct cell editing

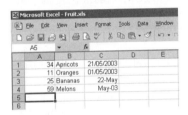

6. With the cursor just to the left of the number 9, type the number **5**, followed by the Return or Enter key on your keyboard. Now you see that the cell A4 reads 59 instead of just 9, as shown in Figure 20.21.

FIGURE 20.21   The result of directly editing cell A4

> If you need to replace the entire contents of a cell, simply double-click with your left mouse button the data displayed in the Formula Bar; all the text is selected. When you then start typing, all the existing text disappears and is replaced by whatever you type. Similarly, if you're using direct cell editing, a double-click with the left mouse button on the contents of the cell selects the contents and allows you to overtype it with replacement data.

7. When entering or editing data, it is quite easy to make mistakes that you might not spot until you have accepted the changes by pressing Return or Enter. Similarly, you might change your mind about a change and simply wish to revert to the previous contents. Fortunately, Excel has a special feature called Undo that can be extremely useful if you make a mistake when entering data. Using your current example worksheet, select Edit ➢ Undo from the menu bar; the contents of cell A4 reverts to the original value of 9 (as it was before you replaced it with the number 59 in step 6 previously), as shown in Figure 20.22.

The actual wording of the Edit ➤ Undo option on the menu bar depends on the last operation carried out by Excel. As a result, the word *Undo* may be followed by other words that describe what the last action was and what will be undone when you execute the command.

FIGURE 20.22   The result of performing an Undo means that the cell A4 reverts to its previous contents.

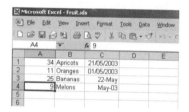

You can access the Undo feature quickly by clicking the Undo icon on the Standard toolbar. Each time you click it, the last action is undone. You can undo several mistakes or previous changes if necessary.

8. As well as the Undo command, Excel has a complementary command called Redo. Where the Undo command effectively cancels the last action, the Redo command repeats the last action. This can be rather confusing, so let's use a brief example to see the difference between the two commands. Select cell E4 and type the word **Good**, followed by the Return or Enter key. Now re-select cell E4 and type the word **Bad**, again followed by the Return or Enter key. Your worksheet should now look like Figure 20.23.

FIGURE 20.23   The result of entering two different words into cell E4

9. If you click the Undo icon on the Standard toolbar, the contents of cell E4 revert to the word *Good*. Now if you click the Redo icon on the Standard toolbar, the word *Bad* reappears. This is because you have instructed Excel to redo the last typing action.

10. Save the current workbook, along with all the changes that you've made so far by either clicking the Save icon on the Standard toolbar or by selecting File ➤ Save on the menu bar.

Duplicating, Moving, and Deleting Cell Contents

Earlier, you saw how to select cells, rows, and columns. Now let's put these procedures to some practical use by looking at copying, moving, and deleting the contents of specific areas in your worksheet.

This section explains how to use the Copy and Paste tools to duplicate cell contents in another part of a worksheet and move cell contents within a worksheet, use the AutoFill tool to copy and increment data entries, move or copy cell contents between active worksheets or workbooks, and delete cell contents in a selected cell range.

Duplicating Cell Contents using Cut and Paste

There are times when you wish to duplicate the contents from one cell in your spreadsheet to another location in your existing document. To do so, take the following steps:

1. If it is not already running, start Excel and open the workbook called `Fruit.xls` that you saved in the `My Documents` folder. Your screen should look like the example in Figure 20.24.

FIGURE 20.24   The Fruit workbook

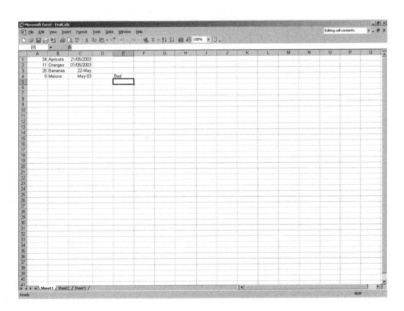

2. Using the cross pointer, select the cells in the range B1:B4. Your worksheet should now look like Figure 20.25.

FIGURE 20.25   Selecting a cell range to copy

3. Next, choose Edit ➢ Copy on the menu bar. This makes a copy of the selected cells in the Windows Clipboard. Click cell C7 once to make it active and select Edit ➢ Paste from the menu bar. An exact copy of the cell range B1:B5 should now appear in the cell range C7:C10, as the example in Figure 20.26 shows.

FIGURE 20.26   Pasting copied cells in a new location

 You may have noticed the dotted, flashing outline that appears around the range B1:B4 when you copy it to the Clipboard. This is called the *marquee*; it is used to indicate which cells have been copied. To remove the marquee, press the Esc key on your keyboard.

4. Next, select the cell range A1:A4 and choose Edit ➢ Cut on the menu bar. Notice that the data in the range disappears, as it has been removed from its original location and placed in the Clipboard. Make cell D7 active and choose Edit ➢ Paste on the menu bar. The contents of cell range A1:A4 now appear in the range D7:D10, as shown in Figure 20.27.

FIGURE 20.27   Moving a cell range using Cut and Paste

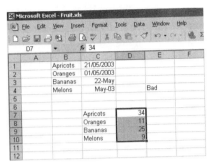

 Instead of using the menu bar to perform the Copy, Cut, and Paste functions via the Clipboard, you can click the appropriate icons on the Standard toolbar: Copy, Cut, and Paste (see Figure 20.26).

5. The Copy, Cut, and Paste functions can also be used to copy or move items to other work-sheets and even to other workbooks. For example, select the range C7:D10 and copy it to the Clipboard using either the Edit ➢ Copy command on the menu bar or the Copy icon on the Standard toolbar.

    Next, click the tab labelled Sheet2 once, near the bottom of the screen. This displays work-sheet Sheet2 in your workbook, which should be blank. Make cell A1 active. Now if you select Edit ➢ Paste from the menu bar, the contents of cell range C7:D10 on Sheet1 will be pasted into the cell range A1:B4 on Sheet 2, as shown in Figure 20.28. Switch back to Sheet1 by clicking the appropriate tab. Notice that its contents are still intact.

6. Moving items to other worksheets or workbooks is simply achieved by using either the Edit ➢ Cut command on the menu bar or the Cut icon on the Standard toolbar prior to performing the appropriate Paste operation. Note that this completely removes the item(s) from the original location.

FIGURE 20.28   Sheet2 after copying a range of cells from Sheet1

7. To copy or move a cell range to another workbook, use the same procedure as described in step 5, but instead of switching to Sheet2 after copying or cutting to the Clipboard, switch to a different workbook. For example, copy the cells C7:D10 on your Fruit workbook Sheet1,

choose File ➢ New on the menu bar, and then click the Blank Workbook option in the Task Pane on the right-hand side of the screen to create a new workbook.

Now select Edit ➢ Paste on the menu bar. The copied range of cells appears in range A1:B4 in the new workbook, as shown in Figure 20.29. To switch back to the original Fruit workbook, select `Fruit.xls` in the Windows Task Bar (normally at the very bottom of your screen), as shown in Figure 20.30.

FIGURE 20.29   Copying between workbooks. Notice that the title of this new workbook is Book2.

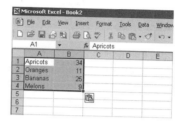

The Windows Clipboard stores only one item at a time. Whenever you choose Edit ➢ Paste Function, whatever was last cut or copied to the Clipboard is pasted; but this might not always be what you intended. Therefore, you should consider Cut and Paste or Copy and Paste as a combined function.

FIGURE 20.30   Switching between workbooks

8. Now that you're back to your Fruit workbook, select the worksheet labelled Sheet1 by clicking the tab at the bottom of the workbook.

9. Re-select cell range B1:E4, as shown in Figure 20.31, and press the Delete key on the keyboard. The contents of the selected range are deleted.

Whilst you can delete the contents of cells by selecting them and pressing the Delete key on the keyboard, you can achieve the same effect by simply omitting the Paste command after performing an Edit ➢ Cut operation.

FIGURE 20.31   Deleting the contents of the selected range

Using Excel's AutoFill Feature

On occasion, you might need to enter the same value in a number of consecutive cells on a worksheet. Whilst you could use Copy and Paste to do this, Excel has another feature called AutoFill that can prove useful and once mastered, is much quicker.

1. For example, select Sheet3 in your `Fruit.xls` workbook by clicking the tab at the bottom of the workbook. Now enter the number **14** in cell A1 and select the cell range A1:A6. Choose Edit ➤ Fill ➤ Down on the menu bar. Excel automatically fills the range with the value entered in cell A1, as shown in Figure 20.32.

FIGURE 20.32   Filling a range of cells using AutoFill

> You can use the four Edit ➤ Fill options to autofill a range of selected cells adjacent to the source cell in four different directions: Up, Down, Right, or Left.

2. Even quicker than using the Edit ➤ Fill ➤ Down option, you can populate a range of cells with identical values using the mouse. For example, delete the contents of cells A1:A6 and

type the word **Grape** in cell A1 and reposition the active cell marker at A1. Now, look carefully at the active cell marker and notice that there is a small black control handle in the bottom right-hand corner called the fill handle, as shown in Figure 20.33. (Note that this image has been magnified so that you can see the fill handle inside the circle more easily.)

FIGURE 20.33   The fill handle

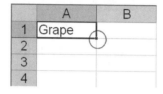

3. Move the normal cross pointer over the fill handle, and it changes to a +-shaped pointer. Now click the fill handle and drag downward with the mouse to A6, as shown in Figure 20.34. When you release the mouse button, the word *Grape* fills the selected cells, as shown in Figure 20.35. Notice the small box that shows you what will be placed in the target cells; this is useful when you are filling a large range and cannot still see the source cell on the screen.

FIGURE 20.34   Using the fill handle to fill a range of cells

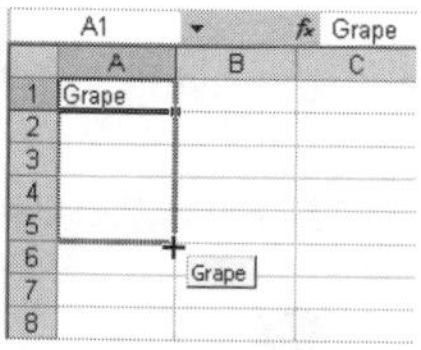

FIGURE 20.35   The selected range filled with the data from cell A1

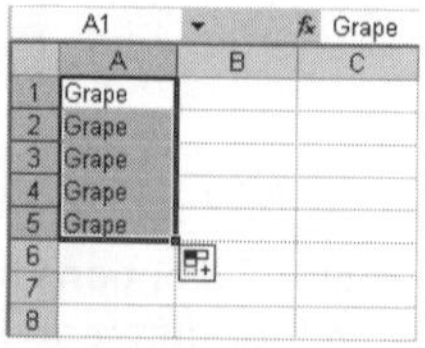

4. Whilst filling a range of cells with identical values is certainly useful from time to time, you often may need to fill a range of cells with a group of consecutive values or a progressive series, for example, a product serial number or a list of employee numbers. Fortunately, Excel comes to your assistance once again with the AutoFill Series feature.

Delete the contents of the cell range A1:A6 and enter the number 140020 in cell B2. This time when you use the fill handle, press and hold down the Ctrl key on the keyboard whilst dragging the mouse to cell B7. When you hold down the Ctrl key, the pointer is supplemented by a tiny + sign.

As you drag the mouse downward, notice that the prompt box displays an increasing series of numbers, as shown in Figure 20.36. When you release the mouse button and then the Ctrl key, the cell range B2:B7 is automatically filled with a series of consecutive numbers through to 140025, as shown in Figure 20.37.

FIGURE 20.36   Using the Ctrl key to fill cells with a series of numbers

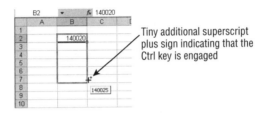

Tiny additional superscript plus sign indicating that the Ctrl key is engaged

FIGURE 20.37   A simple number series created in a range of cells

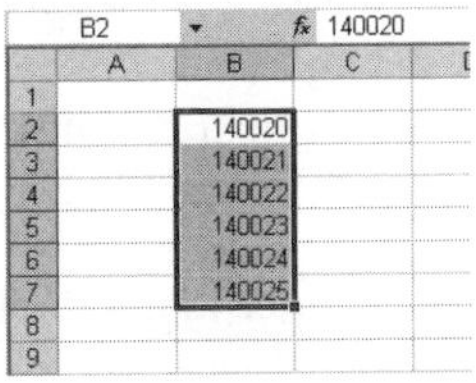

5. You can also apply the AutoFill Series feature to text. The most frequent use of this facility is when you wish to type in consecutive days of the week or months of the year. For example, delete the contents of the cell range B2:B7 and type the word **Sunday** in cell B2. Now drag the fill handle to cell H2, and when you release the mouse button, notice that the other days of the week have been automatically entered into consecutive cells, as shown in Figure 20.38.

FIGURE 20.38   Using the AutoFill Series feature to quickly enter the days of the week

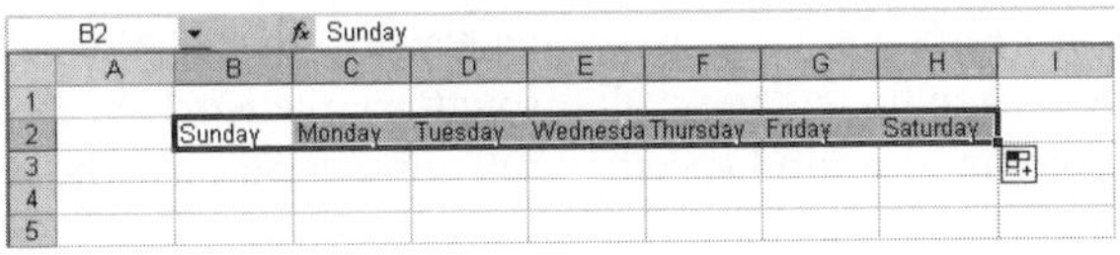

You don't have to hold down the Ctrl key to generate the days of the week because this is a standard feature in Excel.

6. As well as using the mouse and the fill handle to insert AutoFill ranges, you can use the Edit ➤ Fill ➤ Series option on the menu bar. This displays a dialog box (see Figure 20.39) where you can fine-tune the way in which a series of cells is automatically filled.

    For example, you may wish to use a negative number in the Step Value box or limit the AutoFill operation to a certain number of cells defined by the Stop Value box.

FIGURE 20.39   Defining how a series will be filled

7. Save the Fruit.xls workbook by choosing File ➤ Save on the menu bar. Then close Excel by choosing File ➤ Exit. You are prompted as to whether you wish to save the changes to Book2, as shown in Figure 20.40. Select No in this instance, because you don't need to keep this workbook.

FIGURE 20.40   Prompt to save changes in the Book2 workbook

Search and Replace

As data is entered into a spreadsheet, it can become quite large, and sometimes it can be difficult to find specific items. Fortunately, Excel has some features that can make the task of finding information much easier than having to scroll through a large worksheet. This section explains how to use the Find command to find specified cell content and use the Replace command to change specified cell content.

Using the Find Command

Using the Find command is one way to find desired information quickly without having to scroll through a large document. To use the Find command, take these steps:

1. If it is not already running, start Excel and open the Fruit.xls workbook. In order to make this exercise more effective, start by copying the cell range C7:D10 to a remote area of the worksheet. Once selected and copied to the Clipboard, make cell BX500 active and paste the contents of the Clipboard into this new position on the worksheet, as shown in Figure 20.41. Use the scroll bars to see the full range of the pasted selection.

FIGURE 20.41   Selection pasted into cell BX500

	BR	BS	BT	BU	BV	BW	BX	BY
485								
486								
487								
488								
489								
490								
491								
492								
493								
494								
495								
496								
497								
498								
499								
500							Apricots	34
501							Oranges	11
502							Bananas	25
503							Melons	9
504								

To go quickly to a specific cell, use the Edit ➤ Go To option on the menu bar, as shown in Figure 20.42. Here, you enter a cell reference, and when you click OK, you're positioned at the desired location.

FIGURE 20.42   Using the Go To option

2. Now return to the previous position in the worksheet by pressing the Home key whilst holding down the Ctrl key on the keyboard. This takes you back to make A1 the active cell. Next, select Edit ➢ Find on the menu bar. The Find and Replace dialog box shown in Figure 20.43 opens.

FIGURE 20.43   Using the Find option

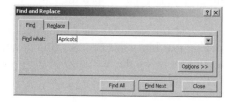

3.   Make sure that the tab labelled Find is displayed, type the word **Apples** in the Find What box, and click the Find Next button. Excel searches for the text string that you've entered and finds it first in cell C7.

Then click the Find Next button, and Excel looks for the next occurrence of *Apples* in the worksheet; it should find it in cell BX500. If you click the Find Next button again, it goes back to cell C7. Note that the Find and Replace dialog box stays on the screen until you close it.

Using the Find and Replace Commands to Replace Cell Contents

Now let's use the Find and Replace commands to replace cell contents using the following steps:

1.   Return to cell A1. This time, select Edit ➢ Find on the menu bar and then select the Replace tab, as shown in Figure 20.44. You can use this option to replace the contents of a cell with something else.

FIGURE 20.44   Using the Replace option

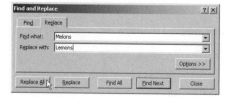

2.   For example, in the Find What box, type the word **Melons**, and in the Replace With box, type the word **Lemons**. Now you can choose whether you want Excel to replace all the occurrences of *Melons* with *Lemons* or just to replace the first occurrence that it finds. For this exercise, let's change all *Melons* to *Lemons*, so click the Replace All button.

3.   A new window opens, confirming completion of the search and stating how many replacements have been made, as shown in Figure 20.45. Click the OK button to close this window

and then click the Close button to close the Find and Replace dialog box. Now notice that all the occurrences of *Melons* read *Lemons*. Go to cell BX503 and check it!

FIGURE 20.45   Confirmation of a search-and-replace operation

You can use the Edit ➤ Replace option to change formulas as well as to change text stored in cells.

Rows and Columns

You've now seen how to move the contents of cells by using the Copy, Cut, and Paste Functions in Excel. However, there is another way to move things around in a worksheet by means of inserting or deleting selected rows or columns. This section explains how to insert rows and columns, modify column width and row height, and delete selected rows or columns.

Inserting New Rows or Columns

When you create a worksheet, you shouldn't be expected to know exactly how many rows or columns your data might need from the outset. If you find that you need to add a row or column, take the following steps:

1. If it is not already running, start Excel and open the Fruit.xls workbook. Select row 10 and then choose Insert ➤ Rows on the menu bar. Notice how the original contents of row 10 are pushed downward to become row 11, and a new blank row 10 has been inserted in the Fruit worksheet, as shown in Figure 20.46.

FIGURE 20.46   Inserting a blank row

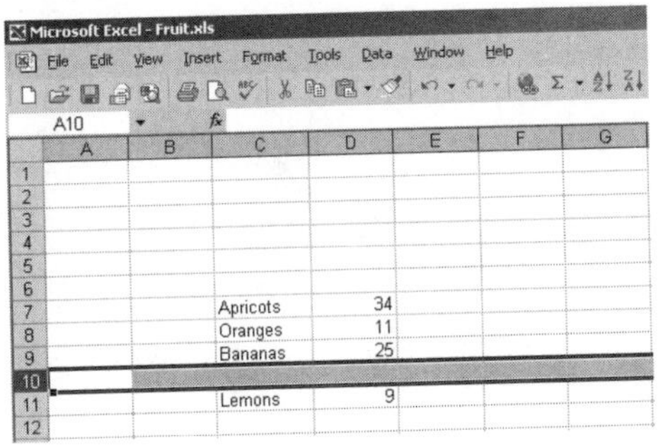

2. You can perform a similar operation with columns. For example, select column B and choose Insert ➤ Column on the menu bar. In this instance, the contents of both columns C and D are shifted over to the right to make room for the newly inserted blank column, as shown in Figure 20.47.

FIGURE 20.47   Inserting a blank column

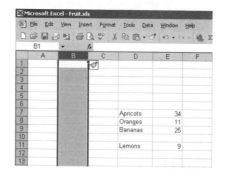

 If you need to insert several additional rows, select multiple adjacent rows and then perform an Insert ➤ Row operation. The equivalent number of new rows are inserted into your worksheet. The same applies to columns as well.

Adjusting Cell Height and Width

So far, you've entered only a short amount of text in cells on your worksheet. But if you select cell D10 and enter the word **Pomegranates**, notice that the text is too wide to fit in the column, as shown in Figure 20.48.

FIGURE 20.48   Text too wide to fit in a cell

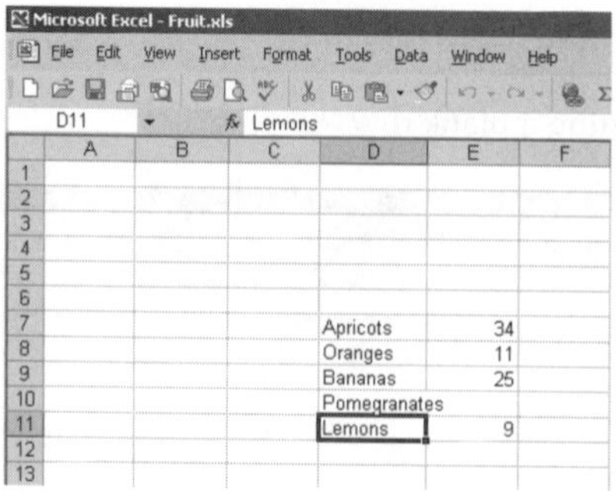

To increase the width of the column to accommodate the extra letters, take the following steps:

1. To increase the width of column D, select the entire column and then choose Format ➢ Column ➢ Width on the menu bar. The Column Width dialog box opens, as shown in Figure 20.49. If you enter a value of **14** and click OK, the width of column D is increased accordingly. See the result in Figure 20.50.

FIGURE 20.49 Setting a column width

FIGURE 20.50 Column D set to width 14

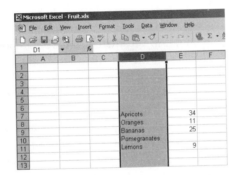

2. You can perform a similar procedure with rows. For example, select row 10 and choose Format ➢ Row ➢ Height on the menu bar. The Row Height dialog box opens, where you should enter a value of **25** and click OK, as shown in Figure 20.51. This time, the height of row 10 is increased, as shown in Figure 20.52.

FIGURE 20.51 Changing the row height

FIGURE 20.52   Row 12 increased to height 25

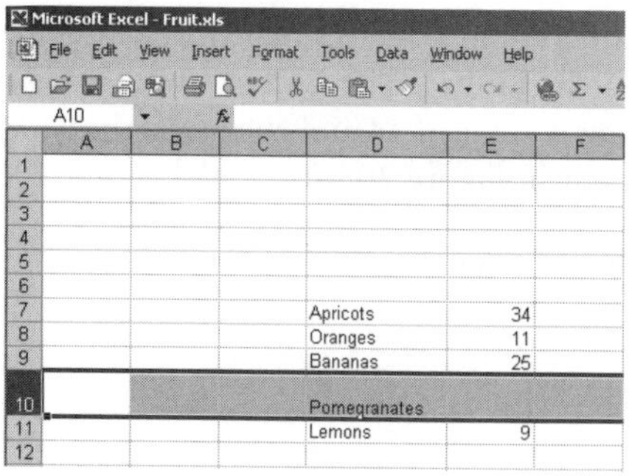

Deleting a Row or Column

Previously in this section you saw how rows and columns can be inserted into a worksheet and the existing data automatically moved to accommodate the changes. The same principle applies when you delete a row or column. However, there is one very important difference: When inserting rows or columns, it doesn't matter whether there is any data already in the row or column selected, because it is simply moved by the action of inserting. But if you delete a row or column containing data, the data is deleted along with the row or column itself.

To see this in action, take the following steps:

1. Select column C in your Fruit.xls worksheet and choose Edit ➢ Delete on the menu bar. The data in the columns to the right of column C is shifted to the left to take up the space vacated by the deleted column, as shown in the example in Figure 20.53. Notice how the data that was originally in cells D7:E11 is now in cells C7:D11.

FIGURE 20.53   The Fruit worksheet after deleting column C

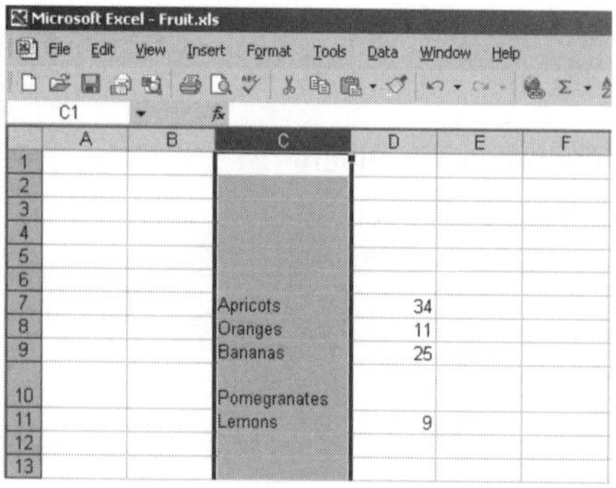

2. However, if you now select column D, which contains the quantities of fruit, and delete that column, the data is also deleted, as you can see in Figure 20.54.

FIGURE 20.54   Deleting columns or rows with data removes the data as well.

Either choose Edit ➢ Undo or click the Undo icon to reverse the column deletion action and reinstate the data.

3. You need to remove the row containing the word *Pomegranates* because you don't need it for the next exercise. So select row 10 and choose Edit ➢ Delete to remove it.

4. Close the Fruit.xls worksheet, saving any changes that you've made so far.

Sorting Data

When people enter data into a spreadsheet, they frequently don't think too much about the order of things. Often, as in your Fruit workbook, for example, items are entered in a fairly arbitrary way. However, sometimes it may be necessary to maintain a list of items in strict alphabetical or numerical order. This section describes how to sort selected data in ascending or descending numeric or alphabetic order.

Sorting Data Numerically

You can sort numeric data easily in Excel using the following steps:

1. Once again, start Excel and choose File ➢ Open to open Fruit.xls, which should now look like Figure 20.55.

FIGURE 20.55 The Fruit workbook

2. Select the cell range D7:D10 and choose Data ➤ Sort on the menu bar. A Sort Warning dialog box opens, as shown in Figure 20.56. This tells you that there is data alongside your selected range that you might wish to include in the sorting operation. For now, ignore the labels next to the numbers and simply sort the numbers themselves. Select Continue With The Current Selection and click the Sort button.

FIGURE 20.56 The Sort Warning dialog box

3. Another dialog box now opens called Sort, as shown in Figure 20.57. Here you specify certain criteria for carrying out the sorting process. For now, just accept the default settings and click the OK button.

FIGURE 20.57 Setting the Sort criteria

4. The Sort dialog box closes, and instantly the list of numbers has been sorted in ascending order, as shown in Figure 20.58. Note that once you've verified that the numbers have been correctly sorted in ascending order, undo the sort operation by selecting Edit ➢ Undo or by clicking the Undo icon on the Standard toolbar.

FIGURE 20.58   Numbers sorted in ascending order

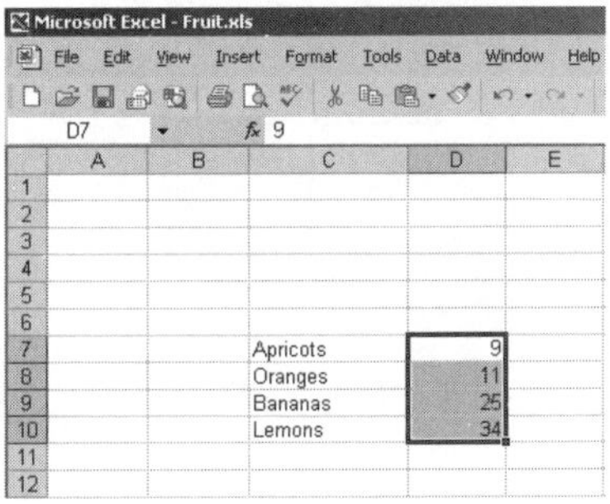

Sorting Data Alphabetically

You can also use the Sort function to sort items alphabetically by taking the following steps:

1. Select the cell range C7:D10 and choose Data ➢ Sort on the menu bar. Notice that no Sort Warning dialog box opens.

2. In the Sort criteria window, make sure that the sort is carried out on the fruit names by selecting Column C in the Sort By drop-down list. Proceed with the sort by clicking the OK button. Once again, the selected range is sorted instantly, with all the fruit and their associated quantities arranged in alphabetical order, as shown in Figure 20.59.

FIGURE 20.59   The sorted list of fruit and quantities

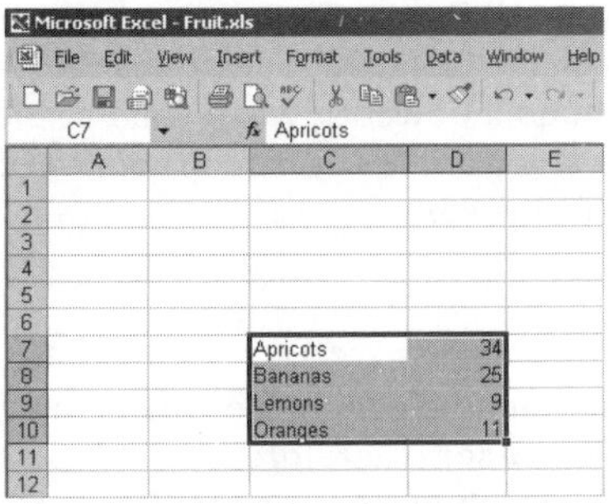

3. With the cells C7:D10 still selected, choose Data ➢ Sort on the menu bar again. However, this time select the Descending option next to the Sort By Column C box, as shown in Figure 20.60. Click OK, and the list is sorted in reverse order, as shown in Figure 20.61.

FIGURE 20.60   Select descending order for a sort.

FIGURE 20.61   The list of fruit and quantities sorted in descending alphabetical order

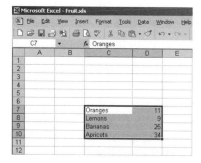

Instead of using the Data ➢ Sort option on the menu bar, you can use the two Sort buttons on the Standard toolbar: the Sort Ascending button and the Sort Descending button. However, when you use these buttons to perform a sort, you are not warned about any data in adjacent cells that you might wish to be included within the sort.

When sorting multiple columns or rows, the sorting order depends on the position of the cursor. Therefore, when you click either the Sort Ascending or the Sort Descending icons on the Standard toolbar, the sort operation is carried out on the column or row that contains the cursor at the end of the selection process.

4. Close the `Fruit.xls` workbook, saving any changes that you've made.

Most sorting within Excel takes place on columnar lists, but you can also sort data in rows. In addition, the more advanced sorting features in Excel allow you to perform multi-level sorting, so for example, you could sort a list of people by age in alphabetical order.

Summary

Excel has a wide variety of tools and facilities to help you enter and edit data in worksheets and manage how it's presented to suit your own particular needs.

In the first section, you saw how numbers, text, and dates can be entered into worksheet cells. Remember that by default, numbers are aligned to the right and text is aligned to the left within cells. You also saw that Excel can automatically format dates, depending on how you enter the data.

You learnt how selecting cells is an important factor when using Excel, and there are several different ways that this can be achieved. Adjacent ranges of cells can be selected, as can adjacent rows or columns. Remember that to select non-adjacent cells, rows, or columns, you must hold down the Ctrl key whilst performing the selection process. You also saw how to quickly select the entire worksheet by just clicking the Select All button.

You learnt how to use the editing facilities in Excel to change or modify the contents of cells. In addition, you saw how to use both the Undo and Redo commands to correct any mistakes that you've made.

Next, you saw how to use the Windows Clipboard combined with Excel's Cut, Copy, and Paste Functions to copy, move, or delete the contents of spreadsheet cells, both within a worksheet or between worksheets or workbooks. You also looked at deleting the contents of cells and using the AutoFill feature in Excel to copy and increment cell values. You might like to practice these procedures so that you become more familiar with the principles involved.

Both the Find and Replace options are extremely useful features of Excel, especially when working with very large spreadsheets. Used wisely, they can save you a considerable amount of time when you need to make repetitive changes to the contents of multiple cells.

Using row or column insert and delete operations is an ideal way of rearranging the data in a worksheet. However, you may need to be careful when deleting rows or columns; you might accidentally delete cell contents. You also saw how to alter the width of columns and the height of rows. This can be useful in helping to make a spreadsheet more readable.

Finally, you discovered that by using the Sort facilities provided in Excel, it's possible to completely rearrange the data stored in cells. This can be extremely useful if you need to maintain, say, a list of people's names in alphabetical order or sort a group of numbers into ascending or descending order of value.

Chapter

21

Worksheets

IN THIS CHAPTER YOU WILL LEARN HOW TO

- ✓ Insert a new worksheet.
- ✓ Rename a worksheet.
- ✓ Delete a worksheet.
- ✓ Duplicate a worksheet within a workbook and between open workbooks.
- ✓ Move a worksheet within a workbook and between open workbooks.

You may remember that, by default, an Excel workbook consists of three separate worksheets that can be identified by the tabs at the bottom of the main Excel window and are labelled Sheet1, Sheet2, and Sheet3. However, as you saw previously when you opened the SAMPLES.XLS workbook back in Chapter 19, "Using the Spreadsheet Application," any workbook can have more than three worksheets in it. In fact, Excel workbooks can contain an unlimited number of worksheets in theory; the number is governed only by available memory.

The ability to be able to insert, rename, and delete worksheets allows you to organise the data within your workbooks more easily. This is especially useful when dealing with large amounts of data that, if it is not split up into logical sections, can be very confusing. For example, let's assume that a workbook is used to record sales data on a monthly basis. It may make sense to have a separate worksheet for each individual month.

It can be easy to get confused when dealing with workbooks and worksheets, so it's best to relate the terms with physical objects. For example, just as a normal book can consist of many individual pages, so a workbook can consist of multiple worksheets. However, if you think in terms of a ring binder, it's easier to envisage the insertion, removal, and reordering of the pages (worksheets) within the binder (workbook).

Imagine a typical office with lots of paperwork. It's often necessary to file certain documents in different binders or box files or to make copies of documents and file them away in different places. If you compare Excel to a manual paper filing system, you often need to move or copy entire worksheets to different locations within a workbook or to entirely separate workbooks.

You have already seen how to insert, delete, duplicate, and move selections of data inside various worksheets. Now you'll learn how to manipulate entire worksheets themselves.

This chapter looks at managing worksheets in general. You'll learn how to insert new worksheets into any existing workbooks, give worksheets meaningful names by renaming them, remove worksheets from workbooks by deleting them, copy an entire worksheet to a new worksheet in the same workbook or to a different open workbook, and move an entire worksheet within the same workbook and between open workbooks.

Inserting a New Worksheet

Once you get going on a document, you might find that you need extra worksheets added to your workbook. To do this, take the following steps:

1. Once again, you'll make use of your Fruit workbook. So, if it isn't already loaded, start Excel and choose File ➢ Open to use `Fruit.xls`, which should now look like Figure 21.1.

FIGURE 21.1   The Fruit workbook

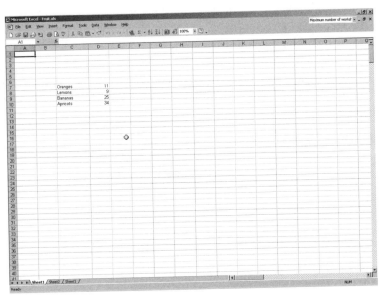

2. As you can see, the workbook has just three worksheets in it, as per the Excel default settings. To insert a new worksheet, select Insert ➢ Worksheet from the menu bar. A new worksheet (labelled Sheet4) appears as a new tabbed section at the bottom of the main workbook window, as shown in Figure 21.2. Notice how the newly inserted worksheet has become the active worksheet in the Fruit workbook.

FIGURE 21.2   The new worksheet inserted into the Fruit workbook

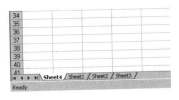

Remember that you can easily switch between worksheets inside a workbook
by simply clicking once on the tabs.

Renaming a Worksheet

Already with just four worksheets in the Fruit workbook, it's proving difficult to remember
what is actually recorded on each one. Therefore, you should give each worksheet a more
recognisable name by taking the following steps:

1. Make Sheet1 active by clicking its tab. You should see the list of fruit as you last left
    it, sorted in descending order, as shown in Figure 21.3. Select Format ➤ Sheet ➤
    Rename on the menu bar. Notice that the Sheet1 tab label has been selected, as shown
    in Figure 21.4.

FIGURE 21.3   Sheet1 active in the Fruit workbook

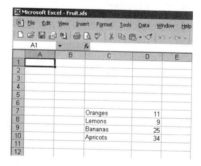

FIGURE 21.4   The Sheet1 tab label selected for renaming

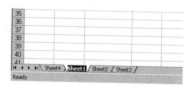

2. Type the word **Sorted** and press the Return or Enter key. Notice that the worksheet has
    been renamed, as Figure 21.5 shows.

FIGURE 21.5   The worksheet Sheet1 renamed as Sorted

Instead of using the Format ➤ Sheet ➤ Rename option on the menu bar to select a work-sheet label tab to rename, you can simply click the tab with your right mouse button and a pop-up menu appears, as shown in Figure 21.6. You can then select the Rename option there.

FIGURE 21.6   Using the right mouse button to rename a worksheet

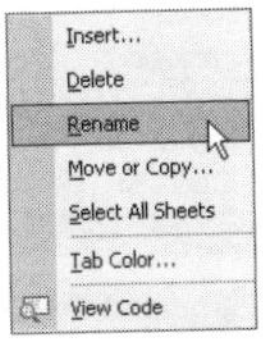

3.   Use the same procedures described in steps 1 and 2 to rename Sheet2 as Unsorted and Sheet3 as Weekly Report. Your worksheet tabs should now look like those in Figure 21.7.

FIGURE 21.7   Sheet2 and Sheet3 renamed

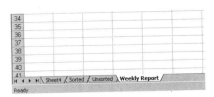

Deleting and Copying a Worksheet

Let's say that you no longer need Sheet4, which you inserted into the Fruit workbook earlier, so you want to delete it. Make Sheet4 active by clicking its tab and selecting Edit ➤ Delete Sheet on the menu bar. The active worksheet is deleted, as shown in Figure 21.8, and the Sorted work-sheet becomes the currently active worksheet.

FIGURE 21.8   The result of deleting Sheet4 from the Fruit workbook

Deleting a worksheet removes any data stored on that sheet, so be careful when using this option. Normally, Excel warns you if you are about to lose data in this way by displaying a dialog box (see Figure 21.9). However, if you accidentally delete a worksheet containing data, you can usually reinstate it by using the Undo option in Excel.

FIGURE 21.9   Warning about deleting worksheets that contain data

To duplicate or copy an entire worksheet within a workbook, follow these steps:

1.   Make the Sorted worksheet active and select Edit ➤ Move Or Copy Sheet on the menu bar. The Move Or Copy dialog box opens (see Figure 21.10).

2.   Make sure that the Create A Copy option is checked and then click the OK button. An exact copy of the Sorted worksheet appears in the worksheet tab area, and the new worksheet is made the current active worksheet, as shown in Figure 21.11. Notice how Excel appends *(2)* to the end of the Sorted tab label; this is so it can be clearly distinguished from the original Sorted worksheet. You can of course change this worksheet name if you wish by using the Rename option after it has been created.

FIGURE 21.10   Making a copy of the Sorted worksheet

When copying worksheets, you can decide whereabouts they are to be placed by selecting the appropriate location in the Before Sheet area of the Move Or Copy dialog window, as shown in Figure 21.10.

FIGURE 21.11   The result of making a copy of the Sorted worksheet

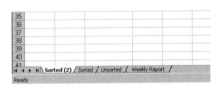

As well as making a copy of a worksheet in the same workbook, you can also copy a worksheet to an entirely different workbook. Follow these steps:

1. With the Fruit workbook still open, open the `Test.xls` workbook (which should be in your `My Documents` folder) by selecting File ➢ Open.

2. Select Edit ➢ Move Or Copy Sheet on the menu bar as you did before, but this time, as well as making sure that the Create A Copy option is selected in the dialog box, click the drop-down list and select the `Fruit.xls` option in the To Book list, as shown in Figure 21.12.

   Now when you click the OK button, an exact copy of Sheet1 from the Test workbook is created in the Fruit workbook, as shown in Figure 21.13. (Note that this image has been edited so that you can see both the contents and the tabbed worksheet area.)

FIGURE 21.12   Selecting a new workbook to copy a worksheet into

FIGURE 21.13   The result of copying Sheet1 from the Test workbook to the Fruit workbook

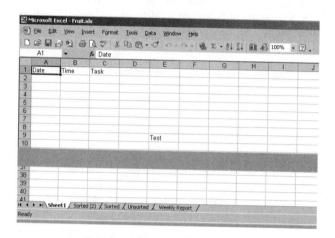

Moving Worksheets

Just as you can shuffle the pages in a physical ring binder, so can you move the worksheets around within a workbook in Excel.

Moving Worksheets within a Workbook

Now that you know how to copy worksheets both inside the current workbook and to other open workbooks, you can use basically the same procedure to move them:

1.   Make the recently copied Sheet1 in the Fruit workbook active.

2.   Choose Edit ➤ Move Or Copy Sheet on the menu bar as you did before, but this time make sure that the Create A Copy option is *not* selected in the dialog box. In the Before Sheet list, click the Weekly Report label, as shown in Figure 21.14.

When you click OK, Sheet1 is moved so that it appears between the worksheets labelled Unsorted and Weekly Report, as shown in Figure 21.15.

FIGURE 21.14   Using the Move Or Copy dialog box to position Sheet1 between
Unsorted and Weekly Report

FIGURE 21.15   The result of moving Sheet1 within the Fruit workbook

To move sheets within the current workbook, you can drag the selected sheets
along the row of sheet tabs. To copy the sheets, hold down the Ctrl key and
then drag the sheets; release the mouse button before you release the Ctrl key.

Moving a Worksheet to a Different Workbook

You can use the same technique to move a worksheet to another workbook by following these
steps:

1. Make the Weekly Report worksheet in the Fruit workbook active. Select Edit ➢ Move Or
    Copy Sheet, and once again make sure that the Create A Copy option is *not* selected in the
    dialog box. Select Test.xls from the To Book drop-down list, as shown in Figure 21.16.
    Also select (move to end) in the Before Sheet list, as shown in Figure 21.17.

FIGURE 21.16 Selecting a new workbook to move a worksheet to

FIGURE 21.17 Using the Move Or Copy dialog box to position the Weekly Report worksheet at the end of the existing worksheets in the Test workbook

2. Now when you click the OK button, the Weekly Reports worksheet is moved from the Fruit workbook so that it appears at the end of the existing worksheets in the Test workbook, as shown in Figure 21.18.

FIGURE 21.18 The result of moving the Weekly Report worksheet from the Fruit workbook to the Test workbook

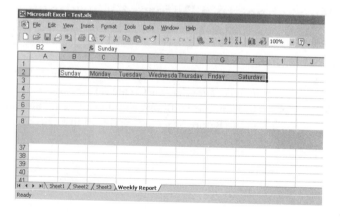

Note that the image in Figure 21.18 has been edited so that you can see both the contents and the tabbed worksheet area.

Be careful when you move or copy sheets, especially between different workbooks. Calculations or charts based on worksheet data might become inaccurate if you move the worksheet. Similarly, if you insert a worksheet between sheets that are referred to by a three-dimensional formula reference, data on that worksheet might be included in the calculation.

3. Save both the Fruit and Test workbooks, along with all the changes you've made so far, by clicking the Save icon on the Standard toolbar or by selecting File ➢ Save on the menu bar in each of the workbook windows. Then close each of the workbooks.

Summary

In this chapter, you learnt a number of valuable lessons. Using the insert, rename, and delete worksheets options means that you can change the overall contents of a workbook instead of using just the three default worksheets generated when Excel creates a new workbook.

In addition, you saw how it is possible to both copy and move worksheets in a workbook and between any open workbooks. This can be extremely useful when you need to use data from an existing workbook in a completely new workbook without having to re-enter it all from scratch.

Chapter

22

Formulas and Functions

IN THIS CHAPTER YOU WILL LEARN HOW TO

- ✓ Use basic arithmetic formulas to perform a range of common calculations.
- ✓ Identify and understand standard error values associated with using formulas.
- ✓ Use relative, absolute, and mixed cell referencing in formulas.
- ✓ Use the SUM, MINIMUM, MAXIMUM, COUNT, and AVERAGE functions.
- ✓ Generate formulas using the logical IF function.

Until now, you've used Excel worksheets only to record data. But the key to any spreadsheet application is its ability to process that data as well. By *process*, we basically mean to use information recorded in spreadsheet cells to generate further data or to modify data in other cells. As well as entering numbers and text in cells, you can enter formulas that can be used to perform calculations.

Excel provides hundreds of formulas that can be used to make many different types of calculations. This is probably the most important feature of a spreadsheet application such as Excel. The ability to perform calculations automatically and to recalculate the results when the underlying data changes makes spreadsheets a practically essential tool for many users, especially in the business world.

As well as formulas, Excel offers a range of functions that can be used to calculate and process spreadsheet data. Formulas and functions work in slightly different ways, so it is important to understand what they are and how they work.

A *formula* is basically an equation that is used to analyse and process the data stored in a worksheet. Formulas can perform very simple operations such as addition, multiplication, subtraction, and division, or they can be extremely complex using sophisticated mathematical, conditional, and logical processing techniques to calculate their results.

Functions are predefined formulas that perform calculations by using specific values, called *arguments*, in a particular order, known as the *syntax*. For example, the SUM function adds values for ranges of cells where the range being totalled is the argument of the function being performed. As with formulas, functions can be either simple or highly complex.

Both formulas and functions can refer to other cells on the same worksheet, cells on other worksheets in the same workbook, or cells on worksheets in other workbooks.

Arithmetic Formulas

This section explains some of the most commonly used formulas in Excel, and you'll learn how to use basic arithmetic formulas to perform a range of calculations in a spreadsheet, for example, addition, subtraction, multiplication, and division. In addition, you'll recognise and deal with some of the standard error messages associated with formulas. You'll also learn how to reference particular cells in a formula.

For this exercise, let's start with a new blank workbook:

1. If it is not loaded, start Excel. A new blank workbook is created. If Excel is already running, close any open workbooks and choose File ➤ New on the menu bar or click the New icon on the Standard toolbar.

2. In your blank worksheet, enter the following data in the specified cells:

Cell Reference	Value
B2	27
B3	49
B4	11
B5	19
C2	50
C3	22
C4	3
C5	6

3. Next, in cell D2, type the formula **=B2+C2** and press Return or Enter on the keyboard.

WARNING   Excel uses the equals (=) key to recognise the fact that you are entering a formula or function in a cell as opposed to numbers or text. If you try entering a formula as just B2+C2, for example, then the actual text "B2+C2" appears in the cell.

4. In cell D3, type the formula **=B3–C3**. In cell D4, type the formula **=B4*C4**. And finally, in cell D5, type the formula **=B5/C5**. Your worksheet should now look exactly like the example in Figure 22.1.

FIGURE 22.1   Performing simple arithmetic in Excel

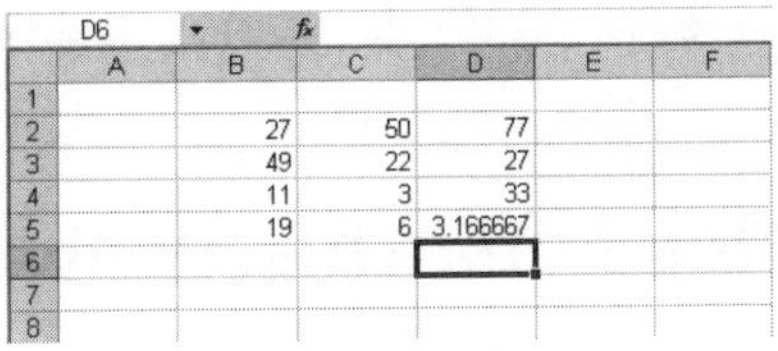

NOTE   Notice how the result of dividing 19 by 6 in cell D5 is displayed as 3.166667. This is because by default, Excel displays numbers to 15-digit precision. But in this instance, the column is not wide enough to display all of the digits, and therefore the number is truncated and automatically rounded down to fit the space available.

As well as actually typing cell references in formulas, you can use Excel to select the cell references and automatically enter them into formulas. Try these steps:

1. Make cell B6 active and type an equal (=) sign. Now using either cursor control keys or the mouse, position the cell marker at B2. Notice that the cell referenced (B2) now appears after the = sign in cell B6. Also notice how a special cell marquee is used to highlight the cell you're selecting, as you can see in Figure 22.2.

FIGURE 22.2   Entering a formula by pointing to cell references

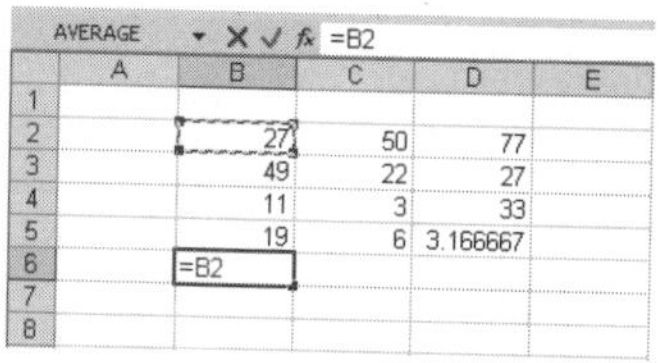

AVERAGE	▾	X ✓ ƒx	=B2		
	A	B	C	D	E
1					
2		27	50	77	
3		49	22	27	
4		11	3	33	
5		19	6	3.166667	
6		=B2			
7					
8					

2. Press the + sign key on the keyboard and then move to cell B3.
3. Press the + sign key again and then move to cell B4.
4. Press the + once more and move to cell B5.
5. Finally, press the Return or Enter key and notice that cell B6 now contains the number 106, which is the result of B2+B3+B4+B5 as per the formula you generated.

Using this method of entering cell references into formulas by pointing to them means that you are less likely to make mistakes than when typing references in via the keyboard. The topic of referencing cells will be covered in more detail in the "Cell Referencing" section, later in this chapter.

NOTE   Excel formulas can contain *constants*, in other words, fixed values for use in calculations rather than just cell references. So it is perfectly valid to enter a formula such as =72*0.2 to calculate 20 percent of 72, giving the answer 14.4.

Using More than One Arithmetic Symbol

Occasionally you may need to combine arithmetic operators in a formula in order to produce certain calculations. When you do, be aware that the order in which you enter mathematical symbols can affect the result of a calculation.

For example, in cell C6 enter the formula **=C2-C3*C4**. Excel calculates the result as –16, because the multiplication is actually carried out before the subtraction, despite the fact that in the formula the – sign appears first. Basically, Excel uses an order of precedence when it comes to calculation. The order used is division, multiplication, addition, then subtraction. Therefore, if in this example you want Excel to perform the subtraction before the multiplication, you have to use parentheses (brackets) in your formula.

Try this out by entering the formula **=(C2-C3)*C4** into cell C7. Notice that although you are referencing the same cells and using the same arithmetic operators, the results are completely different; the new calculation using the parentheses produces the result 84, as shown in Figure 22.3.

FIGURE 22.3   Using parentheses to change the calculation order within a formula

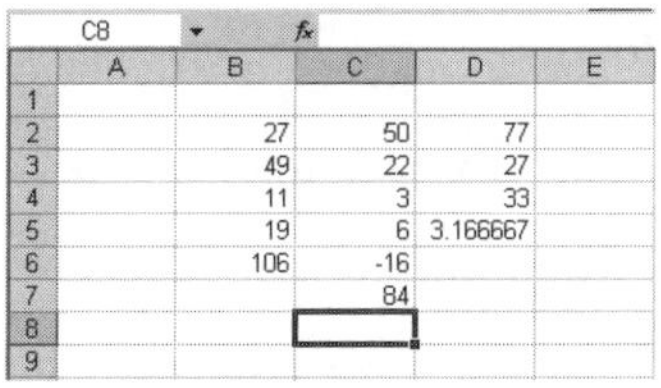

Error Values in Excel

When you enter a formula, Excel checks to see if it is syntactically correct. If it detects a mistake, an error value is generated. Error values can be the result of using text where a formula expects a numeric value, deleting a cell that is referenced by a formula, or using a cell that is not wide enough to display the result. For example, in cell B8 on your worksheet, enter the formula **=B6+I0**, where what looks like the digit 1 is in fact a capital letter I, which is a common typing error. When you press the Return or Enter key, an error is generated. Instead of the expected result, the cell B8 displays #NAME?.

Now move the active cell marker back to B8 and notice a small icon (exclamation point within a diamond) known as a *smart tag* on the left-hand side. If you place your mouse pointer on this icon, a brief explanation of the error is displayed, as shown in Figure 22.4. This particular error is because you mixed text in with numbers in the formula, and Excel cannot resolve the calculation.

FIGURE 22.4   An error resulting from an invalid formula

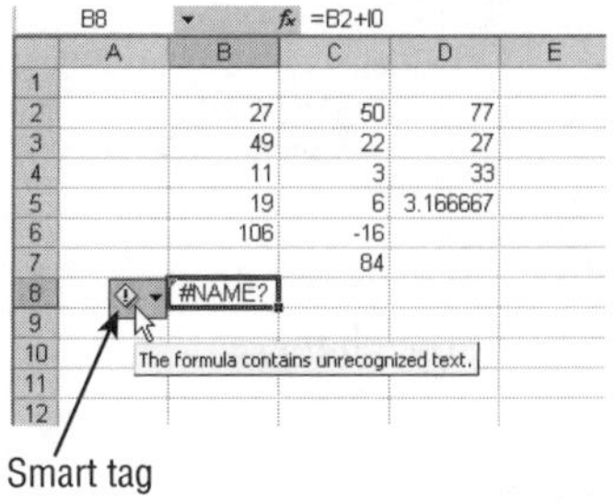

Some of the common error values that you might encounter and their typical causes are as follows:

Error Value	Typical Cause
#NAME?	Text not recognised in a formula.
#REF!	The cell being referenced is not valid.
#VALUE!	The wrong type of argument or operand is being used.
#NUM!	An error in a number used in a formula.
#N/A	The value being used in a formula is not available.
#NULL!	The two areas referenced do not intersect.
#########	The result calculated is too long to display in the cell.
#DIV/0	Division by zero is not allowed.

After encountering an error, if you don't fully understand what has caused it and how to rectify the problem, simply click the alert icon and select the Help on this error option, as shown in Figure 22.5.

FIGURE 22.5   Getting help on a specific type of error

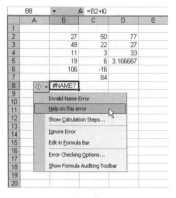

Close the workbook without saving the changes.

Cell Referencing

You've seen that Excel basically uses column and row coordinates to reference the location of cells within a worksheet. However, Excel is capable of recognizing two distinct types of such coordinates or references to identify a cell's location. The first method, and most commonly used, is the *absolute* cell reference. This approach is similar to using a grid reference on a map that identifies a location by specific coordinates, for example, 50 degrees west and 23 degrees north from a single base coordinate or meridian.

The second method is known as *relative* cell referencing; this can use different starting points in order to point to a specific location. For example, from the church, move 120 metres east and 64 metres south to a point that is *relative* to the position of the church (or starting point). In this example, you don't actually need to know precisely where the church is, as you are already starting from its specific location and moving relative to it.

Relative Cell Referencing

The following steps will help you understand relative cell referencing. For this exercise, start with a new blank workbook:

1. Choose File ➢ New on the menu bar or click the New icon on the Standard toolbar.

2. So far, when you have been entering cell references in formulas, you've typed things such as **B2, C6:C10**, or **A1:D9**. This format is called *relative addressing*; it means that when a formula is copied across a range of cells, the formula in each cell changes automatically to reflect the new source cells. In your blank worksheet, enter the following data in the specified cells:

Cell Reference	Value
B2	45
B3	12
B4	62
C2	23
C3	102
C4	19

3. Next, make cell B5 the active cell and double-click the AutoSum icon (the one with the Greek symbol sigma, Σ) on the Standard toolbar. This should result in the total 119 being displayed.

The *AutoSum* icon utilises the SUM function. The use of functions themselves is explained in more detail in the following section.

4. Now, drag the fill handle to autofill cell C5. When you release the mouse button and select cell C5, you'll see that the formula that was copied has automatically adapted itself to refer to the range C2:C4, calculating the appropriate total of 144, as shown in the Formula Bar in Figure 22.6.

If you can't remember how to use the fill handle to autofill a range of cells, then refer back to Chapter 20, "Cells."

FIGURE 22.6   An example of relative addressing

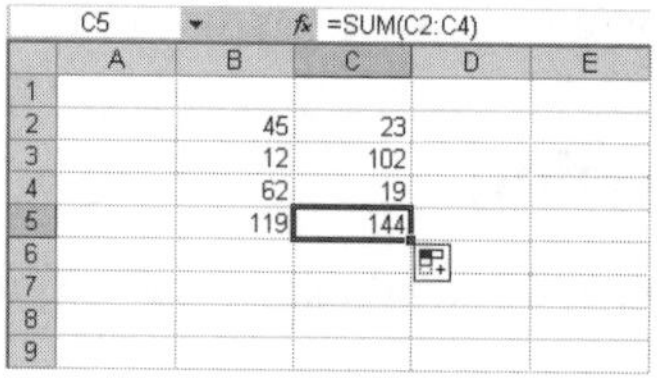

	A	B	C	D	E
1					
2		45	23		
3		12	102		
4		62	19		
5		119	144		
6					
7					
8					
9					

C5   =SUM(C2:C4)

Normally, this action is precisely what you require Excel to achieve; on most occasions, relative addressing is the appropriate format to use. However, sometimes you need to use a specific fixed cell reference in a range of formulas. This can be done in Excel by using a technique known as *absolute addressing*.

Using Absolute Addressing

For the following steps, let's assume that you wish to calculate the tax on a range of values in cells:

1. Close the existing workbook without saving the changes and then open a new blank workbook. In the blank worksheet, enter the following data in the specified cells:

Cell Reference	Value
A1	0.175
B2	10
B3	60
B4	45.95
C2	=B2*A1

2. Make cell C2 the active cell and use the fill handle to autofill the cell range C3:C4. When you do this, something strange happens. Instead of the new formulas calculating the tax correctly, the values of 0 have appeared. This is because the formula in C2 is using a relative address for the reference to the tax rate in cell A1, and the cells C3 and C4 are referring to cells A2 and A3 respectively, which are empty. Hence, the wrong results have been produced, as shown in Figure 22.7.

FIGURE 22.7   Incorrect tax calculations

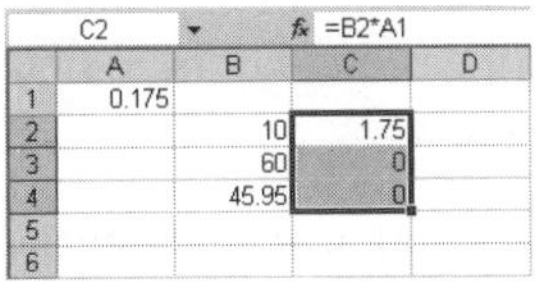

3. You can correct this error by using absolute addressing in the formula in cell C2. To use an absolute address, you need to use $ signs in the cell reference. So, replace the formula in cell C2 with **=B2*$A$1**; this refers to cell A1 as an absolute cell address. Now, when you use the fill handle to autofill cells C3:C4, the correct tax values are calculated, as shown in Figure 22.8.

FIGURE 22.8   Using absolute addressing to perform a correct tax calculation

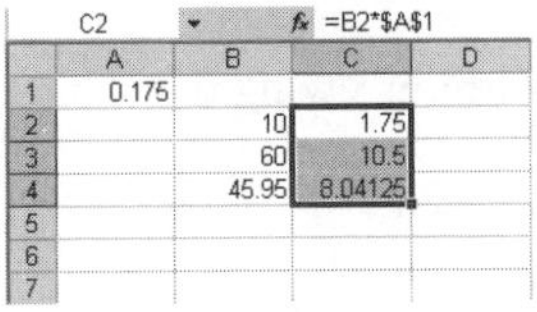

Mixed Cell Referencing

A *mixed reference* has either an absolute column and relative row, or an absolute row and relative column. An absolute column reference takes the form $A1, $B1, and so on. An absolute row reference takes the form A$1, B$1, and so on. If the position of the cell that contains the formula changes, the relative reference is changed and the absolute reference does not change. If you copy the formula across rows or down columns, the relative reference automatically adjusts, and the absolute reference does not adjust. For example, if you copy a mixed reference from cell A2 to B3, it adjusts from =A$1 to =B$1.

As you just saw by using an absolute reference in a formula, you can ensure that the correct cell is always used. However, you can extend this technique a little further by combining a relative and an absolute address to form what is known as a mixed reference. Let's illustrate with an example:

1. Say you want to calculate varying tax amounts for a given value. Modify your existing worksheet as follows:

Cell Reference	Value/Action
B3:C4	Delete contents
A2	0.2
A3	0.25
C3	=$B$2*$A1

Note that this calculation uses a mixed reference $A1 for the multiplication factor.

2. Make cell C2 the active cell and use the fill handle to autofill the cell range C3:C4. The result this time is that the list of varying tax rates in column A are used to perform the calculations, as shown in Figure 22.9.

FIGURE 22.9 An example of using mixed referencing to perform multiple tax calculations

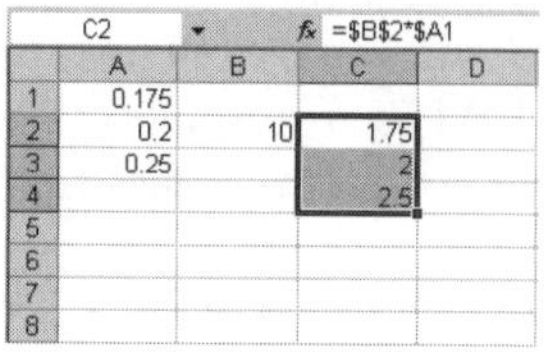

C2		f_x =$B$2*$A1	
	A	B	C	D
1	0.175			
2	0.2	10	1.75	
3	0.25		2	
4			2.5	
5				
6				
7				
8				

3. Close the existing workbook without saving the changes.

TIP In the example tax worksheet, you could simply put a constant value in the formula to calculate the tax, such as =B2*0.175. This would work perfectly well in most circumstances, but if the tax rate changes, you would need to edit the formulas in the spreadsheet. This is why you have designated a specific cell that holds the value of the current tax rate and refers to it in the formula. In this way, if the tax rate changes, you have to change it only in one place in the spreadsheet. This is precisely why absolute addressing can be useful.

Working with Functions

As mentioned earlier, functions are a type of in-built formula that can be used to perform calculations in a similar way to normal formulas. Excel provides a huge range of functions, both general purpose and more specialist, covering areas such as engineering, statistics, finance, mathematics, and trigonometry. This section explains how to generate formulas using the SUM, COUNT, MINIMUM, MAXIMUM, and AVERAGE functions.

Using the SUM and COUNT Functions

As you saw earlier, the SUM function adds up the values of a set of designated cells. You can also use the COUNT function to add up the number of cells. Try these steps:

1. If it is not open, start Excel and a new blank workbook is created. If Excel is already running, close any open workbooks and create a new one.

2. Enter the following into your blank worksheet:

Cell Reference	Value
A1	67
A2	42
A3	117
A4	89
A5	20

3. Make cell A7 the active cell and enter **=SUM(A1:A5)**. The total of the numbers (335) is displayed, as shown in Figure 22.10.

FIGURE 22.10 Using the SUM function

4. Delete the contents of A1:A7, because you will not need them for the rest of this exercise.

5. In cell B2, enter the number **1989**. Using the AutoFill feature, generate a series of sequential numbers in the cell range B3:B22, finishing with the number **2009**. (Remember to hold down the Ctrl key to increment the values.) Next, make cell D10 the active cell and select Insert ➢ Function on the menu bar. A dialog box called Insert Function opens, as shown in Figure 22.11.

FIGURE 22.11 The Insert Function dialog box

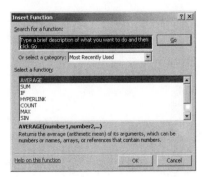

6. Select the specific function you want to use from the list. Choose the COUNT function and click the OK button.

> Instead of selecting Insert ➤ Function on the menu bar, you can click the Insert Function icon on the Formula Bar. The Insert Function icon is a lowercase *f* with a subscript *x* next to it.

7. When you click OK in the Insert Function box, the dialog box closes and a new type of pop-up dialog box opens, called Function Arguments, as shown in Figure 22.12.

FIGURE 22.12 The Function Arguments dialog box, which opens after selecting the COUNT function

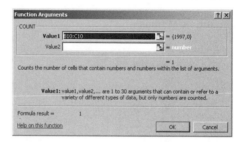

8. The Function Arguments dialog box can now be used to enter the arguments for the COUNT function. In the Value1 box, enter **B2:B22** and then click OK. The dialog box closes, and you'll see that the cell D10 now contains the answer 21, which is the number of items in the list B2:B22, as shown in Figure 22.13.

FIGURE 22.13 The result of using the COUNT function on the list of numbers

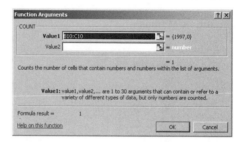

When using a pop-up window to enter the arguments for a function, you can use the mouse to select cells and ranges on the worksheet itself rather than typing in cell references. However, you might find that the pop-up window is obscuring the area of the worksheet containing the cells that you wish to select. If this is the case, you can move the pop-up window out of the way by clicking anywhere on the grey background and then dragging the window to a new position.

9. You might argue that counting a list of numbers is easy, especially because there are row numbers to help you. However, the COUNT function can also be used to count the entries in any range of cells. For example, make a copy of B2:B22 in both A2:A22 and C2:22. Now, redefine the COUNT function in D10 so that the range being counted is **A2:C22**. (You can do this by simply editing the COUNT formula in the Formula Bar after selecting cell D10.)

Notice that the result of the COUNT function is now 63, as shown in Figure 22.14.

FIGURE 22.14 Using the COUNT function on a larger cell range

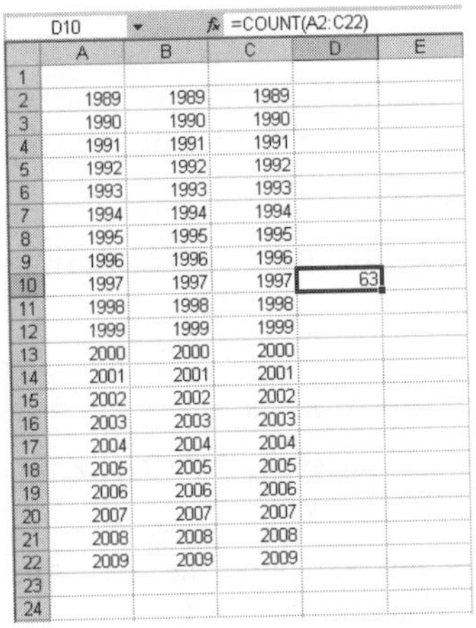

	A	B	C	D	E
				=COUNT(A2:C22)	
1					
2	1989	1989	1989		
3	1990	1990	1990		
4	1991	1991	1991		
5	1992	1992	1992		
6	1993	1993	1993		
7	1994	1994	1994		
8	1995	1995	1995		
9	1996	1996	1996		
10	1997	1997	1997	63	
11	1998	1998	1998		
12	1999	1999	1999		
13	2000	2000	2000		
14	2001	2001	2001		
15	2002	2002	2002		
16	2003	2003	2003		
17	2004	2004	2004		
18	2005	2005	2005		
19	2006	2006	2006		
20	2007	2007	2007		
21	2008	2008	2008		
22	2009	2009	2009		
23					
24					

10. Delete the contents of cells A5, A13, B8, B18, C3, C10, and C21. Notice how the cell D10 now shows the answer 56, as shown in Figure 22.15. This is because the COUNT function counts only cells that contain numbers. Similarly, if a cell in a range being counted contains text, it will be ignored.

FIGURE 22.15   Any gaps in the cell range are ignored by the COUNT function

	A	B	C	D	E
				D10 ▾ *fx* =COUNT(A2:C22)	
1					
2	1989	1989	1989		
3	1990	1990			
4	1991	1991	1991		
5		1992	1992		
6	1993	1993	1993		
7	1994	1994	1994		
8	1995		1995		
9	1996	1996	1996		
10	1997	1997		56	
11	1998	1998	1998		
12	1999	1999	1999		
13		2000	2000		
14	2001	2001	2001		
15	2002	2002	2002		
16	2003	2003	2003		
17	2004	2004	2004		
18	2005		2005		
19	2006	2006	2006		
20	2007	2007	2007		
21	2008	2008			
22	2009	2009	2009		
23					
24					

Using the AVERAGE, MINIMUM, and MAXIMUM Functions

Now that you've seen how to use the COUNT function, let's explore some of the other commonly used functions in Excel using the following steps:

1. In cell E10, type the word **Count**.

2. Make cell D11 the active cell. You'll use the AVERAGE function to work out the average value of all the numbers in the range A2:C22.

3. Select Insert ➢ Function on the menu bar or click the Insert Function icon on the Formula Bar. The Insert Function dialog box opens.

4. In the Insert Function dialog box, select the AVERAGE function. The Function Arguments dialog box opens.

5. In the Function Arguments dialog box, enter the range **A2:C22**, as shown in Figure 22.16, or select the range using the mouse in the worksheet area.

FIGURE 22.16   Using the AVERAGE function

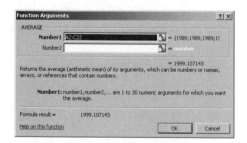

6. Click OK. Notice that the average value of all the numbers in the selected list has been calculated as 1999.107, as shown in Figure 22.17. Notice how, like the COUNT function, the AVERAGE function ignored the cells without any numbers in them.

FIGURE 22.17   The result of using the AVERAGE function on a range of cells

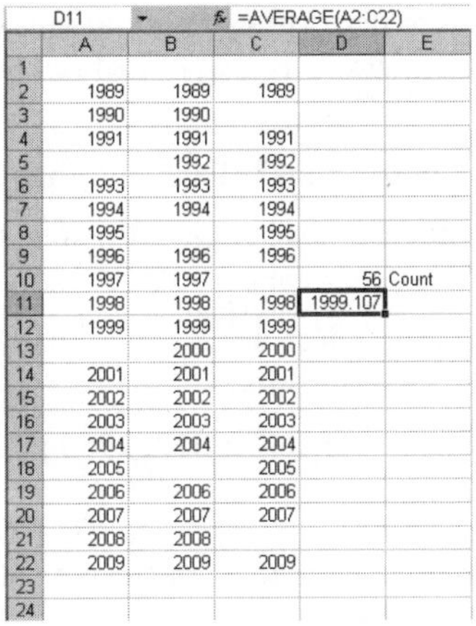

7. In cell E11, type the word **Average**. Using the same procedures as in steps 2 to 6, use the MINIMUM and MAXIMUM functions to calculate the lowest and highest values in the range A2:C22. Place your new functions in cells D12 and D13 respectively, and enter appropriate labels in column E. Your worksheet should now look like Figure 22.18.

FIGURE 22.18   The result of using the MINIMUM and MAXIMUM functions on a range of cells

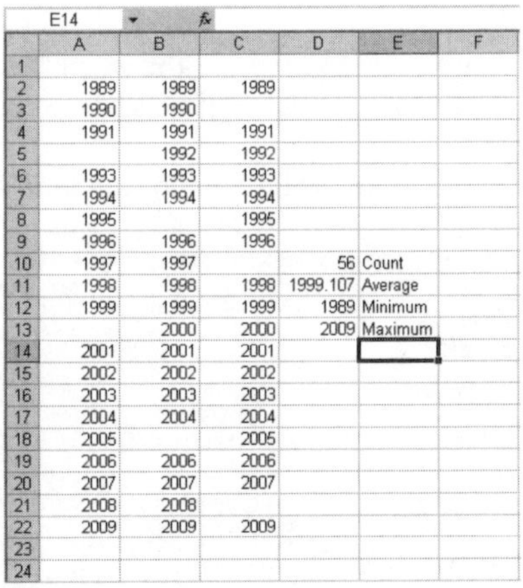

Using the IF Function

Whilst the basic functions described in this section can be extremely useful, there are occasions when you may need to do something a little more sophisticated. For example, suppose you want to display some text in a cell if there were any years earlier to 1990 in the range A2:C22. You could use Excel's IF function to test cell D12, which you used to find the minimum value in the range. The IF function can be used to perform what is known as a *conditional* or *logical test* on a cell and then, depending on the result of the test, one of two specific actions occurs. Let's see it in action:

1. In cell E15, enter the words **Conditional Test** and then make cell D15 active.

2. Select Insert ➢ Function on the menu bar or click the Insert Function icon on the Formula Bar. The Insert Function dialog box opens.

3. In the Insert Function dialog box, select the IF function. The Function Arguments dialog box opens.

4. In the Function Arguments dialog box, enter **D12=1989** in the Logical_Test box, as shown in Figure 22.19.

FIGURE 22.19 Using the IF function to enter the logical test

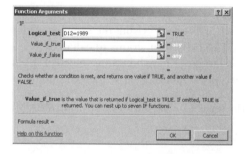

5. Also in the Function Arguments dialog box, enter the word **"Earlier"** in the Value_If_True box and enter the word **"Later"** in the Value_If_False box, as shown in Figure 22.20.

FIGURE 22.20 Entering the other arguments for the logical test

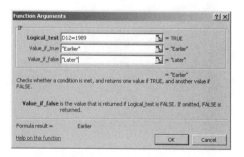

6. When you click OK, cell D15 displays the word *Earlier*, as shown in Figure 22.21. This is because the test condition is True.

FIGURE 22.21   The result of entering the IF function in cell D15

	A	B	C	D	E	F
			fx	=IF(D12=1989,"Earlier","Later")		
1						
2	1989	1989	1989			
3	1990	1990				
4	1991	1991	1991			
5		1992	1992			
6	1993	1993	1993			
7	1994	1994	1994			
8	1995		1995			
9	1996	1996	1996			
10	1997	1997		57	Count	
11	1998	1998	1998	1999.123	Average	
12	1999	1999	1999	1989	Minimum	
13	2000	2000	2000	2009	Maximum	
14	2001	2001	2001			
15	2002	2002	2002	Earlier	Conditional Test	
16	2003	2003	2003			
17	2004	2004	2004			
18	2005		2005			
19	2006	2006	2006			
20	2007	2007	2007			
21	2008	2008				
22	2009	2009	2009			
23						
24						

7. Now if you select row 2 and press the Delete key, you'll see that the text in cell D15 changes from *Earlier* to *Later*, as shown in Figure 22.22. This is because the value 1989 no longer exists within the range A2:C22, and consequently, the condition of cell D12 has changed. The IF function has automatically detected this change, and because the test condition is now False, the original test is replaced. If you click the Undo icon, the cell changes back to *Earlier*.

FIGURE 22.22   The result of a change to the data being tested

	A	B	C	D	E	F
	A2		fx			
1						
2						
3	1990	1990				
4	1991	1991	1991			
5		1992	1992			
6	1993	1993	1993			
7	1994	1994	1994			
8	1995		1995			
9	1996	1996	1996			
10	1997	1997		54	Count	
11	1998	1998	1998	1999.685	Average	
12	1999	1999	1999	1990	Minimum	
13	2000	2000	2000	2009	Maximum	
14	2001	2001	2001			
15	2002	2002	2002	Later	Conditional Test	
16	2003	2003	2003			
17	2004	2004	2004			
18	2005		2005			
19	2006	2006	2006			
20	2007	2007	2007			
21	2008	2008				
22	2009	2009	2009			
23						
24						

8. Close the existing workbook without saving the changes.

Summary

After finishing this chapter, you should now have an appreciation of how important formulas and functions are when using a spreadsheet package such as Excel.

In effect, the use of formulas is a bit like programming the worksheet, because once they have been entered correctly, the recalculation of their results is completely automatic. This is what makes applications such as Excel so useful. When entering complex formulas, it is quite easy to make mistakes; you should now understand some of the types of error values that you may encounter in Excel.

You have seen how the AutoFill facilities provided in Excel can be used on formulas as well as on ordinary data to save time entering repetitive calculations. You have also learnt the differences between relative and absolute addressing and seen why you might need to use the different types of cell referencing within formulas. In addition, you learnt that relative and absolute addresses can be used in combination in the form of mixed referencing.

The functions in Excel are even more powerful and sophisticated than the formulas and, as you've seen, they can be put to very effective use. However, whilst functions such as SUM, COUNT, and AVERAGE are fairly easy to use, some of the more specialist functions in Excel such as the IF function require a significant amount of in-depth knowledge in order to use them efficiently and correctly.

Chapter

23

Formatting Cells and Worksheets

IN THIS CHAPTER YOU WILL LEARN HOW TO

- ✓ Format text, dates, and numerical data.
- ✓ Alter the appearance of cells and the ranges of cells.
- ✓ Change the alignment of data in cells.
- ✓ Add border effects to cells.

The ability to format various aspects of a spreadsheet enables you to dramatically change its appearance. In fact, some Excel worksheets end up looking just like word-processed documents, web pages, or data entry forms—anything but a normal spreadsheet. This is useful when you need to present the results of an analysis or calculation in, say, a formal report or publish it in the form of a sales brochure. Basically, you can change the format of a cell or range of cells using either the Format menu or the Formatting toolbar.

Setting Up a Sample Worksheet

However, before proceeding further, you need to create a new workbook with a wide variety of data so that it can be used for the exercises in this chapter. The following instructions are designed to produce a basic invoice layout that you'll format using varying techniques so that eventually it looks distinctly more presentable and interesting. Take these steps to set up your worksheet:

1. If it is not open, start Excel and a new blank workbook is created. If Excel is already running, close any open workbooks and choose File ➢ New on the menu bar or the New icon on the Standard toolbar.

2. Next, enter the following data in the specified cells:

Cell Reference	Value
A1	Acme Trading Company
A2	12 High Street
A3	Newtown
A4	Anywhere
A5	ZZ9 9XX
A7	Tel: 0119-989898
A8	Fax: 0119-898989
E1	A
E2	C
E3	M
E4	E

Cell Reference	Value
C10	Invoice
A12	Customer:
A13	A/C No:
A14	Oder Date: (Note that this is a deliberate spelling mistake.)
A15	Invoice No:
B12	Mr. Smith
B13	S001
B14	12/05/03
B15	5678
D12	Delivery Address:
D13	97 Main Road, Fieldstone, Yorkshire, YY88 8WW
A19	Item Code
B19	Description
E19	Qty
F19	Unit Price
G19	TAX Rate
H19	TAX
I19	Item Total
A20	C001
A21	D005
A22	L089
A23	B012
B20	Chair
B21	Desk
B22	Lamp
B23	Catalogue
E20	12
E21	6

Cell Reference	Value
E22	15
E23	30
F20	55
F21	158
F22	63
F23	6.95
G20:G22	0.175
G23	0
H20	=(E20*F20)*G20
H21:H30	Autofill from H20
I20	=(E20*F20)+H20
I21:I30	Autofill from I20
H31	Total
I31	=SUM(I20:I30)

Once you have entered all the data as specified, your spreadsheet should look like the example in Figure 23.1.

FIGURE 23.1   The Invoice.xls spreadsheet prior to formatting

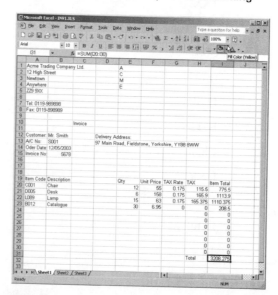

3. Save this workbook in the My Documents folder using the name Invoice.xls.

Formatting Numbers and Dates

Spreadsheet cells containing numbers or dates can be formatted in various ways in order to make them more understandable, for example, as follows:

- To display different number styles such as the number of decimal places, the number of zeros after the decimal point, with or without commas to indicate thousands
- To display different date styles
- To display different currency symbols
- To display numbers as percentages

In the following steps, you'll format the invoice you just created so that it looks more professional and business-like:

1. If it is not loaded, start Excel and open the workbook Invoice.xls. Select View ➢ Toolbars ➢ Formatting to display the Formatting toolbar.

> The Formatting toolbar displays a range of icons that can be used for a variety of formatting tasks. You may find it quicker and easier to use these tools rather than the menu bar options when completing this exercise.

2. Select cells H21:I31. Next, choose Format ➢ Cells on the menu bar. The Format Cells dialog box opens, and six tabbed options are displayed.

3. Click the Number tab if it is not already selected. Under Category, select Number; this allows you to change the way that numbers are displayed, as shown in Figure 23.2.

FIGURE 23.2   Choosing a category under the Number tab in the Format Cells dialog box

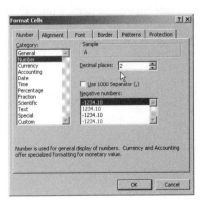

4. Make sure that the Decimal Places option is set to 2 and that there is a tick in the box next to Use 1000 Separator (,), which can be used to ensure that large numbers are displayed with commas indicating the thousands. Click OK. The numbers in the selected range are now displayed to two decimal places.

5. Select cell B14 and using the Number tab in the Format Cells dialog box again, choose Date in the Category list. In the Type list, select *14-March-2001; this formats the date using the month name rather than the month number. Click OK.

Excel allows you to format dates in a variety of different styles. For example 4/3/03 can be displayed as 04/03/03, 04/03/2003, 4-Mar-03, 04-Mar-03, 4-Mar, Mar-03, March-03, 3 March 2003, or March 4, 2003, depending on which type you choose under the Number tab in the Format Cells dialog box. Note that the date formats presented may depend on your country and language settings in the Windows operating system.

6. Select cells H20:I31. Using the Number tab in the Format Cells dialog box again, click Currency in the Category list. In the Symbol list, select the desired currency character (£, $, and so on). Click OK.

Formatting numbers as currency is a frequent requirement. There is a Currency icon on the Formatting toolbar that you can use to quickly format any selected range of numbers to be displayed using the default currency settings.

7. Finally, select cells G20:G30. Using the Number tab in the Format Cells dialog box again, click Percentage in the Category list. Set the number of Decimal Places to 1; this formats the tax rate cells as percentages with a single decimal place.

If you use the % icon on the Formatting toolbar, you may find that the numbers formatted as percentages are rounded either up or down to the nearest whole number. In either case, you can readjust them using the Number tab in the Format Cells dialog box.

8. Click OK and your Invoice.xls worksheet should now look like the example in Figure 23.3.

FIGURE 23.3   Invoice.xls after formatting numbers

9. Select File ➤ Save on the menu bar or click the Save icon to save the changes you've made so far.

Formatting Cell Contents

The text data in a spreadsheet can be formatted in a similar way to how text is formatted in a word-processing document. Formatting is frequently used for column headings and labels. Different types of formatting can be used to emphasise text or to make it more readable, as in the following examples:

- Using different font types
- Using bold, italic, underline, or double underline formatting
- Using different text font colours
- Using various colours/patterns as a background
- Using various text orientations (right, left, centre)

In the following steps, you'll continue formatting your invoice to make it even more presentable:

1. If it is not already loaded, open the workbook `Invoice.xls`.

2. Select cells A19:I19 and choose Format ➢ Cells from the menu bar. The Format Cells dialog box opens.

3. If it is not already displayed, choose the Font tab. This tab allows you to change the way the selected text is displayed, as you can see in Figure 23.4.

   Text consists of a font, point size, and a style, for example, Arial font, 16 point, bold, italic, underline. Each of these settings is called a *text attribute*, and you can use them to alter the way that text appears both on the screen and when it is printed out.

FIGURE 23.4   The Font tab in the Format Cells dialog box

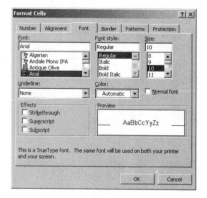

4. Under the Font Style list, select Bold Italic and click OK. The column headings are now emphasised and stand out from the remaining text. Perform the same procedure on cells A12:A15, D12, and H31.

The Formatting toolbar can be used to quickly change text attributes. Simply select the target cells and click the appropriate icons on the toolbar.

5. Now it's time to add a little colour. Select cells A1:A8 and then go to the Font tab in the Format Cells dialog box. Choose from the Color list any of the colours listed and the text changes accordingly. Perform the same procedures on cells C10 and E1:E4.

6. Re-select cell C10. Change the font to Times New Roman, increase the font size to 20, and in the Underline box, select Double. Click OK. Notice how the row height has been automatically adjusted to cater to the increased point size of the text.

7. Next, select the range E1:E4, and using the Patterns tab in the Format Cells dialog box, select an appropriate colour to be used as the background for these cells.

The use of colour can be an extremely effective way of highlighting certain areas of a spreadsheet. However, certain combinations of font and background colours can produce text that is very difficult to read. In fact, it is possible to set both the font and the background to the same colour so that the text is effectively invisible!

As well as changing the background colour of cells, you can also add shading patterns to create some very effective colour schemes.

8. Let's change the orientation of some text. Select cell E1 and choose Format ≻ Cells on the menu bar again. The Format Cells dialog box opens.

9. In the Format Cells dialog box, choose the Alignment tab. On the right, you'll see the Orientation control, as shown in Figure 23.5. Click the red diamond at the end of the pointer and drag it downwards so that the Degrees indicator shows –90 and release the mouse button. Set both the Horizontal and Vertical alignment boxes to Center, as shown in Figure 23.5.

FIGURE 23.5   Changing the orientation of text

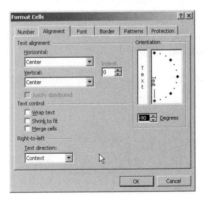

10. Click OK. The letter "A" should now appear on its side in the centre of the cell, as shown in Figure 23.6. In order to apply the same formatting to the rest of the word ACME, use the Format Painter tool on the Formatting toolbar. With cell E1 still selected, click the paintbrush icon and select the cell range E2:E4. The formatting is applied automatically to those cells.

FIGURE 23.6   The result of changing the orientation and alignment of text in cell E1

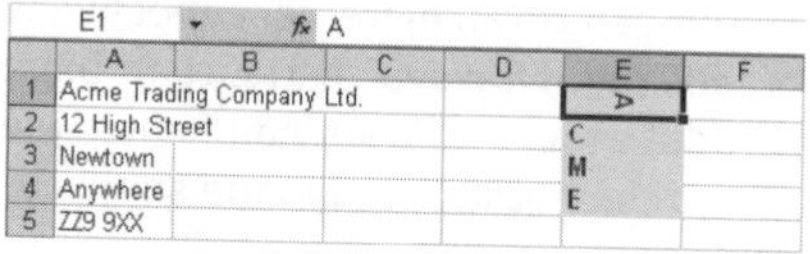

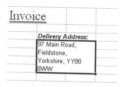

NOTE   Changing the orientation of text within cells is a useful way of reducing the width of columns where the heading is much longer than the data being stored. Simply align the text vertically and it will take up less column width.

NOTE   You might want to apply some other attributes such as colour, pattern, and point size to make this section of the spreadsheet appear more like a company logo. (Note that you cannot see the actual colours used in this formatting example, but you should notice that the coloured areas are slightly darker.)

11. Look carefully at cell D13. Notice that the text overlaps cells to the right. You can change this by forcing the text to "wrap" inside cell D13. Select the cell range D13:E16 and choose Format ➤ Cells on the menu bar again. The Format Cells dialog box opens.

12. In the Format Cells dialog box, choose the Alignment tab (shown earlier in Figure 23.5). In the Text Control area, select both the Wrap Text and Merge Cells options. Click OK. Now the text should look like Figure 23.7.

FIGURE 23.7   Using the Wrap option to align text in a cell

13. However, there is a slight problem because the first part of the postcode "YY88" should be on the bottom line. You can correct this problem by clicking the text in the Formula Bar and positioning the cursor immediately before the first letter "Y" in the postcode. Hold down the Alt key on your keyboard and press the Return or Enter key. Now release the Alt key and press Return or Enter by itself. The entire postcode "YY88 8WW" should now be on the last line of the cell.

14. Your `Invoice.xls` worksheet now looks like the example in Figure 23.8. Don't worry about the colours, as you have been left free to use any colours you choose.

FIGURE 23.8   The `Invoice.xls` worksheet after formatting the text

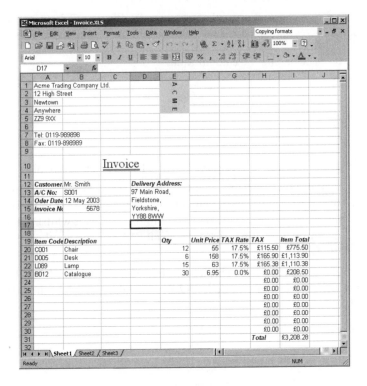

15. Select File ➢ Save on the menu bar or click the Save icon to save the changes you've made so far.

Alignment and Border Effects

When you enter text into cells, it is aligned toward the left by default. Numbers, on the other hand, are by default aligned to the right within cells. However, you can change the alignment of data within cells both horizontally and vertically. You can also format ranges of cells in other ways:

- Centre and align cell contents in a selected cell range: left and right; top and bottom.
- Centre a title over a range of cells.
- Add border effects to a selected cell range.

Using Alignment Techniques

Let's finish formatting the invoice by taking these steps:

1. Open the workbook Invoice.xls if it is not already loaded.

2. Select column A and choose Format ➢ Column ➢ Width. The Column Width dialog box shown in Figure 23.9 opens. Set the width of column A to **16** and click OK.

FIGURE 23.9 Formatting the column width

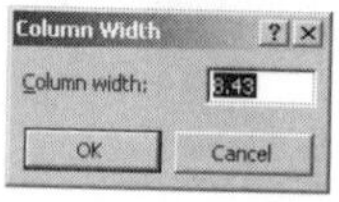

3. Select cells A12:A15 and choose Format ➢ Cells. The Format Cells dialog box opens.

4. Choose the Alignment tab in the Format Cells dialog box (shown earlier in Figure 23.5). In the Horizontal list, select Right (indent). Click OK. The text in these cells is now aligned toward the right-hand side of the column. However, whilst the adjacent text in cells B12:B13 now looks fine, the date in cell B14 and the number in cell B15 look decidedly misplaced.

5. Select cells B14:B15 and align them both to the left using steps 3 and 4, but this time choose Left (indent) in the Horizontal list. Cells A12:B15 in your spreadsheet should now look like Figure 23.10.

FIGURE 23.10 Aligning cells

6. Select row 19 and click the Center icon on the Formatting toolbar. This aligns the column heading text centrally within their cells. However, the title "Description" is centred only within cell B19; it would look better if it was aligned centrally across columns B to D. You can do this by selecting cells B19:D19 and then clicking the Merge and Center icon on the Formatting toolbar.

7. You might as well merge the cells where the actual descriptions of the goods appears underneath the title so that any long descriptions do not overlap adjacent cells. Select the range B20:D20 and choose Format ➢ Cells again. The Format Cells dialog box opens.

8. Choose the Alignment tab in the Format Cells dialog box (shown earlier in Figure 23.5), select the Merge Cells option in the Text Control area, and click OK. Use the Format Painter tool to copy the format to the range B21:D30.

9. The cell contents in a selected cell range can also be aligned vertically. Select cell C10 and increase the height of the row to **50** in the Row Height dialog box (choose Format ➢ Row ➢ Height). Notice how the text is aligned toward the bottom of the cell.

10. Select Format ➢ Cells and choose the Alignment tab in the Format Cells dialog box (shown earlier in Figure 23.5). From the Vertical list, select Center and click OK. You can adjust the column width to fit the text by selecting cell C10 and then choosing Format ➢ Column ➢ AutoFit Selection from the menu bar. The word *Invoice* is now neatly central within the row height and the column width, as shown in Figure 23.11.

11. Note that you can also align text vertically within a cell so that it appears at either the Top or Bottom by selecting the appropriate option from the Vertical list on the Alignment tab.

FIGURE 23.11 Vertical alignment within a cell

Adjusting the width of columns and the height of rows can be achieved quickly and easily by moving the appropriate column or row boundary using the mouse. When you position the mouse cursor over a column boundary, clicking and dragging allows you to adjust the boundary width, as shown in Figure 23.12.

FIGURE 23.12 Adjusting a column width using the mouse

	A	B	
1	Acme Trading Company Ltd.		
2	12 High Street		
3	Newtown		
4	Anywhere		
5	ZZ9 9XX		
6			
7	Tel: 0119-989898		
8	Fax: 0119-898989		

C10   Width: 18.71 (136 pixels)

Adding Borders to Cells

Your last bit of tidying up involves formatting the borders of the ranges of cells using the following steps:

1. Select cells A19:I30 and then choose Format ➢ Cells to open the Format Cells dialog box again. Choose the Border tab and select both the Outline and Inside buttons in the Presets area, as shown in Figure 23.13.

FIGURE 23.13   Using the Border tab to add borders around selected cells

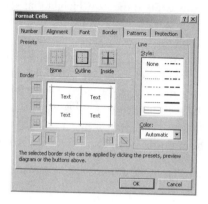

2. Click OK and notice that the area you selected on the worksheet now has borders around each of the cells, as shown in Figure 23.14.

FIGURE 23.14   Thin borders around cells

	Item Code	Description	Qty	Unit Price	TAX Rate	TAX	Item Total
18							
19	Item Code	Description	Qty	Unit Price	TAX Rate	TAX	Item Total
20	C001	Chair	12	55	17.5%	£115.50	£775.50
21	D005	Desk	6	158	17.5%	£165.90	£1,113.90
22	L089	Lamp	15	63	17.5%	£165.38	£1,110.38
23	B012	Catalogue	30	6.95	0.0%	£0.00	£208.50
24						£0.00	£0.00
25						£0.00	£0.00
26						£0.00	£0.00
27						£0.00	£0.00
28						£0.00	£0.00
29						£0.00	£0.00
30						£0.00	£0.00
31						Total	£3,208.28
32							

3. Select cells H31:I31 and this time in the Border tab, select the thickest border in the Style box in the Line area, which is the second-to-last choice. Choose only the Outside button in the Presets area, as shown in Figure 23.15. Click OK.

FIGURE 23.15   Choosing an alternative border style

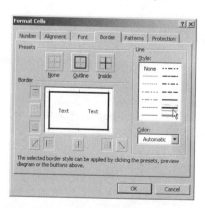

The Totals cells now have a thicker border around them, as shown in Figure 23.16.

FIGURE 23.16 Thick borders around cells

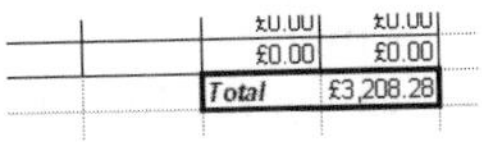

	£0.00	£0.00
	£0.00	£0.00
	Total	£3,208.28

4. Finally, select cells D12:F17, choose Format ➢ Cells, and select the Border tab in the Format Cells dialog box again. Click the double line in the Style list in the Line area (which is the last choice) and then click only the Outline button. This creates a double-line border around the Delivery Address box on your invoice.

5. The complete `Invoice.xls` worksheet should now look like the example in Figure 23.17. Select File ➢ Save on the menu bar or click the Save icon to save the changes you've made so far.

FIGURE 23.17 The `Invoice.xls` worksheet after the final formatting exercise

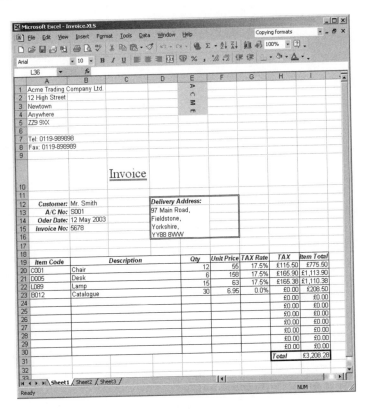

Summary

This chapter described the various ways that certain elements within a spreadsheet can be formatted as a means of enhancing its appearance. Both numbers and text can be altered to produce different effects, and you can apply formatting options to a range of cells to enhance their appearance.

In addition, you learnt how it is possible to add background colour and borders around cells to enhance the look of a worksheet.

As you can now appreciate, there are numerous options and choices regarding how you can format a spreadsheet. With a little practice, you can produce some really professional-looking results.

Chapter

24

Charts and Graphs

IN THIS CHAPTER YOU WILL LEARN HOW TO

- ✓ Produce different types of charts and graphs from spreadsheet data.
- ✓ Edit or modify a chart or graph.
- ✓ Format a chart or graph in a variety of ways.
- ✓ Change the chart type.
- ✓ Resize, duplicate, move, and delete charts or graphs.

So far, you've looked at ways that you can use Excel to produce spreadsheets containing text, numbers, formulas, and functions. But there are some more advanced features of the package that allow you to be much more creative. Typically, one of the primary uses of spreadsheet packages is to process large amounts of numerical data. However, analysing numbers stored in a spreadsheet can frequently be very difficult and, even taking into account Excel's powerful formulas and functions, it can be quite daunting looking at row after row and column after column of figures.

Fortunately, Excel has some excellent features for creating graphs or charts based on the data stored in worksheets so that information can be presented in a more easily understood format.

Using Charts and Graphs

The facilities in Excel for producing charts and graphs are extensive and powerful. This section explains how you can create and modify charts and graphs to produce a variety of visual effects.

Using the Chart Wizard

Creating charts in Excel is easy, thanks to the Chart Wizard, which guides you step by step through the four-step process of producing a chart. Excel is capable of creating a wide variety of different types of charts; you select the appropriate type from Step 1 of the Chart Wizard. Using the Chart Wizard, you can create column charts, bar charts, pie charts, line charts, area charts, and many others. In addition, most charts have sub-types, so you can, for instance, have a three-dimensional bar chart or a pie chart with the segments split up.

To learn how to use the Chart Wizard, you'll need some spreadsheet data that is suitable for analysing and turning into a graph. Let's get started:

1. If it is not loaded, start Excel; a new blank workbook is automatically created. If Excel is already running, close any open workbooks and choose File ➤ New on the menu bar or click the New icon on the Standard toolbar.

2. Enter the following data in the specified cells:

Cell Reference	Value
B2	ACME Trading Company Ltd
B4	Monthly Sales
B6	Jan
C6	Feb
D6	Mar
E6	Apr
B7	1025
C7	998
D7	1147
E7	723

3. Before graphing the data, save the workbook in the My Documents folder with the name Sales.xls.

4. Your worksheet should now look like the example shown in Figure 24.1.

FIGURE 24.1   The initial Sales.xls worksheet

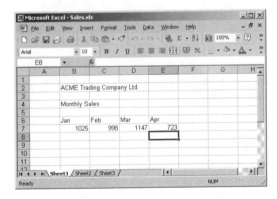

Charts in Excel can be created in two different forms: as an object embedded in a worksheet or as a separate chart worksheet within a workbook. The procedure for creating these two types of chart is basically the same; when you use the Chart Wizard, you are asked which type of chart you wish to create.

5. The first thing to do is to decide on the data to be used to create the chart. In the Sales.xls example, you want to plot the sales figures for the four months. Therefore, select the cell range B6:E7 and then choose Insert ➤ Chart. The Chart Wizard automatically starts at Step 1 with the Chart Type window shown in Figure 24.2.

FIGURE 24.2 Step 1 of the Chart Wizard: Choosing the chart type

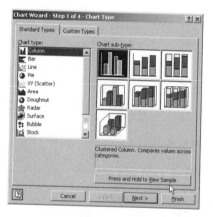

You can also start the Chart Wizard by clicking the Chart Wizard icon on the Standard toolbar.

Note that the Chart Wizard automatically prompts you to enter the correct information that is directly relevant to the type of chart being created.

6. Step 1 of the Chart Wizard allows you to select both the type and the sub-type of the chart you wish to create. For the moment, simply accept the defaults presented, which is a clustered column chart. Because you selected your chart data before you started the

Chart Wizard, you can use the Press And Hold To View Sample button, and a preview of your chart is displayed. Click Next to proceed.

7. Step 2 of the Chart Wizard displays the Chart Source Data dialog box, as shown in Figure 24.3. Here you specify the cells where the data for the chart can be found. But you've already done this, so proceed to the next step. Click Next to proceed.

FIGURE 24.3   Step 2 of the Chart Wizard: Selecting the data source

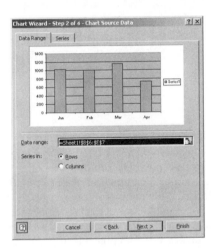

8. At Step 3 of the Chart Wizard, the Chart Options window opens, as shown in Figure 24.4. This multi-tabbed dialog box allows you to specify a whole range of chart options such as titles, axis labels, gridlines, legends, data labels, and whether the chart should include a data table. For the moment, ignore these options and proceed to the final step of the Chart Wizard. Click Next to proceed.

FIGURE 24.4   Step 3 of the Chart Wizard: Specifying chart options

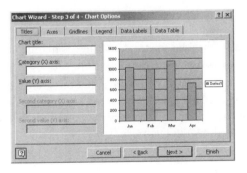

9. Step 4 of the Chart Wizard is the Chart Location window, as shown in Figure 24.5. Here you decide whether you want the chart to be created as a new sheet with the sheet name Chart1, or as an object in your currently active worksheet (Sheet1). In this instance, opt for the latter, so select As Object In if it is not already selected. Click Finish.

FIGURE 24.5   Step 4 of the Chart Wizard: Deciding on the chart location

An *object* is any element on a worksheet that is not contained in a cell. Objects can be created with Excel itself by, for example, using the drawing tools. Alternatively, objects can be imported from external sources by choosing Insert ➢ Object. Whichever method is used to incorporate an object into a worksheet, it is treated as a discrete element that is separate from the worksheet but stored in the workbook when it is saved. You can resize and move any type of object, but if an object is imported from another file, you cannot edit its contents unless you start the underlying application that was used to create it by double-clicking the object itself.

10. As soon as you click Finish in the Chart Wizard, the dialog box closes and the newly created chart appears as an object in the centre of your worksheet, as shown in Figure 24.6. As well as the chart object, a "floating" Chart toolbar also appears. For now, close the toolbar by clicking its Close control button.

    The chart object is already selected, so you can use the box size control handles and the mouse pointer to resize and move the chart object to a different position on the worksheet if you wish. Notice also that the source data range is highlighted with special coloured borders, but as soon as you deselect the chart object, these borders disappear.

11. Just as formulas change dynamically when you alter the source data, charts in Excel do the same. For example, on the Sales.xls worksheet, select cell C7 and type in the value **200**. As soon as you press the Return or Enter key to accept the change, the chart changes to reflect the new data, as shown in Figure 24.7.

FIGURE 24.6 The new chart embedded as an object in your worksheet

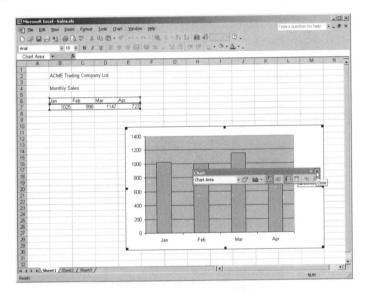

FIGURE 24.7 Charts change when the source data changes.

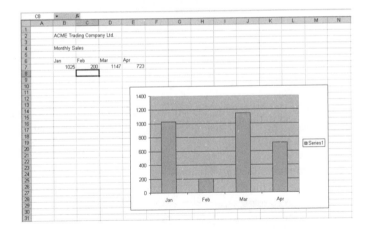

The first step in the Chart Wizard allows you to decide which type of chart to create and you are free to choose a bar, a line, or a pie chart instead of the default column chart. However, deciding on the type of chart to create can be rather difficult as the actual data being graphed may not be suitable for every format. Fortunately, as you will see later in this chapter, if a particular chart type proves to be unsuitable, it is a relatively simple matter to change it into something more appropriate.

Modifying Charts and Graphs

Once your chart is created in Excel, you can go back and modify various characteristics of it by taking the following steps:

1. Select the chart on the worksheet. (If the Chart toolbar opens, simply close it or drag it out of the way for the time being.)

2. Choose Chart ➢ Chart Options on the menu bar. The Chart Options window that you originally saw in Step 3 of the Chart Wizard (see Figure 24.4) opens. You can use this tabbed window to change various characteristics of your chart.

3. Make sure that the Titles tab is selected. In the Chart Title box, type **Product Sales by Month**; in the Category (X) Axis box, type **Month**; and in the Value (Y) Axis box, type **Units** (see Figure 24.8). Notice that when you make these changes, the chart preview window updates automatically.

FIGURE 24.8 Entering the chart titles

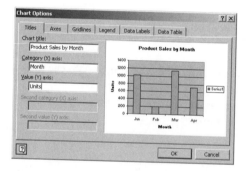

4. Select the Legend tab in the Chart Options window and uncheck the Show Legend tick box. In the preview window, the legend disappears and the chart resizes itself to fill the space available, as shown in Figure 24.9.

FIGURE 24.9 Removing the chart's legend

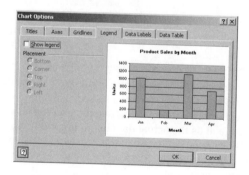

5. Select the Data Labels tab in the Chart Options window and then check the Value option in the Label Contains section. In the preview window, the unit values appear just above the columns on the chart, as shown in Figure 24.10.

FIGURE 24.10   Adding the data labels to your chart

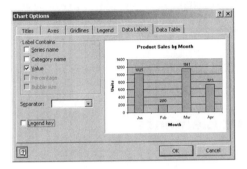

6. Finally, click OK. The Chart Options dialog box closes, leaving the chart embedded in the worksheet, updated with the changes that you've made, as shown in Figure 24.11.

FIGURE 24.11   The embedded chart after changing various chart options

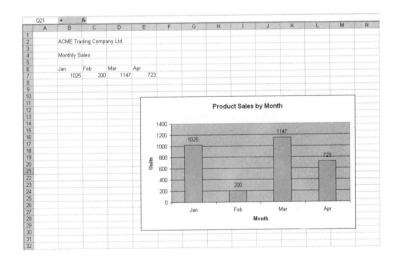

When you resize a chart object on a worksheet, the image either shrinks or expands. Note that the scaling of the X or Y axis does not alter. If you need to rescale the axis on a chart, select the axis and then choose Format ➤ Select Axis. Using the Scale tab in the Format Axis dialog box, adjust properties of the axis such as the maximum and minimum values and the major and minor units used in the axis. In addition, you can reverse the plotting order of the values or apply a logarithmic scale if necessary.

7. Before proceeding further, select File ➤ Save on the menu bar or click the Save icon to save the changes you've made so far.

Formatting Chart Elements

A chart consists of many different elements such as the plotted data series, the axes, and the data labels. Each of these elements can be formatted in their own right to change the look of a chart.

Suppose you want to change the colour or shading pattern used for the columns in the Sales.xls chart. You can do this by following these steps:

1. Select the columns with a single click with the left mouse button. Now if you select Format ➤ Selected Data Series on the menu bar, the Format Data Series dialog box opens, as shown in Figure 24.12. Here you can select any of the colours shown to replace the existing column colour and then click the OK button. Similarly, you can change the colours of bars, lines, and pie slices in other types of charts by using the same technique.

FIGURE 24.12   Changing the formatting of the data series

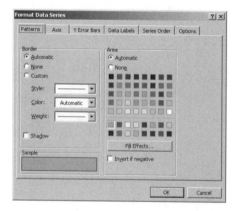

2. On the Patterns tab in the Format Data Series dialog box, click the Fill Effects button. A new dialog box called Fill Effects opens, as you can see in Figure 24.13.

FIGURE 24.13   The Fill Effects dialog box

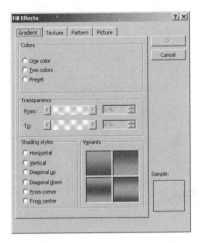

3. Select the Pattern tab in the Fill Effects dialog box and choose a prominent pattern to use, such as diagonal lines, as shown in Figure 24.14.

FIGURE 24.14   Selecting a fill pattern

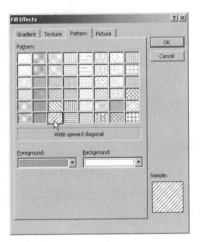

Don't get confused between the Patterns tab in the Format Data Series window and the Pattern tab in the Fill Effects window—they are different. The former allows you to change the way the borders around elements of a chart appear and the colours used. The latter enables you to change the actual shading pattern used within a chart element such as a column or a pie slice.

4. Click OK to close the Fill Effects window and click OK again to close the Format Data Series window. Your chart should now look like the example in Figure 24.15.

FIGURE 24.15 Patterned columns

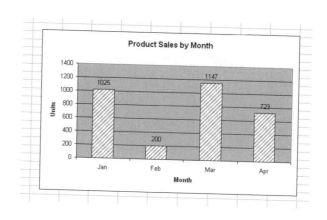

5. Before proceeding further, select File ➢ Save or click the Save icon to save the changes you've made so far.

As well as changing the colour and pattern used for the bars in your chart, you can alter its background. Follow these steps:

1. Select the Chart Area by clicking an area just inside the border. (Note that if you accidentally select an element of the chart, such as the title or the plot area, simply move your mouse pointer and click again until the whole chart has been selected.)

2. This time you'll use the Chart toolbar to make the changes to the chart. So select View ➢ Toolbars ➢ Chart. The Chart toolbar opens, as shown in Figure 24.16.

FIGURE 24.16 The Chart toolbar

Format Chart Area

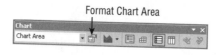

3. Click the Format Chart Area icon. The Format Chart Area dialog box opens, as shown in Figure 24.17.

FIGURE 24.17   The Format Chart Area dialog box

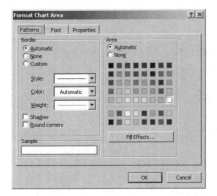

4. Select any colour displayed in the Area section and click OK. Your chart now has a coloured background, as shown in Figure 24.18.

FIGURE 24.18   The chart with a coloured background

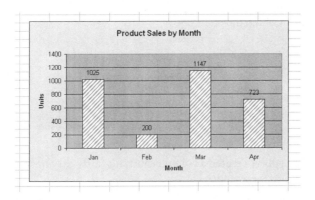

As well as changing the background colour of charts, you can also add shading patterns to create some very effective colour schemes. However, certain combinations of background and foreground colours and patterns can produce somewhat garish-looking charts. Be prepared to experiment with different formats and styles until you achieve the desired result.

It should now be apparent that charts consist of several different elements or components such as the background, the title, the legend, and the axis labels. Each of these can be formatted in a variety of different ways. In the case of the title or the axis labels, you can edit the text as well, by taking these steps:

1. For example, click the chart title "Product Sales by Month" once to select it, as shown in Figure 24.19.

FIGURE 24.19   Selecting chart elements—in this case, the chart title

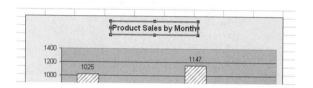

2. Now if you click inside the object selection box, a vertical flashing cursor appears so that you can edit the text. Change the chart title to read "Monthly Sales," as shown in Figure 24.20. Click anywhere outside the chart title area to complete the editing process.

FIGURE 24.20   Editing the chart title

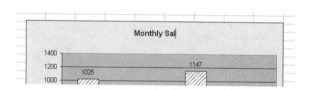

Despite the fact that you've created a column chart, it's fairly easy to change the type of chart to something else. Follow these steps:

1. Select the chart object and choose Chart ➤ Chart Type on the menu bar. This displays the Chart Type dialog box that you originally saw in Step 1 of the Chart Wizard (see Figure 24.2, shown earlier). You use this tabbed window to select the new type of chart.

2. Click Pie in the Chart Type list, and in the Chart Sub-Type window, select the top centre three-dimensional sub-type, as shown in Figure 24.21.

FIGURE 24.21 Changing the chart type

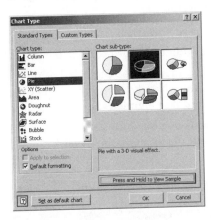

3. In the Options section, select the tick box labelled Default Formatting, as shown in Figure 24.22.

FIGURE 24.22 Using the default formatting for a chart

4. Click OK. Your embedded chart changes to a three-dimensional pie chart, like the example in Figure 24.23. Notice that the chart title has disappeared; this is because you used the Default Formatting option when you converted the chart to a pie format.

FIGURE 24.23 The Sales.xls chart changed into a three-dimensional pie chart

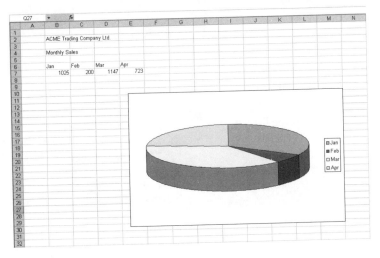

Duplicating, Moving, Resizing, and Deleting Charts

You learnt earlier that charts can exist as either objects on a worksheet or as separate chart worksheets within a workbook. In the following, you'll see how you can duplicate, move, resize, and delete a chart. To convert your embedded chart into a chart sheet, take these steps:

1. Select the chart object and then choose Chart ➤ Location from the menu bar. If you remember, this displays the Chart Location dialog box that you originally saw in Step 4 of the Chart Wizard (see Figure 24.5, shown earlier).

2. When the Chart Location dialog box opens, it shows the current chart placement as an object in Sheet1. To change the location, simply click the As New Sheet option, as shown in Figure 24.24.

FIGURE 24.24   Changing the location of a chart

3. Now, when you click OK in the Chart Location dialog box, the chart switches from an embedded object to become a separate chart sheet labelled Chart1 within the Sales.xls workbook, as shown in Figure 24.25.

FIGURE 24.25   The Sales.xls chart as a chart sheet

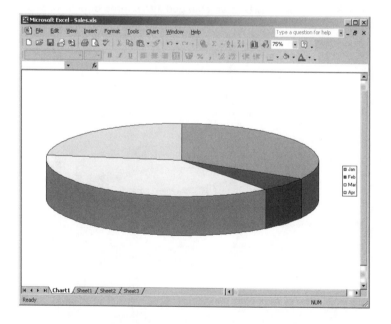

To move, resize, and duplicate your chart object on a worksheet, follow these steps:

1. Reselect Chart ➤ Location from the menu bar and set the chart location As Object In Sheet1 again. Select the chart and, using the mouse, drag it from the centre of the sheet toward the left-hand side, just below the data. Using the resize handles, make the chart object approximately 50 percent smaller. Your worksheet should now look similar to Figure 24.26.

FIGURE 24.26 Positioning and resizing the chart object on Sheet1

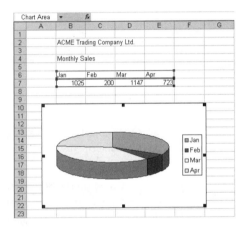

2. With the chart object still selected, use the Copy and Paste tools on the Standard toolbar to make a copy of the chart and position it alongside the original, as shown in Figure 24.27.

FIGURE 24.27 Two copies of the same chart on Sheet1

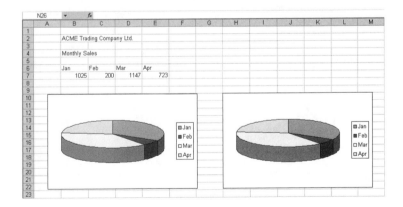

3. Now select the right-hand pie chart and convert it into a three-dimensional line chart. Select cell C7, enter the value **4500**, and press the Return or Enter key. Notice how both the charts change automatically to reflect the new value. Your worksheet should now look like Figure 24.28.

FIGURE 24.28 Two different types of charts on Sheet1

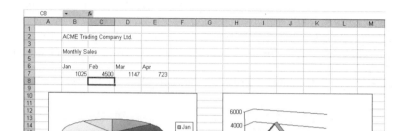

As well as duplicating a chart on the same worksheet, it is entirely possible to copy or move a chart from one worksheet to another, or from one open workbook to another. Follow these steps:

1. Open a new workbook by clicking the New icon on the Standard toolbar. Go back to the Sales.xls workbook and select the three-dimensional line chart.

2. Using the Cut and Paste buttons on the Standard toolbar, move the chart onto the new Book2.xls Sheet2, as shown in Figure 24.29.

FIGURE 24.29 The result of moving the three-dimensional line chart from the Sales.xls workbook to the new Book2.xls Sheet2

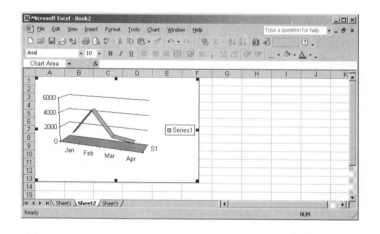

Charts embedded within worksheets are just like other objects in that you can move and resize them in the same way. To delete an embedded chart, simply select it and press the Delete key on the keyboard. The source data from which the chart was created remains untouched. If a chart has been created as a separate worksheet in a workbook, you simply delete the entire worksheet to remove it, as explained in the section "Deleting a Worksheet" in Chapter 21.

3.   Finally, close the Sales.xls workbook, saving any changes made. Close the Book2.xls workbook, but *do not save it.*

Summary

In this chapter, you saw how various types of charts can be generated from source data in an Excel worksheet. You learnt how to format charts in lots of different ways and how to convert a chart from an embedded object into a chart sheet within a workbook. In addition, you saw how charts can be resized, duplicated, moved, and deleted.

Creating charts in Excel can be very rewarding. Once you start exploring the capabilities available, you can produce some extremely useful and professional-looking results. The best advice is to experiment with all the various formatting options just to see exactly what is possible.

Chapter

25

Preparing Outputs

IN THIS CHAPTER YOU WILL LEARN HOW TO

✓ Modify the margin settings of a worksheet.

✓ Change the worksheet orientation.

✓ Adjust the document setup to fit on one page or on a specific number of pages.

✓ Add or modify headers and footers on a worksheet.

✓ Insert fields into headers and footers.

✓ Check for spelling and other errors.

✓ Use the Print Preview tool prior to printing a spreadsheet.

✓ Select the appropriate printing options.

✓ Apply automatic title rows for printing on every page.

✓ Print all of a worksheet, multiple copies, a predefined cell range, or a selected chart.

So far, everything that you've done has been in relation to how spreadsheets appear on the computer screen. However, one of the primary uses of spreadsheets is in the preparation of data to be produced in a printed form for distribution. Therefore, you now need to learn how to prepare and format a spreadsheet for printing and getting the results of your work onto the page.

This section starts by making use of the Invoice.xls worksheet that you created in Chapter 23, "Formatting Cells and Worksheets."

The steps in this section assume that the PC that you are using to perform the following exercises has a suitable printer attached to it and that it is properly configured for use by the Windows XP operating system. Should this not be the case, any tasks that require you to actually print a worksheet in this chapter should be modified to print the output to a file instead.

Worksheet Setup

Before actually printing your invoice, it is important to understand how you can control the way that a spreadsheet is printed. In this section, you'll learn how to modify a document's margins and orientation as well as how to modify the header and footer.

Modifying the Margins of a Worksheet

Margins are used to control the blank borders around a printed spreadsheet on the page. They can be adjusted so that the data printed is positioned neatly on the page. Frequently, you may need to reduce the margins so that more of a spreadsheet can be printed on a page. Take these steps to modify a worksheet's margins for printing:

1. If it is not already open, open the workbook Invoice.xls.

2. Choose File ➢ Page Setup from the menu bar and select the Margins tab in the Page Setup dialog box, as shown in Figure 25.1.

3. The printed page has four margins: top, bottom, left, and right. You can adjust the various margin settings by typing in new values (in cms) or by using the up/down control buttons to increase or decrease the values. You can click the Print Preview button in order to see the results of any changes that you make.

Adjusting the margins to get the data printed exactly in the middle of the page can be fiddly. However, there are two check boxes in the Center On Page section on the Margins tab. These check boxes are labelled Horizontally and Vertically. If you select both of these, the printed data is automatically centred on the page for you.

FIGURE 25.1   The Margins tab in the Page Setup dialog box

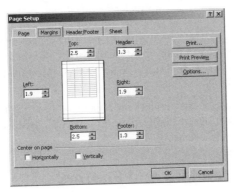

Change Worksheet Orientation

The *orientation* refers to how the worksheet appears on the page, vertically or horizontally. Take these steps to change a worksheet's orientation:

1. Click the Page tab in the Page Setup dialog box, as shown in Figure 25.2. Here you set the orientation of the printed page as either Portrait (this is the default) or Landscape. Because many spreadsheets are often wider than they are long, printing them out in Landscape format is a useful feature of Excel.

FIGURE 25.2   Switching between Portrait and Landscape orientation

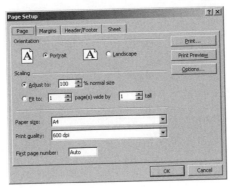

2. Just below the Orientation section on the Page tab is a section called Scaling, as shown in Figure 25.3. These settings can be used to adjust the size of the print on the paper.

FIGURE 25.3   Adjusting the scale of the print

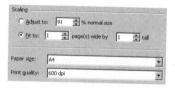

For example, you can increase or shrink the print by a percentage using the Adjust To control, or you can force the print to fit on a specific number of pages using the Fit To controls. Click the Fit To radio button to select this option to print on a single page, as shown in Figure 25.3.

Also on the Page tab are boxes to select the paper size and the print quality that you want to use. However, the settings available in these two drop-down lists depend on the type and model of printer that you are using.

Setting Up the Headers and Footers

Excel has two special areas called the *header* and the *footer*, which are reserved for use when printing out worksheets. As you can probably deduce, the header appears at the top of printed pages and the footer appears at the bottom. Headers and footers are a useful method of ensuring that specific information is always printed on each page. This information can be constant in the form of a company name, or it can be a variable in the form of a sequential page number.

Take these steps to set up headers and footers in a worksheet:

1. Select the Header/Footer tab in the Page Setup dialog box, as shown in Figure 25.4.

FIGURE 25.4   Setting up the headers and footers for a worksheet

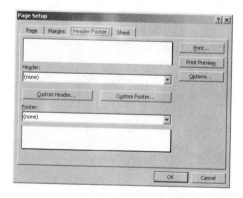

2. Headers and footers can be printed automatically on every page generated when you print your spreadsheet. This is especially useful when a spreadsheet spans several pages. On the Header/Footer tab, there are a selection of predefined headers and footers that you can choose from. Using the drop-down list, select the last item, which inserts "Prepared by *User Name Date*, Page 1" into the header, as shown in Figure 25.5.

FIGURE 25.5   Inserting a predefined header into your worksheet

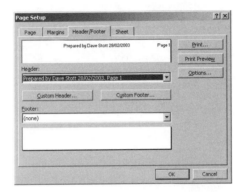

Note that headers and footers that are created in the Page Setup options do not appear in the actual worksheet itself. But they can be seen in the Print Preview view, and they do print out on the page.

3. As well as using the predefined settings for headers and footers, you can define your own headers and footers by clicking the Custom Header or Custom Footer buttons. Click the Custom Footer button; a new window called Footer opens, as shown in Figure 25.6.

FIGURE 25.6   Creating a custom footer

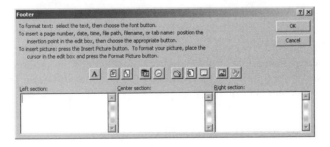

4. In the Left Section, type the words **Customer Invoice** and then click the Right Section box. Here you should insert the time by clicking the small clock icon, as shown in Figure 25.7. Click OK to complete the process of customising the footer.

FIGURE 25.7   Inserting details into a custom footer

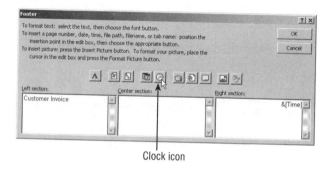

Clock icon

5. The Page Setup window should now look like the one shown in Figure 25.8, but with your own username in the header details.

FIGURE 25.8   The result of modifying headers and footers

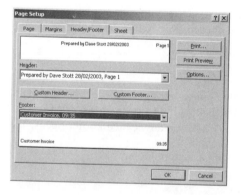

WARNING   When using date and time fields in headers or footers, Excel uses the current date and time values provided by the Windows operating system when the document is printed.

6. Save any changes made to the Invoice.xls workbook.

Preparing the Worksheet for Printing

Now that you've performed the document setup procedures, you need to prepare the worksheet for printing your invoice. This section explains how to properly prepare your worksheet prior to printing and how to preview the document to ensure that it prints in the desired format.

Checking for Spelling Mistakes and Other Errors

Just as when using a word processor to produce documents, it is important to ensure that all the words in a spreadsheet are spelt correctly if you are to create a good impression. Take these steps to check your worksheet:

1. If it is not already open, open the workbook Invoice.xls.

2. Excel has a spelling checker that can be activated by either clicking the Spelling icon on the Standard toolbar or selecting Tools ➢ Spelling from the menu bar.

3. When triggered, the spelling checker checks the entire spreadsheet or the currently selected range of cells. Therefore, to check the whole of the spreadsheet, make sure that the active cell is A1.

4. When the spelling checker encounters what it thinks is an incorrectly spelt word, it highlights the cell and displays a Spelling dialog box, as shown in Figure 25.10.

FIGURE 25.9   The Excel spelling checker in action

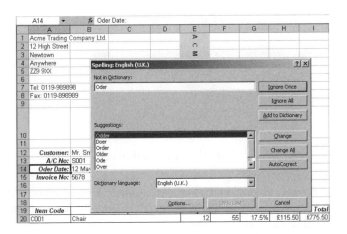

5. In Figure 25.9, you can see that the word "Order" has been typed as "Oder." The spelling checker presents a list of suggested corrections. If the correct spelling is listed as a suggestion, simply double-click it to accept it. However, if the correct word has not been suggested, type the correct spelling in the Change To box and then click the Change button.

6. If the word is not found in the dictionary but you know that it is spelt correctly (for example, it is a trade name or a foreign word), click the Ignore button (or Ignore All button if there is likely to be more than one occurrence of the word).

7. When you either change or ignore an incorrectly spelt word, the spelling checker then moves on to search for the next possible incorrect word in the spreadsheet. At the end of the spell-checking process, a small window appears to confirm that it is complete, as shown in Figure 25.10. You can simply click OK to continue.

FIGURE 25.10   The spelling checker notifies you when it has completed.

8. Save any changes made to the workbook.

As well as checking the worksheet for spelling mistakes, Excel also allows you to check for any errors in your formulas. You learnt about formulas in Chapter 22, and there shouldn't be any formula errors in your Invoice.xls worksheet. Therefore, let's introduce an error temporarily for the purposes of demonstrating the error-checking capabilities of Excel. In cell H12, enter the formula **=test*99**. Naturally, this automatically generates an error as soon as you press the Enter or Return key; Excel offers to correct the error for you, as shown in Figure 25.11. However, for the moment, reject the proposed correction and click No.

FIGURE 25.11   Forcing Excel to ignore an error when entering it

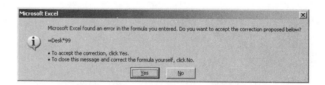

As you saw in Chapter 22, an error label is created in cell H12. To continue checking for formula errors, follow these steps:

1. Select Tools ➤ Error Checking on the Standard toolbar. Excel searches through the worksheet until it encounters an error. If it finds one, the Error Checking dialog box appears, as shown in Figure 25.12.

FIGURE 25.12   The Error Checking dialog box

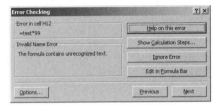

2. You now have several different options: Help On This Error, Show Calculation Steps, Ignore Error, and Edit In Formula Bar. Seeing as you generated this error on purpose, simply click the Ignore Error button; a small window appears to confirm that the error check is complete.

3. Click OK to continue. Once you are back to the `Invoice.xls` worksheet, delete the contents of cell H12.

Whilst Excel can check for errors in formulas, this is not the same as checking the validity of your calculations. For example, if you make a mistake and multiply something when you really meant to divide, this is not an error as far as Excel is concerned. The formula is entirely correct, but the mistake was created by you. Therefore, it's entirely up to the user to check whether or not the calculations are valid for the intended purpose.

4. Save any changes made to the `Invoices.xls` workbook.

Previewing a Worksheet Prior to Printing

You can preview the page(s) of a worksheet before actually printing it by either selecting File ➢ Print Preview from the menu bar or by clicking the Print Preview icon (a sheet of paper with a magnifying glass) on the Standard toolbar from within the worksheet itself. If you do this, you'll see that whilst all the details of the invoice are shown, the projected printout does not really look like a proper invoice, because both the cell reference headings and the gridlines around the cells are printed as well, as shown in Figure 25.13.

FIGURE 25.13 Print Preview of `Invoice.xls` showing gridlines and cell reference headings

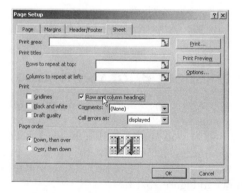

You can prevent these elements from being printed by turning them off in the Page Setup dialog box. Follow these steps:

1. Select File ➢ Page Setup from the menu bar and then select the Sheet tab in the Page Setup dialog box. Notice that both the gridlines and the row and column headings boxes are selected by default. Click each box to turn them off, as shown in Figure 25.14.

FIGURE 25.14 Removing gridlines and row and column headings prior to printing

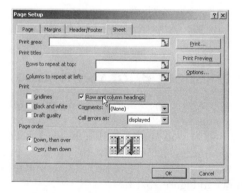

2. Now, when you preview the printed output using the Print Preview option, the page being printed looks more like a proper invoice, as shown in Figure 25.15. Close the Print Preview window, and you are returned to the normal worksheet view.

3. Save any changes made to the workbook and then close it.

FIGURE 25.15   Print Preview showing the removal of gridlines and row and column
headings prior to printing

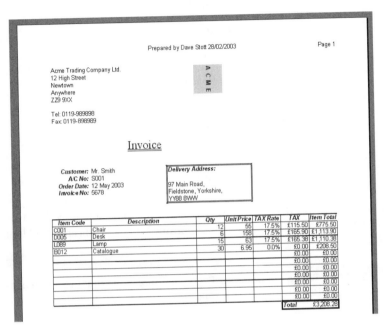

Printing Column Headings

So far, you've dealt only with worksheets that contain a fairly small amount of information, in other words, no more than can fit on a single page when printed. However, many spreadsheets—typically long tables—contain large amounts of data that result in many pages when printed. As a result, it may be necessary to print column headings in a worksheet at the top of every page to aid the reader in identifying the contents of columns. Note that this is not the same as printing page headers, which was covered earlier in this chapter.

Follow these steps to print column headings:

1. For this exercise you'll use a fresh worksheet. Choose File ➢ New on the menu bar or click the New icon on the Standard toolbar.

2. Enter the following data in the specified cells:

Cell Reference	Value
A1	Date
B1	Day

Cell Reference	Value
C1	Serial No.
D1	Prod. Code
E1	Description
A2	01/03/2003
B2	Sat
C2	1000001
D2	AAAA
E2	BBBBBBBB

3. Using the mouse, select the cells A2:E2, click the fill handle, and drag downward with the mouse to E300 before releasing the mouse button. Your worksheet should look similar to Figure 25.16.

FIGURE 25.16   Filling the range A2:E300 with data. Note that the figure uses a split window to show the top and bottom of the range.

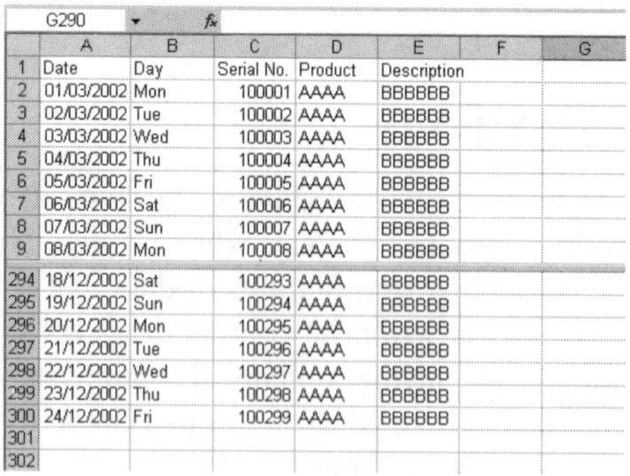

4. Select File ➤ Page Setup and click the Sheet tab in the Page Setup dialog box. Click once in the Rows To Repeat At Top box and then select row 1 in the worksheet behind the Page Setup window, as shown in Figure 25.17. Click OK.

5. Now if you perform a Print Preview, you'll see that the row you selected appears at the top of every page, as shown in Figure 25.18. Use the Next and Previous buttons in the Print Preview window to check this out. Then close the Print Preview window.

FIGURE 25.17 Selecting a row to use as a print title

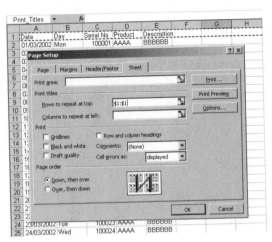

FIGURE 25.18 Page 3 of your worksheet showing the title row at the top of the page

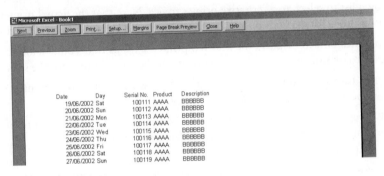

6. Close the Book1 worksheet without saving any of the changes; you no longer need it.

Printing a Worksheet

Now that you've performed the worksheet setup and the preparation procedures, you can think about printing your invoice. In this section, you'll learn how to use the printing options to print all or just part of a worksheet.

Using the Printing Options

For this final exercise, you'll need both the Invoice.xls workbook and the Sales.xls workbook:

1. If it is not already open, open the Invoice.xls workbook.

2. Select File ➤ Print on the menu bar. A Print dialog box such as the one shown in Figure 25.19 appears. This dialog box can be used to control the actual printing of a worksheet.

FIGURE 25.19   Controlling a print job

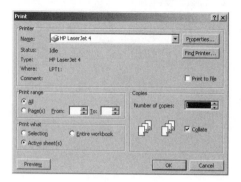

3. In the Printer section, select the specific printer that you want to use for this particular print job; normally, the current Windows default printer is shown here. If necessary, use the drop-down list to select an alternative printer to use. Note that the actual printers available in the drop-down list depends on what printers have been installed in your Windows system.

4. The Properties button displays the selected printer settings that you can alter; this is generally used to set things such as the print quality or the paper source for the selected printer.

5. In the Print Range section, define how much of the worksheet is to be printed by selecting All or by specifying one page or a range of pages.

6. In the Copies section, specify how many copies of a worksheet you want to print and whether you want to collate (assemble in order) the copies.

7. Finally, in the Print dialog box, there is a section labelled Print What. Here you specify whether you want to print a worksheet selection, the current active worksheet(s), or the entire workbook.

8. Once you're satisfied with the various settings controlling the print job, simply click OK to start the printing process.

9. If there isn't a printer available on your system, you may have to print to a file instead. If this is the case, make sure that there is a tick in the Print To File box in the Print dialog box. Then when you click OK to start the printing, you are asked to provide an Output File Name in the Print To File dialog box, as shown in Figure 25.20.

FIGURE 25.20   Request for an output filename

Instead of using the File ➤ Print option from the menu bar, you can simply click the Print icon on the Standard toolbar. However, if you do this, you forego the opportunity to change any print settings; the printout is produced using the default settings, which are the current default Windows printer, print all pages, print one copy, and print the active sheet(s).

Assuming that you are using A4 paper and that you print using the default settings, when you print the `Invoice.xls` worksheet, it may print on two pages, with the Item Total column on the second page. This is because the `Invoice.xls` file is too wide to fit on a single sheet of A4 paper in Portrait format. If you experience this problem, simply select Landscape orientation on the Page tab in the Page Setup dialog box and print the document again.

Before you actually produce any printed pages, you can, if you wish, look at a preview of the document by clicking the Print Preview icon on the Standard toolbar. This opens a new window that displays the document as it will appear on the page, as shown in Figure 25.21.

FIGURE 25.21 The Print Preview window controls

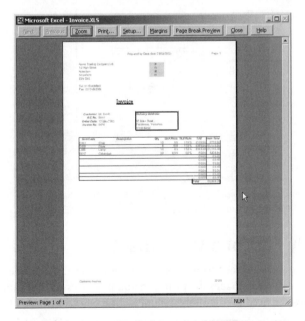

The Print Preview window has a series of nine control buttons running along the top:

- The Next button displays the next page if the document has more than one page.
- The Previous button displays the previous page if the document has more than one page.

- The Zoom button allows you to magnify or shrink the page image being displayed.

- The Print button opens the Print dialog box.

- The Setup button displays the Page Setup dialog box.

- The Margins button overlays the page image with the current margin settings so that you can see what the printing boundaries are and adjust the margins using the mouse.

- The Page Break Preview button is probably the most useful button. When you click it, Excel displays the current worksheet with the page boundaries or print area shown, as in Figure 25.22. To return to the normal worksheet view, select View ➢ Normal on the menu bar.

- The Close button closes the Print Preview window and returns you to your normal worksheet view.

- The Help button gives you more detailed information about the Print Preview window.

FIGURE 25.22   The Page Break Preview display for the `Invoice.xls` worksheet

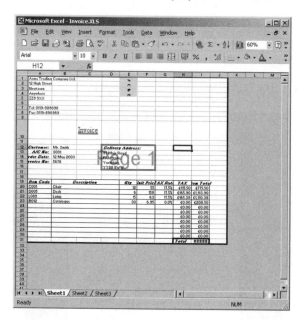

Printing Only Part of a Worksheet

Normally when printing, you need to print an entire worksheet. When the document being printed is quite large, Excel manages the print job and produces the relevant number of pages. However, sometimes you need to print only a small section of a worksheet. Here's how to do that:

1. Select the range of cells that you want to print, for example, D12:F17 in the `Invoice.xls` worksheet.

2. Choose File ➢ Print Area ➢ Set Print Area on the menu bar. This defines the area to be printed based solely on the cells selected in the worksheet. Now, if you perform a Print

Preview, notice that just the Delivery Address box on your invoice will be printed, as shown in Figure 25.23.

FIGURE 25.23   Print Preview of a selected area of the `Invoice.xls` worksheet

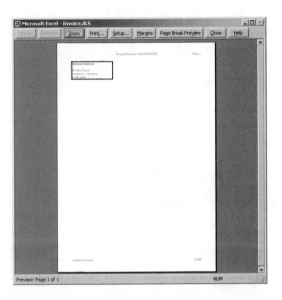

3. Close the `Invoice.xls` workbook without saving any of the changes, because you no longer need it.

Before you finish with the printing capabilities in Excel, you might on occasion need to print out a graph or chart. Follow these steps:

1. Start by opening the `Sales.xls` workbook. Click the pie chart, as shown in Figure 25.24.

FIGURE 25.24   Selecting a chart to print

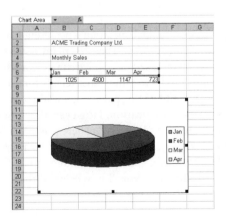

2. Select Print Preview and notice that just the selected chart will be printed, as shown in Figure 25.25.

FIGURE 25.25   Print Preview of a selected chart area of the Sales.xls worksheet

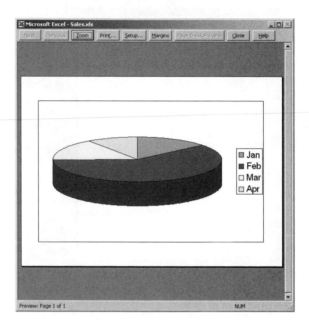

3. Close the Sales.xls workbook without saving any of the changes, because you no longer need it.

Summary

Printing worksheets is pretty much an essential operation when using Excel. In this chapter, you learnt how to control and manage the printing process. There are many issues to consider, for example, the printer settings, the page settings, the print settings, and even the worksheet settings. Fortunately, the Print Preview option allows you to check everything on screen before committing anything to paper.

Now that you have reached the end of this part, you should have gained a good insight into the principles of using a spreadsheet application. However, this module is not intended to be a fully comprehensive training manual for Excel XP. There are many features of Excel that were not covered in this book. Excel is the type of application that the more it is used, the more varied tasks you'll find it can tackle. Therefore, you are encouraged to further explore the capabilities and features of Excel in order to broaden your knowledge of the software.

If you have access to the Internet, start by visiting the Microsoft Excel website, where you'll find plenty of additional information about the product:

`http://www.microsoft.com/office/excel/default.htm`

If you don't have access to the Internet, or if you are happier learning from a book, there are numerous published training guides for Excel that cover every single facet of using the software.

Module Review Questions

1. What is the difference between a worksheet and a workbook?

2. Which two toolbars are displayed on screen by default in Excel?

3. How do you enter a series of numerical digits into a cell so that they are treated as text?

4. Whereabouts on the screen would you click with the mouse to select an entire
   - Row?
   - Column?
   - Worksheet?

5. How do you increase the width of a worksheet column?

6. How can you ensure that a worksheet is copied rather than simply moved?

7. What is the difference between a formula and a function?

8. What type of error causes #NAME? to be displayed when entering a formula?

9. What is the difference between the relative addressing and absolute addressing of cells?

10. How can you specify the number of decimal places that a value in a cell should display?

11. What procedure do you use to produce vertical text in a cell?

12. How do you convert a pie chart to a column chart?

Answers to Module Review Questions

1. The term workbook refers to the actual spreadsheet file and a workbook can consist of a number of separate worksheets. In other words, a workbook is a collection of worksheets.

2. The Standard toolbar and the Formatting toolbar are displayed by default.

3. Place a single quote (') character at the beginning of the numbers you wish to enter so that they are treated like text.

4. To select an entire row, click in the vertical row headings on the left-hand side of the worksheet. To select an entire column, click in the horizontal column headings at the top of the worksheet. To select an entire worksheet, click once with the cross pointer on the small grey box called the Select All button at the junction of the row numbers and column letters.

5. Either choose Format ➢ Column ➢ Width from the menu bar or use the cursor on the column heading area to stretch or shrink the column width.

6. Select Edit ➢ Move Or Copy Sheet from the menu bar, make sure that the Create A Copy option is selected in the dialog box displayed, and then click the OK button.

7. A formula is basically an equation that is used to analyse and process the data stored in a worksheet. Functions are predefined formulas that perform calculations by using specific values, called *arguments*, in a particular order, known as the *syntax*.

8. This type of error occurs if you have mixed text in with numbers in your formula and Excel cannot resolve the calculation.

9. An absolute cell address is the single coordinate that defines its position within a worksheet. A relative address refers to a cell's position in relation to another cell's position. A cell can have many different relative addresses but only one absolute address.

10. Select the relevant cells and choose Format ➢ Cells from the menu bar. Click the Number tab if it is not already selected and under Category, select Number. Use the Decimal Places option to set the number of decimal places required.

11. Choose Format ➢ Cells from the menu bar. In the Format Cells dialog box, click the Alignment tab and then use the Orientation control.

12. Select the chart object and then choose Chart ➢ Chart Type from the menu bar. This displays the Chart Type dialog box. You can use this tabbed window to select a new type of chart to be displayed.

ECDL Module 5: Databases

PART

V

Chapter

26

An Introduction to Databases

IN THIS CHAPTER YOU WILL LEARN HOW TO

- ✓ Define and describe data and information.
- ✓ Explain the need for and the advantages of databases.
- ✓ Describe some applications of databases.
- ✓ Explain the organisation of a database.
- ✓ Describe the basic principles of a relational database management system.
- ✓ Explain the storage of data in tables.
- ✓ Define the roles of queries, forms, and reports.
- ✓ Start up and close down Access.
- ✓ Recognise the important features in an Access window.
- ✓ Open and close an existing database.
- ✓ View a database in various different ways.
- ✓ Modify a database record.
- ✓ Select and modify the toolbars.
- ✓ Use Access Help.
- ✓ Save the database.

This module is intended to help you develop your skills in both building and querying databases in order to obtain useful information in the form of reports and other types of output. We do not assume any previous exposure to databases, and we will avoid most of the technical background that underpins database systems. By the end of this part of the study guide, you will have covered all the skill sets and task items defined for the ECDL Module 5 and be ready to pass the practice-based test.

The best way to learn about a new subject is usually to do something practical. We will adopt this approach throughout this part by developing a simple database to store information about a collection of music CDs. We will also use a sample database provided by Microsoft that shows what can be achieved when you have attained a good level of familiarity with Access, Microsoft's database management system.

ECDL focuses on Access for databases in just the same way it uses Microsoft Word for word processing.

Introduction to Databases

The module is divided into five chapters and covers the major components of Access.

Work through these chapters in sequence, because each chapter builds on the information in the previous chapter. Use the sample CD database as the core of your practical work.

Data, Databases, and Information

First we need to define what we mean when we talk about data and storing it in databases. Let's start with a definition of a database: A *database* is a collection of related data.

This helps, but might still leave you unclear about what is meant by *data*. We tend to use this word in normal conversation in a very general way, without being too concerned about what it actually means. A further definition clarifies the meaning: Data is known facts about something that can be recorded and stored. To record something means that you have taken a fact and written it down on paper or turned it into some electrical signals that can be stored in a computer system.

In our definition of a database, we talked about related data. This emphasises that the collection of facts is not just a random collection of facts about anything. They must be organised and focussed on a particular topic area. We'll keep referring back to this idea of organising data in this module, because it is fundamental to understanding databases.

A collection of facts is not particularly useful on its own. It's like a pile of bricks delivered off the back of a lorry. You have to arrange the bricks in some sensible way in order to get a building. You could actually produce lots of different buildings from the same pile of bricks. The same is true of data. You can apply this analogy to see how you use a collection of data to build useful information.

Information is derived from data and is useful in solving problems. Information is the meaning that a person assigns to data by means of the known conventions used in its representation.

This means that data becomes useful information when you put it together to solve a real problem. The facts that you have stored are not really useful in themselves, but they become information when you apply what you know about the facts to draw conclusions from them.

This is a very important idea. Databases store data, but they are really only useful when you can extract information from them in a useful way. Three full chapters of this module are devoted to the ways in which you can carry out this extraction process.

Database Management Systems

We have defined the term *database*, but you know already that there are database programs such as Access. Are these databases in the way that we have defined them? The answer is no; Access is not a collection of related data. Programs such as Access are really database management systems. A *database management system (DBMS)* is a collection of programs that enables users to create and maintain a database.

Taking the pile of bricks analogy a little further, think of a DBMS as the tool that you need to put together a useful building using the bricks.

Another way of thinking about a DBMS is to compare it with a word processor. You use a word processor to put together and maintain a document. The word processor simply gives you the tools needed to type, organise, store, and print words. A DBMS such as Access does exactly the same thing for a collection of data.

Database management systems have been around for a long time, far longer than PCs have existed. There is more than one type of DBMS, but most recent systems use a similar approach to the way that they structure and relate data. They are based on simple yet powerful ideas and rules that work well for most business applications of databases.

The most important of these ideas is that you can store and organise data in tables. Database management systems that use these simple table-based ideas are called *relational database management systems (RDBMS)*.

Access is an RDBMS, and it shares many of its basic ideas with a lot of other database management systems that run on all kinds of computers, from PCs up to enormous mainframes. This doesn't mean that you could run Access on such machines!

Many people believe that the word relational comes from the fact that you are storing collections of related data. This is not so. The word relational comes from the underlying theory of this type of database management system that is based on the mathematical word for a table, which is a relation.

Uses of Databases

We've defined a database as a collection of related data, but we recognise that for a database to be useful, you must be able to extract information from it in a variety of different ways. Some databases are used just as a place to deposit data and return it as information at a later date. A more useful way of employing a database is as the foundation for a more complete computer application, an application that is designed to carry out a significant business function.

Typical business applications for databases are as follows:

- A personnel system keeping records about employees, their grades, training, and employment history.

- An accounts system that keeps data about all the transactions that a company makes. An accounts system produces a wide variety of reports and automates some functions such as the calculation of Value Added Tax (VAT).

- A customer relations management system that keeps records of a business's current and potential customers. The system reminds salespeople when they should follow up a sales lead and records what information has been sent to all the potential customers.

Each of these three applications would normally be built on top of a database. This gives the system designers a lot of help and avoids them having to re-create a lot of standard building blocks. Writing computer programs that work with databases goes beyond the syllabus for this module, but be aware that this is very common and that Access provides a rich set of tools for creating an application in this way.

Try to think of an application that is likely to use a database. Hint: These applications usually use a lot of data.

Relational Databases

You've already seen that most modern database management systems are based on the relational model. You don't need to understand all the theory that led to the relational model, but you certainly need to understand the basic ideas.

Relational model is just a sophisticated way of saying "based on tables."

All data in a relational database is organised in tables. Each row in a table contains a single set of facts about a thing that you're interested in. All the rows in a table are laid out in the same way with the same columns. Each column specifies a different part of the fact that you are recording. To illustrate this, consider an employee table that might be part of a personnel database, as shown in Figure 26.1.

FIGURE 26.1   An employee table

First Name	Initials	Last Name	Social Security Number	Grade
John		Williamson	1285TN1	3
Marie	S	Dupont	6589AF7	1
Luigi		Moretti	8762KQ9	3
Henry	N	Porter	5672HF2	2
Wilma	W	Wimble	8712DE4	3

Notice that each row represents facts about a different employee. For example, the first row says that you have an employee called John Williamson with a Social Security number of 1285TN1 and a grade of 3. The first column is called First Name and contains the first name of every employee. Every column has a name, and all the rows in that column contain the same type of information. For example, the Social Security Number column contains only Social Security numbers and nothing else. In a table, you have only one piece of data at the junction of every row and column. Don't try to cram everything into one or two columns—this is important.

In some cases, the values in a column may be optional or may not apply in every row, in which case the junction of a row and column is empty. The Initials column is a good example of this.

A relational database consists of a series of such tables. Each table stores a set of facts about a separate thing, and every table has a name. This simple idea is powerful enough to enable you to build extremely complex databases. In Chapter 27, "Creating a Database," you'll decide what tables you need for a database and how you can set up these tables in Access.

Queries, Forms, and Reports

Storing data in tables is the basis of the relational model, but you need to be able to get information from those tables to make a database useful. You also need to add to and change the data in the tables.

Ideally, you want to see information in a more attractive and familiar form than just plain tables. You can achieve all of these objectives by using queries, forms, and reports.

A *query* extracts the data that you want from one or more tables and presents it to you as another table. You should notice that a query works with tables and produces tables. This is in line with the relational thinking that insists that all data in the database is stored in tables and nothing else. You can design queries to extract the data that you require and then store the query for future use any time you need that data again.

A *form* is used to enter, change, view, and print data in one or more tables or queries. You can design forms so that they resemble paper forms, or you can make them much more interactive, with pictures and even sounds if you wish. Forms are the human face that your database presents to the people who use your database whilst sitting in front of a screen.

A *report* is a printed output from a database, suitable for people who need information away from a computer screen. You can use a lot of imagination in the design of reports. Access provides excellent tools for producing professional-looking reports. In a business context, reports are an essential feature of any database management system.

The last three chapters of this module cover queries, forms, and reports.

If you are not yet familiar with the general use of a Windows-based application, please review Module 2 before going on with this chapter. You will need to know the basic use of scroll bars, menus, icons, and other Windows features before continuing.

Getting Started with Access

In this section, you'll take your first steps to being competent with Access. You will concentrate initially on opening and looking at a database and then shutting it down again correctly.

Access must be installed on your PC in order to make use of this module. If you are unsure if Access is installed, try the actions in this section. If you can't find the program, try reinstalling the software or seeking assistance.

The most certain way to start up Access is to click the Start button at the bottom left-hand corner of the screen and then click All Programs. Microsoft Access should be listed, alongside its typical icon, a key. This looks something like Figure 26.2.

FIGURE 26.2   Starting Microsoft Access

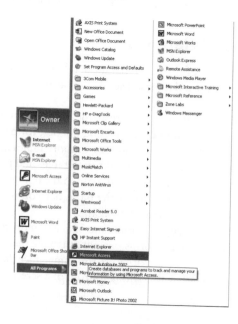

It may be more convenient to set up Access as a shortcut on your screen, because you'll be starting and stopping it many times during this module. Once Windows has started up Access, you should see a window resembling Figure 26.3.

FIGURE 26.3   The opening screen for Microsoft Access

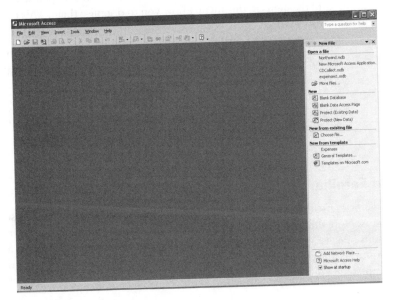

At the moment you don't want to open an existing database, so simply close this window using the Close control button at the top right of the window.

Exploring the Access Window

Open Access again and take a look at the window in Figure 26.3; this is where you'll spend most of the time in exploring Access. At the top of the window, notice the typical Windows menu bar just underneath the Access title bar. Most of the menu items will be familiar from other Windows applications:

File   The File menu is used to open new and existing databases, to close databases, and to exit from Access. It also provides some save functions, but these are not quite the same as those in other Office applications.

Edit   The Edit menu performs useful functions such as cutting and pasting data from one place to another.

View   The View menu is very important. It gives you different ways of looking at a database, which is particularly useful when you are building a new database.

Insert   The Insert menu might appear to be useful for adding data to your database, but its primary role is to help you to add new functions (such as reports and forms) to your database.

Tools   The Tools menu contains a collection of useful functions, some of which, like spell check, may already be familiar to you. Some other functions are rather specialised, and you won't use them in this module.

Window   The Window menu is all about manipulating the various windows that you might have open at the same time. Access allows you to have several windows open within the main application window, and the items in this menu allow you to organise them. This is exactly like all the other applications in Office.

Help   The Help menu is another familiar menu item. You'll use this quite frequently during this module. Help behaves just like the Help capabilities in other Windows applications.

Access is not like Word where you can have several documents open at once. Each Access window can contain only one database at a time.

Becoming Familiar with Access Menus

Explore the facilities provided by the menus by clicking them and then selecting some of the possible options. Note that some menus have further options, indicated by a small arrow. The range of options open to you is limited at this stage, because you have not opened a database. Many of the options are greyed out and not selectable, although you can still read them. Once you have completed exploring the window, exit from Access by choosing File ➢ Exit.

Opening a Database

Now that you've seen how Access looks without a live database, you can progress to trying it with a real database. You aren't going to create a new database at this stage; you're just going to look at a sample.

Fortunately, Microsoft provides a sample database that is ideal for your needs. The database is a file called `Northwind.mdb`. You should keep the Northwind database safe so that you can always return to the original version. Other people may want to use the same PC after you, so it's important that you return everything to the original state when you finish.

An easy way to do this is to make a copy of the Northwind database. To do this, open Windows Explorer from the Start menu and browse to the folder that contains the Northwind database. Typically, this is in `C:\Program Files\Microsoft Office\Office\Samples`. (Your PC may use a different location. If you can't find this database, contact your system administrator for advice.) Select the `Northwind.mdb` file, choose Edit ➢ Copy, and then choose Edit ➢ Paste. This makes a copy of the database. You can copy this back to the original `Northwind.mdb` any time to bring it back to the original condition.

To open the database, start up Access as you did before, but this time select File ➢ Open. In response to the Open window, browse to select `Northwind.mdb`. A graphic containing a lighthouse appears; click OK to clear this. A window entitled Main Switchboard also opens. Close this with the Close control button in the top right-hand corner of the window. You should then see a window similar to Figure 26.4.

FIGURE 26.4   The Northwind database

Notice that the Northwind database window has buttons down the left-hand side. These buttons are labelled Tables, Queries, Forms, Reports, Pages, Macros, and Modules. We will not be concerned with macros, pages, and modules in this guide, but by the time you finish, you'll be familiar with the other four buttons.

Review the menus that you looked at before you opened the database, navigating through all of the options. Don't change anything—just look at the range of options. Did you notice that there is now a much wider range of options? This is because (as with all other Office applications) the menus change when you have opened a file, or in this case, a database.

If you see a double downward-pointing arrow at the bottom of a menu selection, there are additional options available. To see them, move your mouse pointer over the arrows.

Make sure that the Tables icon is selected. You should see a list of tables displayed: Categories, Customers, Employees, and so on, as shown in Figure 26.4. As discussed earlier, a database typically consists of a number of linked tables, and the Northwind database has eight tables.

Viewing a Table

Take a look at the Employees table by double-clicking the Employees table icon. The result should look like Figure 26.5.

FIGURE 26.5   The Employees table in the Northwind database

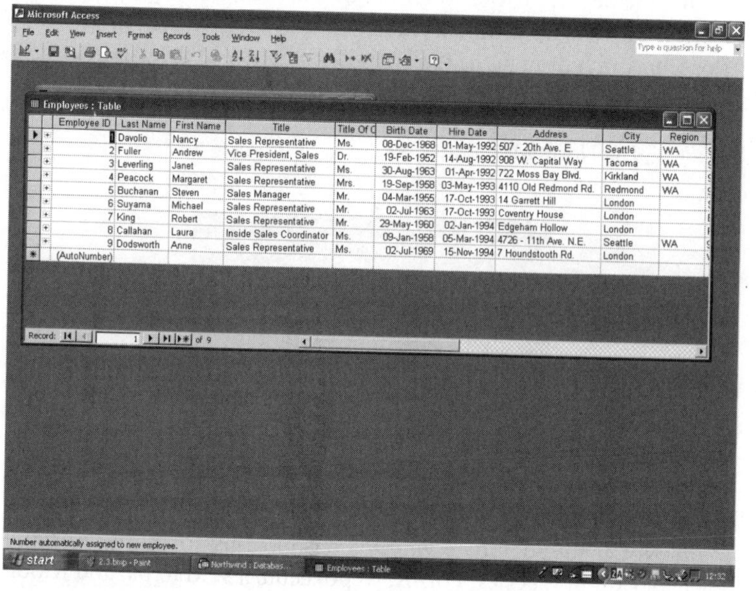

The layout of the Table window may look familiar if you've ever used a spreadsheet such as Excel. Access shows tables in exactly the same way—as a series of rows and columns. The similarity to Excel is really only superficial. Under the surface, the system is entirely different.

Each rectangle contains a single item of data. You can move around the table using the cursor key and the mouse. Your PC screen may not be large enough to display the entire table at once. If that's the case, you can use the scroll bars at the side and bottom of the window to scroll it into view.

We need to introduce some new terminology at this stage to make sense of what Access tells you. A *data field* (or just *field*) is the single item of data in each of the cells in the table. A *record* is an alternative way of describing a row in a table.

> **WARNING**
>
> Neither of these definitions would really stand up to close examination by a computer scientist, but they are acceptable for our purposes.

Navigating the Table

The bottom of the Table window contains some record navigation buttons. These use the same icons as a video recorder. You can move up or down in the table one row (record) at a time, or you can skip directly to the first or last row. The record counter displays which record number you are currently viewing. You can also skip directly to a record by typing the row number in this box and pressing Enter.

Use the cursor keys to scroll from the left-hand side of the table to the right-hand side. Use the mouse to move from one row (record) to another. Use the video recorder-style buttons to move from one record to another and to the top and bottom of the table.

Modifying a Record

You can change the data in a table just by typing in the new data. For instance, let's say Steven Buchanan has a new telephone extension number. You need to find the old number and change it to 3890. Take these steps:

1. Start by scrolling down to the row that contains Steven Buchanan's details, (employee id 5).

2. Scroll to the right using the keyboard arrow keys until you reach the Extension column.

3. Type in the new extension number.

Saving a Database

You're used to the idea of saving a document that you're working on with an application such as a word processor. Usually any change that you make to the document is stored to a file on your hard disk only when you save the document.

Access does not work in quite the same way. Whenever you change the data in a record, the data is saved immediately without you needing to execute any Save command. This is an important part of the database management system's function. If Access has any problems saving data after you enter or change it, it tells you.

However, there are some types of changes that Access does not automatically save for you. If, for example, you create a new table in a database, Access does not save it automatically; you must do this yourself. Access reminds you to do this, so it's not a big problem.

The difference between the things that are saved automatically and those that are not is quite simple. Access automatically saves all the data that you put in the database. Access does not automatically save changes in the structure of your database; you must do this yourself.

Saving structural changes is easy. Choose File ➢ Save, and the current database is saved in the original filename. You should now appreciate why you made a copy of the original database file at the outset.

In common with all the other Office applications, you can save time by using the key combination Ctrl+S to save the database. If you have not used such combinations before, the shorthand Ctrl+S means "press the Ctrl key, then the s key, and then release both keys." This technique is much faster than reaching for the mouse and going through the menus.

Access View Options

You've viewed a table, but what about the other parts of the database? You can look at these in the same way that you viewed a table—through the Northwind window.

Viewing Queries

Click the Queries button in the Northwind window. A window appears containing about 18 different queries. Double-click CurrentProductList. Were you surprised with the result?

The queries look just like tables, but they aren't real tables containing real data. What you see is the result of running a query on a real table. This is subtle, but important; the result of a query on a table or tables is another table, but Access doesn't store that table as real data. It just works out what the table should look like every time you ask for it. This means that if you change the real tables, the results of a query on those tables changes automatically. This is a very powerful feature.

Viewing Forms

Now let's look at forms. As you've probably guessed, you do this by clicking the Forms button. Click the Forms button and look for the Employees entry. Double-click the Employees entry, and a form appears. Navigate to the record for Steven Buchanan and check his extension number. What does this tell you about using a form?

A form is another way of looking at a table or at more than one table. The simple spreadsheet approach is fine, but you wouldn't want to use that all the time in a real database. A form is much more convenient. You could have changed the extension number using the form much more easily than you did in the raw table view. In case you're wondering, you can create forms on the tables that are produced by a query just as easily as if they were real tables.

This form contains photographs. Go back to the Table view, open the Employee table, and find out which column is used for the photos.

The photos are included in the Photo column. This is quite important; it tells you that you can store different types of data in a table. Pictures, text, and numbers are just a few of the possibilities.

Viewing Reports

Finally, let's look at the reports for the Northwind database. You can reach these by clicking the Reports icon in the Northwind window. Take a look at the Summary Of Sales By Year report. What table did this data come from? The data actually came from several tables, and some of it was calculated, not stored in any table. This is typical of reports.

Working With Access Features

You've now seen all the main parts of the Northwind database, but you haven't learned how to create tables, queries, forms, and reports. Let's take a quick look at this now and then return to this topic in detail in later chapters.

Make sure that you've closed any open forms, queries, tables, or reports. Click the Tables button and then select Employees with a single click. Now click the Design button at the top. You should see a window like that in Figure 26.6.

FIGURE 26.6   A table showing the Field Name, Data Type, and Description columns

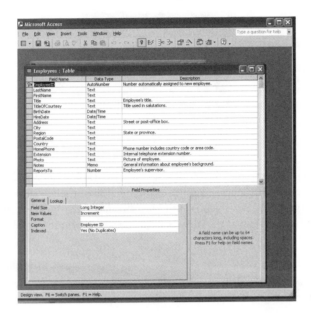

Look at the Field Name column. Each of these is a column in the Employee table; this Design View allows you to design a table by specifying what goes into each column.

The Data Type column allows you to specify what type of data is stored in each column of the table. Look down the column to see the various different types of data. These are fixed in advance as part of the design of Access, so you simply choose what you require.

The Description column allows you to describe what each column in the table is used for. Notice that some of the columns have no descriptions; this information is optional. Don't change anything; you're simply looking at this stage.

Now close the table and look at the Design Views for the queries, forms, and reports. In each case, what you see in the Design View is the set of tools used to construct or modify that type of object.

Normally, you don't want people to be able to change the design of a database once it has been completed. This could lead to all kinds of confusion, or worse. In normal day-to-day use, people do not use the Design Views at all, and if you are the database designer, you can stop them from seeing these.

Let's conclude this chapter by looking in more detail at the View menu. Click this menu now to look again at the options, shown in Figure 26.7.

FIGURE 26.7 Options available in the View menu

Choosing one of the Database Objects options to select tables, queries, and so on works the same way as clicking one of the icons on the left-hand side of the window in Figure 26.4.

Try using the Large Icons, Small Icons, and List options on the View menu. Notice how they present a slightly different view of the objects in the database window. You can use whichever of these you prefer.

If you don't see "Large Icons," roll the mouse pointer over the double arrow at the bottom of the list.

Selecting and Modifying Toolbars

The View ➤ Toolbars option allows you to choose the toolbars displayed at the top of the window. There's a lot of choice in Access, but this is not immediately visible. To get a wider choice of toolbars, choose Customize and then select the Toolbars tab. This displays a list of available toolbars (about 29 of them). You can choose any selection of these. A tick next to the toolbar name indicates that it will be included in the display. If you wish to remove a toolbar from your display, simply select it a second time to remove the tick.

It's also possible to change the toolbars, adding or removing icons from them. Given the wide selection of available toolbars in Access, this should not be necessary for normal use.

Using Access Help

Access Help follows the usual Microsoft Office approach. Click Help to see the available options. The Microsoft preferred tool is Microsoft Access Help. If you use this option, Access opens a small Office Assistant window. The Office Assistant can assume a variety of different characters such as Einstein or a paper clip. Call up the Office Assistant by clicking Microsoft Access Help and then typing a question in the What Would You Like To Do window. The Office Assistant then displays a number of topics that are related to what you entered. This may help with your problem.

WARNING Then again, it may not. The purpose of the Office Assistant is to be friendly and helpful, but it relies on understanding what you are asking; sometimes this doesn't work too well.

Once you've worked through even a small part of this module, you'll probably prefer to get much more direct answers from Help. To do this, disable the Office Assistant by choosing Help ➤ Options and deselecting Use The Office Assistant. Now, when you use Help, you'll get a more conventional window.

A good starting point is the Contents tab in the Help window. The Contents tab is organised into a series of topics that you can choose and is useful when you cannot remember (or do not know) how to carry out a specific task.

Sometimes you need to be even more specific. You can get help based on a particular word by choosing Help ➤ Index. This allows you to search for specific words or for Help pages.

Closing a Database

To close a database, choose File ➤ Close. This closes the currently open database but leaves the Access application window open, allowing you to open a different database if you wish.

Closing a database is not quite the same as closing most Office documents such as a Word file. In the case of Word, you would be asked whether you wish to save changes when you close a file (assuming that there are any unsaved changes). In Access, changes to the data in a database are automatically "saved" as you make them.

Summary

This chapter covered a lot of details that you need to bear in mind as you read the rest of this module. It started by spending some time defining some concepts that seem very familiar until you try to relate them to computer usage. Understanding data, information, databases, and database management systems is fundamental to your success with this study guide and with this particular ECDL module.

Access is a relational database management system. You learnt the big idea that is at the heart of a relational database, that you store data in simple tables. A real database is composed of at least one and often many tables.

The next section explained how to start up Access, open, close, and save databases and use various tools to view an existing database.

There are Design Views for all of the main database objects such as tables, queries, forms, and reports. In the next chapter, you'll start to use these Design Views to create a new database.

Chapter

27

Creating a Database

IN THIS CHAPTER YOU WILL LEARN HOW TO

- ✓ Design and plan a database.
- ✓ Recognise the different types of data.
- ✓ Create a new Access database.
- ✓ Create an Access table.
- ✓ Use validation rules.
- ✓ Add and delete data in a record and use the Undo command.
- ✓ Save an Access table.
- ✓ Delete an Access table.
- ✓ Add a column to a table.
- ✓ Select and use primary keys.
- ✓ Set up an index on a table.
- ✓ Modify a table design.
- ✓ Set up default values and display formats.
- ✓ Set up relationships between tables.
- ✓ Understand the need for referential integrity and how to ensure it.
- ✓ Delete a relationship between tables.
- ✓ Use filters on tables.
- ✓ Search a table for a word.
- ✓ Sort data in a table.

In the last chapter, you gained some familiarity with Access, in particular, its basic tools for viewing databases. Using a database is only part of the skill set that you need. It's also important that you can create a new database from scratch, based on your understanding of a business requirement. This chapter is all about the process of designing a new database and implementing it using Access.

Designing Tables

A database consists of one or more tables, but how do you decide what tables you need and what columns they should contain? This is a critical issue.

A database is designed to solve a particular problem. It may be to do with business or perhaps personal data recording, but before you can make any progress, you need to think about that problem.

The first stage is to decide which are the important things about which you need to record data. This is hard to do in an abstract fashion, so let's use a simple example.

Creating a CD Collection Database

Imagine that you want to build a database to record data about your extensive music CD collection. You keep all your CDs in a series of racks, and when necessary, you buy a new rack. They are all the same design but of different sizes, so they look nice in your living room. You sometimes forget which rack you've used to store a CD, so you number the racks so that you can find a CD quickly. You want to be able to find which particular named tracks or songs are on which CD, so you need the database to record this. Similarly, you want to record the artist or band that performs on each CD.

Given this statement of your interests, try to produce a list of the main things that your database must be concerned with. Don't get bogged down in details—just go for the important things. If you find it difficult, looking at an actual CD might help.

One answer to this exercise might be the following things:

- CD
- Artist or band
- Track
- Rack

Now you need to decide what data you want to record for each of these different things. Let's do the first two together, then you can try the third and fourth for practice. Your answers might be different. Don't worry about this; there is a degree of subjectivity about the design based on what you think might be important.

The CD has a title, and it is produced by a record company. Because you are a really serious collector, you are also interested in the CD's catalogue number. Notice that you do not include the tracks or the artist with the CD because these are different things.

The artist or band has a name. You may also want to record their date of birth and some brief notes about their history, but only for those artists that really interest you. Date of birth sounds a little strange for a band or group, but there is no reason why you can't use this to actually mean the date that the group was first formed.

Now try the same process for each track on the CD. Think of the data that you want to record about a particular track. Look at a real CD for inspiration. Each track has a number, a name, and a duration in minutes. This is almost always provided on the sleeve notes.

The rack is simple. All you need is its rack number, and perhaps the number of CDs that it can store so you can quickly see when it is becoming full.

To summarise: You want to store the following things and the most important data fields for each:

- CD
  - Title
  - Record company
  - Catalogue number
- Artist
  - Name
  - Date of birth (DOB)
  - History
- Track
  - Number
  - Name
  - Duration
- Rack
  - Number
  - Capacity

Establishing Primary Keys

Each thing that you decide to store in a database needs to be identifiable in a reliable manner. The next stage is to decide on the best way to identify each of the four things that you've decided are important. You want to use one of the data fields that you've selected, but it's important that you choose something that you know will have a different value in every row and that this unique value will remain so forever.

Derived Data

You might want to know the total number of minutes of recording on a CD. This data is not included in the initial design, but it could be added to the CD table. However, adding it to the CD table would be a poor design decision. The total playing time of a CD is derivable data; that is, it can be calculated by adding together all the play lengths of all the tracks on the CD. Except under very special conditions, you should never include such derivable data in your tables. There are two main reasons for this:

1. You should aim to store a fact about something in one place and in one way only. Storing it in two ways means that there is the potential for them to disagree, which could result in inconsistent information being produced from your database.

2. Storing derivable data wastes space. Admittedly, the amount of space used is minimal in this case, but in a large database, it can be an important factor.

You might think that calculating the total playing time would take a significant amount of time. This is not really true; the calculation would be almost instantaneous, but finding all the track records takes a little longer. Even though there might be a small penalty in speed, this is worth accepting, knowing that the database can't give inconsistent information.

For example, you might think that you could identify every CD by means of its name, but that would lead you into difficulty. There are dozens of recordings of each of the Beethoven symphonies, even multiple recordings by the same orchestra, so the title would not be enough to identify any one of them. You may have only one of these recordings at the moment, but you might well buy a second one at some future date. A much better choice would be the catalogue number, because the recording companies work hard to ensure that these are truly unique—it makes their life easier.

The artist's name should be easier, because the artist's or band's name should be enough to uniquely identify them. But further thought shows that this is not always true—there is at least one famous example of a singer who deliberately changed his name. There is another problem with an artist's name as an identifier—you need to spell it correctly and consistently every time you enter the data. If you don't, you don't get correct results when you try to get information from the database at a later stage. Yet another consideration is that where possible, it's better to make the identifier short and numeric; the database usually works faster like that. All of these factors suggest that the artist's name would work as an identifier, but is not the best choice. In this case, an artist number—unique for every artist—is a better choice.

This situation occurs fairly frequently. Access provides a special kind of number that is good for making identifiers in these situations. The number is increased by one every time you add a row to the database, so Access guarantees that it is always unique.

Track appears to be simple—use the track number. A little thought shows that this doesn't really work. Every CD has a track 1 on it, so the track number is not unique. You could use the track name, but that's not guaranteed to be unique. It's possible that there are two entirely different CDs with the same name for a track. In fact, this is likely to happen frequently because artists tend to cover (in other words, produce their own versions) of each other's tracks. It also suffers from the same problem as the artist's name—it's potentially too long and difficult to keep typing. Even the combination of track number and name is not guaranteed to be unique. There is an obvious way to fix this problem, and that is to use the CD catalogue number, in combination with the track number. This absolutely guarantees that you can uniquely identify each track. The identifier will therefore be a combination of two fields.

For rack, you can use the rack number. This has no problems, especially as you can ensure that every time you buy a new rack, you give it a new, unique number.

The technical term for the unique identifiers is a *primary key*. To record your choices, you can italicise the primary key, so your design to this point is as follows:

- CD
  - Title
  - Record company
  - *Catalogue number*
- Artist
  - *Artist number*
  - Name
  - Date of birth (DOB)
  - History
- Track
  - *Catalogue number*
  - *Track number*
  - Name
  - Duration
- Rack
  - *Rack number*
  - Capacity

Types of Data

Now you need to decide what type of data you require for each of the data fields. As you'll find later, there are a lot of possibilities, but for the present, let's use only the basic types that Access provides. These are as follows:

Text   Text is used for fields that contain alphabetic data, usually a single word or a short phrase.

Memo   Memo is used for much larger amounts of textual data, perhaps a description of the data.

Number   This data type is used for numbers. If you think you might need to do sums with a data field, use the Number data type.

Date/Time   If you want to store dates and/or time, use this data type. Access recognises dates and allows you to do useful, date-related things with them.

Currency   Use this data type when you want to store amounts of money.

AutoNumber   This is useful when you want Access to create a series of numbers that automatically increase whenever you add a new record.

    AutoNumber is exactly what you need to make an identifier for the Artist table.

Yes/No   Sometimes you just want to store information that can only have one of two possible values. For example, you might want to store a person's gender. This can only be male or female.

Determining the Appropriate Data Type

Next, decide on the most appropriate data types for your CD database design, recording the type alongside each field. Reasonable choices would be as follows:

CD

Title	Text
Record Company	Text
Catalogue Number	Text

Artist

Artist Number	AutoNumber
Name	Text
Date of Birth (DOB)	Date/Time
History	Memo

Track

Catalogue Number	Text
Track Number	Number
Name	Text
Duration	Number

Rack

Rack Number   Number

Capacity   Number

Notice that you're using the Memo data type for the History field. This is because sometimes you may want to write lengthy notes, and at other times, nothing at all. Memo is a good choice for this type of situation.

There is a final check that you should carry out on your database design before you're ready to start working with Access. Look at each of the things that you've decided are important (CD, artist, and so on). Decide whether the whole of the primary key identifies uniquely (on its own) the values of all the other fields, and that none of the other fields can do this either singly or in combination. Ask yourself the following questions, for example:

- If you know the CD catalogue number, is there only one possible CD name and record company? The answer is clearly yes.

- Can you tell unambiguously what the CD name is if you know only the record company? The answer is clearly no; only the primary key determines the CD name.

Apply this test to all of the things that you've identified. If you find something that does not satisfy the test, then take a close look at your design. Probably you have two separate things mixed together. Try to separate them out.

This test may seem rather mysterious, but it's important. Passing the test means that your database design should work well and not give you any strange results. Designs that don't pass the test could eventually cause surprising effects or lose data altogether.

> **NOTE** The process just described is technically described as *normalisation* and is an essential part of the process of designing a database. There is a great deal more to this process than we've described here, but you can gain most of the benefits by applying the tests described. Another way of stating the tests for normalisation is a variation on the oath sworn by witnesses in court: "Does every field depend on the primary key, the whole of the primary key, and nothing but the primary key?"

Choosing Appropriate Number and Date Formats

Two data types—Number and Date/Time—come in a variety of different forms. You need to choose the most appropriate for your design. One of the reasons why Access provides all this choice is that storing data requires disk space. Some forms of numbers and dates require a lot more space than others, so there is a big advantage in choosing the most economical type of format for your needs.

Another reason why Access provides different types of numbers is that there really are different types of numbers in everyday use. *Floating-point numbers* are used for measuring values that can change smoothly in value and have a decimal point. *Integers* are used for counting whole items that never come in fractional parts.

NOTE This may seem a rather artificial distinction, but it does matter. Using the wrong type of number can lead to silly answers or the loss of data.

Here are some examples of the use of different types of numbers:

- Integers are used for counting people, CDs, books, and cars. 0.35 people does not make sense, and neither would 0.76 of a car, but 3 students and 25 cars with no decimal points seems reasonable.

- Weight is measured in kilograms, so a person might weigh 70.42 kilograms. You do not think of weight as being limited to whole numbers of kilos, so you naturally use floating-point numbers to record weight.

In addition to dividing numbers into integers and floating-point numbers, Access also has numbers that are capable of storing large values with a lot of accuracy and numbers that can store only small numbers with limited accuracy. Each of these different types of numbers has a different name. These are all listed in Table 27.1.

TABLE 27.1   The Different Types of Numbers Used by Access

Name	Type	Decimal Places	Range
Byte	Integer	None	0 to 255
Integer	Integer	None	−32678 to 32678
Long Integer	Integer	None	Very large
Single	Float	7	Typical numbers
Double	Float	15	Enormous

First, decide whether you need an integer or a floating-point number. Then choose the number with the smallest range that you are quite certain can hold the largest possible value that the data field could ever have.

WARNING If you get this wrong and choose a number type that is too small, Access gives you a warning when you try to enter a larger number in that field. If you continue, you may lose data. This loss can also have a knock-on effect on other tasks that you might want to use that number for, such as calculations. If you're unsure, choose a larger number type.

Access provides a variety of date and time formats. These provide a range of different types of date/times that can be used to suit your requirements. The following table shows the main types of date and time formats with some examples of how they may look. You should, however, recognise that the way that dates and times are displayed depends on local regional preferences.

TABLE 27.2   Date Formats

Name	Usage	Example
General Date	If the value of the data is just a date, then only the date will be displayed. If the value of the data is only a time, then only the time is displayed.	13/2/2004 or 15:43
Long Date	Provides the same results as the Windows Regional setting. This means that the date will be displayed in full detail according to how your Windows system is configured.	Friday, February 13, 2004
Medium Date	Provides a more compact version of the Long Date	13-Feb-04
Short Date	Provides the same results as the Windows Regional setting for short dates. This is usually a very compact date representation.	13/2/04
Long Time	Provides the same results as the Windows Regional setting. This means that the time will be displayed in full detail according to how your Windows system is configured.	5:25:12 PM
Medium Time	Provides a shorter version of the Long Time.	5:25:12
Short Time	Provides the most compact representation of time.	5:25

Indexes

You use indexes all the time in normal life without thinking about them much. For example, this book has an index that allows you to find pages that contain specific topic words. To use the index, you scan through it until you find the word; then you open the book at the page number shown. You can scan the index quickly because it's always in alphabetic order. Just consider the alternative; without an index, you would have to read through large parts of the text to find where a topic was covered. In the extreme, you might have to read a whole book just to find out what a particular small topic was all about.

Databases can have *indexes* as well. An index helps Access find rows in a table much more quickly. You don't have to define any indexes when you first design a database; you can add them later if you really need them. Access, like any good relational database, delivers results whether or not you define any additional indexes. You might think that if indexes speed up the retrieval of data from the database, you should obviously set up indexes on every field. Unfortunately, it isn't as simple as that, because indexes on the wrong fields can actually slow things down a lot and greatly increase the size of the database. This is because keeping the indexes up to date absorbs computer power and requires extra data, sometimes very significantly.

The best approach to adopt, at least until you have more experience with databases, is to follow these guidelines:

- Only set up indexes on fields that hold text, numbers, currency, or dates.

- Only set up indexes on fields that will be used a lot.

- Only set up indexes on fields that will contain a lot of different values.

- If in doubt, don't set up an index unless and until you're sure that your database isn't working quickly enough.

Access automatically sets up indexes on primary keys for you. This makes sense because primary keys have different values in every row, are used a lot, and are usually numbers, dates, or short text fields.

Access Database Wizards

Access (and any other DBMS) supplies you with some sample database designs that you can use without having to go through the processes described in this chapter. To use these, start Access in the normal way, but when you see the Microsoft Access window, select File ➤ New ➤ New From Template ➤ General Templates ➤ Databases. Access displays a list of database templates. If you select one of these, Access takes you through a series of windows in which you can make various choices about the layout of the database.

Database wizards are ideal if your requirements are met by the supplied templates. Unfortunately, the templates are rarely an exact fit, so you have to either compromise your requirements or modify the database design. We will cover such modifications later in this chapter, but for the present, let's assume that you want to build a database that meets your exact requirements.

The Table Design Toolbar

Access provides a set of toolbars that are tailored to match all the major design tasks. This module will describe these toolbars as you need them.

Most of the Access toolbars come in pairs. Typically, the first of these provides all the major tools that you need to create and change something such as a table, and the matching toolbar is intended to help you use the object that you have created (such as a table). You can flip between the Design View and the User View with the Flip To button. This is really useful when you are learning Access, because you can try out a change in the Design View and then immediately flip to the other view to check your changes.

Figures 27.1 and 27.2 show the toolbars that are available for table design. Access normally displays these toolbars when you work with a table, but if for any reason they're not visible, choose View ➤ Toolbars and select the toolbar that you need.

FIGURE 27.1   The Table Design toolbar

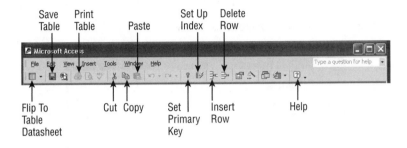

FIGURE 27.2   The Table Datasheet toolbar

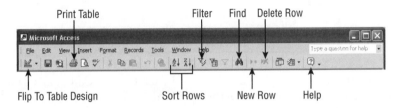

The Table Design toolbar has all the usual Save, Print, Cut, Copy, and Paste buttons. There are also some special-purpose buttons that you'll use during this chapter and that you should look out for:

- Set Primary Key is used to tell Access which column or columns are the primary key for the table.

- Set Up Index is used to define which columns should have an index to speed up the retrieval of data.

- Flip To Table Datasheet moves you from the Table Design View to the Table Datasheet View.

The Table Datasheet toolbar also has some special-purpose buttons:

- Sort Rows allows you to sort the rows into a different sequence.

- Find helps you locate a particular number or a word within a table.

- Filter helps you by displaying only those rows that meet particular criteria. This is very useful with large tables.

Note that help is available on both these toolbars (and on every other toolbar).

Creating a New Database

Now that you've determined your design and learned a little bit about the tools that Access has available, you're ready to create a new database. The first task in implementing your database design in Access is to set up a new blank database. Start up Access and select Blank Database. The File New Database window opens, as shown in Figure 27.3.

FIGURE 27.3 The File New Database window

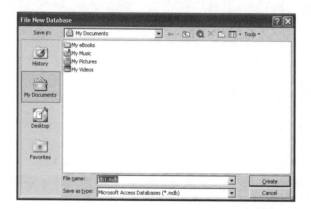

Choose a suitable name for your database and click Create. Call your CD database `CDCollect.mdb`. The `.mdb` extension is the standard Microsoft file ending for Access databases in the same way that `.doc` is used for Microsoft Word documents.

Next, the familiar Database window opens (see Figure 27.4), with CDCollect in the title bar. You're ready to start creating tables.

FIGURE 27.4 Creating a new table

Each of the items that you decided were important in your design will become a table and each of the fields will be a column. Start with the CD table. Double-click Create Table In Design View.

Note that there is a Table Wizard that can help you create some standard types of tables, but just as with the Database Wizard, these do not match your requirements exactly, so use the

Design View. A blank Table Design window opens, similar to that shown in Figure 27.5. Access thoughtfully provides a Table Design toolbar as well.

FIGURE 27.5 A blank Table Design window

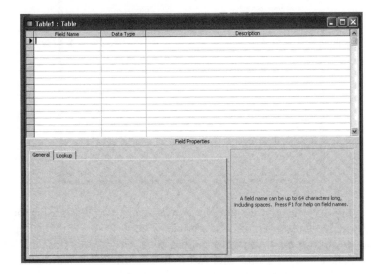

Adding Fields

Type in the first field name, **Title**, in the first row of the table, then press the Tab key to move to the next column, Data Type.

The Tab key is a quick way to move between fields in many different situations.

Notice that Access provides a drop-down list to choose the data type, so click the arrow and select Text. Tab to the next column and type in a description of this field, something like **The title of the CD**.

Press Tab again to go to the next row and enter the remaining data fields. Finally, you need to tell Access which of your fields is the primary key. This is the italicised field in your design. Select the Catalogue Number field and then click the Primary Key button on the Table Design toolbar. This button looks like a small key. Access indicates the primary key by inserting a small picture of a key just to the left of the Catalogue Number row.

You should finish up with something that looks like Figure 27.6.

FIGURE 27.6   The result of an initial table design

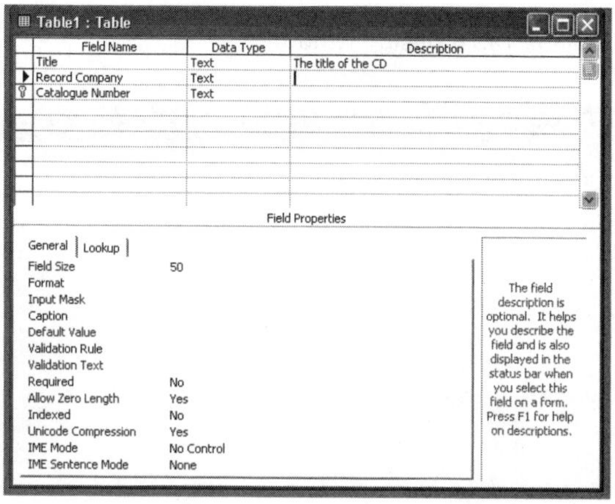

Now you need to save the table design. The simplest way to do this is using the Save button on the Table Design toolbar (see Figure 27.1, shown earlier), the one with the floppy disk icon. When you click this, Access prompts you for a table name. The name of this table is CD, so type that in and click OK. Close the Table window by clicking the Close control button in the top right-hand corner. This brings you back to the Database window. You can add further fields to a table at a later date in just the same way.

Set up the other tables (Artist, Track, and Rack) in just the same way as for the CD table.

You can add additional fields to a table at any time using exactly the same approach as described earlier.

If you find that you frequently need to add new fields to existing tables, you should take a good look at the resulting database design. It is very easy to produce a design that will not provide reliable and consistent results when you modify and query data.

Choosing Field Options

Once you have some basic tables defined, start adding some more detail to your fields. You may have noticed that there are a number of additional options at the bottom of the Table Design window. These add a great deal to the usefulness of the database, so you should use them where appropriate. The additional options are as follows:

Field Size   This is the maximum length of the field, measured in characters, or the selection of the number types discussed earlier in the section "Choosing Appropriate Number and Date Formats."

Format   The Format option allows you to decide how the field will be displayed.

Input Mask   Mask might seem a rather mysterious term, but it simply means the things that are validated when data is entered in the field. This is very important because specifying an input mask helps to ensure that only valid data is added to the database.

Caption   This is a label that can be used in a form or a report; again, it's useful to define this.

Default Value   The Default Value is a value that is automatically supplied when a new record is created unless data is entered for this field.

Validation Rule   The Validation Rule is a means of ensuring that only correct data can be entered. These can become very sophisticated, but this module considers only simple validation rules.

Validation Text   You can enter some text here that will prompt a user for what type of data must be entered.

Required   Some fields must always be filled with data. Others may not require an entry in every record. If a field is marked as Required = Yes, it must have data entered.

Allow Zero Length   This allows a text field to have no characters in it.

Indexed   This defines whether or not an index is created on this field. You can set up an index simply by selecting Yes. You must choose whether duplicate values will be allowed for this field.

Access always sets up an index for the primary key with no duplicates allowed. This is because Access can use the index to make it easy to check for unique values. In addition, most access to the table will be through the primary key, so an index speeds up data retrieval significantly.

If you look at the Artist table and the Name field, notice that some of these properties are already set, but they are not really appropriate for your design. Let's correct or add all the useful details for this table (as shown in Figure 27.7); then you can do the same for the other tables and fields:

- The Name field size is probably set to 50 characters. This is a little generous, but leave it alone, because it's possible that a band name might approach this number of characters.

- The Format and Input Mask options are currently not set, and because there is no real pattern to the name of an artist or band, there is no advantage in specifying a format in this case.

- Captions are useful so enter **Artist/Band**.

- There is no sensible Default Value, Validation Rule, or Validation Text for this field, so don't enter this data.

- You'll always require an artist or band name, so mark this field as required. Similarly, you don't want to allow the field to contain no characters, so disallow zero length.

FIGURE 27.7   Choosing the field options in the Artist table

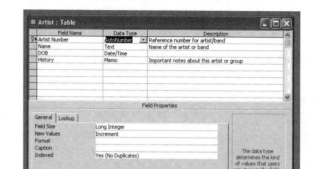

Let's continue the same process for the DOB field.

- Format does not show a length of field, because Access already knows that this is a date field. If you click the Format field, you see a range of possible date formats:

    - General Date
    - Long Date
    - Medium Date
    - Short Date
    - Long Time
    - Medium Time
    - Short Time

    You don't need a really accurate date/time, so Short Date is a suitable choice.

- Input Mask also presents options that are suitable for a date field. Click the drop-down arrow to display these and choose. Make sure that the date format matches your local country standards; otherwise, users cannot enter data in a familiar format. You are guided through your choice of an input mask by a small wizard, which is very useful in this case.

- Add a suitable caption as before, but don't bother with the Default Value, Validation Rule, or Validation Text options.

- You won't require data to be entered in this field (some singers may be coy about their age!), nor do you need an index.

Now carry out the same process for all the other fields in your CD database. You should not have had any major problems completing this section, but if you later decide that you need to change anything, you can simply go back to the Design View for that table and alter it.

Creating a Simple Validation Rule

You can use validation rules to define what data can be entered into a field. These rules can become very elaborate, but we will consider only some simple examples for number, text, date/time and currency fields.

To create a validation rule, click the Validation Rule field in the Table Design window. You can now type in some simple code that will control what can be entered in the field. You will probably need to use Access help (Press F1) to get the full details of all the operators and functions that you use, but the following table will give you some starting examples.

Field Type	Validation Rule	Effect
Number	<=500	Allows only numbers less than or equal to 500 to be entered.
Number	<>0	Will allow only non-zero numbers to be entered.
Text	Like "B???"	The value must be exactly four characters long and must begin with the letter B. The ? stand for a single character.
Date/Time	>#1/1/2004#	The date must be in or after 2004.
Currency	>= 250.20	The money amount entered must be at least 250.20.

We will see more examples of the use of special characters such as ?, >, =, and < when we consider searching databases later in this chapter.

Setting Up Relationships

As you saw in Chapter 26, "An Introduction to Databases," most databases store data about more than one thing, and there is useful information in the way those things are related to each other.

Take your CD database as an example. You now have tables for CDs, artists, racks, and tracks, but these are all entirely separate. This does not actually tell you a great deal about your collection. You cannot, for example, say which artists perform on which CDs, nor can you find out where you've put a particular CD, because there are no connections at all between these different types of records. You have to add those connections to your database.

To do this, you need some further analysis of your design. Ask the following question of the items in your database: How many of this item could be related to some other item? An example makes this obscure question more understandable.

How many CDs could an artist be a performer on? Answer: at least one and possibly a lot.

How many artists could appear on a single CD? Strictly speaking, the answer could be several artists, but this is unusual. For your collection, assume that only one artist or band performs on a CD. If you really do have a collection of artists, call the artist "Various Artists."

This is a bit of a simplification, but accept it as part of the business rules that govern your database.

Expressing this in database terms, one artist is related to many CDs, but any single CD has only one artist. This type of relationship is called a *one-to-many* relationship and is by far the most common form of relationship that you need to set up.

Use some judgement about defining relationships. In a more extensive database design, you could define an enormous number of relationships, most of which would be irrelevant to your application. It is important that you keep in mind the questions that you want to ask of your database and define the relationships that are essential for that purpose.

Occasionally you may encounter relationships that are one-to-one rather than one-to-many. This means that one item is related to at most one example of some other item, never many of them. An example could be the relationship between a person and a driving licence. You could say that a person can have at most one driving licence and that a driving licence is owned by exactly one person. If this is true, then you have a one-to-one relationship between person and driving licence. However, this would not be true if you allow a person to have an international licence in addition, and you want to record this fact. Then there is a one-to-many relationship. The type of a relationship depends on your interpretation of the business rules that apply to the situation that you want to record in your database.

Access supports one-to-one relationships in just the same way as one-to-many relationships.

If you think that your database design has a lot of one-to-one relationships, you're probably doing something wrong. They are relatively unusual, so take a close look at your thinking about types of relationships. You'll probably find that you have some slightly "fuzzy" ideas about the thing that you want to record in your database, or that what you thought were one-to-one relationships are actually one-to-many.

Clarifying Relationships

To make relationships clear to Access, you need to add some details to the database.

First, you need to add the primary key from the one side of the relationship (in this case, Artist) to the many side (CD). This is shown in Figure 27.8.

Notice that you don't have to use exactly the same name for the added field. In fact, it's probably better in this case to spell out the name as you've done so there is no confusion. Notice also that the Artist Number field has been set to Required = Yes, meaning that you must always say what band or artist performs on a CD.

Now you need to connect these matching fields so that Access knows that the Artist Number field in the Artist table is connected to the Artist Number field in the CD table.

FIGURE 27.8 Adding the primary key from the one side to the many side

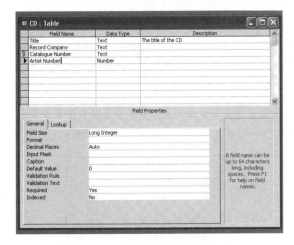

To do this, choose Tools ➢ Relationships from the main Access menu. The Relationships window opens. This window displays the relationships between tables in a graphical manner. You should also see a Show Table window that displays the names of all the tables that you have defined so far. If you don't see this window, click the Show Table button on the toolbar. Click each table in turn and click Add. A new small window representing each table opens, so your screen (after closing Show Table) looks like Figure 27.9.

FIGURE 27.9 Preparing to connect matching fields

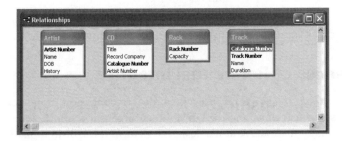

You may need to resize some of the windows and move them around to get a tidy layout. Notice that Access has provided you with a new toolbar called Relationships (the name of the toolbar is not displayed).

To make the connection, click the primary key on the one side of the relationship Artist:Artist Number and drag it to the corresponding field on the many side—CD:Artist Number. Notice that the mouse cursor changes shape as you do this, and the Edit Relationships window opens. This is used to define the nature of the relationship. Most of the work is already done for you, but one important additional action is to select the Enforce Referential Integrity box. This makes Access ensure that the relationship you have defined is always maintained, so the database won't let you enter a new CD without saying who the artist is.

 After you have gained further experience with databases, you may decide not to enforce referential integrity, but for the present, let Access handle this for you.

The result is a Edit Relationships window that looks like Figure 27.10.

FIGURE 27.10 Example of a Edit Relationships window

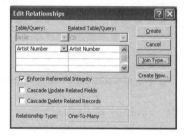

The Edit Relationships window in Figure 27.10 shows that the relationship type being created is a one-to-many-relationship. In nearly every case, this is what you will want. If, however, you need a one-to one-relationship, Access will create this for you automatically but only when a specific set of conditions are met:

- Both of the fields selected are primary keys; or

- Both of the fields selected have a unique index.

If these conditions are met, Access creates the one-to-one relationship for you. You can confirm this by checking the Relationship type in the Relationship window.

Consequences of Referential Integrity

The idea of *referential integrity* can cause a great deal of confusion, so it's useful to describe some of the consequences of asking the DBMS to enforce it for you. Referential integrity is usually exactly what you want. And it's desirable to have the DBMS look after it for you, rather than relying on the users of the database to maintain integrity. To see why this is so, consider some possible scenarios:

- You want to add a new CD to your database, one by an artist that you have not seen before. The DBMS will not let you enter the data for the CD without first entering the data for the artist. This prevents you from having an "anonymous" CD.

- The DBMS does not let you delete an artist whilst there are CDs in the database that were recorded by that artist. This is also to avoid an "orphan" CD without a valid artist.

You can ask Access to take actions when you try to breach referential integrity. For example, you can set a relationship in the Edit Relationships window to Cascade Delete Related Records.

If you do this, then when you attempt to delete an artist from the database, the DBMS looks for all the records in related tables that are by that artist and "cascades" the deletion to those records also. This makes sure that the database is always valid.

Similarly, you can ask Access to Cascade Update Related Fields In this case, if you update the primary key of a row, for example, the Access updates that value in all related tables automatically.

Establishing Links between Tables

Click the Create button in the Edit Relationships window to complete the process of establishing the link between the tables. The link is shown as a line joining the appropriate fields, with a number *1* adjacent to the Artist table and ∞ (infinity) at the other end of the link. This is a visual cue to remind you that this is a one-to-many relationship between artist and CD.

Now complete your analysis of the CD collection database design to decide what other relationships need to be represented, and which end of each relationship is one and which is many.

There are two more relationships:

- One CD can have many tracks.
- One rack can contain many CDs.

 When you define the relationship between CD and track, you'll find that you already have the primary key of CD as a field in the Track table, so you don't need to add it again. This helps to confirm that you made a good choice at an earlier stage.

Add these relationships to your Access database and then rearrange the table windows so that it looks tidy. The actual arrangement of the tables in the Relationships window does not matter. You should have noticed that as you drag the tables around, the links remain connected. The arrangement in Figure 27.11 shows how it might look, but you may have used different names for the additional fields in CD.

FIGURE 27.11 Your Relationships window should look something like this.

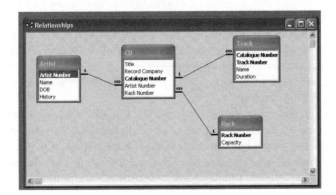

Deleting Relationships

You can delete a relationship by right-clicking the line representing the relationship, then selecting Delete. Note that this removes the relationship, not the data in either of the tables.

Data Entry

Now that you have a working database, test it by entering some data in the tables. This will serve two purposes:

- You'll learn the details of data entry into tables, particularly where these tables are related.

- You can test the design of the CD database.

You will use the simple Datasheet View, and you'll be working with the CDCollect database. Start from the CDCollect:Database window. Select the CD icon and click Open to open this table in the Datasheet View. The result should look like Figure 27.12.

FIGURE 27.12   Opening the table in Datasheet View

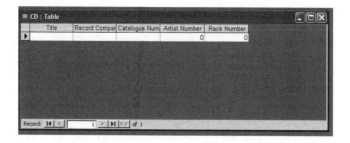

Facilitating Data Entry

Entering data into a table is simple. Click the cell of the table where you want to add data and then just type in the data that you need.

If you want to add an entirely new record, choose Insert ➤ New Record. This will take you to a blank row in the table where you can type in the new data. You can use the Tab key to move from one field to the next as you enter data.

You can immediately see that you need to make some changes to the layout in order to simplify data entry. The problem is that the columns have a uniform width, and in two cases, you cannot read the titles at the top of the columns.

The Datasheet View behaves in a similar way to a spreadsheet. We can drag the column boundaries to enlarge the column.

To resize a column, move the mouse cursor until it lies on the title area of the column on the vertical column boundary. At this point, the cursor changes shape to a double-headed arrow. Press down the left-hand mouse button and drag the column boundary to the required position.

Resize all the columns so that they are a sensible width for data entry. Because the first three fields are all fairly large, you can't make the columns the full width of the fields, but choose a comfortable size.

Entering Data into a Table

Now you insert some real data to the database by adding the following data to the CD, Artist, and Rack tables:

Title:	Blood On The Tracks
Record Company:	Columbia
Catalogue Number:	COL 4678422
Artist Name:	Bob Dylan
DOB:	24 May 1941
History:	Born Robert Allen Zimmerman, Duluth Minnesota. First record, 1962. Serious motorcycle accident 29 July 1966. First movie part in *Pat Garrett & Billy the Kid.*
Rack Number:	8, which can store 100 CDs
Tracks:	
1 Tangled Up In Blue	5.66
2 Simple Twist of Fate	4.30
3 You're a Big Girl Now	4.60
4 Idiot Wind	7.90
5 You're Gonna Make Me Lonesome When You Go	2.90
6 Meet Me In The Morning	4.32
7 Lily, Rosemary and the Jack Of Hearts	8.83
8 If You See Her, Say Hello	4.77
9 Shelter From the Storm	4.98
10 Buckets of Rain	3.48

Enter the data for this CD, starting with the CD table. If you encounter any problems, make a note of the messages from Access and try to work out what has gone wrong. Close each table as you finish entering data in it.

You probably got a message stating, "You can't add or change a record because a related record is required in table Artist." The Help button provides a more detailed explanation.

This tells you that you can't add a record to the many side of the relationship until the matching record exists on the one side of the relationship. Translating this into simpler language, Access does not let you create a database record for a CD without first entering the data for the artist. A similar problem exists for the rack. This problem exists because you chose to enforce referential integrity when you set up the relationships between tables. If you try to get around this problem by ignoring the messages, you'll receive further messages, and finally Access says that it cannot save your changes. If you don't fully understand what is happening, take a look back at the "Setting Up Relationships" section.

The simplest way around this problem is to enter the data in the following order:

1.   Artist

2.   Rack

3.   CD

4.   Track

This fills all the tables on the one side of each relationship before the many side.

Try entering the data using this sequence. Make a note of anything that you found difficult or clumsy.

Figure 27.13 shows what the Track table should look like when you have finished. You may have found that entering the Track table data was a little laborious and wondered whether it was strictly necessary to provide some of the data.

FIGURE 27.13   The completed Track table should look like this.

Catalogue Num	Track Number	Name	Duration
COL 4678422	1	Tangled Up In Blue	5.66
COL 4678422	2	Simple Twist of Fate	4.3
COL 4678422	3	you're A Big Girl Now	4.6
COL 4678422	4	Idiot Wind	7.9
COL 4678422	5	you're Gonna Make Me Lonesome When you Go	2.9
COL 4678422	6	Meet Me In The Morning	4.32
COL 4678422	7	Lily, Rosemary And The Jack Of Hearts	8.83
COL 4678422	8	If you See Her, Say Hello	4.77
COL 4678422	9	Shelter From The Storm	4.98
COL 4678422	10	Buckets of Rain	3.48
*	0		0

Record: |◄ ◄ | 8 | ► ►| ►* | of 10

For example, why do you have to enter the track number in each case? Surely Access knows that if you enter the tracks in sequence, the track numbers should follow that sequence? The answer to this is rather important. Access is a *relational database*, and with any relational database, the sequence or order of rows in a table is not relevant and may not be maintained by the database. You cannot rely on being able to obtain the track number from the sequence of rows in the table, so you need to enter it.

Why do you need to keep entering the catalogue number for each record? Just because you entered all these records together does not mean that Access associates them automatically with the same CD; the catalogue number is essential for each record.

You can significantly reduce the effort and potential for error when entering the same data again and again by using the clipboard. Type in the first value and then select the entry by dragging the cursor though it. Choose Edit ➢ Copy to copy it to the clipboard. Now every time you need to enter that data, press Shift+Insert on your keyboard to insert a copy.

Now enter the data for the following CD, using what you have learnt. The Artist table data is not repeated, because it is the same as before:

Title:	Blonde On Blonde
Record Company:	CBS
Catalogue Number:	CDCBS 22130
Artist Name:	Bob Dylan
Rack Number:	6, which can store 75 CDs
Tracks:	
1 Rainy Day Women Nos 12 & 35	4.58
2 Pledging My Time	3.72
3 Visions Of Johanna	7.50
4 One Of Us Must Know (Sooner Or Later)	4.92
5 I Want You	3.11
6 Stuck Inside Of Mobile With The Memphis Blues Again	7.07
7 Leopard-Skin Pill Box Hat	3.85
8 Just Like A Woman	4.68
9 Most Likely You Go Your Way And I'll Go Mine	3.24
10 Temporary Like Achilles	4.82
11 Absolutely Sweetmarie	4.78
12 4TH Time Around	4.46
13 Obviously 5 Believers	3.52
14 Sad Eyed Lady Of The Lowlands	10.75

Take a look at the tables after you have entered the data. Notice that you made a small error in the table design—one of the tracks has such a long name that it has exceeded the size of the field that you allocated. You can correct this error quite simply by closing the table and reopening it in Design View. Change the field size to 55 characters, solving the problem. Close the Design View and then reopen the table in Datasheet View and correct the name that was truncated. This kind of change can be made to the table design after data has been entered in the table.

WARNING Access is very forgiving of this kind of change, but there are some changes that might cause your existing data to become invalid, so be cautious when making design alterations.

Figure 27.14 shows how the tables should look after all these changes. Don't bother arranging your table windows like this—just check them one by one.

FIGURE 27.14 Tables resulting from additional data entered and the changes made

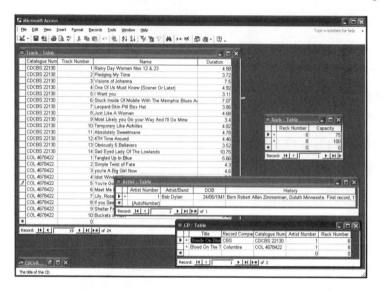

Deleting Data in a Table

Deleting a row from a table is easy. Select the record that you wish to delete by clicking at the far left-hand side of the row as you see it in the Datasheet View. The whole row goes black, indicating its selection. You can now use the Delete key on the keyboard or choose Edit ➢ Delete Record to delete the row. Access warns you, "You are about to delete one record(s)." If you click Yes, the record is deleted and you will not be able to undo this action. This message gives you a useful clue that you can delete several rows at the same time with this method if you wish.

 Access maintains referential integrity when you add new records. The same is true when you delete records. If you try to delete a record that is at the one end of a one-to-many relationship, Access will not let you; it displays a warning with a Help button to give you further guidance.

It is also possible to delete records using forms, and this is the typical way that users carry out this action.

Editing Data in a Table

Editing data in a table is very easy. Make sure that the table is displayed by clicking the table name in the Access window. You can navigate to the row that you wish to change using the navigation bar, or by using the arrow keys on your keyboard. To alter data in a field, simply click in the field and then type the new value that you wish to store. You can use the cursor control keys on the keyboard to move around in a field, and the Backspace and Delete keys on the keyboard allow you to remove existing data.

Access provides an Undo feature that behaves in just the same way as it does in the other Office tools. If you click the Undo button on the toolbar, the last editing change is undone.

Remember that Access saves your changes as you leave the field, the row, or the table.

Organising Data

Once your data is in the table, there are many ways to change its presentation to make it more convenient to work with. You can also use some tools to make it easy to find and change data in a large table.

Sorting Table Data

You probably notice that the Track table no longer displays the tracks in the order they were entered. You can change the order in which the rows of a table are displayed to make it easy to work with the data.

 Changing the ordering of the rows in a table has no effect on any applications, queries, reports, or forms that you may use. Remember, relational databases do not make any use of the sequence of the rows in a table.

You might want the tracks displayed in alphabetical order. Left-click on the name at the top of the column. The entire column is highlighted. Now right-click the mouse and notice the Sort Ascending and Sort Descending options. Sort Ascending sorts the data in alphabetical order, putting the As at the top and the Zs at the bottom of the column. If you look closely at the menu icons, you will see that this is represented graphically. Select the Ascending option, re-sort the table based on Track Number, and then re-sort again on Catalogue Number. Did you get the result that you expected?

Rearranging Table Columns

The order of the columns in a table datasheet can be changed quite simply. This is purely a cosmetic change. Relational database theory states that the sequence of columns in a table has no significance. The only way that the DBMS can normally get at the data is through the column name, so the sequence of columns is unimportant.

To move a column, take the following steps:

1. Click the column title bar to select the whole column, which goes black to indicate the selection.

2. Make sure the mouse cursor is on the title bar and then click and drag the column to the right or the left until the desired column position is reached.

3. Release the mouse button. The whole column is moved to the new position.

4. It is conventional (but not required) to put the primary key fields in the leftmost position in a table. Rearrange the tables so that this is the case.

Changing the ordering of the columns in a table has no effect on any applications, queries, reports, or forms that you may use. In theory, relational databases do not make any use of the sequence of the columns in a table, only their names. In practice, Access uses the number of the column in a table for some purposes, but reordering the columns does not change this numbering.

Using Find and Replace

Once tables start to become large, it is necessary to use more sophisticated tools to manage the data held in them. The Find and Replace commands are extremely valuable in helping you to maintain your data.

If you are used to Word, these tools operate very similarly, but this also is a drawback because there is a crucial difference. By default, the Find and Replace commands operate only within the selected column, not across the whole table or the whole database. This can cause some confusion unless you are aware of it.

To find text within a column, take the following steps:

1. Open the table in Datasheet View.

2. Click the title bar of the column that you wish to search. The column goes black to show it has been selected.

3. Choose Edit ➢ Find and type in the text that you wish to find. This could be a whole field that you wish to match, or a word, or even part of a word.

4. If you want your text to match part of a field, select Any Part Of Field in the Match box. The other options are Whole Field, which only matches your text against the whole field contents, or Start Of Field, in which case your text will match only the start of the field.

5. You can search the whole of the column, or from the top to the bottom (Down), or vice versa (Up). This is important when you expect to find more than one row that matches your search text.

6. Look In Name Of Column is probably selected. If you really want to search all columns in this table, select the whole table.

7. Click Find Next. This finds the next row that matches your search text. You can repeatedly use Find Next to step through all of the records that match in turn.

Replacing text works in the same way, except that you specify the search text and the text that should replace the search text. You can use Replace All if you want Access to go ahead and make all the changes without stopping. This is a quick and efficient way to change a lot of data in your database.

Choosing Replace All is also a good way to destroy a lot of data if you use it incorrectly. Access helps you avoid the worst by giving you a warning when you change data in this way, but until you are fully familiar with Replace, it's better to step through changes one at a time so you can fully appreciate what's happening.

You can search for any kind of data (numbers, text, dates, and so on) using this approach. When you want to search for dates and other types with complex formatting, you need to be careful with the way that you enter the data. If, for example, you enter a date in the Find What field as 19/09/1958, but the dates in the table are formatted as 19-Sept-1958 and the Search Fields as Formatted check box is selected, the search will not succeed in finding the matching record. If you want to search in this way, uncheck this box.

Using Wildcards

The Find and Replace facility can be made a lot more powerful with the use of *wildcards*. A wildcard character is a special symbol that can stand for one or many characters. You can use a mixture of ordinary and wildcard characters in your search text. Here are the wildcard characters and their usage:

Character	Use	Examples
?	Matches any single character	?ob matches Rob or Bob.
*	Matches any number of characters	win* matches window, wink, and winter.
#	Matches any single numeric character	#1 matches 11, 21, 91, and so on

Deleting Tables

You can delete an entire table from a database. This is a drastic type of deletion, and if the table in question has relationships with other tables, Access may well give you messages that ask about referential integrity. Clearly it makes no sense to maintain relationships with tables that no longer exist.

To delete a table, select the table in the Access window and then click the Delete icon.

Checking the Spelling in Text Fields

Access provides some simple spell-checking tools. These can find simple spelling errors in text fields, but, of course, they can't correct some of the rather unusual words that you would typically find in song lyrics. The tables shown back in Figure 27.14 contain some spelling mistakes. To find them, choose Tools ➢ Spelling. A Spelling window appears that is identical to those provided in the other Office applications. Click Ignore or Change for each of the words that are found, depending on whether they are really mistakes or simply unusual words.

Filtering Rows

A *filter* allows you to select which rows you wish to see within a table. It is very important to recognise that a filter does not change any of the data in a table; all the rows are still there, even though they may not be visible. A filter is a good idea when you want to do the following:

- Work with just a small number of rows in a big table, and you don't want to hunt through all the table for those rows. In a big table, you might easily miss a few.

- Look at the data in a table in a special way based on the contents of one or more columns.

You can set up a filter from the table Datasheet View. Open the table and click the data value that you want to select for viewing. Right-click the mouse. A small window opens, displaying at its top a list of filtering options. Click Filter By Selection. The datasheet is redisplayed, showing only the rows that have the same value as the one you first selected.

Apply a filter to the Tracks table so that only the tracks from Blonde on Blonde are displayed. The result should look like Figure 27.15.

FIGURE 27.15 Applying a filter to the Tracks table

Catalogue Num	Track Number	Name	Duration
CDCBS 22130	1	Rainy Day Women Nos 12 & 23	4.58
CDCBS 22130	2	Pledging My Time	3.72
CDCBS 22130	3	Visions of Johanna	7.5
CDCBS 22130	4	One Of Us Must Know (Sooner Or Later)	4.92
CDCBS 22130	5	I Want you	3.11
CDCBS 22130	6	Stuck Inside Of Mobile With The Memphis Blues A	7.07
CDCBS 22130	7	Leopard-Skin Pill Box Hat	3.85
CDCBS 22130	8	Just Like A Woman	4.68
CDCBS 22130	9	Most Likely you Go your Way And I'll Go Mine	3.4
CDCBS 22130	10	Temporary Like Achilles	4.82
CDCBS 22130	11	Absolutely Sweetmarie	4.78
CDCBS 22130	12	4TH Time Around	4.46
CDCBS 22130	13	Obviously 5 Believers	3.52
CDCBS 22130	14	Sad Eyed Lady Of The Lowlands	10.75

You remove the filter in the same way. Click a value in the column that has the filter. Right-click the mouse and choose Remove Filter.

Filters can also be used with forms.

Printing Tables

It is possible to print tables, just as they appear in the Datasheet View. This is of limited value, but it can be useful for checking batches of data as you add records. Much better printing facilities are available when you design a report (see Chapter 30, "Producing Reports").

1. Choose File ➢ Page Setup to select the size of paper that you wish to use and the margins. These can be adjusted in the same way as for any other document. Once you've set up the page correctly, click OK.

2. Choose File ➢ Print Preview to see a visual representation of your table. This is useful, because when your tables become much larger, you can check the number of pages that will be printed before you start wasting paper. To do this, navigate to the last page by clicking the buttons in the navigation bar at the bottom of the window. The number of pages is displayed at the bottom of the Print Preview window. You should also check that everything else is in order before you start printing.

    Close the Print Preview window using the Close control button on the toolbar when you are satisfied with how the table looks.

3. To actually print the table, choose File ➢ Print, making sure that the correct printer and printing options are selected. Click OK to start printing.

You can print specific pages rather than all pages by specifying the beginning and ending page numbers in the standard Print dialog box. If you want to print only certain records in the table, you can set up a filter on the table and then print the result rather than the whole table. Use Print Preview to ensure that you have correctly chosen the result that you want to see printed.

Further Organisation of Your Database

Imagine that you have a lot of classical CDs in your collection. For these CDs, you're interested in the composer and the conductor as well as the artist (orchestra). You would really like to record the same type of details for a composer as you have for an artist, in other words, the date of birth and some historical notes. For a conductor, you don't really want the date of birth, but the ability to store some notes is still useful. Remember that you won't always want to record the name of the conductor and the composer for all CDs; this wouldn't make much sense for a typical pop CD.

Change your database design to allow for these extra features. Don't forget to make the necessary additional relationships. Follow these steps:

1. You need two new tables, one for the conductor and one for the composer. You could create these tables from scratch using the same approach used earlier in this chapter, but

you may have noticed that they are both very similar to the Artist/Band table you started with. You can quickly create copies of a table:

- Select the table in Database View.

- Choose Edit ➢ Copy to copy the table to the Clipboard.

- If you then select Edit ➢ Paste, you can choose to paste the new table as structure only or with all its data. Clearly you require only the table's structure.

2. You also need to supply new names for the new tables. Once the new tables have been created, change the names using the same approach used earlier in this chapter. Delete the Date Of Birth field from the Conductor table.

3. There is slight problem with the Date Of Birth field for the Composer table in that you probably don't know the full date of birth for many of them, just their birth year. For now, you can get around this problem by entering the date as 1 January in the relevant year.

4. A composer can compose the music on many CDs, but for your purposes assume that each CD has only one composer. A conductor can conduct different pieces of music on many different CDs, but let's assume that one CD features only one conductor. Both of these assumptions are reasonable, but might occasionally be invalid for a few special cases.

   Figure 27.16 shows the Design View for all three tables. Notice that you have not made the Composer and Conductor fields in the CD table required, because you don't want to have to provide this data for all CDs.

FIGURE 27.16   Design View for the CD, Conductor, and Composer tables

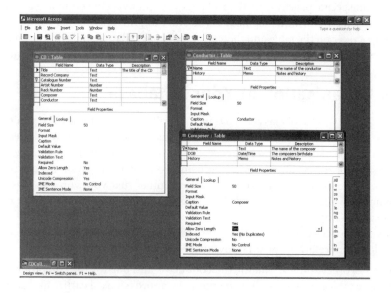

Based on this analysis, both of these new tables have a one-to-many relationship with the CD table, so you need to add new fields to the CD table to represent the links to the new tables.

5. Once this is done, use the Relationship tool to make the relationships between the tables clear to Access, as shown in Figure 27.17.

FIGURE 27.17   Creating new relationships for the new tables

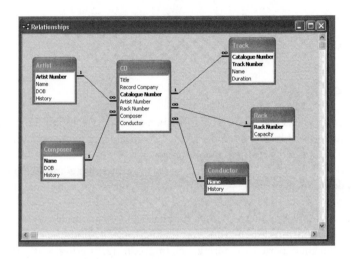

Before continuing, you need to add a bit more data to your sample database to facilitate the lessons of the next chapters. Add the data for the following CD. Notice that data is not provided for some of the fields:

Title :   Brandenburg Concertos 2 & 3

Record Company: HMV

Catalogue Number: HMV 7 67606 2

Artist Name: Academy of St Martins in the Fields

Conductor: Neville Marriner

Composer: J.S. Bach

Date of Birth: 1685

Rack Number;   1, which can store 150 CDs

Tracks:

1 Brandenburg Concerto No 3	13.58
2 Concerto for Two Violins	16.92
3 Sheep May Safely Graze	4.53
4 Jesu Joy of Man's Desiring	5.20
5 Suite No 3 in D	18.58
6 Brandenburg Concerto No 2	15.23

Summary

This long chapter covered some of the most difficult aspects of developing a database. You need to carry out an analysis of business requirements before starting to create tables, and this analysis is the key to creating a useful, reliable database.

Access provides a useful set of tools for setting up the tables that compose your database, but you need to make full use of these—especially primary keys and relationships—to build an effective database.

In this chapter, you were able to create a database and create tables within that database. You established relationships among those tables and learned about the consequences of referential integrity. You got experience entering, deleting, editing, filtering, and sorting data in your database. You learned how to delete tables, find and replace text in a table, spell-check your data, and print a table.

All the remaining chapters in this guide build on what you have learnt in this chapter. It is important that you are fully confident before you proceed, so do not hesitate to review the material before moving on.

Chapter

28

Retrieving Information Using Queries

IN THIS CHAPTER YOU WILL LEARN HOW TO

- ✓ Create a simple query.
- ✓ Create a query based on more than one table.
- ✓ Find a record based on given criteria.
- ✓ Save a query.
- ✓ Edit a query.
- ✓ Delete a query.
- ✓ Create a query with multiple criteria.
- ✓ Select and sort data based on l ogical operations.
- ✓ Print the results of a query.

You've now seen how you can design a database, implement that design in Access, and populate the tables with some data. However, databases are much more than simply a container for storing data. Chapter 26, "An Introduction to Databases," emphasised how the retrieval of data from a database in such a way that you can solve real-world problems was an important goal. To achieve that goal, you need to be able to query a database.

Creating Queries

The previous chapter put a lot of effort into getting a good design for your database. One of the reasons for that effort was so that you would be able to ask a range of questions about your data—some of which could be very complex—and obtain correct answers.

A *query* is a request to the DBMS to retrieve some data. One of the fundamental ideas underlying the theory of relational databases is that all queries work on tables and every query produces a table. This is helpful, because you already know a lot about tables and how they behave.

Keep this model of a query in mind as you work through this chapter. A query can draw data from one or more than one table and combine it together to produce a result table, which Access calls a *dynaset* (see Figure 28.1).

FIGURE 28.1   A query combining data to produce a dynaset

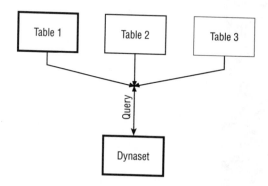

Queries are very important in making Access useful for real business applications. So far you have worked with data at the raw table level, but you would not want to work in that way all the time. You can design queries and then save the query to be run again.

We phrased the last sentence in a rather specific manner to emphasise an important point. When you save a query, you are saving the *definition* of the query, the question you are asking of the database. The result of running the query—the dynaset—is not saved. This is regenerated every time you use the query, so the results are always up to date.

These queries can then be used to construct forms and reports, which are essential for real business applications. This chapter is therefore an essential building block for the last two chapters in this module.

There are a variety of ways in which you can construct a query, but Access uses a simple but powerful approach called Query By Example (QBE). QBE is easy to learn because instead of needing a new language to define a query, you essentially show Access an example of the data that you want and QBE finds the data for you.

Queries are the second major part of Access that you have investigated (the first being tables), so let's start in the same place—the Database View. This view has a button for queries, just below the Tables button. A query can be constructed starting from this window. Click the Query button and then click the New button. The New Query window displays, which should look like Figure 28.2.

FIGURE 28.2   The New Query window

On the right-hand side of the window is a list of five tools that can be used to construct queries. If you click any of these once, a short explanation appears in the left-hand side of the window. These five tools perform the following tasks:

Design View   The Design View is the main tool you use for constructing queries.

Simple Query Wizard   The Simple Query Wizard provides a simple step-by-step wizard-based approach for building queries, but like all wizards, if you want to do something a little different, this is not the tool to use.

Crosstab Query Wizard   The Crosstab Query tool is used to construct a very specialised type of query that we will not consider in this book.

Find Duplicates Query Wizard   This is a useful tool for defining queries that can find rows with duplicated values. We won't cover this tool, but you should remember that it is available and use it if you find it necessary.

Find Unmatched Query Wizard This wizard helps you build a query that can locate rows in one table that do not have related rows in another table. This is again a useful tool, but not one that you will need to use for constructing a simple database.

Let's start by considering queries based on a single table. These are much simpler to construct, and this will help you learn about the different tools. We'll return to queries that take in more than one table later.

Using the Simple Query Wizard

The Simple Query Wizard is a good starting point for simple queries. The first stage of the Simple Query Wizard (see Figure 28.3) prompts you for the fields that you will use in your query. Select the table in which the fields can be found. The wizard then displays the names of the fields in the Available Fields list.

FIGURE 28.3 The first stage of the Simple Query Wizard

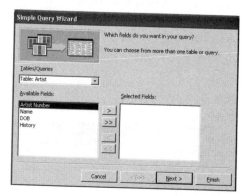

Select the fields you need by double-clicking their names, or by clicking the right arrow button. The field name then appears in the Selected Fields list on the right-hand side.

If you need all the fields, click the double right arrow button. If you make a mistake and select the wrong field, use the left arrow button to put it back into the Available Fields list. If you want to put all the fields back, use the double left arrow.

The next section of the wizard asks you to name the query. You can use any name you like, but it is useful to follow a consistent naming scheme so that you can quickly recognise a particular query.

The wizard asks you if you wish to open the query to view information or to modify it. These two options correspond to the Table Datasheet and Table Design Views used in the previous chapter. The same facilities are presented for queries.

Just as you saw for table design, the wizards are useful, but you also need to understand how to construct a query using the Design View.

Creating a Simple Query

Before you started to implement your CD database in Access, you first spent some time designing the database. This is also a good strategy for creating queries. A little time thinking about what you need can save a lot of work. When you design a query, you can specify the following:

- The tables from which data will be extracted. For a simple query, let's work with only one table.
- The fields within these tables that will be involved in the query.
- The specific rows that you require. You can limit the result to rows that meet a particular criterion.
- The order in which rows should appear in the result.
- Calculations based on data in the tables that you specify.

You'll use your CD database as the basis for exploring queries.

An obvious query would be one that found all the tracks for a particular CD, putting them in sequence. Using the analysis above:

- The table required is Track.
- You want to see data from the Catalogue Number, Track Number, Name, and Duration fields of the Track table.
- You want to select rows based on the Catalogue Number field.
- The result should be put in order of the Track Number field.

Now you're ready to implement this query using Access.

Start from the CDCollect:Database window. Click the Queries button. You should see one query already in the window; this is the one you created earlier with the Simple Query Wizard. Click New and this time select Design View (see Figure 28.4).

FIGURE 28.4   The Design View window is used for selecting tables.

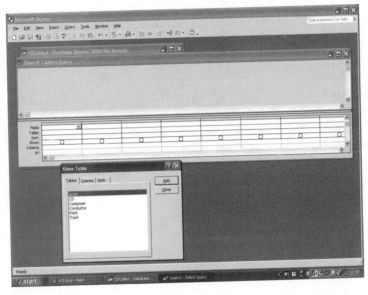

The Show Table window allows you to select the tables to be used in this query. You want only the Track table so select this, click Add, and then click Close to remove the Show Table window. You can always add further tables if you want to change a query later.

> You may have noticed that Show Table has three tabs: Table, Queries, and Both. This is because you can use both tables and queries to build new queries. Remember that a query produces a dynaset, and this can be used like any other table in a query. You don't need to use this capability at the moment.

Now you need to select the fields to use in the query. The available fields are displayed in the upper part of the Query window, shown in much the same way as in the Table Design View. The bottom part of the window is the working area in which you assemble these fields to create your query.

This area consists of a number of columns, each of which can contain a field. Double-click the required field in the upper part of the window. Access displays this field in the next available column. Carry on doing this until you have all the relevant fields in the bottom part of the window.

> If you prefer, you can drag the fields from the top part of the window to the lower working area.

Editing the query is very simple:

- You can change the sequence of the fields. Click the bar at the top of the column and then drag the column to the left or the right. This changes the sequence of the columns as they are presented in the resulting dynaset.

- You can edit a query in place by clicking the cell and typing in the changed text. Use the Backspace and Delete keys on your keyboard to remove characters that you do not need.

- You can delete a column from the query working area by clicking the top bar and then pressing the Delete button on the keyboard.

- You can control whether a column forms part of the resulting dynaset or is hidden by selecting or deselecting the Show parameter for that column.

- You can add new fields to a query at any time by using the Query Design window and adding further fields exactly as we did in the initial query design stage.

You don't really want to see the catalogue number on each row of the dynaset, so uncheck the Show box in this column.

You want the dynaset sorted in ascending order based on the value of the Number field. Click in the Sort row of the Track Number column and select Ascending. You can sort on number or text fields in just the same way. Sorting a text field in ascending order means that text at the start of the alphabet will be at the top of the list. Sorting numbers in ascending order means that lower numbers will be at the top of the list. The opposite is true in both cases if the sort order is descending.

To test your query, ask Access to extract only those tracks that belong to the catalogue number CDCBS 22130. Type this in the Criteria box for the Catalogue Number field. Notice that Windows puts double quotes around this input for you. At the end of this, your query should resemble Figure 28.5.

You can remove a criteria by selecting the criteria field and then deleting the criteria text using the Delete or Backspace key.

FIGURE 28.5 Your query should look like this.

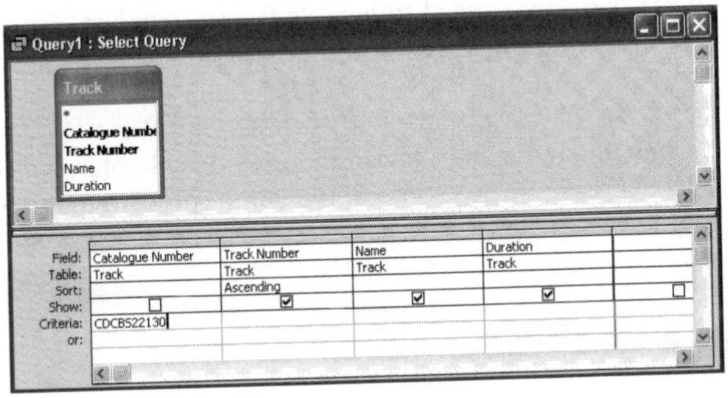

Close the window and when prompted, give the query a suitable name, such as TotalTime. You can also save the query by choosing File ➢ Save and File ➢ Save As. The Save As option allows you to save an edited query under a different name.

You can now test the query by selecting it in the CDCollect:Database window and then clicking Open. This forces Access to run the query and present the results to you, which should look like Figure 28.6.

FIGURE 28.6 Presentation of query results

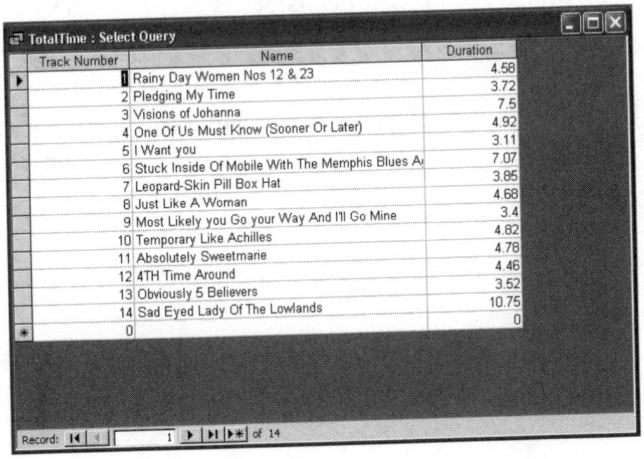

The result of running the query is a dynaset, and as you can see, it looks just like a table. Now you know how to construct a simple query. Everything else covered in this chapter can be tackled in easy stages, building on this foundation.

Specifying Criteria and Using Expressions

First you need to be able to select rows rather more flexibly than just typing in the whole of a value such as CDCBS 22130. This would quickly get tedious, and certainly doesn't help when you want to select rows according to a comparison with another value, a technique that you'll find especially valuable.

To understand criteria better, you need to be able to put together *expressions*. These vary according to the type of data that you have stored in a field.

You may find it useful to revisit the previous chapter, which discussed wildcards. Expressions use some of the same wildcard features.

Let's start with the simple wildcards:

Character	Use	Examples
?	Matches any single character	?ob match Rob or Bob.
??	Match any two characters	he?? match help, head, and heat.
*	Matches any number of characters	win* match window, wink, and winter.
ar	Match any number of characters at the start of the word and any number at the end	*ar* match March, garden, and embargo.
#	Matches any single numeric character	#1 match 11, 21, 91, and so on

You can do comparisons:

Character	Meaning	Examples
<	Less than	< 1024 matches rows with values less than 1024.
>	Greater than	> 5 matches numbers greater than 5. > Bill matches all words that are alphabetically higher, for example, car, door, elephant, and so on.
>=	Greater than or equal to	>= 10 matches 10 and all higher numbers.
<=	Less than or equal to	<= 10 matches 10 and all lower numbers.
<>	Not equal to	<> 20 matches all numbers except 20.
Between…and	A range of values	Between 12/10/95 and 12/12/99 matches all dates between these dates.

Notice that you can use these comparisons with dates, numbers, and text. Mixing different types of data does not usually make sense, so if you have a date field, comparing it to "California" would not be useful.

You can connect bits of expressions together to create more complex expressions. To achieve this, you use a form of English based on a few keywords:

Word	Meaning	Examples
Or	Either value	Bill or John matches any row that has the value Bill or the value John.
And	Both values	>= 1/3/99 and <= 1/12/99 selects all the dates that are later than or equal to 1 March 1999 and earlier than or equal to 1 December 1999.
Not	Opposite to	Not B* selects only those rows that do not contain a word beginning with B.

NOTE   Query Designer provides a lot more functionality in putting together criteria than we can cover in this book, but you can achieve a great deal using just the tools described in this section. This is one area where Access Help is an essential source. Look for "Creating Queries" in Help topics and "criteria" and "wildcards" in the Help Index for more information and starting points for more advanced techniques.

Let's modify the TotalTime query so that it selects only tracks 2–6 inclusive for all the CDs in your collection and does not include the names of the tracks, but does show the catalogue number. Make the catalogue number the first column. Call this query MiddleTracks. Then test the query by opening the dynaset.

The query should look like Figure 28.7, and the dynaset should look like Figure 28.8.

FIGURE 28.7   Your MiddleTracks query should look like this.

FIGURE 28.8   The dynaset resulting from the MiddleTracks query

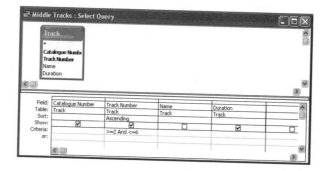

Using Queries

Now you've seen the basics of designing a query, you can begin to make use of some of the features that Access provides to make life easy. One of the most important of these is the Query Design toolbar.

The Query Design Toolbar

The Query Design toolbar, like the other Access toolbars, is displayed automatically when you are carrying out query design activities. If it's not visible, you can display it by choosing View ➤ Toolbars. An annotated view of the Query Design toolbar is shown in Figure 28.9.

FIGURE 28.9   The Query Design toolbar

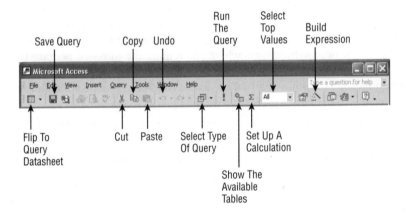

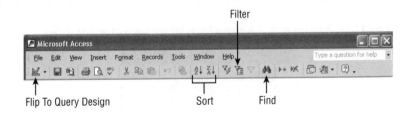

You will not use all of these buttons in this module, but here's a short description of some of their functions (omitting the obvious ones such as Save, Cut, Paste, and so on).

Undo   Undo may allow you to undo the last change made to a query.

Select Type Of Query   This function helps to select the type of query you are building—a select query, a crosstab, and so on.

Run   The Run button causes Access to run the query that you have designed and display the result as a datasheet. It flips the toolbar to the Query Datasheet toolbar, which is shown below the Query Design toolbar.

Show The Available Tables   This function displays the window containing the names of tables.

Select Top Values   This function is useful where a query could return a vast number of rows. It allows you to specify that you want only the top 10 rows (for example) from the dynaset. We will not cover this feature in detail.

Build Expression   The Build Expression button opens a window that helps you to build an expression easily.

Adding Calculations to Queries

Chapter 27, "Creating a Database," warned against including derived or calculated data in your database tables. By using a query that contains a calculation, you can obtain that calculated data without having to store it permanently. This is a good technique because you can be sure that the result of the calculation always reflects the current values of data in the tables.

A typical example of a calculation is where you require the sum—or perhaps the average—of a selection of rows grouped according the value of one of the fields. For example, you might want to obtain the total duration of all the tracks for your CDs, grouped or collected by the CD catalogue number. This is easy to achieve with the Query Design window:

1. Starting from the CDCollect database window, select Queries, and then click New and Design View.
2. Select the Track table and the two fields you require: Catalogue Number and Duration.
3. Click the Σ button. This introduces a new Total row to the Query Design view.
4. Select Group By for the Catalogue Number field, so that the totals are grouped by the CD catalogue number.
5. Select Sum for the Duration field. The resulting query should look like Figure 28.10.

FIGURE 28.10   An example of a query for total duration of all CD tracks

6. Save the query as CalcTotal, and then click the Run button to test it. The dynaset should look like Figure 28.11.

FIGURE 28.11   The dynaset resulting from CalcTotal query

7. Modify CalcTotal so that it calculates the average track length per CD rather than the total playing time.

Adding a Filter

Filters can be used with queries in just the same way as for tables. Review the "Filtering Rows" section in Chapter 27 for details of how to use filters in that context.

To see how this works, return to the TotalTime query and open it with the Query Design View. Run the query to display the dynaset. Click the first row, which has a track number of 1, and then click the Filter By Selection button. The dynaset is filtered so that only those rows with track numbers equal to 1 are displayed.

Saving a Query

Queries are not data, so Access does not automatically save changes in queries as you make them. You should save your query periodically by using the Save button on the toolbar. If you forget to save, Access prompts you to do so when you leave the Query window and attempt to do something else with your database.

Deleting a Query

You can delete a query just like any other database object such as a table or a form. Select the query that you want to delete in the Access window, and then click the Delete button in the toolbar or press the Delete button on the keyboard.

You may have forms and reports that depend on the existence of a query. In this case, Access asks you before it deletes the query. Be careful about using this feature—if you're careless about deletion, you may lose a significant amount of work.

Queries Based on More than One Table

Whilst queries based on one table are useful, it is vital that you can construct simple queries based on more than one table. These types of queries are the basis for much of the work that you will do with the forms and reports in Chapter 29, "Using Forms," and Chapter 30, "Producing Reports."

Queries can be based on two, three, four, or even more tables, but the vast majority of multiple table queries use just two tables; this is the type that you will investigate. As well as the number of tables, the way you put the tables together in the query can vary a great deal, and this can become very complex. You will only use the simplest way of joining tables in a query.

WARNING You should gain experience with these simple two-table queries before trying anything more adventurous. When you feel you're ready to try more complex queries, first do some general reading on relational database theory. A good general database textbook is *Fundamentals of Database Systems*, 4th Edition, by Ramez Elmasri and Shamkant B. Navathe (Addison-Wesley, 2003).

Chapter 27 explained how to set up a relationship between two tables. You will base your two-table queries on those relationships. An example will help to illustrate this idea. You need a query to display the title of a CD alongside its total playing time. So using the same step-by-step approach as before, follow these instructions:

- The tables you need are Track and CD.

- You want to see data from the CD:Title and Track:Duration fields.

- You want to select rows based on the Catalogue Number field, which is shared between the two tables.

- The result should be sorted in order of the Catalogue Number field.

Use the Query Design View to create a new query. Select the required tables from the Show Table window. Notice that the two tables are shown in the same way as in the Relationships window, with the connection between the Catalogue Number field in the CD table and the Catalogue Number field in the Track table.

Add the required fields to the lower part of the window. These fields are Title from the CD table and Duration from the Track table.

Click the Σ button from the toolbar to open up the Total row and then add Sum to Duration and Group By to Title. The query should look like Figure 28.12.

FIGURE 28.12 An example of a two-table query

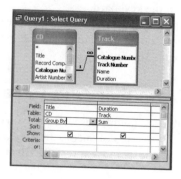

Save the query as JoinTable and run it. You should see a result similar to Figure 28.13.

FIGURE 28.13   The result of the JoinTable query

Do you think it matters that the SumOfDuration column is displaying so many decimal places? What might you do about this?

Printing the Results of Queries

When a query is run, the result is a dynaset. You can print a dynaset in just the same way as you print a table. To review table printing, look at the "Printing Tables" section in Chapter 27.

You can print specific pages rather than all pages by specifying the beginning and ending page numbers in the standard Print dialog box.

If you want to print only certain records in the table, you can set up a filter on the table and then print the result rather than the whole table. Use Print Preview to ensure that you have correctly chosen the result that you want to see printed.

Summary

This chapter explained how you can create a query based on one or more tables that form the core of your database. Queries play a central role in extracting data from those tables in a flexible way and can also carry out simple calculations on numeric and date data. The results of using Access queries is a table that's known as a dynaset.

You learnt about the different ways to create queries, including using the Query Wizard. You learnt how to save, edit, and delete queries, and how to add calculations to queries. You specified criteria for your queries and sorted and printed the results. You also now understand how to add filters to your queries.

In the last two chapters of this module, you'll apply what you've learned to produce screen-based forms and printed reports.

Chapter

29

Using Forms

IN THIS CHAPTER YOU WILL LEARN HOW TO

- ✓ Open an existing form.
- ✓ Use the Access Form Wizard to create a simple form.
- ✓ Create a form using the standard Access tools.
- ✓ Save a form.
- ✓ Delete a form.
- ✓ Arrange objects in a form.
- ✓ Use a query as the basis for a form.
- ✓ Enter data using a form.
- ✓ Format form text.
- ✓ Add and modify text in form headers and footers.
- ✓ Change the background colours and appearance of a form.
- ✓ Use graphics in a form.
- ✓ Print a form.

Paper forms are a part of everyone's working lives. You're used to filling in forms for such activities as taxes, insurance, orders for products and services, and general enquiries. Such paper forms are usually (eventually) typed into computer systems by data entry staff.

A much better approach is to do away with the paper and to enter the data directly onto a form displayed by the computer. This has the following significant advantages:

- The screen form can be made to look similar to an existing paper form, making it easy for people to switch from paper to computer use.

- The computer-based form can check what is entered as it is entered, so that only accurate data is processed.

- Using computer-based forms to replace paper preserves resources (trees) and saves on storage costs.

Forms are an important and often indispensable part of many databases. Access provides tools that can be used to create extremely versatile forms, and you'll find working with these tools both easy and creative.

Form Basics

In order to understand how forms work, you first need to recognise some basic ideas.

A form is built from a number of different components.

Controls are areas where data can be entered or displayed by the computer. Some controls can be *bound* to fields in the database. This means that they automatically display the value of the underlying database field, and if the data is changed in the control, it is changed in the underlying database. Some examples of the controls covered in this chapter are as follows:

Text box   A text box is a control that displays text.

Command button   A command button is a control that issues a command to the database.

List box   A list box is a control that displays a list of items and allows the user to select one of them.

Labels   Labels are textual descriptions that can be used anywhere within a form, but are often attached to a specific control to inform the user what should be entered in that control.

Graphics   Graphics can be as simple as lines and boxes, or as sophisticated as full colour pictures.

Form-formatting features   These include headings and page breaks that can be used to give a form a recognisable structure. These features are very important for forms that fill more than one screen.

Figure 29.1 illustrates many of these form features. This form is part of the Northwind sample database. You can investigate the design of this form at any time to see how the various effects have been achieved.

FIGURE 29.1   Examples of form features

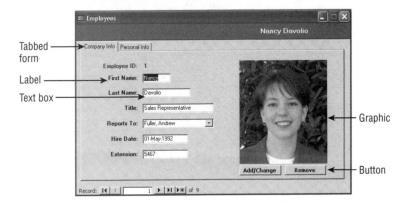

Types of Access Forms

Access supports three main types of forms. These are described as follows, together with some examples taken from the Northwind sample database:

Single-column form   A single-column form (see Figure 29.2) displays all the fields in a single column, with each field on a single line. This is about as simple as form layout can get, but it's quite acceptable for many purposes.

FIGURE 29.2   An example of a single-column form

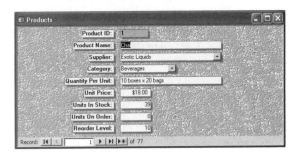

Tabular form A tabular form (see Figure 29.3) is really just a form representation of the familiar Datasheet View. Each row in the table or query appears as a row in the table. The table column titles are used as column titles in the form. This type of form—like the single-column form—is easy to set up.

FIGURE 29.3 An example of a tabular form

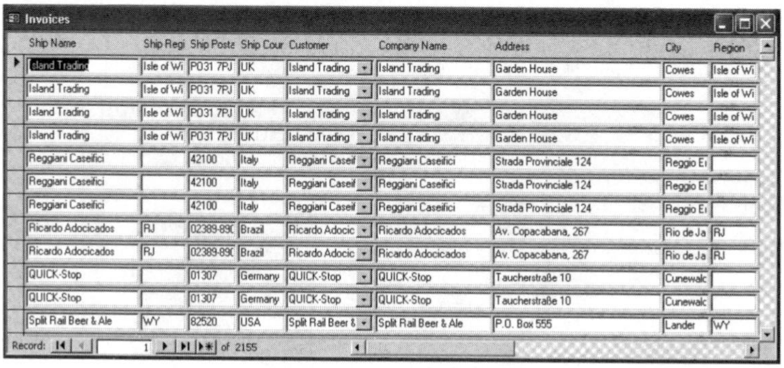

Datasheet form A datasheet form (see Figure 29.4) looks exactly like the familiar table that you saw in previous chapters.

FIGURE 29.4 An example of a datasheet form

Getting Started with Forms

In Chapter 26, "An Introduction to Databases," we had an introduction to forms. We now need to look at this topic in much more detail. You can use a form to carry out all the main data entry and editing database functions. Forms are the preferred way of carrying out these activities with Access.

Opening a Form

Open a form by clicking the Form button and then selecting the form that you wish to use. You can practice this with the Northwind database.

Navigating in Forms

Forms use a navigation bar to help you move between records. This navigation bar was covered in Chapter 26, but to reiterate, the buttons on the bar behave just like a video recorder or a CD player. You can use the left and right buttons to move forward or backward one record. Similarly you can move to the first or last record with the buttons provided. The record number is displayed in a small window; you can go directly to a particular record by typing the required record number in this window.

Entering Records

To enter data in a record, simply type the data into the fields that the form provides. The validation rules that we previously discussed will define the range and type of data that can be entered.

If the form does not display a blank set of fields for you to enter data, click the New Record button; this is the button on the navigation bar with an asterisk (*) in it. Alternatively, you can navigate to the last record and click the Next Record button.

Modifying Records

To modify the data in a record, navigate to the required record, then type the new data over the old, deleting old data as required with the Backspace or Delete key.

Deleting Records

To delete a record when using a form, navigate to the record that you wish to delete and then click the Delete Record button on the toolbar.

Sorting Data in Forms

You can sort data in a form in the same way that we sorted data in tables. Right-click the field that you want to sort by and then select either Sort Ascending or Sort Descending. This will work with both text and numeric fields. You can remove a sort by right-clicking the same field and selecting Remove Filter/Sort.

Saving and Closing Forms

Forms behave just like other database objects such as tables and queries. You need to save any changes that you make to the structure of a form; the Save button on the toolbar does this for you. If you forget to save, Access reminds you when you close the form in Design View. The data that you enter using a form is saved immediately and automatically by Access. You do not need to explicitly save this data.

Forms are closed by using the normal Windows Close button that you find in the top right-hand corner of the Form window.

Deleting Forms

You can delete forms that you no longer require by using the Delete key on the keyboard. This does not delete the data that you entered using the form.

Creating a Form

As you've already discovered in earlier chapters, there is some benefit in doing some analysis before you start to work with Access, and working with forms is just the same. Think about the following points:

- What process is the form meant to support? Don't try to design a do-everything form. This is usually very hard for other people to use. Try to divide up the use of your database into two or three significant tasks that need to be carried out, perhaps by different people. Each of these people might need a unique form.

- Who will use the form? If the typical user is a computer expert, you may be wasting your efforts producing a form that has a lot of visual frills. In contrast, if the typical user normally works with a paper form, then it's probably sensible to put a lot of effort into making your Access form look similar.

- How often will the form be used? If data entry is needed only once a year or perhaps once a month, it may not be necessary to design a form at all. As you saw in Chapter 27, "Creating a Database," simple data entry can be done directly into a table. If a form will be used frequently and by a large number of people, then it's probably necessary to create a form.

Designing the Form

Given the previous thoughts, start your analysis of a new form by writing down the following:

- The names or roles of the people who will be using the form
- The name of the process that the form will support
- The tables and fields that will be involved
- The way in which these fields will be used, for display only or for input

Now draw out the form roughly on a piece of paper. Put the fields in a logical sequence and sketch in any graphical aids.

   A form can be larger than a single screen. If you do design a large form, Access displays scroll bars so you can move around it.

   Although it is possible to build large forms, this is usually a bad design.

Creating a Form with the Form Wizard and AutoForm

As you've seen earlier, wizards are a simple way to create standardised components of a database. A similar facility is available for forms, but this is supplemented by AutoForms. This tool allows you to build a form based on a single table automatically. The forms created by

AutoForm or Form Wizard can be modified to meet your needs, so this is a convenient starting point for your requirements. Let's see how you use both of these facilities:

1. Start with the CDCollect:Database window and click the Forms button and then click New. This displays the various ways in which you can create a new form. Figure 29.5 shows the New Form window, and descriptions of the options follow.

FIGURE 29.5   Options for creating a new form

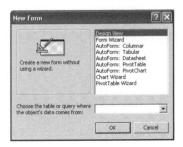

- Design View is the standard tool view, allowing you to build a form from scratch or to modify an existing form.

- The Form Wizard takes you through form design in a conversational manner.

- AutoForms are available for five different types of forms.

- The Chart Wizard helps you to build a graph as part of a form in a conversational process. We will not cover this tool in the module.

- The PivotTable Wizard builds a form based on a pivot table. We have not covered pivot tables in this module. This type of form, whilst useful, is best ignored until you gain more experience with Access.

2. Select the Form Wizard and click the arrow in the drop-down list. A list of all the tables and queries that you have defined in CDCollect appears. The Form Wizard can work with either queries or tables. Select Artist and click the OK button.

3. The Form Wizard displays a window asking which fields you wish to use in the form. This should be familiar from your work with queries. Select all the fields by clicking the right-facing double arrow, and then click Next.

4. The Form Wizard displays a window asking which type of table you require. The choices are

- Columnar

- Tabular

- Datasheet

- Justified

The first three should be familiar, but the fourth type is new.

5. Click the bullet and note how Access shows you a picture of a typical justified layout.

6. You will use a justified table for this form, so select this and click Next.

7. The next window asks what style you would like. There will be at least 10 different styles available through this window. As with the form type, you can click the type and see a depiction of the form. Try this for all the styles.

8. Select Standard and click Next.

9. The final window asks for a form title. Call your form Artist and click Finish to see the completed form, which should be as shown in Figure 29.6.

FIGURE 29.6   The completed Artist form

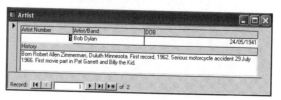

Using AutoForm is even easier than the Form Wizard. Start from the CDCollect:Database window. Click New and select AutoForm:Columnar and the Composer table. Click OK to create the table.

Creating a Form Using Design View

Because using Form Wizard and AutoForm is so easy, why do you need to use anything else? If you need to produce a form that looks like a paper version, or you need to produce a form that is based on two or more tables, you need to use the Form Design View.

Make sure that the Form Design toolbar is displayed. Figure 29.7 shows the main features of this toolbar and the corresponding Form View toolbar.

FIGURE 29.7   The main features of the Form Design toolbar

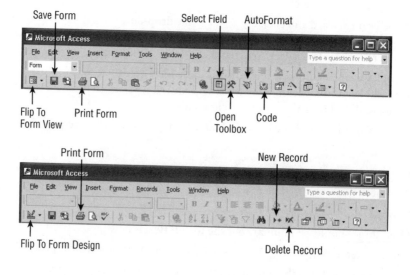

Most of these buttons will be familiar, but the following buttons are significant:

Select Field   The Select Field option selects the fields that you can use in the form. Drag the required field to the correct position on the form.

Open Toolbox   The Open Toolbox option opens an additional toolbar containing icons useful for designing the form. Click this icon if the toolbox is not visible.

AutoFormat   The AutoFormat option provides part of the functionality of the Form Wizard. It is useful for applying a consistent format to a series of forms.

Code   The Code option is used for programming purposes. We will not cover any aspect of this significant but complex component of Access in this book.

Take the following steps to create a form using Design View:

1.   Start from the CDCollect:Database window. Click New and select Design View. You'll base your form on the Track table, so select this in the table box.

2.   Access displays a blank form with a grid layout, as shown in Figure 29.8. The grid is the pattern of dots and squares. If your form does not have a grid, choose View ➢ Grid to switch this on.

FIGURE 29.8   A blank form with a grid layout

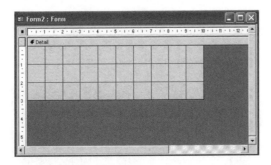

The grid is very useful for rapidly lining up the different elements of a form. These elements snap to the nearest grid point, making it easier to get a professional-looking layout.

As well as a grid, your form should have a ruler. This is the measurement scale displayed along the top and left-hand side of the window. The ruler can be used to place parts of your form at a precise measured position.

Let's start by placing some text boxes on the form. These text boxes will be bound to the fields that belong to your selected table.

3.   If a Customer field list is not displayed, click the Field List button on the Form Design toolbar.

4.   Now select Catalogue Number and drag it onto the blank form. Place it at the bottom of the first row of squares. If you do not get it in the correct position on the first attempt, drag it into position.

5. Notice that you have actually placed two components. The right-most part is a text box, which is bound to the Catalogue Number field. The left-hand part is a label.

6. You can change the size of the text box by dragging on the corners. The label displays the caption if one is defined for the field. When you designed the Track table, you supplied a caption for this field, so Access displays it. You probably need to change the size of the label to make it look tidy. Figure 29.9 shows how it should look.

FIGURE 29.9   The Catalogue Number label

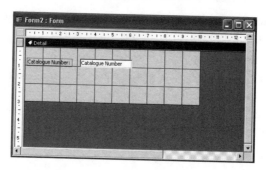

7. Add the other fields from the Track table to the form, keeping them lined up and providing better text labels where required.

   The end result should be a layout such as Figure 29.10.

FIGURE 29.10   Your form layout should look like this.

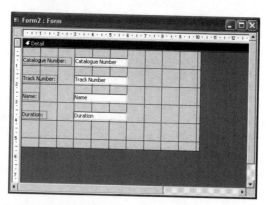

8. All the boxes are the same size in this design, but you need a much larger box for the track name, so extend this box to the right by dragging its right-hand control handles (the little black squares) so that you can see a sensible amount of text. The Track Number box is too big, so fix this also.

9. Now you're ready to test your form. Display it by clicking the View button on the toolbar. The result should look something like Figure 29.11.

FIGURE 29.11   The result of the form creation using the View button

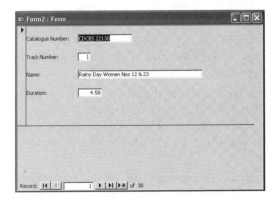

10. Test the form using the navigation buttons at the bottom of the window. The boxes displayed in the form are bound to the fields in the table, so you can modify the rows in the table by typing in new data. Test this by modifying the text of one of the track names. Add some extra data by typing into the new form. Access provides all the usual facilities for editing data in the form's boxes. You can also delete entire records through the form—use the Delete button on the toolbar.

The form works, but it doesn't look very professional. The boxes for Number and Duration are still a bit too big, and you could really use a heading at the top of the form. Close the form and reopen it in Design View to make the modifications:

1. First, modify the form to reduce the size of the relevant boxes. To add a header to the form, right-click in the grid area of the form. In the pop-up window, select Form Header/Footer. This opens new form areas at the top and bottom of the form, as shown in Figure 29.12.

FIGURE 29.12   New form areas at the top and bottom of the form

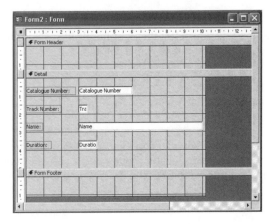

2. Now you need to add a title in the header area. Click the Toolbox button to make the Toolbox window visible. Click the label icon and then drag a rectangular area in the header. This opens up a text box.

    This looks superficially like the text boxes that you can see in the Detail part of the form. But this box is unbound; it is not attached to any row in the database's tables. This means that it will not change as you look through the tracks.

3. Fill the box with some suitable text by typing in the box. Check the results by clicking the View button on the Form Design toolbar. The results probably won't inspire much enthusiasm. You need to increase the size of the text—perhaps use another font—and some colour would be welcome. Go back to the Design View by clicking the View button on the Form Design toolbar.

4. Check whether you have a Formatting toolbar with the usual font tools visible. If not, choose View ≻ Toolbars and select Formatting (Form/Report). This displays the Formatting toolbar, as shown in Figure 29.13.

FIGURE 29.13   The Formatting toolbar

We will not describe this toolbar in the same detail that we have for the other toolbars, because it is so similar to the toolbars used for the other applications in the Office suite.

5. Select the label in the Form Header area and then pick a larger font size in the toolbar (about 20–24 points would be a good choice). While you are working with the text, try some different fonts.

6. Change the font colour using the Font colour button. Right-click in the grid area of the header. Select an appropriate background colour from the menu.

WARNING   Make sure that you select the right-hand side of this button so that you get access to the full set of available colours.

Your finished form might look like Figure 29.14.

TIP   Don't forget that you can copy and paste a whole form from the database window. This is very useful if you need a series of forms that use a similar layout. Just make copies of the first form, then add and remove fields to get the desired results.

Your form is now looking a little more acceptable, but it could be made even tidier. Experiment with fonts for labels and try adding some explanations to the footer.

FIGURE 29.14   Your finished form might look like this.

Working with Forms

Now that you've got your basic form in place, let's take a look at some final tasks involving forms.

Adding Graphics to Forms

You can add graphics to a form by simply pasting in a picture from another application. A good source of such graphics is the Office Clip Art Gallery. Choose Insert ➤ Object and select Microsoft Clip Art Gallery. Choose your clip art and then click Insert. You can move and resize the clip art graphic to achieve the desired effect.

Using Filters with Forms

In Chapter 27, we saw how you can use a filter with a table to restrict the set of records that you wish to view. As you might expect, you can use filters in just the same way with forms. When you click the Filter By Selection button on the Form toolbar, the Form window will display only the records that match the value of the currently selected field.

You can remove the filter by right-clicking the selected field and selecting Remove Filter.

Printing a Form

It is possible to print a form. This is often very useful, because a form can be used to retrieve data from one or more tables, and the resulting information may need to be used away from the computer screen.

To print a form, make sure that the required data is displayed and then click the Print button on the toolbar, or choose File ➤ Print on the main menu. The Print Preview option is also available if you want to see how your form will look before you print it.

You can print specific pages rather than all pages by specifying the beginning and ending page numbers in the standard Print dialog box. If you want to print only certain records, you can set up a filter on the form and then print the result. This will include only the records that match the filter. Use Print Preview to ensure that you have correctly chosen the result that you want to see printed.

If you find that you need to print out a lot of records, printing forms is a clumsy and time-consuming approach. It's much better to design a report and let Access do most of the repetitive work for you.

Summary

Access forms make entry of data into your database very easy. A computer-based form can look just like a paper form, it can validate user-entered data automatically, and it can save the environmental and storage costs associated with paper forms.

Forms are easy to produce, and the Form Wizard can help a great deal. A form can be based on one or more tables or queries.

You now know how to create, save, and delete forms. You learnt how to format and lay out forms, enter data onto forms, arrange objects on forms, and add text to a form's header and/or footer. You can produce forms that use different fonts, backgrounds, and graphics.

Chapter

30

Producing Reports

IN THIS CHAPTER YOU WILL LEARN HOW TO

- ✓ Open and use an existing report.
- ✓ Use the Access Report Wizard to create a simple report.
- ✓ Sort data for presentation in a report.
- ✓ Modify reports.
- ✓ Use graphics in a report.
- ✓ Create and customise headers and footers.
- ✓ Group data in report totals and subtotals.
- ✓ Use simple expressions in reports.
- ✓ Print a report.

Database management packages usually provide tools to help you generate printed output from the database, and Access is no exception. This final chapter in this module investigates the types of report that you can produce and the ways in which you can arrange information within them.

Using Reports

A *report* presents information drawn from a database. The key idea is that a report takes indigestible data (rows from tables) and turns it into information that is usable for a particular problem or requirement. You can present the same data in a host of different ways to suit different needs.

Some examples of reports are as follows:

- Mailing labels ready to stick on envelopes.

- Mail merge letters using data drawn from a database.

- A summary, grouped into categories, with subtotals for each category and a grand total for all categories. This is typical of management reports and accounts.

- A graph showing how data varies over time. Prices are often shown in this way.

You typically use reports where you want to present information in a formal way, as a document that will be printed and perhaps bound. To meet this requirement, you need all the typical features of a document, including page layout, margins, headers, footers, and page numbers. Access reports provide all of these features for you in an easy-to-use tool.

Reports are similar to forms, and you construct them using some of the same types of tools, but they have a different primary objective. Forms are mainly intended for use through a computer screen, but reports are designed for printing. This does not mean that you cannot print forms (you saw how to do this in Chapter 29, "Using Forms") or view reports on screen, but that is not their main objective.

Some Examples of Reports

To illustrate the typical uses of reports, return to the Microsoft sample database, `Northwind.mdb` that you viewed earlier. Open the database and select Reports in the Database window. At least four different reports are displayed.

Note the top button on the left of the window. Instead of the Open button that you've seen for tables, queries, and forms, you see a Preview button. This is because when you view the report on screen, you are essentially previewing the printed report. This reinforces your view that reports are mainly intended for reading on paper.

Select the Sales Total By Amount and click Preview. You should see the first page of a multi-page report, as in Figure 30.1.

FIGURE 30.1   Viewing a report using Preview

Page through the report using the video-style controls at the bottom of the window. Now print the report using the printer icon in the toolbar. Take a close look at the report. It uses heading and subheadings and is divided into sections by value of sales in thousands of dollars. A subtotal is provided for each page. It is perhaps dubious whether a calculated total by page is really useful, but it illustrates a capability of Access reports. Each page has a footer with a page number and the total number of pages. Access has calculated the number of pages before printing the report.

Using the Report Wizard

As you've come to expect, Access provides a wizard that can produce a report layout with minimal effort. Use the CDCollect database to try this out:

1. Close the Northwind database and open CDCollect.mdb. Click the Reports tab and then click New. In the New Report dialog box, Access presents the familiar choices shown in Figure 30.2. Select the Report Wizard and the Track table.

FIGURE 30.2   Selecting the appropriate report option

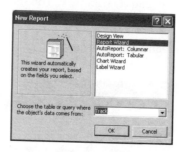

2. The first stage of the Report Wizard follows exactly the same pattern that you saw for queries and forms. Select all the fields and click Next. You should see a window resembling Figure 30.3.

FIGURE 30.3   Selecting how to present your report information

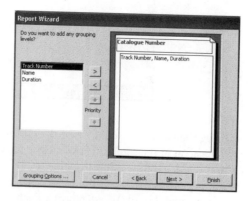

This window is concerned with how your report groups information together. The picture in the right-hand side of the window shows how the report will present the information. The wizard has already decided that you want to group information by catalogue number, which is very sensible, but it's offering you the opportunity to change this and to select a subgrouping if you need this. In this case, it doesn't make sense to group by any of the other fields, so ignore this and continue to the next part of the Report Wizard.

3. The next Report Wizard section helps you to decide how the information in your report will be ordered and what subtotal you will use. You would really like the tracks to be put in track number sequence, but no further ordering is necessary. If it was, you could select up to three further levels of ordering. The report would sort the information on the first field, then sort the records that have the same value for that field using the second-level field, and so on. In most cases, one or two levels of sorting is sufficient. The Ascending/Descending button adjacent to each field allows you to specify whether you would like the data sorted in ascending or descending order.

> You have already used a similar Ascending/Descending facility in Chapter 27, "Creating a Database." Revisit that section for more information.

4. Click the small arrow to drop down the list of fields for the first sort criteria and select Track Number (see Figure 30.4).

FIGURE 30.4   Sorting data in a report

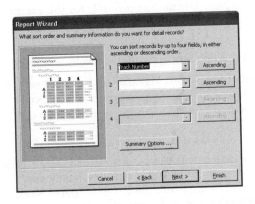

5. You want the Report Wizard to calculate the total playing time for the CD. To do this, click the Summary Options button and select Sum as the Summary Option for Duration. Click OK to return to the Report Wizard.

> Notice that you can also select other arithmetic functions at this stage such as Average, Maximum, and Minimum.

6. Click Next to move to the next stage of the Report Wizard, which is concerned with the layout of data on the page (see Figure 30.5).

FIGURE 30.5 Deciding on the layout of data

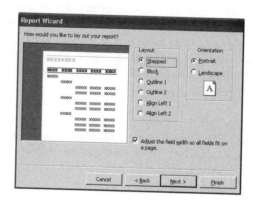

7. The diagram representing your final report is very helpful in understanding all the options. Try each of the layout styles in turn while observing the diagram. It is largely a matter of taste which of these styles you select, because each displays the same information, but in different places on the page. Use the Stepped style for this example.

There is a small tick box that allows Access to adjust the field width to make the information fit on the page. This is a sensible option for most reports, but you can always repeat the wizard process if this does not give you the results you need.

The right-hand side of the Report Wizard window contains the familiar paper orientation selections. Make your choice based on how you expect your report to be read. Most document-oriented reports use portrait orientation.

Access uses the default paper size for your copy of Microsoft Office. By default, this is often set to Letter size, which is mainly used in the USA. You probably want your reports to use the European paper sizes, in particular, A4. If your reports don't fit the paper properly, make sure you have the default paper size set correctly.

8. Click Next to move to the next Report Wizard stage, which should look like Figure 30.6.

FIGURE 30.6 Selecting a report style

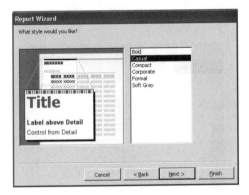

As in the previous wizard stage, you can select different styles for your report. But in this case, it is the font, associated rulings, and patterns that are made available. Try each of the bulleted options to find one that suits your needs. You are developing a report for personal use with a CD collection, so you don't want anything too formal. Choose Casual and click Next to move to the next stage of the Report Wizard.

9. The final stage of the wizard allows you to select a title for the report and to preview or modify it (see Figure 30.7). Call the report MyCDTracks.

FIGURE 30.7 Selecting a title for the report

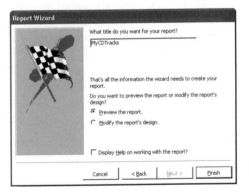

You've spent a little longer with the Report Wizard than with some of the other wizards you encountered earlier. This is because it will probably be an appropriate tool to use for most of your reports. When a minor variation is needed, it is easier to use the Report Wizard to produce a report and then modify it than to start from scratch.

10. Click Finish to see your report, which should look like Figure 30.8.

FIGURE 30.8   The final layout of the MyCDTracks report

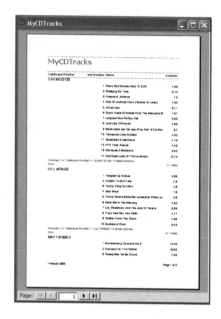

The resulting report is not quite perfect. The Duration column needs a little more space and the Track Name column is too small. The column headings are not very informative.

One way to change the column titles would be to edit the report, but you can achieve the same result in a different way that is probably more useful. In Chapter 27, you set up the field options for the tables in the database. Amongst these options was Caption. If you change the field Caption to the column title that you want, then it will be used automatically on all reports unless you specify something different.

Report Design Toolbar

The Report Design toolbar, shown in Figure 30.9, is similar in most respects to the Form Design toolbar that you saw in the previous chapter.

As you would expect, the Report Design toolbar is paired with the Print Preview toolbar. You can switch between them by using the buttons on the far left-hand side of each toolbar.

As with the Form Design toolbar, AutoFormat allows you to use parts of the Report Wizard in your own reports. This can be very useful, avoiding a lot of detail work but still giving you the freedom to design reports the way you want them.

FIGURE 30.9   The Report Design toolbar

Save Report   Toolbox AutoFormat

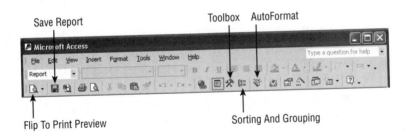

Flip To Print Preview   Sorting And Grouping

Zoom

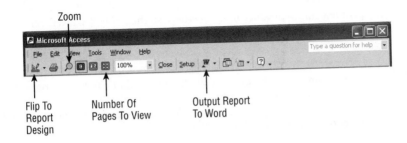

Flip To Number Of Output Report
Report Pages To View To Word
Design

Creating a Report Using Design View

To create a report using Design View, take these steps:

1. Start from the Database window and click the Report button. Click New to see the New Report window, as shown in Figure 30.10.

FIGURE 30.10   The New Report window

You've already used the Report Wizard, but there are five other options:

- The Design View allows you to build a report from scratch; you'll explore this shortly.

- There are two AutoReport options, one for columnar layouts and one for tabular layouts. We will not review these options, but you should investigate these when you've gained some familiarity with reports. They can be a big timesaver in the same way as the Report Wizard.

- The Chart Wizard is useful for preparing reports that contain a chart such as a graph. This again is well worth investigating if you need to produce this type of report occasionally.

- The Label Wizard is focused on producing mailing lists. This is a very specialised wizard, but many people want to produce mailing labels, so the Label Wizard is very helpful. We will not review this wizard in detail.

If you plan to use the Label Wizard, you will find it helpful to decide on your label format (size and number per sheet) by selecting from one of the popular commercial label types. The Label Wizard recognises these label numbers, so by choosing one of these, most of the work is done by the wizard.

2. To use the Design View, select the table or query that you wish to use and click OK. Use the Artist table for your example, arranging the report in a simple tabular fashion. An empty report opens, as shown in Figure 30.11.

FIGURE 30.11 An empty report produced under Design View

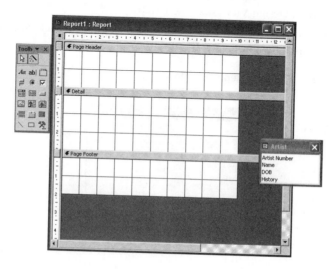

The report has three sections, just like the form. Concentrate on the Detail section first, which will contain information about artists, one row for each artist.

3. You should have a window displaying the fields available from the Artist table. Select only Name, Date Of Birth, and History from the list. Click each one in turn and drag them to the Detail section of the report. Line them up one on top of each other to begin with, so the result looks like Figure 30.12.

FIGURE 30.12   Selecting the report components

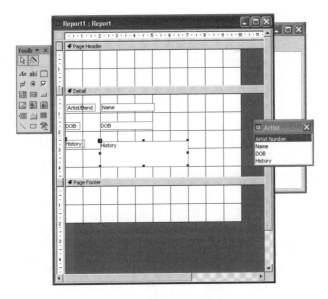

4. The fields are all bound to the underlying database table, exactly as you require, but the labels are not where you want them. For a tabular layout, they should be at the top of each column, not immediately to the left of each field.

5. You can fix this very easily. Drag through the labels, selecting only the labels and not the fields. Now select Edit ➤ Cut from the main Access menu. The labels disappear from the Detail section. Now click inside the Page Header area and choose Edit ➤ Paste from the main Access menu. The labels are pasted into the header area, without disturbing the fields.

WARNING   You might think that you can simply drag the labels to the header area. Unfortunately, this does not work—you must use the Edit ➤ Cut and Edit ➤ Paste routine.

6. Now line up the fields and labels so that they take up an appropriate amount of space and line up with each other. The History field could contain a lot of text, so give this plenty of page width. While you're working with the Page Header area, add a suitable report title. Assume that this report will be printed on a monochrome laser printer, so you don't need special colours.

7. Your report design should look something like Figure 30.13.

FIGURE 30.13   Your report design should look like this.

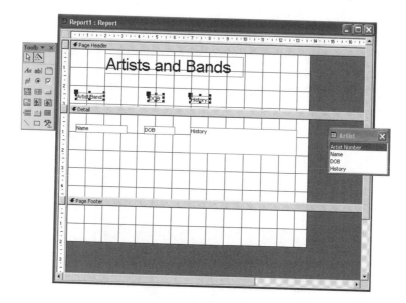

8. Now test your report by clicking the Print Preview button. The report is basically correct, but you may find that the Date Of Birth field is too narrow for the date to be fully displayed. You could fix this by increasing the width of the field, but a better way is to change the display properties for the field so that you no longer see all the details of the date. To do this, right-click the field and select Properties. This window contains all the details of how the field is to be displayed. Change the format to General Date and retest the report.

The Properties window is useful for adjusting all aspects of field display. Explore all its capabilities when you've gained some experience with reports. The same capabilities are available for forms as well.

Sequence and Group Information in Reports

You saw how the sequence of data can be specified using the Report Wizard. You can achieve the same result when you design your own reports.

Click the Sorting And Grouping button on the toolbar. Access displays a Sorting And Grouping window, which combines these two functions in one, as you can see in Figure 30.14.

FIGURE 30.14   The sorting and grouping functions combined

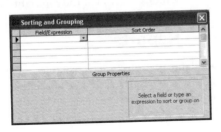

In the Field/Expression column, you place the fields that you want to use to sequence the report. You want the artists in alphabetical order by name, so click the down arrow and select Artist Name. The Sort Order is already set to Ascending, so you don't need to change this.

You can also use an expression instead of a field name. See the "Specifying Criteria and Using Expressions" section in Chapter 28, "Retrieving Information Using Queries," to revise expressions if you need this.

You can also group together records based on the value of the field. Each group can be given a group header and footer. You can see the options for grouping in the lower part of the Sorting And Grouping window. You don't need any grouping of data in this case, so leave the options unchanged.

You have not defined any rules about how to record the name of an artist. You probably should have insisted that all names be fully spelt out. You also have another more serious problem. Your report is sorting artists based on the their name starting with the left-most letters. This means, for example, that you're sorting Bob Dylan on B then on O. This may be what you want, but it might be better to have entered the data as Dylan, Bob, so that the records are sorted in the way you would expect. Go back to your Artist table and change the data to reflect this.

Now go back and modify the report that you created at the start of this chapter with the Report Wizard. Fix the problems that you saw with the field widths. While you're doing this, take note of the way that the Report Wizard has achieved its results. You should be able to replicate most of these manually using the skills that you've learnt in this chapter.

Using Graphics in Reports

You can use graphics in reports in just the same way that you did for forms. You can add more excitement to your design by using graphics in the Page Header and Detail areas. Any graphic added to the Page Header area appears only in the header, but a graphic added to the Detail area is repeated for each and every record. Obviously, you don't want to use large and elaborate graphics for each record, but a simple symbol can add a lot of visual appeal to a report.

Try adding an appropriate graphic to the header section of the MyCDTracks report that you've been editing. Test the results to ensure that it operates as you expect.

Opening and Closing Reports

Reports are opened and closed in the same way as all other database objects such as tables, queries, reports, and so on. To open a report, double-click the appropriate named report icon. To close a report, click the Close Window button at the top right-hand corner of the window.

Saving and Deleting Reports

Reports behave just like other database objects such as tables, queries, and forms. You must save the changes that you make to reports; the Save button on the toolbar does this for you. If you forget to save, Access reminds you when you close the report in Design View.

You can delete reports that you no longer require using the Delete button on the keyboard.

Printing Reports

To print a report, choose File ➤ Print. You can print specific pages rather than all pages by specifying the beginning and ending page numbers in the standard Print dialog box.

Summary

Reports are one of the public expressions of your skill in designing a database and are designed primarily for use as printed documents. They are used by people in meetings and for decision-making, so it's important that they communicate information easily and clearly.

This chapter explored a little of the large toolset that Access provides for constructing reports, including designing reports, and laying out, sequencing, and grouping the data in reports. Most of the reports that you'll need can be created using the Report Wizard, but this chapter also described the facilities that you need to use in order to create a report from scratch or to edit a report produced manually or through the Report Wizard.

With the conclusion of this chapter, you have now covered all the skills that you need in order to meet the requirements of the ECDL Module 5.

Module Review Questions

1. How do you start Access from the desktop?

2. What is a database query?

3. Choose the correct answer. When you enter data into an Access table, it is:
    - Not saved until you use the Save command.
    - Not saved until you close the database.
    - Saved after you have entered nine more changes.
    - Saved automatically.

4. In an employee table, which of the following would be a good choice for the primary key?
    - Employee first name
    - Employee initial
    - Employee date of birth
    - Employee Social Security number

5. Choose the correct answer. What is a Memo data field used for?
    - To store memorandums
    - To store textual data where the quantity of text varies and could be large
    - To store large numbers
    - To store data that you need to remember

6. Choose the correct answer. You should consider using an index only when:
    - The field will frequently be used to select records.
    - The field is a Memo field.
    - The field contains derived data.
    - The field contains a graphical image.

7. What is a field's default value used for?

8. What types of relationship are you likely to encounter when designing an Access database? (Choose all that apply.)

9. When does Access check referential integrity?

10. How does a grid help when designing forms?

11. How can you print a form containing data?

12. How can you delete an unwanted report?

Answers to Module Review Questions

1. Click the Start button on the Taskbar and select the All Programs option, followed by the Access option. If there is a shortcut on your desktop, you can start Access directly by double-clicking its icon.

2. A database query extracts the data that you want from one or more tables and presents it as another table.

3. Saved automatically.

4. Employee Social Security number.

5. To store textual data where the quantity of text varies and could be large.

6. The field will frequently be used to select records.

7. A default value is a value that is automatically supplied when a new record is created unless data is entered for this field.

8. The correct answers are one-to-many and one-to-one.

9. Access checks referential integrity when entering, deleting, or modifying data.

10. All the different form elements such as controls snap to the grid, making it easy to achieve a professional-looking layout.

11. Ensure that the form is displaying the required data and then select File ➢ Print.

12. Select the report in the Access database object window and then press the Delete key on the keyboard.

ECDL Module 6: Presentation

Getting Started with Presentation Tools

IN THIS CHAPTER YOU WILL LEARN HOW TO

- ✓ Open and close a presentation application.
- ✓ Open one or several presentations.
- ✓ Create a new presentation using the default template.
- ✓ Save a presentation to a location on a drive.
- ✓ Save a presentation under another name.
- ✓ Save a presentation in another file type.
- ✓ Switch between open presentations.
- ✓ Use the available Help functions.
- ✓ Close a presentation.
- ✓ View presentations in different ways.
- ✓ Add new slides to a presentation.
- ✓ Change between different slide layouts.
- ✓ Change the background colour on specific slides or on all slides.
- ✓ Use PowerPoint's design templates.
- ✓ Use PowerPoint's Slide Master facility.
- ✓ Insert and remove a picture, image, and drawn object on a Master Slide.
- ✓ Add text in the footer of specific slides or all slides in a presentation.
- ✓ Apply automatic slide numbering and dates into footers of specific slides or all slides in a presentation.

Module 6 of the ECDL qualification is concerned with the subject of presentation applications and is based on Microsoft's Power-Point XP software. Before embarking on the task of learning how to use PowerPoint, it is important to understand what presentation packages are and what role they play in modern PC-based computing.

Presentation graphics software is a tool that can be used to create, edit, modify, and display information in a structured and controlled manner as an aid to communication. You have all probably seen presentations using equipment such as flip charts, white boards, or overhead projectors. A presentation graphics program allows you to utilise PC technology to deliver presentations effectively and professionally.

Like most other presentation graphics packages, PowerPoint XP is based on the *slide show* metaphor. In essence, it can be used to produce "virtual" slides that can subsequently be displayed on a PC screen or on a large screen via the use of an electronic LCD projector attached to a PC. However, PowerPoint is not solely designed for displaying slides on screen; you can use it to create actual 35mm slides via a bureau service, printed black-and-white or full-colour overhead transparency sheets, speaker notes, audience handouts, and presentation outlines. In addition, presentations can be converted into web pages for use on the Internet.

If you intend to use PowerPoint to create overhead transparency sheets, make sure that you use the correct materials specifically designed for your printer. In particular, you must use film sheets that are guaranteed heat-proof when using a laser printer.

Presentations can come in all shapes and sizes—both formal and informal—and many organisations make extensive use of presentations to provide effective communication of ideas, concepts, or factual data. Typically, presentations are used as an adjunct to tasks such as product marketing, product sales, training, education, and committee or board meetings—basically any situation where a speaker needs to deliver information to an audience.

Microsoft PowerPoint XP has some key features that make it suitable for generating a wide variety of presentations, and we shall cover a number of these in this module. Using PowerPoint, you can perform the following tasks:

- Create, edit, and save presentations.
- Modify existing presentations.
- Publish presentations as Internet web pages.
- Create slides containing text, images, audio, and video.

- Copy, move, delete, or rearrange slides or slide elements.

- Modify and format text and borders.

- Draw lines, boxes, and other shapes on slides.

- Include organisational and other types of charts on slides.

- Incorporate information from other packages on slides.

- Print slides, presentation outlines, speaker notes, and audience handouts in various formats.

- Apply animation to various objects on slides.

- Set up special transitions between slides when displaying presentations.

- Control and navigate through on-screen slide shows.

This part of the study guide is structured into chapters that are designed to be followed in a logical sequence. You are advised to work through the guide one chapter at a time from the beginning. At the end of this module, there are some review questions so that you can verify that you understand the principles involved correctly.

First Steps with PowerPoint

Before you begin, check whether Microsoft PowerPoint XP is already installed on your PC. Choose Start ➢ All Programs; you should see a list of installed programs. PowerPoint may be listed here, or it may be under the Microsoft Office option, depending on how your system has been set up (see the example in Figure 31.1).

FIGURE 31.1   Starting PowerPoint from the Start menu

Note that there may be other Microsoft Office programs installed on your PC such as Word, Access, or Excel. However, it should be fairly obvious whether PowerPoint is installed or not.

If Microsoft PowerPoint is not already installed on your PC, follow the instructions for setting up the software as detailed in the Office XP *Getting Started* guide. These instructions are quite straightforward, but if you have any difficulty installing the software, seek advice from your computer supplier or system administrator.

Assuming that PowerPoint is installed on your PC, you're now ready to start using it to create and edit presentations.

PowerPoint is an extremely flexible package and can be used to create a wide variety of presentations for different purposes. Your PowerPoint presentations can be as simple or as complicated as you like. You will soon learn how to create basic presentations that can be enhanced to produce interesting and dynamic-looking slide shows. In this initial section, you will learn some basic procedures.

Opening a PowerPoint Presentation

This section explains how to start PowerPoint, open and save presentations, and switch between open presentations. Take the following steps to open an existing presentation:

1. Open PowerPoint by choosing Start ➤ All Programs from the Taskbar, as you saw earlier in Figure 31.1. Each time you start PowerPoint, you'll see a window like the one in Figure 31.2.

FIGURE 31.2   The main window displayed when PowerPoint is started

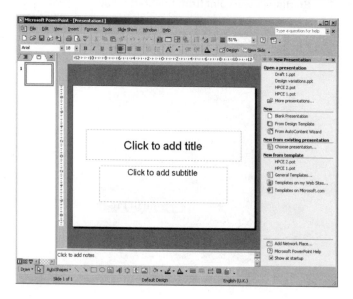

PowerPoint automatically starts with a new blank presentation ready for you to use. However, using the Task Pane on the right-hand side of the screen, you can choose to create another new presentation or open an existing presentation.

2. For the moment, let's ignore the creation of new presentations. Select File ➢ Open, or click Presentations in the Task Pane, or click the Open icon on the toolbar at the top of the screen. The Open dialog box is displayed, and by default, the folder My Documents is open, as shown in Figure 31.3.

FIGURE 31.3   The Open dialog box showing the My Documents folder

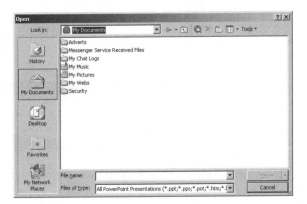

Don't be alarmed if there are no presentations displayed for you to open. The chances are that if this is the first time you have run PowerPoint, there won't be any presentations in the My Documents folder. You need to look somewhere else to find some existing presentations to open.

3. Using the Look In drop-down list, select the C:\Windows\Program Files\Office\Office10 \1033 folder. Once selected, you should see a file called QUIKANIM.PPT. Select this and click Open. The PowerPoint QUIKANIM presentation is loaded, and your screen should look like Figure 31.4.

The preceding instructions assume that when Microsoft Office XP was installed on your computer, the standard default locations were used. If this is not the case, the file QUIKANIM.PPT may be located somewhere else; use the Find options in the Open dialog box to locate it. If the file does not exist on your hard disk, open it from the Office folder on the Microsoft Office XP CD-ROM.

FIGURE 31.4   Slide 1 of the PowerPoint QUIKANIM presentation file

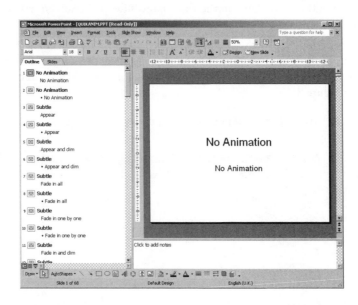

Before proceeding further, make a copy of the presentation QUIKANIM.PPT by saving a new version of it in the My Documents folder using the following steps:

1.   On the menu bar, choose File ➤ Save As. The Save As dialog box opens, as shown in Figure 31.5.

FIGURE 31.5   The Save As dialog box with the filename highlighted

2.   Select the My Documents folder using the Save In drop-down list and type the filename **PowerPoint1** in the File Name box. Check that the Save As Type box says Presentation and click Save.

Microsoft PowerPoint also allows you to open several different presentations at the same time. Try it out using these steps:

1. With the `PowerPoint1.ppt` presentation still open, choose File ➢ Open on the menu bar. A new window called the Task Pane opens on the right-hand side of your screen, as shown in Figure 31.6.

FIGURE 31.6   The Task Pane window

2. The Task Pane lists the tasks that you can perform, in this case, opening an existing presentation or creating a new presentation. Click the Blank Presentation task, and a new empty presentation is created, as you saw earlier in Figure 31.2.

    Notice that the original `PowerPoint1.ppt` presentation has disappeared. However, it is in fact still there, but it is no longer the *active* application. If you look at your Windows Taskbar (normally at the very bottom of your screen), there are now two versions of Microsoft PowerPoint running, with a presentation open in each one, as shown in Figure 31.7. Make sure that `PowerPoint1.ppt` is the active presentation before proceeding.

FIGURE 31.7   The Taskbar showing two PowerPoint sessions running

As with other applications, you can have many copies of PowerPoint running at the same time. You switch between them simply by clicking the appropriate item on the Windows Taskbar.

Saving a PowerPoint File

In the previous section, you saw how to do a simple save of a PowerPoint presentation. In this section, you'll see some of the options that PowerPoint gives you for saving files.

Saving PowerPoint Files in a Different Format

PowerPoint uses its own file format with the filename extension .ppt for storing presentations. However, there may be occasions when you need to save a presentation in a different format, for example, to transfer text into a word processing package or to use a presentation as a web page. As well as being able to specify a filename and a location (folder) for saving the presentation, you can also specify the file type or file format by clicking the drop-down list in the Save As Type box, as in Figure 31.8.

FIGURE 31.8   Use the Save As Type option to save a presentation in a different file format.

PowerPoint allows you to save a presentation in the following file formats:

Save as Type	Extension	Used to Save
Presentation	.ppt	A typical Microsoft PowerPoint presentation
Windows metafile	.wmf	A slide as a graphic
GIF (Graphics Interchange Format)	.gif	A slide as a graphic for use on web pages
JPEG (Joint Photographics Experts Group file format)	.jpg	A slide as a graphic for use on web pages

Save as Type	Extension	Used to Save
PNG (Portable Network Graphics Format)	`.png`	A slide as a graphic for use on web pages
Outline/RTF	`.rtf`	A presentation outline as an outline document
Design template	`.pot`	A presentation as a template
PowerPoint slide show	`.pps`	A presentation that always opens as a slide show presentation
Web page	`.htm; html`	A web page as a folder with an `.htm` file and all supporting files
Web archive	`.mht; mhtml`	A web page as a single file, including all supporting files
PowerPoint 95	`.ppt`	A presentation to be used by PowerPoint 95
PowerPoint 95, 97–2002 presentation	`.ppt`	A presentation to be used by PowerPoint 95, 97–2002

Saving PowerPoint Files for Use on the Web

In addition, you can save the data in a PowerPoint presentation in a format that is suitable for publishing web pages on the Internet by following these steps:

1. Choose File ➢ Save As Web Page, and the Save As dialog box shown in Figure 31.9 opens.

FIGURE 31.9   Use the Save As Web Page option to save a presentation as a web page.

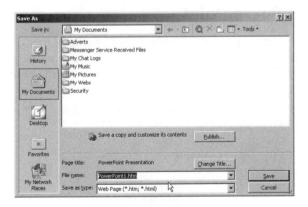

2. Click the Publish button, and in the Publish As Web Page dialog box, you see the various options that enable you to save the presentation in different ways on the Web, as shown in Figure 31.10.

FIGURE 31.10 The publishing options for saving a PowerPoint presentation as a web page

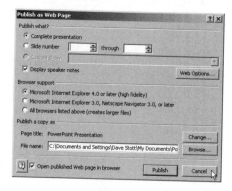

3. Press the Cancel button to return to the PowerPoint1.ppt presentation.

Closing a PowerPoint File

To close a presentation, choose File ➤ Close on the menu bar. PowerPoint itself should remain open with a blank presentation active. If this is not the case, just start PowerPoint again from the Start button on the Taskbar.

If you have made any changes to an open presentation, then when you try to close it, you're asked whether you wish to save the changes you have made to the file.

If you click Yes, the file is saved with the existing filename, overwriting the original version. However, if you wish to keep the original version of the file, click No and choose File ➤ Save As to save the current open presentation with a different filename from the original.

Using Help in PowerPoint

This section examines the Help facilities available in PowerPoint that can provide you with online assistance when you need it. There are several different ways to trigger the Help functions within PowerPoint, and this section describes each method in turn. Take the following steps to use the Office Assistant:

1. When you start PowerPoint, you may notice a small window, as shown in Figure 31.11. This is the Office Assistant.

FIGURE 31.11 The Office Assistant

The Office Assistant is designed to provide you with help if you encounter problems when using the program. You may have encountered the Office Assistant in other Office XP modules such as Word or Excel. The Office Assistant—like the normal Microsoft Help facilities—is context-sensitive, which means it tries to provide help based on what you are doing at the time.

If the Office Assistant does not open when you start PowerPoint, you can activate it by choosing Help ➤ Show The Office Assistant in the menu bar.

As you've learned with other Microsoft Office programs, there are several different characters available to act as Office Assistants, depending on how your version of Microsoft Office has been configured. To review the details of Office Assistant, see Chapters 14, 19, and 26.

2. If you click the Office Assistant, the pop-up dialog box in Figure 31.12 is displayed.

FIGURE 31.12   The Office Assistant asks you what you would like to do.

As you can see from the example in Figure 31.12, one of the best features of the Office Assistant is that you can simply type in a question, and it tries to find the most appropriate help for you. For example, type in the words **Saving my work** and click Search. The Office Assistant displays a list of topics similar to that in Figure 31.13 for you to choose from.

FIGURE 31.13   Performing a query using the Office Assistant

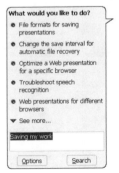

Clicking an item in this list displays the relevant Help topic.

As well as the Office Assistant, you can access Help by choosing Help ➤ Contents And Index on the menu bar. This opens a Help window with three tabbed sections: Contents, Answer Wizard, and Index (see Figure 31.14).

FIGURE 31.14 The Microsoft PowerPoint Help window with the Contents tab showing sub-sections

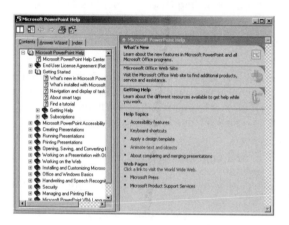

The Contents tab presents you with a list of help topics to select from. Note that the main sections may have sub-sections, as shown in Figure 31.14. Clicking any of the labels displays the results on the right-hand side of the Microsoft PowerPoint Help window.

The Index tab displays a list of indexed keywords that are available in the PowerPoint Help system. You simply type in the index word that you want and click the Search button, as shown in Figure 31.15.

FIGURE 31.15 You can search for keywords in the Index section.

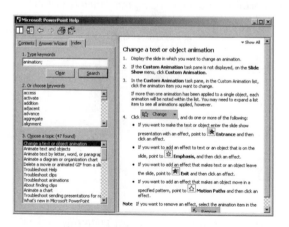

The Answer Wizard tab allows you to search for any word or phrase, and the Help system then shows you any matches that it finds. Once again, just click any topic and then click Search to see the details, as shown in Figure 31.16. Note that if your computer is connected to the Internet, you can also search for help using the Search On Web button in the Answer Wizard tab.

FIGURE 31.16   The Answer Wizard section lets you look for any words or phrases.

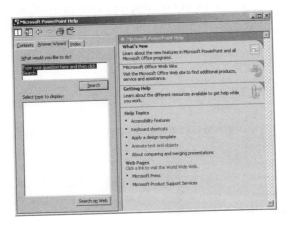

 Help is always available in PowerPoint no matter what task you are performing. The quickest way to get help is to press the F1 key on your keyboard.

Whichever method you use to access the Help system in PowerPoint, you can see step-by-step help on most topics, as shown in Figure 31.17.

FIGURE 31.17   A specific Help topic on how to open a presentation

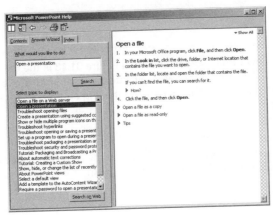

Adjusting Settings in PowerPoint

Now that you know how to start PowerPoint and open and save files, you need to investigate the main PowerPoint screen in more detail. In this section, you'll learn how to adjust the view, display and hide toolbars, and modify basic options and preferences.

You can alter the way that PowerPoint displays information, and you can alter the appearance of PowerPoint itself. If it is not already open, start PowerPoint and open the PowerPoint1.ppt file you saved in the My Documents folder in the preceding section. If you see the warning about macros, simply click Disable Macros. Your screen should look something like Figure 31.18.

FIGURE 31.18   The PowerPoint screen after opening the PowerPoint1 presentation

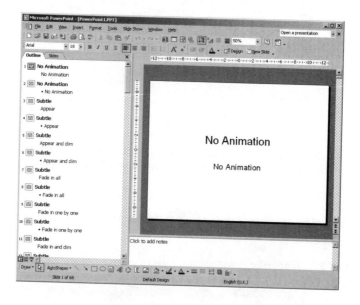

 The PowerPoint screen shown in Figure 31.18 is the default view of a presentation. The main window is split into three separate areas: the Slide pane on the right, the Outline/Slides pane on the left, and the Speaker Notes pane at the bottom.

If the Office Assistant is displayed, close it by choosing Help ➢ Hide The Office Assistant. Similarly, you might have the Task Pane displayed on the right-hand side of the main window, which you can close by clicking the Close control button.

Adjusting the Magnification/Zoom

Let's look at the use of the magnification/zoom tools in PowerPoint. Click any blank area of the slide. Controlling the magnification or zoom level can be achieved in two ways:

- Use the Zoom control drop-down list on the Standard toolbar, as in Figure 31.19.

FIGURE 31.19   Using the Zoom icon to change magnification

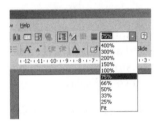

- Choose View ➢ Zoom from the menu bar, which opens the Zoom window, as shown in Figure 31.20.

FIGURE 31.20   The Zoom control window

Adjusting the Toolbars in PowerPoint

PowerPoint has a total of 5 separate toolbars available. By default, three of these are displayed, two at the top of the screen and one at the bottom of the screen (see Figures 31.21, 31.22, and 31.23):

FIGURE 31.21   The Standard toolbar (at the top of the screen by default)

FIGURE 31.22   The Formatting toolbar (at the top of the screen by default)

FIGURE 31.23   The Drawing toolbar (at the bottom of the screen by default)

You can control which of the 5 toolbars are visible by choosing View ➢ Toolbars. The toolbars that are currently displayed are shown with a tick next to them, as shown in Figure 31.24. To hide a toolbar that is currently displayed, simply select it again, thus removing the check mark and the toolbar from your display.

FIGURE 31.24   Selecting the toolbars to be displayed

Setting Other Preferences

PowerPoint has a series of options that are used to specify preferences for things such as the name of the user, where to look for presentations to open, and which folder to save files in. Take the following steps to set these options:

1.   Choose Tools ➢ Options, and the Options dialog box opens (see Figure 31.25).

FIGURE 31.25   The Options dialog box

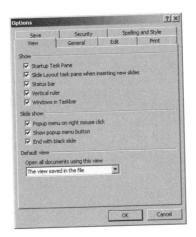

2. By default, the View tab is shown. Click the General tab, as shown in Figure 31.26. Notice the Name field in the User Information area; the Name field identifies the author of any presentations created.

FIGURE 31.26   The General tab in the Options dialog box

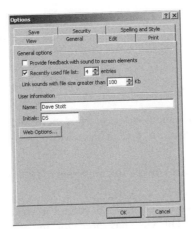

3. Click the Save tab as shown in Figure 31.27. The Default File Location box specifies where presentations are opened from and saved in. Normally this is C:\My Documents, but it could be set to any folder. Click Cancel to close the Options window.

FIGURE 31.27   The Save tab in the Options dialog box

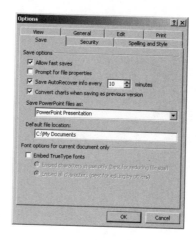

4.   Close the PowerPoint1.ppt file by choosing File ➢ Close.

Developing a Presentation

Now that you have a general understanding about how PowerPoint works, you shall now expand on this knowledge by looking at some basic operations that will help you create your own presentations.

Presentation Views

Microsoft PowerPoint has three main views: Normal view, Slide Sorter view, and Slide Show view. You can select a view, based on these main views, to be your default view in PowerPoint. Try the following steps:

1.   If it is not already open, start PowerPoint and open the PowerPoint1.ppt file saved in the My Documents folder.

Normal view is the main editing view, which you use to write and design your presentation, as shown in Figure 31.28. This view has three working areas:

-   On the left, tabs that alternate between an outline of your slide text (Outline tab) and your slides displayed as thumbnails (Slides tab)

-   On the right, the Slide pane, which displays a large view of the current slide

-   On the bottom, the Notes pane

FIGURE 31.28   The default Normal view

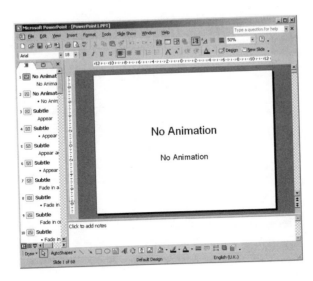

2. You can change the way a presentation is displayed on screen by using the View control buttons situated in the bottom left-hand corner of the main window, as shown in Figure 31.29.

FIGURE 31.29   The View control buttons

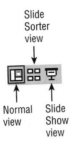

3. From left to right, these buttons allow you to select the following views:

- Clicking the Slide Sorter View button displays all the slides in a presentation in miniature, as shown in Figure 31.30. Use this view to rearrange or add transition effects to your slides.

FIGURE 31.30 The Slide Sorter view

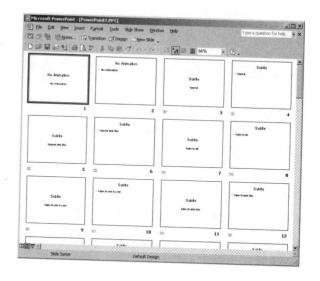

- Clicking the Slide Show View button displays a presentation as a series of slides on screen, as shown in Figure 31.31. Use this view to check the appearance of your slides and to run through a presentation on screen. (Note that to exit from the Slide Show view, you press the Esc key on your keyboard.)

FIGURE 31.31 The Slide Show view

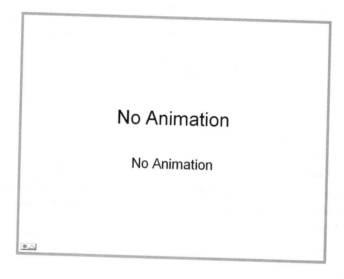

When using the Slide Show view, you can control the slide show by clicking the small control icon in the bottom left-hand corner of the screen, as shown in Figure 31.31.

- Apart from the three views accessible by clicking the icons in the bottom left-hand corner of the screen, there is a fourth view available in PowerPoint that you can access by selecting View ➤ Notes Page. This view displays the current slide with any speaker notes underneath, as shown in Figure 31.32.

FIGURE 31.32   The Notes Page view

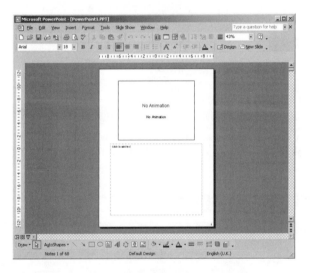

Working with Slides

Up until now, you have been using the QUIKANIM.ppt and PowerPoint1.ppt files for carrying out your exercises. Whilst these have been useful in the early stages of understanding Power-Point, it's time you created your own presentation from scratch.

This section describes how to create a new presentation and add slides, look at the options available for the automatic laying out of slides, modify the slide layout, and change the background colour of slides.

For the purposes of this and subsequent sections, you will create a new presentation designed as a guide to "Buying a House." It doesn't matter whether you know anything about this subject—it's just an example of the types of tasks that presentation software such as PowerPoint can be used for. We will keep things fairly simple to start with, and you will be told what information should appear on each slide of the presentation.

Creating a New Presentation and Adding Slides

If it is not already open, start PowerPoint and make sure that there are no existing presentations open. Take the following steps:

1.   Choose File ➢ New. The Task Pane opens (see Figure 31.33).

FIGURE 31.33   Using the Task Pane to create a new presentation in PowerPoint

2.   Click the Blank Presentation option to create a new blank presentation. Your display should now look like the example in Figure 31.34. If the Office Assistant is displayed, close it by choosing Help ➢ Hide The Office Assistant.

FIGURE 31.34   A new blank presentation in PowerPoint

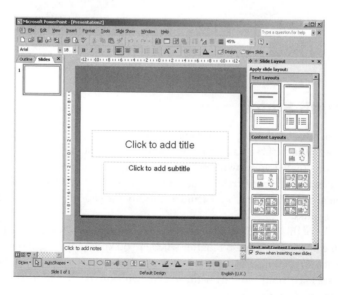

When you create a new presentation, PowerPoint always creates a new slide to start off with. This new slide is created using the standard Title Slide layout by default.

3. Select Insert ➢ New Slide, and a new slide appears underneath the existing slide in the Slides tab on the left-hand side of your screen, as shown in Figure 31.35. The new slide uses the Title And Text layout from the Slide Layout Task Pane on the right-hand side of the main window. This layout has a separate area for the Title and a Text area in which a bulleted list can be created.

FIGURE 31.35   The result of adding a slide to a presentation

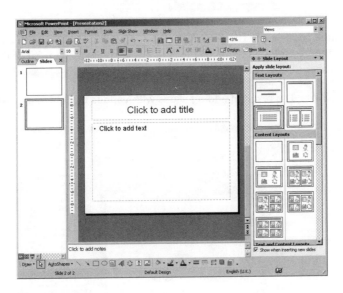

4. You can also add slides from the Slide Layout Task Pane by selecting Insert New Slide from the drop-down list next to a particular slide layout thumbnail, as shown in Figure 31.36.

FIGURE 31.36 Inserting a new slide using the Task Pane

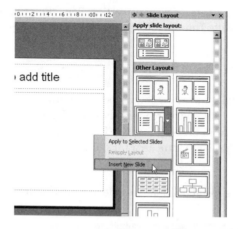

5. Use the method described in the preceding steps to insert new slides with a Blank layout, a Title, Text, and Chart layout, and a Title And Table layout, for a total of five slides. Your presentation should now look similar to Figure 31.37.

FIGURE 31.37 The result of adding slides with various layouts to a presentation

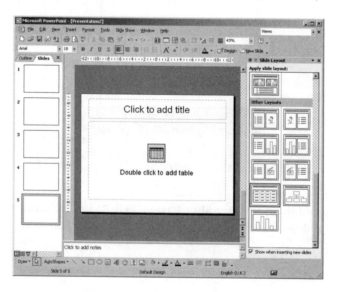

Changing the Layout and Background Color of a Slide

You can change the layout of an existing slide quickly and easily in PowerPoint using these steps:

1. Select slide 3 (the blank slide) by clicking the thumbnail in the Slides tab on the left of your screen. This displays the actual slide in the Slide View area. Next, click the Title And Text layout in the Slide Layout Task Pane. Slide 3 automatically changes to the new layout, as shown in Figure 31.38.

FIGURE 31.38   Changing the layout of an existing slide

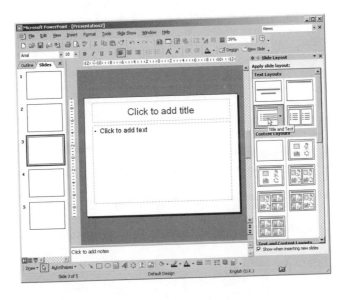

 A *thumbnail* is the term used to describe a small graphical image of a slide as used in the Slides tab or in the Slide Sorter view.

2. With slide 3 still selected, choose Format ➢ Background. The Background window opens, as shown in Figure 31.39.

FIGURE 31.39 The Background window

3. If you now click the drop-down list control in the Background Fill area, you see several colours to choose from, as shown in Figure 31.40. Select one and then click Apply in the Background window.

FIGURE 31.40 Selecting a background colour

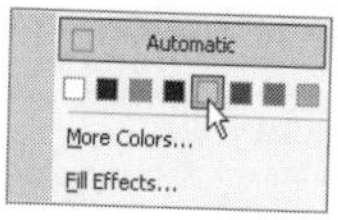

Your slide now has a coloured background, as shown in Figure 32.41.

FIGURE 31.41 Slide 3 with a background colour applied

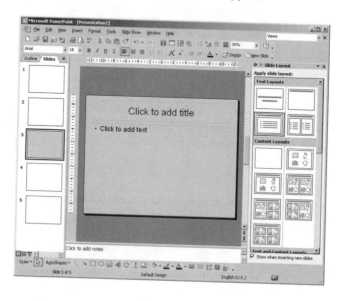

4. When changing the background colour, you can click the Apply To All button, and all the slides in a presentation will have the same colour background applied to them. Do this now so that all the slides in your presentation have the same background colour.

5. Before going any further, save the work that you have done on your presentation so far. Choose File ➤ Save and save the presentation with the filename House in the folder My Documents.

Using Design Templates

As well as adjusting the layout and background colour of slides, PowerPoint offers you the ability to apply design templates to specific individual slides or to all the slides in a presentation. This section explains how to apply a design template to a presentation and change between available design templates.

PowerPoint comes with a wide range of *templates* that you can use to create your own presentations. These are useful because that they can save you a considerable amount of time designing fancy layouts and colour schemes.

Take the following steps to work with design templates:

1. With slide 3 selected, choose Format ➤ Slide Design. The Task Pane on the right-hand side changes to display a series of design templates in the form of thumbnails for you to choose from, as shown in Figure 31.42.

FIGURE 31.42   The Slide Design Task Pane

2. You can apply a particular slide design to all slides or to selected slides by choosing the appropriate option from the drop-down list next to a particular thumbnail, as shown in Figure 31.43.

FIGURE 31.43 Applying a slide design to all slides in a presentation

3. Select whatever you think is a suitable slide design from the list of those available and chose Apply To All Slides. However, don't pick anything too fancy—try either Clouds.pot or Textured.pot, for example.

> Just as with slide layout and background colours described earlier, you can change the slide design for any or all of the slides in a presentation at any time.

4. Choose File ➢ Save and save your presentation.

Using a Slide Master

Each PowerPoint presentation has a special slide known as the Slide Master. The Slide Master's purpose is to let you make a global change—such as inserting an image or adding a footer—and have that change reflected on all the slides in your presentation.

The *Slide Master* is an element of the design template that stores information about the template, including font styles, placeholder sizes and positions, background design, and colour schemes.

> As each design template has its own Slide Master, a presentation can have multiple Slide Masters, depending on how many design templates have been used throughout it.

This section describes the procedures for inserting an image onto a Slide Master, adding a footer to a Slide Master, and setting automatic features to a footer in the Slide Master. Take the following steps:

1. If it is not already open, open the House presentation by selecting File ➢ Open. Your screen should look similar to Figure 31.44, depending on which slide design you have chosen.

FIGURE 31.44   The House presentation

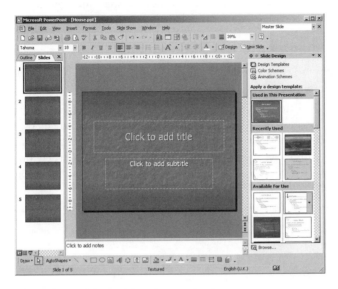

2. Select View ➢ Master ➢ Slide Master, and the Slide Master appears in the slide area, as shown in Figure 31.45. Notice how there are *two* Slide Masters shown in the slide pane on the left-hand side; this is because you applied a slide design to your presentation earlier.

FIGURE 31.45   The Slide Master in your House presentation

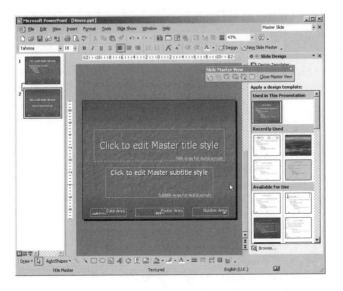

3. However, you don't actually need two Slide Masters in this presentation, so you can get rid of one of them. Select the lower of the two Slide Masters and press the Delete key on your keyboard; the second Slide Master is deleted.

Inserting an Image onto the Slide Master

To insert an image onto your Slide Master so that it appears on every slide in your presentation, take the following steps:

1. Choose Insert ➤ Picture ➤ Clip Art, and the Task Pane changes to display the Insert Clip Art options, as shown in Figure 31.46. When you select Insert ➤ Picture on the menu bar, you are given several options as to where PowerPoint should source an image from. For example, From File... means using an existing picture that is stored somewhere on your computer.

FIGURE 31.46   The Insert Clip Art options in the Task Pane

2. Type the word **House** in the Search Text box and click the Search button. The Task Pane changes again to display any images that match the search text, as shown in Figure 31.47.

FIGURE 31.47   Clip art images displayed in the Task Pane

The actual images that you see in the Insert Clip Art Task Pane depend on what clip art files are stored on your computer. If for some reason there isn't a clip art image of a house available, just use any clip art image.

3. Select any suitable image and double-click it with the left mouse button. A copy of the image is placed on the Slide Master, as shown in Figure 31.48.

FIGURE 31.48   Newly inserted clip art images appear in the centre of a slide

4. Now you can use the box size control handles and the mouse pointer to resize and move the image to an appropriate position on the slide, as shown in Figure 31.49.

FIGURE 31.49   The image after it has been resized and repositioned

 To remove or delete an image from a slide, simply select it with the mouse and press the Delete key on your keyboard.

 As well as clip art, PowerPoint allows you to insert other types of objects onto a slide. For example, you can insert photographs from a file, a drawing created in another application, or a graph or table from a spreadsheet such as Excel. You can even insert audio or video clips if you so wish.

Adding Information to a Footer via the Slide Master

To add some text to the footer of the Slide Master so that it appears on every slide in your presentation, take these steps:

1. Select View ➢ Header And Footer. A Header And Footer window opens, as shown in Figure 31.50.

FIGURE 31.50   The Header And Footer window

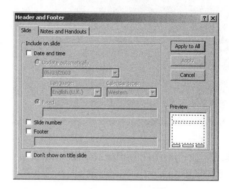

2. Click the Slide tab, and you'll see three check boxes in the Include On Slide section. Click the Footer check box and type the words **Buying a House** in the text box, as shown in Figure 31.51.

FIGURE 31.51   Inserting text into the footer

3. As well as inserting text in the footer area, you can also use the Slide Number check box to apply automatic slide numbering to your presentation, so select this option as well. Similarly, the Date And Time check box allows you to include the date, time, or both on slides. If you click the Date And Time check box, choose whether to set the date and time to update automatically or not. If you opt for Update Automatically, choose the format you want the date to appear in by selecting from the drop-down list. Alternatively, if you opt

for Fixed, you can type the date and time in the box instead. For this exercise, select Update Automatically and choose any format you like, as shown in Figure 31.52.

FIGURE 31.52   Inserting the slide number and the date and time into the footer

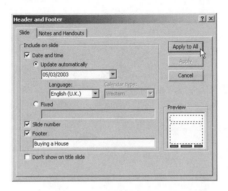

4. Once you have made the changes in the Header And Footer window, click the Apply To All button, and the Slide Master is modified accordingly. Note that header and footer information can be applied to specific slides in a presentation rather than to *all* slides by clicking the Apply button. However, in this instance, because you are amending a single Slide Master, this option is not available.

When using the Update Automatically option for the date and time fields in headers or footers, PowerPoint uses the current date and time values provided by the Windows operating system whenever the slide show is viewed or printed.

5. As an alternative to using View ➢ Header And Footer to apply text to a slide, click <footer> within the Footer area of the slide and type your text directly into the box, as shown in Figure 31.53.

FIGURE 31.53   Inserting text directly into the Footer area of a slide

6. Select View ➢ Normal. Your presentation should now look like Figure 31.54, with the inserted image and the footer information displayed on every slide.

FIGURE 31.54   The Normal view after modifying the Slide Master

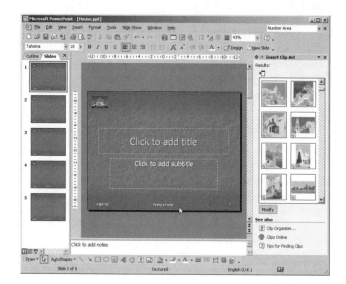

7.   Choose File ➤ Save and save the presentation.

Summary

This first chapter on PowerPoint covered the procedures necessary to start the application and to open any existing presentation files. You also learnt how to save presentations and how to use both the Office Assistant and the Help system to obtain help relevant to the procedures being carried out.

Fortunately, these basic tasks are common to all the modules in Microsoft Office, so once you've mastered these procedures in PowerPoint, you should be able to cope with the same tasks in the other applications such as Word or Excel.

You learnt how to use the Zoom controls to increase or decrease the size of an image being viewed. In addition, you looked at how to control the displaying of toolbars, and you saw how the various PowerPoint options/preferences can be set or adjusted.

The final section of this chapter described how to use the various different views in Power-Point, such as the Slide Show view and the Normal view. You started to create your own presentation by inserting several slides with different slide layouts and applying design templates to slides. You used the Slide Master to insert footer information and an image on all the slides in your presentation.

You should now have a better understanding of the main elements of the PowerPoint screen and how to control and manage the display and saving of information.

Chapter

32

Using Text and Images in PowerPoint

IN THIS CHAPTER YOU WILL LEARN HOW TO

- ✓ Add text to a slide in either Normal or Outline view.
- ✓ Edit slide content.
- ✓ Change text appearance, font type, and size.
- ✓ Apply text formatting such as bold, italic, and underline.
- ✓ Apply case changes to text.
- ✓ Apply different colours to text.
- ✓ Apply shadow effects to text.
- ✓ Align text left, right, and centre.
- ✓ Adjust line spacing for bulleted or numbered text.
- ✓ Change between bullet and number styles.
- ✓ Use the Undo and Redo commands.
- ✓ Insert a picture and an image into a slide.
- ✓ Duplicate text, pictures, and images within a presentation and between open presentations.
- ✓ Move text, pictures, and images within a presentation and between open presentations.
- ✓ Resize pictures and images on a slide.
- ✓ Delete text, pictures, and images on a slide.

One of the main tasks of creating a presentation is entering text on slides and applying different types of formatting to that text. PowerPoint provides the ability to change the appearance of text and text boxes on a slide. By using different fonts, styles, colours, and other attributes, you can enhance the look of slides and make them much more attractive and interesting. You can change the format of text in a text box either by using the Formatting toolbar or by using the options on the Format menu. However, the actual text boxes themselves can only be altered using commands on the Format menu.

This first section explains how to input, edit, and format text, modify spacing and list styles, and use the Undo/Redo commands.

Text Input and Formatting

Text on a slide is always contained within a place holder called a *text box* or an *AutoShape*. When you create a new slide, a number of Autoshapes are generated automatically, depending on which slide layout you choose. In addition, you can add a text box to a slide by choosing Insert ➤ Text Box and then simply drawing the boundaries using the mouse.

Existing text can be formatted in several ways:

- Change the font type.
- Centre text, align text: left and right, top and bottom.
- Apply italics, bold, underlining, and case changes to text.
- Apply shadow to text.
- Use subscript and superscript text.
- Apply different colours to the text font.
- Adjust line spacing.
- Change the type of bullets in a list.

Text consists of a font, point size, and a style, for example, Arial font, 16 point, bold, italic, and underline. Each of these settings is called a *text attribute*, and you can use them to alter the way that text appears both on the screen and when it is printed out.

Adding Text to a Slide

Now that you have defined the layout, design, and Slide Master for your Buying a House presentation, take the following steps to input and format the text on the individual slides:

1. Open the presentation file `House.ppt` and make sure that you are positioned on slide 1.

2. Click the text Click To Add Title at the top and type **Buying a House**, as shown in Figure 32.1.

FIGURE 32.1   Inputting a title on a slide

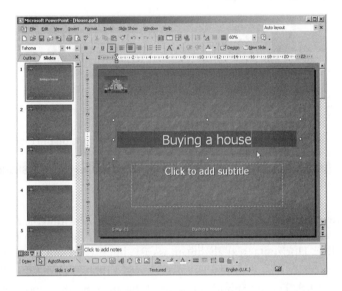

3. Select the text with the mouse and then choose Format ➢ Font. The Font dialog box opens, as shown in Figure 32.2.

FIGURE 32.2   The Font dialog box allows you to change text attributes.

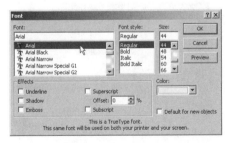

Also in the Font dialog box, *subscript* positions text slightly below the line, whilst *superscript* positions text slightly above the line.

4. Select Arial from the Font list and click OK. The text is now displayed in Arial font, as shown in Figure 32.3. As well as changing the font itself, you can use the Font dialog box to change the point size to make the text larger or smaller.

FIGURE 32.3   The text shown in Arial font

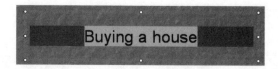

The Formatting toolbar can be used to quickly change text attributes. Simply select the target text and click the appropriate icons on the toolbar. For example, click the Bold icon to change text to bold, click the Italic icon to change text to italic, click the Underline icon to underline text, or click the Shadow icon to produce shadowed text.

When you first entered this text, it was automatically centred within the AutoShape frame. But you can change the alignment by choosing Format ➢ Alignment or by using the Formatting toolbar. Horizontal text alignment is easy, but if you want to align text vertically within an AutoShape or a text box, you need to use a slightly different technique.

5. Click the text Click To Add Subtitle underneath the main heading and type **A simple guide for first time purchasers**. Then select Format ➢ Placeholder. The Format AutoShape dialog box opens. Select the Text Box tab, as shown in Figure 32.4.

FIGURE 32.4   Aligning text in the middle of a text box

6. In the Text Anchor Point list, select the Middle setting and click OK. The text is now centred vertically within the AutoShape box, as shown in Figure 32.5.

FIGURE 32.5   Text aligned in the middle of a text box

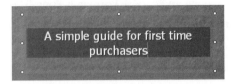

7. Text attributes or styles such as bold, italic, or underline can be easily applied to selected text by using either the Formatting toolbar or by choosing Format ➤ Font. However, PowerPoint has another neat feature that allows you to quickly change the case of any selected text.

8. Select the heading text on your slide and select Format ➤ Change Case. The Change Case dialog box opens, as shown in Figure 32.6.

FIGURE 32.6   The Change Case option box

9. Select the UPPERCASE option and click OK. The heading is now in all capital letters.

Other text attributes that can be applied to text include Shadow, Subscript, and Superscript. Shadow can be applied by clicking the Shadow button on the Formatting toolbar, but you need to choose Format ➤ Font to apply or remove Subscript or Superscript on selected text.

When you make any adjustments using the Format AutoShape dialog box, you can check the effect by simply clicking the Preview button. This allows you to easily change your mind before clicking OK to accept the changes.

10. Once again, select the heading text and click the Shadow button on the Formatting toolbar. Your heading should now look like Figure 32.7.

FIGURE 32.7   Applying the shadow effect to text

Adding Colour to Text

The use of colour is one of the most effective ways of emphasising text; PowerPoint allows you to change the colour of any selected text. Try it out using the following steps:

1.   Select your heading text again and choose Format ➢ Font. The Font dialog box opens.

2.   In the Color list, select More Colors and the Colors dialog box opens. Make the Standard tab active, as shown in Figure 32.8.

FIGURE 32.8   Selecting different colours for fonts

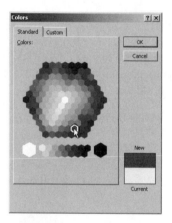

3.   Click the colour you want and click OK. The text changes accordingly.

If you can't see the colour that you want on the Standard tab in the Colors dialog box, you can mix your own using the Custom tab.

Editing Existing Text and Adding Lists

As well as inputting text, you can also edit existing text on a slide using these steps:

1.   Position the mouse cursor exactly between the words "for first" in the subtitle and click once. This activates the text box for editing. You can now type **all** in between "for" and "first," as shown in Figure 32.9. You can use this method to add any words or characters that you wish. Click anywhere outside the subtitle box, and the editing is complete.

FIGURE 32.9   Editing text on a slide

2. Move to the second slide in your presentation and enter the text in there. (Click slide 2 in the list of slides on the left-hand side of the main window.) Notice how this slide uses a different slide layout—the Title And Text layout that uses bullets in the lower AutoShape, as shown in Figure 32.10.

FIGURE 32.10   Slide 2 in House.ppt

As well as entering text by clicking the relevant AutoShape text boxes on the slide itself, PowerPoint allows you to enter text using the Outline tab on the left-hand side of the main window.

3. Click the Outline tab, and you see a small flashing cursor next to the slide icon for slide number 2. Type **First Steps**, and the text appears on the slide itself, as shown in Figure 32.11. Click anywhere on the slide area to finish entering the text.

FIGURE 32.11   Entering text via the Outline tab

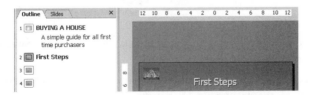

4. Click Click To Add Text on the slide, enter **Set your budget**, and press the Enter key on your keyboard. Notice how a bulleted list is automatically generated. Now enter the following phrases, pressing the Enter key after each line:

> **Decide on a location**
>
> **Define your basic requirements**
>
> **Research the market**
>
> **Start looking at properties**

When you have finished, click anywhere outside the text box. Slide 2 should now look like the one in Figure 32.12.

FIGURE 32.12   Slide 2 after entering bullet points

When adding text to a bulleted list, each time you press the Enter key, a new bullet appears automatically. Press the Backspace key to delete any unwanted bullet points. If you press the Tab key, a new bullet level is created so that you can have indented bulleted text, as shown in Figure 32.13.

FIGURE 32.13   Creating multiple levels of bulleted lists

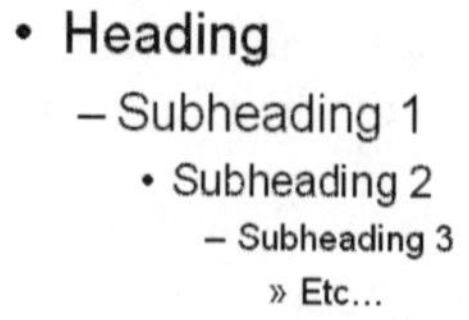

- **Heading**
  - Subheading 1
    - Subheading 2
      - Subheading 3
        » Etc...

To return to the previous level of indented bullets, hold down the Shift key and press the Tab key on your keyboard.

5. The actual bullet points generated in the previous step are the default ones for this particular slide design. However, you can change the style of these bullets fairly easily. Select *all* the text in the bulleted list and choose Format ➢ Bullets And Numbering. The Bullets And Numbering window opens; on the Bulleted tab you can choose a different style to use, as shown in Figure 32.14.

FIGURE 32.14   Selecting an alternative bullet style

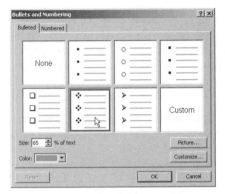

6. Click the Numbered tab, and notice the various styles of automatic numbering that can be applied to a list, as shown in Figure 32.15. Select any one of these numbering styles and click OK. Your slide should now look like the one shown in Figure 32.16.

FIGURE 32.15   Selecting an alternative number style

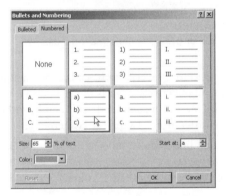

FIGURE 32.16   Slide 2 with a numbered list

Using Undo and Redo

When entering or editing text or formatting a slide, it's quite easy to make mistakes that you might not spot until you have accepted the changes by pressing the Enter key. Similarly, you might change your mind about an edit and simply wish to revert to the previous format. Fortunately, PowerPoint, like other Microsoft Office products discussed in this study guide, has a special feature called Undo that can be extremely useful if you make a mistake when editing or formatting. Take these steps to see how it works:

1. Using your current example slide 2, choose Edit ≻ Undo. The numbered list reverts to the original settings using the default bullet points, as shown earlier in Figure 32.12.

 The actual function of the Edit ≻ Undo menu option depends on whatever the last operation carried out by PowerPoint was. As a result, the word Undo could be followed on the menu by other words that describe what the last action was and what will be undone when you execute the command, for example, Undo Bold or Undo Typing.

 You can access the Undo feature quickly by clicking the Undo icon on the Standard toolbar. Each time you click it, the last action is undone. You can undo several mistakes or previous changes if necessary.

2. As well as the Undo command, PowerPoint has a complementary command called Redo. Where the Undo command effectively cancels the last action, the Redo command repeats the last action undone by the Undo command. This can be rather confusing, so let's use a brief example to see the difference between the two commands.

3. On slide 2, click the second line in the numbered list and type **Good** between "a" and "location." Then click outside the text box. Now change the word "Good" to "Bad," and again click outside the text box to complete the edit. Your slide should now look like Figure 32.17.

FIGURE 32.17 Slide 2 following the second edit

4. If you click the Undo icon on the Standard toolbar, the contents of slide 2 revert to the word "Good." Now if you click the Redo icon on the Standard toolbar, the word "Bad" reappears.

This is because you have instructed PowerPoint to redo the last typing action. Re-edit the slide to remove either the word "Good" or "Bad" from the second line of the bulleted list.

5. The bulleted list on slide 2 uses PowerPoint's default setting for the spacing between the lines of text. However, this line spacing can be adjusted by selecting all the text and then choosing Format ➤ Line Spacing. The Line Spacing window is displayed where you can adjust the overall line spacing and the amount of space before and after paragraphs, as shown in Figure 32.18. Play around with the various settings to see what they do and use the Preview button to check the effects. When you have finished, click Cancel to return to the Normal view.

FIGURE 32.18   Adjusting the line spacing between text

6. Using the procedures you have learnt previously, create the five slides as shown in Figure 32.19 to appear as slides 3 to 7 in your presentation. Choose Insert ➤ New Slide as necessary to create any additional slides required.

FIGURE 32.19   Five new slides created in House.ppt. Note: In the interest of clarity, the following slides are shown without the use of the slide design or background.

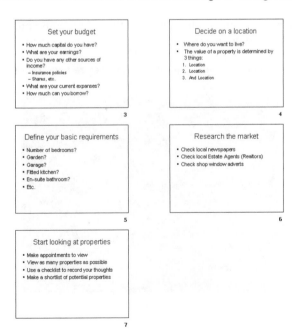

7. Choose File ➤ Save and save your presentation.

Using Images in PowerPoint

Earlier in this chapter, you saw how to insert a clip art picture into the Slide Master. You can also insert pictures and images into specific individual slides as well, so try out these steps:

1.   If it is not already open, open the presentation file House.ppt and make sure that you are positioned on slide 4.

2.   Select Insert ➢ Picture ➢ Clip Art, and the Task Pane changes to display the Insert Clip Art options. Type **Globe** in the Search Text box and click the Search button. The Task Pane changes again to display any images that match the search text, as shown in Figure 32.20.

FIGURE 32.20   Clip art images displayed in the Task Pane

3.   Select any suitable image and double-click it with the left mouse button. A copy of the image is placed on the slide. Resize and position the image, as shown in Figure 32.21.

FIGURE 32.21   The new image after it has been resized and repositioned

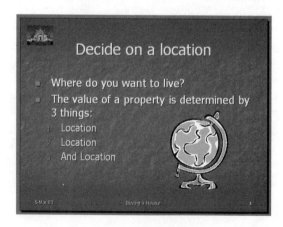

You can use the box size control handles and the mouse pointer to resize and move an image to an appropriate position on a slide.

As well as clip art, PowerPoint allows you to insert images such as photographs from a file.

4. Go to slide 5 and choose Insert ➤ Picture ➤ From File. This time, the Insert Picture window opens, where you can choose an image to insert, as shown in Figure 32.22.

FIGURE 32.22   The Insert Picture window where you can choose an image file to insert

PowerPoint supports a wide variety of graphics file formats, so you can insert most types of images easily. However, if you don't find any suitable files in your My Documents folder, you may wish to try the My Pictures folder instead. If you fail to find any image files to insert, seek advice from your computer supplier or system administrator.

5. Select any suitable image file and double-click it to insert it into your slide. Resize and reposition the image; your slide should now look like Figure 32.23.

FIGURE 32.23   Slide 5 after inserting an image from a file

6.   Choose File ➢ Save and save your presentation.

Duplicating, Moving, and Deleting Content

Editing slides in a presentation is one of the most fundamental aspects of using PowerPoint to create presentations. Most elements of a presentation (text and images) can be duplicated, moved, or deleted. This section explains the procedures for doing so.

Using Copy, Cut, and Paste in PowerPoint

As with other Microsoft Office applications discussed in this book, you can use the Copy and Paste tools in PowerPoint to duplicate text and images within the presentation or active presentations using the following steps:

1.   If it is not already open, open the file House.ppt and make sure that you are positioned on slide 1.

2.   Double-click the word "House" in the top text box to select it, as shown in Figure 32.24.

FIGURE 32.24   A portion of text selected is shown as white on black.

3. Choose Edit ➢ Copy to copy the selected text to the Clipboard.

Instead of using the menu bar to perform Copy, Cut, and Paste functions via the Clipboard, you can click the appropriate icons on the Standard toolbar.

4. Click just to the left of the word "purchasers" in the lower text box to establish an insertion point, as shown in Figure 32.25.

FIGURE 32.25   Marking the insertion point

5. Now if you select Edit ➢ Paste, the text that was copied to the Clipboard (the word "House") is inserted just before the word "purchasers," as shown in Figure 32.26.

FIGURE 32.26   Slide 1 after inserting the word "House"

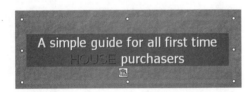

Notice that the original selected text "House" remains where it was in the top-most text box. If you want to move the word "House," select it, choose Edit ➢ Cut to remove it from its original position, and then select Edit ➢ Paste to insert it wherever it is required. You can also simply delete the word "House" by either selecting it and pressing the Delete key on the keyboard or by omitting the Paste function after choosing Edit ➢ Cut.

6. Now select the word "House" that appears between "time" and "purchasers." Delete it using the Delete key on the keyboard, choosing Edit ➢ Cut, or clicking the Cut icon.

The Windows Clipboard stores only one item at a time. Whenever you choose Edit ➤ Paste, whatever was last cut or copied to the Clipboard is pasted—this might not always be what you intended. Therefore, consider Cut and Paste or Copy and Paste as a single function.

Using the Copy, Cut, and Paste functions along with the Clipboard not only allows you to move, copy, and delete selected items within an individual presentation, but it also enables you to move and copy them between any active (open) presentations as well. Follow these steps:

1. Select all the words in the title on slide 1 by choosing Edit ➤ Select All and copy the words to the clipboard by selecting Edit ➤ Copy.

2. Choose File ➤ New, and the Task Pane is displayed. Click the Blank Presentation option to create a new blank presentation. Your display should now look like the example in Figure 32.27.

FIGURE 32.27   Creating a new presentation in PowerPoint

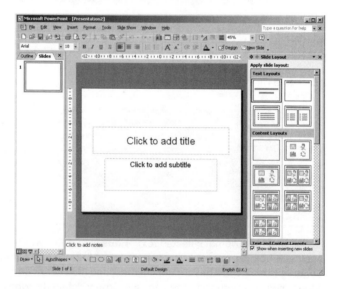

3. Select the Click To Add Title box and then click the Paste icon on the Standard toolbar. The title from the House presentation (slide 1) is copied into the new presentation, as shown in Figure 32.28.

FIGURE 32.28   Copying text between open presentations

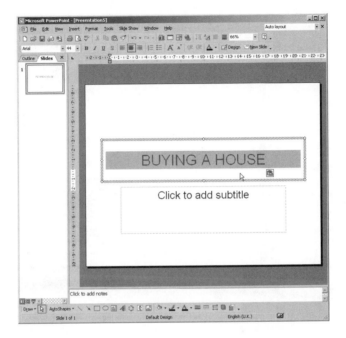

 You can have many copies of PowerPoint running at the same time and switch between them simply by clicking the appropriate item on the Windows Taskbar.

Modifying Graphics in a Presentation

You can use the same technique to insert and copy any graphics images. PowerPoint also allows you to resize images in your presentation. Try out the following steps:

1. Return to the House presentation and click slide 4. Select the image of the globe and copy it to the Clipboard. Now, switch back to the new presentation and paste the image onto the slide, as shown in Figure 32.29.

FIGURE 32.29 Copying images between open presentations

Using the Windows Clipboard is an ideal way of creating a new presentation quickly by copying and pasting elements or components from any existing presentations.

2. You can resize the image that you have just pasted onto the slide by dragging on the box size control handles, as shown in Figure 32.30.

FIGURE 32.30 Resizing an image on a slide

3. You can move the image about on the slide to reposition it by clicking it and dragging it with the mouse, as shown in Figure 32.31.

FIGURE 32.31   Moving an image on a slide

4. Finally, delete the image by simply selecting it and pressing the Delete key on your keyboard.

5. Close the new presentation without saving it and switch back to the House presentation. Save any changes that you've made to the House presentation and close it.

Deleting Text and Images

Deleting text, pictures, or images from a slide is simply a matter of selecting the object to be deleted and then either pressing the Delete key on the keyboard or choosing Edit ➢ Cut from the standard menu bar.

Summary

This chapter first described the various ways that text can be entered and edited in PowerPoint. In addition, you saw how text can be formatted in order to enhance its appearance. This ability to apply formatting to such elements is one of the key features of PowerPoint, and it allows you to be creative in the design of your presentation slides. The vast range of options and choices available can be a bit bewildering at first, but if you are prepared to experiment, you can produce some very interesting results.

You saw how to insert both clip art pictures and images from files onto a selected slide. Pictures and images are an excellent way to enhance the look of a presentation.

The final topic in this chapter explained the various ways that both text and images can be duplicated, moved, and deleted on a single slide, between slides in a presentation, and between separate presentations.

Chapter

33

Charts, Graphs, and Drawn Objects

IN THIS CHAPTER YOU WILL LEARN HOW TO

✓ Create different kinds of charts such as bar charts and pie charts.

✓ Change the background colour of a chart or graph.

✓ Change the colour of a chart or graph column, bar, line, and pie slice.

✓ Change the chart or graph type.

✓ Create an organisational chart with a labelled hierarchy.

✓ Change the hierarchical structure of an organisation chart.

✓ Add or remove managers, co-workers, and subordinates in an organisation chart.

✓ Add different types of drawn objects to a slide: line, free-drawn line, arrow, rectangle, square, circle, oval, and text box.

✓ Change the background colour, line colour, line weight, and line style of a drawn object.

✓ Change arrow start and finish styles.

✓ Apply shadow to a drawn object.

✓ Rotate or flip a drawn object in a slide.

✓ Align a drawn object: left, right, centre, top, and bottom of a slide.

✓ Resize a chart, graph, or drawn object within a presentation.

✓ Bring an object to the front or back.

✓ Duplicate a chart, graph, or drawn object within a presentation or between presentations.

✓ Move a chart, graph, or drawn object within a presentation or between presentations.

✓ Delete a chart, graph, or drawn object.

As well as inserting pictures and images in PowerPoint, you can include other graphical elements like charts or graphs on slides. These elements can be created in another application such as a spreadsheet and then imported into your presentation, or they can be created directly within PowerPoint itself.

Using Charts and Graphs

One of the most common uses of applications such as PowerPoint is to present numerical information in the form of a graph or chart. This section explains how you can

- Create and modify different types of in-built charts or graphs in a slide.
- Change the background colour in a chart or graph.
- Change the column, bar, line, and pie slice colours in a chart or graph.
- Change between different kinds of charts such as a bar chart, a pie chart, and so on.

Creating and Modifying a Chart

In this section, you will create a new presentation called Charts using the following steps:

1. If it is not already open, start PowerPoint and make sure that there are no existing presentations open.

2. Choose File ➤ New and create a new blank presentation. Select Insert ➤ Chart. Your slide should look like the one shown in Figure 33.1. This is the default chart type that Power-Point uses, but you'll see shortly how you can change the type of chart or graph. For the moment, use this chart type.

Creating a chart in PowerPoint involves the use of a table known as a *datasheet*, as shown in Figure 33.2. This datasheet stores the data values used to generate the plotted points (columns in this case) and the labels used for both the X and Y axes. Datasheets are similar to spreadsheets, except they cannot be used to calculate formulas.

You can change any of the data values and axes labels in the datasheet. As you do so, the changes are automatically reflected in the chart itself. For example, change the value in location A2 to read 12 and the label "North" to read "South." Your chart should now look like Figure 33.3.

FIGURE 33.1 Creating a chart in a presentation

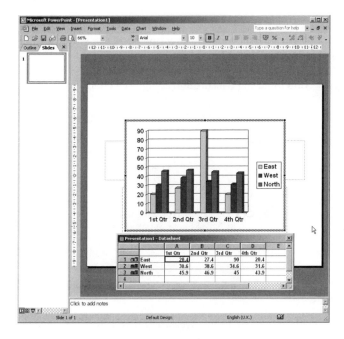

FIGURE 33.2 The datasheet used when creating or modifying a chart in a presentation

Presentation1 - Datasheet

		A	B	C	D	E
		1st Qtr	2nd Qtr	3rd Qtr	4th Qtr	
1	East	20.4	27.4	90	20.4	
2	West	30.6	38.6	34.6	31.6	
3	North	45.9	46.9	45	43.9	
4						

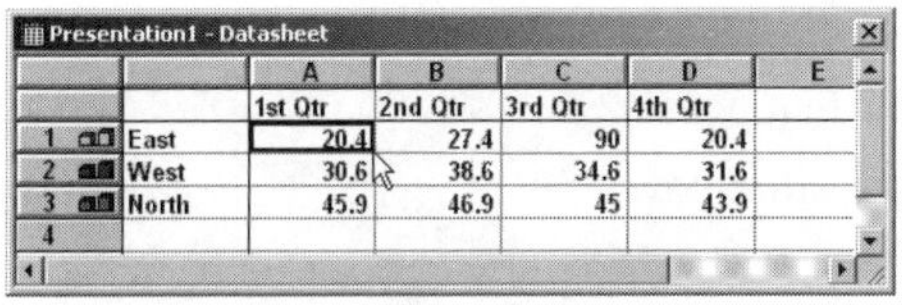

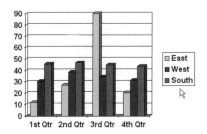

FIGURE 33.3 Changing the values and labels in a chart

As well as changing the data values and labels, you can change the background colour on a chart. Follow these steps:

1. Click the chart itself once to select the chart area. Now choose Format ➤ Selected Chart Area, and the Format Chart Area window opens. Make sure that the Patterns tab is selected, as shown in Figure 33.4.

FIGURE 33.4   Changing the background colour in a chart

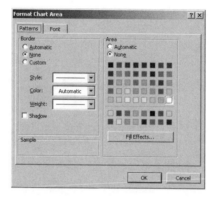

2. Select any of the colours shown in the Area section and click OK. The background of your chart has now changed to the colour that you selected, as shown in Figure 33.5.

FIGURE 33.5   The chart with the new background colour

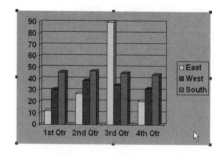

In addition to changing the chart background, you can also change the colours of the actual columns in your chart. To do this, follow these steps:

1. Click any of the columns once, and all the columns for a particular data series are selected, as shown in Figure 33.6.

FIGURE 33.6   Selecting columns in your chart

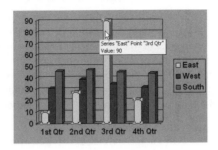

2. Choose Format ➢ Selected Data Series to open the Format Data Series window. Make sure that the Patterns tab is selected. Click your desired colour and click OK. The columns change colour automatically, as shown in Figure 33.7.

FIGURE 33.7   Columns with the colour changed in your chart

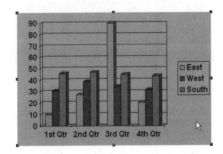

Similar procedures can be used to change elements of other types of charts, such as pie slices, lines, or bars. You can also change the entire chart type quite easily. Try these steps:

1. Select the chart by clicking the chart area once and choose Chart ➢ Chart Type. In the Chart Type window that opens, you can choose from a wide variety of chart types (see Figure 33.8).

FIGURE 33.8   Selecting a new chart type

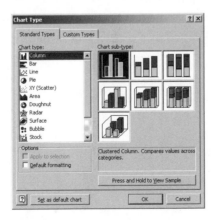

WARNING   Certain types of charts are designed to plot only a single data series; for example, pie charts. This means that if you change the chart type, not all of the selected data may be plotted. For instance, in the example in this section, the data for the chart shown in Figure 33.2 has three separate series for each of the regions. If you convert the column chart to a pie chart, only one of these regions is plotted. Therefore, take care when converting between different types of charts, because sometimes the results might not be what you expected.

2. Select the Area chart type, and various chart sub-types appear in the Chart Sub-Type section. Select the Stacked Area type (centre top row) and click OK. Your chart should now look like the one shown in Figure 33.9.

FIGURE 33.9   The column chart converted to an area chart

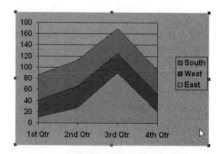

Save the presentation in the My Documents folder with the name Charts.

Creating and Modifying Organisation Charts

PowerPoint can also be used to create hierarchical organisation charts that are ideal for, say, graphically depicting the staffing structure of a company. In this section, you'll learn how to create and modify an organisation chart.

For this exercise, continue to use the Charts presentation and take the following steps:

1. Choose Insert ≻ New Slide and then a blank slide layout, as shown in Figure 33.10.

FIGURE 33.10   Inserting a new blank slide

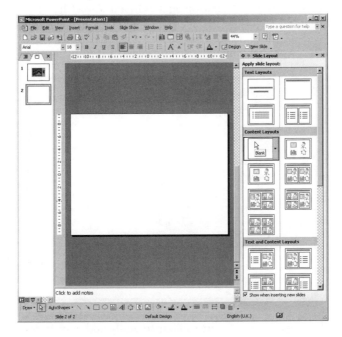

2. On the menu bar, choose Insert ➤ Picture ➤ Organization Chart. A new object appears on your blank slide, as shown in Figure 33.11.

FIGURE 33.11   Creating an organisation chart

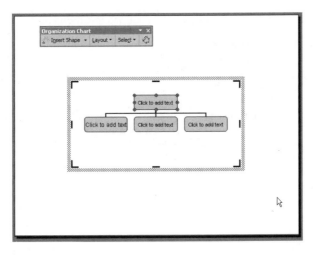

3. Here you can see the default format for organisation charts in PowerPoint. You can change this format by clicking the Layout button on the Organization Chart toolbar. Select the Left Hanging option, and your organisation chart should look like Figure 33.12.

FIGURE 33.12   A left-hanging organisation chart

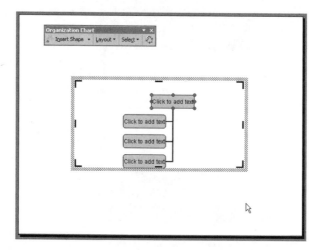

4. You can use the Organization Chart toolbar to easily add new boxes for subordinates, co-workers, or assistants to your organisation chart. For example, to add a subordinate, click the lowest box in your chart and select Insert Shape ➢ Subordinate on the Organization Chart toolbar. A new box opens underneath the original box with a link showing it as a subordinate, as shown in Figure 33.13.

FIGURE 33.13   Adding a subordinate to your organisation chart

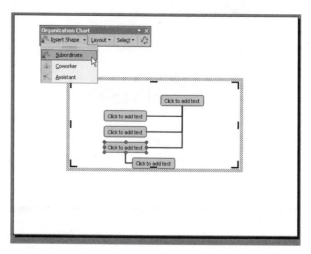

5. Similarly, you can add a co-worker or an assistant to an existing chart by clicking the appropriate option in the Insert Shape drop-down list. In addition, you can add any text to a box and format the text, boxes, and connecting lines to a certain degree. Figure 33.14 contains an example of the sort of organisation chart that you can create. To remove a box from an organisation chart, simply select the box and press the Delete key on your keyboard.

FIGURE 33.14 An example of a formatted organisation chart

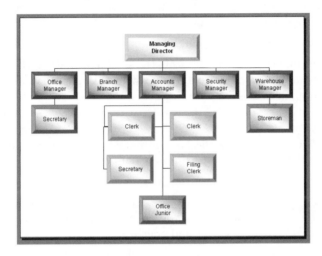

6. Save the Charts presentation, along with any changes you have made.

Drawn Objects

So far you have dealt only with pre-drawn objects such as clip art, pictures, images, charts, or graphs. PowerPoint allows you to create your own drawn objects from scratch.

You may have already noticed the Drawing toolbar, which by default appears at the bottom of the main PowerPoint window. If it isn't displayed on your screen, choose View ➤ Toolbars ➤ Drawing to display it. Using the drawing capabilities of PowerPoint, you can embellish and enhance your presentation slides by adding graphical objects such as lines, boxes, circles, and other shapes.

With drawn objects you can

- Add different types of drawn objects to a slide.

- Change a drawn object's appearance.

- Change the start and end arrow type of lines.

- Apply a shadow to a drawn object.

- Rotate or flip a drawn object in a slide.

- Align a drawn object: left, right, centre, top, or bottom.
- Resize a drawn object.
- Bring a drawn object to appear in front of or behind other slide elements.

Adding and Modifying a Drawn Object to a Slide

In this section, you will continue to use the Charts presentation to add and modify drawn objects to slides. Take the following steps:

1. Create a new slide with a blank layout.

2. On the Drawing toolbar, click the Line icon. Using the mouse, draw a line anywhere on the slide. Drag with the mouse to create the line at whatever length you want. When you release the mouse button, the line is drawn.

If you want exact vertical or horizontal lines, hold down the Shift key on the keyboard whilst you are drawing them with the mouse.

3. If you select a line that you have drawn, you can move it to a new position when the cursor changes to a cross by simply clicking and dragging.

4. When a drawn line is selected, it has control handles at either end that can be used to either resize the line or to change its orientation, as shown in Figure 33.15.

FIGURE 33.15 Resizing and changing the orientation of a drawn line

5. Whilst the line is selected, you can alter its appearance by choosing Format ➢ AutoShape to open the Format AutoShape dialog box, as shown in Figure 33.16. Here you can select different line colours, line styles (for example, double), dashed lines, line weights (thickness), and arrows (on either end of the line or both ends), as shown in Figure 33.17. Experiment with these settings, using the Preview button to check the results. Once you are happy with your changes, click the OK button.

FIGURE 33.16   Formatting a line (AutoShape)

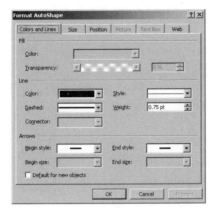

FIGURE 33.17   Examples of different types of line formats and styles

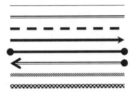

PowerPoint refers to drawn objects such as lines, boxes, and ovals as *AutoShapes.*

6. As well as drawing lines on your slides, you can use the Drawing toolbar to draw a variety of other simple objects such as rectangles, squares, circles, and ovals, as shown in Figure 33.18. For example, to draw a box on a slide, click the Rectangle icon and then click anywhere on the slide and drag with the mouse to create the AutoShape at whatever size you want. When you release the mouse button, the AutoShape is drawn. You can use the control handles to resize the AutoShape and use the cursor to position the AutoShape on the slide as required.

FIGURE 33.18   Examples of simple rectangles, squares, circles, and ovals

 To draw perfect squares or circles, hold down the Shift key on the keyboard whilst drawing a rectangle or oval.

7. If necessary, you can choose Autoshapes ➢ Lines from the Drawing toolbar to draw various types of freehand shapes and lines on a slide with the mouse. In addition, you can add text boxes to a slide by selecting the Text Box tool from the Drawing toolbar and then drawing a suitably-sized rectangle to contain the text.

 When positioning or resizing objects such as AutoShapes, it is perfectly possible to place them either spanning the edges of slides or outside the slide boundaries completely. But be aware that only the parts of an object that are inside the slide boundary are displayed during a slide show.

Changing the Appearance of Drawn Objects

Once you have drawn an object on a slide, you can choose Format ➢ AutoShape to use the Format AutoShape dialog box to change the object's appearance. You can change an object's fill colour, fill pattern, fill texture, line colour, line weight, or line style. With a bit of practice, it's possible to create almost any desired basic drawn object using the tools provided, as shown in Figure 33.19.

FIGURE 33.19   Changing the appearance of drawn objects

It is possible to alter and enhance a drawn object in other ways as well. For example, try these steps:

1. On a new blank slide, draw a simple rectangle and then select it. You can now use the Shadow icon on the Drawing toolbar to add special shadow effects. There are several effects to choose from, as shown in Figure 33.20; experiment with these to see how they can change the look of an object.

FIGURE 33.20   Different shadow effects are available for drawn objects.

2. As well as adding shadow effects to a drawn object, you can rotate an object using the Size tab in the Format AutoShape dialog box and adjusting the rotation angle, as you can see in Figure 33.21. Alternatively, you can free rotate using the special green-coloured control handle for the object, as shown in Figure 33.22.

FIGURE 33.21   Using the Format AutoShape dialog box to rotate an object

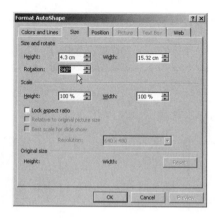

FIGURE 33.22   Using the Free Rotate handle to rotate an object

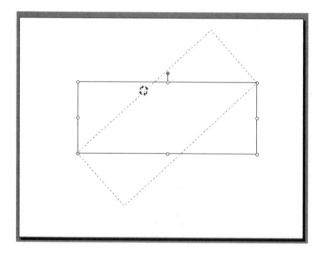

To constrain the rotation of the object to 15-degree angles, hold down Shift key while you drag the rotate handle.

3.   It is also possible to flip a drawn object so that it becomes a mirror image of itself. However, to actually see this effect, you must use a non-symmetrical AutoShape such as an arrow or even better, a more complex AutoShape such as a block arrow, a flowchart symbol, or a banner. Select a suitable AutoShape such as the U-Turn Arrow, as shown in Figure 33.23, and draw it on a blank slide.

FIGURE 33.23   Selecting a complex AutoShape

4. To flip a drawn object, first select it. Then on the Drawing toolbar, choose Draw ➢ Rotate Or Flip and either Flip Horizontal or Flip Vertical as required. The drawn object flips to produce a mirror image of itself. You might need to experiment with this to carry it out confidently.

5. One problem that often arises when dealing with drawn objects is aligning them relative to the slide. Fortunately, PowerPoint comes to the rescue again by means of the Draw ➢ Align Or Distribute option on the Drawing toolbar. To see this in action, simply select a drawn object on a blank slide and choose Draw ➢ Align or Distribute ➢ Align Center, as shown in Figure 33.24. The drawn object is moved automatically to the horizontal centre of the slide.

FIGURE 33.24   Using the alignment options to align a drawn object

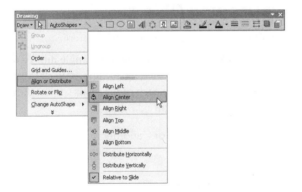

WARNING   Note that the alignment options only work either horizontally or vertically at any one time. In other words, you cannot simply centre a drawn object in the exact middle of a slide with a single alignment command; you have to use two separate functions.

6. Resizing drawn objects or charts on slides is simply a matter of using the control handles, as described in Chapter 32, "Using Text and Images in PowerPoint," which dealt with the resizing of pictures and images, or using the Size tab in the Format AutoShape window, as shown in Figure 33.25. Using this window, you can resize a drawn object or chart by adjusting its size measurements or by altering its scale. Adjustments can be made to either of the two dimensions (height and width) independently. However, if you select the Lock Aspect Ratio check box, any adjustment affects both dimensions simultaneously.

FIGURE 33.25 Using the alignment options to align a drawn object or chart

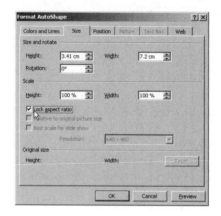

Controlling Overlapping Objects

Take these steps to control overlapping drawn objects:

1. Start by creating a new blank slide and drawing a rectangle and two ovals on it. Fill each type of drawn object with different contrasting colours, say, dark grey for the ovals and light yellow for the rectangle. Now move each of the ovals so that they overlap one separate corner of the rectangle, as shown in Figure 33.26.

FIGURE 33.26 Objects overlapping one another

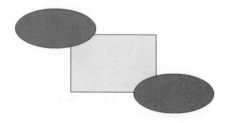

2. You can change the way that these drawn objects overlap by choosing Draw ➢ Order on the Drawing toolbar. First select the rectangle and then choose Draw ➢ Order ➢ Bring To Front on the Drawing toolbar, as shown in Figure 33.27. The rectangle is now displayed in front of the two ovals (see Figure 33.28).

FIGURE 33.27   Bringing an object to appear in front of other objects

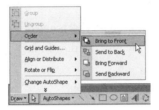

FIGURE 33.28   The rectangle is brought to the front.

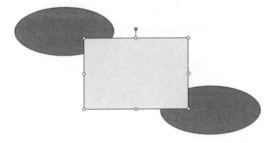

3. With the rectangle selected, choose Draw ➢ Order ➢ Send To Back on the Drawing toolbar. The rectangle is now displayed behind the two ovals, as shown in Figure 33.29.

FIGURE 33.29   The rectangle is sent to the back.

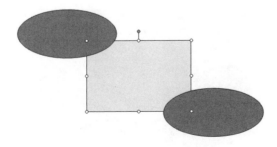

4. Save the Charts presentation, along with any changes you have made.

Duplicating, Moving, and Deleting Objects

You have seen previously how elements of a presentation such as text and images can be either duplicated, moved, or deleted. The same is true for charts, graphs, and drawn objects.

Using Copy and Paste with Charts and Drawn Objects

To try out the Copy and Paste functions with charts and drawn objects, take the following steps:

1. If it is not already open, open the presentation Charts.ppt and make sure that you are positioned on slide 1.

2. Click the chart to select it, as shown in Figure 33.30.

FIGURE 33.30   Selecting a chart to copy into the Clipboard

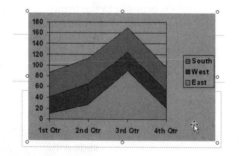

3. Choose Edit ➤ Copy to copy the selected chart into the Clipboard.

4. Choose Edit ➤ Paste, and a copy of the chart is displayed overlapping the original, as shown in Figure 33.31.

FIGURE 33.31   Two copies of the same chart on slide 1

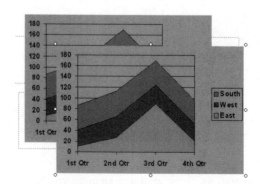

5. Now if you select slide 2 and choose Edit ➤ Paste, a copy of the chart is displayed overlapping the organisation chart, as shown in Figure 33.32.

FIGURE 33.32   A copy of a chart pasted onto another slide

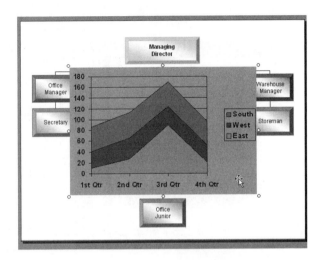

Once a chart, graph, or drawn object has been copied into the Windows Clipboard, it can be pasted as many times as you like into many different locations such as the same slide, a different slide within the same presentation, or a slide in a different presentation.

6. Using the Copy, Cut, and Paste functions along with the Clipboard allows you to not only move, copy, and delete selected items within an individual presentation, but it also enables you to move and copy them between any active (open) presentations as well. Select File ➤ New, and the Task Pane opens. Click the Blank Presentation option to create a new blank presentation.

7. Click the Paste icon on the Standard toolbar. The chart, which was copied from slide 1 in the Charts presentation, is copied into the new presentation, as shown in Figure 33.33.

Remember, you can have many copies of PowerPoint running at the same time and switch between them simply by clicking the appropriate item on the Windows Taskbar.

FIGURE 33.33 Copying a chart between open presentations

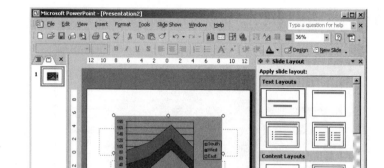

To move a chart, graph, or drawn object to a new location rather than copying it, simply use the Cut icon on the Standard toolbar rather than the Copy icon. This removes the chart, graph, or drawn object from its original location and places it in the Windows Clipboard, thereby allowing you to paste it to a new location. Similarly, you can use the Cut icon to effectively delete a chart, graph, or drawn object.

 If you use Cut to remove a chart, graph, or drawn object from a slide, remember that it remains in the Windows Clipboard until it is overwritten with a subsequent Cut or Copy operation. Therefore, it is generally better to select a chart, graph, or drawn object and then press the Delete key on your keyboard to remove it entirely from a slide.

Close the new presentation without saving it and switch back to the Charts presentation. Save any changes you made to the Charts presentation and close it.

Summary

This chapter explained how to create and modify charts in PowerPoint. You looked at the various ways that you can change the background colour and column colours, and you saw how easy it is to change chart types in PowerPoint.

You learnt how to create and modify organisation charts in PowerPoint, and you now understand how easy it is to insert and remove additional assistants, co-workers, and subordinates in an organisation chart.

PowerPoint provides you with several ways to create and modify various types of drawn objects. There are many different types of AutoShapes available in PowerPoint, and the ability to change their appearance opens up enormous possibilities for designing slides.

The final section of this chapter described the various ways that either a chart, graph, or drawn object can be duplicated, moved, and deleted on slides, between slides in a presentation, and between separate presentations. Using the Windows Clipboard is an ideal way of creating a new presentation quickly by copying and pasting elements or components from any existing presentations.

Chapter

34

Slide Show Effects

IN THIS CHAPTER YOU WILL LEARN HOW TO

- ✓ Add pre-set animation effects to entire slides.
- ✓ Change pre-set animation effects on specific text or images.
- ✓ Add slide transition effects.
- ✓ Change slide transition effects between slides.

So far, you have only seen the basic slide show facilities that can be used to display your presentations in a simple sequence of slides. However, PowerPoint has some very flexible animation and slide transition features that you can use to make your slide shows much more dynamic and exciting.

Pre-Set Animation

One technique that you can use to liven up your presentations is to apply movement or animation to either entire slides or to certain individual elements on your slides.

Adding Pre-Set Animation Effects

Take these steps to apply some of PowerPoint's pre-set animation effects to objects on slides:

1. If it is not already open, open the presentation House.ppt and make sure you are positioned on slide 1. Your first slide should look something like Figure 34.1, but don't worry if it isn't exactly the same, so long as it is roughly similar.

FIGURE 34.1   Slide 1 should look similar to this.

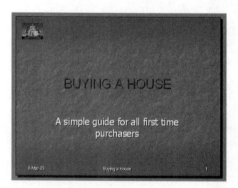

2. Let's start off by animating the entire slide contents. Select Slide Show ➤ Animation Schemes, and the Task Pane on the right-hand side of the screen changes to display a list of pre-set animations for you to choose from, as shown in Figure 34.2.

FIGURE 34.2   Animation schemes that apply to entire slide contents

3.   Click any animation scheme to select it and provided that the AutoPreview box is checked, you will see the animation effect on your slide in the slide area. If you want to see the animation effect again, simply click the Play button. Try out the various animation schemes to see what they do.

Changing Pre-Set Animation Effects on Specific Text or Images

You can also apply animation effects to individual elements on a slide, in fact, to any object, by taking the following steps:

1.   Start by selecting the desired object and choose Slide Show ➢ Custom Animation. For example, select slide 5 and then select the title. Using the Add Effect button, choose any of the Entrance effects, and you should see the title animated on your slide. Notice how the title has been given a numbered label, as shown in Figure 34.3. This is used to indicate the object's position in the animation sequence.

FIGURE 34.3   Applying an animation effect to a single text box

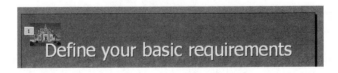

2.   Select the image and once again using the Add Effect button, choose a different Entrance effect for this element of the slide. Now press the Play button, and you should see the title animate first, followed by the image animating, as shown in Figure 34.4.

FIGURE 34.4   The effect of an animation on an image, in this case, the Blinds effect

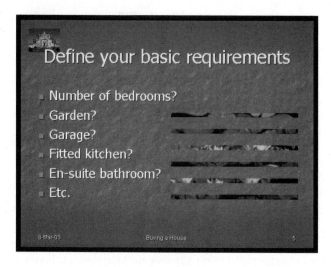

3.   To change the animation effect for an element on a slide, first select the existing effect in the Custom Animation list. Then click the Change button, as shown in Figure 34.5.

FIGURE 34.5   Changing an animation effect

4.   Save the House presentation along with any changes you have made.

Slide Transitions

Not only can you animate objects on individual slides, but PowerPoint also allows you to define how the changes between separate slides take place during a slide show. These are known as *slide transitions*.

Adding and Altering Slide Transition Effects

Try these steps to add and alter slide transition effects:

1. If it is not already open, open the presentation House.ppt and make sure that you are positioned on slide 1.

2. Select Slide Show ➢ Slide Transition. The Task Pane displays a list of options, as shown in Figure 34.6.

FIGURE 34.6   Selecting a slide transition option

3. In the Task Pane, you can select from a wide variety of different slide transition effects. Provided that the AutoPreview box is checked, you can see the transition effect on your slide in the slide area. If you want to see the transition effect again, simply click Play. Try out the various slide transition effects to see what they do.

4. Once you've decided which transition effect you want to use, you can either use the same effect between all the slides in the presentation by clicking the Apply To All button, or restrict the transition effect to appear only when the currently selected slide is displayed in a slide show. Notice that you can also decide whether slides appear on a mouse click or automatically after a specific number of seconds. Lastly, you can modify the slide transition to govern its speed and apply a sound to the transition, specifying whether it should play just once or loop until the next transition.

You cannot actually remove a slide transition from a slide in the same way that you can remove custom animation from a slide element. Instead, you must select the No Transition option in the Slide Transition Task Pane.

5. Changing the transition effect for a slide is simply a matter of selecting it and choosing an alternative slide transition from the Task Pane.

6. Save the House presentation, along with any changes you have made.

Summary

By using the PowerPoint animation features to animate text and images, you can really add some pizzazz to your presentations. There are numerous options and combinations of effects to play with, and it can be easy to get distracted by the animation effects available.

This chapter explained how to set up different types of transitions between slides and control how the changing of slides can be triggered. Once again, it's best to try out various transition effects to see which ones work best for your particular presentation.

Chapter

35

Preparing PowerPoint Outputs

IN THIS CHAPTER YOU WILL LEARN HOW TO

- ✓ Select the appropriate output format for a slide presentation.
- ✓ Spell-check the text content of slides and amend where necessary.
- ✓ Add notes to slides to assist the presenter.
- ✓ Change the orientation of a slide to either landscape or portrait.
- ✓ Duplicate or move slides within a presentation or between presentations.
- ✓ Delete slides.
- ✓ Print presentations in various ways and output formats.
- ✓ Hide or show slides.
- ✓ Start a slide show, either from the first slide or from a specific slide.

Now that you have created some presentations, you need to think about the printing and distribution of the material. Whilst many presentations are given as slide shows on the computer itself, PowerPoint has some useful features that can help you prepare presentation materials in different formats for different purposes such as outlines, handouts, and speaker notes.

WARNING This chapter assumes that the PC you are using to perform the following exercises has a suitable printer attached to it and that it is properly configured for use by the Windows XP operating system. Should this not be the case, any tasks that require you to actually print a presentation should be modified to print the output to a file instead.

Preparing a Slide Show for Printing

You can print all or part of your presentation (the slides, outline, speaker's notes, and audience handouts) in colour or in black and white, and no matter what you print, the process is basically the same.

This section explains how to change the slide orientation to either landscape or portrait, use the spell-check program and make changes where necessary, and add notes to slides for the presenter. You'll also see how to duplicate or move slides within the presentation or between open presentations, and delete slides when necessary.

Basic Preparation

To prepare your slide for printing, you will return to your Buying a House presentation and take the following steps:

1. Open the presentation House.ppt and make sure that you are positioned on slide 1.

2. The first thing you have to do is tell PowerPoint what it is you want to print. Choose File ➢ Page Setup, and the dialog box shown in Figure 35.1 opens.

FIGURE 35.1   Setting up the page format before printing

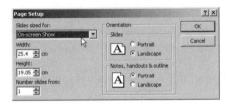

3. You can use the Slides Sized For drop-down list to select the type of printout you want. In the example shown in Figure 35.2, A4 size paper is selected.

FIGURE 35.2   Selecting the output media

4. On the right-hand side of the Page Setup dialog box is a section headed Orientation, as shown in Figure 35.3. Here you select whether to print your slides in either Portrait or Landscape mode. Similarly, you can instruct PowerPoint to print your notes, handouts, or outline in either Portrait or Landscape layout.

FIGURE 35.3   Determining the orientation for printing

5. Once you are happy with your Page Setup settings, click OK to accept them. When you subsequently print your presentation, these values will be used.

Checking the Spelling in Your Slide Show

Before you actually print your presentation, you need to check whether there are any spelling mistakes or typos that could detract from the quality of a professional-looking piece of work.

As you have seen with other Microsoft Office applications, there is a built-in spelling checker in the PowerPoint program. Take these steps to use it:

1. To check the spelling in your slide show, click the Spelling icon on the Standard toolbar or choose Tools ➤ Spelling. This starts the spelling checker. If any incorrectly spelt words are found, the Spelling window shown in Figure 35.4 opens.

FIGURE 35.4   The PowerPoint spell-checker has found what it thinks is an incorrectly spelt word.

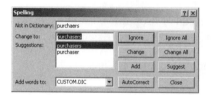

2. In the Spelling window, you can accept any of the suggested spellings by clicking the Change or Change All buttons; type in your own word(s) in the Change To box; ignore the incorrectly spelt word by clicking Ignore or Ignore All; or add the word to the CUSTOM.DIC (dictionary) by clicking the Add button.

Rather than checking the spelling for an entire presentation, you can constrain the spell-check by selecting an area of text first.

PowerPoint can be set to check your spelling as you actually type text. If you select Tools ➤ Options and click the Spelling tab, you can turn this feature on or off. When active, any words that the spelling checker thinks are incorrectly spelt are underlined with a squiggly red line.

3. After the entire presentation has been checked for spelling errors, the box shown in Figure 35.5 appears. Click OK to return to your presentation.

FIGURE 35.5   The spell-check is complete.

Adding Additional Information Via Notes

In order to aid either the presenter or the audience, consider whether you need to provide additional information to supplement the text on the slides themselves in the form of handouts. You do this by using the Notes facility within PowerPoint. To add notes to your slides, choose View ➢ Notes Page, and the display changes so that the current slide is at the top, with a text box area for adding notes underneath, as shown in Figure 35.6.

FIGURE 35.6   Adding notes to a slide in the Notes Page view

You can also enter and edit any notes by selecting the Notes area at the bottom of the main window when in the Normal view, as shown in Figure 35.7.

FIGURE 35.7   The Notes area in the Normal view

Controlling Print Output

You can control the way that your handouts are printed out by taking the following steps:

1. Choose File ➢ Page Setup. Using the Page Setup window that opens, you control the size of the paper to print your handouts on by selecting the appropriate option in the Slides Sized For drop-down list. Also in this window, you specify whether the handouts should be printed in either Portrait or Landscape orientation, as shown in Figure 35.8.

FIGURE 35.8   Controlling the way your handouts are printed

2. Clicking the Slide Sorter View button displays all the slides in a presentation in miniature, as shown in Figure 35.9. Use this view to move, duplicate, or delete any slides within your presentation prior to printing. You can also use the Slide Sorter view to move or duplicate slides between any open presentations.

FIGURE 35.9   Using the Slide Sorter view to prepare a presentation prior to printing

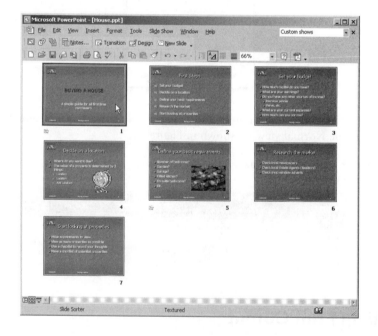

Printing Your Slide Show

Before you commit your presentation to paper, you may need to preview the output to make sure that what you are printing is exactly what you require. Basically, you should preview a printout so that you don't waste reams of paper printing the presentation in the wrong format or layout.

This section explains how to preview the presentation document using the Print Preview option. You'll also see how to print an entire presentation, specific slides, handouts, notes pages, an outline view of slides, or multiple copies of a presentation.

Using Print Preview

For the following steps, you will once again use your Buying a House presentation:

1. If it is not already open, open the presentation `House.ppt` and make sure that you are positioned on slide 1.

2. You can preview the different types of printouts by selecting the appropriate view by choosing File ➢ Print Preview or by clicking the Print Preview icon on the Standard toolbar. This displays your document exactly as it will appear on the printed page, as shown in Figure 35.10.

FIGURE 35.10   Using the Print view to see exactly what will be printed

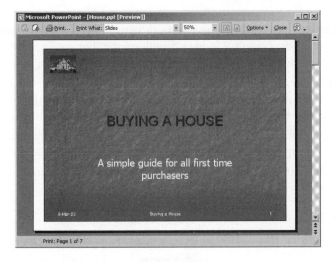

Setting the Desired Print Options

As you have seen with other Microsoft applications, there is a Print dialog box in Power-Point where you can designate specific print options. Take the following steps to set these options:

1. To print a presentation using a certain layout, choose File ➢ Print. The Print dialog box allows you to select various printing options, as shown in Figure 35.11.

FIGURE 35.11 Controlling the printing of a presentation

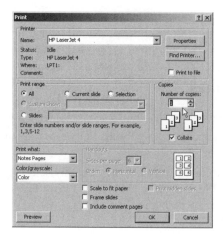

2. This is quite a complicated dialog box, with numerous options, so you need to examine it in detail:

- At the top is the Printer area where you can select which printer you wish to use. This always displays the current Windows default printer, but you can change it if you wish using the drop-down list.

- The Print Range area allows you to specify which parts of the presentation you want to print. For example, you can select all slides, the current slide, the currently selected slides, a custom show, or a specific range of slides.

- In the Copies area, you can set the number of copies to be printed and whether the printed pages are to be collated or not.

- Lastly, at the bottom, the Print What drop-down list allows you to select what you want to print, as shown in Figure 35.12.

FIGURE 35.12 Selecting what you want to print

3. Once you have made your choices, simply click OK to start the printing process.

You may need to experiment with the various options for printing so that you become familiar with the types of printouts that PowerPoint can produce.

If there isn't a printer available on your system, you may have to print to a file instead. If this is the case, make sure that there is a tick in the Print To File box in the Print window. Then when you click OK to start the printing, you are asked to provide a filename in the Print To File dialog box, as shown in Figure 35.13.

FIGURE 35.13 Request for a filename

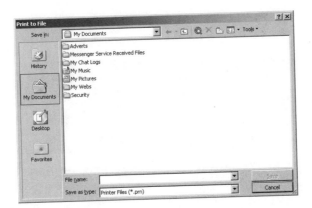

 Instead of choosing File ➢ Print, you can simply click the Print icon on the Standard toolbar. However, if you do this, you forego the opportunity to change any print settings. The printout is produced using the default settings, which are the current default Windows printer, print all pages, print one copy, and print the entire set of slides in the open presentation.

Delivering a Presentation

Now that you've done all the hard work in creating, editing, and enhancing your presentation, it is time to learn how to use PowerPoint to manage the delivery of the presentation.

PowerPoint has several different tools that you can use to prepare a presentation for showing to an audience. In this section you will learn how to start a slide show, how to hide and show specific slides, and how to start on any desired slide.

Starting the Slide Show

To start a slide show, take the following steps using your Buying a House presentation:

1. If it is not already open, open the presentation House.ppt and make sure that you are positioned on slide 1.

2. Occasionally, you might want to hide a slide or a group of slides so that they do not display during a slide show. You can do this from the Slide Sorter view by selecting a slide and then choosing Slide Show ➢ Hide Slide. The Slide Sorter view then shows any hidden slides with a diagonal line through the slide number, as shown in Figure 35.14.

FIGURE 35.14 Slide Sorter view showing a hidden slide on the right

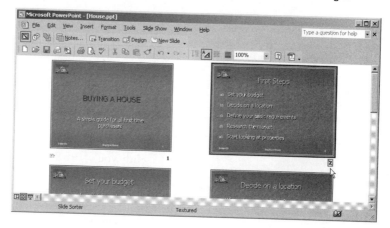

3. Also in the Slide Sorter view, you can select multiple slides by holding down the Ctrl key on the keyboard whilst clicking slides with the mouse. Once multiple slides have been selected, you can hide them by selecting Slide Show ➤ Hide Slide.

4. To show or unhide slides, merely repeat the preceding procedure; the diagonal line through the slide number disappears.

5. When you start a slide show by selecting Slide Show ➤ View Show, PowerPoint displays each slide in sequence, starting at the first slide in the presentation by default. However, you can control precisely the range of slides to be displayed by choosing Slide Show ➤ Set Up Show, which displays the Set Up Show dialog box shown in Figure 35.15.

FIGURE 35.15 Setting up a slide show

6. In the Set Up Show dialog box, you can choose the Show Type, specify the start and end slides, and decide whether slides should change manually or after pre-set timings. The

timings between slides can be set using the slide transition options described in Chapter 34, "Slide Show Effects."

When running a slide show in manual advance mode, you can either click once with the mouse or press the spacebar on the keyboard to move to the next slide in the sequence. You can also use the Page Up ➢ Page Down or Up and Down arrow keys to move forwards and backwards, one slide at a time through the slide sequence. To stop the slide show at any time, press the Esc key on the keyboard. If you press the F1 key during a slide show, a list of controls appears.

When running a slide show, if you move the mouse slightly you may notice that a small icon appears on the slide in the bottom left-hand corner (see Figure 35.16). This is called the *onscreen control button*.

FIGURE 35.16   Use the onscreen control button to display a shortcut menu with slide show navigation options.

Clicking this icon with the mouse causes a small shortcut menu to appear on screen, as shown in Figure 35.17.

FIGURE 35.17   The shortcut pop-up menu

If you choose Go ➢ Slide Navigator, a Slide Navigator window like the one in Figure 35.18 opens.

FIGURE 35.18   Using the Slide Navigator to go to a specific slide

In the Slide Navigator window, you can select the title of any slide in your presentation as the one to move to next when you press the Go To button.

You can terminate a slide show at any time. Press the Esc key on your keyboard, and you are returned to the PowerPoint screen exactly as you left it.

During a slide show, if you need to display a hidden slide, you must position yourself at the slide immediately preceding the hidden one, click the onscreen control button and select Go ➤ Hidden Slide from the pop-up shortcut menu. Alternatively, click the onscreen control button on any slide in a presentation, choose Go ➤ Slide Navigator, and then double-click the slide you want in the Slide Navigator window. Numbers in parentheses designate hidden slides, as shown in Figure 35.19.

FIGURE 35.19 The Slide Navigator showing hidden slides with numbers in brackets

If you opt to reveal a hidden slide during a slide show, it then remains revealed for the duration of that show, so if you move backwards and forwards, you will see it. However, rerunning the slide show causes any slides marked for hiding to be hidden once more.

You have now reached the end of the final exercise. You can close the Buying a House presentation, saving any changes you made, and close PowerPoint itself.

Summary

This chapter explained how you can open the presentation you want to print and choose whether you wish to print slides, handouts, notes pages, or an outline in the Page Setup dialog box. In addition, you can specify the orientation of the printed output.

You have seen how you can provide aids to the presenter by adding speaker notes, and you have learnt how to use PowerPoint's spelling checker to identify and correct any incorrectly spelt words in your presentation. You saw how you can use the Slide Sorter view to arrange your slides prior to printing. Using these facilities should help to ensure that your presentation is as accurate and professional-looking as possible.

There are several different ways that you can print information from your presentations. Most importantly, you can use the Print Preview option to see exactly how the printed page(s) will look before committing yourself to actually printing them.

PowerPoint provides you with numerous ways in which you can control and manage the presentation of a slide show, by specifying a range of slides to display, by navigating through the sequence of slides, and by temporarily hiding slides so that they are not displayed.

As usual, you are advised to experiment and play around with these options so that you become familiar with their capabilities and how they work.

Now that you have reached the end of this module, you should have a good insight into the principles of using PowerPoint. However, this guide is not intended to be a fully comprehensive training manual for PowerPoint XP; there are many aspects of the package that have not been covered. You are encouraged to further explore the capabilities of PowerPoint in order to broaden your knowledge of the software.

If you have access to the Internet, start by visiting the Microsoft PowerPoint website, where you can find plenty of additional information about the product:

`www.microsoft.com/office/powerpoint/default.htm`

If you don't have access to the Internet or if you are happier learning from a book, there are numerous published training guides for PowerPoint that cover every single facet of using the software.

Module Review Questions

1. How many different toolbars are available in PowerPoint?

2. How do you change the layout of a slide?

3. What is the principal use of the Slide Master in PowerPoint presentations?

4. How can you make sure that the current date appears on all slides in a presentation?

5. How do you change a bulleted list to an automatically numbered list?

6. There are two different ways that you can add movement to a presentation. What are they?

7. When animating an object on a slide, how can you see the effect without actually running the slide show?

8. What procedure would you use to print audience handouts in Landscape mode?

9. How do you check what a printout will look like prior to actually printing a presentation?

10. How can you instruct PowerPoint to print on a particular printer?

11. How can you make a slide show start on a particular slide?

12. How can you make a slide show end on a particular slide?

Answers to Module Review Questions

1. PowerPoint has a total of 5 separate toolbars available.

2. Select the slide whose layout you wish to change by clicking the thumbnail in the Slides tab on the left of your screen. This displays the actual slide in the Slide view. Next choose Format ➢ Slide Layout and then select the appropriate layout from the Task Pane on the right-hand side of the screen.

3. The Slide Master is used to set the format and layout of any new slides that you create in a presentation. The Slide Master also lets you make a global change—such as inserting an image or adding a footer—and have that change reflected on all the slides in your presentation.

4. Display the Slide Master and click the Date area at the bottom of the slide. Select Insert ➢ Date And Time and choose the desired format to be displayed.

5. Select the contents of the bulleted list, choose Format ➢ Bullets And Numbering, and then click the Numbering tab in the window that is displayed. Here you can choose which numbering style you wish to apply to the text.

6. You can add movement to a presentation by adding transitions between slides that are displayed in a slide show or by adding animation effects to various elements on a slide.

7. First select the object on the slide that has been animated. Then click the Play button at the bottom of the Custom Animation Task Pane.

8. Choose File ➢ Page Setup and then select Landscape in the Notes, Handouts, & Outline area of the Orientation section.

9. If you choose File ➢ Print Preview, then a new view opens, showing you exactly what will be printed.

10. When you choose File ➢ Print, a window is displayed where you can select a specific printer to use from the drop-down list of printers available on your system.

11. Select Slide Show ➢ Set Up Show to specify which slide number the slide show starts from.

12. Selecting Slide Show ➢ Set Up Show to specify which slide number the slide show ends with. Alternately, you can terminate a slide show at any slide simply by pressing the Esc key on your keyboard.

ECDL Module 7: Information and Communication

Chapter

36

The Internet

IN THIS CHAPTER YOU WILL LEARN TO

✓ Connect your PC to the Internet.

✓ Understand and distinguish between the Internet and the World Wide Web (WWW).

✓ Understand the terms HTTP, URL, hyperlink, ISP, FTP, cookie, and cache.

✓ Understand the makeup and structure of a web address.

✓ Identify a web browser and understand what it is used for.

✓ Recognise a search engine and understand what it does.

✓ Appreciate the security implications of using the Internet.

✓ Understand the first steps of using a web browser.

✓ Adjust the settings in a web browser.

Unless you have been hibernating in a cave for the last 10–15 years, you cannot have failed to notice the emergence of a new phenomenon known as the *Internet* that has revolutionised global communications. But what exactly is the Internet? Basically, it is a sprawling collection of computer networks that spans the globe, connecting government, military, educational, and commercial institutions—as well as private citizens—to a wide range of computer services, resources, and information.

The Internet is constructed in such a way so that it appears to the user as a single large network, even though the computers that are linked together use many different hardware and software platforms. Most importantly, it provides access to an enormous quantity of information covering every conceivable subject. As a result, the Internet has become the single most valuable research tool the world has ever known.

Connecting to the Internet

If you already have an Internet connection established on your PC, skip this section and proceed straight to the next section, "Internet Basics."

In order to connect to the Internet using your PC, you must have three basic things:

- A telephone line

- A modem

- An account with an Internet service provider (ISP)

Whilst the vast majority of people connect to the Internet via a standard telephone line, there are other ways of connecting. For example, many cable TV companies offer Internet access via their cable infrastructure using a device called a *cable modem*. Similarly, telephone companies such as BT, Deutsche Telecom, and France Telecom offer a service known as *broadband*, which provides high-speed access to the Internet, usually by means of a technology called *asymmetrical digital subscriber line (ADSL)* that uses an ADSL modem.

Let's look at each one of these items in turn:

The telephone line   A *telephone line* is used to make a dial-up connection to the Internet. Most standard domestic voice telephone lines allow you to access the Internet. However, if you are in any doubt, speak to the company that provides your telephone service. If you intend to connect to the Internet via an office switchboard, you may need to speak with the switchboard equipment supplier first.

The modem   A *modem* is a special piece of equipment that allows your computer to transmit and receive data over a dial-up connection. There are basically two main types of modems: internal and external. An internal modem is a small PC expansion card that is installed inside the computer and has a single cable that plugs directly into a telephone wall socket. External modems are small boxes that are designed to sit on your desk. They require a power connection and have one cable connected to the PC and another cable connected to the telephone wall socket. All modems come with software that is used to install and configure them for use. Nowadays most PCs are supplied with internal modems already fitted. If your PC doesn't have a modem, talk to your computer supplier before proceeding.

The ISP account   Generally, you need to connect to the Internet via an *Internet service provider (ISP)*, unless the company you work for already has an established Internet connection. An ISP is effectively a gateway to the Internet, whereby your computer dials into the ISP computer that is already connected to the Internet itself. However, in order to gain access to the ISP's computer, you (the user) must have an existing account that verifies your permission to access it. Due to massive competition in the marketplace, there are many ISPs to choose from. The majority of ISPs offer free accounts to users, so generally you have to pay only for the cost of telephone calls in order to access the Internet.

WARNING   If your PC is part of a local area network (LAN), talk to the network administrator or supervisor about establishing a connection to the Internet.

First-Time Internet Connection

Assuming that you have a suitable telephone line and modem available, you can begin to set up an Internet connection. Don't worry if you don't have an existing account with an ISP; you can register for an account online during the setup procedure, if necessary.

In order to connect to the Internet for the very first time, you need to use the *New Connection Wizard*, which is a standard feature of Windows XP. Running the Windows XP New Connection Wizard sets up your computer to use Internet Explorer to browse web pages and Outlook Express to send and receive e-mail. After completing the steps in the wizard, you should just be able to double-click the Internet Explorer icon on your Desktop to connect to the Internet.

The New Connection Wizard may appear as an icon on your Desktop, as shown in Figure 36.1, in which case you can simply double-click it to start it.

FIGURE 36.1 Double-click here to start the New Connection Wizard.

New
Connection
Wizard

 As discussed in other modules, a *wizard* within a Microsoft application is a special feature that is designed to guide the user step by step through a complex process. Generally, when you run a wizard, you see a series of dialog boxes that ask you questions. Depending on your answer, the wizard configures your system accordingly.

If there is no icon on your Desktop, you start the New Connection Wizard as follows:

1. Click the Start button and select the All Programs option.

2. Select the Accessories menu option, followed by the Communication option. The New Connection Wizard opens. Click this option, as shown in Figure 36.2.

FIGURE 36.2 Starting the New Connection Wizard from the Start button

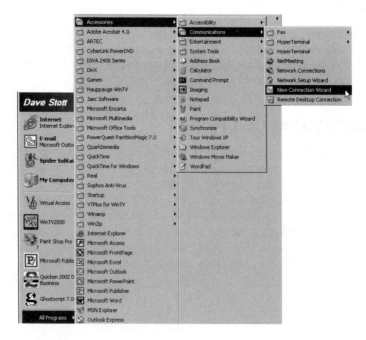

3. Once started, the New Connection Wizard displays a Welcome screen, as shown in Figure 36.3.

FIGURE 36.3   Using the New Connection Wizard to sign up for a new Internet account

4. Follow the instructions provided. When you have successfully completed the New Connection Wizard process, your Internet connection should be configured and ready for use.

Internet Basics

Assuming that you have either successfully established an Internet connection with your chosen ISP or that you already had an existing Internet connection, this section explains some of the most common concepts and terms associated with using the Internet, including

- The difference between the Internet and the World Wide Web (WWW)
- The terms HTTP, URL, hyperlink, ISP, FTP, cookie, and cache
- The makeup and structure of a web address
- What a web browser is and what it is used for
- What a search engine is and what it is used for

The Internet and the WWW

The Internet is a global network of computers that has been developing and evolving since its initial conception in the late 1960s, when the U.S. military decided to build a network of computers that would be resistant to any form of nuclear attack.

In 1969, the Defense Advanced Research Projects Agency (DARPA) developed a resource-sharing environment called the ARPANet. The ARPANet provided communications links between major computing sites at government, academic, and industrial laboratories involved in defence-related work.

The Internet has now become a vast collection of more than 100 million interconnected computers, with an estimated 605 million users worldwide, and is growing at a rate of over 100,000 people every day. It is also estimated that there are in excess of two billion web pages currently available online. Therefore, it is not surprising that the Internet represents such an important resource for research purposes.

In addition, because it operates on a global scale, the Internet has proved to be an extremely valuable and fast method of international communication, with an estimated 200 billion individual e-mail messages transmitted annually.

The *World Wide Web (WWW)* is the term used to describe the overall concept of using web pages to deliver information to users of the Internet. The WWW is based on an idea first developed in 1991 by Tim Berners-Lee, who, whilst working at Conseil Européen pour la Recherche Nucléaire (CERN), decided to use a system of hyperlinks within electronic documents to allow users to find related information stored as further electronic documents. This idea was revolutionary, and it quickly became adopted as the preferred method of presenting information on the Internet. And so the WWW was born.

Many people refer to the Internet simply as "the Net" or even as "the Web," and often these two terms are used interchangeably. In either case, it is generally safe to assume that reference is being made to the Internet as a whole.

Common Internet Terms

As with most things to do with computers and technology, the world of the Internet is strewn with highly technical terms, abbreviations, and acronyms. As such, it can be extremely unnerving for the first-time user when confronted by so much jargon and techno-speak.

Therefore, it is important to at least establish a grounding in a few of the most common concepts and terms associated with using the Internet.

The Internet relies on a series of *protocols* or standards that are specially designed to enable the electronic transfer of data reliably. There are a whole range of protocols in common use on the Internet, many of which you may never encounter. The principal ones are listed in Table 36.1.

TABLE 36.1   Common Internet Protocols

Protocol	Full Name	Brief Description
TCP/IP	Transmission Control Protocol/Internet Protocol	This is the base set of protocols used by the Internet to establish connections between linked computers and networks for all the transmission of data.
HTTP	Hypertext Transfer Protocol	This is the primary protocol used by the WWW to enable the transfer of web pages from web servers to client computers.

TABLE 36.1   Common Internet Protocols *(continued)*

Protocol	Full Name	Brief Description
FTP	File Transfer Protocol	This protocol is used to enable the transfer of complete data files of various types from FTP hosts to client computers.
SMTP	Simple Mail Transfer Protocol	This protocol is used to transfer e-mail to and from mail servers and to and from client computers.
HTTPS	Hypertext Transfer Protocol Secure	This protocol uses encryption to transfer sensitive information to and from secure hosts. HTTPS is mainly used for conducting e-commerce.

As well as protocols, there are several other common terms and concepts that you may need to be aware of:

URL   A *Uniform Resource Locator* is the address used to locate web pages and other files on the Internet. A URL is sometimes just referred to as a *web address*. We'll describe web addresses in more detail in a later section.

Hyperlink   A *hyperlink* is the method used to link between related web pages. Normally, hyperlinks are designated by coloured text that is underlined. However, any element, including graphical images on a web page, can be a designated hyperlink.

Cookie   A *cookie* is a special file that is automatically stored on your computer when you visit a particular web page. When you subsequently revisit the same web page, the information in the cookie is sent back to the web page server. This information is frequently used to personalize your return visit to a web page.

Cache   A *cache* is an area on your computer's hard disk that stores web pages that you have recently visited so that they can be re-viewed without having to transfer the information across your Internet connection again.

Web Addresses

As noted earlier, Internet web pages are referenced by means of a special address called a Uniform Resource Locator (URL). This is what appears in the browser's Address box when a particular page is being displayed.

A URL consists of two mandatory parts and three optional parts. The parts in a URL always appear in the following sequence:

Protocol   This can be `http`, `https`, `ftp`, and so on. The most common, which every Internet website URL begins with, is `http` (Hypertext Transfer Protocol).

Server name   This is the Internet address of the computer or file server where the source (generally a web page) is stored; for example, `www.sybex.com`.

Port number (optional)   Port numbers rarely appear in a URL, because the majority of file servers are located at the Web's default port, which is 80.

Filename (optional)   This is the name that the file or web page has on the server. If the file is in a directory or subdirectory on the server, the path to the file and the name of the file appear. If no filename is specified, the default file that web browsers look for and load is `index.html`.

Anchor (optional)   An anchor is a named bookmark within an HTML (Hypertext Markup Language, the language used to "write" web pages) file.

The following are examples of typical URLs or web page addresses:

```
http://www.bbc.co.uk/
http://info.isoc.org/guest/zakon/Internet/History/HIT.html
http://www.altavista.com/
http://msn.co.uk/homepage.asp
```

Notice that whilst most web page addresses incorporate the letters WWW, this is not always the case.

Web Browser

The key element is accessing the WWW is an application known as a *web browser*. This is a software program that runs on your PC and accepts requests in the form of URLs and then subsequently displays any web pages that it finds at an address. One of the browser's primary capabilities is its ability to activate hyperlinks so that when you click a hyperlink, the relevant page is displayed. Indeed, most sessions on the WWW involve jumping or linking to several different web pages and browsing their contents, hence the name "browser" for this type of application.

Web pages generally consist of a mixture of both text and graphics, but there can be other elements associated with a web page such as audio, animation, or video. A web browser must be able to cater to various types of data and either display or process it accordingly.

There are several different web browsers available such as Netscape, Opera, and Mozilla. Each has their own benefits and drawbacks, but most people use the standard Internet Explorer (IE) web browser, which is included in Windows XP.

Search Engine

With in excess of two billion web pages, the WWW is huge and growing all the time. As a result, it can often be difficult to pinpoint particular information. It's fine if you know a specific URL that you can simply type in your browser, but frequently you have no idea where to look for the information that you require.

Fortunately, the WWW itself comes to the rescue, as there are facilities widely available that you can use to search for information on the Internet. These facilities are known as *search engines,* and they maintain huge indexes to web pages on the Internet that allow you to pinpoint whatever it is you are looking for.

Search engines are just like other web pages, but they allow you to enter search terms in text form, which the system then searches for, displaying the results on a new web page. You can then click any of the hyperlinks displayed to take you to specific web pages that match your search criteria.

Security Considerations

One of the most important aspects of using the Internet is security, as there is the need to control access to information and to protect any confidential information that may be vulnerable.

Consequently, there are several security issues that need to be considered when accessing the Internet.

Access Control

Whilst the majority of the WWW is freely accessible, many websites contain confidential or commercially valuable information, and therefore access to such websites is strictly controlled. The most common way that this is achieved is by requiring the user to register with the website before granting access. Usually this means that the user has to fill in a web page form, providing the website with basic details such as their name, their e-mail address, and their country of origin. In return for this information, the user is issued a *username* and an associated *password* that subsequently allow the user to log in to the restricted website.

Such protected websites are not uncommon when conducting any e-commerce or financial transactions on the Internet, and it is quite easy for the user to build up a whole range of different usernames and passwords that are required to access protected websites.

Digital Certificates

As well as using login procedures to control access to certain websites, many online systems use digital certificates to provide extra security when conducting commercial or financial transactions.

The need to authenticate a user is crucial to secure communications. Basically, users must be able to prove their identity to those with whom they communicate and to verify the identity of others. The authentication of identity on a network is complex, because the communicating parties do not physically meet as they communicate. This can allow an unethical person to intercept messages or to impersonate another person or entity.

The *digital certificate* is a common credential that provides a means to verify someone's identity. A trusted organisation such as a bank assigns a certificate to an individual or to an entity. The individual or entity to which a certificate is issued is called the *subject* of that certificate.

When you visit a secure website (one whose address starts with "https"), the site automatically sends you its certificate. The *digital signature* component of a security certificate is your electronic identity card. The digital signature tells the recipient that the information actually came from you and has not been forged or tampered with.

Using digital certificates can protect your security when dealing with personal or financial transactions on the Internet, because they bind the identity of the certificate owner to a pair (public and private) of electronic keys that can be used to encrypt and sign information digitally. These electronic credentials assure that the keys actually belong to the person or organisation specified.

Encryption

Closely linked with the concept of digital certificates is a technique known as *encryption*. Most information that is transferred around the Internet is plain text, which can be read and understood by anyone who either intercepts it or receives it in error in, say, an e-mail. This is just as you might be able to overhear someone else's conversation in a crowded restaurant or read someone's newspaper sitting next to you on a train. Naturally, this can have severe implications when it comes to the security of, for example, financial transactions on the Internet. Therefore, when necessary for security, plain text is frequently encrypted or specially coded in a way that means it cannot simply be read without first being decrypted or decoded.

Most websites that are used for either online shopping or financial transactions use some form of encryption to ensure that the data transmitted is protected from any prying eyes.

This sounds very complicated, but fortunately the task of encrypting and decrypting coded text is generally handled automatically by your web browser. As far as the user is concerned, the process is completely transparent.

Viruses

As you saw in Part 1, computer viruses pose a major security problem for users of the Internet. Whenever an e-mail containing an attached file is received or a file is downloaded from a website, there is the potential of your computer system becoming infected by a virus.

A *virus* is a program or piece of code that is loaded onto your computer without your knowledge and runs against your wishes. Whilst many viruses are harmless, a significant portion are designed to cause severe disruption to computer systems by either deleting or corrupting files on the hard disk. Viruses can also replicate themselves, so that a virus makes a copy of itself over and over again and subsequently spreads from one computer to another via the Internet.

There are two important ways that you can protect yourself from virus infections when using the Internet:

- Make sure that you download files only from reputable websites, and be wary of any unsolicited e-mails containing attached files sent from people you don't personally know.

- Make sure that your PC has an appropriate anti-virus program installed and that this is kept up-to-date.

Fraud

We have briefly mentioned e-commerce and online shopping, which are popular uses of the Internet. Both secure websites and authentication go a ways toward ensuring that information sent over the Internet is relatively safe. However, most online shopping systems require the user to use a credit card in order to pay for goods being purchased. This opens up another security risk.

Unlike normal face-to-face credit card purchases that you make in a shop, online trading takes place remotely, which means that both the seller and the purchaser can be anywhere in the world. This naturally poses certain problems. For example, you as the buyer cannot be sure that the seller is in fact a bona fide business, and you may pay for something and never actually receive the goods. The same goes as far as the seller is concerned, whereby they cannot be certain that the credit card being used is not stolen or copied. However, these risks are present with both mail order and telephone-based shopping, so the Internet is not unique in this respect.

As with any other sensitive or confidential transaction, online shopping should not be a major security risk if you take the following precautions:

- Always purchase from reputable companies and make sure that any online shopping website provides comprehensive contact details about the company that you are dealing with such as telephone numbers, registered business address, and membership of any applicable trading organisations.

- Only deal with companies that use secure websites for online shopping, that is, websites that use `https` protocols for transactions.

- Be particularly wary of companies that allow you to specify an alternative delivery address other than the address of the credit card holder.

 Never send your credit card details in e-mail as plain (unencrypted) text. If such an e-mail were to be intercepted, your credit card details are too easily read.

Firewalls

Finally, in this section on security considerations, it is important to understand what is meant by the term *firewall* and what firewalls are used for.

When accessing the Internet, a wide range of different data traffic passes backwards and forwards between your PC and your ISP. Most of this traffic is fairly innocuous and poses no security threat to your computer system. However, it is perfectly possible that unknown to you, a person can gain direct access to the data stored on your PC. In order to prevent such unauthorised access to data, many organisations and some individuals use a device known as a firewall, which effectively blocks any attempts to access private data.

There are generally two types of firewalls: a special hardware device that sits between the PC and the connection to the Internet or a piece of software that runs on the PC itself. Both types of firewall are designed to check on both outgoing and incoming data and block any messages that do not meet specified security requirements. For example, any requests to transmit a file from your PC to someone else on the Internet that you have not explicitly instructed the computer to do are stopped by the firewall hardware or software.

Firewalls are particularly important when a PC is permanently connected to the Internet, as in the case with most broadband connections. A PC that is left unattended for long periods whilst still connected to the Internet is particularly vulnerable, and therefore should always be protected by a firewall device or software.

First Steps with the Web Browser

Now that you understand the concepts and terms associated with the Internet and looked at the security considerations, it's time to get on with some of the practicalities of accessing the Internet.

Assuming that you have either successfully established an Internet connection with your chosen ISP, or that you already had an existing Internet connection, you can proceed with the task of understanding the first steps of using a web browser.

In this initial section, you will see some basic procedures that allow you to

- Open (and close) a web browser application.

- Change the web browser home page.

- Display a web page both inside the current window and in a new window.

- Stop a web page from downloading.

- Refresh a web page.

- Use the available Help functions.

Opening a Web Browser

This section makes use of the Microsoft Internet Explorer (IE) version 6 software, which is supplied standard with Windows XP, to look at web pages. Follow these steps to open IE:

1. On your Windows Desktop, there should be an Internet Explorer icon, as shown in Figure 36.4. Double-click this icon with the left mouse button to start the application. If this icon is not on your Desktop, you can start the program by clicking the Start button on the Taskbar and choosing All Programs ➢ Internet Explorer.

FIGURE 36.4   The Internet Explorer icon on the Desktop

2. After starting IE, your system establishes a connection to your ISP. Normally, this is achieved using a utility called Dial-Up Networking (DUN), and depending on how your DUN program has been configured, you might see a window like the one shown in Figure 36.5. Enter the username and password that were assigned to you when you opened your account with your chosen ISP and click the Dial button to continue.

FIGURE 36.5 The Dial-up Connection window

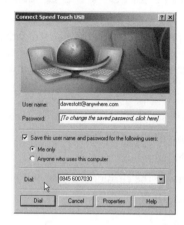

Once the connection has been established, you are logged on to the ISP's computer and the Dial-Up Connection box closes.

Internet Explorer now displays your home page, which is basically your starting point for browsing the World Wide Web (WWW). Normally, your home page is your ISP's default starting page (see Figure 36.6), but as you will see shortly, you can change this if you wish.

FIGURE 36.6 The Internet Explorer main window displaying a typical home page

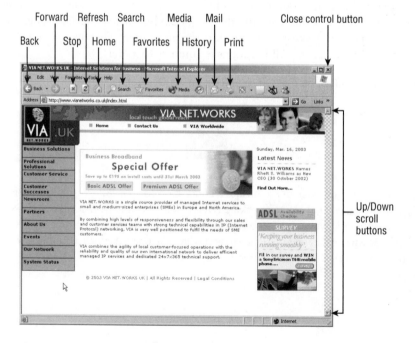

The buttons in your browser perform the following tasks:

Back The Back button takes you to the previous web page viewed.

Forward The Forward button takes you to the next web page (where applicable). Note that you can use the Forward button only if you have previously used the Back to move to a web page that you viewed earlier.

Stop The Stop button stops a web page from loading.

Refresh The Refresh button reloads the current web page.

Home The Home button takes you to your current home page.

Search The Search button opens a search pane on the left-hand side of the main window.

Favorites The Favorites button displays your saved favorite websites in a pane on the left-hand side of the main window.

Media The Media button displays the media control pane on the left-hand side of the main window.

History The History button displays a list of web pages that you have previously visited.

Mail The Mail button links to your e-mail software, generally, Outlook Express.

Print The Print button prints the currently displayed web page.

As noted earlier, Internet web pages are referenced by means of a special address called a URL. This is what appears in the Address box when a particular page is being displayed. You can type the address of a specific page for IE to find and display. For example, type `http://www1.bcs.org.uk` in the Address box and press the Enter key on your keyboard. This takes you to the British Computer Society website and displays the default start page, as shown in Figure 36.7.

FIGURE 36.7   The BCS home page displayed in Internet Explorer

Address box ⟶

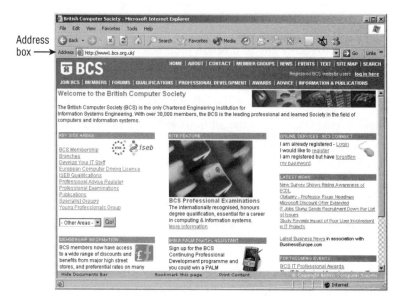

Changing Your Home Page

As mentioned previously, Internet Explorer uses a home page, which it displays each time the application is started. Whilst this is normally the start page of your chosen ISP, you can change it if you wish. Take the following steps to change your home page:

1. Make sure that the page you want to use as your new home page is already displayed in Internet Explorer, and then select Tools ➢ Internet Options on the menu bar. The Internet Options dialog box opens (see Figure 36.8).

FIGURE 36.8   Setting a new home page

2. Click the Use Current button and then the OK button to set your new home page to the page currently displayed by your browser.

Alternatively, from any web page, you can go to the Internet Options dialog box (Tools ➤ Internet Options) and type in the address of a web page to use as your home page in the Address box in the Home Page section and click OK. The next time you start Internet Explorer, it displays your new home page as your starting point for web browsing.

When typing in URLs in the Address box in Internet Explorer, you don't have to type the http:// at the beginning—this is the default. If you just type **www.microsoft.com**, the http:// is added automatically when you press the Enter key on your keyboard.

The Internet is extremely dynamic in nature, and things are changing all the time. Web pages in particular are being constantly updated, modified, and replaced. Therefore, you cannot always expect a particular page to appear exactly the same each time you visit a site. Don't be surprised if any of the examples used in this guide look completely different when you open them in Internet Explorer.

Using the Browser

One of the first things that you notice when using Internet Explorer is that as you move your mouse pointer around on a web page, it changes shape.

Normally, the mouse cursor is a simple arrow similar to the one you see in many applications. However, as you move across any hyperlinks, the cursor changes into a hand-shaped pointer to signify a link to another web page or to a different website. Try clicking a few hyperlinks on the BCS web page to see what happens.

By default, every time you click a hyperlink, the new web page is displayed in the same Internet Explorer window. However, you can force a hyperlink to open a new Internet Explorer window by holding down the Shift key on the keyboard whilst clicking a hyperlink with the mouse.

Whilst clicking a hyperlink normally opens the new web page in the same window, this is not always the case. The author or developer of the web page may instruct Internet Explorer to open a new window automatically when a hyperlink is used.

Using the Stop and Refresh Buttons

As mentioned previously, web pages frequently contain a mixture of text and graphics. In fact, some web pages do not contain any text and consist entirely of a single graphic image or multiple images. Simple text-only web pages download and display in your browser reasonably quickly, but more complex web pages with high-resolution graphics often take some time to download (depending on the speed of your Internet connection). Consequently, there may be occasions when you are waiting for a web page to download and you decide to cancel the download instead. You can do this by either pressing the Esc key on your keyboard or clicking the Stop button on the Internet Explorer toolbar, as shown in Figure 36.9. Notice that when you stop a web page from downloading, some of the text may already be displayed and maybe one or two images, but as in the web page shown in Figure 36.9, the information is incomplete.

FIGURE 36.9 Stopping a web page from downloading

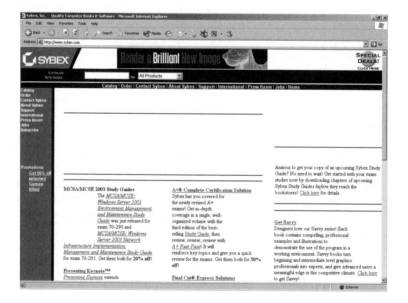

You can restart the web page download and display its entire contents by clicking the Refresh button on the IE toolbar. Figure 36.10 shows the same web page as Figure 36.9 after it has been refreshed and allowed to download completely.

FIGURE 36.10   Refreshing a web page

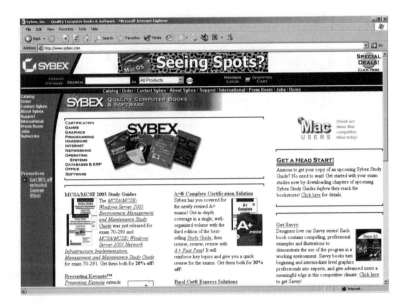

Certain web pages, especially those containing online news, are updated every two or three minutes; you may need to use the Refresh button frequently to see the latest updates.

Using the Help System in Internet Explorer

If you get stuck when using Internet Explorer, and you don't know how to perform a particular task, there is an in-built Help system where you might find an answer to your problem. Take the following steps to learn how to use IE Help:

1. You can access Help at any time by pressing the F1 key on your keyboard or by choosing Help ➢ Contents And Index. This displays a window with four tabbed sections: Contents, Index, Search, and Favorites. In addition, there is an easy-to-use web page–type interface on the right-hand side, with hypertext links to other Help pages, as shown in Figure 36.11.

FIGURE 36.11 The Internet Explorer Help system

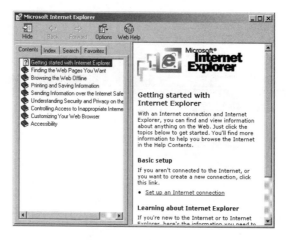

2. Clicking the Contents tab presents you with a list of Help contents for you to select from. Note that the main Contents sections may have sub-sections, as you can see in Figure 36.12.

FIGURE 36.12 The Help Topics Contents tab showing sub-sections

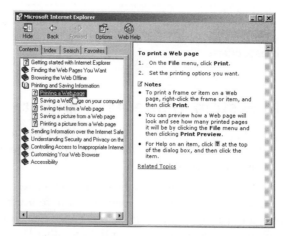

3. Selecting the Index tab displays a list of indexed keywords that are available in the Help system. Click the index word you want and then click the Display button, as shown in Figure 36.13.

FIGURE 36.13   You can search for keywords in the Index section.

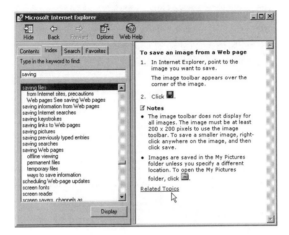

4. Clicking the Search tab allows you to look for any word or phrase, and the Help system then shows you any matches that it can find. Type a word or phrase such as **URL** in the box provided and then click the List Topics button. Once again, you simply select any topic that is found and click the Display button to see it, as in Figure 36.14.

FIGURE 36.14   The Search section lets you look for any words or phrases.

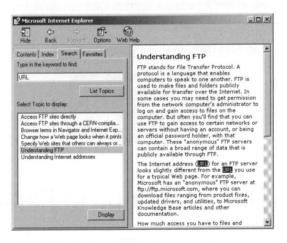

5. The Favorites tab allows you to save any Help topics for future reference, as shown in Figure 36.15.

FIGURE 36.15 The Favorites section lets you save any help topics for future reference.

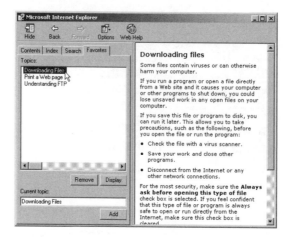

Closing Internet Explorer

To close Internet Explorer, choose File ➢ Close or click the Close control button in the main window. If you are connected to your ISP when you close Internet Explorer, you may see an Auto Disconnect dialog box asking you whether you want to stay connected or not, as shown in Figure 36.16. Normally you click the Disconnect Now button to terminate your telephone call. But you can, if you wish, click Stay Connected, so that if you start Internet Explorer again, you don't have to wait for a connection to be established before continuing to view other web pages.

FIGURE 36.16 The Auto Disconnect dialog box

Adjusting Basic Settings in Explorer

Now that you have seen how to start Internet Explorer, view web pages, and use the Help system, it's time to look at some of the basic settings that allow you to control and manage the application. In this section you will learn how to

- Modify the toolbar display.
- Display or hide images on a web page.

- Display previously visited URLs using the browser Address bar.
- View and delete browsing history.

Modifying the Toolbar Display

You can make adjustments to the toolbar options to customize Internet Explorer by taking the following steps:

1. If it is not already open, start Internet Explorer by double-clicking the icon on the Desktop or by choosing Start ➤ All Programs ➤ Internet Explorer. Once started, your current home page is displayed.

2. We've briefly mentioned toolbars in passing. If there is a tick next to a toolbar in the menu, then that toolbar is currently being displayed. If you wish to turn off a toolbar, simply select it again, removing the tick and removing the toolbar from your display. Choosing View ➤ Toolbars from the menu, you can turn the display of the Standard toolbar and the Address toolbar on and off. In addition, there is a toolbar called Links (which are predefined web page addresses). You can see all three toolbars in Figure 36.17.

FIGURE 36.17   All three Internet Explorer toolbars displayed

 You can quickly switch between the Normal and Full Screen views of a web page by pressing the F11 key on your keyboard.

Adjusting the General Display

Many web pages consist of a mixture of text and graphics. However, text downloads and displays itself far quicker than graphics, and there may be occasions when you wish to view a web page without displaying the graphics. Fortunately, you can do this in Internet Explorer by choosing Tools ➤ Internet Options and then clicking the Advanced tab, as shown in Figure 36.18. Under the Multimedia section, there is an option labelled Show Pictures. If you deselect this check box, then when you view a web page, the graphics are not displayed, as shown in Figure 36.19. To view the current web page without displaying the graphics, simply click the Refresh button on the Standard toolbar.

FIGURE 36.18 Preventing graphics from being displayed

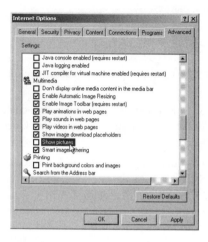

FIGURE 36.19 The BCS web page without graphics

The term *download* or *downloading* refers to the process of data transfer from a host computer such as a web server to a client computer such as your PC. The opposite is, of course, *upload* or *uploading*, whereby you are sending data from your PC to the host system.

Notice that when you turn off the Show Pictures option, the graphics themselves are no longer displayed, but the boxes that hold the images are still visible, as shown earlier in Figure 36.19. If you want to remove these image placeholders, as they are called, reselect the Show Pictures check box and deselect the Show Image Download Placeholders instead, as shown in Figure 36.20.

FIGURE 36.20   Removing the image placeholders

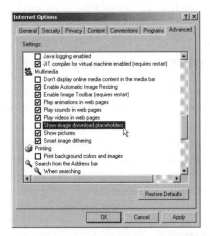

This then removes all the image boxes from the page, leaving just the text, as shown in Figure 36.21.

FIGURE 36.21   The BCS page without placeholders

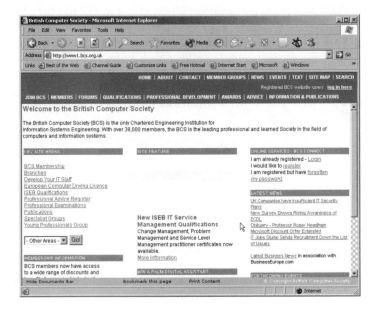

Certain pictures on web pages contain hypertext links to other web pages so that you can click them to display more information. If you turn off the displaying of graphics, these hypertext links will still be there on the page, and you can still use them in the same way. The only difference is you cannot easily see whereabouts on the page the links are without the graphics to guide you.

Using Internet Explorer's History Features

Internet Explorer keeps track of where you have been and has several features for making it convenient to find previously visited sites. Try out the History feature using the following steps:

1. Internet Explorer automatically keeps track of all the URLs that you type into the Address bar. You can use the drop-down list to select any of the web pages that you have recently visited and so return to them quickly and easily without having to retype the address. Click the drop-down list control on the right-hand side of the Address bar and select one of the URLs that you have previously visited, as shown in Figure 36.22.

FIGURE 36.22   Using the Address bar drop-down list to revisit a web page

2. A record of all the web pages that you visit is placed in a special History folder. You can view the contents of the History folder by selecting View ➢ Explorer Bar ➢ History or by clicking the History icon on the Standard toolbar. This displays a new window on the left-hand side of the screen, detailing all the web pages that you have visited over a specific time period, as shown in Figure 36.23.

FIGURE 36.23   The History folder displays all web pages that you have visited.

3. By default, Internet Explorer retains 20 days of records in the History folder, but you can adjust this time period if you wish. Similarly, you can clear or delete the contents of the History folder by selecting Tools ➢ Internet Options. On the General tab, click the Clear History button, as shown in Figure 36.24.

FIGURE 36.24 Deleting the contents of the History folder

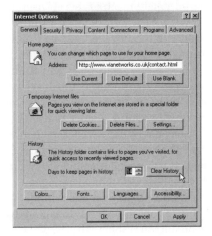

Summary

The first section of this chapter explained what you need in order to access the Internet and how to set up your PC to connect to an ISP. You also learnt some of the main concepts and terms associated with using the Internet and the differences between the WWW and the Internet.

There are several security considerations associated with using the Internet; you need to be aware of issues related to access control, digital certificates, encryption, viruses, fraud, and firewalls. Whilst security is an important factor in using the Internet, if the necessary precautions are taken, the risks associated with accessing the Internet are all manageable.

You learnt how to start Internet Explorer and display web pages by typing in URLs in the Address box. You now understand the makeup and structure of web addresses and how to display a given web page using both the Stop and Refresh buttons. Internet Explorer uses a home page when it starts; you learnt how to change this to any web page you like. If you get stuck, you can access the Internet Explorer Help system in order to solve problems. When you close Internet Explorer, you are given the option of disconnecting from your ISP.

Internet Explorer provides several options for controlling how a web page is displayed. For example, you can prevent graphics from being displayed and even stop the image placeholders from appearing on a web page.

You can control the display of the various toolbars available in Internet Explorer and use both the Address bar and the History folder to quickly and easily return to any web pages that you have visited in the past.

Chapter

37

Web Navigation

IN THIS CHAPTER YOU WILL LEARN HOW TO

- ✓ Go to a URL.
- ✓ Activate a hypertext or image link.
- ✓ Navigate backward and forward between web pages.
- ✓ Complete a web-based form.
- ✓ Make use of bookmarks.
- ✓ Organise bookmarks.

Now that you understand the basic principles of connecting to the Internet and viewing web pages with Internet Explorer (IE), you need to look at the various ways in which you can navigate around the WWW.

Accessing Web Pages

This section looks at accessing web addresses in more detail, and you will learn how to perform the following tasks:

- Open a URL (Uniform Resource Locator).

- Activate a hyperlink or image link.

- Navigate backward and forward between previously visited web pages.

- Complete a web-based form and enter information in order to carry out a transaction.

Basic Web Navigation

You'll begin your web-navigation exercise by using the Address bar, hyperlinks, and toolbar buttons to move between web pages. Take the following steps:

1. If it is not already open, start Internet Explorer either by double-clicking the IE icon on the Desktop or by choosing Start ➤ All Programs ➤ Internet Explorer. As soon as you have established an Internet connection and your current home page is displayed, you are ready to proceed.

2. As mentioned previously, most web pages contain hypertext links or hyperlinks that you can click to display further information. A hypertext link can take you to a different part of the same page (especially if it is a long page), a new page on the same website, or even a page on a completely different website (usually related in some way). For example, go to the BCS main page again by typing the address **www1.bcs.org.uk** in the Address box and pressing the Enter key on your keyboard or clicking the Go button.

3. Notice how some of the text on this page is displayed in blue and underlined. These are the hypertext links. Clicking them takes you to different web pages. As you move the mouse pointer over these hypertext links, the pointer changes from an arrow to a "pointing finger" symbol to indicate that this is a link that you can click to go somewhere else. On the BCS main web page, click the link called Branches, as shown in Figure 37.1.

FIGURE 37.1   Clicking a hypertext link to view another web page

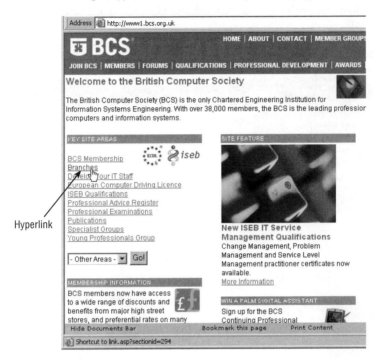

4. Click the List Of All Branches hyperlink on the left side or the Click Here hyperlink (see Figure 37.2) to display a complete list of BCS branches.

FIGURE 37.2   Selecting a hypertext link

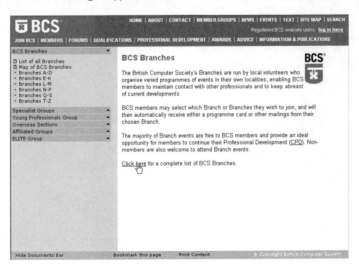

5. On the List of All Branches page, click the hyperlink for Manchester (see Figure 37.3). The BCS Manchester Branch page opens. Click the Manchester Branch Website hyperlink (see Figure 37.4).

FIGURE 37.3 Selecting another hypertext link

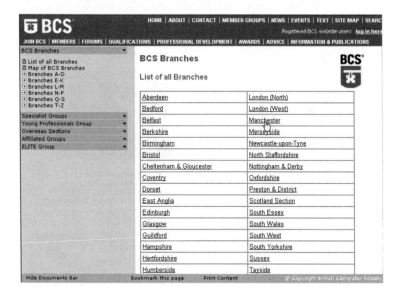

FIGURE 37.4 Selecting the last hypertext link in a chain

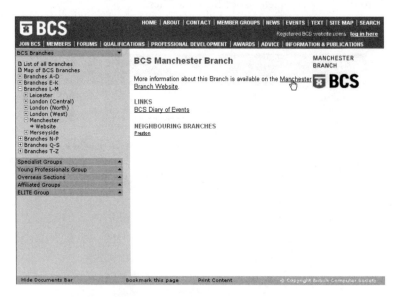

6. When the Manchester Branch home web page is displayed, notice in the Address bar that you have been taken to a completely different website at `http://www.ksap.demon.co.uk/bcs/`, as shown in Figure 37.5.

FIGURE 37.5   The www.ksap.demon.co.uk/bcs/ web page

7. To return to the previous web page, click the Back button on the toolbar. Once you have viewed a number of web pages, you can use the Back and Forward buttons to step through the web pages that Internet Explorer has previously displayed.

You've seen how hypertext links work, but images on web pages can also act as hyperlinks as well. For example, go back to the BSC home page using either the Back button on the toolbar, or select its URL from the Address bar drop-down list. This time, position your mouse pointer over the ECDL logo and click once, as shown in Figure 37.6.

FIGURE 37.6   Using an image hyperlink

When you click the ECDL image, you are taken to the BCS web page that displays information about the ECDL, as shown in Figure 37.7.

FIGURE 37.7 The BCS EDCL web page

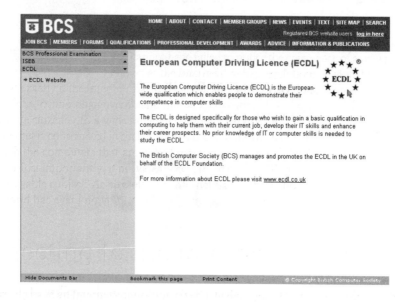

 When viewing a web page, it's not always obvious whether any images displayed actually have hyperlinks associated with them. The best approach is to sweep across any images using the mouse; any hyperlinks are indicated by the fact that the cursor changes from a simple pointer to a hand-shaped cursor.

Completing Web-Based Forms

Chapter 36, "The Internet," mentioned the fact that certain websites restrict access to either confidential or commercially valuable information, and many websites require a user to register with them before full access can be gained. The BCS website is an example of this. If you return to the BCS home page, notice on the right-hand side a section called Online Services – BCS Connect. Take these steps to register with the BCS:

1. Click the word Register, as shown in Figure 37.8.

FIGURE   37.8   The BCS hyperlink to register

2. Whilst BCS members can gain access to all the online services on offer, non-members can also register to gain limited access to certain services. So click the word Register in the Non Members section, as shown in Figure 37.9.

FIGURE   37.9   Starting the registration process

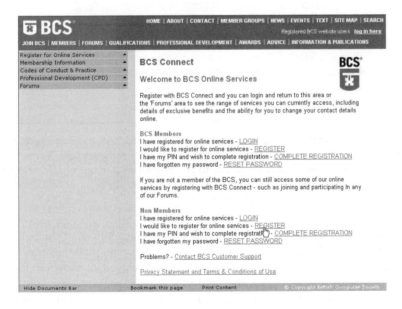

3. On the next page, click the New Details box to begin the registration process.

4. Look at the online form shown in Figure 37.10. Fill in the boxes with your details, making sure you scroll down to complete the whole form. Notice that certain fields are mandatory, and you cannot leave them blank. Also, if you point to the ? symbols, a tip is provided as to what to enter in a particular field. When you have finished entering all your details, click the Save button at the bottom of the page.

FIGURE 37.10 Entering details using an online form

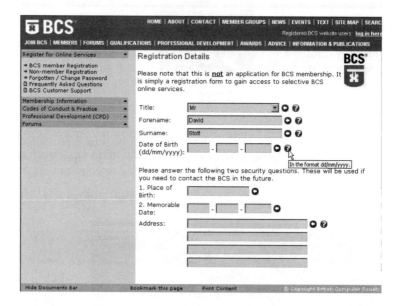

 Most online forms are pretty straightforward, and you just need to click each separate box with your mouse to enter the necessary text. Some boxes have drop-down lists to allow you to select from a list of options, for example, country or job title. Generally, you can use the Tab key on your keyboard to move to the next box (field) on a form.

5. Once you have completed the form and clicked the Save button at the bottom, your details are processed by the BCS. Assuming that you have not made any mistakes such as omitting a mandatory field, a confirmation page is displayed, as shown in Figure 37.11. You receive your Reference Number and PIN in two separate e-mails to the e-mail address you specified. You can subsequently use these details to log in to the BCS Online Services.

FIGURE 37.11   Confirmation after completing the BCS online form

Using Bookmarks

As you have seen previously, you can type a URL in the Address box in Internet Explorer. Provided that the page is currently available, it is displayed on your screen. However, web page addresses can be long and complicated, and it is very easy to make a mistake whilst typing an address. Fortunately, Internet Explorer has a feature known as Favorites that allows you to "bookmark" a page so that you can visit it again easily.

In this section you will learn how to

- Bookmark a web page.
- Display a bookmarked web page.
- Organise your bookmarks.

Creating a Favorite

The *Favorites* option in Internet Explorer enables you to bookmark a web page and subsequently open a bookmarked web page. Bookmarks or favorites are extremely easy to create, and any web page can be bookmarked for future reference using the following steps:

1. To create a favorite, you need to have the actual page that you want bookmarked displayed in Internet Explorer. Go to the page by typing the URL in the Address box and pressing the Enter key on the keyboard or by clicking a hypertext link from another web page.

2. Once the page you want to bookmark is displayed, select Favorites ➢ Add To Favorites. The Add Favorite dialog box opens, as shown in Figure 37.12.

FIGURE 37.12   Adding a specific web page to your list of favorites

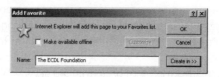

3. The Name box is automatically filled in with the page's title. However, you can overtype this suggestion with anything that you like.

4. Click the OK button, and the bookmark is saved in your Favorites list.

5. To open a bookmarked page, click the Favorites menu option and a drop-down list of your current favorites appears, as shown in Figure 37.13. Simply select the one you want, and Internet Explorer takes you to that page automatically.

FIGURE 37.13   Selecting a bookmarked favorite

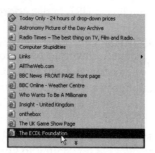

There is an alternative way to create and make use of bookmarks in Internet Explorer. Select View ➤ Explorer Bar ➤ Favorites from the menu or click the Favorites button on the toolbar. This opens a window on the left-hand side of the Internet Explorer main window that displays all your favorites. You can select any item in the list to activate the hyperlink to that web page, as shown in Figure 37.14. You can also add bookmarks by clicking the Add button at the top of the Favorites window.

FIGURE 37.14   Using the Favorites window

Organising Bookmarks

When you create a new bookmark, it is placed in the main Favorites folder by default. However, you can if you wish store a bookmark in a folder that you have created. Using folders can help you keep related bookmarks together and organised. Try these steps:

1. With the Add Favorite dialog box open, click the Create In button and a list of existing folders is displayed, as shown in Figure 37.15. Select the target folder and click OK.

FIGURE 37.15   Storing a favorite in a specific folder

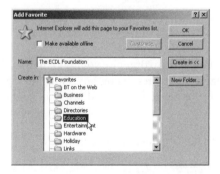

2. If you want to create a new folder to place your bookmark in, click the New Folder button and the Create New Folder dialog box opens, as shown in Figure 37.16. Type the name of the new folder and click OK.

FIGURE 37.16 Creating a new folder

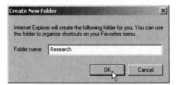

3. Note that any new folders are created in relation to where in the folder hierarchy (tree structure) you actually start from. In this example, the Research folder appears as a subfolder of Education, as shown in Figure 37.17.

FIGURE 37.17 The tree structure of folders

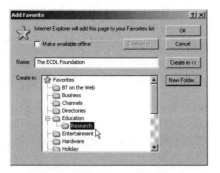

4. Internet Explorer also allows you to organise your bookmarks. Select Favorites ➤ Organize Favorites, and the Organize Favorites dialog box shown in Figure 37.18 opens. Here you can create folders, rename or delete folders and favorites, and move a folder or favorite to another folder.

FIGURE 37.18 Using the Organize Favorites window

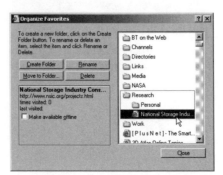

5. Finally, select an item in the scrolling list and click the Delete button. The Confirm Folder (or File) Delete window opens, as shown in Figure 37.19, and you're asked to confirm that you indeed want to delete that file or folder.

FIGURE 37.19   Confirming a deletion

Summary

In this chapter, you saw how it is possible to navigate through the WWW using hypertext links and the Back and Forward buttons on the toolbar. You also looked at how to complete any online forms that may be required in order to register with a website to gain access to restricted areas.

This chapter also described the various procedures required to create and use bookmarks or favorites. This feature is extremely useful if you intend to return to a particular web page sometime in the future—you don't have to remember the actual URL, which can be quite long and complicated.

Obviously, the more bookmarks that you have, the more likely you are to need to organise them properly. As a result, the facilities provided by Internet Explorer for organising your bookmarks are very useful in helping with this task.

Chapter

38

Web Searching and Printing

IN THIS CHAPTER YOU WILL LEARN HOW TO

- ✓ Make use of a search engine.
- ✓ Search for specific information by keyword or phrase.
- ✓ Duplicate text, images, and URLs from a web page to a document.
- ✓ Download and save web pages and web elements.
- ✓ Prepare Internet Explorer to print a web page.
- ✓ Print web pages.

With in excess of two billion web pages, the WWW is huge and growing all the time. As a result, it can often be very difficult to pinpoint specific information. Fortunately, the WWW itself comes to the rescue, as there are facilities widely available that you can use to search for information on the Internet. Whilst much of this information is likely to be viewed on screen, this chapter also describes how to produce printed hard copy as well.

Using a Search Engine

Search engines are just like other web pages, but they allow you to enter search terms in text form. The search engine then searches for these terms and displays the results on a new web page.

Initiating and Refining a Search

Internet Explorer (IE) has its own built-in Search capability, which can be accessed by clicking the Search button on the toolbar; by default, this feature uses the MSN search engine. This section uses a search engine called All the Web throughout the following exercises. Try it out using the following steps:

1. If it is not already loaded, start Internet Explorer by double-clicking the IE icon on the Desktop or by clicking the Start button on the Taskbar and selecting All Programs ➢ Internet Explorer.

2. Type **http://www.alltheWeb.com/** into the Address bar and press the Enter key on your keyboard. You should now see a web page similar to the one shown in Figure 38.1.

FIGURE 38.1   The All the Web search engine main page

3. You are going to use the All the Web search engine to look for information about collecting postage stamps and in particular, the Penny Black stamp featuring the head of Queen Victoria. Start by entering the word **stamps** in the Search box and clicking the Search button. A new page is displayed showing the results of the search. In this example, over six million web pages have been found containing the word "stamps," as shown in Figure 38.2.

FIGURE 38.2   Initial search on stamps

4. This is obviously far too many web pages to look at in detail; you need to narrow your search down a little. So add the words **Penny Black** after *stamps* in the Search box and click the Search button again. This time, the results displayed have been reduced to a little over 210,000, as shown in Figure 38.3. Whilst this is better, it is still too many websites to look at in detail.

FIGURE 38.3   Narrowing down your search

5. You can refine your search even further by adding more words. This time add "**Queen Victoria**", including the double quotes, which tells the search engine to look for the exact two words in combination rather than the word *Queen* and the word *Victoria* separately. This time, your results are even smaller, with fewer than 13,000 web pages found, as shown in Figure 38.4.

FIGURE 38.4   Refining your search

6. Notice how each of the words you entered as your search criteria is highlighted in bold in the results displayed, which helps you decide whether a particular web page is relevant. Click any of the hyperlinks listed, and that specific page is displayed. Use the Back button on the toolbar to return to the search results page.

7. Each time you refine your search criteria by adding extra words or when you enclose words in double quotes to form search phrases, you reduce the number of web pages that the search engine finds. You can also exclude specific words from your search to reduce the number of results. For example, enter "**The Planets Suite**" (make sure you surround the phrase with double quotes) in the Search box and click the Search button. As you might

expect, nearly every one of the 900-odd results contains a reference to the composer Holst, as shown in Figure 38.5.

FIGURE 38.5   Search for "The Planets Suite"

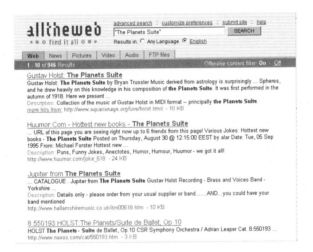

8. However, if you exclude the word *Holst* by changing the Search box to read "**The Planets Suite**"-**Holst** (note the use of the minus sign), the number of web pages found is dramatically reduced to less than 90, as you can see in Figure 38.6. This is an example of using a logical operator in a search engine. Different Internet search engines use different techniques to achieve the same sort of results. Generally, on each search engine website, there is a hypertext link to a Help page that gives you specific instructions on how to use the system effectively.

FIGURE 38.6   Using a logical operator to reduce search results

There are many different search engines available on the WWW, and each offers its own particular features and benefits. Some of the most popular ones are listed here for you to try out:

```
http://www.altavista.com
http://www.askjeeves.com
http://www.excite.com
http://www.alltheWeb.com
http://www.google.com
http://www.hotbot.com
http://www.inktomi.com
http://www.lycos.com
http://search.msn.com
http://search.netscape.com
http://www.Webcrawler.com
http://www.yahoo.com
```

Using and Saving Search Results

Displaying information and images in your browser is obviously very useful, but occasionally you might want to incorporate some part of a web page in a document that you are writing in another application. Or you may wish to save your search results as a file on your computer you can refer to later.

Duplicating Web Information in Microsoft Word

Let's see how to duplicate text from the Web into Microsoft Word using the following steps:

1. Start by going to the ECDL home page by typing **www.ecdl.com** in the Address bar (or select it from your list of Favorites if you have bookmarked this page). As you can see from the example in Figure 38.7, this page consists of a mixture of both text and graphic images.

FIGURE 38.7   The ECDL home page

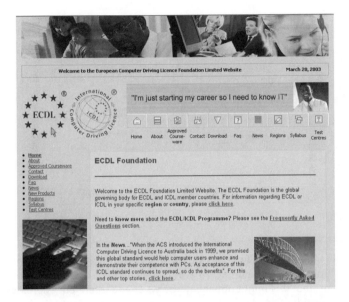

2. In order to duplicate a part of this page in a Word document, you first need to select whatever it is you want to copy. Using the mouse, click and drag the mouse pointer across an area of text, and it is highlighted, as shown in Figure 38.8.

FIGURE 38.8   Selecting text on a web page

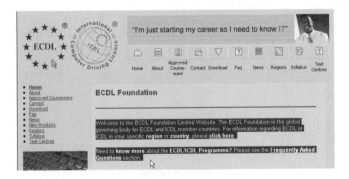

3. Next, with the area of text still selected, choose Edit ➢ Copy. This copies the text into the Windows Clipboard. Now if you start Microsoft Word with a new document, you can duplicate the copied text from the Windows Clipboard into your document by choosing Edit ➢ Paste, as shown in Figure 38.9.

FIGURE 38.9   Duplicating text from a web page in a Word document

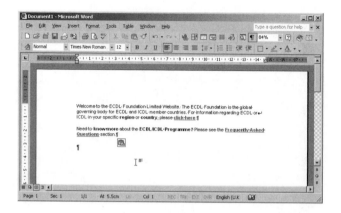

 WARNING   The Windows Clipboard stores only one item at a time. Whenever you use the Edit ≻ Paste function, whatever was last cut or copied to the Clipboard is pasted; this might not always be what you intended. Therefore, you should consider Cut and Paste or Copy and Paste as a single function.

You can do the same with graphic images on a web page, but the method of selecting an image is slightly different from selecting text:

1. Deselect the text that you selected in step 2 by clicking a blank area of the web page. Now, use the right-hand mouse button to click the image at the top of the ECDL home page. A pop-up menu opens, as shown in Figure 38.10.

FIGURE 38.10   Selecting an image to copy into the Windows Clipboard from a web page

2. Click the Copy option and the image is copied into the Windows Clipboard. You can now switch back to your Microsoft Word document and choose Edit ➢ Paste to insert a copy of the image into your document, as shown in Figure 38.11.

FIGURE 38.11 Duplicating an image from a web page into a Word document

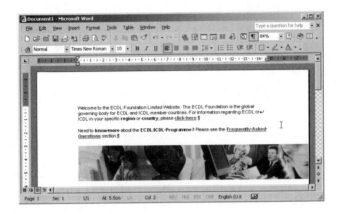

 If the text or image that you select on a web page for duplicating contains a hyperlink, then when you right-click it with the mouse, you are given the option of copying the shortcut (the actual URL) rather than just the selected text or image itself. You can then paste the shortcut into a document, and it becomes what is known as an *embedded hyperlink*.

Saving Results for Offline Use

In order to access and view a web page, you must be online to the Internet so that the information can be retrieved from the appropriate web server. However, it is also possible to view web pages that are stored locally on your own PC. Therefore, Internet Explorer gives you the option of saving a web page so that you can view it when you are offline. This can be useful if you wish to keep a particular web page for future reference, or if you wish to avoid paying for the telephone call in order to read a long, detailed page of information. Try out these steps:

1. Make sure that the ECDL home page is displayed in your browser. Choose File ➢ Save As, and the Save Web Page dialog box opens, as shown in Figure 38.12.

FIGURE 38.12 The Save Web Page dialog box

2. By default, Internet Explorer uses the My Documents folder to store any web pages that you save, but you can select a different folder using the Save In drop-down list. Internet Explorer also uses the actual web page name as the filename for the saved page; you can change this if you wish. To save the page, click the Save button and the Save Web Page window closes.

To open a web page that you have previously saved, follow these steps:

1. Choose File ➢ Open, and the Open dialog box like the one in Figure 38.13 opens.

FIGURE 38.13 The Open dialog box

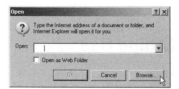

2. Click the Browse button, select the My Documents folder, and click the Open button. Select the file that you want to open, as shown in Figure 38.14, and then click Open again. The web page you selected is displayed in Internet Explorer.

As well as saving web pages as HTML documents, you can also save them as plain text files by using the drop-down list in the Save As Type box in the Save Web Page window shown earlier in Figure 38.12. However, if you do this, the text file that is saved cannot contain any graphics and cannot be subsequently opened in Internet Explorer. You can open web pages saved as text files in other applications such as WordPad or Microsoft Word.

FIGURE 38.14   Opening a saved web page

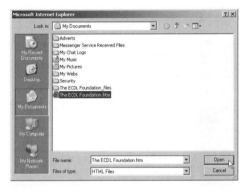

You have just seen how you can save web pages for viewing when offline, but there are other ways that you can collect data from web pages. For example, try these steps:

1. Enter **metalab.unc.edu/wm/paint/auth/vinci/joconde/joconde.jpg** in the Address bar and press the Enter key on your keyboard. You should now see a picture of the Mona Lisa. If you position your mouse pointer over this image, you see a small box with four icons in it. Click the leftmost icon, which has the symbol of a disk, as shown in Figure 38.15.

FIGURE 38.15   Saving an image file from a web page

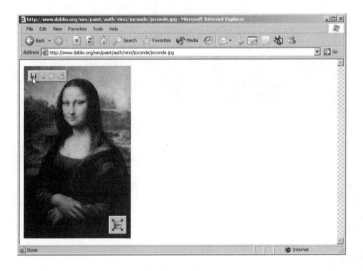

2. A new Save Picture window opens that allows you to save the image as a file. Type the words Mona Lisa in the File Name box and click Save, as shown in Figure 38.16. Also notice that when you place the mouse pointer over the image, another button appears in the lower-right corner; this can be used to enlarge the image on the web page.

FIGURE 38.16 Saving an image as a file

Downloading Files from the Internet

Certain web pages offer the option of downloading information in the form of files. This uses a special Internet feature called the File Transfer Protocol (FTP) to transfer data from a website and enables you to save a file directly to your PC's hard disk. Take the following steps to download a file from the Internet:

1. Go back to the ECDL home page and click the Download icon, as shown in Figure 38.17.

FIGURE 38.17 Selecting the ECDL Download icon

2. You are given the option to download two different files. Select the Acrobat Reader file to download, as shown in Figure 38.18.

FIGURE 38.18   Selecting the Acrobat Reader file

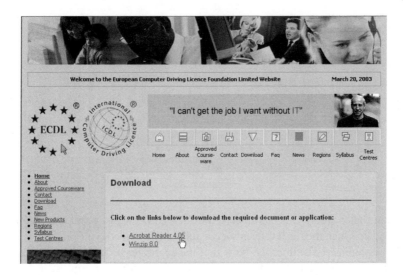

 Many documents on the WWW are stored as Acrobat files, and you need a copy of Acrobat Reader installed on your PC in order to display such files.

3.   When you click this hyperlink, a File Download window opens, as shown in Figure 38.19.

FIGURE 38.19   Saving a download file to disk

4.   Select the option to save the file, and the Save As window opens asking you where you wish to save the file, as shown in Figure 38.20. Select an appropriate location and click Save.

FIGURE 38.20   Specifying a location for saving a file download

5.   When you click Save, the file is transferred from the host website and is saved on your local PC hard disk. Once the file has been successfully downloaded, you can access it even when you are not online to the Internet. Note that the example you have downloaded is an application that needs to be installed (set up) on your PC before you can use it.

There are wide variety of files that you can download from the WWW, including plain text, images, sound, video, and software files. However, when downloading files from web sites, there are three issues you need to be aware of:

Copyright   Certain information on the Internet—whether it is text, graphics, audio, or video—is subject to copyright restrictions. Therefore, before you download anything, you should check whether an item is copyright protected.

Large files   Many image, audio, and video files are extremely large, and consequently, they can take a long time to download (especially if your connection to the Internet is slow). Downloading large files can be an expensive procedure, but fortunately you can cancel the operation at any time.

Viruses   Any file that contains executable code—a program or a document with macros in it—can contain a virus that may damage or delete any data stored on your hard disk. Therefore, you should use appropriate anti-virus software to check any files that you download from a website before running them.

WARNING   Make sure that you are aware of the possible dangers, responsibilities, and complications that might arise from downloading files from the Internet.

Printing Web Pages

Whilst most users of the Internet tend to view information solely on the screen, there may be occasions when you want to print some information from a web page.

This section assumes that the PC that you are using to perform the following exercises has a suitable printer attached to it and that it is properly configured for use by the Windows XP operating system. Should this not be the case, any tasks that require you to actually print a web page should be modified to print the output to a file instead.

Preparing to Print a Web Page

Before actually printing anything from Internet Explorer, there are one or two things that you need to do to prepare the output:

1. If it is not already open, start Internet Explorer by either double-clicking the IE icon on the Desktop or by choosing Start ➤ All Programs ➤ Internet Explorer. As soon as you have established an Internet connection and your current home page is displayed, you are ready to proceed.

2. Any web page that is currently being displayed in Internet Explorer can be printed. However, before you print, you may wish to see what the actual printed page will look like. You can do this easily by selecting File ➤ Print Preview. This displays the web page in a new window, as shown in Figure 38.21.

FIGURE 38.21   The Print Preview window showing how a web page will be printed

3. The Print Preview window shows you how the web page will be printed. If the output would result in multiple pages being printed, you can display each page by clicking the Next Page or Previous Page icons as appropriate. Click the Close button when you have finished previewing the page, and you are returned to the normal browser view of the web page.

4. Prior to printing, you may need to adjust the setup options for the page. To do this, choose File ➢ Page Setup, and the Page Setup dialog box opens (see Figure 38.22).

FIGURE 38.22 The Page Setup dialog box

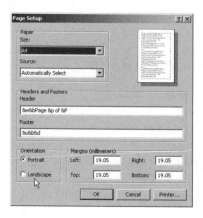

5. Here you can specify the paper size you intend to use; define any headers or footers to be printed on each page; select either portrait or landscape mode for the printed pages; and adjust the page margins. You can also select a specific printer to use. Once you are satisfied with your chosen page settings, click OK to close the dialog box.

Printing Web Results

Once you have done the necessary preparation, it's relatively simple to actually print a web page. To print a web page, choose File ➢ Print, and the Print dialog box opens, as shown in Figure 38.23. Here you can select the page range and specify the number of copies you want to print. Click the Print button to start the print process.

FIGURE 38.23   Controlling the printing process

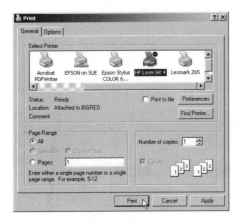

If there isn't a printer available on your system, you may have to print the web page to a file instead. If this is the case, follow these steps:

1. Make sure there is a tick in the Print To File box in the Print window, as shown in Figure 38.24.

FIGURE 38.24   Opting to print to a file if no printer is available

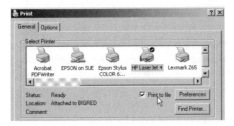

2. When you click Print to start printing to a file, you are asked to provide an filename, as shown in Figure 38.25.

FIGURE 38.25   Specifying a filename for printing

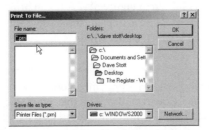

Occasionally you might wish to print a specific area of a web page such as the results from a search engine. You can do this by following these steps:

1. Select an area on the currently displayed web page by clicking with the left mouse button and dragging the pointer across this area, which turns blue as you select it, as shown in Figure 38.26.

FIGURE 38.26 Selecting an area of a web page for printing

2. Choose File ➢ Print and click the Selection option in the Print Range area. Only the area selected on your web page is printed.

Because they are primarily intended to be displayed on a monitor, many web pages make extensive use of colour graphics and patterned backgrounds. You may find that if you print them out using a monochrome printer, they can be quite difficult to read.

Many web pages use a system of *frames*, which are a bit like static borders that stay the same when you click a hyperlink to another web page. As well as selected areas of text to print, you can also choose to print specific frames on a web page. You do this by following these steps:

1. Click the Options tab in the Print window.

2. Select one of the following options: As Laid Out On Screen, Only The Selected Frame, or All Frames Individually, as shown in Figure 38.27. If you print the BSC home page with the option All Frames Individually, you will print three separate pages, with a frame on each page rather than the single web page as a whole.

Instead of using the File ➢ Print menu option, you can simply click the Print icon on the Toolbar. However, if you do this, you forego the opportunity to change any print settings. The printout is produced using the default settings, which are the current default Windows printer, print all pages, and print one copy of the current web page.

FIGURE 38.27   Choosing to print separately all frames of a web page

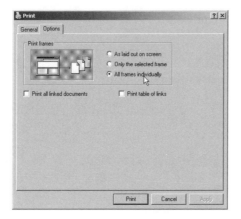

Close Internet Explorer by selecting File ➤ Close or by clicking the Close control button on the main window. If you are connected to your ISP when you close Internet Explorer, you may see an Auto Disconnect dialog box asking whether you want to stay connected or not. Click the Disconnect Now button to terminate your telephone call.

Summary

This chapter explained how you can use search engines to find specific information on the Internet. By including more words and using double quotes around words and phrases, you can reduce the results of a search in order to home in on whatever specific information you are looking for. In addition, you can use logical operators to refine your searches so that they are more accurate. As with most things to do with the WWW, you should explore the Internet and experiment with different search engines to see which ones best suit your needs.

You have seen how you can duplicate parts of a web page in a word processing file and how to download certain files for use locally. You've also seen how to use the Print Preview option to see what a printed web page will actually look like on paper before it's printed. You learnt the various ways that you can customise the printed output by, say, printing in landscape orientation or adjusting the margins on the page.

The final topic of this chapter described how easy it is to print any web page that is currently displayed in Internet Explorer. You can control the page setup and the print process by using the options on the menu bar. If necessary, you can also select specific areas of a web page to be printed.

Chapter

39

Electronic Mail

IN THIS CHAPTER YOU WILL LEARN HOW TO

- ✓ Recognise the makeup and structure of an e-mail address.
- ✓ Appreciate the advantages of e-mail.
- ✓ Value the use of network etiquette.
- ✓ Appreciate the security implications of using e-mail.
- ✓ Take the first steps in using an e-mail application.
- ✓ Adjust the settings in an e-mail application.

Now that you understand the essential elements of using Internet Explorer to access the WWW, it's time to look at a completely different aspect of using the Internet: electronic mail, or e-mail as it is generally known.

For this part of the guide, we will be using Microsoft Outlook Express version 6, which is supplied as standard with Windows XP.

Essentially, *e-mail* is a mechanism for sending text messages from one computer user to another. This was one of the first real business applications used extensively on the Internet. Even today, e-mail is still the most widely used application on the Internet. A basic e-mail message consists of the recipient's address, an optional subject line, and a message body containing lines of text.

Over the last few years, the use of e-mail has exploded and now over 33 billion e-mail messages are sent each day. This growth in e-mail use is likely to continue, and it has been predicted that by 2006, there will be over 60 billion e-mail messages sent daily. Just to put this into context, the U.S. Postal Service, the world's largest carrier of conventional mail, handled 203 billion packages and letters during the whole of 2002, or the equivalent of around six days' worth of e-mail messages.

Used properly, e-mail is an extremely efficient and effective form of communication. From its early beginnings, e-mail has evolved from being able to send short, simple, text-only messages into a versatile communications medium that can be used to transmit all kinds of electronic data. This versatility has effectively killed off previously well-established technologies such as the Telex and the fax machine. Therefore, it's not surprising that it has grown in popularity at a phenomenal rate.

Setting Up Outlook Express

With an Internet connection and *Outlook Express*, you can exchange e-mail messages with anyone on the Internet. But first you need to set up Outlook Express to access the e-mail account provided by your chosen ISP. Take the following steps:

1. On your Windows Desktop, there should be an Outlook Express icon, as shown in Figure 39.1. Double-click this icon with the left mouse button to start the application. If this icon is not on your Desktop, you can start the program by choosing Start ➤ All Programs ➤ Outlook Express.

FIGURE 39.1   The Outlook Express icon on the Desktop

2. When you start Outlook Express for the very first time, you see a Welcome screen like the one in Figure 39.2. If there are no mail accounts already in existence, you must run the Internet Connection Wizard to set up a new mail account before proceeding any further. If the Internet Connection Wizard does not start automatically when you start Outlook Express, you can access it by choosing Tools ➤ Accounts from within Outlook Express itself. An Internet Accounts window opens, as shown in Figure 39.3.

FIGURE 39.2   Running Outlook Express for the first time

FIGURE 39.3   Creating a new mail account

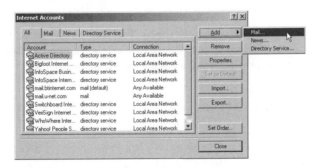

3. Click the Add button in the Internet Accounts window and select Mail. The Internet Connection Wizard starts.

4.   The Internet Connection Wizard helps you connect to one or more e-mail servers. You need the following information from your Internet service provider (ISP) or local area network (LAN) administrator: your account name and password and the names of your incoming and outgoing e-mail servers. The wizard guides you through the process step by step, and once completed, you have an e-mail account set up to use with Outlook Express.

E-mail Basics

Before using an e-mail application, let's start by explaining some of the most common concepts and terms associated with using e-mail. This section discusses the following topics:

- The makeup and structure of an e-mail address
- The advantages of e-mail
- The importance of network etiquette (netiquette)

E-mail Addresses

An *e-mail address* consists of two distinct parts, a name followed by a location in the format:

name@location

The @ sign is used as a separator between the recipient's name (username) and their location (*host name* or *domain name*) on the Internet.

The name part of an e-mail address refers to the recipient's mailbox and can take a variety of different forms such as

```
SmithJ
J.Smith
John.Smith
John_Smith
JOHNSMITH
```

The location part of the address refers to the mail server, the computer where the recipient has an electronic mailbox. It's usually the name of the user's ISP or a company or organisation that runs its own domain on the Internet, as in the following examples:

```
@microsoft.com
@bbc.co.uk
@u-net.com
@galaxy.net
```

Generally, e-mail addresses can consist of any combination of alphanumeric characters and can be either uppercase or lowercase characters, or a mixture of the two. Whilst full stops are usually allowed, spaces are not, hence the use of the underline (_) character to denote a space.

The Advantages of E-mail

Without doubt, the primary advantage of e-mail over conventional letter post is the speed of delivery. Even allowing for transmission delays and holdups associated with busy servers, an e-mail sent from the U.K. can arrive in a recipient's mailbox in, for example, Australia, in just a couple of minutes. It is this relative immediacy that has revolutionised communications, particularly in the commercial world.

The second most significant advantage that e-mail has is cost. Typically, the cost of sending a conventional letter is related to the physical distance involved, so it's more expensive to send a letter from Paris to Tokyo than it is to send the same letter from Paris to Lyon. With e-mail, this distance-related cost does not apply, and it costs the same to send an e-mail from anywhere in the world to anywhere else in the world. Similarly, the cost of sending a letter to several recipients is generally a straightforward multiple of an individual mail cost, but with e-mail you can send the same message to several recipients at no extra cost. Lastly, mail charges for letters often depend on their weight, but generally there are no additional costs when sending large e-mails.

The third major advantage of e-mail over conventional mail is one of convenience. With many physical mail systems, your mail is delivered to your specific address, which is fine if you are there to deal with it. But if you are away, the mail has to be redirected or forwarded to you at another location, which takes time. E-mail, on the other hand, uses the mailbox model, so you can collect your e-mail from a mail server from wherever you happen to be at the time. Most importantly, you don't have to physically go to your mailbox in order to collect your e-mail; you merely have to send an instruction to the mail server to send any e-mail to your PC running your e-mail software. Some e-mail services even allow you to store and manage your e-mail online via the WWW.

Network Etiquette

The Internet is a vast global community, with a whole range of user types from businessmen to academics to schoolchildren, and, over the years, accepted methods of communicating via e-mail have evolved. These are commonly referred to as *network etiquette* or *Netiquette*. As with any other form of written communication, it is not just the actual words you use, but the way in which you present things that is important. Therefore, Netiquette or good manners are essential elements of e-mail.

Whilst there are no strict rules regarding Netiquette, there are certain recognised recommendations that you should consider when using e-mail:

- If you access the Internet as part of your job, check with your employer about their policy regarding the use of e-mail.

- Don't assume that e-mail is completely secure. Never put in an e-mail message anything you would not put on a postcard. In other words, do not use offensive language or resort to any form of racial, sexual, or religious abuse.

- If you are forwarding or reposting a message, don't change the original wording. Always quote the original in its entirety. However, you may delete the original message provided that you indicate that it has been cut out.

- If you are replying to a message, quote only the relevant parts. The sender already has a copy of the original, so there is generally no need to repeat its contents back to them.

- Never send chain letters, as they merely waste other people's time and simply increase Internet traffic.

- Do not send heated or extremely argumentative, personally critical messages (also known as *flames*). If you receive such a message, it is best to simply ignore it.

- Take care with addressing mail. A mistake of even a single character can mean the e-mail is sent to the wrong recipient.

- Despite the relative speed of e-mail, always allow time for mail to be received and replied to, keeping in mind time differences around the world and other people's busy schedules.

- Keep your e-mail messages short and concise. Don't make them too long, unless the receiver is expecting a verbose message. Most e-mails are less than 20 lines in length; anything over 100 lines is considered long.

- Remember the Internet is a global community, and other people's values and outlook on life may be different to your own. Be tolerant of other cultures and try to avoid slang or phrases that may not be understood in another country.

- Always use mixed case. Using solely lowercase and lack of line breaks or punctuation makes messages very difficult to read. UPPERCASE LOOKS AS IF YOU'RE SHOUTING.

- All e-mails should have an appropriate subject header that reflects the content of the message.

- Always check your spelling and grammar, as this reflects on your attitude towards the recipient.

- Unsolicited e-mail advertising is unwelcome (and forbidden in many countries). So never forward or resend any junk e-mail that you receive.

- When attaching files, don't send any larger than about 50KB, unless you have made prior arrangements with the recipient.

- Bear in mind that like most other forms of written communication, e-mail cannot convey context clues such as body language or intonation. Choose your words carefully and try to make your message as clear as possible.

Abiding by the preceding recommendations should ensure that you never upset any intended recipients of your e-mail messages. This will enable you to use e-mail as an effective method of modern communication.

E-mail Security Considerations

One of the most important aspects of using e-mail is security, and there are certain issues that you need to consider to protect any confidential information that may be transmitted via the Internet.

Unsolicited E-mail

Whilst the ease with which e-mail can be sent via the Internet is one of its main advantages, it is also a possible drawback when it comes to the problem of unsolicited e-mail. Just as you cannot prevent anyone sending you advertising material in the form of junk mail through the normal mail system, so you cannot stop anyone sending you junk e-mail via the Internet. Indeed, direct marketing, as it is known, is a huge worldwide business, and it's only natural that businesses and individuals would exploit the ability of mass e-mailing in order to reach a large potential audience cheaply. However, economics aside, junk e-mail has become a major problem on the Internet, and it is generally frowned upon.

Spam is an alternative name for junk (mass unsolicited) e-mail. This term is now fairly common, and it derives from a British TV comedy programme called Monty Python's Flying Circus, first broadcast in the late 1960s. The actual sketch involves a restaurant that serves all its meals with lots of Spam (a spiced ham product), and the waitress repeats the word several times in describing how much spam is in the items on the menu. And so the word *spam* has become associated with something that is repeated ad nauseum such as junk e-mail.

How does junk e-mail work, and why is there so much of it on the Internet? Basically, marketing companies (or individuals) either buy or acquire extremely large lists of e-mail addresses (a CD-ROM can often store 600 million e-mail addresses) and then blindly sent out junk e-mail messages to them in the hope of either selling something or simply promoting their business. Many e-mail addresses are also collected via registration forms for accessing websites, and once you are on someone's e-mail list, you are a potential target for junk e-mail.

Most junk e-mail is just fairly innocuous advertising, but it may contain offensive material such as pornography or even illegal material. Therefore, you need to be wary of any dubious unsolicited e-mail; the best approach is to simply delete it unread.

Many junk e-mails give you the option of removing yourself from a list by replying to a specific address. However, you should *not* respond to such requests to be removed from a list, as it frequently just notifies the sender of the junk e-mail that your e-mail address is legitimate and being actively used.

Viruses

The other major security problem associated with using e-mail concerns the issue of computer viruses. Whenever an e-mail containing an attached file is received, there is the potential that your computer system may become infected by a virus.

There are two important ways that you can protect yourself from virus infections when using e-mail:

- Be wary of any unsolicited e-mails containing attached files sent from people you don't personally know.
- Make sure that your PC has an appropriate anti-virus program installed and that it is kept up-to-date.

Digital Signatures

As more people send confidential information by e-mail, it is increasingly important to be sure that messages sent in e-mail are not forged, and to be certain that messages you send cannot be intercepted and read by anyone other than your intended recipient.

One way of achieving this is to make use of what are known as *digital signatures* or *digital IDs*, which effectively prove the identity of a sender in the same way that your signature does on a physical letter.

By using digital signatures, you can prove your identity in electronic transactions in a way that is similar to showing your driver's license when you cash a cheque. You can also use a digital signature to encrypt messages, thus keeping them private.

First Steps with E-mail

Now that you understand the general concepts and terms associated with using e-mail and looked at the security considerations, it's time to get on with some of the practicalities of sending and receiving e-mail messages. In this section, you will learn how to

- Open an e-mail application.
- Open a mail inbox for a specified user.
- Open mail messages.
- Switch between open messages.
- Close a mail message.
- Use application Help functions.
- Close the e-mail application.

Opening Outlook

Assuming that you have successfully set up an appropriate e-mail account in Outlook Express, let's start by looking at the Outlook Express window in detail using the following steps:

1. If it is not already open, start Outlook Express by double-clicking the Outlook Express icon on your Desktop or by choosing Start ➢ All Programs ➢ Outlook Express. A window appears similar to that in Figure 39.4.

This section assumes that only a single mail account has been set up for Outlook Express to use. If this is not the case, you have to select the appropriate account to use throughout this and the following exercises. To do this, choose Tools ➢ Accounts from the Outlook Express menu bar and click the Mail tab. Select the appropriate mail account to use and then click the Set As Default button. Finally, click the Close button to exit the window and return to Outlook Express.

FIGURE 39.4   The Outlook Express window

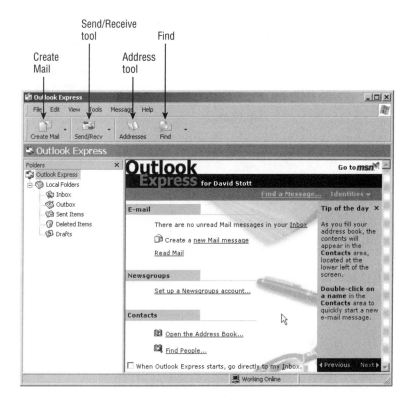

2. Click the word Inbox, which is listed in the Folders section of the main window. (If the Folders section is not visible, choose View ➢ Layout and make sure that there is a tick in the Folders list box.) Your screen should now look similar to Figure 39.5.

If you are using Outlook Express for the first time, it's highly unlikely that you will have any e-mail messages in your Inbox to view. There are two ways that you can solve this problem: Ask a friend or colleague to send you some sample e-mail messages to the e-mail address that you used to set up Outlook Express, or send yourself some sample e-mails using the procedures described in the upcoming "Sending Messages" section.

FIGURE 39.5 Viewing the contents of your Inbox

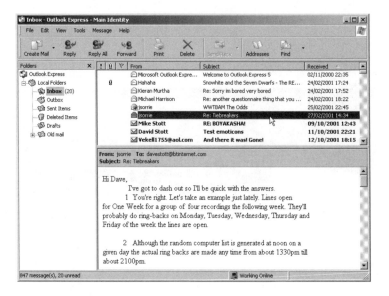

Viewing E-mail Messages

The main Outlook Express window is split into two areas. At the top is a list of e-mail messages that have been received in the order in which they arrived. Next to each e-mail message is a small envelope icon that indicates mail that has been read, and any messages that are unread. Take the following steps to view your e-mail messages:

1. To read an e-mail message, simply click the message header that appears in the top window, and the body of the message is displayed in the bottom window. The envelope icons change automatically as you read each mail message. To the right of the envelope icon is the sender's name or e-mail address, followed by the subject line and the timestamp indicating when the message was received. At the bottom of the window is a preview of the actual e-mail message whose header is selected in the window above.

2. If you double-click a message header, a new window opens up that displays both the e-mail header and the message itself, as shown in Figure 39.6.

3. Using the option to display a message in a separate window means that you can select several different messages and view their contents at the same time, as shown in Figure 39.7. The various message windows can be minimised so that they appear on the Taskbar at the bottom of your main Windows screen, where you can switch between each one individually to view them.

FIGURE 39.6 Viewing an e-mail message in the message window

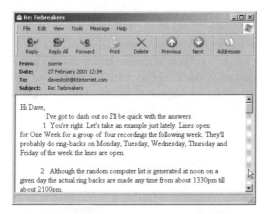

FIGURE 39.7 Opening several messages in separate windows at the same time

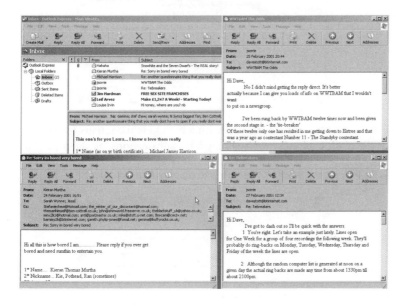

4. To close a message window, click the Close button in the top right-hand corner of the appropriate window.

Using the Outlook Express Help Feature

As with other Microsoft applications covered in this book, Outlook Express has a Help feature to help when you need it. Take these steps to learn how to use it:

1. If you get stuck when using Outlook Express, you can access the online Help system at any time by pressing the F1 key on your keyboard or choosing Help ➢ Contents And Index. This displays a window with three tabbed sections: Contents, Index, and Search. In addition, there is an easy-to-use, web page–type interface on the right-hand side with hypertext links to other help pages, as shown in Figure 39.8.

FIGURE 39.8 Accessing Help in Outlook Express

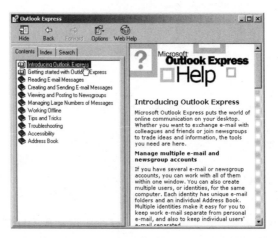

2. Clicking the Contents tab presents you with a list of Help contents for you to select from. Note that the main Contents sections may have sub-sections, as shown in Figure 39.9.

FIGURE 39.9 Using the Help Contents to display a help topic

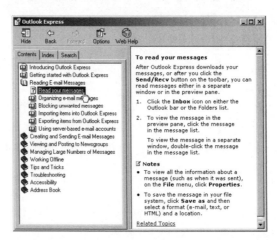

3. Selecting the Index tab displays a list of indexed keywords that are available in the Help system. Click the index word you want and then click the Display button, as shown in Figure 39.10.

FIGURE 39.10 The Index tab lists all the indexed keywords in the Help system.

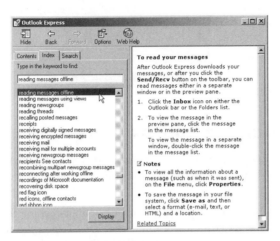

4. Clicking the Search tab allows you to look for any word or phrase, and the Help system then shows you all of the matches that it can find. Type a word or phrase in the box provided and then click the List Topics button. Once again, select any topic that has been found and click the Display button to see it, as shown in Figure 39.11.

FIGURE 39.11 The Search tab allows you to look for relevant help.

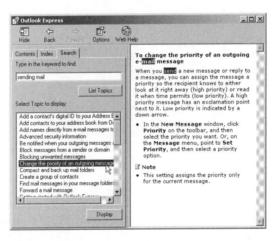

5. Close Outlook Express by choosing File ➤ Close or by clicking the Close button on the application main window. If you are connected to your ISP when you close Outlook Express, you may see an Auto Disconnect dialog box asking you whether you want to stay connected or not, as shown in the example in Figure 39.12. Normally, you click the Disconnect Now button to terminate your telephone call.

FIGURE 39.12   The Auto Disconnect dialog box

Adjusting Settings in Outlook Express

Now that you've seen how to start Outlook Express and view e-mail messages, it's time to look at some of the basic settings that you can use to control and manage the application. Try out the following steps:

1.   If it is not already open, start Outlook Express by double-clicking the icon on the Desktop or by choosing Start ➢ All Programs ➢ Outlook Express. After the application has started, click the Inbox folder in the Folders list to display its contents.

2.   You can change the appearance of Outlook Express by selecting View ➢ Layout. The Window Layout Properties dialog box opens (see Figure 39.13).

FIGURE 39.13   Changing the appearance of Outlook Express

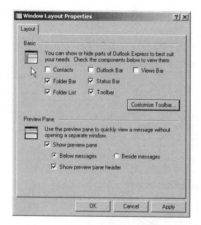

3.   This window is split into two sections: the Basic settings at the top and the Preview Pane settings at the bottom. Let's start by hiding all the various parts of Outlook Express by unchecking all the tick boxes in the Basic section. After doing this, click the Apply button followed by the OK button. Your Outlook Express window should look something like the one in Figure 39.14. Notice how you have removed all the components, leaving just the e-mail message headers at the top, with the message preview window at the bottom.

FIGURE 39.14   The most basic Outlook Express layout, with just the e-mail headers and the Preview Pane

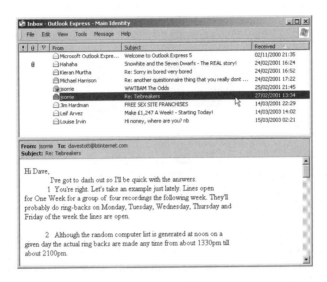

4. Next, reverse the process and display all the basic components to see what happens. To do this, choose View ➢ Layout again, check all the tick boxes in the Basic section, and click the Apply button followed by the OK button. Now, as you can see in Figure 39.15, there are lots of different window sub-sections displayed. Decide which of these is the most suitable combination for your particular way of working and then hide any components that you don't need displayed.

FIGURE 39.15   Using the layout options to display all components in Outlook Express

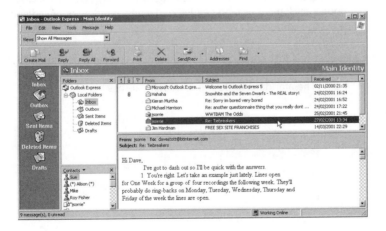

5. As well as using the Window Layout Properties dialog box to alter the layout of the main Outlook Express window, you can choose View ➢ Columns to change how the various columns are displayed in the message header window, as shown in Figure 39.16.

FIGURE 39.16   Changing the columns displayed in the message header window

6. Notice that you can decide which columns are displayed and the order in which they appear from left to right. In addition, you can specify the width of each column. If you display all the available columns, your message header window will look like the example in Figure 39.17.

FIGURE 39.17   The message header window with all columns displayed

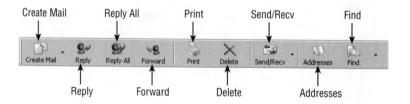

To view the contents of a mail message when there is no Preview Pane displayed, double-click the message header, and a new window opens, displaying the full message content.

The standard toolbar in Outlook Express looks like the example in Figure 39.18.

FIGURE 39.18   The standard toolbar in Outlook Express

Here is a basic description of what each of these buttons does:

Create Mail   The Create Mail tool is used to write e-mail messages.

Reply   The Reply button is used to send a reply to the selected e-mail.

Reply All   The Reply All button is used to send a reply to all recipients in the selected e-mail.

Forward   The Forward button is used to send a complete copy of a selected e-mail to designated recipient, in other words, not the original sender.

Print   The Print button is used to print out a copy of a selected e-mail.

Delete   The Delete button is used to delete the selected e-mail message.

Send/Recv   The Send/Recv tool is used to send or receive e-mail to and from your ISP.

Addresses   Click the Addresses button to manage your e-mail address book.

Find   The Find button is used to search for specific messages in folders.

Customising the Outlook Express Toolbar

Generally, your Outlook Express toolbar closely resembles the one shown earlier in Figure 39.18. However, by choosing View ➤ Layout, you can change this default toolbar by clicking the Customize Toolbar button, which displays the Customize Toolbar dialog box (see Figure 39.19).

FIGURE 39.19   Customising the Outlook Express toolbar

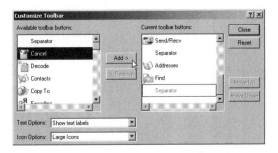

Using the Customize Toolbar dialog box, you can add or remove toolbar buttons, move toolbar buttons to new positions, and if necessary, reset the toolbar to the default standard layout. When you have finished customising the toolbar, click the Close button and then click the Apply button, followed by the OK button in the Window Layout Properties dialog box.

Summary

This chapter described the main concepts and terms associated with using e-mail and explained how important it is to abide by certain guidelines to ensure a degree of acceptable manners and behaviour in its use.

You also learnt about the major security issues associated with using e-mail and identified several areas that you need to be aware of. Whilst security is an important issue when using e-mail, so long as you take the necessary precautions, the risks are manageable.

You learnt how to start Outlook Express and select a specific mail account for use. You looked at the Outlook Express Inbox and saw how to open and read any e-mail messages that have been received. If you have difficulties, you can use the Help system at any time to find a possible solution to your problem.

You saw how it is possible to customise the main window layout within Outlook Express so that different components are visible. You can display or hide the Contacts window, the Folders list, and any of the control or information bars. In addition, you can alter the way in which the columns in the message header window area display information. Finally, you are able how to modify or customise the standard Outlook Express toolbar to add or remove the various tool icons available.

Chapter

40

E-mail Messaging

IN THIS CHAPTER YOU WILL LEARN HOW TO

- ✓ Read e-mail messages.
- ✓ Reply to received e-mail messages.
- ✓ Send e-mail messages.
- ✓ Duplicate, move, and delete e-mail messages.

Obviously, the most important use of Outlook Express is for reading, sending, and receiving messages to and from other e-mail users. You will now look at Outlook Express's messaging capabilities in more detail.

Reading and Replying to Messages

Of course, one of the primary tasks you'll be doing with Outlook Express is reading incoming messages. Outlook Express provides tools for systematically doing so. The program also allows you to reply to a message. This section explains how to use Outlook Express to

- Flag an e-mail message and remove a flag mark from an e-mail message.

- Mark a message as read or unread.

- Open and save a file attachment to a location on a drive.

Reading and Flagging E-mail

Let's start with reading a simple incoming e-mail message, taking the following steps:

1. If it is not already open, start Outlook Express by double-clicking the icon on the Desktop or by choosing Start ➤ All Programs ➤ Outlook Express. After the application has started, click the Inbox folder in the Folders list to display its contents.

2. When checking your e-mail, you have three options: Send And Receive, Receive Only, or Send Only. To collect any incoming e-mail, select Tools ➤ Send And Receive, or Tools ➤ Send And Receive All, or click the Send/Recv icon on the toolbar.

3. Any new incoming messages appear in your Inbox. Here you can mark or highlight a message for future attention by choosing Message ➤ Flag Message from the toolbar. When you do this, a small flag marker appears next to the message header, as shown in Figure 40.1.

FIGURE 40.1   A message flagged in the Inbox

!	0	⚲	From	Subject	Received	
			Kieran Murtha	Re: Sorry im bored very bored	24/02/2001 16:52	
			Michael Harrison	Re: another questionnaire thing that you really dont ...	24/02/2001 17:22	
			jsorrie	WWTBAM The Odds	25/02/2001 21:45	
	⚑		jsorrie	Re: Tiebreakers	27/02/2001 13:34	
			Jim Hardman	FREE SEX SITE FRANCHISES	14/03/2001 22:29	
			Leif Arvez	Make £1,247 A Week! - Starting Today!	14/03/2003 14:02	
			Louise Irvin	Hi noney, where are you? nb	15/03/2003 02:21	

4. You can flag as many messages as you like; if you want to flag multiple messages, simply hold down the Ctrl key on your keyboard, click each message header that you want to flag, and then select Message ➤ Flag Message from the toolbar. All the selected messages are flagged, as shown in Figure 40.2.

FIGURE 40.2 Flagging multiple messages

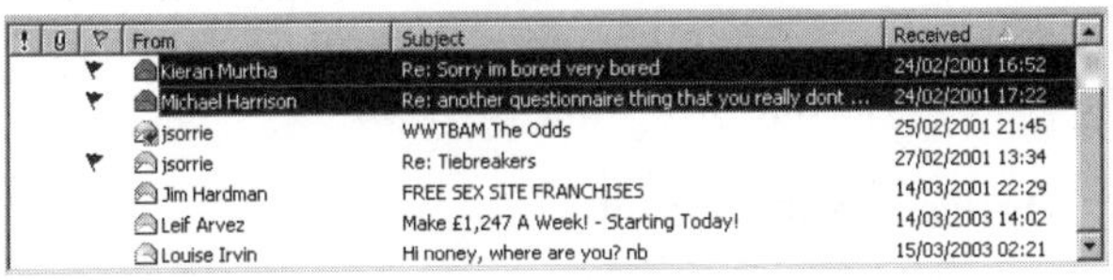

5. To remove a flag from a message, select the message header and then select Message ➤ Flag Message. The flag is removed. Alternatively, you can click once with the mouse pointer directly on the Flag icon itself, and the flag is removed, as shown in Figure 40.3.

FIGURE 40.3 Removing a flag by clicking the Flag icon

6. Outlook Express uses envelope icons next to message headers to signify whether a mail message has been read or not. A sealed envelope means that the message hasn't been read yet, and an opened envelope means that a message has been read. However, you can change the status of a mail message so as to make read messages appear as unread and vice versa. To do this, click a message header that has been read and select Edit ➤ Mark As Unread. The opened envelope next to the message header changes to a sealed envelope, as shown in Figure 40.4. Notice at the same time that the subject line is formatted in bold to help you identify unread messages. Marking a read message as unread is the same, except you choose Edit ➤ Mark As Read instead.

FIGURE 40.4 Marking a read message as unread

Handling E-mail Attachments

Occasionally you might receive an e-mail from someone that contains a file attachment such as a photograph or a chapter of a book. An e-mail that contains an attachment is evident by the appearance of a small paper clip icon next to the message header. Take these steps to handle e-mail attachments:

1. To open an attachment, click the Attachment icon to the right of the message header in the message Preview Pane. A drop-down menu opens, as shown in Figure 40.5. Simply double-click the attachment that you want to open.

FIGURE 40.5   Opening an attachment

  There are two very important things to consider when dealing with any file attachments that have been sent to you via e-mail. First, in order to open any attachment, you must have the appropriate software installed on your PC. This means that if someone sends you, for example, an Excel spreadsheet, you must have the Excel application installed on your system to be able to open the file. Second, certain documents and files may contain a virus, and these could easily corrupt or delete the data stored on your hard disk. There-fore, use appropriate anti-virus software to check any files that you receive as attachments before opening them, especially if they have come from an unknown source.

2. As well as opening file attachments, you can save them in a folder on your hard disk. To do this, select File ➢ Save Attachments or click the Save Attachments option on the drop-down menu from the Attachment icon to the right of the message header in the message Preview Pane. A Save Attachments dialog box like the one in Figure 40.6 opens, and you can select any attachments to a message and save them in an appropriate folder.

E-mail works by using a system of mailboxes, similar to the way that the conventional postal service works. You create your e-mail message on your PC and then post it by sending it to the mail outbox that resides on your ISP's computer. Just like when you post a letter, the delivery of the message takes place automatically once you have posted or sent it.

FIGURE 40.6 Saving attachments

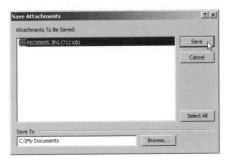

However, there is one important difference between e-mail and the postal service when it comes to receiving messages. With the standard postal service, letters are delivered to your address by the postman, you don't normally know that you are going to receive anything until it drops through your letterbox. With e-mail, however, you have to check your incoming mailbox to see if you have received anything and request it to be sent to your computer. This is similar to the situation where you have a P.O. box at the post office—unless you physically go and check its contents, you do not know whether you have received anything. Don't just expect new e-mail messages to appear on your PC by magic; instead, check for incoming e-mail on a regular basis by using the Receive Mail options in Outlook Express.

Replying to Messages

Another common task you need to perform when using Outlook Express is to reply to messages that you have received. The simplest reply goes directly back to the sender with the address information filled in automatically by Outlook Express. Take the following steps to reply to a message:

1. In your Inbox folder, select an e-mail message that you have received by clicking the message header. To reply to the message, select Message ➤ Reply To Sender or click the Reply icon on the toolbar.

   A new message window opens with the recipient's address and the subject line already filled in, preceded by *Re:* to signify that this message is a reply. In addition, the text of the original message appears in the new message body, as shown in Figure 40.7.

2. If a mail message has more than one recipient, choose Message ➤ Reply To All or click the Reply All icon on the toolbar to send a reply to all the original recipients of the message. When you do this, the individual e-mail addresses are automatically added to the To address box in the new message, as shown in Figure 40.8. Notice also that *Re:* has been inserted in front of the subject to indicate that this is a reply to an original message.

FIGURE 40.7   Replying to a received message

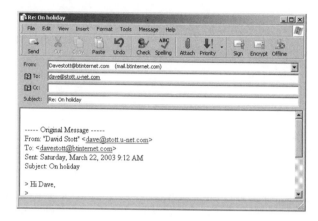

FIGURE 40.8   Replying to all original recipients of a message

3. Note that by default, Outlook Express includes the text from the original message in your replies. You can of course delete this text if you wish by selecting it in the message text area with your mouse and pressing the Delete key on your keyboard. However, if you don't want it to be included automatically in the first place, choose Tools ➤ Options to open the Options dialog box. On the Send tab, uncheck the tick box next to Include Message In Reply option, as shown in Figure 40.9, click Apply, and then click OK. Now, whenever you reply to a message, none of the original text is automatically inserted.

FIGURE 40.9   Preventing the original text from appearing in replies

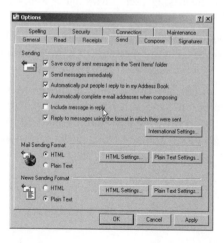

Sending Messages

Of course, you may find that you want to initiate a message to a new recipient. This section explains how to create a new message, address messages, use spell-checking, set a message priority, and attach a file to a message.

Creating a New Message

To create a new message, follow these steps:

1. If it is not already open, start Outlook Express by double-clicking the icon on the Desktop or by choosing Start ➤ All Programs ➤ Outlook Express. After the application has started, click the Inbox folder in the Folders list to display its contents.

2. There are two ways to create a new message in Outlook Express: choose Message ➤ New Message or click the New Mail icon on the toolbar. Whichever method you choose, a New Message dialog box opens (see Figure 40.10).

FIGURE 40.10   Creating a new message

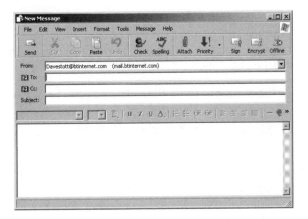

   If you are using Outlook Express for the very first time, you may not have anyone's e-mail address to enter in the To box. However, you can always send an e-mail message to yourself in order to test the system and see if it is working properly—simply enter your own e-mail address in the To box.

3. The first task is to enter the recipient's e-mail address in the To box. This can be any valid e-mail address, generally in the format *name@somewhere*, where the first part is the user's name and the second part after the @ sign is the user's location, as shown in Figure 40.11.

FIGURE 40.11 Entering an e-mail address

4. As well as sending a message to an individual, you can send a message to multiple recipients by simply adding them to the To box, separating each address by a semi-colon (;), as shown in Figure 40.12.

FIGURE 40.12 Entering multiple e-mail addresses in the To box

5. Alternatively, if you want to copy someone with an e-mail message that you are creating, enter an e-mail address in the Cc box, which stands for carbon copy, as shown in Figure 40.13.

FIGURE 40.13 Using Cc to send a copy of a message to other recipients

Note that if you use Cc, all the recipients of your message know that a copy of the message has been sent to other parties, because the message header contains the Cc details, as you can see in Figure 40.14.

FIGURE 40.14 The message header shows that a Cc has been sent to another party.

6. There is a way of sending a copy of a message to other recipients so that they are unaware of anyone else receiving the message using what is known as a *blind carbon copy*. However, the Bcc box is not visible in the New Message window by default; you have to choose View ➤ All Headers to display it. Now you can type in the e-mail addresses of anyone who you want to send a blind carbon copy of the message to, as shown in Figure 40.15.

FIGURE 40.15 Sending blind carbon copies of a message

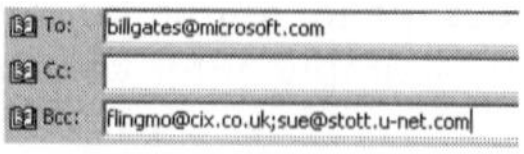

7. Next, enter a subject or title for the new message in the Subject box. Simply type something relevant concerning the message you are sending, as shown in Figure 40.16.

FIGURE 40.16   Entering a subject or title for a new message

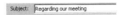

8. Note that the subject is optional, and you don't have to enter anything in this box if you don't really want to. However, if you don't type in a subject, you will receive a warning message like the one shown in Figure 40.17 when you try to send the new message.

FIGURE 40.17   A warning message displays when a mail message has no subject.

9. After you have completed the To and Subject boxes, you can enter the text of the message in the main area of the New Message window, as shown in Figure 40.18. Notice that when you click the message area, a new toolbar appears that allows you to format the text that you type in a variety of different ways.

FIGURE 40.18   The completed new message prior to sending

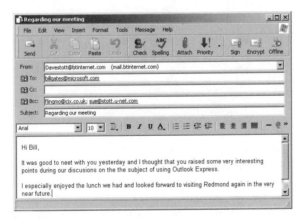

10. After you have typed the body of your new message, you can get Outlook Express to check for any spelling mistakes by choosing Tools ➢ Spelling from the New Message menu bar or by clicking the Spelling icon on the toolbar. If any incorrectly spelt words are found, a Spelling dialog box like the one in Figure 40.19 opens, and you can make any corrections.

FIGURE 40.19   Checking the spelling in a new message

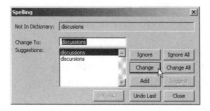

Spell check will also catch repeated words in your message; if you have repeated words, the Change button shown in Figure 40.19 will read Delete, and clicking it will remove one instance of the repeated word.

11. Occasionally, you might want to send someone a document or other type of file that you have prepared using another application such as a spreadsheet. This is known as a *file attachment*, and it allows you to send a file, along with a normal text mail message. You can do this by choosing Insert ➢ File Attachment from the New Message menu bar or by clicking the Attach icon on the toolbar. An Insert Attachment dialog box opens (see Figure 40.20). Select a file and click the Attach button to complete the process.

FIGURE 40.20   Attaching a file to a new message

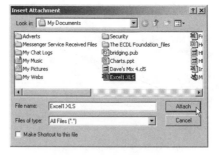

If you intend to send someone an e-mail with a file attachment, you should, as an act of common courtesy, check with them beforehand. Not only does the threat of viruses make people wary of receiving e-mail with file attachments, but if the recipient has a very slow Internet connection, they may be reluctant to accept large file attachments without prior agreement.

> It is also possible to use Outlook Express to send an e-mail message to a distribution list. However, in order do this, you need to make use of the Outlook Express Address Book facilities, which are covered in detail in Chapter 41, "E-mail Management."

12. Once you have composed your entire message, checked the spelling, and attached any necessary files, send your e-mail by either choosing File ➢ Send Message or by clicking the Send icon on the toolbar in the New Message window. If you are online to your ISP at the time, the message is sent immediately. If you are not currently online, the message is placed in the Outbox folder and sent from there the next time you click the Send/Receive icon or choose Tools ➢ Send And Receive on the Outlook Express toolbar when you are connected to the Internet.

When you send a new message or reply to a message, you can assign the message a *priority* so the recipient knows how urgent the message is. There are three levels of priority you can set: Low, Normal, and High, with Normal priority the default. To set the priority for a new message, choose Message ➢ Set Priority from the New Message menu bar or click the Priority icon on the toolbar and choose the level you require. A new line appears in the New Message dialog box showing the priority if it is set to anything other than normal, as shown in Figure 40.21.

FIGURE 40.21 A complete message with a file attachment and High priority set

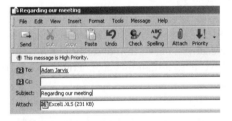

Forwarding a Message

As well as replying to a message you have received, you can forward a copy of any message to someone else using the following steps:

1. Select the message you want to forward in your Inbox and then choose Message ➢ Forward or click the Forward icon on the toolbar. This procedure works in a similar way to replying to a message.

2. When you forward a message, you need to specify a recipient in the To address box, as shown in Figure 40.22. Notice also that *Fw:* has been inserted before the subject to indicate that this is a forwarded message.

FIGURE 40.22   Forwarding a message

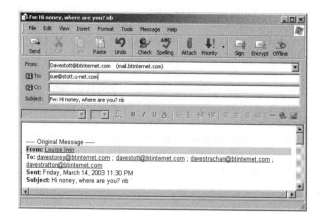

3. Choose File ➢ Send Message or click the Send icon on the toolbar in the New Message window.

Editing Messages

When you are creating a new message to send to someone, there are a few tools you can use to help you edit the text more easily. This section describes how to use standard Copy, Cut, and Paste methods for editing text in an e-mail message. You'll also learn how to delete text and attachments from a message.

Duplicating, Copying, and Deleting Text

When you are composing messages, you may find that you need to adjust the text in your e-mail. Outlook Express provides easy ways to do so. Try them out using the following steps:

1. Select File ➢ New Mail Message or click the New Mail icon to open the New Message dialog box. Enter an address and subject and then type some text in the main body of the message, as shown in Figure 40.23.

2. Select some of the text in the body of the message by using the left mouse button and dragging the pointer across an area of text. The selected text is highlighted in black, as shown in Figure 40.24.

FIGURE 40.23   Sample message

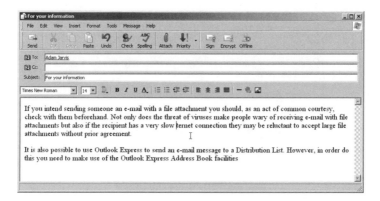

3. Select Edit ➢ Copy to copy the selected text into the Clipboard. Position the cursor somewhere else in the message, and now if you select Edit ➢ Paste, the text that was copied to the Clipboard is inserted, as shown in Figure 40.25. You can use the same procedure to copy text from any messages that you have received into any new messages that you are sending. You can have several messages open in their own windows at any time by simply double-clicking the message header. Similarly, you can create more than one new message at a time in separate windows. This means that it is relatively easy to use Copy, Cut, and Paste to duplicate or move text between active messages. Similarly, you can use the Copy and Paste tools along with the Clipboard to copy text from other applications such as a word processor into your messages.

FIGURE 40.24   Selecting text in a message

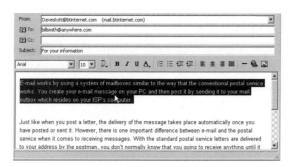

FIGURE 40.25   Pasting copied text elsewhere in a message

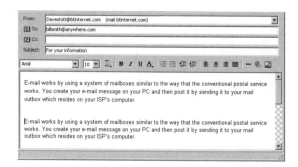

 TIP   Instead of using the menu bar to perform Copy, Cut, and Paste functions via the Clipboard, you can click the appropriate icons on the toolbar.

4.   To remove text from a message, first select it using the mouse and then delete it using the Delete key on the keyboard, using Edit ≻ Cut, or clicking the Cut icon on the toolbar.

 WARNING   The Windows Clipboard stores only one item at a time. Whenever you use the Edit ≻ Paste function, whatever was last cut or copied to the Clipboard is pasted—this might not always be what you intended. Therefore, you should consider Cut and Paste or Copy and Paste as a single function.

Removing an Attachment

If you have attached a file to a new message and then you change your mind and wish to delete the attachment, Outlook Express provides a simple way of doing so using the following steps:

1.   Highlight the filename in the Attach box, as shown in Figure 40.26, and press the Delete key on the keyboard.

FIGURE 40.26 Selecting a file attachment to remove from an e-mail message

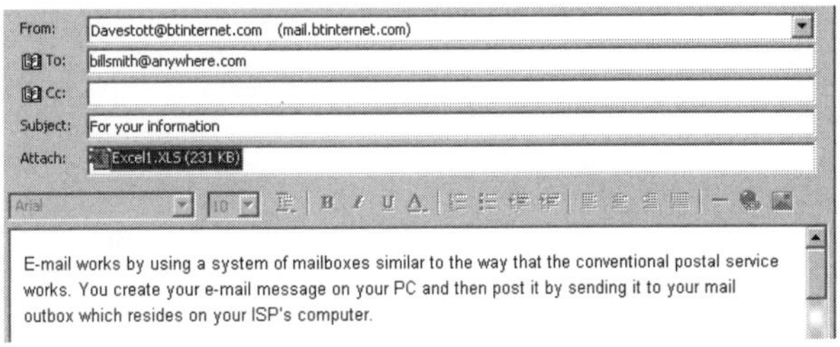

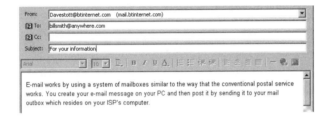

2. The Attach box disappears from the New Message window, as shown in Figure 40.27.

FIGURE 40.27 A file attachment removed from a message

Summary

This chapter reviewed several tasks involved in e-mail messaging, from reading e-mails to marking or flagging messages for your future attention. You saw how easy it is to mark messages as read or unread and vice versa. You looked at how to view and save any file attachments that you have received.

Replying both to individuals or multiple original recipients of a message is simple and efficient in Outlook Express. However, remember that by default, the text from the original message is inserted into your replies, but you can turn off this option if you wish.

There are several options available when you wish to send an e-mail message. Whilst the address of the recipient is mandatory, everything else regarding the message is optional. You can add a subject, attach a file, and set the priority when creating new messages. You can even check the spelling before you send a message.

This chapter also described how to use the Copy, Cut, and Paste tools in conjunction with the Windows Clipboard. This allows you to edit messages easily, include text from other applications, and delete any text. In addition, you saw how you can delete any file attachments if you change your mind about sending them.

Chapter

41

E-mail Management

IN THIS CHAPTER YOU WILL LEARN HOW TO

✓ Make use of some of the techniques to manage e-mail effectively.

✓ Use address books.

✓ Organise e-mail messages.

✓ Prepare and print e-mail messages.

As time goes by, you will probably accumulate a significant number of both incoming and outgoing e-mail messages. As a result, your Inbox and Outbox can become rather full. Therefore, you need to identify some of the techniques that you can use to manage your e-mail messages easily and effectively.

Basic E-mail Management Techniques

E-mail is starting to become the preferred method of communication for both the business world and the individual private user. As a result, the volume of e-mail messages that people need to be able to manage have increased substantially over the last few years.

Fortunately, applications such as Outlook Express provide several facilities to help users organise and manage their e-mail messages quickly and efficiently. In addition, there are various techniques that can be employed to make dealing with large quantities of e-mail messages less of a problem:

Mail folders   Although Outlook Express provides five folders for handling e-mail messages by default, you are not limited to just these few. In fact, you can create any new folders or subfolders that you feel might be necessary to organise and manage your messages efficiently. The only exception is that you cannot create any subfolders underneath the `Deleted Items` folder.

Moving messages   Once you have created any additional folders, you can move or copy any messages between folders so that they are better organised according to your needs. For example, you may wish to keep all your business-related e-mail messages together in a specific folder.

Deleting messages   As well as moving or copying mail messages between folders, you can, of course, delete them. This is especially useful if you receive a large amount of junk e-mail or spam. You should go through your various folders from time to time and delete any old messages that you no longer need.

Using address lists   Because e-mail has proved to be an efficient way to communicate with several different people at the same time, you will find the use of address lists or distribution lists an invaluable facility in Outlook Express. Address lists are particularly useful if you need to communicate with groups of people on a regular basis.

Message rules   When it comes to managing large volumes of incoming e-mail, Outlook Express allows you to set up message rules to automatically sort incoming messages into different folders.

However, this technique is fairly complicated and is beyond the scope of this book, so the procedures required for setting up and using message rules are not covered here.

Using Address Books

As you start to use Outlook Express regularly, you will probably send and receive mail messages from a number of different people. Each time you create a new message, you have to enter a suitable e-mail address (unless you are replying to one that you have received). Fortunately, Outlook Express provides an *address book* where you can record all sorts of details about the people you are in regular contact with. Most importantly, it allows you to record their e-mail addresses for future use.

This section explains the basic features of the Outlook Express address book. In particular, it describes how to add an e-mail address to an address book, update an address book from incoming e-mail, delete an e-mail address from an address book, and create a new address list/distribution list.

Try out these steps to learn how to use address books:

1. There are two ways you can add an e-mail address to your Outlook Express address book.

    - If you have received an e-mail message from someone, you can select the message by clicking the message header and then choosing Tools ➤ Add Sender To Address Book. The new address then appears in the Contacts window if it is currently displayed, as shown in Figure 41.1.

    - Alternatively, you can select Tools ➤ Address Book or click the Addresses icon on the toolbar, which displays the address book, as shown in Figure 41.2.

FIGURE 41.1   Adding a contact to the address book from a message received in the Inbox

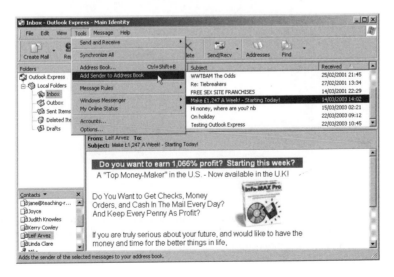

FIGURE 41.2   The address book

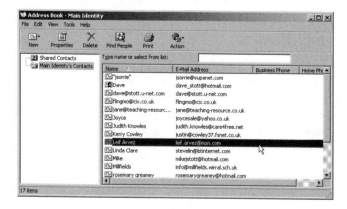

2. If you've used the second method, in the address book, select File ≻ New Contact to add someone's e-mail address. A Properties window opens, as shown in Figure 41.3. Here you can simply fill in the required boxes, click the Add button, and then click the OK button when you have finished. There are several other tabs on this window that allow to you record comprehensive details about a particular contact if you so wish.

FIGURE 41.3   Adding a new contact to the address book

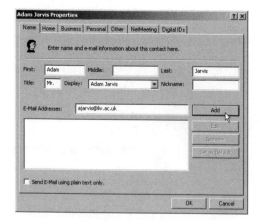

    By default, there is an option on the Send tab in the Options window (Tools ≻ Options) that automatically puts people that you reply to in the address book. You can turn this option off if you wish.

3. You can delete a contact by selecting it in the Contacts window or in the address book and then pressing the Delete key on your keyboard, selecting File ➤ Delete, or clicking the Delete icon on the toolbar. Whichever method you choose, a warning message appears asking you to confirm the deletion process, as shown in Figure 41.4.

FIGURE 41.4   Confirming that you want to delete a contact from your address book

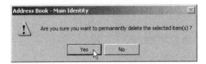

Creating a Group in Your Address Book

There may be occasions when you want to send the same e-mail message to a number of people at the same time. You can do this by typing multiple e-mail addresses in the To box when creating a new message, separating each one by a semi-colon or a comma.

However, there is a better way, particularly if this is something that you want to do on a regular basis; you can set up a *distribution list* or *group*. Take the following steps to do this:

1. Open up the address book (Tools ➤ Address Book or click the Addresses icon on the toolbar) and select File ➤ New Group; this displays the Group Properties dialog box. Enter an appropriate name for your new group in the Group Name box, as shown in Figure 41.5.

FIGURE 41.5   Creating a new group in your address book

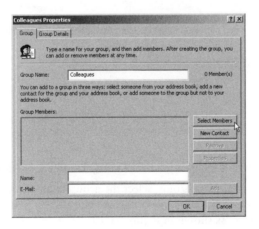

2. Next, click the Select Members button. The Select Group Members dialog box opens, where you can choose which of your current contacts should be members of this group, as shown in Figure 41.6. Once you are satisfied with the makeup of your group, click OK and then click OK again on the previous Group Properties dialog box. You are returned to the Address Book window.

FIGURE   41.6   Selecting contacts to become group members

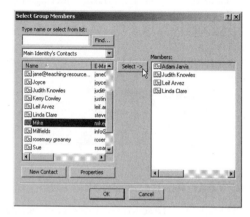

3. If you now select View ➢ Folders And Groups from the Address Book menu bar, a list of folders and groups is displayed on the left-hand side of the window (see Figure 41.7).

FIGURE   41.7   A group in the address book

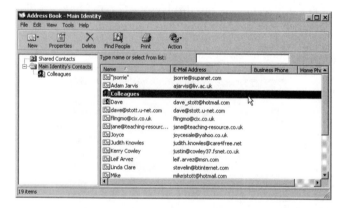

4. Clicking a group name displays a list of the group members, as shown in Figure 41.8.

5. To send an e-mail to an entire group, select the group name from your Contacts window by double-clicking it (see Figure 41.9). Alternatively, add the group to the To box on the New Message window, as shown in Figure 41.10.

FIGURE 41.8   Displaying a list of group members

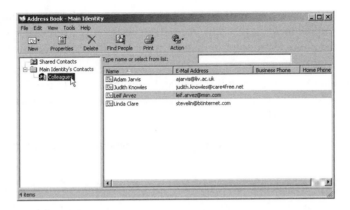

FIGURE 41.9   A group name in the Contacts window

FIGURE 41.10   Sending an e-mail to a group

Organising Messages

As you accumulate mail messages over time, your Inbox can become quite full, which means that it can be difficult to find certain messages easily. Therefore, the ability to search for text is quite important, as is the use of additional folders for storing messages away for future reference.

This section explains how to search for a message by sender, subject, or mail text content; create new folders for storing mail; move messages between folders; and sort messages. You'll also learn about the features associated with deleting messages.

Searching for a Message

When you have accumulated a large number of messages in your Inbox, you might find it difficult to locate a specific message that you received, especially if you received it a long time ago. Outlook Express provides features for finding them that you can experiment with by taking the following steps:

1. Make sure that Outlook Express is started and your Inbox is selected. In this case, choose Edit ➤ Find ➤ Message or click the Find icon on the toolbar. This displays the Find Message dialog box (see Figure 41.11).

FIGURE 41.11   Using Outlook Express's Find capability to locate specific messages

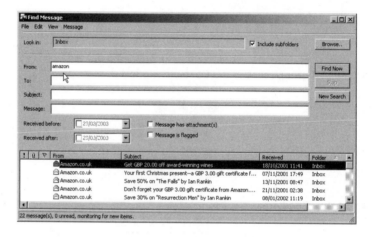

2. In the Find Message dialog box, you can enter various details about the message you are trying to locate. Obviously, the more specific the detail you enter in the various boxes, the more likely you are to find precisely the message(s) that you are looking for, so enter as many details as you can.

If you know approximately when the message that you are looking for was received, you can set the Received Before and Received After dates in the Find Message window to restrict your search. This is particularly useful if your Inbox is extremely large, as it can speed up searches quite dramatically.

Creating E-mail Folders

Whilst by default, all incoming messages end up in your Inbox, you can if you wish create other folders in which to store various messages. To create a new folder, take the following steps:

1. Select File ➤ Folder ➤ New. The Create Folder dialog box opens (see Figure 41.12).

FIGURE 41.12   Creating a new folder to store messages in

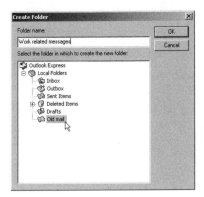

Note that new folders are created within the existing hierarchical folder tree structure. In this example, the folder `Work Related Messages` is created as a subfolder of `Old Mail`, which was originally created as a subfolder of `Local Folders`, as shown in the Folders window illustrated in Figure 41.13.

FIGURE 41.13   The new folders structure

2. Once you have created some new folders to store your messages in, you will probably need to move some messages from their existing folders to new locations. To do this, select the message you want to move by clicking the message header and then select Edit ➤ Move to Folder. The Move dialog box opens (see Figure 41.14).

FIGURE 41.14 Moving a message to another folder

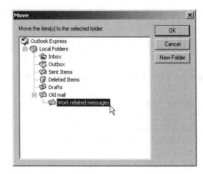

3. In the Move dialog box, you can select a target folder for the message to be moved to. Note that you can also choose File ➢ Copy To Folder; this leaves the original message intact whilst making a copy of it in the target folder.

Sorting Messages

When organising messages within folders, choose View ➢ Sort By to automatically sort messages into a specific order. For example, you can sort by Priority, Attachment, Flag, From (Sender), Subject, or Received Date in either ascending or descending order, as shown in Figure 41.15.

FIGURE 41.15 Sorting messages within folders

 To sort messages in a folder quickly and easily, click the individual column headings. The messages are sorted based on that column. Clicking the same column heading a second time reverses the sort order.

Deleting Messages

You may eventually find that you need to delete some messages; you may also find that you wish you hadn't. Outlook Express gives you ways of deleting messages, restoring messages from the `Deleted Items` folder, and emptying items from the `Deleted Items` folder altogether.

To remove a message from the Inbox or any other folder, select the message header and press the Delete key on your keyboard or click the Delete icon on the toolbar. This procedure doesn't actually delete the message immediately; instead, it moves the message to the `Deleted Items` folder, as shown in Figure 41.16. If you make a mistake and delete something accidentally, you can copy or move it from the `Deleted Items` folder to the original folder or to a different folder if you wish.

FIGURE 41.16   The Deleted Items folder

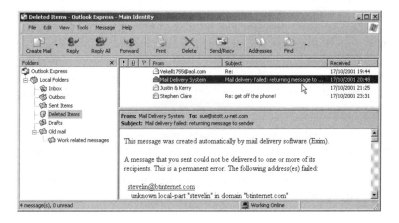

However, if you wish to remove a message entirely, you can delete it from the `Deleted Items` folder itself. Note that if you delete a message from the `Deleted Items` folder, it is removed completely—you can't retrieve it. In fact, you will see the warning message as shown in Figure 41.17, which cautions you regarding this fact.

FIGURE 41.17   Warning shown when deleting messages from the Deleted Items folder

You can also clear the entire contents of the `Deleted Items` folder by selecting the Edit ➢ Empty 'Deleted Items' Folder menu option.

When selecting a message to move or copy to another folder, if you hold down the Ctrl key on the keyboard, you can select multiple messages at the same time. You can also move messages between folders quickly and easily by selecting them and dragging them to a new location using the mouse.

Printing Messages

Whilst many people only ever view their e-mail messages on screen, there are occasions when you might need to print an entire message or part of a message. Unfortunately, for some reason, Microsoft has not provided all of the various menu options to control printing within Outlook Express that are available in other applications in the Office XP suite. Specifically, there is no menu option for Print Preview, so you cannot see how a mail message will look on the printed page before actually printing it. Similarly, there isn't a Page Setup option on the menu, so you cannot adjust the page margins from within Outlook Express prior to printing. Nevertheless, there are some basic settings that can be used to control printing that are covered in this section.

This section assumes that the PC that you are using to perform the following exercises has a suitable printer attached to it and that it is properly configured for use by the Windows XP operating system. Should this not be the case, any tasks that require you to actually print a message or part of a message should be modified to print the output to a file instead.

Preparing to Print

Let's look at some of the basic Print options available. Take the following steps:

1. Make sure that Outlook Express is started and your Inbox is selected. Before you actually commit to printing a message or part of a message, choose File ➤ Print to adjust various settings that control the printing process. This option displays the Print dialog box seen in Figure 41.18.

If there isn't a printer available on your system, you may have to print to a file instead. If this is the case, make sure that there is a tick in the Print To File box in the Print window, as shown in Figure 38.24 in Chapter 38. Then when you click the OK button to start the print, you are asked to provide a filename, as shown in Figure 38.25.

FIGURE 41.18   The Print dialog box

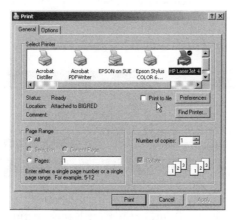

2. Using the Print window, specify which printer to use (assuming that you have more than one printer attached to your PC) and choose the number of copies you want to print by either typing a number in the appropriate box or by using the control buttons. To start the printing, click OK.

3. By default, Outlook Express always prints the entire message, no matter how long it is. You can specify a page range to print by checking the Pages button and entering values in the associated box, as shown in Figure 41.19. However, because there is no option to preview the pages before printing, it is very difficult to tell which parts of the message would be printed on which page(s). Therefore, using the Page Range option can be a bit of a hit-and-miss affair.

FIGURE 41.19   Printing a range of pages

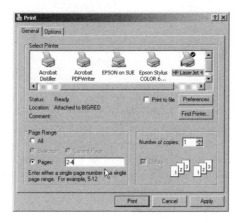

4. Rather than using the Page Range option, you can print part of a message by selecting the actual text in the message and clicking and dragging your mouse across the area of text you want to print, as shown in Figure 41.20.

FIGURE 41.20 Selecting text within a message for printing

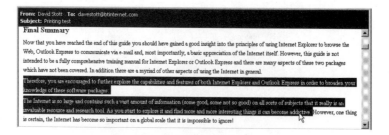

5. Now when you select File ➢ Print, in the Page Range section of the Print dialog box, click the Selection button, as shown in Figure 41.21. Only the text that you have selected within the message is printed when you click OK.

FIGURE 41.21 Printing a selection of text from within a message

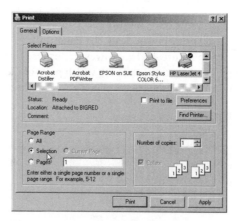

 Whilst you cannot adjust the page margins from within Outlook Express, it is possible to set them another way. Outlook Express uses the Internet Explorer print engine, so you can choose File ➢ Page Setup within Internet Explorer to adjust the page margins. When you return to Outlook Express, those settings are used.

6. You can choose to print more than one copy of a message. Simply adjust the number in the Number of Copies box by either using the arrows to move up or down or typing the desired number of copies directly into the box. If your e-mail is more than one page long and you choose to have multiple copies, you can also select the Collate check box to ensure that the printed pages come out in the correct order.

You have now reached the end of this final exercise, so close Outlook Express by selecting File ➤ Exit on the menu bar or by clicking the Close control for the main application window.

Summary

This chapter covered the various techniques you can use to manage large numbers of e-mail messages easily and effectively. Much of the advice is common sense, and if you adopt these techniques from the outset, then as the volumes of e-mail messages that you have to deal with increases, you will be better equipped to cope.

You also learnt how, by using the Address Book features in Outlook Express, you can maintain a list of regular contacts so that you don't have to keep typing in their e-mail addresses when you want to send them a message. You can add contacts to the address book in various ways and set up groups with specific members that you can use as a distribution list.

You can use the Find option to search for messages stored in folders. To help in organising messages, you can create new folders, move and copy messages between folders, delete messages, and sort them into various ascending or descending orders.

The final section described how to adjust the various settings that control how mail messages are printed. Although the printing controls within Outlook Express are rather limited, you can at least print selected text from within messages.

Now that you have reached the end of this module, you should have gained a good insight into the principles of using Internet Explorer to browse the Web, using Outlook Express to communicate via e-mail and, most importantly, a basic appreciation of the Internet itself. However, this guide is not intended to be a fully comprehensive training manual for Internet Explorer or Outlook Express; there are many aspects of these two packages that have not been covered. In addition, there are a myriad of other aspects of using the Internet in general that you will no doubt encounter as you gain more experience over time.

Therefore, you are encouraged to further explore the capabilities and features of Internet Explorer and Outlook Express in order to broaden your knowledge of these software packages.

The Internet is so large and contains such a vast amount of information (some good, some not so good) on all sorts of subjects that it really is an invaluable resource and research tool. As you start to explore it and find more and more interesting things, it can become addictive. However, one thing is certain—the Internet has become so important on a global scale that it is impossible to ignore it.

Module Review Questions

1. What is a home page?

2. What is meant by the term *download*?

3. What is a hypertext link or a hyperlink?

4. What is a bookmark?

5. What is a search engine?

6. Which menu bar option do you use to control the layout of a printed page?

7. How can you adjust the width of message header columns?

8. What happens if you don't include a subject line in a new e-mail message?

9. How can you send copies of an e-mail without other recipients knowing?

10. Why should you check your e-mail post box on a regular basis?

11. You have received an e-mail message from someone that you have not communicated with before. How can you add their e-mail address to your list of contacts?

12. What happens when you delete an e-mail message from your Inbox?

Answers to Module Review Questions

1. A home page is the default web page that a browser loads automatically when it is started.

2. Downloading refers to the transmission of data from a server to a client.

3. A hyperlink is the method used to link between related web pages. Normally, hyperlinks are designated by using coloured text that is underlined. However, any element—including graphical images on a web page—can be a designated hyperlink.

4. A bookmark is a reference to a web page (URL) that can be stored in your Favorites list in Internet Explorer so that you can revisit a website quickly and easily.

5. A search engine is just like other web pages, but it allows you to enter search terms in text form. The search engine then searches for these terms and displays the results on a new web page.

6. Select File ➢ Page Setup and then specify the various options.

7. Choose View ➢ Columns to change how the various columns are displayed in the message header window.

8. You receive a warning message when you try to send an e-mail message without a subject line.

9. To send copies of an e-mail without other recipients knowing, use the blind carbon copy (Bcc) field rather than the carbon copy (Cc) field.

10. E-mail is not automatically sent to you—you have to collect it from your ISP. Therefore, you should check your e-mail post box on a regular basis to stop it from filling up and causing potential storage problems on the e-mail server.

11. To add the sender of an e-mail message to your address book, click the message header and then select Tools ➢ Add Sender To Address Book.

12. The deleted message is moved to the `Deleted Items` folder, where it remains until you delete it from there.

Index

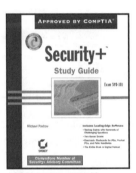

TELL US WHAT YOU THINK!

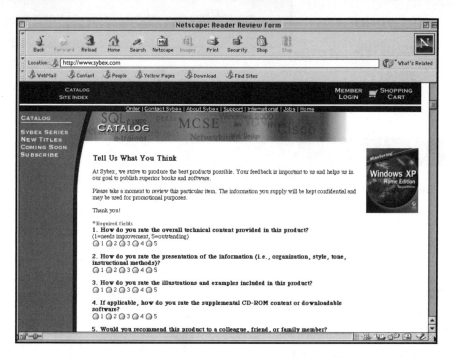

Your feedback is critical to our efforts to provide you with the best books and software on the market. Tell us what you think about the products you've purchased. It's simple:

1. Go to the Sybex website.
2. Find your book by typing the ISBN or title into the Search field.
3. Click on the book title when it appears.
4. Click **Submit a Review.**
5. Fill out the questionnaire and comments.
6. Click **Submit.**

With your feedback, we can continue to publish the highest quality computer books and software products that today's busy IT professionals deserve.

www.sybex.com

SYBEX Inc. • 1151 Marina Village Parkway, Alameda, CA 94501 • 510-523-8233